A TREASURY OF MEXICAN FOLKWAYS

A TREASURY OF

MEXICAN FOLKWAYS

By Frances Toor

THE CUSTOMS · MYTHS · FOLKLORE · TRADITIONS

BELIEFS · FIESTAS · DANCES · AND SONGS

OF THE MEXICAN PEOPLE

Illustrated with 10 Color Plates

100 DRAWINGS BY CARLOS MERIDA

AND 170 PHOTOGRAPHS

CROWN PUBLISHERS, INC. • NEW YORK

ISBN: 0-517-502925

Thirteenth Printing, November, 1973
Printed in the United States of America

TO MY FAMILY

PICTURE CREDITS

For Photographs 1-168 following page 298

PREFACE

Although Mexico is just across our southern border, we knew less about its people until recently than about others from more distant lands. And a good deal of what we "knew" was wrong and untrue. The notion prevailed that the majority of Mexicans were primitive and inferior. Few North Americans were visiting Mexico, and the Mexicans who came to this country were mostly the unskilled workers brought by contractors looking for cheap labor. And because they were poor and different, many thoughtless persons despicably called them "greasers" and treated them rudely.

Since about 1930, however, hundreds of thousands of North Americans are visiting Mexico annually—tourists, pleasure-seekers, businessmen, professionals, scientists, students—and practically all of them are impressed with the culture, artistry, and dignity of the poor Mexicans. The aim of this book is to present a composite picture of their life. They are that portion of the population—perhaps over half of the twenty million—still preserving the arts and traditions of their pre-Conquest ancestors or those still living in a folkloric state of civilization as compared to the modern. They are the people in whom I have been chiefly interested during my twenty-five years of residence in Mexico.

The book is divided into five parts—the Introduction is a simplified account of the most important of the ancient races; Part One describes the economic life of the people; Part Two, their social and religious organization; Part Three, music and the dance; Part Four, their literature in all its forms. The music, songs, and illustrations add much reality to the picture and I think that the reader will be wise to look at the photographs before starting to read the book.

The customs which I am describing exist at the present time. My own experiences in the field have been continuous since 1922, and the sources with which I am supplementing personal investigations have been checked with present conditions.

In instances where present-day customs appear directly connected with those of ancient times, I am indicating them. However, I am not trying to separate the aboriginal from the Spanish elements. For the purposes of this book such a classification is unimportant and would be practically impossible under any circumstances. There has been little research along these lines and human traits cannot always be classified on a racial basis. We shall see that many of the religious beliefs of the pagan Mexicans were similar to those of the Catholic Spaniards; also that their ethics and laws were not much different from our own.

Racially, Mexico is about thirty or forty percent of purely aboriginal extraction, the bulk, *mestizo* or mixed, and about fifteen or twenty percent pure white. There are no exact figures in this respect, as the last census was taken on a cultural basis—how the people lived and dressed and what languages they spoke. About forty percent of the folkloric population spoke the native languages, in many cases also a little Spanish; a small percentage of *mestizos*, who spoke only Spanish, were also living in the folkloric manner.

It has been customary to speak of the population living in a folkloric way as "Indian," but that is no longer possible because many of the so-called Indians have adopted modern ways of living. Since there are no exclusive terms with which to designate the folkloric peoples, I am using racial names, "native" and "folk," to distinguish them from the modernized ones, to whom I refer as "mestizo," "ladino," or "citified."

Because of the enormity of subject matter much has had to be omitted, but I hope I have succeeded in making the picture human and alive.

ACKNOWLEDGMENTS

A book of this kind requires much co-operation. Many persons have been kind, and I am grateful to all of them, even though it is possible to mention only the names of those to whom I am most indebted:

Professor Alfredo Barrera Vázquez, Maya scholar, for stories, riddles, and sayings;

Dr. Ralph L. Beals, Chairman of the Department of Anthropology, University of California at Los Angeles, for the use of his unpublished Cherán manuscript and other material;

Dr. Ralph S. Boggs, of the University of North Carolina, authority on Latin American folklore, for reading Part One of the manuscript;

Dr. Daniel Rubín de la Borbolla, Director of the National Museum of Mexico, for lending me valuable books;

Dr. Alfonso Caso, Mexico's most distinguished archæologist, for help with the introduction and permission to use any of his material;

Dr. Howard Cline, Instructor in Mexican History at Harvard University, for reading parts of the manuscript and for data;

Donald B. Cordry, ethnologist and photographer, for data and for the use of his excellent photographs;

Crown Publishers, for making my book beautiful, and all the persons of the Company who worked on it, for their warm co-operation;

Dr. Gordon F. Ekholm, specialist in Mexican archæology and Assistant Curator of the American Museum of Natural History of New York, for reading the manuscript of the Introduction;

Dr. George M. Foster, anthropologist of the Smithsonian Institution of Washington, for the use of his notes on Tzintzuntzan, Michoacán, and other material;

Prof. Julio de la Fuente, ethnologist and Assistant Director of the Department of Indian Affairs of the Federal Ministry of Education, for the use of his "Yalalag" manuscript and other data;

Raoul Guerrero, musician and ethnologist, for music and data on dances;

Dr. Calixta Guiteras Holmes, ethnologist, for her notes on the villages of Cancúc and Chenahló and for much valuable help;

Carlos Merida, well-known artist, for his beautiful illustrations and deep interest in all aspects of this book;

Concha Michel, collector and singer of folksongs, for giving generously of her rich store;

Dr. Robert Redfield, formerly Dean of the Division of Social Sciences of the University of Chicago, now Chairman of its Department of Anthropology, for material and for helpful advice;

Alfonso Villa R., anthropologist of the Carnegie Institution, for his notes on Oxchuc and other data;

Herbert Weinstock, author of books on music, who knows Mexico well, for reading the galley proofs;

Ben Meiselman, for preparing the Index;

Henrietta Yurchenco, who made records of folk music in various parts of the Mexican hinterland, for the use of her reports and verbal communications;

And to my brothers—Herbert E. Toor, for setting the machinery in motion for the writing and publication of this book at the present time; Harold O. Toor, for generously helping with facilities for part of the work.

The Institutions I am indebted to for material are—the Mexican Ministry of Education, the Instituto Indigenista Interamericano, the Mexican National School of Anthropology, the Cultural Department of the State of Chiapas, the University of Chicago, and the Carnegie Institution, the last four having patronized the research in Chiapas.

I must also include in this expression of heartfelt thanks the good friends who helped most when I was publishing "Mexican Folkways," a goodly part of the preparation for this book. Among them were Drs. Caso and Redfield, mentioned above. Others were:

Carleton Beals, author and authority on Latin America;

Jean Charlot, artist and author;

Carlos Chávez, conductor and composer;

Miguel Covarrubias, artist, author, and archæologist;

Francisco Domínguez, musician and composer;

René d'Harnoncourt, artist and author; now one of the Directors of the Museum of Modern Art, New York;

Salvador Novo, poet and author;

Jose J. de Nuñez y Domínguez, poet, author, diplomat;

Diego Rivera, artist;

Esther Toor Rosedale, honor graduate of Cornell University, teacher and mother;

William P. Spratling, architect, artist, author.

IN MEMORIAM

Herbert Croly, founder and editor of the *New Republic;*

José Frias, poet and Head of publications of the Ministry of Education, 1924-28;

Professor Pablo González Casanova, philologist and author;

Miguel Othón de Mendizábal, social anthropologist and author;

Dr. Elsie Clews Parsons, anthropologist and author;

Dr. Moises Saenz, educator, author, diplomat, and Sub-Secretary of Education, 1924-28.

Mexico City, April 1947   FRANCES TOOR

CONTENTS

PART ONE

WORK AND WORSHIP

PART TWO

SOCIETY — CUSTOM — FIESTA

PART THREE

MUSIC — VERSE — DANCE

SONGS AND DANCE MUSIC

PART FOUR

MYTHS – TALES – MISCELLANEA

LIST OF ILLUSTRATIONS

COLOR PLATES

(Following page 124)

DRAWINGS

Drawings throughout the text, not separately listed.

MAP

Ethnographic map of Mexico facing page one.

PHOTOGRAPHS

(Following page 298)

INTRODUCTION

The Ancient Cultures

For a better understanding of the folk with whose ways this book is concerned, it is necessary to know something of their past. Although native groups of the Indian races have been treated and considered as of low caste since the coming of the white man, they are the descendants of noble races. Among them were great artists, architects, engineers, and men wise in astronomy, who were builders of strange and brilliant civilizations.

The written history of Mexico began with the Conquest. The reconstruction of the development of the civilizations prior to that event has been a difficult task and is still incomplete. There are the early chronicles containing much valuable information on the history and cultures of the conquered peoples, especially the Aztecs, the dominant race at that time. The rest has been furnished by historians, anthropologists, and particularly by archaeologists, who have deciphered hieroglyphs and the picture-writings of the codices, studied monuments, artifacts, and all related sources. However, their conclusions are necessarily subject to change whenever new, important material is unearthed.

Since most archaeological deductions are speculative, there is seldom agreement with respect to dates. But more excavating and research has been done in recent years than ever before, and archaeologists are now agreeing along the general lines, which I shall follow in this brief summary.

It is believed that man did not originate on the American continent, but that this continent was first populated by tribes coming from Asia across the Bering Straits or the Aleutian Islands, some fifteen or twenty thousand years ago; that these tribes were nomads, living by hunting, fishing, and the gathering of edible foods from trees and in the fields; that they possessed the arts of fire-making, basketry, and stone-chipping in a rudimentary form.

Although the first tribes to settle in Mexico were at the same cultural level and had a common heritage, there were between them differences which were accentuated by the conditions of their new environment. In order to obtain sufficient food, the large tribes had to divide into small groups and to disperse. Often they were separated by mountains, ravines, streams, or long distances. and so were unable to keep in contact. Later, it is also possible that peoples came from areas other than Asia, introducing different cultural elements. Thus the differences in language and customs were more intensified. At the time of the Conquest, there were over a hundred self-governing tribes, speaking as many different tongues, whose customs were also different.

After thousands of years in the land, and having become familiar with its climatic conditions and soil, the nomads evolved a better way of life by discovering or learning from others how to grow staple foods like corn, squash, beans, and others. Corn, or maiz, is the most important and is believed to have been developed in Mexico or farther south by experimenting with a plant called teocentli. After their sources of food were assured, the nomads were able to settle down and to develop their complex ceremonial cultures.

Nothing has been found to date of the remains of the nomadic tribes. The first civilization unearthed, which has been called Archaic because it is the oldest, was that of a people leading a sedentary life. This culture extended from northern Mexico through parts of Central America, but it undoubtedly did not develop at the same time nor at the same level at all points. In the Valley of Mexico, where the Archaic remains are most evenly distributed, a period ranging from one to several thousand years is attributed to it. At some time around the beginning of the Christian era, the dominance of Archaic man came to an end and his culture was transformed into a higher one.

Archaeologists speak of the different civilizations in terms of "cultural horizons"—Archaic, Toltec, and others. "Horizons" refers to the layers of objects found under the soil belonging to any one of the cultures, objects which furnish clues with respect to sequence and characteristics. However, the dates arrived at through a combination of evidences are only approximate, with the exception of some of those of the last few centuries before the coming of the Spaniards.

Many archaeological excavations have been made in Mexico since 1910. In the environs of Mexico City, four cultural horizons of agricultural peoples have been discovered. The deepest of these was that of the Archaic, consisting of stone and bone implements, many clay figurines, crude stone statues, and relatively simply modeled and painted pottery.

In 1917 an ancient cemetery of Archaic man was found in the quarry of Copilco, under the Pedregal, or lava flow, on the outskirts of Mexico City. The Federal Archaeology Department turned it into a museum in which the bodies remain in the positions in which they were found, with the funeral offerings near them in attractive pottery bowls, together with many figurines. At the opposite end of the Pedregal stands the Pyramid of Cuicuilco, the oldest on the continent. It is an oval adobe construction of several terraces faced with cobblestones and with an open altar at the top. Cuicuilco in Aztec means, "Place of song and color."

These and several other sites have contributed greatly to our knowledge of the Archaic civilizations. The figurines are particularly interesting because they shed light on the customs of that epoch. They are apparently portraits of either the living or the dead or both, for they show dress, adornments, musical instruments, and occupations. They are about five inches more or less in height, flat, and modeled in clay, gouged and incised with pointed instruments, the bodies often painted and with indications of tattooing. Shirts, skirts, and aprons are painted on or incised with geometrical designs; a variety of earrings and nose-rings are modeled on, as well as turbans, fillets and various objects coquettishly perched on the side of the head. Some of the men are shown throwing the atlatl or spear, or using clubs; others, beating drums and conch-shells; women nursing children and carrying water. The garments are an indication of loom-weaving, while the many nude females symbolize fecundity, and were probably offerings for good crops. Although these figurines are crudely made in comparison with those of the later, higher civilizations, they are very expressive. One can find among them the gamut of all human types.

Since 1940 excavations in the southern part of Vera Cruz have unearthed an extraordinarily creative art, referred to as the Olmec. From the standpoint of time, the Olmec style seems to be as old as the Archaic period and may have influenced the development of the great Maya art. At Tres Zapotes a huge, strongly carved basalt head, seven feet high, with Negroid features, wearing a curious headdress in the form of a helmet, was found, together with many fine small sculptures. At another place, called La Venta, in the jungle forests, there were discovered various handsomely carved monuments, numerous heads, four immense stelae with sculptures of distinguished personages, altars, and many unusual small pieces, some being statuettes of the finest green jade ever seen in Mexico.

Following the Archaic epoch, a series of cultures rose and fell on the Central Plateau and in the south. The reasons for their disappearance are various and can only be surmised. There were, undoubtedly, a combination of them in most instances—exhaustion of the food supply because of primitive methods of agriculture, epidemics, oppression by the ruling classes, strife between rival and confederated cities, and the invasions of barbarians from the north or from the tropical forests of the south.

Some few centuries after the Archaic, the highest of all the Mexican cultures began, the Maya Golden Age or the Maya Old Empire, flourishing between the third and tenth centuries, A.D. The Mayas have been called "The Greeks of the New World." Their civilization was magnificent, brilliant, comparable in esthetic achievement to the highest in the world. Artists of today marvel at their art, and scientists at their calendar.

The Maya Old Empire extended from what is now southern Mexico, through Guatemala, British Honduras and the northwestern part of the Republic of Honduras. The ruins of many superb stone cities of that epoch are to be found in that region. Those belonging to Mexico are in the State of Chiapas. Yaxchilán and Palenque are the most outstanding. Palenque, in fact, is considered the finest of all the Maya area, the most advanced architecturally, while artistically it is unrivaled in its stucco relief and low-relief stone carvings.

Situated in a tropical forest of the Tumbala foothills, Palenque is still overwhelmingly beautiful. There on terraced plazas rises the imposing palace with its three-story tower. Lovely small temples stand out against a background of trees reaching to the heavens. The place is full of tropical wild flowers, shrubs and bushes, and through the grounds flows a stream that blends its music with that of many birds. It must have been a wonder-world when it was alive with people and color and music.

While the Old Empire lasted, the Mayas not only constructed those dazzling cities, but also made notable progress in the arts and sciences. They invented an advanced system of hieroglyphic writing by which they were able to record events and dates. (Unfortunately, as yet archaeologists do not agree in the correlation of the Maya dates with ours.) They even had a sign for zero long before the Europeans. Maya astronomers evolved a year count as perfect as ours, even though it was more complicated. There were two calendars— one of eighteen months of twenty days each, plus five additional days at the end of the year, based on the seasons; the other, known as the tzolkin, consisted of thirteen months of twenty days each, totaling only 260. The latter did not correspond to any natural period and was used for ceremonial purposes only. All the civilizations that followed based their calendars on the Mayan count of eighteen months of twenty days, the Aztecs also having a book of days, called the Tonalamatl.

In the field of sculpture, the artists of the Old Empire reached a high degree or sophistication in their hieroglyphs, as well as in the human figures. Temples and palaces were painted both inside and out in brilliant colors and exotic motifs. The minor arts—pottery, jewelry, weaving, and others—were varied and beautiful.

Sometime in the tenth century, the Mayas abandoned their great ceremonial centers, leaving them to the mercy of the elements and to the jungle. All that is known now of the makers of that stupendous civilization must be deduced from the mute evidence of their pyramids, temples, and palaces, the sculptures of priests, rulers, and slaves, hieroglyphs and paintings; pottery, jewels, masks, carvings.

Mexico, because of its geographical situation, is the passageway between the great continental areas of the north and south; and, together with Central America, was one of the two important cultural sources of the Americas, the other being in the Andes. The regions in which the greatest number of high civilizations flourished were in the south and in the Valley of Mexico. The Valley, with its lakes, mountains, and fine climate, attracted all the tribes coming from the north, who settled there, the strongest of them ruling until others came along to wrest away their power.

Contemporaneously with the Golden Age of the Mayas, the splendid Teotihuacán civilization flourished in the Valley of Mexico, possibly with influences from the south. Teotihuacán, in Aztec "the dwelling place of the gods," was the most magnificent ceremonial center of the Valley. Its pyramids, palaces, courts, sculptures, fresco paintings, figurines, and pottery are still mute witnesses to its past greatness. For some unknown reason the brilliant Teotihuacán epoch also came to an end in the ninth century, when the Toltecs came into power.

AZTEC CALENDAR

The two great Toltec centers are Tula—formerly Tollan, "Place of Reeds"—in the State of Hidalgo, and Cholula in the State of Puebla. Recent excavations in Tula have uncovered pyramids, a ball court, many magnificent sculptures, some fifteen feet high, and paintings in black and white as well as in color. The ruins in both places, together with sculptures, pottery and other objects belonging to them, attest to a very high culture.

QUETZALCOATL
(From the Borbonic Codex)

The god of the Toltecs was Quetzalcoatl, about whom many legends exist. He is said to have been the creator of man, the discoverer of corn, the inventor and patron of the arts and crafts, and the originator of the calendar and the priestly ritual. The fall of the Toltecs in the twelfth century was undoubtedly due to the advancing hordes of Chichimecas, but legend attributes it to the departure of Quetzalcoatl. It is said that after giving laws to his people he departed eastward. Upon reaching the sea, he took off his feather dress and snake mask, after which he sacrificed himself on a funeral pyre, his soul becoming the morning star. As god of the morning star, his calendrical name was ce acatl, "one reed," one of the dates marking the periodical appearances of Venus.

Another account has it that he sailed away toward the east, promising to return on a similar future day.

According to another legend, the promise of Quetzalcoatl to return in a year ce acatl is supposed to have favored the Spaniards in their conquest of Mexico, for their coming coincided with that date. As Quetzalcoatl was thought to be white and bearded in his human form, Cortés was taken for him.

During the centuries of power of the Toltecs, the Mayas were living through another glorious epoch, even though of less brilliance than the first. After a dark age of readjustment on the Peninsula of Yucatán, they built their second Empire, this time completely separate from the Mayas of Central America. In the tenth century three of the leading cities formed a league, Chichén Itzá, Uxmal, and Mayapan.

When the power of the Toltecs was waning, some found their way into Yucatán and had a strong influence on the Mayas. Quetzalcoatl became the Maya Kukulkan, and the Mayas adopted Toltec ideas in their architecture, customs, and methods of warfare.

For several centuries, until the end of the twelfth, Chichén Itzá was the great pilgrimage city of Yucatán, and peace reigned. Then strife began between the cities of the league. Mayapan, with the help of Mexican mercenaries, won over Chichén Itzá. The wars continued until Mayapan was completely destroyed in 1461. Shortly afterwards a great hurricane swept the Peninsula, causing much damage. The population was still large and vigorous, and might have recovered, but new disasters came in the form of epidemics and more wars. When the Spaniards arrived, about seventy-five years later, there was nothing left of the ruling theocracies. Today, Chichén Itzá and Uxmal are still wonder cities, Uxmal the older and smaller, because of its marvelous sculpture, and Chichén Itzá because of its impressive grandeur. There are various other beautiful ruins of that period, among them Tulum on the eastern coast and Labna and Sayil in the interior.

During the time of the great cultures in the south and in the Valley of Mexico, other high civilizations, whose influence extended over vast areas, flourished in the intermediate regions. In Vera Cruz the important ceremonial center was El Tajin, the pyramid that stands in the jungle forests near Papantla, with terraces and handsome sculptures. It is believed to have been constructed by the Totonacs during the time of the Maya Old Empire. The attractive sculptures of laughing boys' heads and the mysterious, richly carved yokes are also attributed to the same people.

During that period of high cultures, from about A.D. 500 to 1000, the Zapotecs of Oaxaca lived their "Golden Age," during which they constructed their magnificent ceremonial center of Monte Alban. It is dramatically situated on a mountain top, dominating the City and

Valley of Oaxaca. The mountain was terraced, and temples and pyramids were constructed on platforms around plazas.

Later the Mixtecs began to wage wars against the Zapotecs and occupied Monte Alban for some time. Judging from the dazzling objects discovered in the famous tomb of Monte Alban in 1931, the Mixtecs were also superb artists. These are known as "The Jewels of Monte Alban" and are now on exhibit in the State Museum of Oaxaca City. They consist of strings of pearls and golden beads, turquoise and jade ornaments, exquisitely wrought golden masks, elaborate necklaces of golden beads hung with little bells. In the collection are also finely carved deer and jaguar bones, objects of shell, onyx, and jade, and a very marvelous rock-crystal goblet.

A few centuries later there was a Zapotec renaissance, during which time the temples and palaces at Mitla were constructed, in the Valley of Oaxaca. The name Mitla is derived from the Aztec word mictlan, meaning "Place of the Dead," which was probably a burial place for kings. The Mitla zone now has one large mound with a superstructure, and a group of handsome temples and palaces on platforms surrounding spacious courts. The buildings are adorned with extraordinarily beautiful mosaics of cut stones in scrolls and greques.

The Zapotec calendar, system of writing, religious practices, and arts resemble those of the Mayas but show independent traits. Their early history is lost in myth and speculation, yet there is no uncertainty concerning the greatness of their architecture and plastic arts. In the end they were probably dominated by the Aztecs.

Throughout western Mexico there were a number of independent cultures, noted for their fine ceramic sculptures. Outstanding among them was the Tarascan in the region of Lake Pátzcuaro, which preserved Archaic traits and attained a very human expression. At the time of the Conquest, the Tarascan Capital was at Tzintzuntzan, "Place of humming birds" in Tarascan, on Lake Pátzcuaro, Michoacán. Among the Tarascan artifacts are fine pieces of sculpture, pottery, and idols. The Tarascans were famous for their weaving with hummingbird feathers. And their men were expert in the art of spear-throwing. Their early history also is lost in myth and legend.

The last of the great pre-Columbian civilizations was that of the Aztecs in the Valley of Mexico. They are called "The Romans of the New World" as the Mayas are the Greeks, because of similarities in traits, achievements, and historical roles. While the Mayas excelled in the arts and sciences, the Aztecs achieved fame as warriors and organizers, availing themselves of the knowledge and experiences of the more civilized peoples who had come before them. Aztec history was short-lived but extraordinarily brilliant. In one century the Aztecs changed from a nomadic tribe to a dominating force in the entire country, and during another they were able to enjoy power and luxury on a splendid scale. Then in one year everything that they had gained in the previous two centuries was tragically wiped out by the Spaniards.

The Aztecs were one of the seven Nahua tribes, known as the Chichimecas or barbarians. According to their own calendar and chronicles they left the caves of their mythical origin in A.D. 1168, to seek a permanent home. After almost a century of adventurous wanderings, they settled on one of the islands of Lake Texcoco in the Valley of Mexico in 1325. Legend has it that they were influenced in their choice by seeing an enormous eagle perched on a nopal, or prickly-pear cactus, holding a serpent in its huge claws, and with wings outstretched to the rising sun. Such an omen their war god Huitzilopochtli told them to look for on the site for their future city. They called it Tenochtitlán, "Place Where Nopals Grow," now Mexico City.

The Aztecs were still at the height of their power when the Spaniards came. Tenochtitlán was a handsome city with palatial homes set in beautiful gardens along canals. The Templo Mayor, or Great Temple, stood on what is now the Zócalo or main plaza. Connected with it were schools for warriors and priests, music and the dance. The ruling classes wore rich garments and unique jewels of gold and precious stones. They lived well, but all phases of their lives, including their sports and entertainment, were dominated by religion. Every activity, from the highest to the lowliest, was under some deity, and over all of them ruled Huitzilopochtli, the god of war.

The gods and priests were numerous and they made constant demands on the people. They were not content with prayers, penance, dramas, chants, food, beautiful dances and music, but exacted human hearts. Thus the Aztecs fought their wars not for territorial acquisition but to capture slaves to offer to their gods, and for tribute.

The Maya and all the other groups were equally under the domination of their gods, but they were less cruel. None of them exacted human sacrifices to the extent of the Aztecs.

The Aztec gods, like those of all the other cultures, were represented not as humans but according to their attributes, partly serpent, animal, or bird or with astral and natural elements. Aztec sculptors were great artists in fashioning their idols to express in stone their conception of life and death, endowing them with such great subjective reality that they were overpowering works of art in their barbaric ugliness.

Some of the Mexican gods were deified for having accomplished notable things, while others were of miraculous origin, and represent the natural elements. In the fantastic legends about them, they are both kindly and cruel, beautiful and ugly.

Huitzilopochtli, usually shown in the dress of a humming bird, is said to have been conceived by his mother, Coatlicue, from a ball of down which fell from heaven and which she placed in her bosom. When her other children, led by the moon, accused her of improper conduct because they doubted the story of the divine conception, Huitzilopochtli sprang from her womb as the sun, armed with a sunbeam to kill the moon and the stars.

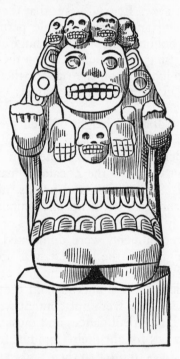

COATLICUE
(Mother of the Gods)

The statue of Coatlicue, the goddess of earth, the sun, moon, stars, and all mankind, in the National Museum of Mexico City, is one of the great Aztec works of art. As her name implies, she wears a skirt of entwined serpents, and the rest of her is a composition of claws, skulls, and snakes, with necklaces of hearts and hands—a fear-inspiring synthesis of the good and bad elements of the earth and mankind.

Huitzilopochtli is the sun, the youthful warrior, born anew each morning from the body of the earth goddess. Each evening he dies again so that the world of the dead may be illuminated by the fleeting light of his passing. Every morning when he comes to life, he fights with his brothers, the stars and the moon, to put them to flight, his victory signifying for man the dawn of a new day of life. Day after day this heavenly struggle is renewed. The sun must be strong and vigorous to meet and vanquish, with sweeps of his gold-tipped spear, his enemies who are the stars of the firmament of the north and south.

Huitzilopochtli, warrior and sun god, must needs be fed to be kept vitally strong, but not with the lowly food of mortals. He must be kept supplied with the stuff of eternal life, chalchihuatl, the magic liquid that flows through the swelling veins of man, where it slowly turns into the terrible nectar of the gods. And it is the duty of the Aztecs, the chosen children of this god, to supply him with the human victims.

When the Great Temple of Tenochtitlán was completed and dedicated to Huitzilopochtli, some authors say as many as twenty thousand slaves were sacrificed, and during all his fiestas human sacrifices were offered him, as well as to other gods and goddesses, although in lesser numbers. This is the great stigma upon the civilization of the Aztecs! Yet which of the civilizations of the twentieth century can point a finger? What religious faith can justify the infinitely greater number of human sacrifices offered now during wars and at other times to our gods of ambition and injustice?

In matters of ordinary conduct, the standards of the Aztecs were as high as ours, but their laws were more rigidly enforced. Since these were practically the same among the Mayas and other groups, it is interesting to quote the opinions of Fray Diego de Landa, first Bishop of Yucatán immediately after the Conquest, who describes life in a more human and intimate manner than other early chroniclers.

Maya men were of pleasing appearance, in spite of the fact that to enhance their good looks their heads and foreheads were flattened and they were made cross-eyed at birth. Often they were bow-legged as a result of being carried astride the mother's hip in infancy. Their ears were pierced and torn by sacrifices. They wore their hair short on top but long and braided below and they never allowed beards to grow. The men were clean, delighting in perfumes, and used bouquets of flowers and sweet-smelling herbs. Only men used mirrors, and they painted their faces and bodies. For breeches they wound a band of cloth a hand wide around the waist, with one end falling in back and the other in front, both embroidered with feathers. Their only other garment was a square piece of cotton cloth, tied over one shoulder. Their sandals were of hemp or untanned deer skin.

The women Landa considered generally better-looking than the Spanish, adding that they did not make up "as our nation does." It was a mark of elegance to file the teeth as sharp as those of a saw, a task performed by older women with certain stones and water. The women bathed often and tattooed the upper part of the body, with the exception of the breasts, but with finer designs than those used by the men. They anointed their breasts, arms, and shoulders as did their husbands, with a red ointment, sometimes adding to it a rare, sticky, scented gum preparation resembling liquid amber. The women took extreme care of their hair, wearing it long and making elegant coiffures. Their one garment consisted of a straight skirt, drawn in at the waist and open at the sides. Some women of other places covered their breasts with a piece of cotton cloth tied under the armpits.

In spite of their semi-nakedness and public bathing, the women were modest and chaste, prudent, sociable, and extremely generous. They had many children and were good mothers. The poorer ones not only worked in the home but also helped their husbands in the fields and in the raising of the animals, often nursing young deer to tame them. Both boys and girls were taught to respect their elders and to fear their gods. Some of the boys were educated outside of their homes by the priests.

ITZAMA, THE SKY GOD OF THE MAYAS
(Dresden Codex)

The Mayas, like the Aztecs, had big monthly festivals to some one of their important deities and various smaller ones for the lesser gods, celebrated with dances, music, special food, and ritual drinking. Both Aztec and Maya men purified themselves for the religious ceremonies by fasting several days, abstaining from salt and pepper in their stews, and from sleeping with their wives. The women had their separate dances but occasionally danced with the men.

Punishments for offenses were very severe. A Maya adulterer was turned over to the offended husband, who had the right to pardon or to kill. The woman concerned was in great disgrace and was often deserted by her husband. Homicides were dealt with by the relatives, who either inflicted death upon the criminal or made him pay in material goods for the life he had taken. Ordinary thieves were reduced to slavery, but if the offender was a noble or leader, he was made to suffer the ignominy of having his face tattooed in public. The rich were dealt the same justice as the poor; money could not buy escape from any hardships. If anything, the Aztecs were even crueler in their punishments.

TLALOC, GOD OF RAIN
(Florentine Codex)

When on the threshold of death, Maya men confessed their sins in the presence of witnesses, either to priests or relatives. Theft, homicide, false testimony, and weaknesses of the flesh were the commonest offenses. If, as sometimes happened, the dying recovered after a confession, there were embarrassing complications, especially between husband and wife.

Returning to the Aztecs, further descriptions of their customs and arts are given throughout the text of the book, since more is known about them than about any of the other pre-Conquest peoples.

The story of the Conquest of Mexico is well known. It was accomplished in a comparatively short time—from 1519 to 1521—but the Spaniards did not achieve it by themselves as is commonly believed, even with their horses and gunpowder. They were clever enough to enlist the help of the enemies of the Aztecs, without whose assistance they might have been defeated. To get an idea of how amazing it all was—the valor and cruelty of the Spaniards and the strange and wonderful world they were fighting in—one must read the story of the Conquest by Bernal Díaz del Castillo, one of Cortés' soldiers, of which there is an excellent translation in English; also, "The Conquest of Mexico" by Prescott.

The story of what happened to the natives after the Conquest is also well known. The Spaniards offered the natives one God, but with many images of Christ, the Virgin, and saints to replace their deities. The new God did not exact human sacrifices, but the Spaniards themselves outraged women, killed and enslaved men, and set up the Inquisition.

There were good priests, like Las Casas, who protested violently against the cruelty and injustice of his own people, and like Motolinía, who established the first school for native boys in Texcoco. There were also some good viceroys and other officials who were intelligent and just. Yet during the three centuries of Spanish domination in Mexico, the natives of all social classes who survived the bloody carnage of the Conquest throughout the country, with some few exceptions, became the peones, practically slaves, of the Spaniards. After Mexico freed itself from the Spanish yoke in 1821, the dominating classes continued the exploitation of the poor.

The Social Revolution of 1910–20 was ostensibly fought to free the oppressed classes. Much has been done in education, social legislation, and other fields to improve conditions, but much remains to be done. This, too, is a familiar story but it will receive further mention in the text.

Now as we begin to turn the pages of the book, we shall meet the descendants of those whose civilizations have been so fleetingly touched upon in this Introduction, and those of many other peoples who were considered "inferior" by such aristocrats as the Aztecs. Many of them are still living in the remote mountain regions of the country on the fringe of the more "civilized" centers of population, in much the same way as they did in pre-Spanish days. There are Aztecs in the Valley of Mexico, and some in other parts of the country; Zapotecs and Mixtecs are still in Oaxaca, Totonacs in Vera Cruz, and Mayas in Yucatán. All of these peoples, who have forgotten about their past greatness, still preserve ancient traditions and customs and the dignity of their ancestors.

PART ONE

WORK AND WORSHIP

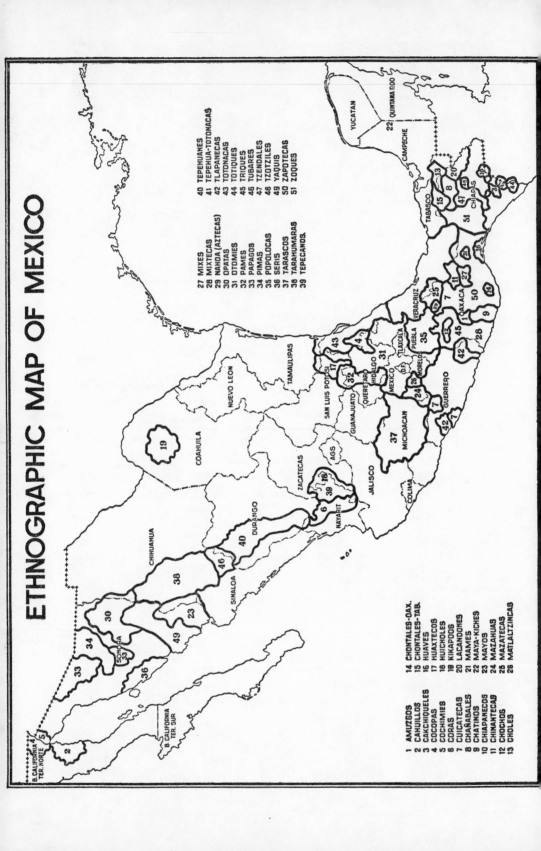

ETHNOGRAPHIC MAP OF MEXICO

27 MIXES
28 MIXTECAS
29 NAHOA (AZTECAS)
30 OPATAS
31 OTOMIES
32 PAMES
33 PAPAGOS
34 PIMAS
35 POPOLOCAS
36 SERIS
37 TARASCOS
38 TARAHUMARAS
39 TEPECANOS.

40 TEPEHUANES
41 TEPEHUA-TOTONACAS
42 TLAPANECAS
43 TOTONACAS
44 TOTIQUES
45 TRIQUES
46 TUBARES
47 TZENDALES
48 TZOTZILES
49 YAQUIS
50 ZAPOTECAS
51 ZOQUES

1 AMUZGOS
2 CAHUILLOS
3 CAKCHIQUELES
4 COCOPAS
5 COCHIMIES
6 CORAS
7 CUICATECAS
8 CHAÑABALES
9 CHATINOS
10 CHIAPANECOS
11 CHINANTECAS
12 CHOCHOS
13 CHOLES

14 CHONTALES-OAX.
15 CHONTALES-TAB.
16 HUAVES
17 HUAXTECOS
18 HUICHOLES
19 KIKAPOOS
20 LACANDONES
21 MAMES
22 MAYA-KICHES
23 MAYOS
24 MAZAHUAS
25 MAZATECAS
26 MATLALTZINCAS

WORK AND WORSHIP

To live by bread alone is generally the lot of the poor, but this does not apply to the Mexican folk. On occasion many of them may lack sufficient food, but nearly always the majority have something beautiful to use—a handsomely hand-woven garment, a lovely pot or bowl. Like their pre-Conquest ancestors, most of the present-day natives are artists, making objects of great beauty. Even the poorest have never completely divorced beauty from utility.

Religion is also closely wedded to utility because the folk believe that nothing can succeed without the help of the gods. The well-known categories into which we divide our lives—economic, social, religious, artistic—do not exist in their world. For them all these aspects are integrated and form a part of daily living.

After the Conquest in 1521, the culture of the country became a mixture of aboriginal and Spanish elements. The natives adopted the materials, techniques, and ideas introduced by the Spaniards, which they were able to utilize and understand, but also preserving their own as much as possible.

For several hundred years after the Conquest, the Mexican markets were supplied chiefly by the handmade goods of the natives. In the nineteenth century, articles from other countries began to reach Mexico and later the manufacture of cotton textiles and some few other products began. Since about the end of the nineteenth century, Mexican markets have been flooded with all sorts of machine-made articles, especially the cheap products from Germany and Japan, which competed with the native handicrafts.

In recent years even some of the most conservative natives have begun to use a few modern household objects and implements. The process has been slow because of lack of means, a natural resistance to change, and fear of the unaccustomed. However, where the village folk are in contact with city ways of life, the progressive ones are adopting new customs and purchasing as many modern objects as they can afford.

Communities

The natives live in communities ranging in size from a few families to hundreds. The smallest places are the rancherías or parajes, both meaning small settlements; the larger, pueblos and ciudades, or villages and cities. As the rancherías are scattered, being located near fields and places of work, their inhabitants gather at a central one or at a village for fiestas, for the administration of the law, and for trade. Such groups, or those living in villages, have different customs. Though they speak the same language, local differences also appear. They consider the area circumscribed by their common religious and secular activities as separate and apart from the rest of the country— it is their own "tierra y patria chica," their own little world and fatherland.

Place names consist of an indigenous one alone or combined with that of the patron saint, but large cities often bear only Spanish names or those of Mexican heroes. The indigenous names are sometimes poetic descriptions of some characteristic of the place. Mixcoac, a suburb of Mexico City, means "The Snake of Clouds," so named because it rains there more than elsewhere in the vicinity. Xochimilco, also a suburb, means "Flower Gardens," as flowers grew there in Aztec days and still do. Texcoztingo means "Laughing Hills," a lovely hillside not far from Mexico City, where the Texcoco rulers built their palaces. Chalco, "Many Mouths," is so called because of its canals.

Many villages consist of scattered huts, often clustering around a fine church. But the older, larger, and more important ones are laid out like the cities—a central plaza with streets radiating from it in all directions. On the plaza are the church, government buildings, and principal stores. The plaza is usually a fine garden spot, shaded by lovely old trees, with a bandstand in the center and seats all around. It is the center for religion, law, commerce, and social life.

The social aspect of the plazas is the most important. It is a meeting place, where the people love to loiter whether for business or pleasure. One or more nights a week, depending upon custom, there are band concerts, called serenatas or serenades. During these, the paseo or promenade takes place, when the more progressive or citified boys and girls circle around to the music, separately but in opposite directions—an opportunity for flirting. On national or religious fiesta days, the plazas are more animated. They are often decorated with colored china paper streamers and additional lights; there are more objects and foods for sale and more music.

Houses and Ceremonies

Primitive houses are simple, inexpensive, picturesque, and often perfectly adapted to their environment. The materials and techniques for construction today are practically the same as before the Conquest. They are made of sticks or thin boards, roofed with palm leaves or grass; of poles or stones set in a mud mortar; of logs, or adobe bricks with thatched or tiled roofs; they are, in fact, made of anything suitable that the locality offers. Floors are made of dried mud; fences, of stones and mud, or organ cactus. Often a simple hut is set in a lovely orchard and many humble houses have flowers and potted plants.

Houses are either round, square, oblong or rectangular, each place having its own style. The poorer ones consist of one windowless room, which serves all purposes. Sometimes a lean-to is added for a kitchen; a simple pen for animals; a troje or corncrib; and where custom demands, a temazcal or aboriginal sweatbath. The latter is low and small, with an opening just large enough to crawl into, and is used principally for therapeutic purposes (Pls. 12, 97, 98, 99).

In the more progressive villages, families of means often build several unconnected, one-room houses around a patio or court—one for a kitchen, one to sleep in, one for work. Some even have such modern features as windows, roofed porches, and outhouses. More modernized, well-to-do families sometimes construct masonry houses, in a style resembling the Mexican-Colonial—walls hard on the sidewalk, long grated windows, and a patio. In the poor neighborhoods of every city there are primitive adobe huts.

Public constructions are the Palacio Municipal or Municipal Palace —so called even if it be only an adobe hut—schools, small chapels, large crosses, and fountains or wells. They are of the best materials available in the vicinity, paid for by the community and constructed with communal labor. In some places the churches are no better than the huts of the people; in others, especially in the central states, they are fine old Colonial edifices. Revolutions and earthquakes have destroyed many churches, so that often one sees them in ruins. Or one may see a hut taking the place of a church, with the handsome old bells hanging nearby.

Masons are sometimes employed for special jobs, but generally a man builds his own house with the help of relatives and friends, whom he helps in return. Occasionally, the helpers even furnish their own food, but there is always a feast and usually a ceremony when the house is about to be occupied. The ceremonies are different in every place, as are the beliefs with respect to making the house strong and free from evil spirits.

In the village of San Pedro Chenahlo, Chiapas, the wood for the new house is cut during the period of the full moon, so that it may last a long time.[1] The friends who help in the construction bring their own food each day, for nothing is offered them until the house is finished. Then a turkey is killed and cooked and a little of the broth is sprinkled from the mouth or spilled from a small gourd vessel around the base of every post, while prayers are being said for the safety of the house and its inmates. Afterwards drinks are offered. Next, an old man lights the first fire in the middle of the house—it has to be an old man, or otherwise the poles of the house will "bite" everyone who enters. Finally, all the guests are invited to partake of food, drinks, and cigarettes.

In Cancuc, another village in the highlands of Chiapas, the friends who help in the building are given simple food each day. When everything but the roof is done, the owner serves a meal of pork just before the grass for the roofing is to be brought in. After the roof is finished, a new cross is placed in the house before which the mistress prays for three days. During that time there is no physical contact between husband and wife. If they did not observe this rule, both would "become ill and die." [2]

To insure a new house and its inmates from harm through envy or witchcraft, in Yalalag, Oaxaca, the proprietor places at the four corners of the foundation small pine crosses, each of which is sprinkled with the blood of chickens previously beheaded for the purpose. The resinous pine of the crosses acts as a defense against real lightning, as well as against the sorcerers who take the form of lightning. Here, also, the wood for the house is cut during the time of the full moon, and friends co-operate in the construction. Not only is their help returned in kind, but food also is served.[3]

In some of the conservative Mixe villages of Oaxaca, the new-house ceremony consists of killing a turkey or rooster and sprinkling the blood over the floor. Then some of the blood is mixed with pinole, a corn powder, and buried in a hole in the center of the house. All those who helped are invited to a feast at which are served the sacrificed fowl and tepache, an intoxicating drink.

The only new-house ceremonies recorded by students of Huichol culture are in connection with the god-houses and temples, which are more important to the Huichols than their dwellings.

For roofing a god-house, the shaman selects the necessary bunches of grass and solemnly places bamboo sticks over them. After this he and his assistant make four grass opossums, which they adorn with parrot feathers, to symbolize prayers for rain, and with macaw plumes, to express reverence for the fire and the sun. When the animals are finished, the shaman spits upon them several times and places his hands over them in a prayerful motion. Next the tempiske tree leaves are tied into a bundle to be hung under the roof to drive away evil. Then four young men climb upon the framework of the roof where they make a ceremonial circuit with great agility and tie the four animals to the rafters, one on each side, with their tails projecting above the ridge.

Before the thatching begins, the shaman presents the bamboo sticks to the four cardinal points, the heavens, and the earth. The same ceremony is repeated before each layer of thatch is put on. When the work is finished, all pray aloud, offering the house to the gods and asking for health in return.

The Otomís of San Pablito, in the sierra of the State of Hidalgo, perform their ceremony some time after they have lived in the house in return for the shelter it has given them. Should they forget to do so, the spirit of the house would become angry and make the owner ill.

A tree trunk of the same kind that has gone into the construction of the house is placed in its center, and on it is fixed an adornment woven of palm leaves, called a "sun." A white paper figure is fastened to the center of the "sun" and the walls of the altar are adorned with others of the same kind and color.

The sorcerer who performs the costumbre, as this ceremony is called, first "cleans" or "sweeps" the place with a magic bundle. While he is engaged in this task, four boys—one in each corner of the room—are shooting arrows at the tlapanco, a sort of wide shelf to keep things on, while four other boys, who are sitting on the shelf, shoot arrows at the ceiling. Finally, the sorcerer, who is also a musician, plays and dances around the tree with the eight boys.

The sorcerer prepares the magical bundles which he uses for all his ceremonies in the following manner. He cuts out several figures from the dark bark paper made by the natives for magical purposes. He places these on the ground in two rows over other paper of the same kind, with perforations forming two crosses or two flowers. These papers are called "beds" or "chairs" because the figures rest on them. In each of the corners of the rectangle formed by the figures, the sorcerer places a lighted candle. Then he prays in Otomí, after which he kills a chicken by cutting its neck with a scissors and sprinkles the figures with its blood, while singing, dancing, and jumping around on them. After this performance, he wraps up the chicken with the papers and figures into a bundle for the "cleaning."

A different kind of ceremony takes place in the Aztec villages of Acatempan and Chapa, Guerrero. When a man is building his house, he looks for padrinos or godparents. On the day it is to be occupied, they come with friends, playing music and bringing two flower-decked crosses, brandy, firecrackers, cigarettes, rosaries of flowers, and wreaths hung with roses made of dough. The gifts are placed on a board carried by two youths, one at each end. As the guests approach the house, they throw firecrackers at it, while the band plays

A—MAKING PAPER   B—FIGURE MADE OF BARK PAPER

lively tunes. The host receives the group at the door with polite and allusive speeches. After everyone has entered, the padrinos place one of the crosses on the altar with a lighted candle on each side, blowing incense over everything from a small pottery censer, and saying prayers. Following this act, one of the group climbs to the roof amid bursting firecrackers and the playing of the band, to place the other cross on its peak. Then, after more polite exchanges between the host and padrinos, they hang the rosaries on each other's necks. The affair ends with a fiesta in the old house, where mole de olla (beef cooked in red chile sauce), drinks, and cigarettes are served. The party continues with music until everyone becomes very gay. It sometimes ends disastrously.

The detail of bread as an adornment is also part of the roofing fiesta in the Tarascan village of Cheran, Michoacán. Here the breads are hung on the long narrow belts used by women and are in the shape of animals, chiefly little bulls. Birds, mules, and other animals are made of painted corn husks, stuffed with pinole (powdered corn). All these are tied together with small thin wheat tortillas (pancakes) and paper flowers.

When the fiesta is well under way with food, drinks, cigarettes, and music, many of the women go with the musicians to bring the wife's relatives, who have been preparing the cuelgas or gifts. When they return, some of the adorned sashes are hung on the houseowner and other men guests, including the master carpenter and relatives. Dancing and drinking continue until late into the night.

In most Catholicized villages, the ceremonies consist chiefly in placing a blessed cross in the foundation or walls or the roof when the house is being built. On completion, the house is blessed by the priest or some pious person, with holy water and incense. Often fiestas take place with food, drinks, cigarettes, firecrackers, and even dancing. In many places the custom exists of looking for padrinos to pay most of the expenses.

House Furnishings

The furnishings of primitive houses are reduced to mere essentials, most of them of pre-Conquest origin. They consist mainly of something to cook on and in, to eat from, and to sleep on.

The most common type of hearth is the tlacuil, formed of three stones to support a comal or clay griddle for baking and toasting. Kitchen utensils are ollas or clay pots for cooking, pottery bowls and mugs for food, or little gourd vessels in regions where the calabash trees grow. Large gourds are shaped into food and water containers. The fingers and pieces of tortilla, a thin corn pancake which is the native's bread, take the place of knives and forks; each piece of tortilla is formed into a spoon and eaten with the food.

Every household has at least one metate, the three-legged stone with its mano or long roller for grinding corn; a molcajete or stone mortar and pestle for chiles and tomatoes; wooden bowls and stirring spoons; the chiquihuites, or aboriginal types of baskets without handles, and some modern ones; clay water jars of various sizes and shapes for carrying and keeping water, although in some places they are replaced by tin cans; and the ubiquitous machete, the long and wide-curved or straight steel knife that serves many purposes. Other accessories depend upon the environment and the occupations of the family. They nearly always include some few primitive agricultural implements, for practically everybody raises corn.

A petate or reed mat spread on the ground in the daytime takes the place of chairs, and at night becomes the bed, mattress, and pillow. Some of the northwest natives sleep on skins, and hammocks are used in the tropics; or the petates are placed on rustic beds made of sticks or boards because it is considered dangerous to sleep on the ground. Such beds are used also in villages of higher altitudes. Wooden boxes, small hammocks, and petates, or nets attached to curved bamboo handles serve as cradles. Occasionally there are a few low stools or benches.

METATE

The note of color in a hut is the household altar. It is a small table, real or improvised, on which stand gayly dressed images or colored chromos or oil paintings of the patron saints of the family. It also contains bright fresh or artificial flowers in vases or bottles; candles, and incense burners. Among the Mayas, the highland natives of Chiapas and those of the northwest, where crosses are used more than images, several small crosses are placed on the altar or one large one is placed in the yard. Often, colored calendars and pictures clipped from papers adorn the walls of huts.

Clothes are either rolled up and put on a shelf, hung up, or kept in wooden boxes. Other valuables are carefully hidden, and where there is much money, it is generally buried; this accounts for so many stories about ghosts coming back to look for hidden treasures.

All sorts of objects hang from the rafters. Sometimes they are the heads and jaws of animals that have been killed in hunting. In Chenahlo, they are kept hanging so that the live animals of the same kind may not be offended and do harm to the man on his next hunting trip. Also, in practically every house in Chenahlo, Cancuc, Oxchuc, and in other villages of the highlands of Chiapas, an ofrenda or offering is hung to Chin-Uch, a tiny almost invisible fly, so that it may not come to spoil the pozole corn dish. The offering consists of various diminutive objects—a ball of pozole wrapped in a banana leaf; a red chile, a tortilla, an ear of corn, a little stick of the kind used for stirring the kernels as they are being toasted; cigarettes, beans,

TLACUIL

salt—all put into a cornhusk.[1] In Catholicized households, blessed palm is hung over the door to keep away lightning and evil spirits.

One is frequently surprised at finding Singer sewing machines in primitive villages, remote from all civilization. But the explanation is that the Singer Sewing Machine Company has a good sales system, and the machine is both useful and fascinating to the natives. Here and there, where least expected, an old fashioned phonograph, perhaps with a flaring horn, is found.

The more progressive families of means have tables, chairs, beds, wardrobes, some china dishes, glasses, a few knives, forks and spoons, and some modern kitchenware. On the other hand, there are families that have money, and others that, although poor, could afford the homemade stools, beds, and other improvements, but prefer not to change their traditional way of living. Such families or persons are called cerrados, meaning "closed to new ideas," and are to be found in all the advanced neighborhoods.

Primitive peoples prefer to sit and sleep either on or close to the ground, but the cerrados of Yalalag rationalize their preferences. They say it is safer to sleep on the ground because the earth is "soft" and "warm" and it is good to maintain contact with it; a high bed makes it possible for the "air" to enter and gives one the sensation of height and the danger of falling; boards are hard and if of pine, the resin makes them "very hot." The ground or low stools are safer, because if one is obliged to sit for any length of time on a bench or chair of ordinary height, he becomes sleepy or may get inflammation in his legs. Shoemakers and other artisans use low seats when working, but officials in discharge of their duties sit on chairs or benches of customary size.[2]

Huts are always unpleasantly dark and smoky because they have no windows or smoke vents, but fortunately in many regions the Mexican climate is such that there is little need to stay indoors beyond the time necessary for eating and sleeping. The poorer people get their light at night either from the hearth fire or a pine stick, while others can afford a candle or kerosene flare.

Food

The basic foods are still corn, beans, and squashes, prepared mostly as before the Conquest. Corn foods are the most important because the natives live on them alone for days and weeks at a time, especially when away from home; also they are preferred for offerings to the pagan gods.

The most prominent of the corn foods are tortillas—the unleavened thin pancakes of different sizes—the bread of the natives for many centuries. They are made of the kernels, cooked slightly and soaked over night in lime water, in which state they are called nixtamal; then they are ground on the metate into a paste called masa or dough. In some places the tortillas are formed on banana leaves, but more generally they are patted with both hands to the desired size and thickness, after which they are immediately baked on the comal. The patting of tortillas is one of the most familiar and vital of all Mexican rhythms.

As tortillas are consumed in great quantities at every meal, the grinding requires long hours of back-breaking work daily. In recent years molinos de nixtamal, or grinding mills, have been established in the larger, more progressive places, where the nixtamal is ground by electricity for a few centavos. But some families cannot afford even this small expenditure, while the cerrados prefer their wives to do the grinding. There is a general belief that when the nixtamal is ground on the metate, the tortillas taste better.

Corn dough is the base for many other foods besides tortillas. There are the different kinds of tamales, which are eaten by the natives chiefly on festive days, but on any day by city people. They are about the size and shape of a small banana, either plain or filled with beans or meats, flavored with chile or sweetened and steamed in corn husks or in banana leaves. Other simple corn foods are atoles or gruels, sometimes flavored with chocolate and generally sweetened with sugar or honey. In Chiapas, Yucatán, and Oaxaca, corn paste mixed with water is called pozole. Men take it to the fields or on long trips in a banana leaf and add water just before eating. Pinole, a powder of toasted corn, serves the same purpose; it is also used in combination with other foods and makes a delicious drink when sweetened with honey.

In addition to the simple corn foods, there are the complicated ones that form part of the diet of the progressive, well-to-do folk as well as of all other social classes. All Mexicans, poor and rich, eat tortillas. Of the complicated corn foods the outstanding ones are the tacos—beans, cheese, or meats, wrapped in tortillas, seasoned with chile and fried; and enchiladas, which are tacos covered with chile sauce to which sour cream is sometimes added. Tortillas fried crisp and covered with similar ingredients are called tostados. Turnovers of corn dough, filled with cheese, potatoes, squash flowers or huitlacoches—the Aztec name for the black mushroom-like growth on the corn—are called quesadillas. All these are among the popular Mexican dishes called antojitos.

The poor prepare their food very simply. Corn cakes, kernels and squash seeds are baked or toasted on the comal; coffee, teas, and meats are boiled near the fire under it. Earth pits are sometimes used for outdoor cooking, and meats for fiestas are either roasted over big fires or cooked in huge clay bowls out of doors.

Warm beverages consist of coffee or a variety of "teas"—boiled water flavored with canela or cinnamon, fusions with the yellow camomile flowers, mint, lemon, dried orange leaves and blossoms, all sweetened with piloncillo, brown sugar or honey. Chocolate, which is a luxury for some, is still beaten to a froth with a wooden beater in the primitive manner.

All cooked foods are well seasoned, and tortillas and beans are always eaten with spicy sauces of chile and tomatoes. *Moles*, from *molli* in Aztec, are the chile sauces in which meats are cooked or served. The richest *moles* are those that go with guajolote, the Aztec name for turkey; they are made of a variety of chiles, spices, sesame seed, ground almonds, and chocolate. There are brown, black, and green *moles*, the seasoning different in every region but always hot and spicy. *Mole de guajolote* is the most festive Mexican dish. It is served in the best restaurants and homes, but only the well-to-do natives can afford it for fiestas.

A favorite Lenten dish in all homes is the leaves of the nopal or prickly-pear cactus, cooked with chile; its fruits, called tunas, are eaten with salt. The white succulent maguey worms, fried crisp in lard, are a delicacy; they are served in the better Mexico City restaurants as are frogs' legs.

Progressive natives of means add white bread and other European foods to their diet, while the daily fare of the poor is mostly tortillas and beans. Some of them, though, who live away from the centers of civilization, like the primitive groups of Chiapas, Oaxaca, Yucatán, and the northwest, eat quite well some of the time. They hunt, fish, gather herbs and wild fruit; plant some vegetables and fruit trees.

But even where these natural foods abound, there are lean months between harvests in some places. Here also custom plays an important part. The basic native foods now, as many centuries ago, are corn, beans, and squash; substitutes do not satisfy them. In some places the federal government, through its rural schools and agricultural agencies, has improved the food situation by teaching truck gardening and modern methods in agriculture.

Natives occasionally fix squash with brown sugar or some other sweet, but they do not make desserts. However, many of them eat the inexpensive dulces or sweets so temptingly displayed at big fiestas and at all times in the larger markets. They are made of fruits, milk, sugar, or seeds in brightly colored bird and animal forms. Mexican food appeals to the eye as well as to the palate.

The festal foods of the progressive natives consist of the more expensive dishes, such as *mole de guajolote*, tamales and as many other good things as they can afford. For the Mayas, Huichols and some other groups, they take on a sacred character. Before fiestas, ceremonial hunts for deer and other wild animals take place, which together with cattle are sacrificed to the pagan gods. When their meats are cooked, they are again offered to the gods before being eaten. The Huichols make tiny tortillas and tamales for their gods; also small corn cakes in animal forms, some of which are strung to form necklaces to hang on altars and prayer arrows.[1] The Mayas of Chan Kom and Quintana Roo prepare their ritual foods in earth ovens or pits in the ground, those for the pagan gods being more numerous and receiving greater care.

Breads in animal and human forms, generally made of white flour, are common everywhere for the Day of the Dead, November 2, when they are offered to the dead and later eaten by the living.[2]

The importance of foods has given rise to various beliefs. Tortillas of yellow corn are preferred in Yalalag because they are considered "more sustaining" than those of other colors; it takes only a few of them to satisfy one's hunger as compared to many of the others. There is a similar belief with respect to water—that from the village fountain quenches one's thirst immediately, which is not so if one drinks from a private well.[3]

The most significant belief in connection with food is its classification as "hot" or "cold." The assignment of foods to these categories has little if anything to do with actual temperature, but rather with the qualities ascribed to them. The Mayas of X-Cacal believe that the easily digested foods which stimulate heat in the body are "hot," those which are difficult to digest and reduce heat are "cold." Some of the foods considered very "cold" by the Mayas of Chan Kom are peccary, wild turkey, rice, boiled eggs, papaya, limes, pork, squash, certain bananas, the meat of large deer; some very "hot" ones are coffee, beef, honey, pinole; intermediate ones are oranges, pineapple, sweet potatoes, domestic fowl, pigeon, tomatoes, sugar cane, beans, atole, meat of small deer, tortillas. The mixture of two opposites produces an intermediate; of two of the same kind, an extreme. Vegetation that stays fresh and green the longest is "cold." The pagan gods of the Mayas prefer "cold" foods, so those prepared for them in the earth ovens are considered "cold" even when they are hot. The classifications may vary somewhat here and there, but they are just as arbitrary. In Yalalag, for example, tortillas are "hot" on the day they are baked even when they have become cold and are not warmed for the next meal.

Persons are also classified as "hot" and "cold" among some of the groups. The X-Cacal Mayas believe that a "hot" person drives away the bees because they do not like the heat; that a "cold" person cannot easily light a fire in the primitive manner. The Zapotecs of Yalalag say the human body is "hot" but not excessively so; that it changes with the temperature—cold in the morning, hot at noon, and cold again at night.

"Hot" or "cold" foods may cause illness or help in cures. There is a general belief among all Mexicans that hot food and drinks are good for chills; cold, for fevers.[4]

Liquors and Ritual Drinks

Every region has its own special intoxicating drinks; pulque, tequila, and mezcal being the most widely known, and imbibed by all social classes. Tequila is manufactured from the small agave plants in the village of Tequila, Jalisco. It is customary to take it with salt and

TLACHIQUERO EMPTYING A MAGUEY PLANT

lemon; one licks a little salt held in the hollow between the thumb and forefinger of the left hand and sucks on a piece of lemon, but good drinkers take it straight. Tequila is said to cure many ills. As a remedy for a cold, one must drink it until he sees double the number of bottles actually before him. Mezcal comes from the State of Oaxaca and is fermented from the hearts of maguey plants after they are baked. There is a popular saying about mezcal—"Para todo mal mezcal y para todo bien también," which translated freely means that mezcal is good for all ills but also for all good times.

Other states have their own special brands of aguardientes or liquors, mostly of sugar cane, bearing such different names as charanda in Michoacán, refino in Vera Cruz, comiteco in Chiapas, sotol in

Nayarit. In Yucatán it is xtabentun, made of flowers of the same name; Toluca, in the State of Mexico, specializes in liquors flavored with all kinds of fruit.

All the commercial liquors are used for fiestas and ceremonies in most places, but the more primitive groups make their own ritual drinks. Among the Huichols and Tarahumaras of the northwest it is a corn beer called tesgüino; in the states of Oaxaca and Vera Cruz, tepache, pulque sweetened with honey or brown sugar; among the highland tribes of Chiapas, chicha of sugar cane. The Chamulas, who are the traders of that region, always sell chicha near a cross adorned with pine needles and flowers, whether along the highways or in the village plazas.

Pulque

Pulque, made from the juice of the agave or maguey plants and called octli before the Conquest, is one of the oldest and most wide-spread of the intoxicating drinks of Mexico. It is said to have been discovered by the Toltecs about the tenth century A.D. and popular-ized by Xochitl, a young woman of high rank. The imbibing of it too freely is one of the various reasons advanced for the downfall of her people.

Among the Aztecs, as now, pulque was both a ceremonial drink and a tipple, but only old men were permitted to become intoxicated with impunity. Drunkenness in young men was severely punished—for an excess of it the poor were clubbed to death in public to serve as an example and the rich were executed privately.

The Aztec goddess Mayauel represented the maguey plants, and her four hundred sons were associated with pulque. Their animal was the rabbit and complete drunkenness was described in the picture writings by the signs indicating four hundred rabbits; lesser degrees by smaller numbers.

Ometochtli or "Two Rabbit" was the most important of the pulque gods, but the best known one at the present time is Tepoztecatl, the tribal god and hero of Tepoztlán, Morelos. On the highest one of the hills surrounding the village stands a temple in his honor, and there are many legends current about him in the region, several of which are included in Part Four.

Pulque was considered sacred by the Aztecs, who used it as an offering to their gods, especially to the god of fire. Vessels contain-ing the drink were placed in front of the fire, or some of it was sprin-kled or spilled around the hearth. Pulque was also used as an offering at weddings and funerals and for medicinal purposes.[1]

Maguey plants grow best on arid lands at high altitudes. In large sections of the states of Mexico, Hidalgo, Puebla, and Tlaxcala, where enormous pulque haciendas are located, one sees vast fields of maguey set in even rows, their strong well-shaped, blue-green leaves rising from the ground in graceful curves—an exotic sight in the bright Mexican sunshine. The magueys are reproduced from shoots that germinate at the bottom of the mature plants. These are cut off and given sun and air treatment and kept in nurseries for a few years until they reach a height of several feet, when they are ready to be transplanted.

It takes from eight to twelve or more years before the plants can be exploited for pulque, those growing in the higher altitudes taking longer but yielding finer juices. The ripeness of the plant is indicated by a slight inward turning and yellowing of the leaves. Then the central leaves are cut off and the heart is pierced with a long knife, the process being technically known as "castration." Nothing more is done to the plant for a few months, during which time the aguamiel, honey-water or juice, has accumulated. Then a bowl is scraped to receive it. After this, the tlachiquero, the man with an acocote or long gourd with a hole at each end, empties the bowl by suction twice a day, scraping it each time with a sharp steel spoon and leaving it carefully covered. The merit of a good tlachiquero lies in knowing how to scrape the bowl so that only a very fine skin comes off the surface, as otherwise the plant will not last long. The skin is called metzal in Aztec and is fed to the pigs.

If the plants are not cut into on time, a tall stalk grows from the center, bearing quiotes or yellow flowers. They are good to eat when fried, but the plant is spoiled for pulque.

A maguey yields a few quarts of juice a day for some six months. After that it is finished for pulque, although it is still useful. Ixtli, the maguey fibre, is twisted into rope or spun into thread for weaving and the leaves are sometimes used in the construction of huts and fences. The same uses of the magueys were made before the Conquest, when, in addition, the thorns served for needles to sew with and for piercing the flesh for penance. The heart of the maguey makes a handsome decoration when cut into floral designs; it is also good to eat when baked with brown sugar. No part of the plant is wasted.

The juice from the plants is taken in pigskin containers to the tinacal or pulque brewery, and emptied into vats made of oxhide or wood. There are some well-equipped, sanitary tinacales, while others are just poorly lighted sheds. However, if good pulque is to be obtained, the process and ritual have to be the same in all of them. Cleanliness and prayers are necessary for success in the fermentation, so the vats are kept clean and every tinacal has its patron saint set upon a colorfully adorned shelf over the vats. When the "pulque-seed" is put into the juice, the men stand around bareheaded in an attitude of prayer; in fact, it is the custom for men to take their hats off on entering a tinacal as if it were a church. The "pulque-seed" is carefully prepared by the tinacalero or head brewer in a vat removed from all the others; it is made by fermenting the juice to putrefaction, the process being kept a secret.

Great care is taken of the vats during fermentation, which takes a few days, and certain taboos are observed. In some places no woman may approach them, especially if with child.

There are certain humorous customs in connection with receiving visitors to tinacales, especially those who come for the first time. In some it is necessary to drink a quart of pulque without stopping to breathe; if one fails, one must try again, thus must drink two quarts instead of one. After this feat, the visitor is invited to drink with all the men, passing the gourd from one to another—a sort of friendship token. The aim in all the tinacales is to get their visitors intoxicated, which is not difficult, for just to smell freshly fermented pulque seems sufficient to produce a hilarious condition.[2]

Pulque has an alcoholic potency about equal to that of beer, so one has to drink a great deal of it in order to get drunk. It is white, thick, and slightly sweet, which gives it a satisfying food quality, and it is even fed to children. Analyses have shown that pulque is rich in vitamins which counterbalance the high protein diet of the poor. In regions where the maguey plants abound, the natives supplement their insufficient diet with many quarts of pulque a day, and men go about befuddled from after the noon meal until the next morning. The men are encouraged to drink all they can pay for and although it is sold cheaply, some owners of pulque haciendas have made fortunes; even small tinacales are profitable.

All social classes drink pulque where there are tinacales, and it is not adulterated like that which is shipped to the cities. Some people "cure" their pulque with fruit juices, but real drinkers prefer it pure.

In cities and towns pulque is sold in pulquerías, where no other kind of drinks are served. Up to less than a century ago, before the days of cabarets, the pulquerías of Mexico City were patronized by writers, artists, monks, sports, soldiers, and gay women. They were immense huts with dirt floors into which men could enter on horseback and leave their horses tied to posts. Food was served, men gambled, and women entertained with singing and dancing.[3]

Now the pulquerías are like any small saloon, visited mostly by the working classes. The outside walls are painted by folk artists with allusive subjects, which sometimes illustrate their humorous and poetic names—"The Lady of the Night," a tragic looking lady in white with a romantic moon in the background; "Los Changos Vaciladores," a group of monkeys enjoying themselves. Other names are "Your Office," "Memories of the Future," "The Loves of Cupid," "Market of Flesh," "Let Us See What Happens," "I Am Laughing," "Wise Men Without Study." Both in the names and the paintings (the latter occasionally excellent works of art) is expressed the Mexican love of bright colors, their irony and their unique mocking humor —always bordering on the tragic—known as the vacilada or laugh with the tongue in the cheek.

When a city pulquería receives fresh pulque, it is sometimes announced by hanging strings of bright vari-colored china paper streamers outside, or even by music.

The natives have a double motive for drinking—one, which they share with all other drinkers, for whatever pleasure it may give; and the other for ritual; so there is considerable drunkenness among them. Their drunkenness is generally pacific, tinged with sadness rather than with hilarity. I have at times been alone at village fiestas where there were many drunks, but have never had occasion for fear. Yet I know that many beat their wives and children when under the influence of drink, who do not do so when sober; also that when drunks get into quarrels with enemies, they use their machetes freely and sometimes fatally. Women also drink both for pleasure and ritual, but not so much as men.

Fiestas generally end up with many drunks but there are some few exceptions. The ritual drink of the Mayas of X-Cacal is an unfermented wine, so there is no drunkenness then even though there may be at other times. And recently some persons who visited the Zapotec village of Lachiguiri in the mountains near Tehuantepec, found a fiesta taking place with everyone perfectly sober; in fact, there were not any alcoholic drinks to be had. When inquiry was made as to the reasons for this unusual condition, it was learned that prohibition had existed there for over twenty years. The school teacher, who had lived among them all that time, had taught them to do without drink and to make their village sanitary and productive. Here and there are villages where there is very little drinking; in the majority there is too much.

Soft Drinks

Refrescos are the soft drinks so popular everywhere in Mexico. Made with fruit, seeds, and even flowers, they are sold on the streets, plazas, and market places of every city and large village, and always at fiestas.

In the cities the refrescos are attractively displayed in large glass jars, each one a different color according to the fruit or seed with which it is flavored. In places where ice is not available, a primitive method of refrigeration is employed—the drinks are served from clay containers kept cool by putting them into wet earth pits. During fiestas, the earth around the jars is sometimes decorated with colored paper flags, flowers, and green leaves.

CLAY CONTAINERS FOR SOFT DRINKS

Refrescos in the smaller, more conservative places are few, mostly made of ground corn and sweetened with brown sugar or honey. Sometimes chía seeds are ground with the corn, as before the Conquest, but more generally they are used alone.

The most common refrescos are those flavored with some kind of fruit and called by its name, and those flavored with seeds. The following are some of the most typical:

Chía is made from the seeds of a herbaceous plant with blue flowers, called chiantzozolli in Aztec. The seeds are put into water and stirred until they form a soft mass. Lemon juice and sugar are added to taste. As chía plants grow practically everywhere, this drink is widespread.

Chicha is an equal amount of toasted corn and raw barley grains soaked in water for two days; flavored with cinnamon, ground pineapple or orange juice; sweetened to taste.

Horchata is made with pepitas or melon seeds, which are ground and passed through a strainer after the water is added; flavored with lemon peels and cinnamon; sweetened to taste.

Jamaica is a delicious drink made of a pretty red tropical flower of the same name. The proportion is twenty flowers to each quart of water, boiled until the water acquires the color of the flower and the slightly acid taste of the calyx. Sugar and fruit juices may be added as well as wine or something stronger.

Tamarinda is made from the pods that grow on the beautiful tamarind trees. The pods are either soaked in water or boiled and the drink is ready. It has a slightly acid taste, so it is necessary to add sugar.

Taxcalate is the popular drink of Chiapas. It is made by grinding toasted corn with cacao and is sweetened with brown sugar. The achiote flowers are added to give it a reddish color.

Tuba is made with the sap from the cocoanut palms and the water from the cocoanuts that grow on them. It is a delicious drink.

Tepache (not the alcoholic drink already mentioned) is a very popular refresco in many states. It is prepared by grinding the whole pineapple and putting it into a clay jar containing three quarts of water; seasoned with pieces of cinnamon sticks and cloves. After two days, boiled barley and brown sugar are added if fermentation is desired. It is strained before serving.[1]

Smoking

Smoking is a pre-Spanish art, indulged in for both pleasure and ritual. Some of the ancients made a kind of cigarette by filling hollow reeds with tobacco, and used clay pipes for ceremonies. When the Spaniards first saw the natives smoking, they thought it the work of the devil; it seemed impossible that anyone could emit smoke from the mouth without burning up inside.

The present-day natives smoke cigarettes chiefly. They roll their own in corn leaves or buy the cheaper factory-made brands. Mixe women of Oaxaca make cigarettes, preparing their own tobacco, but using Barcelona paper imported from Spain. In the hot southern states both men and women smoke homemade cigars.

Cigarettes are always served at fiestas and are never omitted from the offerings to the gods, as well as to both the good and evil spirits. The acceptance of a cigarette from someone who is asking a favor implies an obligation; and smoking together, friendship. When the Chamulas of Chiapas invite a stranger to smoke with them, they fill a small otate reed vessel with tobacco and narcotic herbs, and perforate it with as many holes as there are smokers, so that all can smoke at the same time, each with his own small reed tube.

The arrieros, mule-pack drivers, perform a charming ceremony in connection with smoking, called la lumbre or asking for a light. It takes place on the road when one of them wants to smoke and he and his companions do not have matches. As there is no place to buy any, he may have to wait for hours until someone comes along. If it is another mule-pack, both stop their animals, who generally welcome the respite and prick up their ears expectantly. The man who wants the light does not ask for it immediately, but first exchanges solemn greetings in the name of God. Then if the one who has the matches is not smoking, instead of offering the box, he lights one of his own cigarettes, touches the brim of his sombrero with the tips of his fingers and removes it with the sweeping gesture of "I am at your service"; he hands the lighted cigarette to the stranger, who in receiving it also bares his head. After lighting his cigarette carefully, so as not to damage or put out the borrowed one, he returns it with polite phrases of gratitude, at the same time offering one of his own. The man refuses it, saying he has plenty, but the recipient of the favor insists, "Take it, señor, it will at least serve for the ear." (Arrieros, truck-drivers, and other men working in this way often carry an unlighted cigarette over the ear.) The man thus importuned accepts the cigarette because it would be an offense not to. Then follow more courteous phrases and with a buen viaje, each caravan goes its own way.[1]

Chews

The natives chew, but neither tobacco nor gum, and not solely for the pleasure of chewing and spitting; they chew to allay hunger, to soothe thirst, to arrest fatigue, as well as for enjoyment. The following are some of their chews:

Sugar cane is, perhaps, the most widespread and popular of all the chews. Bundles of the long green canes are a familiar sight at practically every fiesta, and in many places the kind for chewing is grown together with the corn.

The hearts of the maguey plants, baked with brown sugar, are sold in the markets and are savory chews. In some villages they are called mezcales.

In the Gulf and Pacific coast states a favorite chew is a small orange-colored fruit that grows on a palm tree, called coyol near the Gulf and coyul along the Pacific. The fruit is peeled and the sweet fibrous meat is chewed for hours until soft; then the pit is cracked and the tiny nut found inside is eaten. Children make chains and toys of coyol pits.

Favorite chews in the states of Morelos and Guerrero are the cayaca, a brown walnut shaped fruit, with a sweet oily meat; also the green pods from the huamuchil trees, very pleasant tasting.

The fruit of the cajinicuil tree, which grows in the tropics, is a sweet and refreshing chew. It is a large green-skinned pod with white cotton-like viscous meat and black seeds.

The highland natives of Chiapas chew finely-chopped tobacco leaves mixed with lime, which they carry in little gourd containers hanging from their belts. In Tzeltal it is called mai and in Tzotzil, pelico. This chew is served together with drinks and cigarettes at fiestas and is very refreshing when one is walking a long distance.

In the State of Mexico, the natives, when tired and thirsty, chew the juicy root of the chinela plant.

Other chews are chicle in its natural state—in the cities everyone chews gum—mesquite, guyaule, and the bark of oak trees.

Among the natives of the northwest the peyote or hikuli cactus plant serves for chews, cures, and as a narcotic. The Huichols consider this plant sacred, going on long and difficult pilgrimages to gather it in the State of San Luis Potosí.[1]

The younger, more progressive folk are beginning to chew gum like the city people of all social classes. Until a few decades ago it was considered improper for girls and women to chew in public. The same opinion prevailed before the Conquest, when only unmarried girls of lower category chewed a kind of gum prepared from resin or bitumen.[2]

Animals

For the primitive races in remote regions, wild animals are still very important because of the excitement and ritual connected with hunting them and because of the meat they furnish, especially for fiestas. The animal most appreciated as a sacred food is the deer, but cattle and fowl are also offered as sacrifices to the pagan gods.

Animals are caught in traps and hunted with guns or bow and arrow. When hunters go out in groups, the men who have no weapons help by surrounding the animals or driving them in the direction of those who are armed. Many know how to attract and deceive their prey by imitating the sounds of animals and bird songs. The aid of either Christian saints or pagan gods or both is invoked by the hunters before every hunt. Prayers, candles, and incense are offered to the saints, but the pagan gods are addressed differently. Huichol hunters hang tiny deer traps on prayer arrows; these are believed to communicate with the gods; or they put beautiful dove and parrot feathers on deer shrines in the mountains so that their prayers may be heard.

Domestic animals are found everywhere—chickens, turkeys, pigs, cows, burros, mules. Few of the poorer natives own horses; when they do, they use them more as beasts of burden than for riding. However, the progressive well-to-do families, especially ranchers, have good horses and ride well.

Some Mayas, Huichols, Tarahumaras, and others raise cattle. In many regions there are sheep for wool, goats for cheese and meat, oxen for ploughing and harnessing to carts. Although large herds are considered as business investments, they produce little profit because they are not cared for scientifically nor are their products sold to advantage. Barnyard fowl are generally kept only for festal food. The skins of the animals are cured in a primitive way and used as well as sold by the owners.

There are few cats among the natives, but many dogs. They are usually scrawny and look badly treated, but that is because their owners are poor. Actually, dogs are the most beloved of all the animals. Aside from the fact that dogs are companions, and help with the herds and in other ways, the pre-Spanish belief that certain dogs swim the dead across a river still exists and is another reason for treating them well. The hairless dogs one sees occasionally are an indigenous breed.

All animals have either Christian or pagan patrons, or both, whose co-operation must be sought for success not only in hunting wild animals, but also in keeping the domestic ones safe and well. The Mayas of Chan Kom and X-Cacal believe that deer are protected by supernatural beings called zip, who resemble the deer so much that the hunters can never catch them. The cattle of these Mayas are also watched over by a supernatural being, whose name is X-Juan-Thul, about whom little is known except that he keeps the evil winds away and expects offerings.

Among the Huichols in the region of Tuxpan, Jalisco, the cattle are blessed by the shaman, who walks around them in a circle making gestures with his beautiful plumes. The blessing takes place just before the rain ceremony, when at the same time the bull to be sacrificed for the feast is made sacred by being brought close to the pictures of the saints, with the shaman pointing from the bull to the saints as if in offering. Animals are also branded during this ceremony; their horns are adorned with colored paper flowers for the occasion and the iron is applied to the accompaniment of violin and guitar music

The Catholicized folk, living in large places including cities, take their animals to church to be blessed on January 17, the day of St. Anthony the Abbot. Dogs, pigs, parrots, burros and others are painted in gay colors or adorned with ribbons and flowers, forming a bizarre and amusing group.[1]

Bee Keeping

Bees have been kept since before the Conquest. Their honey is highly prized as a sweetener and for medicinal purposes, and the wax for ritual candles. Occasionally the more primitive natives get honey from wild bees, but domesticated ones are kept everywhere. The keepers of the more populated centers often make a business of selling honey to stores.

Bees are generally respected and well treated because of their industry, products, and their Christian or pagan patrons. According to the Huichols, bees were created by the gods of the sea for the purpose of securing wax for candles when the wooden ones would not light. Tata Dios watches over the bees for the Tarahumaras; the Mayas of Chan Kom believe their bees are protected by pagan deities to whom offerings must be made for taking their honey. The Virgin Mary takes care of the bees for the Mayas of X-Cacal, who make her offerings of zaca or corn meal upon taking the honey from the hives; they also offer zaca to the wild bees when they take their honey, as otherwise the bees might inflict punishment upon them by causing a tree to fall or an ax to slip.

The natives of Amecameca, a large Aztec town near Mexico City, have an interesting method of domesticating bees. Several men go out together to get them, one going ahead ringing a small bell and wafting incense as they do during Mass in church. Another man has an ayate or a square fibre carrying-cloth. When the comb is taken from the tree it is placed in the middle of the cloth and carried by the four ends. Upon reaching the house, the comb is put in a box and the bees settle in it to the ringing of the little bell. After they reproduce, the queens with their bees are put into separate hives. Flowers and water are placed near the apiaries; when there are no flowers the water for the bees is sweetened.

Making a Living

A village native tries to be economically self-sufficient and to spend as little cash as possible for his living. He generally raises his own corn, beans, squashes, and other things, depending upon space, climate, and soil. Many households weave the necessary blankets or cloth for the family. Some objects are secured through barter.

There is, however, always a need for money, which is earned in numerous ways. Men hire out as laborers in agriculture and other fields, but employment is generally seasonal. Even the skilled workers in the larger places—masons, carpenters, barbers, shoemakers— usually have to work at other jobs part of the time. The only specialists who keep busy at their own trades most of the time are the artisans who supply city markets and stores with handicrafts.

In Chiapas, men leave their homes to work on coffee fincas; in Tabasco, on banana plantations; in Quintana Roo, in the chicle industry, and so on, for the length of time necessary to satisfy the need for ready cash—sometimes for one or more years. Since the Social Revolution of 1910–20, new jobs have been opened to villagers, especially road building. But of all the kinds of work, old and new, agriculture and the handicrafts are still the most important in the native economy.

Wages are still low, varying from thirty centavos to three pesos a day—five to sixty American cents—so the poor remain poor. Only those natives who own a fair amount of land or cattle, or who are engaged in home industries or trade, have any surplus money to bury under the ground or to use for better living conditions.

AGRICULTURE AND CEREMONIES

Mexico is an agricultural country, producing many important crops, but for the natives corn is the principal one.

The majority of the natives, who depend on corn for sustenance, believe the plant is of supernatural origin. As the growing of it is the chief concern of their lives, they spend much time on ceremonies to please the deities, who have the power to help assure the success of the crops.

Practically every native, no matter what else he may do for a living, has his own milpa, or cornfield. Some own considerable land; others rent land and work it on shares; but those who live on the margins of civilization utilize the unclaimed land on the mountain sides and elsewhere. Since 1920, the federal government has expropriated many large haciendas in order to give ejidos, or parcels, to the peasants to work individually or in co-operatives.

Among the primitive groups the raising of corn occupies most of the time of the men. The "cleaning"—felling and burning of trees and bush—begins in the late fall, and the planting with the first rains.

As in most cases a field has to rest after each crop, the work of "cleaning" new land has to be done often.

Progressive natives of means are now using some modern agricultural implements, but the old-fashioned primitive ones introduced by the Spaniards hundreds of years ago are still extensively utilized, together with such aboriginal tools as the coa or planting stick.

Even large haciendas have been and still are utilizing primitive implements because human labor is less costly than modern machinery. Yet these haciendas had employed speed-up methods long before they were introduced into modern industry.

Planting on haciendas near Toluca, State of Mexico, is done by men and women after the fields have been tilled with a wooden plow drawn by oxen. The man uses a stick with a small flare on one end with which he brushes the surface, holding it so that he can turn it around rapidly to make a hole for the seed with the other pointed end. The woman follows with a fibre bag of seeds hanging from her shoulder, dropping them into the holes and covering them quickly and mechanically with her feet as she walks along.

Women also help in harvesting, but only the young and strong are so employed. They are mostly Otomí near Toluca and they come to their work attractively dressed—a full homespun wool skirt, embroidered shirt, and big sombreros to protect them from the sun. Hanging down their backs is a soft reed basket, suspended from the chest by a sort of strap called a tumpline, to receive the corn. Each one has a small lance, a few inches long, attached to the third finger, called the pizcador or gleaner, used for opening the leaves around the husks so that the ear may be cut more easily.

Upon entering the field, the pizcadoras, or women gleaners, take their places along the furrows assigned them, but do not commence work until the mayordomo or overseer says, "Ave María Purísima," to which they answer in chorus, "Conceived without sin." After this no more time is lost.

As soon as a basket is filled, it is emptied into a costal, or sack, carried by men called costaleros, who take them to the conveyances that transport them to the threshing floor.

Shortly after the work has started, and at regular intervals thereafter, the voice of the mayordomo is heard—"Hurry it up, girls, hurry! Move those hands! Don't leave anything behind! Move those lines, keep moving! . . ."

The admonitions of the mayordomo are followed by the voices of the costaleros who are standing nearby with their bags waiting for the girls to come to fill them—"Come to empty your baskets, girls, or the costalero will leave; the costalero is tired standing . . ." And when the costaleros are slow in returning with their empty bags and

the girls have their baskets full, they begin calling, "Costalero, costalero . . ." In spite of the watchful mayordomo, the pizcadoras and
costaleros find time for romance, with resulting unions.[1]

A less pleasant type of speed-up was practiced until some fifty or
more years ago by mayor domos, who used to ride through the fields
on horseback, dealing out lashes with a long leather whip to those
who were slow.

The chief events in the agricultural cycle are planting and harvesting. For these, as in house building, reciprocal labor is the custom and
festal foods are offered by the owner. There is little real work to do
in the fields in the intervening time, but constant attention is necessary. Besides having the weeds picked out occasionally, the crop must
be protected from evil spirits that often take the form of animals, as
well as from the real enemy animals and birds of prey. But what is
most important in securing a good crop is to keep the gods content
so that they may send the necessary amount of rain and order the evil
spirits to stay away.

The milperos, men who own and work the cornfields, and their
families do not leave everything to the gods, but help watch over
their fields from tiny huts or platforms on high stilts. When I visited
Palenque, the famous archaeological site in the tropical forest of
Chiapas, I rode out one afternoon with the villagers on horseback to
their cornfields for the purpose of frightening off the magpies which
come in swarms to steal corn. We climbed the tapancos, or platforms,
from which we shouted and waved at the pretty little green, red-
bellied thieves until they all flew past. Unfortunately, not all the
robbers are so charming nor so easy to scare off.

Catholic Customs

In Catholicized communities, seeds are blessed in the churches, generally on Candlemas day, February 2. At planting time, crosses
are often set up and the fields blessed with incense and holy water;
prayers are said, and offerings of candles and incense are made to
the saints in the churches and at home.

At harvest time, the first fruits of the fields are brought to the
churches and thanksgiving fiestas held. On haciendas, it is the
custom for the owners to give a fiesta to the workers, with food,
drinks, music, and dances.

To invoke rain, an image of the most miraculous saint is taken out
in procession, the people carrying flowers, lighted candles, and lighted
censers. Fireworks are shot off because the natives believe they pro-

duce rain clouds. The image of San Isidro, patron saint of the farmers, is taken to the fields in villages of the State of Mexico and others. Masses are said either before or after the processions. Wherever a fiesta is given to San Isidro as patron of a village, his altar is adorned with agricultural offerings and the oxen used for ploughing are decorated with flowers, branches, and gay paper streamers for the procession.

The days of important saints are considered good for planting; as is May 3, the Day of the Holy Cross.

With some variations, this is more or less the pattern of Catholic agricultural ceremonies, but by scratching the surface a little, much paganism may be discovered. A rural school teacher told me he saw a procession for rain in a village on the Pacific coast of Oaxaca. As the rain did not fall immediately, the natives became angry. They disrobed the saint and left him abandoned near the church, continuing the procession with a stone idol in his place. In the month of June 1944, when I was visiting the resort city of Cuernavaca, capital of the State of Morelos, the natives of adjoining villages were very much worried over the drought that was threatening their crops. They had offered prayers, candles, incense, and Masses to the saints, whom they had also taken out in procession. When all these efforts failed to bring rain, they undressed the saints and put them in the fields to swelter in the tropical sun, to see if suffering from it would make them listen to their prayers. When it rains too much, they put their saints in the streams so that they, also, may suffer from too much water and make the rains stop.

Pagan Ceremonies [1]

Most of the pagan ceremonies are not free from Catholicism, but the Christian influence is not sufficient to change their character. Among some of the tribes, they are very elaborate and require a great deal of time. The beliefs are often charmingly poetic, as for example, those of the Mayas concerning the gods, birds, and animals; their ceremonies, too, are very interesting with their magic and drama.

Maya Beliefs and Ceremonies

The Mayas of X-Cacal and Chan Kom believe in the same pagan deities. They existed among the ancient Mayas and still bear the same names. Generically, they are the Yuntzilob, or the "Lords" or "Patrons." Although these Mayas believe in God and the saints, the

Yuntzilob are much closer to them, because it is they who have the power to make the cornfields fertile, to control the rains and winds, the animals and the birds. So the ceremonies are all in their honor, and there are many.

The Yuntzilob are divided into three groups, each having different functions; (1) the balams who protect the cornfields, men, and villages; (2) the kuil-kaaxs who take care of the forests; (3) the chaacs who control the rains. They are thought of as spirits and sometimes as "little people, only made of air." When they are seen in the cornfields, they appear as tiny old men, with white hair, dressed like the natives, with sandals and sombreros.

The balams of the cornfields are believed to be stationed in the four corners, from whence they can see the entire field. When animals approach, they make noises to drive them away, and they handle thieves severely. But if they do not receive offerings from the owner, they will abandon his field.

The rain chaacs are first in the devotion of the natives, because rain is a prime necessity. Those of X-Cacal believe that when Jesucristo wills that there be rain, the chaacs ride through the skies on slender horses, carrying the rain in a fountain calabash whose water is never exhausted. Sometimes they are accompanied by the Virgin Mary, who rides a black horse from which the water falls in torrents. But there is no danger of floods from this water because it flows into two subterranean channels leading to two underground wells unknown to man, which can never be filled.

The chaacs are so numerous that they form a hierarchy. The four great ones who stand at the cardinal points come first, the one at the eastern point being regarded as the most powerful. After these come all the others, each group named after their specific meteorological functions—"distributor-sky" chaacs, those who produce the persistent rains; "flooding-sky" chaacs, who cause heavy downpours; "lightning-sky" chaacs, who cause lightning; "sweeper-sky" chaacs, who go about cleaning the sky after the rains.

When the chaacs are not occupied in making rain, the lesser ones are believed to be in the bush, hiding in the caves and cenotes or underground wells. At other times, they live like men in villages which are invisible. The most important of them, perhaps, live somewhere in the eastern sky; the shooting stars sometimes seen in that direction may be the light from their cigarette butts. It is there that the chaacs receive their orders before going out to water the world. The signals for such meetings are the first thunders which are heard coming from the east early in April.

The Mayas of Chan Kom believe that there are animals and birds which are good and bad in connection with rain and the growing of corn. The frog, toad, bat, and tortoise that are to be found in the cenotes and caves frequented by the chaacs should not be killed. There is special sympathy for the tortoise. When there is plenty of rain he is never seen, but when there is drought and there is danger that the crops may fail, men meet him, looking dry and hot, with tears in his eyes. It is said that he weeps for men and that his tears draw rain. Thus it is a good omen to see one. When the bush is being burned, the peasant always warns the tortoise, crying out, "Save yourselves, tortoises! Here comes the fire!"

The birds that frequent the cornfields, taking little of the corn, are considered as belonging to the Yuntzilob—the white-winged and white-breasted doves and the red-billed pigeons. The small hawk, who from a tree-top yells at the blackbirds when they try to steal the corn, is called chuy or "the guardian of the cornfield." The x-kol or sweet-voiced bird sings for the corn plants so that they may be happy. And there is one little bird that "stretches the corn-plants"; it jumps from plant to tree and back again, singing and jumping to make the plants grow. As soon as the ears are formed, the work of these birds is done and they leave. Then comes the "horse-catcher" bird who whistles to summon the horses which the chaacs ride for making the rain. None of these birds can be harmed or killed, for they belong to the Yuntzilob.

The Mayas of the X-Cacal group of villages perform agricultural ceremonies continuously, individually and in groups; at harvest time they ocasionally overlap. The first two of the three following ceremonies seem to be unique in Yucatan, as similar ones have not been described elsewhere excepting in Chan Kom.

1. Ceremony After the Land Is Selected

After the milpero or peasant has selected the land for his cornfield, he sets up a small cross and places before it five small gourd vessels of zaca (corn meal) and water. Then he calls to the gods of the fields to come to partake of his offering, which is an indication to them that the man who is to use the land is a friend. After that, they will drive away all the snakes and other harmful animals. At the same time, the trees become aware that there is an atmosphere of friendliness and make no resistance to being felled and do no harm to the milpero. Some believe that the trees fall upon a person of their own volition to hurt him for cutting them down. The milpero, therefore, must be careful not to fell any more trees than necessary for his purpose.

II. Ceremony for Burning the Bush

In this ceremony seven dishes of zaca, the sacred corn gruel, are placed in front of the cross; where the bush is remote and little known the number is increased to thirteen. The milpero then makes the invocation and, kneeling, recites the six Christian prayers of the Payalchi, asking Jesucristo to command the strong wind that blows in a spiral to cover the entire field with flame so that the burning may be effective. If the rains come before the field is cleared, the opportunity to plant may be lost.

The Mayas believe this special wind is composed of the souls who have committed sins of the flesh on earth and are now paying for them by fanning the flames for the milpero.

III. The Okotbatam or "Petition"

This ceremony, which is the most important of all, is also an interesting example of the simultaneous performance of pagan and Christian rites without any conflict. It is offered to all the gods and the spirits, taking place in August or September, for during that period the cornfields require the co-operation of all of them for successful ripening. If the petition were not made, the gods would consider themselves neglected and might do harm.

The ceremony begins in the evening with a collective deer hunt. The following morning some of the men go to the bush for firewood, while others erect the altar in the church for the pagan gods. Meanwhile the women are cooking the meat and thick broth, called kol, in nearby houses, each one contributing a dish of zaca and one of ground spices. The men dig the pit for the earth oven and prepare for the pagan gods the sacred bread, which must not be touched by women.

While the bread is baking, the h-men, the pagan priest, offers zaca from thirteen small gourds to the Yuntzilob, sprinkling some of it in the four directions and saying—"Here I offer you your holy table in the presence of God, the Father, and I deliver thirteen holy gourds of the holy refreshing beverage." An additional larger dish is dedicated to Jesucristo. Before it is taken out of the oven the bread is blessed by the chief of the tribe by tossing over it some consecrated zaca in a gesture forming a cross.

The dedication of the offerings to the gods is the most important moment. To the Christian God it is made with Catholic prayers before the altar in the "Gloria" by the chief who has placed on it food, three black wax candles, and incense of rosemary and lavender.

The dedication to the Yuntzilob, which takes place simultaneously, is presided over by the *h-men*. He has also placed food and three wax candles on the pagan altar, but the incense is of copal, on banana-tree bark laid on burning coals. The *h-men* recites both Christian and pagan prayers on this occasion, kneeling for the former and standing for the latter. To conclude the ceremony of the offerings, he rises and mentions each of the sacred breads by name, as well as the rest of the foods. Then the chief and acolytes kneel at the pagan altar and recite Christian prayers.

The women are permitted to kneel outside of the enclosure of the "Gloria" and they eat apart from the men. Food is sent to each of the crosses guarding the principal entrances to the village.

When a village Okotbatam does not secure a good harvest, another is celebrated in X-Cacal, the sacred capital, with all the group participating, with more food, music, and a big Mass. During the morning some of the men perform the penitential act called "ask pardon," crawling on their knees seven times a distance of seven meters from the altar upon which stands the patron cross.

The first fruit and harvest ceremonies continue during weeks and overlap those first described. One can easily imagine their unique charm, with the participants all dressed in white and not intoxicated.

Rain Ceremony in Chan Kom

When a long period of drought threatens the crops and all individual and collective prayers have failed to bring rain, a ceremony takes place in which every man in the village participates. It is performed out of doors, the *h-men* officiating, and lasts three days, during which time all work is suspended.

At noon of the first day the men go to bring "virgin" water for the sacred bread from a cenote situated in the depths of the woods, unknown to women, where the chaacs come to fill their calabashes for watering the corn plants. From that time on they are expected to stay away from their wives until the ceremony is over, as otherwise the sanctity of the proceedings would be defiled and of no avail.

Each man contributes zaca, candles, spices, and hens; and his gifts are received and recorded by the *h-men* and his two assistants.

At dawn of the second day the *h-men* mixes a jar of zaca with "cold holy water" to place on the altar as an offering to the Yuntzilob, and while he prays every man is served a dish of it. A few hours later, he prepares three more jars of zaca, placing them in gourd-carriers to hang on a tree near the altar. These are offered in turn to

San Gabriel, San Marcelino, San Cecilio, the guardians of the forest, and to the zip, who watch over the deer, with prayers for "virgin animals." The zip are asked not to warn the deer of the approach of the hunters. The *h-men* then consults his crystals and tells the hunters where to go. If they return without deer, he blames the zip and sends them off in another direction. When an animal is brought in, it is cooked in the earth-oven and placed on the altar for the men to eat. Twice during the night they are given zaca. During the intervals between ceremonies and refreshments, the men amuse themselves by telling stories and eating toasted squash seeds.

The principal part of the ceremony takes place on the third day. At dawn, the *h-men* fills thirteen small gourd vessels with balche, the ritual drink, offering them to the gods with a prayer. Afterwards four men selected by him sit on a bench in front of the altar to chant a prayer to the chaacs and balams for rain. Then the assistants serve balche to everyone.

Next the *h-men* sanctifies and dedicates the hens to the gods, putting balche into the beak of each one and praying. The prayer, consisting of nine parts, begins with offering a "holy virgin animal" to the chaacs and to St. Michael. As the *h-men* recites the following eight parts, he puts more liquor down the hens' throats. Then they are handed over to the assistants to have their necks wrung.

Between ceremonies, the *h-men* rests in his hammock, from which he arises from time to time to pray and asperge the cross and the altar with balche. He does this thirteen times, each time offering the consecrated balche to the men, who after drinking it, give formal thanks —"Thrice be saluted, Sir."

Following the offering of the feast to the gods and the saying of the explicit prayer for rain, the *h-men* ties the right leg of each of the four boys who are to impersonate the frogs to the four posts of the altar table and selects one of the older men to represent the kunku-chaac or chief of the rain gods. Then the assistants carry this chief to a cleared space east of the altar to the "trunk of heaven," where the kunku-chaac is supposed to dwell. The men do this carefully and reverently, without turning their backs to the altar because they believe the balams are gathered there.

The kunku-chaac is given a calabash, symbolizing those used by the rain gods for watering corn, and a wooden lelem or blade with which they produce lightning. The *h-men*, with an assistant at each side, kneels at the altar to pray. He summons the gods and mentions various place names. Then as he continues praying, his assistants sprinkle the altar with balche and add grains of copal to the incense in the small burner. The frogs croak on a special note and the kunku-chaac stands up from time to time to imitate the sound of thunder with his voice and the flash of lightning with his lelem.

After the gods and men have finished their banquet, the *h-men* pours balche on the head of the kunku-chaac, saying, "In the name of God, the Father; God, the Son; God, the Holy Ghost; Amen!" Then the kunku-chaac goes to sit among the "frogs" who are busy eating. The rest of the food is then divided among all present, thus concluding the ceremony with the usual feast.

The feasting over, the *h-men* offers thirteen dishes of zaca to the deities with the same prayer used in the morning; the assistants help him take down the altar, and he sanctifies the place with a sprinkling of balche, to convey persons and things from the secular world to the sacred and back again. For when balche is sprinkled on the altar, it becomes fit for the gods to approach, and the same act consecrates the fowl. On the other hand, the kunku-chaac and the place where the ceremony is held are asperged with balche so that they may be safe again for ordinary life.

At rain ceremonies in the settlements of X-Koptiel and Santa María, four men impersonate the four chaacs of the cardinal points. They stand at the four corners of the altar, each with a calabash and a machete. While the *h-men* prays, the chaacs dance around the altar nine times, brandishing their machetes, which they do again when the balche and food are offered. In addition to the four boys acting as frogs, four others are put in the underbrush to imitate the sounds made by the chachalacas—the birds whose cries are believed to presage rain. These ceremonies end with the *h-men* and assistants joining hands in a circle into which each man passes in turn and is gently beaten with habin branches as he turns around nine times.

All the other primitive groups also have interesting agricultural ceremonies but space will permit only a few more. However, there are a sufficient number to give an idea of their fantasy and significance.

Cave Ceremonies, District Oxchuc, Chiapas

When the planting has been finished in the month of April, the officials of each settlement organize the "Mass of the Cornfield," for which every owner contributes one peso. This money is sufficient for an abundant amount of brandy, an explosive bomb, some firecrackers and paraffin candles. Thus supplied, the officials and everyone else who wishes to accompany them, go to Oxchuc to say Mass to Santo Tomás, patron of the Municipality. This act is called sacar la misa, "to take the Mass outside," for which a priest is not required. Both in going to and returning from the village, the group is headed by two musicians—one playing a drum, the other a flute.

As soon as the men have returned from the village, they go to the cave where the patron cross of the settlement is housed, to spend the night there, drinking and burning firecrackers. The musicians are joined by a harpist and guitarist. At dawn, the group abandons the cave, first burning the bomb at the entrance. Then a procession is formed for the purpose of praying in each one of the smaller caves that house crosses of secondary importance.

During the ceremony, the officials light four candles before the cross in each small cave, put incense into a little burner on live coals, and kneeling, pray in Tzeltal, each holding a rosary. They remain for some time on their knees and without ceasing to pray, change position so that their foreheads almost touch the ground. Shortly afterwards, still praying, they return to their original positions. While the prayers are being said, the musicians play the harp and guitar and a firecracker is shot off from time to time.

Afterwards, the officials stand up, and taking a gourd-rattle on a deer bone handle, begin to dance to a tune played by the musicians. It is a primitive Yucatán melody, similar to the Xtoles. After a pause in the dance, the tune is changed. The dance is very simple, the men marking the rhythm with their feet and with rattles to that of the music.

After the dance the procession continues to the next cave. It appears that the prayers in these caves are dedicated to the Christian saints, because the act is designated as "To go to pray in the caves." On the other hand, these natives believe that the caves are inhabited by lightning, which comes out to attack the hail and the hurricanes that can harm the cornfields.

The following prayer, reconstructed from the Tzeltal, does not indicate whether it is addressed to the Christian saints or pagan gods, but it has the childlike quality of all their prayers and is typical of those said on all occasions:

"Here we come to bring you food, to light candles and to burn incense for you; to play the flute, to play the drum, to play the harp, to play the guitar for you. Here we come to make a fiesta for you, so that you may be content and not abandon us.

"We have planted our cornfields; the seed is in the ground. Father, do not abandon us. Let there be plenty of rain—not too much nor too little. Let there be sun and clouds, so that the earth be content.

"Father, keep the hail from coming; stop the wind; let there be no locusts; keep away the harmful animals; make the thieves stay away, so that they do not rob us and leave us in misery.

"Father, let this be a good year! Let there be a good corn crop! Let there be plenty of beans! Keep us well. Keep us from anxieties! Father, the food has been eaten; the prayers have been said. . ." (The prayer ends with the sign of the cross.)

Ceremonies Among the Western Mixes of Oaxaca

In many of the villages, large and small, offerings are still made to the spirits of lightning and the wind to secure rain and good crops. The conservatives of Ayutla kill a turkey in the middle of the field just before planting; dig a small round hole in the ground in which they bury tortillas and tamales, sprinkled with the blood of the sacrificed fowl. As they cut off the head of the turkey, they pray to Tata Dios and the Earth, "Now that we are sowing, do us the favor of giving us corn."

In the village of Yacoche before planting time a man sleeps apart from his wife, after which he goes to church to pray. Then he takes to the field thirteen perfect ears of corn and all the double-pointed ones, which he has saved from the previous harvest, and sprinkles all the ears with blood and pinole or powdered corn. The blood and pinole are buried in the field and the head of the turkey is passed over the seed in a counter-clockwise motion. The ears sprinkled with the blood are saved until the first flowers appear on the corn plants, when they are ground and made into tortillas and tamales. At the same time more blood is sprinkled on the new green leaves, which are taken as an offering to the summit of Zempoaltepec, the highest peak of the sierra.

The Ceremony Among the Populuca of Vera Cruz

A man and his wife must not sleep together for seven nights before planting; otherwise the seeds will be eaten by rats and raccoons. On the day of the sowing, the seeds are smoked with copal and a prayer is said to the Virgin of Carmen of Catemaco or to mok santu, the corn god. After the sowing, the field is smoked with incense by someone walking over it with a clay censer full of burning copal; again when the corn is knee-high, and once more when the tassels and tiny ears appear.

When the ears are ready for roasting, the man and his wife go to the field before dawn, smoke it with copal, and cut seven ears, which are later made into tamales to be eaten at midnight. After this ceremony, ears may be cut at any time.

After the grains have become hard, seven ears are taken home, smoked with copal, and lighted candles are placed near them. This is done to keep away harmful insects and to prevent the corn from moulding. After the corn is harvested, it is given a final smoking with incense and there is feasting.

The natives believe mok santu to be only three feet tall, with corn-silk hair. While the corn is growing, he is young with golden hair, but when it is ripe, he changes into a wizened old man with dry brown hair.

The Huichol Purification of the First Fruits

This is the most important of the Huichol fiestas because the people cannot make use of their new crops until after it has taken place. Every one attends, as the persons who are going to consume the crops have to be "purified" together with the first fruits.

The altars are adorned with beautiful sacred paraphernalia—prayer arrows, plumes, god-discs, gourd votive bowls, candles, flowers, and young corn.

The ceremonies begin in the evening with the straining of the tesgüino, the ritual beer, and all night long the people stay awake to listen to the shaman's recital of the myths explaining the creation of the world and the functions of all the gods, to pray, and to eat and drink.

The chief participants are the women. At dawn they put on their best costumes and dress their children, adorning their heads with new hair ribbons, into which they stick shaman's plumes, to indicate that they are taking part in a sacred ceremony, and "god-eyes" to symbolize prayers for health and long life. The women also weave wreaths for their heads of the yellow and red flowers that bloom in the cornfields in the fall, interspersing them with orchids, and paint their faces with circles and those of their children with linear designs with a yellow root from peyote land. Meanwhile the women without children take care of the altars and prepare the food. An effigy of the corn goddess, formed of a small chair piled with corn husks and dressed in women's clothes and finery, is a sacred symbol.

The shaman in his best ceremonial costume takes his place near the altar behind his drum, which is decorated with chains of yellow flowers and tufts of cotton to symbolize prayers for rain. On each side of him sits an assistant, and in front on the ground the women and children form a semi-circle, all having gourd-rattles. The shaman begins singing passionately and is soon weeping. The assistants, women and children repeat phrases of the song, marking the rhythm of the

drum with their rattles. Excepting interruptions for prayers, ceremonies, and food, the singing goes on in this way throughout the whole
day and night and part of the following day.

Shortly after the singing starts, the young hunters file into the patio
before leaving for their deer traps in the mountains. The shaman puts
an eagle feather on each one of their arrows, which are stuck in the
ground so that they may ask the gods for success, while the shaman
sings loudly at the altar.

Next the dedication of the children to the sun takes place. The
mother lights her magical candle at the altar, its flame symbolizing life.
While one of the shaman's assistants lifts the child, the other holds the
rattles, god-eyes, and plumes over its head. The singing increases in
vehemence; the assistant keeps time with the rattle, as everyone looks
at the sun. The ceremony ends with one of the singers sticking a
yellow flower in the child's hair ribbon and the mother extinguishing
her candle at the altar with sacred water.

After another interval of singing, the women leave their children on
the ground and approach the altar to offer their best beads to the
gods. All the candles are lighted again and live coals put in the censers,
causing the incense to rise in waves. The women break one of the
strings they are wearing and drop a few beads into each votive bowl.
Then they return to their squatting and singing.

If deer have been killed, the men fill little votive bowls with their
blood for annointing the paraphernalia on the altar and the bunches of
green corn. After dark, food is served—one bowl of cold corn gruel
and another with pieces of meat—and everyone relaxes to chat and
laugh.

After the feasting is over, the comisario or head of the community
is led into the circle of women by two young men. He is seated facing the shaman, and all the guardians of the votive bowls of the place
follow to squat behind him. He recites a long prayer to which the
shaman answers, revealing the will of the gods. The people all listen
reverently.

By the time that is over, it is night again and the ceremonial fires
are lighted. Once more the shaman, assistants, women and children
are in their places and the dancing is resumed. This time the dancers
perform a running step with a few backward steps in the direction of
the cardinal points, stomping their sandals to attract the attention of
the gods. Both men and women take part, the men dancing more
vigorously. From time to time some drop out and others take their
places informally. At intervals during the night, the dancers stop to
march around the patio five times, carrying green corn and squashes.

At dawn, when the women and children are again in their places
singing, a number of persons bring out bundles of green corn and

squashes from the god-houses, which are adorned with red and yellow flowers and orchids. Then a procession is formed, the people carrying lighted candles. The women walk along on the outside, sprinkling the corn and those carrying it with sacred water from flowers.

Next all file into the temple and crowd around the burning fire, upon which two huge pots of green corn are cooking. The men, praying quietly, remove the flowers from the corn, while the women sprinkle them and their corn. Then the men offer their corn to Grandfather Fire and do not lift their bundles until the tips are smoldering. Another baptism is then given to men and corn and all file back to the patio where the corn is laid on the ground near the altar. Afterwards, the ribbons holding together five ears—their sacred number—are untied and the corn is offered to the people. While the women and children are receiving the corn, their heads are sprinkled with the sacred water from bunches of yellow flowers. Several women go around the circle to give this baptism. With the sprinkling, the people and corn are "cleansed" and the eating of the corn is safe.

This is generally the last ceremony, after which the people are free to enjoy themselves as they please. The women enter the temple and throw cold water at the men hugging the fire and afterwards serve them tortillas and ears of corn from the bundles. The eating, drinking and fun continue until it is time to leave. Then men and women take their paraphernalia to the god-houses to put away until the next fiesta.

THE FOLK ARTS

The Mexican folk arts are among the most varied and beautiful in the world. Every region has its own kinds, styles, and designs. Humble objects are touched with beauty.

Before the Conquest the minor arts reached a high degree of perfection. The artist craftsman of today have inherited and kept alive the skill of their ancestors, but their arts have changed to satisfy a new world. They are no longer purely indigenous, but a fusion of Spanish and native elements transformed into a Mexican pattern.

The development of the folk arts since the Conquest has naturally been influenced by economic forces. Fore some time afterward, when practically all the nobles had been either killed or enslaved, there was little demand for the finer things. But within a century, thanks to the wealth of the Mexican lands and mines, there was the new Spanish aristocracy to supply, and the folk arts flourished. It was during that epoch which lasted for over a hundred years that the finest things were made. A decline began in the nineteenth century, with the importation of competing objects—cloth, dishes, glassware, jewelry. The lowest level was reached during the Díaz dictatorship, when everything foreign was the fashion, while the finest art manifestations at home were looked upon with indifference.

Since the Social Revolution of 1910–20, the folk arts have entered a new phase. A great wave of nationalism swept the country in the early twenties. The first Revolutionary-Reconstruction Government became the patron of all the arts. While some artists were painting the first frescoes on the walls of educational institutions, others were collecting handicrafts for an exhibition, patronized by the Ministry of Commerce, Industry and Labor, held in Mexico City in 1922. The beauty of the objects exhibited was a revelation to the people. Afterwards it became quite the fashion among the well-to-do families, especially those connected with the government, to have a Mexican room, decorated with native crafts.

More recently the folk arts have acquired even greater prestige as well as economic interest. The hundreds of thousands of tourists who have been flocking to Mexico since about 1933, have fallen in love with these products, and the visitors from the United States are taking them home literally by the carload. As a result, numerous shops have been established in the favorite tourist centers and the sales have been increasing by leaps and bounds.

At the same time the demand for Mexican handicrafts in the United States has been growing. At first small shops showed them here and there; now the best department stores are carrying them. Thus practically over night, the export end of this business alone has increased from thousands to hundreds of thousands of dollars.

This enormous increase in volume of turnover in the native arts must of necessity have its effects on both the craftsmen and the crafts. One unacquainted with the facts would immediately imagine that the craftsmen were the first to be benefited, but that is true only to a limited extent. The poor Mexican has never been a good bargainer. As a common or skilled worker his wages have been notoriously low. Generally an artist craftsman earns less than a common laborer. He has no union to support him and is not considered in the minimum wage law. As a business man the native craftsman is usually also a failure. His earnings have always been so low that he does not know the value of time in a handmade object, and is glad to obtain a little above the cost of his raw materials. It is true that the greater demand for the handicrafts means steadier employment but in the last analysis the only gain is an opportunity to work harder and less happily. The majority of craftsmen have not bettered themselves economically.

In larger quantities the handicrafts sell more cheaply, so that profits are not sufficient to improve their low standard of living. And the necessity of having to make many pieces of the same kind and often having to turn them out in a hurry, kills the artist's joy in creation.

On the crafts the effects of the increased demand is generally bad. Some dealers exact excellent workmanship and respect the taste of the craftsman, but the majority, perhaps, care only for profits. They acept orders which have no relation to any kind of art, and sell anything without discrimination. When the new things that are constantly being made for city people are left to the taste of the craftsmen, they have artistic merit or at least they are objects of good taste. But unfortunately only too often outsiders interfere in the selection of the decorations.

Weaving in Wool and Cotton

Weaving is one of the oldest as well as one of the most important of the handicrafts. Probably it was begun together with or shortly after agriculture, thousands of years ago.

As wool was unknown before the Conquest, all fabrics were woven of the fibres from the cotton plants, cactus, and magueys. Spinning was done on a clay whorl called malacate, and the weaving on a horizontal loom with one end tied to a post and the other on a belt encircling the waist of the weaver (Pl. 101).

It appears from reproductions in the codices that only one heddle

PRE-CONQUEST LOOM (FROM MENDOCINO CODEX)

was used, yet the weavers were able to make the most intricate designs. They learned the art of making dyes of insects, plants, and shells—scarlet from the cochineal, blue from the indigo plant, fine purple from the murex (a sort of snail) shells. They made indescribably beautiful patterns in their textiles by massing a great variety of feathers of the humming and other birds, such as the toucans, macaws, blue jays, scarlet tanagers, and the marvelous quetzal. The Spaniards had never seen anything like it; no wonder they were dazzled!

Since the Conquest the natives have been using the spinning wheel and upright loom, but they have never abandoned their own horizontal loom and spinning whorl. Many beautiful old whorls, ornamented with modeled and engraved designs, are still being used, and new ones are made of clay and wood. (Pl. 100).

For a long time after the Conquest all cloth was handwoven and colored with natural dyes. It was not until the nineteenth century, after the first large textile mills were established, that the natives began to use machine-made cottons. But they still weave practically everything they use in wool, as well as some cotton cloth, so that even

A   B

A—SPINNING WHORLS   B—GIRL SPINNING (FROM MENDOCINO CODEX)

at the present time weaving is one of the most widespread of the handicrafts.

Together with the old techniques, certain beliefs have been preserved. Before the Conquest there were deities that watched over the weavers; now it is the patron saint. But many do not rely on the saints alone. A young weaver from Acaxochitlan, Puebla, told me that he and his friends make offerings of dyed strands of wool, colored paper ribbons, and food to the earth, the trees, and bushes from which they take their dyes. They also dress themselves in the colors they are making and say prayers in Aztec so that their work may turn out well.

Serapes

Serapes or blankets, generally of pure wool, are among the showiest and most useful of the handwoven objects. They are worn by men and boys only, for whom they serve as overcoats, for adornment, as wedding cloaks, and in the end for shrouds. At night they are used for covers and in the daytime to spread things on in the market place; also to stretch over poles for shelter from the sun or rain. Serapes are favorites with tourists, who use them for rugs, couch covers, and lap robes.

Serapes are woven everywhere, generally by men, on upright looms, and everywhere they are different. Even in serape-weaving villages that supply markets and stores, where many weavers use the same colors and patterns, no two are alike. Yet one with experience can recognize the regions they are from. The following are some of the most outstanding styles.

The Texcoco serapes from the village of San Miguel de Chiconcuac, are heavy, of firm weave, blue background with a diamond-shaped geometrical design of contrasting colors in the center called a bocamanga, black and white stripes at the edges, with here and there a touch of red. Other colors are also used. Serapes from villages near Toluca are of lighter weight and looser weave, mostly of natural wool colors, some with all-over designs (all places in the State of Mexico) (Pl. 103).

The best known serapes from the State of Puebla are from the village of Santa Ana Chautempan. Here some of the designs are similar to those of Texcoco, but of different colors and lighter weight. Some of them are made especially for tourists with colors that shriek to the heavens. And they sell well! (Pl. 102)

Typical serapes from Oaxaca are those made in the village of Teotitlán del Valle. They are light weight, loosely woven, some with stylized animal designs on soft gray centers, with black and white striped borders; others have a plain red center with the Mexican flag or flowers at the sides; some have blue and black designs on a white background. Here, too, they make a tourist specialty in shrieking colors, adorned with an idol or calendar stone.

Around Lake Pátzcuaro, Michoacán, and Silao and Dolores, Guanajuato, the serapes are of dark colors, coarse weave, with very simple but pleasing designs in red. In Jocotepec, Jalisco, some of the weavers make very handsome serapes of dark natural wool colors, with red floral designs in the center and at the edges. The Mayos of Sonora weave a very attractive, heavy, one-piece serape—all the other full-sized serapes are woven in two lengths—with lovely blue, black and brown simple decorative motifs. From around San Luis Potosí and Aguascalientes come the very fine, tightly woven serapes, with all-over polychrome patterns of crosswise stripes, the kind the Mexican charros love to sport (Pl. 103).

In San Miguel Allende, Guanajuato, where serapes were once made that compared with the fine ones from Saltillo, Coahuila, the weavers produce good heavy ones, of natural wool colors, mostly for home consumption.

There are innumerable styles of serapes of beautiful texture and very simply adorned, that are never seen except on the backs of natives. Notable among these are the Tarahumara serapes, heavy and roughly woven, of natural wool colors, mostly unadorned, which possess that peculiar beauty derived solely from texture and simplicity (Pl. 102).

Carefully hidden away in ancient family chests one still finds some of the highly-treasured, exquisitely woven and beautiful century-old Saltillo serapes. Occasionally one may be purchased at a very high price. In comparison, the serapes made now seem very inferior, yet there are a sufficient number of good ones among them to demonstrate the fact that the weavers of today are also excellent craftsmen and artists.

Woolen and Cotton Cloth

Most of the cloth woven for commerce is of wool and comes from Toluca, Santa Ana, around Lake Pátzcuaro, and from León, Guanajuato, and Guadalajara. It is either in plain colors or has contrasting crosswise stripes or checks. None of it is so fine as that woven by the women for their own use. The cotton homespuns sold in stores and markets are chiefly for the table. Oaxaca specializes in a great variety of dinner, tea, and bridge sets in plain or combined colors, embroidered with birds or idols. Everywhere in the country women weave

and embroider napkins and cloths for their own use, which are usually
of better quality than those for sale.

Sashes

Sashes or girdles—fajas or ceñidores in Spanish—are worn as well
as woven by both men and women, but mostly by women. They
vary from one and a half to five inches or more in width and from one
to several yards in length. In every region they are of different
widths, lengths, colors, and designs. Most of the cotton sashes are
long and wide and worn by men; red is the preferred color. The
Otomís of Hidalgo weave sashes of very fine dark cotton thread in
attractive all-over patterns. Around Toluca, the Otomís make theirs
of red wool with very pleasing designs. In Milpa Alta, D. F., the
Aztec women use narrow and wide sashes, with charming inwoven
woolen designs of stylized birds, flowers, and butterflies. Oaxaca has
a great variety of sashes. Those from the mountain regions are mostly
narrow, of red wool, with simple designs. In a few villages of the
Sierra de Juárez, the natives weave long, wide sashes of crude silk in
beautiful shades of purple and red, of an extraordinary heavy texture;
some of wool in the same colors are made in Mitla. Women around
Patzcuaro use several very narrow sashes at the same time, of different
colors and designs. The most interesting of all the sashes are those
worn by Huichol men. They are long, fairly wide, of natural wool
colors, brown and white predominating, beautifully woven with
simple primitive designs.

Woolen Bags

Bags, bolsas or morrales, are made in all sizes. The majority of bags
used are woven of fibre. The most interesting ones of wool are those
of the Coras of Nayarit and of the Huichols of the same state, and
also of Jalisco; the Huichols using strings of tiny ones around the
waist and larger ones to hang from the shoulders. Other beautiful
bags are those made by the Otomís of Ixmiquilpan and Zimapán,
Hidalgo, with inwoven designs of stylized birds, animals, and flowers
in various colors, chiefly reds, blacks, and blues. No matter how
lovely the bags are, they are for ordinary use. I once asked an Otomí
to sell me a beautiful bag he was carrying wrapped around some tortillas and he answered, "No señorita, this bag is for service."

Rebozos

The rebozo or shawl apparently had no counterpart before the Conquest. It seems to have its origin in the necessity that a woman cover her head with something soft in the Christian temples. Mexican women never wear hats in church.

The rebozo is of the same importance to the woman as the serape to the man. It is her hat and coat; serves as a cradle for the baby on her back and as a blanket when it is lying beside her; for a market basket, as a cover for a large clay pot of tamales on the street; when twisted on the head, as a stand for a basket or water jar. Often young girls wear rebozos folded over the shoulders and crossed in front for adornment.

Rebozos for adults are about a yard wide by two and a half long; smaller ones are made for children. Rebozos are generally woven on horizontal looms by women, occasionally by men, but the women always make the intricate fringe. As they are used principally by the poor, nearly all rebozos are of ordinary cotton thread and conservative colors—dark blues, grays, browns, all with fine white pin-point designs. The patterns are achieved in the dyeing and require great skill. The weavers take balls of white thread and form skeins with the help of a wheel. Then they tie the thread at certain points so that it does not take the dye, thus forming the design.

As almost all rebozos are similar in color and design, the regional differences are very subtle, with the exception of those of Michoacán. Here they have a plain dark blue background with a white lengthwise stripe and often bright colors in the fringe, which is sometimes of feathers. Occasionally rebozos are made of silk or rayon in gay colors for holidays.

The loveliest of all the rebozos are those that are woven of such fine thread that the saying is they can be pulled through a ring. They are of the same colors and designs as the cheaper ones and are seldom made now. But some of the old ones—over a hundred years old—are still in existence from the famous rebozo-weaving centers of Santa Maria, San Luis Potosí and Tenancingo, Mexico. Some rebozos recently made in Tenancingo are extraordinarily fine, with knotted designs in the fringe of birds and flowers, taking months to make (Pl. 105).

As the rebozo does not interest city people or foreigners to any great extent, it has not changed much and has remained a typical folk garment. Young girls know how to use rebozos so as to enhance their charm and women, their dignity.

Petates

Petates, Aztec for reed mats, are as primitive, and their use is as widespread as before the Conquest. They are woven by hand—some of a coarse reed called tule; the finer ones of palm leaves. The most common designs are—cuadrado or square, costilla or ribbed, jaspeado or variegated.

Whether on the ground or on a bed, the native nearly always sleeps on a petate. He comes into the world on a petate and often leaves it

PETATE DESIGNS

rolled in one. Petates are used to sit on, to spread things on, to receive gifts on. In Tuxpan, Jalisco, a new petate is carried to church by one of the bridal party as a symbol of union (Pl. 76).

There are petates of all sizes; they are made wherever tule and palms grow and are sold everywhere. The finer palm petates come from the States of Puebla, Guerrero, and Oaxaca. These are generally decorated with geometrical designs in reds, blues, yellows, and violets. The tule petates are never dyed; they are coarsely woven and because of their simplicity are the most attractive and cheapest.

The Lerma River and lagoons in the Toluca Valley furnish much tule and many petates are made there. The entire village of Tultepec is devoted to petate making. The natives of this region also make amusing petate figures of soldiers, horses and other animals, charming birds and rattles. Similar toys are made of the palm petate; in addition large purses are made with two sections fitting into one another, which city women like to use as sewing baskets. The round baskets, without handles, called tompeates, are also made of palm; similar ones of tule are called chiquihuites, the latter serving for tortilla containers.

The important and intimate character of the petate has given rise to a number of popular sayings. To describe an undertaking started with great enthusiasm and suddenly dropped—llamarada de petate, or a petate flame. Instead of saying a person has died—se petateó, or he has taken himself off in a petate. Ya lió su petate, or he has rolled up his petate, means that someone has moved elsewhere. To indicate that someone is of lower rank than yourself—esas pulgas no brincan en mi petate, or those fleas do not jump on my petate. El que nace en un petate siempre anda eructando a tule, or he who was born on a petate always belches tule, is a figurative way of describing a vulgar person.

Sombreros

Sombreros, or the Mexican style of hat, are made by hand of palm leaves in all textures, shapes, and sizes. Everybody in the native male world wears a sombrero, and occasionally women also wear them as a protection against the sun.

Sombreros are made everywhere and everywhere they are different, the differences being found in the shape and size of both crown and brim. Those from Morelos are distinguished by their very wide brims; those from Papantla, Vera Cruz, by their very tall crowns and narrow brims. Huichol sombreros have flat crowns and ordinary sized brims similar to the Chinese hats, and they are adorned with red wool, tropical feathers and, for fiestas, also with orchids. Chiapas has a variety of interesting sombreros, adorned with ribbons and wool. Finely woven horsehair, leather or braid bands are also used around the crown. The finest palm sombreros come from Yucatán and Tabasco. City charros or riders wear felt sombreros, trimmed with braid. The variety of Mexican sombreros is infinite (Pls. 15, 33, 106, 140, 141).

Baskets

Canastas or baskets are the first products of an agricultural people, hence they are among the oldest of the handicrafts. They also show regional differences. Those from San Juan del Rio, Querétaro, are of the natural color of the palm, beautifully woven, with a wide brown band near the top. Among the most popular are the Toluca baskets, made in the nearby village of Santa Ana. The palm is dyed in a great variety of colors and designs of animals, and figures are inwoven with the background white, or vice versa. These baskets are made in all sizes and shapes, with and without covers, for clothes, paper, sewing.

Fibre Objects

The fibre of a squat maguey is spun and made into rope and string. The Otomís of Hidalgo weave ayates or carrying cloths of fibre; some are coarse and loosely woven while others are so fine that they could be used for curtains. Sometimes ayates are beautifully embroidered with colored wool. Around Toluca, the ayates are heavier, of tighter weave and richly embroidered in bands of stylized animals, birds, and flowers. The best ones are used for altar cloths and for carrying flowers and candles on pilgrimages to miraculous shrines.

Hammocks of palm or ixtli, the maguey fibre, are used a great deal in the hot regions, principally as beds. Guerrero produces fine palm hammocks as well as colorful fibre mats to put under saddles. In Yucatán the hammocks are of sisal fibre and the finest ones of cotton thread, frequently mixed with rayon.

Oaxaca natives make an unusually attractive fibre bag, called a *red* or net, adorned with gayly colored bands of purple, blue, cerise, yellow, and undyed ixtli. Simple ixtli net bags are much used in Chiapas and in other parts of the country.

There are many uses for reed, palm, and fibre. A handful of fibre, called estropaje, is used for a wash cloth or for ordinary scrubbing of dishes and other objects; or fibre is made into small brushes, for the same purpose, with colored handles. The bottoms and backs of chairs and benches are woven of palm or tule. Petate fans are used for starting the fire in the brasero stoves. Women use petate or palm belts under their wool or cotton sashes in some places. Picturesque palm-leaf rain-proof capes are worn by natives. Sandals are made of fibre rope (Pls. 43, 64).

Embroidery

Embroidery before the Conquest went together with weaving as it does now, and was patronized by the same goddess. Since then it has been enriched with new materials and designs and is very popular with all Mexican women. Among the natives it is used by men also.

Native women embroider shirts, blouses, skirts, bed-covers, napkins, bags; in fact, anything and everything that lends itself to such adornment, often combining embroidery with inwoven designs in solid or cross-stitch patterns, using floral, bird, animal or other motifs, such as objects used in the church—a candelabra, the tree of life, even a horned devil. Whether they copy their designs from samplers or do them from imagination, women and girls work them without tracing, selecting their own colors. Some of the results are very beautiful. In Almoloya del Rio, Mexico, native women make tea and bridge sets, bags, centerpieces, and coats of unbleached cotton, embroidered with black or blue silk thread in attractive all-over designs for the markets and stores.

The most elegant Mexican embroidery is that done with fine silver and gold thread on church vestments and bullfighters' costumes (Pl. 104).

Hand-Drawn Work

Native women do very fine hand-drawn work, but it is always on ordinary white cotton cloth because Mexico does not produce linens. Aguascalientes, Irapuato, Celaya and Guanajuato supply stores with centerpieces, doilies, and handkerchiefs. City stores often purchase imported linens and hire women to do the work on them.

Bead Work

Fine bead designs on cloths, napkins, bags, cigarette-cases, and hat-bands were popular in the eighteenth century; they were made but not used by the native women. At the present time this type of

WOOLEN BAG FROM IXMIQUILPAN, HIDALGO

adornment is used by them chiefly around the necks of blouses and the ends of homespun hair ribbons. Huichol women make bracelets and earrings of very fine blue and white beads for their men, and rope chains and earrings for themselves. Beads of all colors and sizes are used to adorn the headdresses of dancers and are worn in strings by women and girls everywhere. Colored spangles are used to adorn costume skirts.

Crocheting and Knitting

Native women and girls crochet laces and yokes, but chiefly to sell. It is sometimes possible to find such objects for sale at market places. The same is true of sweaters and socks, the latter sometimes knit by men as they sit in the markets trying to sell them.

Pottery Making

Pottery and weaving are the two most ancient, important, and varied of the folk arts. But while there are no pre-Conquest examples of cloth because of its perishable character, we have many examples of pottery of all the races and epochs. Thus we know that the potters of ancient times utilized almost all the known technical processes and obtained beautiful results.

ANCIENT TRIPOD BOWLS (BRITISH MUSEUM)

The tripod bowl with cascabel feet was one of the characteristic forms. Others were vases with globular bodies, supported on three feet; plates, short-necked bottles, vessels in the form of animals, and so on. The potters also made many little figures and figurines, some with small whistles in back; these shed light on the clothing and ornaments worn by the people. The pottery was painted in beautiful colors and designs, as well as decorated by incision, impression or engraving.

The Spaniards introduced the pottery-wheel, glazing, and a more efficient method of firing through a well-constructed kiln. But as in weaving, the primitive techniques, processes and forms persist along with the European and modern. Also as in weaving, entire families and villages specialize in the production of pottery. In some large cities there are pottery factories in which the work is specialized but all done by hand.

Pottery-making is a slow process in Mexico, even in the large, well-equipped potteries, as so much is done in the primitive way because of low wages—men and boys knead the clay by treading on it all day long; all the decoration and other work is done by hand. The potters who work at home are even slower. They have to bring their sand from long distances, carrying it on their own backs or on burros, and they work without conveniences. Even their ovens are usually improvised for each baking, with stones, sherds, and grass.

It is difficult to classify and describe all the various regional types of pottery because they are so numerous. But all of them can be divided into two classes—the corriente or common type used by the natives and the better, more expensive, kind made for city people. Although the common pottery is often the chief industry in a village, it is produced by isolated potters throughout the Republic. The finer pottery is made chiefly at the present time in the states of Puebla, Oaxaca, Michoacán and Jalisco, but its best period ended long ago. Common pottery, on the other hand, because it is not a product for city people, has preserved its purity and good taste to a greater degree.

Potters, like weavers, have patron saints in their homes and shops. They make offerings to them as well as to the elements and pagan gods so that they may have luck in their work.

Pottery-making gives the artist-craftsman ample scope to express talent and originality, especially if he is working at home.

The first steps are to bring the sand and to prepare the clay, generally the work of men. Women sometimes make the clay in the same manner as they do tortilla dough, on their grinding stones (Pl. 79). Four processes are employed in forming the pieces—modeling, moulding, modeling parts on a piece that has been moulded, and modeling with the wheel.

There are three types of finish on Mexican pottery—the unglazed which is simply baked, the polished, and glazed. On the unglazed the decoration is applied after the pieces have been dried in the sun and baked; on the other two, after the pieces have been slightly baked, and then they are baked again to fix the colors, or are polished. The decorators use earth colors and brushes made of dogs' hair. The glaze for the better pottery is composed of fine sand, tin, and lead, and of lead alone for the ordinary pottery.

Common Pottery

Common pottery is generally glazed, inexpensive but usually very attractive. It is made in all the forms necessary for dishes, cooking utensils, and water containers. There are little mugs for children, larger ones for adults, soup bowls, lovely ordinary-sized and huge water jars, large deep bowls for cooking meats, and so on. The colors vary from an orange yellow to a dark ochre, with decorative touches in yellow and black of lines, flowers, animals, a verse, a name—a tender thought from the humble maker to the equally humble user. However, common pottery is found in all Mexican kitchens, even in those of the rich. Toys and ritual objects made of this ware will be described later.

Unglazed Pottery

There are villages here and there that produce an inexpensive but very beautiful unglazed primitive type of pottery, which reaches regional markets only, as it is too brittle to transport long distances. The best examples are the large water jars and smaller pieces with interesting decorative motifs in brown on a light background from Guerrero; water jugs from Hidalgo and Chiapas; light brown pieces of various sizes and styles with all-over designs in red, and the plain black jugs and delightful toys from Oaxaca (Pls. 111, 113, 114).

Puebla Talavera

Puebla has always been a famous pottery center. Soon after the city was founded in 1532, the Spaniards taught the natives, who were descendants of the great Toltec potters, the technique of the Spanish Talavera. But contrary to the usual experience, this pottery did not take on a Mexican character at once. Throughout the Colonial period the industry was dominated by the Spaniards, who obliged the potters to make faithful copies in form and color of the Talavera de la Reina or the Talavera of the Queen—white glazed background with blue designs. As the native craftsmen are not good at copying, this pottery was inferior artistically, but it was considered among the best during the eighteenth and nineteenth centuries, when the rich used pottery dishes.

After Mexico won her independence from Spain in 1821, the Toltec spirit of the potters also rebelled. They began creating a more Mexican type of Talavera, with added colors and different designs. It was then that it became internationally known as the Talavera de Puebla.

Even though the Puebla Talavera took on a more Mexican character in its best epoch, it was and still is more hybrid than other types, showing marked foreign influence in form and decoration—Italian, Spanish-Moorish, and even Chinese. The best and most beautiful pieces are those made by talented potters who combine the Talavera technique with Mexican forms, colors, and motifs.

The Puebla Talavera of today is of good quality—perhaps the best and least breakable of any made in the country—well finished and made in a great variety of forms, such as dinner and tea sets, vases, flower pots, and huge jars resembling the Chinese; also a great variety of tiles. The churches of Puebla, Cholula, and others of the region are noted for their tile domes in all colors, principally of the Spanish Talavera—white, blue, and yellow. Some of them also have beautiful tiled façades (Pl. 115).

Semi-Talavera Types

In the late eighteenth and early nineteenth centuries, the patriot Father Hidalgo gave impulse to the pottery industry of his State of Guanajuato and it became a rival to Puebla. The potteries there made beautiful vases, large plates, bowls, dishes, utilizing the Talavera technique in combination with Mexican decorative motifs—flowers in greens, sienna, reds and brown on white and light brown glazed backgrounds. Some of this type of ware is still being made in the City of Guanajuato but it is not comparable to the old. Green glazed pottery of pleasing styles is made now in Dolores Hidalgo, Guanajuato.

Aguascalientes is now making good-looking pottery, similar to the Guanajuato semi-majolica type in quality and decoration, in vases and sets of dishes; some of the same kind is also being made in La Paz, San Luis Potosí.

Oaxaca Pottery

The best Oaxaca pottery is that which is being made in the capital in dinner sets, vases, bowls and other pieces, simply but charmingly decorated with flowers, birds, and butterflies in reds, greens, browns, and blues on a burnt-orange or white glazed background. The green glazed ware from Santa María Atzompa is also very attractive; it consists of toys and tableware, suitable for use in city homes.

Michoacán Pottery

Michoacán has beautiful red earth and produces, perhaps, more lovely unspoiled pottery than any other state at the present time. Examples of all of it may be found in the Popular Art Museum in Patzcuaro.

A simple but pleasing type of pottery is produced in Patzcuaro. In Tzintzuntzan, the ancient seat of Tarascan kings, the potters make attractive sienna, unglazed jars, some with faces like the ones made there before the Conquest; small bowls and other pieces, with a cream-colored background, adorned on the inside only, with figures, birds, and flowers. The typical Santa Fe pottery has a very dark, almost black background and is painted with very gay stylized flowers. Michoacán kitchens are often hung with strings of tiny pitchers of this colorful ware (Pl. 96).

Many other villages produce interesting types of pottery. Outstanding among them is Huancito, one of the eleven of the picturesque Cañada. From there come lovely polished ochre jars with primitive stylized designs in black, white, and red; toys and other pieces.

Capula and Santo Tomás make similar pottery—graceful, highly polished, plain dark jars; vases, pitchers, and attractively glazed brown dishes. Villa Morelos produces beautiful large bowls, glazed in black on the inside only; handsome jars, the covers decorated with fish and figures.

The most beautiful pottery comes from Patamba, a mountain village. It consists of dark green glazed plates, with all-over lighter floral and geometrical designs; also of jars of the same style in lovely forms, and other pieces. The pieces made by the Contreras family are fantastically adorned with stylized owls, deer with strange horns, surrealistic flowers and forms, in whites on greens or dark brown backgrounds. Family traditions in styles and techniques come to an end when there is no one to carry them on, often a great tragedy (Pls. 108, 119).

Jalisco Pottery

Jalisco is another state in which some of the very best and most beautiful pottery has been made, and during its best epoch it was exported to foreign countries. As the pottery villages are near Guadalajara, the state capital, the ware is always referred to as Loza de Guadalajara.

The outstanding pottery villages were Tonalá, Tlaquepaque, and Santa Cruz, each making distinctive styles. In recent years the Santa Cruz potters joined those of the two other villages, and later the best potters from Tonalá were hired by Tlaquepaque potteries. Now, although differences in style still exist, they are not so well defined.

Tonalá used to be the most important of the three villages. The potters modeled their pieces and painted them with great talent and fantasy, producing the most beautiful clay objects since the Conquest. These were in the form of handsomely shaped covered and uncovered jars, vases, bowls, water bottles, cups, and so on, with unglazed backgrounds either in soft grays or reds, decorated with indigenous motifs and colors—geometrical designs, stylized flowers, plants and birds, in grays, grayish blues, rose, ochres, reds, and black. All the earth colors were found in the vicinity, the only imported item being the carbonate for the white. A characteristic of this ware was its pleasing scent when it was wet, which was achieved by applying a light coat of varnish of tierra de Sayula—a clay from the village of that name—and firing with jara or rock-rose, a process still applied to the unpolished pieces, known as loza de olor or the scented ware (Pl. 109).

Tlaquepaque used to make a limited assortment of glazed pottery, among which the clay toys were outstanding. But because it is nearer to Guadalajara, it has become much more important than Tonalá, especially with respect to quantity production. All the expensive ware is now made in this town; however, it is not what it was even as recently as fifteen years ago. Merchants and exporters have so rushed the potters and interfered with their good taste, that only now and then does one come across a fine unglazed or even glazed piece, decorated in the beautiful Tonalá manner. Now the large jars are made in moulds, and although the decorators still use indigenous motifs, they lack the beauty of the older ones. So in Tlaquepaque also, the inexpensive pottery remains the best. The specialties here are the famous painted pigs, animal toys, clay fruit of all kinds and colors, religious figures and those of native types in regional dress, bullfighters and others, and dinner sets of pleasing styles (Pls. 111, 112).

Ritual Pottery

Ritual pottery is always in use, but special objects are made for the three most important religious festivals. As this type of pottery is in the nature of an offering to the gods, some of it is especially beautiful.

For Holy Week it is customary to decorate the altars with tender shoots of corn and other plants for which new pots are always utilized.

The Atzompa potters make some in the form of angels, frogs, pigs, and deer, which are partly glazed in green. In some churches the natives reproduce the orchard where Christ is supposed to have been arrested, and put all sorts of clay animals in the grass.

The Day of the Dead, November 2, is the next holiday for which much new pottery is made. Although censers and candlesticks are used every day of the year, special ones are made for this occasion; they are generally of black glazed clay, ornately adorned with modeled angels, birds, and flowers. In Ocotlán, Oaxaca, the censers are more primitive—of brown unglazed clay, supported by three feet, and surrounded with figures called ánimas or souls. Many allusive toys are made for this holiday—papier-maché skulls, skeletons, masks, and coffins—which delight the children (Pls. 41, 45, 117, 118, 119).

The third festival is Christmas. Many elaborate mangers are set up in homes and churches, adorned with clay Biblical figures, animals, shepherds, regional native types, bullfighters and others. The holy figures are especially interesting because the potters represent them in the robes they see on the saints in pictures or in church and add a Mexican touch by modeling a sombrero on their backs. Occasionally one finds a very charming Adam and Eve under a tree with the apple, or some other expression of the native's imagination (Pl. 46).

Hand-blown Glass

Glass blowing is one of the various crafts taught by the Spaniards, but by this time Mexican glass has achieved a character and reputation of its own not only in Mexico but also in the United States, where it is sold in the best stores. Complete dinner and tea sets as well as pitchers, glasses, and jars are made of it in lovely forms and colors.

Village natives seldom use glasses, but the city poor can afford native glasses because they are less expensive than the ugly commercial ones. The attractive dark green ribbed pitchers and glasses are the least expensive but, on the whole, handmade glass is a luxury even in Mexico.

Many of the glass blowers are artists and do not limit their productions to utilitarian objects. They make perfectly formed diminutive horses with riders on their backs, other animals and birds, about an inch in height; intricate miniature chandeliers, candlesticks, and complete sets of dishes in tiny glass closets.

Glass factories in Mexico City and Guadalajara supply most of the city stores. The work is dangerous and poorly paid but fascinating to watch. The glass is melted in a huge oven and the blowers take some of the molten mass on the ends of long iron tubes to blow it into a simple or intricate form before it cools. The scene makes one think of hell, as the blowers run about with points of fire.

Gold and Silver Work

The ancient Mexicans wrought marvelously beautiful and wonderful objects of gold and some of silver and copper, the only metals they had before the coming of the Spaniards.

Among the presents sent to Cortés by Moctezuma were gold jewels, diadems, ducks, lizards, dogs, soles for sandals, all beautifully wrought; a wheel of fine gold as large as a cartwheel, engraved with the sun and other designs, and a larger silver wheel in imitation of the moon.

Many extraordinary objects may still be seen in Mexican and foreign museums. In the Monte Albán collection on exhibition in the State Museum of Oaxaca, are gold, pearl, and turquoise necklaces, ex-

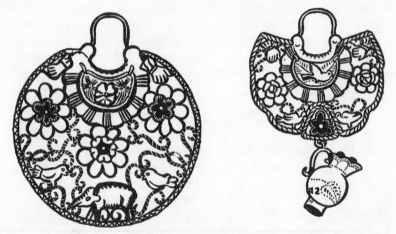

SILVER EARRINGS

quisitely made gold pendants, tiger heads, masks, a cup of a natural mixture of silver and copper, a rock crystal goblet and other marvels.

After the Conquest the native gold and silver smiths continued making gold jewelry for the wealthy, and silver objects for the churches. There was much silver and it was used lavishly. It is said that the foundation of the handsome La Valenciana Church of Guanajuato was laid with silver from the rich mines of that city. Huge silver candlesticks, goblets and other objects filled the churches and even altar rails were made of silver. Wealthy families used heavy silver table-ware, candlesticks, boxes, goblets, cigarette cases and other objects. Silversmiths also made tiny silver toys. In Puebla it was the custom to make presents of silver matracas or rattles in Holy Week.

The present-day natives use very little gold and silver jewelry, so for a long time their smiths had very little work. But since about 1933, Mexican silver tableware and jewelry have become very popular with the well-to-do and tourists, and are being sold both at home and abroad in enormous quantities. The silversmiths use indigenous motifs for jewelry and some of them produce some beautiful pieces.

Iron—Steel—Copper—Tin

Iron was introduced by the Spaniards who taught the natives how to work it. Everywhere in Mexico one sees handsomely wrought iron fences, especially around old churches; window grilling, banisters, immense door-nails, knockers, locks, keys, and adornments on carved chests. The best iron work dates from the Colonial period; very little of it has been done since.

Steel, which was also brought by the Spaniards, is often used in

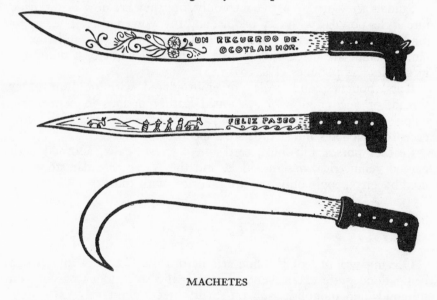

MACHETES

combination with silver for bridle bits and spurs. Amozoc, Puebla and León, Guanajuato, are both noted for this kind of work. But the most popular and widely used steel object is the machete or long wide straight or curved knife. The machete is the native's inseparable companion. He uses it for cutting wood, to clear away the bushes in the jungle, for cutting sugar cane and for other work, as well as for self-protection and aggression. There are machetes of various kinds and prices, some very fine ones etched with attractive decorations, enclosed in handsome leather cases. Nearly all of the better ones have some allusive saying on the blade—"Don't unsheath me without reason nor replace me without honor," "If this reptile bites you, there is no cure in the drugstore," and others.

Copper was known and used before the Conquest. It is still mined primitively and is inexpensive. Fine hand-hammered copper kettles and other objects are often used by the poor. In Santa Clara del Cobre, Michoacán, the coppersmiths used to make some very beautiful copper pots and deep trays; for tourists, they now make many small objects, such as ash trays and pots, and some very nice serving trays.

Leather Work

Leather work came to Mexico through the Spaniards and is, therefore, a post-Conquest art. Leather is made into bags, saddles, belts, coats, and sandals; it is carved, tooled, embroidered, and appliquéd.

Sandals are worn by native men only, but they are now being made into styles popular with city people; and for women also. The largest sandal production centers are Oaxaca City, Guadalajara and Mazatlán, but some are made everywhere. León, Guanajuato, is noted for its saddles and pouches (Pls. 107, 136).

Belts, pouches, and coats are embroidered with gold or silver thread, or decorated with appliquéd leather designs in contrasting colors. Saddles as well as other objects are also adorned. Handsome cases for machetes and swords are a specialty.

Leather purses, bill-folds, card and cigarette cases, adorned with carved geometrical designs, idols, and the Aztec calendar stone are used by city people only and are favorites with tourists.

Carving

Carving was one of the fine arts before the Conquest and is still being done quite extensively. There is the stupendous carving on pyramids and monoliths and on small objects constantly excavated. Many such, of jade, bone, metals and other materials, are now in museums.

After the Conquest native artists did an enormous amount of beautiful carving in colonial churches and homes. The choir stalls of the Mexico City and Puebla Cathedrals and the seats of San Agustín, which are now in the National Preparatory School, are but a few of the many excellent examples. Everywhere in Mexico one sees beautiful carving done by nameless native artists.

Carved objects for popular use are the metates and mortars, some in the form of animals like the ancient ones. Spoons and combs are carved of wood, the latter with charming bird designs on the handles. The wooden chocolate beaters are especially attractive. They are turned on lathes, burned and carved with geometric and bird designs. The same process and type of adornment is applied to wooden boxes, salt and pepper shakers, tooth-pick and powder containers made for city people. Paracho, Michoacán, produces these objects; also villages around Toluca.

In the City of Puebla native craftsmen make many attractive onyx novelties in the form of strings of beads, inkwells, paper-cutters, pen-holders and other objects.

Horn objects are scarce but here and there one sees a lone vendor selling them on the city streets. The horns of young bulls are cleaned and with the aid of acids are formed into graceful birds, desk accessories, chessmen and other articles.

In every large seaport one finds numerous shell novelties—combs, earrings, necklaces, trays and other objects.

Feathers—Straw—Horsehair

The art of feather work has practically disappeared. Before the Conquest the natives embroidered their fabrics with colorful feather designs and wove feather garments. The only use made of this kind of adornment now is on New Year, place, and bridge cards, but feathers are still used on the headdresses of indigenous dancers.

Colorful cards and pictures, demonstrating skill and imagination, are made of popote or broom straw. And there are the many funny brooms and dusters.

Horsehair is dyed and woven into little purses, cigarette cases, a great variety of small baskets, brush handles, belts, and hatbands, the latter of natural colors.

Prisoners in the Mexican penitentiaries make horsehair and carved objects, among them chess sets, which they sell to visitors.

Lacquer

Lacquer is a pre-Spanish art, believed by some investigators to have been introduced by the Chinese, who visited Mexico long before the Conquest. In support of this theory there is the coincidence that the important lacquer centers are in the Pacific Coast states of Michoacán and Guerrero, in which the Chinese first landed; also, there are similarities to the Chinese technical processes and stylization of flowers.

But whoever may have introduced the lacquer art, it soon acquired a definite Mexican character.

Lacquer, like the other important handicrafts, began to decline in the nineteenth century and has now been revived because of the tourist demand. Spanish influence did not improve the process but enriched the palette with new colors and increased the demand by utilizing a greater number of objects—chests, sewing boxes, litters for images. For themselves the natives made only bateas or large deep trays, jícaras or small gourd bowls, and other small containers. Many fine examples of all the objects of the best period have been preserved in private households and museums.

Uruapan, one of the oldest lacquer centers of Michoacán, is still the most important. It is situated in the vicinity where the tzirimu wood for bateas and other pieces is found. Here, too, the Tarascans discovered that they could extract oil from the chía seeds of the salvia chian; also from a worm called aje, which makes the lacquer hard, unbreakable, and waterproof, giving it a unique quality. And the earth of the region furnishes all the necessary colors.

The decorative process typical of Uruapan is that of incrustation. First the background, generally black, is lacquered on the object and permitted to dry. Then the design is cut into the coat of lacquer with a fine steel point, after which each color is applied separately and rubbed in with the palm of the hand, and must dry before another is rubbed on. In Pátzcuaro and Quiroga, the designs are mostly painted. Formerly gold and silver dust were mixed with the colors.

The Michoacán lacquer of today has degenerated greatly. Most of the workers are substituting linseed oil for the natural, and prepared dyes for the earth colors, and most of their decorative motifs are stilted and ugly. One is no longer sure of the quality of even the most expensive pieces, and the small boxes, bowls, pin-trays, powder boxes and other objects made to supply modern needs are seldom incrusted.

In Pátzcuaro, however, the Popular Art Museum has had a good influence. Some of the lacquer workers are reviving old techniques and designs and using pure materials (Pl. 121).

The most important lacquer center in Guerrero is the village of Olinalá, interesting but difficult to reach. It is picturesque, with a church dating from the sixteenth century, which the lacquer workers have painted with religious subjects in the dorado or gold process, for which they were famous at one time. Guerrero has most of the necessary raw materials for lacquer and an especially fine aromatic wood, called olinalau, of which boxes are made.

In Olinalá the workers decorate with rayada or grooving technique. First one color is lacquered on the piece and left to dry, after which another contrasting one is applied. After the second one has dried.

designs of stylized birds, butterflies, and flowers are grooved with a fine steel point, leaving the first color exposed.

Some of the designs are also painted here. About a hundred years ago they made very beautiful painted baules or chests, with either red or black background, decorated with flower arabesques, birds, and eagles. Often scenes from postcards or pictures were used as decorative motifs, but the artists transformed them in such a way that they became quite Mexican. These chests still exist and occasionally one may be found for sale.

Among the inexpensive but charming Olinalá lacquered objects are the jícaras or gourds, painted with lovely bird and flower designs, which at one time were used as dippers and were never faded by the water. Others are tropical fruit of natural sizes and colors. Graceful birds are made by gluing together various suitable gourds—a fat one for the body, a slender one for the neck; also natural-looking fish. [1]

Masks

Before the Conquest, the Mexicans used a variety of masks beautifully wrought of rich materials, chiefly for ritual and magical pur-

YAQUI MASK

poses. Priests wore masks with the facial characteristics of the deities during fiestas in their honor; and dancers, those representing the animals they wished to kill in the hunt. On occasion masks were placed on idols and effigies of the dead. For the latter they were of stone but for human beings they were of wood or mosaics, some with hair and golden crests. Many splendid masks have survived the Conquest. In the National Museum of Mexico City there is one of diorite, encrusted with turquoise and mother of pearl.

The use of masks, which has continued down to the present time, has greatly decreased with the degeneration of the primitive and religious dances. However, a great many are still being made and worn. In Guerrero there are several dances in which masks are worn, the most interesting being that of the tigers for which expressive masks are made with spots, hair, and tusks. Michoacán produces a great variety of interesting masks, among them some black lacquered ones. The Yaquis and Mayos of Sonora make many original masks of wood. Oaxaca, Puebla and other states in which traditional dances have been preserved also produce good masks. Saltillo, Coahuila is noted for tin masks.

Masks are made of wood, cloth, leather, clay, paste, tin, and paper, sometimes with genuine hair and teeth. They are painted, lacquered or left in a natural state. The features are subordinated to the materials and one finds in them the same plastic vigor as in the best and most primitive sculptures.

Even the paper masks, made in quantities and selling at ten centavos or two cents a piece, show imagination, fantasy and great decorative talent. Of these, special ones are made for the Day of the Dead in the form of skeletons and skulls; for carnivals, to represent French and Spanish types; for other times, kings, birds, monkeys, as well as all sorts of fanciful faces, which delight youngsters and adults.

If you were to ask a native why he wears a mask in a dance or at any other time, he would very likely reply, "Es costumbre," "It is the custom." Yet the present-day natives are motivated in their use of masks by the same reasons as their ancestors—magic and the desire to achieve a facial expression for which they feel their own features inadequate (Pls. 2, 22, 23, 77, 78, 84, 90, 91, 92, 124).[2]

Fireworks

Gunpowder and fireworks were unknown in Mexico before the coming of the Spaniards. The latter appealed so to the imagination of the natives that they have incorporated them into their ritual. At important festivals, the patron saint is greeted at dawn with songs of praise and salvos of fireworks. The poorest villages save all year long to gather a few hundred pesos to pay for a fireworks castle for the big fiesta, which constitutes a fortune to be burned up in twenty minutes of dazzling beauty.

Every district has its own artist fireworks makers. The work is poorly paid and dangerous but they love it. Between festivals they work in the fields or at other occupations, because only in the larger places is the work fairly steady.

The most beautiful and intricate of the fireworks pieces are the castles. They are about a hundred feet high, made in sections to represent saints, crowns, crosses, flowers, birds and other forms. Each section goes off separately, the whole taking from twenty minutes to a half hour and ending in a shower of dazzling light. There are also

WHEEL OF A FIREWORKS CASTILLO

daylight castles, with humorous figures of animals and dolls that embrace and dance while the fireworks go off.

Among the favorite pieces are the small bulls, which men wear over their heads to play at bullfighting with the boys as the fireworks shoot out at them. It is a dangerous feat but fun for the crowds. The Judases, which are burned on the streets after the Mass of Glory on Saturday before Easter Sunday, are also fun. They are made of papier-maché, from one to ten feet high, with funny expressive faces; the storekeepers hang things on them for which the boys scramble, after the figures are shot off and fall to the ground.

There is no limit to the variety of objects the fireworks makers invent—from the simplest to the most intricate pieces, even naval battles. The Taxco fireworks makers reproduced a modern air battle during the war, with planes attacking and being attacked.[3]

JUDAS

Toys

The Mexican toy world is full of delightfully fantastic objects and peopled with fanciful animals. It is paradoxical but true that although native children become adults at the age of eight or sooner, dressing like their parents and working with them, they never outgrow their childish pleasure in the simple, amusing things. Thus the craftsmen who make the toys, do so con cariño or with affection, as the Mexicans say when someone loves his work. They, also, love toys.

If all the types of toys could be gathered in one place, they would constitute a great ensemble of beauty, grotesqueness, and humor. There would be clay, glass, and petate insects, birds and animals of all sizes and colors, some with whistles in their tails; animals playing instruments, pigs adorned with gay flowers, petate and tin rattles, and many other amusing things.

Some of the clay animals have slits in their backs, being intended for banks. However, the toy makers often forget to make them big enough for a penny to pass through, which is never discovered by most owners because they have nothing to save. But that does not interfere with their delight in the forms, colors, and comical expressions.

In addition to the every-day toys, there are many seasonal toys that afford fun for the children—for Holy Week, the little Judases and wooden rattles; for the Day of the Dead, cardboard coffins from which a skeleton can be made to jump by pulling a string, masks, and candy skulls; for Christmas, Biblical figures, shepherds, and animals.

There are many household toys—furniture of all kinds, tiny, perfectly formed sets of dishes, metates, mortars, and stoves. Dolls are generally made of cloth or rags and dressed like the adults of the region; there is also a better class of dolls made for city stores. Marionettes made from rags into fantastic personages are very popular. In some regions, as in Guerrero, original wooden dolls are made.

Not all the native children can afford many toys but some even of the poorer families can sometimes buy those made in their own villages; and children are clever at inventing substitutes. They make them of stones, bones, sticks, and rags. Their make-believe world is generally like the adult world, filled with beliefs in magic and miracles (Pls. 41, 45, 111, 112, 113, 128).[4]

Painting and Sculpture

For centuries after the Conquest, the fine arts were forbidden to native artists, so that now one finds many excellent unsigned works in churches and convents; also some splendid eighteenth and nineteenth century portraits in private homes and museums. But painting and sculpture in connection with the folk arts were permitted because they did not compete with the work of Spanish artists.

The most conspicuous works of the folk painters are the decorations on the outside walls of fondas or hole-in-the-wall eating places, butcher shops, and pulquerías. The first are always painted with peaceful scenes but the butcher-shop themes give the animals an opportunity to revenge themselves by cutting up and weighing the butcher and even cooking him. The best and most interesting murals are on the pulquerías, but they are not so good as they were some few decades ago (Pl. 127).

Retablos or votive offerings are the most important and popular aspect of folk painting at the present time. They depict miracles—a man falling down a shaft of a mine is rescued by his saint; someone is dying and is saved by the household, or some other, saint to whom prayers were offered. The persons thus benefited show their gratitude by going to a painter of miracles and ordering the best pictures they can afford of what has happened, painted on tin, copper or canvas. They then hang them in the church, near the saint who has been invoked at that particular time. Many of these retablos—realistic pictures of super-realistic events—are painted with great sensitivity and profound recognition of a truth that makes a miracle of reality and of reality a miracle. Some are works of art (Pls. 125, 126).

Sculpturing at the present time is practically limited to masks and religious images. Some very excellent masks and images are carved of wood which the village sculptors do not paint (Pl. 122). The Huichols carve gable-cap stones and god-discs of soft volcanic rock, with designs in relief for their god-houses; also animal effigies in wood. Sculpturing is done to some extent by practically all the primitive groups for their own rituals and ceremonies.[5]

Furniture

Even though very little furniture is used in primitive houses, folk carpenters manufacture it for the more progressive families of their own communities and for city people. One of the major industries in Tenancingo, Mexico, is the making of chairs, benches, and stools, with reed bottoms and backs attractively painted with gay flowers. Equipales, an indigenous type of armchair, with seat and back of cowhide, come from Guadalajara, Jalisco. Those made in Nayarit are of bamboo sticks and palm leaf, undoubtedly the materials that were used before the Conquest. Folk carpenters also make inexpensive trasteros, or shelves, for dishes and toys, carved with birds and other designs, and much expensive carved furniture for the well-to-do (Pls. 95, 96).

Votive Offerings and Church Decorations

Votive offerings are, perhaps, the most significant expression of the folk arts for the natives, and are, therefore, the most beautiful. Through them they express their relationship with supernatural beings; the gratitude for the miracles that make their lives bearable.

The folk love color, so their offerings are always colorful. They generally make costly robes for their saints, embroider altar pieces, make beautiful candles and adorn them. For festivals the churches are decorated with gay paper streamers and flowers. And when the saints have helped the people in their troubles, they bring painted pictures or silver reproductions of the miracles performed for them.

There is a great variety of handsome candles of rich yellow and black beeswax, some thick and tall as a person, which for special occasions are adorned with flowers, ribbons, and tin-foil. Flowers, birds, and little animals are also made of wax.

The natives from the flower growing villages around Mexico City and elsewhere make handsome arches around church entrances and special decorations for the interiors, one type being tapetes, or rugs, of

CHURCH ORNAMENT OF TIN (DESIGNS IN COLOR)

flowers combined with seeds to form the image of the saint for whom they are intended, or with some other attractive design. They also make beautiful arches for graves for the Day of the Dead. They will spend their last pennies for flowers to offer to the saints. When natural or wild flowers are not available, they make artificial ones.

China paper decorations are very popular during fiestas, both in and outside of the church. Vari-colored paper is cut into streamers and perforated with images of saints, flowers, and various other designs.

They are strung across the streets near the church in great quantities, lending gayety to the scene.

Religious amulets are sold daily at the large and much-visited churches and during fiestas at all of them. There are attractive rosaries made of colorful seeds, sometimes combined with strands of wool or ribbons, with a silver cross or a medallion; silk medallions on ribbons or cords; pictures of the saints on pins, and colored ones in painted frames; sacred hearts and other objects. Everyone tries to buy something that has been blessed by the priest.

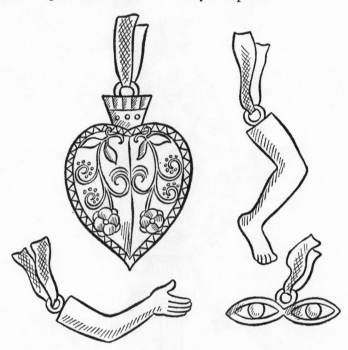

SILVER MILAGROS

Among the various other objects are the silver milagros or miracles, which are reproductions of parts of the body, animals or persons helped in some way by a miracle. The recipient of the favor will buy a corresponding part and hang it in the church near the saint whom he believes responsible. The milagros are hung either on a red or black velvet cloth and the more miraculous saints have enormous amounts of them. Those of St. Anthony are principally of hearts because he is the patron of the broken ones. Formerly these milagros were heavy and beautifully wrought by hand; now they are usually made in moulds of thin silver.

The decorations and votive offerings described above are the most common ones in Catholicized communities, but those of the primitive groups are quite different and more beautiful, as exemplified by the following.

Huichol Ritual Art

The Huichols, whose dress and personal adornments are outstanding, are also unique in the fantastically imaginative objects they have invented with which to speak to their gods. So far as is known, they excel all other present-day primitive groups in this respect, even those of their neighbors who use similar paraphernalia.

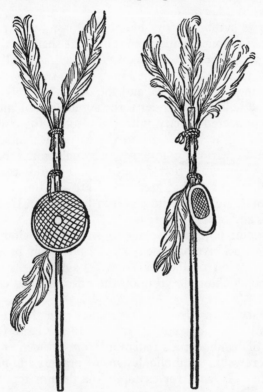

HUICHOL PRAYER ARROWS

The prayer arrows, which seem to be the most important of their ritual objects, are both magical and poetic. They are like those used for hunting, but decorated with faces, lines, colors—symbols of the gods to whom the prayers are addressed and of the supplicants' wishes. Longitudinal lines indicate direction; zigzags, speed; red, the blood of the deer; green, corn or peyote. Many of the symbolical objects made in miniature to offer to the gods are attached to the arrows; for example, a tiny pair of sandals to express a woman's prayer for a husband or merely to symbolize the stomping in the dances intended to call the attention of the gods; or tiny deer traps asking for success in the ceremonial hunt.

The most beautiful objects attached to the arrows are the plumes of the birds connected with the gods; for instance, to the arrows for Grandfather Fire those of the royal eagle and the gorgeous fiery ones of the macaw. The plumes are believed to increase the arrows' strange power and speed. But the Huichols, who have a fine dramatic sense, do not spoil the beauty of their symbolism by shooting them at the gods; they simply lay them on the altars or stick them into the ground so that the arrows themselves may communicate directly with the gods.

As the arrows symbolize the Huichols' most fervent prayers and may be offered without the intervention of the shaman, they are made in great quantities to use in ceremonies as well as at all other times. Thus one finds them wherever the Huichols go to pray—in mountain caves, near springs, rivers, lakes, and the ocean.

Not only poetic but also tender is the symbolism of the "god-eyes" because it is connected chiefly with the prayers for children—good health, long life. The "eyes" are in the form of a square woven of wool or twine of various colors, set diagonally on a bamboo stick. The wish they express is that the eyes of the gods rest with favor on their supplications. The "god-eyes" are laid on altars, attached to prayer arrows, and after the children have worn them, are taken to cave shrines and others (Pl. 19).

Many interesting objects are made to place on the altars, all of them symbolizing prayers. Among the most conspicuously beautiful are the god-discs, also called nealíka or "sight"—again the symbol of the eyes of the gods looking down upon the offerings and ceremonies of the mortals.

The discs vary in size from a few inches to eighteen in diameter, the small ones to hang on prayer arrows and the large for the altars. The frame is of bamboo rods radiating from the center, interwoven with colored crewel in symbolic designs of prayers and gods. On one to Grandmother Growth, for example, the designs represent a cornfield, a squash vine, and bean plants; also the birds and animals connected with her paraphernalia. On the reverse side are snakes and a winged serpent, all connected with growth. Another disc to the same goddess symbolizes prayers for rain on one side and the results desired on the other—a good crop of corn, beans, and squashes. After the ceremonies are over, the discs are thrown into the sea as an offering to the gods so that there may be plenty of rain, but some have been saved for museums.

Around the god-disc which occupies the center of the altar are placed votive bowls with sacred candles and at the edges others containing the ritual beer and foods. The bowls are made from small gourds, lacquered in red or green on the inside and adorned with the conventional symbols of man, deer, snake, birds—all formed with masses of colored beads on a beeswax base. Other adornments are grains of corn, artificial flowers, and even plumes. These pretty gay

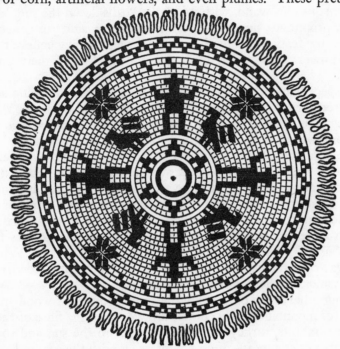

NEALIKA

little bowls are also believed to be endowed with magical powers: they convey prayers—Grandmother Growth, especially, can communicate with her goddesses through them.

The votive bowls are considered too sacred to stand on the altar table without a base, so they are placed on a circular piece of walnut wood, adorned with strings of beads and crewel of various colors, attached with beeswax. Some are made with the center wholly of beads —one half in blue for the sky, the other in white for the clouds.

The votive candles are believed to be symbols of life and are especially associated with Grandfather Fire, but they are also offered to all the pagan gods and Christian saints. They are decorated with paper flowers and rosettes, beads, and the symbols of the gods for whom they are intended.

Censers are simple clay mugs, filled with glowing pieces of oak for the burning of the copal. Women, whose duty it is to offer the incense, carry little bags of it in powdered form hanging around their necks—a little sprinkled on the coals sends up clouds of smoke.

Among the important ritual objects used by the shaman are his plumes. They consist of a few feathers, generally from the tail or wings of the red-tailed hawk, which hang from a small handle on brightly colored crewel. The shaman puts his plumes on altars, attaches them to his wand, with which he "calls down the sun," blesses animals, prophesies, heals, and performs much magic. In general, the Huichols use feathers profusely in their ritual, for they believe that the mystic power with which birds are endowed is in their plumage (Pl. 4).

The special chairs in which the shamans sit when officiating are also considered sacred. They are made of bamboo and palm like the pre-Conquest equipales. The stool part of the chair is believed to represent the flower of the sotol century plant from which a native brandy is made. To suggest the flower, a roll of sotol leaves is attached to the edge of the seat. Tiny objects, symbolizing prayers, are also hung on these chairs (Pl. 3). And there are chairs reproduced in miniature for the gods; these are put on the altars and hung on prayer arrows.

Besides the paper flowers, which are connected with Christianity and considered sacred, the Huichols make handsome flowers from a squat maguey plant with incurving, shiny green leaves. Wherever magueys grow, the natives use the leaves or hearts for decorative purposes, fashioning them into artistic designs.

Among other ritual objects are the animal effigies of wood and clay chiefly for mountain shrines; others are woven of the fibre of the sotol plant into rabbits, turkeys, snakes—to offer to the sun and to tie to prayer arrows as a means of communicating with the sun god. These, too, are left in the mountain shrines as prayers for deer, rain, health and long life.

For the god-houses the most sacred objects are the idols of the gods and their discs with which the sacred holes are covered, also the nealíka or "sight"; both are carved of soft volcanic rock in relief designs with symbols of the gods to whom the house is dedicated, and sometimes painted with their colors—red and yellow for the dry season gods, blue and green for the wet.

One of the ancient ritual objects which has survived is a diminutive staircase or ladder made of sandstone, about twelve inches long, three wide, and two thick, into which six steps have been carved. These little ladders are so old that there is no longer any agreement as to their symbolism—some say they represent the ladder on which Sun-father came out of the sea when he was born; others, the climbing of Great Grandfather Deer-tail and Grandfather Fire on their journeys to peyote land; still others believe that the stairs represent the steps of life or the heights the Huichols try to reach before falling down into death.

There are similar ladders of bamboo, like the mats made for the altars, sometimes adorned with symbols in colored crewel, which the peyote hunters hang on their arrows as prayers for help to climb their steep trails leading to the sacred peyote land; these are left there as an offering to the Sun-father for peyote.

The foregoing is merely a very condensed account of the most outstandingly beautiful of the Huichol ritual-symbolic objects. Before concluding it, however, it is necessary to mention some of the interesting things that are worn and used in the peyote fiestas.

First, the faces of both sexes are painted for the occasion with the yellow roots brought back from the peyote country (Pl. 1). Sometimes instead of paint the red petals of the plumería flower are cut into small designs and stuck on the cheeks.

A youth who has returned from his first pilgrimage may wear squirrel tails on his hat as a reminder of the reason for the origin of the peyote hunt, which was the stealing of the first fire by the squirrel; or the feathers of the buzzard because this animal aided the wounded deer-peyote to escape from the wet season hunters; or the feathers of the eagles or hawks, since these birds belong to the Sun-father, who was enabled to shine because of the success of the first peyote hunt of the dry season gods led by the mighty Grandfather Fire. After adults have made their first trip to peyote land, they use tobacco gourds for the fiesta as well as at all other times, stringing several over the shoulder.

The returned pilgrims and their wives wear a fan-shaped adornment on their heads, as do the singers for the peyote dance when beating the drum.

Among the foreign objects incorporated into the ritual paraphernalia, a curious one for the peyote fiesta is an ordinary maguey fibre brush used for scrubbing, which can be found in every market. The peyote pilgrims buy them in San Luis Potosí. They prefer those with the red handles and consider them highly sacred, as they are used by the wives for combing their husbands' hair after the ritual bath which permits them to resume marital relations.

The most beautiful of the special objects for these fiestas are the staffs carried by the peyote dancers, which symbolize the rattlesnakes of the Sun-father, enabling the sun god to hear their prayers. The staffs are made of bamboo sticks, about four feet long, filled with small hard seeds which make a rattling noise, and they are carved and painted with designs to resemble the snakes' backs. Sometimes beautiful blue jay plumes are tied to these staffs by the shaman, who uses them as he does his wands for magical purposes.[7]

Dress and Adornment

Dress is being included with the folk arts because it is one of their highest expressions. For the natives, dress is not only a prime necessity but an art. When they were masters in their own land before the Conquest, they dressed in colorful garments, painted their faces, and wore jewels of gold and precious stones. The priests, the nobles, and the rich, naturally, used costlier materials and adornments than the poor but even the clothes of the poor were handmade and beautiful.

The centuries of suffering and poverty of these people since the Conquest, as well as other circumstances, have affected their manner of dress. Yet many of the present-day costumes, although comparatively impoverished and sombre, still preserve some of the ancient beauty and picturesqueness.

The costumes of most of the primitive groups of today are quite extravagant as compared with the rest of their material possessions. However, they are never ostentatious but of good quality and taste— worn naturally, with dignity. They are made of excellent wool or cotton homespuns, some being elaborately and beautifully adorned with colorful embroideries in cotton, wool or beads. Such costumes are not only an expression of group custom but also of individual taste, for they are different in every village, and every garment of the same style in the same village is a little different.

Many of the natives who are still living in the old tradition are going through a state of change and their dress is one of the indications; but there are always exceptions. Some who have adopted a more progressive style of dress, are exceedingly conservative in their customs, like the Yaquis and others. But these groups are generally poor in the folk arts, many of which go into the making of the interesting costumes still in existence.

Women's Apparel

Many women, perhaps the majority, wear old-fashioned calico dresses—a full skirt reaching to the ankles or sweeping the ground, with or without flounces; waist plain or with yoke, hanging outside of the skirt. Some use a sleeveless camisa or shirt of white cotton, embroidered with silk thread or beads; these are always worn inside the skirt. Such outfits are often graceful and attractive, especially when made of brightly colored materials like those of the Seri women (Pls. 31, V).

Children's dresses are like their mothers', but many young girls living in large progressive places, are beginning to wear modern dresses of cheap colorful prints, for sale in every city market. In contrast there are villages in which all or most of the women wear beautiful costumes reminiscent of pre-Conquest days.

The two pre-Spanish styles of blouses are still in use—the quexquemetl, made of two rectangular pieces of cloth so joined that they form to points, which hangs over the shoulders like a cape; the huipil,

QUEXQUEMETL

square-necked, sleeveless, loose and shapeless, of varying lengths. The enaguas or skirts are also of two styles—the enredo or wrap-around, of straight pieces of cloth sewed together and folded around the waist in the manner of those shown in the codices; and the ones made of many yards of homespun wool, laid in deep pleats at the waist either in front or back each time they are put on and fastened with one or more long fajas or long homespun sashes or belts.

Some of the Otomí women from villages around Toluca, capital of the State of Mexico, wear a handwoven woolen skirt called a chinquete in their language, which is pleated in front and held on by a wide red wool sash with attractive inwoven designs; the blouse is either a quexquemetl or a sort of embroidered cape. The material of the skirt has a narrow white crosswise strip on a dark blue or purple background. Formerly it was possible to tell the village a woman was from by the color of her skirt and the width of the stripe. It still is possible to some extent but the majority no longer use the costume. Otomí women of Ixmiquilpan and Actopan, Hidalgo, use the full calico skirts, often with a small quexquemetl of dark colors and sashes of the same cotton thread with the same finely inwoven designs. In other villages of the same state the quexquemetl are made with red woolen bands and are worn with full red woolen skirts, or white cotton or woolen ones with blue bands, as in San Pablito.

Near Teziutlán, Puebla, Aztec women wear handsome dark woolen long-sleeved huipils, skirts and shawls, embroidered in cross-stitch with gay flowers. Tephua women of the same region weave very fine open-work white cotton quexquemetl with inwoven red wool bands, which are embroidered with flowers and animals at the points; their sashes of blue homespun wool are blue on one side and white on the other. The long blouses of heavy white cotton homespun with full sleeves worn by the Aztec women of Chahuatlán, Vera Cruz, are very modern looking. Other interesting costumes of the same state are those of Chicontepec, consisting of a loosely-hanging camisa or blouse with fine red, green, and blue embroidery and a heavy white homespun skirt with a three-inch brown band around the bottom, adorned with rosettes of wool in contrasting colors. The Aztec women of Amatlán wear long handsome embroidered huipils of white cotton homespun and, underneath, a petate belt with embroidered ends which never show. The Totonac women of Papantla make their quexquemetl and skirts of white machine-made embroidered material; formerly they were of homespuns, elaborately embroidered. Aztec and Huesteca women of San Luis Potosí also wear attractively embroidered quexquemetl (Pls. 59, 60, 61, 143, 144).

In nearly all the villages around Lake Pátzcuaro and others near Uruapan, Michoacán, Tarascan women wear a rollo or skirt of many yards in width of either red or black homespun wool, with pleats falling fanwise in back over several long, narrow belts of different colors and designs, and embroidered shirts (Pl. IV). The skirts of the Aztec women of Tuxpan, Jalisco, are similar but always of black wool, fastened with only one long narrow belt; their short huipils are of plain white cotton, unadorned. For church these women wear a similar white huipil on their heads and look stunning in groups.

Huipils of various lengths are worn in many parts of the country. The mestizas, as the Maya women of Yucatán are called, ordinarily wear long white cotton machine-made and embroidered huipils, but for holidays the well-to-do make them of fine materials and embroider them by hand, sometimes wearing them shorter so that the lace flounces on their skirts may show (Pls. 131, 133).

In the highlands of Chiapas, native women wear a variety of attractive huipils of white cotton or woolen homespuns, often beautifully embroidered. But the Chamula women of the same region make their huipils and skirts of heavy black homespun wool, the only adornment on the huipil being a red silk tassel—a most striking outfit (Pl. 138).

Chinantec women make beautiful long huipils of red or purple homespun wool, embroidered in contrasting colors with inwoven and embroidered designs; Mixtec, Trique, and Mazatec women also wear long huipils, generally of white cotton homespuns, with red crosswise bands, embroidered in blue, yellow, and other color combinations (Pls. 34, 35, 39, 40, II).

The Zapotec women of the mountain village of Yalalag weave heavy white cloth for their handsome huipils, which are adorned with a machine-stitched yoke and a red or white silk tassel at the neck; those for holidays are sometimes embroidered along the seams. Their skirts are of the same material but with narrow light brown crosswise stripes; they are pleated in front and held on with a palm-leaf belt (Pls. 36, 50). The costumes of the Mixe women from nearby villages are most extraordinary—a full tunic with long sleeves, over plain full skirts, both of heavy dark green or blue homespun cotton.

The gayest Oaxaca costumes are those of the Tehuanas from the town of Tehuantepec, and of the women of Juchitán, and Ixtepec, who are famous for their good looks. Their huipils are waist length, mostly of vivid cottons, embroidered by machine or hand with geometrical or floral designs. Some of the older women and young girls wear wrap-around skirts of homespun cotton with crosswise stripes of various colors, but the majority use the full calico skirts with white flounces at the bottom. For holidays their huipils are sometimes of silk or even velvet; skirts are of the same materials, both richly hand embroidered. To cover the head for church a different type of huipil is used; this is made of lace and starched to form a frame for the face. When worn for adornment it hangs from the top of the head down the back. This huipil grande, or the one for the head, has tiny adornments attached to it that look like the sleeves of a baby's dress. There is much speculation as to its origin but nothing more definite has been discovered than that it may have been copied from a lace baby dress that was found in a trunk of a wrecked vessel off the coast at Salina Cruz. The Tehuanas carry fruit, vegetables, and flowers on their heads in gayly painted gourd bowls called xicapexli. As they walk regally along the unpaved streets in their colorful dresses, with bare feet, they look like exotic queens (Pls. 42, 47, X).

Other women from the Isthmus of Tehuantepec wear similar huipils with wrap-around cotton skirts. Those from villages near Minatitlan have wide crosswise stripes of bright reds and yellows on a dark background. Many of these women go about nude from the waist up and wear natural flowers in their hair.

Young girls generally wear their hair loose or in braids hanging down their backs; married women either wind their braids around their heads or coil the hair in the back. Some weave their own ribbons of wool and adorn them with beads at the ends or simply use strands of colored wool or silk ribbons, which they braid into the hair and tie in big bows at the ends or on top of the head.

Yalalag women use a fantastic coiffure. It is called a rodete or roundlet of plaited hair, formed by dividing the hair into two parts and winding into it strands of black wool, which hang down the sides when the rolls of hair are crossed in front. The difference in the rodete of the unmarried from that of the married women is that the latter cross the hair in back before taking the rolls to the top of the head. Some Mixe women use rodetes with red wool and the Aztec girls and women of Cuetzalán, Puebla, use purple wool in theirs (Pl. 60).

Many women take pride in their looks and take good care of their hair, combing and adorning it daily; others go about disheveled and unkempt most of the time.

No matter how elegantly dressed native women or girls may be, they are generally barefoot, while the majority of men wear sandals; shoes are sometimes used for dances.

Occasionally a woman working in the fields or walking in the sun may wear a man's sombrero but neither women nor girls ever use "ladies' hats." [8]

Men's Apparel

The majority of men wear unbleached cotton suits. Generally shirts and trousers are of the same color, but occasionally the shirt is pink, rose color, orange, purple or yellow. Regional differences are to be found in the cut of the trousers and the style of the shirt—some trousers are fuller than others or pleated at the sides; some shirts are plain while others are made with yokes and pleats, and some are adorned with cross-stitch or solid embroidered designs. Often men wear long wide sashes of homespun wool or red cotton, which they wind around the waist several times. Many who mingle with city people are now discarding these traditional suits for overalls but still wear the straw sombrero.

There are some villages in which men wear unusual costumes. Costumes from lower Mixteca, Oaxaca, consist of short trousers and a full blouse of white homespun cotton, both embroidered, the trousers long enough to form a sort of bag around the waist. The costume is completed by a low-crowned, wide-brimmed black felt or palm hat (Pl. 38).

The natives of the highlands of Chiapas wear short cotton trousers and shirts, which are sometimes embroidered, covered by a plain white or striped homespun wool chamarra or small blanket, belted with crude leather strips (Pls. 139, 141, 142).

The men from San Bartolomé de los Llanos, a village of the lowlands of Chiapas, dress in full long trousers, confined at the ankles, of heavy white cotton homespuns, embroidered all over with figure eights of red wool. Sometimes they wear a beautifully embroidered red cloth on the head in turban fashion (Pl. VIII). Men from other villages use cotton homespun checked kerchiefs, either white or red, tied loosely around the neck or under their hats.

The suits usually worn by the Mayas of Yucatán and Quintana Roo are of white cotton—straight trousers and a jacket; workers often wear just a cotton shirt and an apron from the waist down, as before the Conquest (Pl. 129).

Men from villages in the lowlands of Guerrero are picturesque, wearing a round green or black broadcloth bag with their white suits. It is tied around the waist with narrow bands of the same cloth and hangs down in front below their loose shirts. The Aztec name for this bag is huicho and it serves as a pocket.

The Totonacs of Papantla wear attractive sport shirts with pleated yoke and open sport collar. The young swains always carry a small comb, a mirror, and a tiny bottle of perfume in their shirt pockets. According to Landa, the ancient Mayas used much perfume, the men more than the women.

The most dressed up male of the species is the Huichol of the sierras of Nayarit and Jalisco. Huichols wear unbleached cotton trousers of varying lengths, loose tunics with long sleeves that are full from the elbow to the wrist. Their suits for festive occasions are beautifully embroidered and worn with a pañuelo or kerchief over the shoulders. The pañuelo has an embroidered center and red border. Below their sashes of natural wool colors, hang strings of tiny colored bags; larger ones are strung over the shoulders. The dress of their women is poor in comparison—cotton quexquemetl with little embroidery and full plain skirts (Pls. 1, 3, 4, 5, 6, 7, 8, 10, 11, 12, 14, 16, 17, 18, 19).

Men and boys always wear palm leaf handmade sombreros of all sizes and shapes, each region having its own styles. Only in some few villages of Oaxaca are felt hats worn.

The man's overcoat is the serape or blanket, always of homespun wool, pure or mixed, of different sizes, colors and designs in every village. Different names are applied to some of them because of different sizes and the way they are worn. The jorongos of medium sizes are generally worn folded over the left shoulder as an adornment; those of red wool are popular in the states of Jalisco, Colima, and Nayarit. Around Toluca, the men wear homespun wool or cotton tilmas or cotones, which are like the chamarras of Chiapas (Pl. 63). The full sized serapes when used for protection against the cold are flung around the shoulders with a dignity that transforms the poorest native into a noble figure.

Some natives still wear their hair long—the Lacandons, Seris, Huichols, Tarahumaras—but never in braids. Occasionally a Huichol will coil his hair in back as the women do. Huichols, Tarahumaras and some few others wear hairbands.

Adornment

Girls and women adorn themselves for the most part with inexpensive beads of all colors, wearing from a few to dozens of strands at one time. Huichol women prefer rope chains of fine blue and white beads of which they also make earrings and bracelets. However, in some places the women still use expensive jewelry. The mestizas of Yucatán wear filagree gold earrings and long rosaries, sometimes combined with red coral; the tehuanas also use gold earrings and long gold chains, strung with United States ten, twenty, and fifty dollar gold pieces. In Papantla and other villages of Vera Cruz and in some of Guerrero the women also wear gold earrings and chains with fancy pendants but not so valuable and elegant as those of the mestizas and tehuanas, whose chains constitute the family fortune. In many villages, especially those around Toluca, interesting silver earrings are worn; there are some old ones that are hung with tiny silver pitchers and other adornments. In Pátzcuaro they use silver fish as adornments on earrings; in Yalalag and other villages of Oaxaca, the women used to wear necklaces, and many still do, of unique silver crosses either on ribbons or coral chains, strung with little silver animals (Pl. 44). Some few women of Amatlán, Vera Cruz, still wear long coral chains with old silver coins.

Huichols and Seris paint their faces with attractive designs and colors as in ancient times (Pls. 1, V). Huichol men wear earrings, bracelets, and hairbands of the fine white and blue beads, made for them by their women. For fiestas they adorn themselves with beautiful tropical plumes, which they put on their heads, and hats. Both the men and women use many flowers for personal adornment on such occasions. Some of the Maya men of Quintana Roo wear one gold earring in the left ear (Pl. 130). Their adornments are most exotic but they always seem appropriate.

Men and women generally have several changes of clothing, one of better materials and more elaborately adorned for fiestas—the more conservative ones do not use underwear. On Sundays and feast days most of them look spic and span but not so on week days. But one cannot expect anything else of people who live so many in one room with no facilities for cleanliness.

Wherever there are streams, their banks are usually alive with women pounding their clothes clean on rocks and bathing themselves and children; men and boys also bathe frequently. But there are many places where water is scarce and has to be carried long distances. In Yucatán, where there is little water, even the poor Mayas bathe often and most of them look spotlessly clean every day of the week. On the other hand, the Huichols even when living near water only take occasional ritual baths and many wear their clothes without washing them until they fall to pieces. As among other peoples, some are dirty when they have facilities for keeping clean, while others are clean in spite of all obstacles.[9]

Riding and dance costumes with their adornments will be described in connection with the occasions on which they are worn.

Musical Instruments

Pre-Conquest musical instruments consisted of wooden drums; clay, bone, wooden or reed flutes; notched deer and human bones and sticks; whistles and conch shells; clay, gourd, and bone rattles as well as some with metal discs between two pieces of wood. A sort of resonant drum of inverted gourds on water was also used; in fact, anything that produced rhythm was fashioned into an instrument.

Some of the ancient drums, clay flutes, rattles, and notched bones have survived the Conquest and may be seen in museums, but others are now made for present-day use together with all the other pre-Conquest kinds of instruments.

The two ancient types of drums are the teponaxtli, a horizontally cylindrical hollow log, with the top slotted to form two tongues; the other, the huehuetl, vertically-cylindrical, hollowed out of a log and the top covered with skin. Both were handsomely carved, the teponaxtli often in the form of a crouching man or animal (Pls. 3, 70).

The huehuetl is now the more used but only among the primitive tribes like the Huichols is it made and played with the hands in the ancient manner. The teponaxtlis are used much less; some few villages have ancient ones hidden away and others make one occasionally; neither are carved as in the past. The huehuetl and smaller

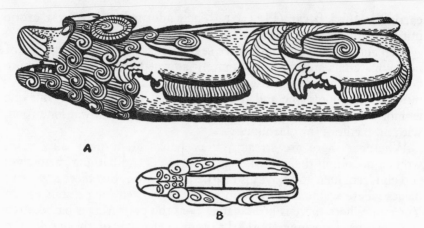

TEPONAXTLI, WITH DETAIL OF SLOTTED TOP (B)

drums together with chirimías or reed, wooden and sometimes clay or tin flutes are played everywhere, even in villages near Mexico City. The use of rattles is also widespread.

The rest of the pre-Conquest styles of instruments are found among the primitive tribes in various regions of the country. The

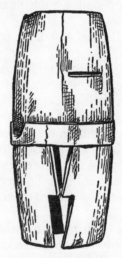

AN OLD HUEHUETL

Yaquis of Sonora use raspadores or notched sticks and gourds inverted over water. The Coras of Nayarit have rattles with metal discs, and the mitote, a curious wooden instrument in the form of an arc, connected with ordinary thin rope. It is played with two sticks, placed on a gourd which rests on the ground, the player holding the two together by placing his foot in the center (Pl. 15).

The musical bow has been found among some of the natives of the northwest. The Chinantecs of Oaxaca have one which consists of a bent piece of light flexible wood, about twenty-five inches long, a cord and small stick being inserted between the bow and string at one end.

In Tehuantepec, Chiapas, and perhaps elsewhere, shells are still played. Drums are sometimes improvised by covering a clay pot with a skin, and there are other rhythmical devices.

After the coming of the Spaniards, the natives began making and playing the stringed instruments which were brought into the country—violins, guitars, harps. They are made everywhere but there are places in which they are a specialty. One of these places is Paracho, Michoacán, where there are many musicians and instrument makers. Among their specialties are well-finished guitars, some of them adorned with bird designs and encrusted with shell. Other typical instruments are large guitars called guitarrones, small jaranas like a ukelele, and conchas or armadillas, so called because they are made of the shells of the armadillo.

The music-loving Huichols make their own guitars and violins, which are crude and tiny, but produce good tones. The Seris of Sonora have a unique, oriental-shaped, one-stringed violin (Pls. 11, 27).

All musical instruments, with the exception of the harp, are made in toy sizes for children, which are sold cheaply and can be played. From the State of Hidalgo come some very tiny ones, about two inches long, beautifully finished and inlaid with shell.[10]

Only the most noteworthy objects have been included in this summary of the folk arts. To describe all the varieties would take volumes. Even in such homely, simple things as petate and palm fans, used for fanning the flames of charcoal burners and stoves, there is an infinite variety of shapes, sizes, and designs. They are used everywhere, and everywhere they are different.[11]

DIVISION OF LABOR

There is no leisure class among the natives—everyone works, adults and children of both sexes. Children begin at the age of eight or earlier and the adults continue as long as they are able. Some work better than others and contribute more, but even the inefficient and lazy have to do something to pay for their living.

Theoretically, the duty of the male consists of doing the hard work in agriculture or other jobs, hunting, chopping wood, carrying the heavy loads, and so on; that of the female, caring for the children, washing, cooking, sewing, weaving, embroidering, bringing water from the well or river, taking care of the domestic animals, helping in the home industries, gardening, and weeding the cornfields. In reality, women often do men's heavy work also, when necessity demands it, while men sometimes do women's work under similar circumstances, but never to as great an extent. Here, as everywhere else in the world, poor women usually work longer hours and harder than men.

Mexican women even do the work of soldiers, for they not only keep house for their men in the barracks but follow them to battle to take care of them and to fight with them. There have been some notable soldaderas, as these women soldiers are called, who have received military titles. However, the majority suffer and fight without any such recognition. The soldaderas often go ahead of the troops to skirmish for food and when their men fall fighting, they pick up their weapons and carry on. They go along with their men on long, difficult marches, often with a babe on their backs. Occasionally, one may drop out to give birth, after which she catches up with the rest as if nothing had happened. A military train is always exciting and picturesque with women, children, bird cages and whatnot. In past revolutions the mess of the Mexican army consisted entirely of women.

Women also share the responsibilities of their husbands in any political or religious offices they may hold.

Children are not expected to work as hard as adults. A father may lift a bundle of wood and remove a few pieces before putting it on the back of his little boy. Older people, too, are not expected to work so hard nor to accomplish as much as the young and middle-aged. But each one contributes according to his capacity for the common welfare of his family and group.

NOTIONS OF WORK AND TIME

The notion prevalent among many people that the natives are lazy is erroneous. They work from sunrise until sunset and even though they take off considerable time for ceremonies and fiestas, are never completely free from work—the preparations in themselves are strenuous and often long journeys on foot, carrying heavy burdens, are involved.

If natives do not turn out as much work as city employers expect, it is not because of laziness but on account of having to change their accustomed rhythm, or perhaps because of chronic malnutrition and sickness. In the tropics everyone suffers from malaria and intestinal troubles and from other diseases in high altitudes, malnutrition being a basic cause.

Time for the natives is endlessly fluid; they never divide it into hours, minutes, and seconds. They have neither watches nor clocks, but tell time by looking at the heavens, by the crowing of the cocks, or other natural signs.

Mañana, tomorrow, for the folk as for all Mexicans, has come to mean any future time. Friends parting without any idea as to when they may see each other again, will say, *hasta mañana*, until tomorrow! So when promises are made for mañana, they should not be taken too literally. There are always more mañanas to come.

It is sometimes exasperating but always amusing to try to find out from a native in the country how long it will take to reach a place. After some experience one learns not to ask, "How far?" or "How long?" but simply "When will I arrive at . . . ?" The answer differs with each individual. One may say, pointing vaguely into space, "It isn't far; just around the little hill—trás lomita." Then you may go on for hours or even a whole day before you find the place "behind the little hill." Another may say in answer to the same question, "Well, if you had started out in the wee hours of the morning, you should be there now." With such vague notions of time, the folk never know how long they have been working or walking.

TRANSPORTATION

Before the Conquest, human beings transported all freight either on their backs or by hauling, and carried the rich on litters. The Spaniards introduced horses, mules, and burros, but the natives continued being beasts of burden. Then came railroads and the paved highways with their trucks and cheap-fare buses, yet one still sees natives with heavy loads on their backs held on with the ancient tumpline from the forehead or chest—not only on steep mountain paths but also on the roads intended for motor vehicles. However, the carrying of heavy burdens on human backs has considerably lessened and will continue decreasing.

Natives not only transport their own merchandise on their backs where modern means of transportation exist, but also do it for others for a mere pittance, especially in the mountainous regions of the country. Some are fortunate enough to own one or more burros or mules to do their carrying.

Although less than formerly, there are still functioning in many regions of the country pack trains of mules or burros, their owners making a business of carrying goods regularly over certain routes.

Those who drive the animals are called arrieros, often a gay colorful lot, noted for their picturesque language and stories; also for their dances at the fiestas of their patron saints, which will be described later.

The places the arrieros stop at along their routes are called mesones, where there are stalls for the animals and beds for those who can afford to pay for them; the rest sleep on their petates on the ground. In Mexico City there is a street that bears the name "Mesones," even though they no longer exist there. But there are many mesones in provincial capitals and other large places still doing a flourishing business. Some are interesting architecturally, especially those of Pátzcuaro, Michoacán.

Wherever there are navigable rivers and lakes, the natives make their own canoes as before the Conquest. They are generally carved out of tree trunks, some attractive in form, and serve for carriers as well as for passengers. On Lake Pátzcuaro there are canoes that can hold more than twenty persons, while others are only large enough for a few.

Natives are becoming accustomed to all sorts of modern means of travel, even planes, which are penetrating into the most remote parts of the country. There are small local lines that carry chicle and other freight in the jungle country of Chiapas and Yucatán and other equally wild regions.

MARKETS

Markets constituted the only pre-Conquest places for trade, so that every product was found in them—from foodstuffs to the very finest of cloths and the most precious of jewels—each kept in a separate section as in our modern department stores. Everything that was for sale, even slaves, was sold in the market places.

Markets were held on fixed days. Among the Aztecs they were made attractive with the celebration of games and fiestas, but also there were laws forcing the people to attend with their wares, and there was a fine for selling them on the way. But the people then, as now, enjoyed going to market; the early missionaries complained that they preferred attending markets to churches.

The custom of fixed market days exists now and the natives prefer markets to stores; in fact, even though they may buy things in a store, they never own one. For them, the markets are not only commercial but also social institutions, where they go to meet old friends and to make new ones; to exchange gossip and to have a good time.

There is a current story which tourists without realizing the psychological reason for it, love to tell about some craftsmen who would not sell their wares even at double the price before reaching the market place. When a native goes to market to sell something, he feels he has no reason for going if he has already accomplished his mission; also his refusing to sell before reaching the market may have some remote connection with the ancient law forbidding such transactions. Customs are often preserved without anyone remembering the reason for their existence. One asks a native why he does something and his laconic reply is, "Es costumbre," "It is the custom."

The present-day markets are also departmentalized, especially the larger ones, where everything is sold, from small objects to supply the kitchen to clothes and personal adornments. The Mexicans, with their innate artistic sense of order and composition, arrange even the vegetables in beautiful patterns. In the markets where there are no stalls, there is an unwritten law which permits each vendor always to occupy the same place and all those selling the same things to sit in groups; and even on the ground, they arrange their wares artistically.

Among the largest, most accessible, most interesting and most visited markets are those of Toluca, Pátzcuaro and Oaxaca, but there are many others both large and small that are interesting and picturesque.

All markets are fascinating and great fun. It is fun just to talk to the natives and to play with them at their game of selling. They begin by asking a price which they know you will not accept. When you comment that it is too high, they respond, "But that is only the asking price; you offer—ofrezca." Then you make another offer, and they continue, "¿Con ganas de comprar, cuánto das?"—"With an honest desire to buy, how much will you give?" And so the conversation goes on with smiling friendliness. But that only happens now in markets not often visited by city people or tourists, who bargain to the bone. In such markets, I have heard vendors say, "This is the price; take it or leave it!" [1]

PART TWO

SOCIETY–CUSTOM–FIESTA

SOCIETY—CUSTOM—FIESTA

The primitive homogeneous groups—also in part the mixed progressive ones—live in a society practically without classes; that is, there are no such divisions as lower, middle, and upper. Usually everyone in the same group lives in the same type of house, similarly furnished; dresses in the same style of clothes, made of similar materials. Even though some individuals may have a few more, or better, garments or jewels than others, or may have money hidden away, their neighbors who have less are not barred from any social functions on that account.

There are persons who enjoy more prestige than others but generally not because of their material possessions. They usually acquire their superior standing in the community—which often implies personal qualifications of leadership—on the basis of service. They hold political offices for which there is no monetary compensation, or religious posts on which they spend most of their savings, even going into debt.

This society without classes is governed by unwritten laws, sanctioned by age-old customs. The outward pattern of life of every individual is much the same; he is received into the world, educated, married, kept in health and finally buried according to a prescribed set of rules. His world is moved to a great extent by magical forces, controlled either by pagan gods or Christian saints or both. Naturally, there are exceptions where modernization is taking place, but otherwise there is very little variation.

Because the will of the gods is dominant in this society, it is necessary to keep in constant touch with them not only by means of prayers and offerings but also through ceremonies and fiestas. Those already described in connection with agriculture in Part One are examples of how exacting the gods are and how much has to be done to please them. In the more primitive groups, because of a greater number of gods to feast, the ceremonies and festivals in their honor sometimes require about one half of a man's working time. Less time is spent on these events in the more progressive, Catholicized places, but they are equally important even in the lives of those people.[1]

The Family

The basic family unit is parents and children, but frequently other relatives are included, such as an older widowed parent, or a married son or daughter with spouse. In some villages it is the custom for a son-in-law to live and work in his wife's house for about a year in payment for the bride, or a newly wedded couple may live temporarily with the parents of either one while their house is being constructed; also a father may want his married son to continue living with the family so that he may help him in his fields or at his trade.

The father is the head of the family but the authority of the mother is also respected. Contrary to the Latin custom of the wife living a sheltered life at home, the native woman is the constant companion of her husband; sharing his responsibilities and pleasures. If he holds a public or church office, she helps him fulfill his obligations. She watches over him at fiestas when he is drunk to keep him from quarreling and getting into jail. If important decisions are to be made, her opinion and consent are solicited. In short, the relationships between a native husband and wife are more like those in the United States than those of the Latin Catholicized population.

Children, as a rule, respect and obey their parents. From about the age of six or seven they begin to help them in their home tasks and industries and accompany them to market places and fiestas. Thus the whole family is closely united in work and play.

When the father dies the eldest son inherits his authority. The property, which in most cases consists of the hut, the land it is on, with its meager furnishings and tools, is divided among the children. Among the Tarahumaras, Zapotecs, and other groups, a woman may have her own property but does not inherit anything upon the death of her husband. The women of the highlands of Chiapas are not permitted to own land but may derive benefits from it through their children while the children remain unmarried. A childless widow usually returns to her family and the husband's sisters and brothers inherit his possessions.[1]

Clans and Kinship Terms

The only clans discovered to date since the Conquest are those of the Tzeltales of Chiapas. They are exogamous and patrilineal. The members of the Cancuc clans are distinguished by their Tzeltal surname, while those of the Municipality of Oxchuc are known by their

Spanish surnames. Among all of them there is a taboo with respect to marriage between a boy and girl bearing the same surname; even though there may be no blood relationship between them, they consider themselves as one family. All the young people of the same clan call each other sister and brother and the parents of one another father and mother. They use different terms for relatives on the mother's side to indicate that they belong to a different clan and show them less affection and courtesies.

When inhabitants of Oxchuc leave their villages to visit others where members of their own clans reside, they can count on receiving hospitality from them even though they may be unacquainted; clanship implies an exchange of duties and favors as among blood relatives. On the other hand, among the clans of this group, only a sorcerer who has the same Spanish surname can work witchcraft on his clan-brothers' families.

Among the Spanish speaking folk in general, kinship terms are the same as our own but they are different in the native groups using their own languages. In some the same term is used for the mother and her sisters, the father and his brothers, and the terms for brother and sister are extended to cousins or even to unrelated persons of the same age. Among the Zapotecs of Villa Alta of Oaxaca, for example, bicha or brother is applied to both parents' brothers, male cousins, nephews and to other male relatives; it may also be extended to every male in the community of the same ethnic group as well as to Zapotec outsiders. Zana, or sister, used by males when speaking to their own sisters or vice versa, is extended in the same way as bicha but not outside of the local group.[1]

Godparenthood

The social relationship of compadrazgo or godparenthood was introduced by the Catholic church, implying sacred responsibilities and duties. The godmother in Spanish is madrina; the godfather, padrino; both, padrinos. A male godchild is ahijado; a female, ahijada; both, ahijados. The relationship thus created between the child's parents and the godparents is very strong, the women calling each other comadre; the men, compadre; co-mother and co-father. In the plural form they are compadres because in Spanish the masculine is given preference. The latter terms are used even among the groups speaking their native tongues, compadre becoming compale; camadre, comale.

There are a great variety of padrinos—for baptism, confirmation, weddings, new-house ceremonies, the "enthroning of a saint" and for

other events. The institution of godparenthood exists among all social classes, the upper having a greater number of occasions, perhaps,
when padrinos can be utilized.

Among the natives the most important padrinos are generally those
of baptism because they often become real co-parents, taking a genuine interest in their godchildren. Some of the worldly-wise folk invite
persons outside of their own social class to act as godparents because
they can afford costlier gifts, but the majority prefer individuals of
their own groups, whom they invite ceremoniously with polite
speeches and gifts. Such invitations are refused only for very good
reasons, and as long as the relationship lasts there is an exchange of
gifts, favors, and hospitality. In some respects the compadrazgo is a
sort of modern clanship, to the extent of having in common the taboo
on sexual relationship and marriage between persons thus related.
When a good Catholic godfather of the upper classes wishes to marry
his ahijada, he must obtain a dispensation from Rome, at a fee which
few can afford.

The Huichols of Tuxpan, Jalisco, have a unique form of compadrazgo in connection with cattle, a ceremony taking place at the time
of the sale. The vendor and the purchaser with their respective wives
go to the casa real or temple in which the Catholic saints are housed.
There they place bowls of ritual beer and tamales on a blanket in
front of the altar. Both couples kneel, making a complicated sign of
the cross five times. On their feet again, the men, holding lighted
candles, say a prayer over the beer and drink from the same bowl as
a token of friendship. Henceforth, they greet each other with the
Mexican embrace and avoid quarreling. They believe if they get
angry and quarrel with one another, their candles will go out during
ceremonies and thus cause their lives to be extinguished.

A similar trade relationship exists among the Tarahumaras, but the
participants are called moráwas instead of compadres, meaning in
their language the joining together of two people who have traded
together. When the goods are cattle, the buyer and seller touch each
other's shoulder, saying, "Dios cuida moráwa," "God protect the
moráwa." And when one moráwa visits another, the guest will be
honored with a stool or goatskin to sit on in a preferred place near
the fire.

Godparenthood among the Mayas is a more sacred relationship than
in some of the other groups. The godparents for baptism and hetzmek, putting the baby astride the mother's hip for the first time, are
the most important. The couple who become godparents for the first
child continue for all the others, as it is considered a sin to change
them for each one. The first choice for godparents are the father and
mother of the husband; if neither one is alive the wife's parents come

next. If none of the grandparents are living, then some very respected couple of the community is asked to serve.

After the couple formally accepts the invitation to become godparents, there is a ceremony "to show respect." The expectant parents go to the home of the godparents to bring them three cooked fowl, a pile of tortillas in a new napkin, and three white candles; to these gifts are sometimes added crackers, chocolate, and sugar. On this occasion the godfather is especially honored as sponsor of the baptism, and a similar ceremony is later performed in honor of the godmother as sponsor of hetzmek.

After several children are born to the couple, they honor the godparents with the ceremony called poh-kap, handwashing; it is very important that this be performed, as the belief exists that otherwise the godparents will have to spend some time in "hell" after death to suffer torture in their hands.

In Quintana Roo, this ceremony takes place in the oratory of the godparents with a maestro cantor, the man who sings and conducts the Christian ceremonies, presiding. It is also necessary that a chapach or trusted friend accompany the parents as a witness.

The oratory is cleaned and the principal entrance adorned with an arch of xiat leaves. On a table in the center of the room, covered with a new cloth, are placed the festal foods, consisting of stuffed turkey, a basket of tortillas, and a gourd of water perfumed with basil leaves for the washing of the hands. On the ground near the table is placed a dish of cooked pork and on the altar about five dishes of turkey with an equal number of piles of tortillas.

At the altar the maestro cantor dedicates the food to the cross, while the couple offering the ceremony kneel to say the prayers of the doctrina. After the Christian rite is finished, the chapach goes to bring the godparents, who are received respectfully and affectionately by their compadres. Then the two couples, the chapach, and the maestro cantor, the only participants, sit on small benches near the table. Next the parents go around the table once on their knees, stopping before the godparents; the man washes their hands and the woman dries them. After the feast is over the same act is again performed, this time the woman washing the hands and the man drying them. After the godparents have left, the parents find a gift of from five to ten pesos on the table as a recompense for some of the expense. The chapach also leaves one or more pesos for the same purpose. The ceremony is finally completed with the sending of a dish of cooked pork by the parents to the godparents.[1]

Relations with Neighbors

The natives are always polite not only with strangers but also among themselves. Children and young people greet elders with great respect, often kissing their hands. Salutations of adults generally express a wish concerning the friend's health and well-being. The handshake is never a clasp but simply a touch of the extended fingers. But even such matters as salutations and other forms of etiquette vary a little in every village.

In Ixmiquilpan and some of the Otomí villages of the states of Hidalgo and Mexico, compadres of both sexes kiss one another's hands whenever they meet, the younger lifting the hand of the elder to his lips first. In Chenahlo, Chiapas, a young person bends his head before an older one who touches it lightly with his fingers. To ask a favor one may kiss another's hand and even kneel. On such occasions the inflection of the voice is slightly higher.

There is always a great deal of reserve between the sexes, especially in the conservative groups. Among the Tarahumaras and many others, a man calling at the home of a friend will make his presence known before approaching the door of the house, and if the woman is alone he does not enter but remains at a distance. Unless there is a close relationship, men and women generally talk to one another only when necessary and then at a respectful distance with averted faces.

We have already seen that relatives, friends, and neighbors help each other to build their houses and in agricultural tasks; they do the same in the life crises, in cases of joy and sorrow, with work, gifts, and money. But it is always a matter of mutual assistance. They never expect anything for nothing from man or God. When natives borrow something, even from relatives, the object is generally returned with a gift; when they ask a favor of a stranger, even a government official, they make him a gift however slight it may be as a token of good will. A promise is always kept, except when made by very corrupt individuals who may be found anywhere.

In small homogeneous groups, centering around one church, there is usually harmony and co-operation between the inhabitants. But life becomes more complicated when there are several barrios, or neighborhoods, in a place, each with its own church. Sometimes serious rivalries and jealousies arise over such matters as the merits of a saint, and sometimes there are old family feuds.

Friendly relations often exist between villages, their inhabitants visiting each others' markets and fiestas. But the fact that there are so many different dialects and customs does not make for close relationships. When there is strife between villages, the bone of contention is usually the boundary lines, which have never been settled definitely in most places. Boundary disputes, sometimes dating from pre-Conquest years, often keep alive a dangerous feud, even between villages of the same ethnic group.

The matter of relations with neighbors becomes even more complicated and serious when outsiders or citified people live among the natives. Such are called mexicanos by some; mestizos or ladinos by others. Often these groups are distinguished from the natives by such flattering terms as gente de razon or people with sense; los correctos, the correct ones, in contrast to los tontos or the fools. When the place is large and there are many ladinos, they occupy the best homes around the plaza and live their lives apart, calling the poor folk inditos and looking down on them as inferior beings. There are, naturally, exceptions among them who are friendly and decent but on the whole the natives dislike them because of their superiority and because they always exploit them.

In the remote villages where there are few outsiders, the natives do their best to get rid of them; in some few places, they have been driven out and those who refused to go had to suffer the consequences. These primitive groups usually have separate temples for their pagan and Christian rites. When it happens, as among the Coras in Jesús María, Nayarit, and elsewhere, that the natives have to use the same church as the ladinos, they avoid going at the same time. In Tenajapa, Chiapas, where there are numerous ladino families living permanently in the village and the natives only come in on market days and for fiestas or official business, the saints of the ladinos are on one side of the church in the usual expensive robes, while the saints of the natives are on the other, resembling them in dress and looks.

Education

Before the Conquest poor children were generally educated at home by their parents. But in the Aztec capital, as elsewhere, there were neighborhood schools for any boys who wanted to enter the army, called "the house of the young." For the children of the nobility and the rich there were day schools of song and dance for both sexes, but the highest schools of learning were the Calmécac, "Row of Houses," connected with the Great Temple. These were boarding schools for boys only, those who wished to train for the priesthood or high official posts.

As all education was religious, it was in charge of priests. The schools of the Calmécac imposed the strictest discipline, making no class distinctions whatever. All the pupils had to rise at dawn, to sweep and clean the houses, cut and bring wood from the hills for the sacred fires and maguey thorns for penance, to work at digging ditches, building walls or in the cornfields. They had to get up at midnight to take ritual baths in cold pools, to pray and go on long pilgrimages as penance to some idol. The older boys would walk for miles to a definite spot in the mountains to leave a bag filled with maguey thorns wet with their own blood as an offering to the deity. Each one would go by himself, wearing nothing but a loin cloth; carrying a clay censer, some firebrands, and a shell instrument to play on the way. There were many fast days when no one ate anything until noon and then only bread and water.

Minor offenses, such as not waking up to bathe and pray, or failure to practice good manners and elegant speech, were punished publicly by pricking all parts of the body with thorns, and whipping with nettles. Drunkenness and carnal sins were considered major crimes and punished with death. Those who became priests had to take vows of celibacy, to eat moderately, to tell the truth always, to live devoutly, and to fear the gods.

At the present time there are public rural schools in all parts of the country but the great majority of native children are still educated at home. At the age of about eight years the fathers begin to initiate their little sons into their occupations; and the mothers, their daughters. A small percentage of the children attend the rural schools and a few even leave their villages for higher education. Since the new system of education was inaugurated by the Revolutionary-Reconstruction Governments, after the Social Revolution of 1910–20, some native boys have become teachers and entered other professions; occasionally girls take up teaching or nursing.

The children like to attend school and the progressive parents permit them to do so during the months when they are not needed in the fields. In some villages a goodly number of girls are found among the pupils, while older boys and men come to night classes. But where the families live in the small scattered settlements and the children have to walk miles to the central village where the school is located, very few are able to attend. Some of the boys arrive late in the afternoon after a hard day's work in the fields and are happy to learn to read and write a little.

The rural schools had a difficult time in the beginning with the reactionary forces—and, in many instances, the natives themselves, who still distrust the white man's teachings—against them. The Municipal President of Putla, Oaxaca, summed up their reasons for not wanting schools to a Federal School Inspector, as follows:

"I shall tell you why we do not want to learn to do the things you do and teach in your schools. In your cities the majority of the people have gone to school. What they learned must be very bad, because many of them lie, take what belongs to others, betray friends, stab a man in the back, and it is seldom that they are ashamed of their acts.

"You are well acquainted with our laws, so you will know that what I am saying is true. If we tell you that we are your friends, it means until death; the same is true when we hate you. But we are incapable of betraying friends as you do. Here we kill one another like men, face to face, and murders are never pardoned.

"Here you have to work whether you are rich or poor, whereas in your cities those who are well dressed and have much to eat do nothing and there is no one who can oblige them to work. Here also your children take care of you when you are no longer able to work, as you took care of them before they were able to herd the sheep, guide the plow, sow the corn.

"If you come here poor, you will be given food and a place to sleep in any house; in your cities when you have no money, you starve and freeze to death because no one will give you a tortilla or a piece of sack cloth to cover up with. And if you are homeless, you will be put in jail.

"When poor women come to us we give them work and do not use language to make them bad.

"We do not want our children to be educated because they will become bad. I have been in Mexico City, where I worked in a hospital and in rich and poor men's homes. I have seen some people working hard, some laughing and abusing; some obeying persons who told them to do bad things.

"This village is poor but healthy. Don't hurt it by making it like your places because it will lose its health, freedom, and happiness. If you love our people, don't teach them anything; don't make them lose faith in their beliefs as I did when I served the priests of a large church. Let them believe so that they may live happily; don't educate them to discover the falseness of their beliefs. Let them respect and love one another; don't spread discord and envy among them." [1]

On the other hand, the authorities of other villages of the same state begged for schools. I saw that happen in 1928, during a long horseback trip in the Sierra de Juárez with the late Dr. Moisés Saenz, who as Sub-Secretary of Education, visited the schools already functioning in that region. The elderly leading men of Chinantec, Zapotec, and Mixe villages came to beseech him for schools and teachers, offering co-operation in their maintenance.

That trip was unforgettable from the point of view of customs, the hospitality of the people and especially the light it shed on Mexico's educational problem. Here, as in many other parts of the country, were natives of the same state, living in the same region, speaking several different languages, yet very few of them speaking or under-standing Spanish. When Dr. Saenz or any one of the school inspectors addressed the people, what he said had to be translated to the audience, and vice versa when one of their leaders spoke. The chil-dren spoke their recently learned Spanish like foreigners. But in so far as we were concerned, we did not suffer from lack of inter-course through language; the customs of these people in receiving us·were utterly charming.

It was fantastic to ride through unpopulated country, emerge from virgin forests, and suddenly hear music and firecrackers. After a while a procession would come into view, headed by the village band, followed by the officials with their silver-tipped canes of authority and school children all in white, who according to an ancient custom, would come to meet the distinguished guests far beyond the limits of the village. Floral arches were set up for us and as we rode under them, the people threw flowers at us, the band playing and fireworks bursting. At the entrance to the village the women were awaiting us, forming a lovely group, their heads covered with dark rebozos, carrying babes in arms. Once inside of the village, we were escorted to the Municipal "Palace," where we were formally and cordially welcomed with dignified speeches, and a symbolical key of the place was offered us. As we left the government house, flowers and confetti were thrown and we were again escorted by the officials and the band to our lodgings, usually the school or some other house where we put up our own cots. Then would follow festal meals and school entertainments. The band would play from early morning until late at night; the musicians would never stop playing, no matter how tired they and we were, without the permission of the authorities.[2]

The people wanted to please Dr. Saenz, so they treated him as if he were a saint; they addressed him respectfully but in the familiar form. They wanted schools for their children, so they brought him gifts—a hen, fruit, corn, a pot made in the region, flowers.

In spite of the obstacles, the rural schools have been progressing and many have done good work. At any rate, they have influenced the ethnography of the people by predisposing them to accept to some extent, even if gradually, modern methods of curing disease, and of work.

Government

The primitive homogeneous communities are practically self-gov-erning; that is, they elect municipal officers from their own people who rule in accordance with their own traditions. Federal and State officials interfere in matters of revenue and major crimes when they are brought to their attention. Even in mixed communities where the folk are obliged to accept outsiders in authority, in their own private matters they are really governed by the elders of the group.

Native officials are usually well-trained civic servants, having to serve in all the lower offices before they are eligible for the higher. In the Sierra de Juárez, for example, the lowest officer is the topil, who is a combination of policeman and general servant of the municipal government officials. Next in rank is the *mayor* or head of the topiles. Then follow the regidores, or councilmen; the alcalde, who acts as judge, with his substitute and secretary; the municipal president and secretary. The latter is generally an outsider and the only paid official. The term of office varies from one to two years but only half of the topiles and regidores are renewed at one time. The outgoing president must account strictly for all the funds that have passed through his hands. If he is unable to do so, he is liable to imprisonment. By the time a man has passed through all these offices, he is ready to join the group of ancianos or elders, whose opinions are still respected.

The same procedure is followed in other places in the matter of eligibility, with variations here and there in details. In the highland villages of Chiapas, there are regional and constitutional sets of officers both working together; they consist of the president, secretary, and judge who are recognized by the state government; the alcaldes, regidores and topiles, who are the traditional officials. Here there is an additional office of síndico, filled by a person educated in Spanish, who knows how to deal with state and federal government officials. There is generally one such official everywhere.[1]

Among other groups, those of the northwest for instance, the highest official is called gobernador or governor. In the Yaqui villages of Sonora the government consists of a governor and his assistants, who are elected on January first and take office on the sixth of the same month, at which time a festal meal is offered them—their only compensation. The governor is also the judge and head of the village military organization, his insignia of authority being a cane tipped with silver or copper. The governors take part in religious processions and go to church every Sunday, accompanied by their assistants and soldiers. The assistant whose duty it is to administer the lashes of punishment carries his rawhide whip with him to church and he is accompanied by the man who sees to it that the lashes are properly administered.

After church services on Sundays, all the governors of the group of villages around Vicam Switch, with their assistants, go to a nearby bench to hold their weekly meeting at which everything of importance concerning the life in the villages is decided. When strangers come among them it is the governors who dictate how they are to be treated. They also form a court to judge all offenses.

One Sunday morning I attended a service at Lencho, one of those villages. The church was only a reed hut, open on the sides. The main altar was covered with a green silk embroidered cloth, on which were placed the crucifixes; on another altar stood the small image of the Virgin of Loreto. Near the Virgin one of the Matachine dancers was playing a drum. A petate was placed at one of the open sides of the church. After the sandals of the governors were removed, they knelt on the petate, holding their canes in front of them, and the whipper his whip, and prayed thus for some time. In the center aisle stood the Matachine dancers, who are called "soldiers of the Virgin." On each side the people were kneeling. On the outside of the church real soldiers stood guard. One of their captains wore a tiger skin and two others, coyote skins hanging down their backs from the forehead, where they were fastened with leather bands, from which sparrow-hawk feathers stuck out.

There is always a procession during a church service, and this time tenanches, the handmaids of the Virgin, wearing their crowns with embroidered cloths falling down their backs, were carrying the statue. The Matachines headed the procession, which went as far as the principal cross and returned. The maestros—there are no resident priests there—preached a little to the governors and soldiers. Then the governors, putting aside their canes, and the captains, putting aside the skins they were wearing, went to the bench for their Sunday council. The people returned to their homes.

Every one of these eight villages has a guardhouse in which soldiers watch night and day. The guard changes once a week, and before the new one enters, they all pray at the cross. The discipline is very strict. Failure to be on duty must be justified or else there is punishment.

It is customary for the guards to sound their drums at dawn, noon, and sunset, when men take off their hats; women and children kneel and their high voices are heard saying, "Ave Maria, the Most Holy, conceived without sin." While the drum sounds near the cross, the guards stand at attention and afterwards they approach it and make a genuflection in a reverent attitude.

The above is an example of the fusion of politics, religion, and militarism. Among the groups where there is no military organization, which is true of most places, the religious and political expressions are generally closely united. High municipal officials fill important religious offices, such as those of the mayordomos or keepers of the saints, who pay most of the expenses of the festivals in their honor.

The higher officials also act as judges and mete out the punishments sanctioned by the traditions of the group. In most places offenders are put in jail or made to work or to pay fines in expiation, but among some of the primitive groups punishments are more drastic. The Yaquis inflict whippings publicly on Sundays so that they may serve as examples. The governor decides the number of lashes—a thief is given twenty-five and threatened with the death penalty if he repeats his offense. A man who rapes a young girl is forced to marry her but not without first receiving his allotted number of lashes. For infidelity both the man and woman are whipped on their naked torsos. When a person is being punished if he or she will say, "Oh, God, pardon me; I will not do it again," the whipping is suspended, but few ever weep or cry out. Men in high positions take their lashes without complaint.

A Yaqui homicide is punished with death. From the moment the culprit is sentenced, he is considered as dead. He is dressed in his burial clothes with rosaries, put under the altar, and watched during the night. The next morning he is taken to church, where he hears the prayers for the dead and all the corresponding ceremonies are performed. A firing squad, consisting of a representative from each village, does the shooting. When it is over the criminal is buried with the usual rites. When a man merely hurts another, he is put in prison. If the wounded man recovers, he may say how many lashes should be given to the prisoner. But if the victim dies, the murderer is shot.

The Huichol governors also act as judges. Formerly they punished offenders cruelly on the whipping posts introduced by the missionaries centuries ago, but recently the State authorities forbade their use. However, they still put drunks in stocks and leave them there until they get sobered up. The whipping-post and stocks are kept in the Casa Real or Christian temple because the Huichols connect them with Santo Cristo and Christianity. During the Catholic ceremonies they, together with other religious paraphernalia, are bathed with sacred water and smoked with incense.

The officials who do most of the work in every village are the topiles, as they have to be ready at a moment's notice to leave their own occupations in order to go on errands for the municipality, sometimes taking days on foot or horseback. But not only those in office serve the community. Every man has to do his share in public works—playing in the band, helping in the preparation of festivals, or in anything that is needed for the welfare of the group.[1]

Communal labor is very important everywhere, the time given to it depending upon how progressive a place may be. In Chan Kom, Yucatán, men gave as much as from one sixth to one quarter of their time when they built their school house and roads in the early thirties.

There, as elsewhere, failure to do one's share is subject to fines or imprisonment.

Among the Chinantecs from around Yoiox, Oaxaca, communal labor becomes a sort of social function. After they are called to work, generally by the beating of a drum on Saturdays or Sundays, the village band comes out to entertain the workers, and the older men furnish drinks.

Religion

The lives of the races before the Conquest were completely dominated by religion. There were exacting gods for every activity, and everything that the people did and created was in the nature of an offering to these deities, to whom they also gave their blood and lives. Thus for those who survived the Conquest, the destruction of their gods and the necessity to accept new ones were great blows. However, they learned to make the best of what they could not help. Some of the natives were sincerely impressed by the miraculous apparitions of the saints, asking for Christian temples wherever an important pagan one was destroyed; others pretended to accept the new religion but went on with the old one in secret. In any case, after over four centuries of Christianity, the natives to this day treat their saints as idols. And there are still pagan traits in Catholic ritual and Christian ones in the pagan—to what extent we have already seen in the ceremonies described. Others still to be written about will bear this out.

As the natives learned more about Catholicism, they found many beliefs and practices in it that were similar to their own. Both religions believed in the plastic representations of their gods—there were about as many images of saints as idols; both believed in baptism, confession, fasting, sexual abstinence, in the chastity and celibacy of their priests and of the women who dedicated themselves to the temples. When Aztecs ate pieces of the statue of their God Huitzilopochtli, made of the wild amaranth seed, they believed they were being identified with the divine body, somewhat as a Catholic believes that communion unites him with the Body and Blood of Christ. All burned incense, but the Mayas even made beeswax candles and believed in one Supreme God. The ceiba, which they worshipped as the tree of life, was the one rising from the trunk in three parts, suggesting the cross. In fact, the religions had so much in common that some of the early important missionaries, such as Friars Sahagún and Las Casas, said that the heathen had been taught the Christian rites by the devil to mock God.

The religious symbol today among many of the primitive tribes—

those of the highlands of Chiapas, Mayas of Quintana Roo, Tara-
humaris, Yaquis—is the cross. However, they do not connect it with
the sufferings of Christ but anthropomorphize it and treat it as a
saint. Among those tribes wooden crosses of all sizes are used; they
are put at the entrances to villages, in the courts of houses and on their
domestic and church altars; in some there are saints also but the crosses
are more important.

Crosses are placed on hilltops, at fords, intersections of roads and
wherever a Christian has died on a trail. In Yolox, Oaxaca, newly
appointed topiles, policemen, have as their first official duty the reno-
vation of the crosses in the town. Travelers often pick flowers and
decorate crosses they find along the way.

In Chenahlo, Chiapas, crosses are dressed in a man's embroidered
tunic with a red kerchief tied at the top. In all that region new houses
have new crosses and individuals have personal ones which are buried
with them. In some villages, as in San Juan Chamula, three crosses instead of one guard the entrance—"one to keep the devil out; one, the
sorcerers; and one, the ladinos."

In Chiapas, as elsewhere, there are individuals who have no fear of
crosses when they want to exploit the people. One form of exploitation practiced there employs the miraculous "talking boxes." These
are made of wood in the form of niches or dolls' houses and each one
has an image or chromo of a saint, which answers questions in a
human voice. Their owners take them from place to place and set
them up in some house, surrounded by curtains so that the person
furnishing the voice is invisible. Generally an admission fee of fifty
Mexican cents or one peso is charged, in addition to which the natives
bring incense, candles, corn and other gifts for the saint. All sorts of
questions are asked, such as how to cure an illness, where to find a
lost or a stolen object, who killed someone. But if anyone wants to
know how much longer he or she will live, there is an extra charge
for the answer.

One of the most famous of the talking boxes in 1942–3, was that of
little St. Michael from the village of Soyaló, which was consulted
not only by the poor, credulous natives, but also by well-to-do city
people. In order to test the authenticity of this box, it was taken out
of doors and set under a tree in plain view of an audience, where it
kept on talking. The skeptical rightly decided that the owner was a
ventriloquist.

The talking boxes increased so rapidly that the Department for the
Protection of the Natives of the State of Chiapas began taking them
away from their owners. At one time there were over fifty in the
offices in Las Casas. No one seems to be able to find out who invented
these boxes but they were operated by both natives and ladinos.

Among the Mayas the cross is the most sacred of their religious symbols; it shares honors with the pagan gods and patron saints of the villages, receiving offerings and festivals. The people put crosses everywhere because of their protective power. They are believed to be the intermediaries between God and man—"the eyes of God."

THE CROSS OF PALENKE

Some crosses are believed to be more miraculous than others, but any kind of cross of sticks, leaves, or even one that is painted on something, wards off danger. A cross placed near burning lime drives away the evil spirits; it helps the bees to produce better honey when cut into the hive. Crosses painted with indigo on a child's forehead and chest keep illness away. In building a house the poles are intersected to form crosses to shut out evil. Even the street intersections are considered crosses, so some acts in connection with magic are performed at street corners. Crosses are placed at the four village entrances so that they may help the balams to protect it. The Mayas know the constellation of the Southern Cross by name because of its symbolism.

However, as seen in the case of the talking boxes, this great reverence for the cross by the Mayas and others has never hindered some individuals from using it as an instrument of deception. About a century ago, a talking cross appeared on a mahogany tree in Quintana Roo. Because of the miracle the site became the shrine village of Chan Santa Cruz and capital of the rebel Mayas in the War of the Castes against the whites, which had been going on for over three centuries. The invention was attributed to a mestizo named Barrera, who employed a native ventriloquist to do the talking for the cross. It said it was the Trinity, sent by God to help the Mayas win the war. The counsels of the cross encouraged the Mayas to fight so much more aggressively that about a year later, 1851, the federal soldiers fell upon the place, destroying the cross and killing the ventriloquist.

Barrera escaped, but returned later to the shrine with the dispersed Mayas to invent another miracle. This time he made the people believe that three crosses, the daughters of the one destroyed, had been sent from Heaven to help them. These crosses also had the power of speech, but as no ventriloquist could be found, they as well as the person talking for them had to be hidden from view. A palm leaf hut was constructed for them. The crosses were clothed in women's huipils and kept on an altar in the inner chamber called La Glória, where only the priest and their patron were permitted to enter. The fact that they could not be seen added mystery, and the cleverly amplified voice inspired awe. These crosses not only talked to express their wishes, but also wrote letters.

The cult of talking crosses spread rapidly. Others appeared elsewhere but those of Chan Santa Cruz remained the most influential. Their priests grew powerful. One of them claimed to be able to enter Heaven to confer with God. The letters said to have been written by the crosses were signed with his name, followed by three little crosses. He referred to himself as the "Son of God" or the "Creator of Christians" or he would say, "I, Jesus Christ of the Holy Cross," until finally the natives confused him with Christ. The Caciques of this group also used the crosses as a means of gaining power over the people and ruled them with an iron hand. For ordinary offenses the penalties were whippings, fettering the feet, and compulsory labor; for witchcraft, murder, or associating with whites, death.

After periods of federal government persecutions, epidemics, plagues, and the invasion of the white man into Chan Santa Cruz, the Mayas left the town about 1930. They split up into two subtribes, one of them that of X-Cacal, which now has the cross of that shrine. It is the tribal patron cross, more powerful than any of the others of the group. It is called La Santísima, the Most Holy Cross, and according to the old tradition, is seldom exposed to public view. It is kept hidden in a wooden box behind a curtain on the altar of La

Gloria of the shrine temple at X-Cacal, where only the priest may enter; an armed sentinel guards it night and day. Neither this nor the other patron crosses are ever taken out in procession: they are represented by a fiadora, or double, in all public rites.

This Most Holy Cross no longer speaks but gives counsel and makes its wishes known by writing letters in Maya, signed "My Father Lord Three Persons," followed by three little crosses because it writes in the name of God, its Father. With persons who have not complied with their devotions the cross indicates its displeasure by blowing out their candles when placed on the altar. That is a serious matter for the owners, who have to find out where they have been negligent and make amends. For serious sins the Most Holy Cross sometimes punishes the entire community with droughts and epidemics. Then all join in giving it a "rogation" fiesta, offering great quantities of food and performing elaborate ceremonies.

Most of the Maya crosses are of cedar but there is a belief that those made of ebony or mahogany by pious old men on Friday are more miraculous. New crosses have to be sprinkled with holy water in the temple at X-Cacal. Then they are dressed in a huipil, the garment worn by the Maya women, adorned with red ribbons, to which little mirrors and glass ornaments are sometimes added. There are domestic crosses of great prestige and power, passed on from father to son like precious heirlooms, patron crosses of villages—a whole hierarchy of crosses—all having personalities and characteristics like persons or saints.

Catholicism increases with the density of population, where the folk live in and near the larger places, but even here it is not free from paganism. However, here the images of saints predominate, but the cross is also important. There are large wooden and masonry crosses in church atriums, on village streets, in the mountains, on hillsides and along the highways, especially to mark places where persons have been killed. There are crosses that have appeared miraculously, like saints. In Tepic, Nayarit, there is a large one of grass, near a chapel on the outskirts of the city, which is an apparition. The day of the Holy Cross is May 3, and in villages where it is patron, the annual fiesta takes place on that day.

The Holy Cross is the patron of masons. On May 3, wherever construction is going on, even on the skyscrapers of Mexico City, the masons set up crosses adorned with flowers and china paper streamers. They and all the other workers on the job stop work just before noon to shoot off firecrackers and to take copitas.

Even for the more progressive, folk religion permeates Catholicism. Every image of the same saint is for them a distinct personality.

Sometimes serious quarrels arise over the superior virtues of one image over the other of the same saint.

The more conservative folk, even though they may be living in Catholicized communities, make very little distinction between saints and idols, using one or the other, according to their "merits." In Huejotzingo, a large village with many churches, on the Mexico City-Puebla Highway, there is a man who rents out his idol to bee-keepers to make the bees produce more honey. A man in Guerrero, otherwise a "Catholic," has an idol in the river near his cornfield in order to keep the waters from overflowing its banks and flooding his field.

To the extent that the people are more primitive, they treat their saints more naturally. In the highlands of Chiapas, the natives pray to saints as well as to crosses. But they do not pray quietly, kneeling with outstretched arms as the folk do elsewhere. They stand up and talk out loud to the saints, argue with them, beg and weep, and offer them liquor from their bottle, spilling a little before them. When a husband and wife have difficulties, they go before an image instead of to court, and each one pleads his case as if before a judge. If the matter that brings them to the saint requires much explanation and they get tired standing, they sit or even lie down. Yet none of this is without due respect. The Huichol mayordomo of Santo Cristo at Tuxpan, Jalisco, when asked by the head of the Federal Cultural Mission why they were preparing a fiesta when they should be preparing their fields for planting, answered affectionately as if speaking of a good friend, "Oh, that so-and-so loves fiestas, so what can we do about it?"

The religious faith of the poor in Mexico, as everywhere in the world, is fraught with profound pathos but, at least, here it is relieved a little by much color and some humor.

During the last twenty-five years, since the Federal Government has been providing more educational facilities for the masses and the influence of labor unions has been growing, I have heard priests complain that the attendance of men in the churches was falling off. But in spite of that, Mexico is still a Catholic country.[1]

THE LIFE CYCLE

Mental and psychological attitudes always are slowest to change. We all know persons who in a crisis return to old beliefs, others who always want to keep on the right side of God, haunted by fear of "in case." In Mexico the expression is "por las dudas"; sometimes one laughingly says, "por las cochinas dudas," "because of those dirty doubts." Thus even the natives who adopt some modern ways of living, preserve religious and life-cycle beliefs because these are among the most vital.

Birth and Infancy [1]

The folk want as many children as possible. Many die but that is "God's will; He sends and takes them away." Those that survive are never burdens. They begin to contribute to the general welfare of the family at an early age. However, fathers and mothers do not look upon their children merely as commercial assets, but love them as other parents do. The work of very young children is an economic necessity; there is no intention of cruelty in it.

Sterility is always blamed on the woman unless proven otherwise, and is one of the most frequent causes for separation. Fortunately for the women, there is very little of it. When children do not come as often as they are wanted or not at all, the woman resorts to medicine, prayers, and magic.

A woman who cannot have a child first takes herb medicines. Sometimes she also goes to a midwife for massages or to a medicine woman for special prescriptions. At the same time she offers prayers and candles to her favorite Virgin; she also tries the magic of objectifying her wish.

When medicines and prayers to local saints fail to bring babies, native women go on long pilgrimages to other more miraculous saints. In Oaxaca, the women generally turn to the Virgin of Juquila. The Zapotecs of Yalalag go with their husbands, walking many days to reach the shrine. They bring candles and make a promise in return for a baby, which usually is to pay for a special Mass. Then they hang on the tree of petitions a crude little cradle, containing a tiny commercial doll, dressed according to the desired sex. If a child is born, the promise is fulfilled. Later the couple return to Juquila to thank the Virgin and to hang something the infant has worn on the petition tree. The Zapotecs of Mitla follow a similar procedure but instead of a cradle, they make tiny tin or wax figures of either sex to put on altars.

Women, as a rule, do not take any care of themselves during pregnancy, interrupting their daily routine of work only for the time necessary to give birth. But the more progressive mothers consult and visit midwives, who give them care and advice. In Cherán, Michoacán, the midwives massage with oil or grease "to keep the foetus in the right position," charging ten centavos or two American cents for each treatment. They advise their patients not to work too much and not to lift heavy burdens; to bathe frequently in cold water —in many places the women bathe in cold streams. However, the expectant mothers, even those who are in a position to have help, continue grinding corn and carrying water because "it is good to keep active."

Abortions sometimes occur but they are seldom voluntary, although medicine women know how to bring them about. In some Catholicized towns, young girls occasionally seek medicine women to help them when they are in trouble before marriage, but normally there is no shame attached to having babies under any circumstances. Contraceptives are unknown among the folk, just as they are among the great majority of other women. Mexico is a Catholic country and the Church does not sanction such measures.

Taboos for pregnant women are widespread; occasionally some are observed by their husbands also. In Cherán, an expectant mother must not tie an animal, or her child may be strangled by the umbilical cord at birth; the same is likely to happen if the father does not untie his load of wood immediately upon bringing it to the house. He should also avoid killing any animal, no matter how small or big it may be; if he does kill one, its spirit will enter the child's nose or mouth and it will be born dead. Here, also, the husband must not work on the day his wife is giving birth. Elsewhere it is believed that an expectant mother can do harm by her mere presence; in Chenahló a baby will become ill if she looks at it.

It is considered bad everywhere for a woman with child to experience an eclipse of the sun or moon; if she does the child will be born with a hare lip or some other facial defect. But the measures taken to counteract the bad effects of eclipses vary. The Tarascan women of Cherán wear a red belt under their clothing; those of Tzintzuntzan place a piece of broken scissors or a knife against the stomach. There is also the belief prevalent among all peoples, that if a pregnant woman wants something to eat, or anything else, and her desire is not satisfied, the child will be born marked in some way; the same will happen if she is frightened by an animal. There are other taboos, but in the last analysis the object of most of them is to keep the mother from disagreeable experiences and in a happy frame of mind for the ordeal and miracle of birth. Such beliefs are as old as the human race. Aztec mothers also avoided eclipses and used similar precautions against their harmful effects.

The mothers do not give birth lying in bed. The most usual position is kneeling but they also squat or stand, always holding on to something for support—a stool, a loop of rope caught in the rafters, the branch of a tree. In most places there are parteras or professional midwives; where there are none, some experienced woman or even a child may help. Occasionally the husband assists, encouraging and applying pressure at the waist or abdomen.

Progressive midwives make some efforts at asepsis. Those of Cherán, besides praying to the saints before the birth, wash their hands and rub them with brandy; they also abstain from smoking and drinking during the ordeal. To hasten the delivery, they sometimes place the mother on a blanket held by four persons, one at each corner, who turn her around gently for about a quarter of an hour. The midwife may also walk from one corner of the room to the other, repeating, "I'm coming; I'm coming." Here the mother stays in bed from one to two weeks and is visited by the midwife daily. After she gets up, she continues taking care of herself until forty days have elapsed from the time of birth, when she resumes normal life and sexual relations with her husband. While a woman is still in a delicate condition, she should not be left alone, as she may be visited by evil spirits or frightened in some way.

In Tepoztlan, Morelos, the midwife generally stays with her patient for a week after the baby is born, eating the same food. At the end of the week, the mother is carried to the temazcal or ancient sweatbath by her husband, where the midwife bathes her and washes her head. Sometimes, all other female members of the family bathe with her, using new fibre washcloths and fresh cakes of soap. It is customary for the mother to stay in bed three weeks longer and to take a similar bath at the end of each week. However, those who cannot afford so much luxury cut the length of time they stay in bed and the number of baths.

Most Maya women are also well cared for during confinement. They are kept in their hammocks in a place especially partitioned off for them, to protect them from contact with persons entering the house who may bring evil winds. Great care is taken of the food served them, as those considered "cold" may cause sterility.

The more primitive women take practically no care of themselves at any time in connection with giving birth to their children. A Tzeltal woman of Cancuc, Chiapas, gives birth in a kneeling position, fully dressed, assisted by a female relative or friend; if she has not had the time to call on anyone else, the husband or an older child will help. After the child is born, the mother is partially undressed and put to bed, where she stays from a few days to a week, depending upon how considerate her husband may be. When she gets up, she bathes in the temazcal and returns to her work. This, more or less, is the way all the other women of the region have their children.

A Tarahumara woman is very shy about giving birth; she goes to some hidden spot away from her house, attended by a woman, her husband or even alone. A nest of grass is prepared to receive the child, over which she stands, holding on to the branch of a tree. She generally resumes her household duties within twenty-four hours, but her husband does not work for three days, fearing some accident to his implements or animals. Three days after birth if the baby is a boy, and four if a girl, a "curing" ceremony is held. Each member of the family kneels before the officiating shaman, while he marks crosses in the air with incense on four sides; then he makes more crosses with three lighted pitch-pine sticks for a boy, and with four for a girl. Next he burns a bit of the hair off the top of the head, and with water from his mouth blows a cross on it. The ceremony ends with the eating of goat meat and drinking of corn beer, dedicated by the shaman. Sometimes the dutuburi dance is also performed. Later two additional ceremonies of the same kind are performed for a boy and three for a girl. A similar ceremony is sometimes performed before birth for the purpose of cutting the invisible wire connecting the foetus with heaven.

A child may be bathed soon after birth or several days later. The umbilical cord, which is believed to have some magical connection with the future life of the child, is never thrown away. That of the girl is generally buried near or under the hearth so that she may become a good housekeeper; that of a boy in the cornfield so that he may be a good farmer. But if the father of a boy wants his son to be a good hunter, he may hang his navel cord on a tree. The Mayas bury the cord under one of the four crosses guarding the entrances of the village, where it remains under the protection of the balam; for if an animal were to eat it, the child would grow up a coward. The Tarahumaras bury the cord in the place where the child is born so that it will not grow up stupid.

Some of the mountain Zapotec, Mixe, and Chinantec groups of Oaxaca believe that a child acquires a tona or animal guardian spirit at birth, to which it remains closely related throughout life, the same accidents or death coming to both at the same time. The animal may be a deer, tiger, fox, small boar, snake or any other. To determine which animal it is, fresh sand or ashes are thrown in or outside of the house where the child is expected, and after it is born the tracks of any animal found upon it are said to be those of the tona. Sometimes a man draws animals on sand while the child is being born. Then the one he has finished when it arrives is the tona. The Chinantecs believe that the child is born with two souls, one staying in the body and the other departing with the tona. Similar beliefs exist among other primitive groups, in Guerrero, Hidalgo, Vera Cruz and elsewhere.

The Huaves of the Isthmus of Tehuantepec, who are fishermen, believe that when an infant is born, an alligator grows simultaneously, and that the lives of both are intimately united. Thus alligators are treated with veneration; no one dares kill one. The people say that no one knows where they die.

The tona is called nagual in some places, as among the Tzeltals, where it seems that only sorcerers are born with them; those born without a nagual cannot perform witchcraft. The Oxchuc sorcerers are said to have two naguales—one is an animal and the other fire. Those of fire are of three different colors, red, yellow and green. The sorcerer who possesses a green nagual always has a green cornfield; a red one is not so good because he makes the cornfields yellowish. These naguales never die because they feed on souls; when those of their owners die, they look for others to live on.

The naguales are believed to be of air, so no one can see them. Thus they can enter houses without being perceived and inform the sorcerers of what is going on in them. The heads of the barrios are also said to have naguales to spy on people. They find out who is hoarding money. Such persons are appointed captains of fiestas in order that they may spend their savings, because it is believed that no one should have more wealth than another.

Here they believe that every person is born with three souls—at death one is eaten by the nagual, another goes to the place of torment, and the third to heaven. The soul which is eaten, if of a child, is as tender as that of a young chicken; of a woman, like a hen; of a man, like a rooster. Sometimes a soul leaves the body and wanders around by itself. If it should happen to come upon a meeting of sorcerers, their naguales eat it and the person to whom it belonged dies. The fire naguales of children fly through the air at night in balls of flame.

Babies are generally baptized as soon after they are born as possible, so that if they die they can become angelitos and go to heaven. In primitive communities where there are no resident priests, the maestro who conducts the Catholic services may perform the ceremony.

Children are usually named after the saint on whose day they are born; sometimes the name of either parent or that of a dead relative is added or a native name. In nearly all of the primitive groups, children are called by nicknames because it is believed that they can be harmed through their real names. In Cancuc, real names are kept a secret to such an extent that some adults never learn what their own names are. The sorcerers cannot perform witchcraft on children so easily when they do not know their names. Among some of these groups—Mayas, Tzeltals and others—many use only native surnames.

In the Catholicized villages of the states of Mexico, Morelos and others, when the baby is forty days old, the mother and godparents take it to church to hear Mass. This is called sacamisa, and commemorates the presentation of the Infant Jesus in the Temple by the Virgin

Mary. It is also an occasion for celebrating the new relationship between compadres—the parents and godparents.

The godparents buy the best outfit they can afford for the baby and pay for the Mass. When the party arrives at the church door, the priest receives and blesses them with holy water. Then they follow him to the altar, the women holding on to the edge of his cape. After this Mass, it is customary for the parents to invite the godparents for a festal meal, which sometimes takes the form of a fiesta with music. When that is the case, the godparents share the expense.

The sacamisa is also observed by city mothers but not exactly on the fortieth day. The poor, who cannot afford the cost of a special Mass, simply go to any Mass with their babies. But there are many who can afford to pay well and do so. The ceremony for them is the same as for the village folk mothers, except that instead of the woman's following the priest and holding his cape, he puts his stole around the neck of the mother and baby. In the cities the feast takes place after the baptism, when the godparents present the baby with a gold chain and medallion; for the sacamisa they make some present to the mother.

The next Catholic ceremony is the confirmation, which admits children of ages varying from a few months to ten or more years old. As it can only be performed by a bishop, not all children are confirmed, because there may be no bishop in the area where they live and the journey is too difficult for them to make. Sometimes new godparents are invited for confirmation—a man for a boy and a woman for a girl.

I once witnessed a confirmation ceremony during a fiesta in a native village near Mexico City. The godparents formed two lines, most of them with babes in arms, all looking clean and dignified. The bishop, followed by his assistant, put a cross of holy oil on each child's forehead and then gave it a slap on the cheek as a reminder of the humility of Christ. By the time he was halfway through there was a loud chorus of protest.

The Huichols perform a "cleansing" and naming ceremony five days after the child is born. At night, while the shaman sings, the name the child is to bear is revealed to him. At dawn, the baby is brought in and the midwife washes it lightly with sacred water and brushes it with the shaman's plumes. When the sun has risen, both mother and child are bathed in warm water. Then the shaman announces what the child will be called. With that the mother is made fit to return to her duties. The navel cord is buried under a century plant, there to live forever.

The next ceremony for a Huichol child is to take it to visit the sacred caves. The people from Tuxpan, Jalisco have to make a long pilgrimage to Santa Caterina, Nayarit, where the caves are situated.

First the child is taken to visit the Mother of the Gods, Father Sun, and the Goddess of Corn. Then it is washed with the water from the most holy of the springs. After this another washing is given the child by the father, with the cold water in the cave of the Goddess of the Eastern Clouds. He holds several arrows of this goddess in one hand as he pours the water with the other. The final baptism is from the principal spring of this cave. Bowls full of cold water are poured over the naked, protesting child, thus insuring the blessings of all the springs of the valley. The children going through this ordeal are sometimes only a few months old. After the final bath, the parents leave gifts for the goddess in the cave—arrows, "god-eyes," or little heads made of tamale dough.

In Oxchuc, Chiapas, a child is named during the first month, preferably the last week. The parents invite someone from the cabildo, a sorcerer or anyone else who knows the prayers, to perform the ceremony. It has to take place on Friday, and the person who is going to say the prayers has to fast for three days—Wednesday, Thursday, and Friday. On Thursday night the person who is going to officiate sleeps in the house of the parents. The next morning at about six o'clock, he prays before the small domestic altar which has been adorned with pine needles and flowers, on which he places five large and three small paraffin candles. It is through these prayers that Santo Tomás is informed that there is a new baby in the house, the cross sending the message. Generally the name is selected by the father after some dead member of the family, those of parents or grandparents being preferred. Sometimes the sorcerer suggests a name of some dead member of his family for the sake of replacing him. His suggestions are usually accepted so that he will not cast spells on the child.

After the ceremony, a breakfast of boiled eggs, tortillas, and beans is served, during which several bottles of liquor are consumed.

As soon as possible after the naming ceremony, the child is baptized according to Catholic ritual, but often the ceremony has to be delayed for years because the people have to wait that long before a priest visits them.

The majority of Mexican babies are carried in rebozos, hanging from the mother's back, but in the hot climes some of them are taken about astride the mother's hip. When Maya babies are old enough to sit on their mother's hip, a ceremony is performed called hetzmek, similar to that which bore the same name among their pre-Conquest ancestors.

Hetzmek in Maya means "the position of being carried astride the hip." The purpose of the ceremony has no relation to the act, but is to perform a ritual which will endow the children with the faculties and skills the parents desire them to possess. Humble food is put into the child's mouth in order that he may learn to adapt himself to what-

BABY CARRIED IN A REBOZO

ever difficult circumstances he may have to experience in later life; agricultural implements are placed in his tiny hands so that he may become a good farmer. A gun put into his hands and fired in his presence will make him a good hunter. If it is a baby girl, the mano for grinding corn, a needle, scissors, or spindle is put in her hands.

The ceremony is performed in the domestic oratory with the family and godparents present. Offerings of food are placed on the altar, and the implements for the child on the ground. The godmother, holding the child, kneels and repeats the prayers of the doctrina, three times. Then she sits the child on her own hip, making a circuit about the place, as she puts into his hands each of the implements in succession, and affectionately explains the purpose of each one and the value of knowing how to use it. In the case of a boy he is carried to a tree and made to touch a high branch in order that he may be good at climbing and extracting chicle. When the godmother returns to the altar with the child still astride her hip, she makes him taste each of the food offerings. Each one is supposed to awaken some faculty implicit in the meaning of their Maya names—eggs, which also means open, are good for the faculty of understanding; the chaya, divided into two pairs, teaches one to weigh the pros and cons of things; pinole makes the memory good; squash seeds cause the memory to flower. After the ceremony is over, the godmother carries the child astride her hip to the homes of relatives and friends to advise them that it has taken place.

Babies are sometimes weaned at the age of two but more generally they continue nursing much longer, often until they are already running about and eating everything; sometimes a mother nurses two children at the same time—the last born and the one next to the baby. During the first year or two of the child's life, it is seldom left alone for any length of time for fear some harm may come to it through animals and evil spirits. The mother or an older sister is always nearby, either watching or holding it, the mother often working with a child in her rebozo on her back, and the little sister playing with it while it is in that position.

Customs similar to those described above existed before the coming of the Spaniards, some of them having been fitted into the present pattern. Among the Aztecs, a pregnant woman had to avoid seeing a man hanged for fear her child might be born with a rope of flesh around its neck; if she looked at an eclipse her baby would have a jagged lip. To counteract the effect, she would put a little stone knife in her bosom. The belief that a woman with child must not be left with a strong, unsatisfied desire also existed.

A midwife took care of the expectant mother for several months before birth, bathing her in the temazcal. The rich turned their daughters over to the midwives with solemn, poetic speeches to which the midwives would answer, promising not to neglect them.

Babies were baptized by the midwife shortly after being born, and named after the day sign on which they were born and after someone in the family. The ceremony took place at sunrise in the patio with prayers and cold water. For a boy a small shield with arrows was made, to which the umbilical cord was tied. This was given to a soldier to bury in a battlefield, so that the boy might become a good warrior. For a girl miniature spinning and weaving implements were prepared, put into a jar, and buried with the navel cord near the hearth to cause her to become a good housewife.

Every four years an ear-piercing ceremony took place for all children born within that period. For this the parents sought godparents, inviting them with ceremonious speeches and presents. The godparents carried the children on their backs to the temple of the God of Fire, where they pierced their ears. Afterwards they took them home, where all ate, drank, and danced together with other children of the neighborhood. On that day even children were permitted to

BATHING IN THE TEMAZCAL

drink pulque, so all were very gay. During the festivities it was customary to lift the children from the ground, holding them at the temples, to make them grow, as now their ears are pulled on the Saturday of Glory for the same purpose.

A ceremony called baptism also existed among the Mayas, the word in their language meaning "to be born anew." Older people were baptized as were children between the ages of three and twelve, when the ritual was more elaborate. Many children were baptized at the same time in the patio of the man who gave the fiesta. The place was freshly swept, spread with fresh leaves, and the evil spirits driven out. One elderly godmother took care of all the girls, and one godfather of the boys. Instead of throwing cold water on the children as among the Aztecs, the priest gave each one in turn a little ground corn and incense to throw into the brazier. Later, the priest, gorgeously clothed, anointed the children's foreheads with virgin water, putting feathers and spices between their fingers and toes. The water was brought from the hollows of trees and rocks in the forest and in it were dissolved pounded cacao seeds and then certain flowers added. Twice during the ceremony the children were threatened—the boys first—with a bone aimed at the forehead, and a second time after the anointment, with a bunch of flowers and a lighted clay pipe, after which each child was given the flowers to smell and the smoke to inhale.

During another fiesta for children, the appliances for all the pursuits were brought, from spindles to equipment for priests. These were anointed with blue bitumen. Each child was then given nine light blows on the joints of the back of the hands with some of these appliances. These were applied by an old woman, clothed in a robe of feathers, who had brought all the paraphernalia. The blows were given to the children to make them skillful in the professions of their fathers and mothers.

Childhood

From the time children are able to run around until they are about eight years old, they usually are left much alone. Most parents do not watch their habits nor do they try to teach them anything. In the hot climes they go about naked or wearing just a little shirt. When they begin to dress, everywhere their clothes are of the same materials and style as those of their parents.

Parents take children of all ages to fiestas, on long pilgrimages, to markets or wherever they may be going away from home. Tiny tots walk long distances, eat anything and sleep anywhere. Notions of comfort or hygiene are non-existent; whatever happens is the will of the gods. All native children are stoics, seldom voicing complaints or permitting themselves the luxury of temper tantrums. Early in life, they learn to respect authority and to obey. They become less well-behaved to the extent that their families become more progressive. Some parents are more affectionate and attentive than others; the majority are kind, punishing only when necessary. In all my travels and stays in villages I have never seen children ill-treated, whereas I have seen children unmercifully beaten by servant-girl-mothers in Mexico City.

Little boys and girls of the same family sleep and play together until about the age of eight. Then they are separated. Then, also, they begin to play apart. A small percentage of the children in larger places are sent to school, the majority of them boys. Many live too far away from schools to attend them.

Whether children go to school or not, the parental education begins. The fathers initiate the boys into adult life, teaching them their occupations, and the mothers do likewise with the girls. Occasionally a few, especially boys, get a higher education and thus enter a different social class from that of their parents. But for the great majority, childhood ends early.

Sometimes orphans or the children of large and poor families begin to work for outsiders when still very young—less than ten years old. Then their lives are very hard indeed. But those who stay at home with their parents generally work only according to their strength. The fathers make small implements and tools for their little sons and give them lighter loads to carry. However, they are not spared long hours or journeys. If the fathers get up at sunrise to go to work in the fields, their little boys accompany them and stay there the full number of hours. They are not expected to do as much work as an adult, but must keep working as long. Girls of eight or younger begin to learn to grind corn, make tortillas, spin, weave, or do whatever household tasks their mothers do. They also take the responsibility of taking care of the younger children.

It is during these formative years that the parents pay most attention to their children, teaching them to become self-supporting, to respect their elders, to take part in the collective life of the community. By the time they reach puberty, their apprenticeship is ended and an adult day's work is expected of them. Soon afterwards, it is time for them to marry. Thus physical and social maturity tend to coincide.

Youth

We have just seen that between the ages of eight and adolescence children are preparing for adult life. The next important event in their lives, following within a short time, is marriage. Thus childhood and youth for native children are much more brief than for those living in a modern way and attending school.

Children are left to learn about the physiological facts of life from observation and experience; it is not the custom for parents to talk to them about such matters. Nor are there any puberty rites. The only ones I have been able to discover are those of the Lacandóns of Chiapas. The fathers offer to the gods in behalf of their young sons a bow and set of arrows, praying that they may become good hunters. After that the boys are permitted to take part in all the rites and to use the loin cloth. The girls of the group indicate their arrival at the age of puberty by wearing a bunch of bright bird feathers tied to the back of the hair as their mothers do. Girls elsewhere sometimes change the style of doing their hair at that time, but their dress remains the same.

With the entire family sleeping in one room, it is natural that boys and girls learn about sex at an early age. But this knowledge does not seem to influence their conduct; the majority marry virgin. They also maintain as much privacy as possible under the circumstances, being careful not to expose their nakedness to the opposite sex.

Young girls in conservative villages are not permitted to go out alone even on household errands. When an older person cannot accompany them, they take a younger sister or brother along. Their mothers watch them even more closely after they begin to menstruate.

Boys enjoy greater liberty than girls during the years between puberty and marriage. They may go out with older men, especially in the larger places, drink with them, play their games and listen to their ribald stories. But they are never permitted to associate with girls, so that there are practically no opportunities for romance and love-making. In some of the more progressive villages, boys and girls take part together in folk dances, the girls returning to their mothers as soon as the dance is over.

Under such conditions marriage is welcome at an early age. It means freedom from parental control for both sexes and general fulfillment. Neither man nor woman can live alone. If one does, he or she is considered abnormal. Marriage is not thought of in terms of pleasure or companionship as among us, but as a necessity. A man needs a woman to keep house for him and to do a woman's work and vice versa. And neither can have any standing in the community alone.

MARRIAGE [1]

Marriages take place at an early age, depending upon the regional customs; the average for girls is about fifteen and for boys, seventeen. They usually marry in their own generation so that the spectacle of an old man married to a young girl is seldom seen. Widows, widowers, and divorcees generally remarry among themselves.

In most cases, marriages are arranged by the parents, in many instances the boy and girl not having spoken to each other before living together. But indulgent parents are sometimes influenced by the wishes of their children in selecting mates for them, especially in the case of the sons. The aggressively romantic boys try to find out in advance if they are pleasing to the girls who attract them, and invent ingenious ways for doing so. Sometimes, as in Ojitlán, Oaxaca, when the girls are coming out of the church, the boys throw pebbles at the feet of the favored ones and watch for their reaction. In other villages, the boys are bolder. They try to get near to the girls returning from the waterholes, gracefully balancing their jars on their heads, to ask for a drink. If they are not rebuffed, then all is well and the fact is communicated to the parents, because it is they who do the formal courting.

The prevailing custom is for the parents of the boy or someone representing them—perhaps a professional marriage-maker—to go to the home of the girl and pedir la novia, "to ask for the bride." The party never makes less than two but more often three or four visits, depending upon the desirability of the girl. Each time they take gifts, consisting of brandy, cigarettes, chocolate, bread, fruit, meat, or whatever the usage of the place requires. The purpose of the call is not mentioned until after much general conversation, even though everyone is aware of it. The matter is treated delicately, the father and mother always making a proper show of reluctance at giving away their daughter. Fathers sometimes even disparage the daughter, as in Chenalhó, Chiapas, saying that she does not know how to make tortillas, weave, embroider; that she sleeps late and is lazy; that they had better look elsewhere for a more suitable mate for their son. Then the boy's parents, kneeling and kissing their hands, answer humbly that it does not matter; that they will teach her everything because "she is the one their son's heart desires." The farce may go on for hours, until in the end a promise to consider the matter is given, both sides having known from the very first that it would be so.

There are two exceptions to the general rule of asking for the bride: (1) when boys and girls, especially those who are marrying for the second time, decide to unite, for which the term is juntarse, without any formalities; (2) robar la novia, "to steal the bride." In some places the term rapto is used, meaning to abduct or rape.

The stealing of the bride takes place even in conservative villages and is gaining in popularity. The boy is usually certain that the girl is willing, and enlists the co-operation of his friends in advance. He may take the girl to the home of a relative, or to the hills for over night. The next morning the initiated meet them with music, fireworks and flowers, as in some villages of Colima. Afterwards the parents are placated and the couple may have a wedding feast or just go on living together.

Civil weddings have been more common recently, although they mean nothing to the natives, who go through the formality only when they are obliged to do so by the authorities. They like church weddings because of the ostentation, but frequently cannot afford the expense or there are no priests in their villages, so a very small number ever marry legally. When they do, certain formalities are observed by all the groups with the differences their customs require. There are always one or two sets of godparents on both sides—sometimes those of baptism serving—who help to pay expenses. If it is a church wedding, it is followed by as sumptuous a feast as the economic circumstances of the groom's parents will permit, with music, good food, much liquor, and often dancing. Advice to the bride and groom is also a feature of formal weddings. It may be given by the judge, some elderly respected relative or member of the community, or the godparents.

Even citified boys and girls, who have an opportunity for courting, preserve some of the customs when they marry legally. The parents of the boy go with gifts to the house of the girl to ask for her. If the families are acquainted, the matter may be settled with one visit but sometimes it takes two or even three. Then a civil wedding takes place, followed by a church wedding if the families are religious and can afford it.

For a church wedding, even of the poor folk living in Mexico City, the proceedings are as follows: Three weeks before the date for the wedding, the "presentation" takes place at the church. The engaged couple, their friends and witnesses go to church, where they are received by the priest, and kneeling before an image of Christ, each one has to state under oath that the boy and the girl are free to marry. Afterwards the girl is asked privately if she is a virgin; if not, she has to do penance.

The day before the wedding, the godparents go to church with the couple for them to confess and receive communion, the godfather accompanying the boy and the godmother the girl. In the evening the parents of both, with their relatives, take leave of the bride and groom at the home of the girl, with admonitions and good wishes, after which light refreshments and drinks are served.

Early the following morning the bride and groom are dressed for the ceremony; each one receives the blessings of the parents while kneeling at the household altar, and sometimes the parents give them some superficial advice.

In addition to the godparents for the wedding, there are three other special sets of them: (1) padrinos de ramo, those who buy the bouquet; (2) padrinos de lazo, those who furnish the white silk cord, the rosary and the Bible; (3) padrinos de arras, those who make a present of the thirteen pieces of silver money and the three wedding rings.

The priest meets the bridal party at the door of the church, where he performs the ceremony. He blesses the three rings, two of which are for the bride and one for the groom. Then the groom takes the arras and lets the pieces slip from his hands into those of his bride as a symbol that he will give her his earnings in the future and that they may be plentiful—this money is usually left in the church for charity. Afterwards the bride and groom, holding the priest's cape, follow him

CARLOS MERIDA

II

COLOR PLATES

III

IV

CARLOS MÉRIDA

V

CARLOS MERIDA

VI

CARLOS MERIDA

VII

VIII

IX

to the altar, where they kneel together during the Mass that follows, with the silk cord around both their shoulders to indicate their union.

Church weddings in other cities are similar, but they are different in the villages. They do not have all those extra godparents; they often rent the arras and wedding rings in the church, and the bride's gown from some store. But they go to church with a band of music, and the whole affair is gayer and more colorful.

Formerly, in La Lechería, Mexico, if the parents found no sign of blood on the sheets, the wedding feast would be broken off abruptly; if otherwise, the fiesta would last a week. In villages around San Juan Teotihuacán, Mexico, if the groom's parents learned that their daughter-in-law was not a virgin, they would show their displeasure by boring holes in the kitchen utensils and cutting napkins in two. In Tehuantepec and other villages of Oaxaca, they used to "dance the sheet" for everyone to see that the bride was a virgin or shoot off firecrackers to spread the good news. If she were not, the groom had a right to leave her. But that seldom happened, when everything else between the couple was right. These customs are dying out. The village folk are becoming modern in this respect.

Chiapas Weddings

The native groups of the Chiapas highlands marry without the sanction of Church or State, but with many drinking feasts. The Tzeltals of the Municipality of Oxchuc have three of them—one after the parents have given their consent, which is called "the first delivery of brandy," for which the boy has to furnish a demijohn of chicha, the sugar cane brandy of the region; a year later another feast takes place with double the amount of chicha, called "an abundance of drink"; and a third takes place at some unstipulated time, with even more chicha. With the third, the marriage contract or "bride price" is finally completed. These feasts have to be attended by the parents of the bride and the most important members of their clan.

Only one feast is reported for the Tzeltals of Cancuc, for which the boy furnishes twenty quarts of chicha. The young couple generally live with the girl's parents, for whom the boy works in payment for his bride—a custom which still exists among many of the primitive groups. During the first two weeks, the couple do not speak to one another, the girl preparing the food and serving her husband in silence. But if all is well on the fifteenth day, the father tells the wife to go to her husband. That night they sleep on the same petate.

Custom sanctions two wives for these natives if they want them, but the second one is acquired with less formality. Occasionally a man has one house in the village and another in a nearby paraje with a wife in each one, so that his friends sometimes jokingly remark, "Lucky man; he has someone to give him his tortillas in both houses." As a rule, where there is more than one wife, they all live together, the women sharing pleasure and work. The second wife is often taken on for reasons other than merely sexual—sometimes the first wife does not know how to weave, or cannot have the desired number of children. Both are equally respected, although the first wife usually has more authority and receives more attentions from the husband. There are no words in the Tzeltal language meaning mistress or concubine.

When a man of Cancuc wants to avoid paying the full "bride price" and the girl he wants has no father or older brother to protect her, he will arrange with the authorities or some important member of her clan to take her by force. Once he has taken the girl into his house, if she stops kicking and scratching and begins to grind the corn, all is well. But when she is not content, she will run away at the first opportunity, the same girl sometimes escaping several times from the same man before he leaves her alone. The fact that she has been forced to sleep with the man is not held against her.

In the Tzeltal village of Tenango, it is the elder of the clan who has to be asked for the bride, and it is he who gives the newlyweds advice at the wedding feast. He says to the groom, "Don't beat her; buy her new clothes, a new outfit every two years." To the bride, "Prepare his pozol, weave his shirt, bear him children to inherit the land of his father, and to care for you both when you are old." When the clans of Cancuc were stronger, the chunel or older member of the clan asked on behalf of the boy. He was never refused because he was also a sorcerer and would have his nagual eat the girl's soul.

The wedding customs of the rest of this highland region are similar, including the "bride price" of many quarts of chicha. If for any reason the wife should leave her husband before bearing him a child, her parents scrupulously return the chicha and all the other gifts they have received for her, but separations are infrequent.

The customs of the Lacandóns, living in the isolation of the jungle forests of Chiapas, are a little different. Here sometimes a young man becomes engaged to a baby cousin and goes to live with his uncle to work for him until the girl is old enough to marry. The marriage ceremony consists of offering pozol and balche, a mild ritual drink, to the gods. Then the newlyweds eat together as a sign that they are husband and wife. After the marriage ceremony neither one will eat again with the parents, even when visiting in their homes. Here, also, polygamy is sanctioned. Sometimes as many as three wives live with one man in harmony, each one doing her share of the work;

usually the first one is the favorite. Occasionally a young man marries a mother and daughter, the older woman to do the cooking and the younger to bear his children. The services of older women are especially important when it is necessary to prepare the ritual food, because only they know how to do it.

Maya Weddings

Maya fathers ask for the brides for their sons in the conventional manner. But if there is a casamentero, or professional marriage-maker, in the village, they may invite him to accompany them or to go by himself to do the pleading. The casamentero is generally an elderly, pious man, sometimes a village functionary, who accepts no fee for his services. He is satisfied with the friendship of his clients, who show their gratitude by helping him in his cornfield and in other ways.

The required number of visits are four, from two to three weeks apart, with gifts of rum, cigarettes, bread, and chocolate, which are consumed by everyone during the evening. If after the first visit a date is set for the next one, it is an indication that the suitor is looked upon with favor. But he is not finally accepted until the third, when the girl's mother specifies what gifts she expects for her daughter from the boy's family. If her demands are too extravagant, bargaining is in order.

The marriage gifts are known as the muhul. In Chan Kom they usually consist of a gold chain, two rings, two hair ribbons, one silk handkerchief, some yards of cotton cloth, rum, bread, chocolate, part of the food for the wedding feast, some money, and the bride's outfit with a specially fine huipil. The chain is the most important object, since it is both an adornment and a symbol of the family wealth. If the bridegroom is able to give his wife additional chains after marriage, it means more prestige and financial security, since these chains are accepted in their community as a draft on a bank is in ours.

The official betrothal takes place with the presentation of the muhul to the girl's parents during the fourth visit, for which relatives are invited. The groom is present on this occasion as a passive spectator, while the bride-to-be is probably asleep in her hammock. The gifts which are placed on a table near a small wooden cross, are offered by the casamentero or chief spokesman with a polite little speech, couched more or less as follows:

"Fulfilling the words of the Señor Dios, who says that every man must take a woman in marriage, the compadres" (indicating the parents and godparents of the boy) "offer you what is on the table, as a sign of gratitude, and in satisfaction of the coming union of their son with your daughter."

The father of the girl thanks them for both himself and his wife, adding, "May the Señor Dios return to you the expenses which you have incurred."

In progressive villages like Chan Kom, the couples are united first by a civil ceremony, attended by the parents, two friends who act as sponsors, and the casamentero, who gives advice to the bride and groom. If a church wedding takes place later, it is attended by the same persons, and a festal dinner is served afterwards by the bridegroom's parents. In the smaller, conservative places, after the four visits and the presentation of the marriage gifts, the couple is either married at home or in church without previously registering with the authorities.

The Mayas of the X-Cacal group in Quintana Roo marry in church. The bridal couple kneel at the entrance on a serape spread on the ground by the sponsors, who give each one a lighted candle. Then kneeling and holding the candles, the bride and groom are obliged to recite seven times the prayers of the doctrina in Maya—Our Father, Hail Mary, the Salve, the Creed, the General Confession, and the Act of Contrition. If either one of them should forget the prayers, the penalty may be twenty-five lashes and a suspension of the ceremony. While the prayers are being said by the couple, Mass is said inside with all the members of the wedding party attending. Afterwards the man acting as priest declares the boy and girl married and gives them counsel regarding their future conduct.

Here and in other Maya villages, the couple lives with the bride's parents for the length of time stipulated as the "bride price," which may be a year or longer.

Weddings in Oaxaca

In this state with its many races there is a great variety of wedding customs, although many follow a general pattern.

Among the western Mixes, who are primitive and poor, even church weddings are without ostentation. In the village of Yacoche, the young man goes with his parents "to ask for the bride," but without the usual formalities. If he is accepted, he takes tamales to her house. The wedding may take place within a month or a year, when it is registered with the civil authorities. If there is a church wedding, it is performed by some functionary who "prays like a priest" but without the chain and arras. The bridegroom presents the bride with a bead collar and a ring. A feast is given in the groom's house, which is decorated with wild flowers brought from the mountains. Tamales and tepache are served. A special feature of the fiesta, which lasts a day and a night, is an eating ceremony. The bride and groom eat first, then their parents, and last the godparents for the wedding. At some time during the fiesta a turkey is sacrificed outside of the house and its blood spilled over cornmeal.

The most formal and elaborate weddings of this group take place at Juquila. The father of the boy asks for the bride. The final answer is given at the second visit, when he takes as gifts two or three cartons of Monarca cigarettes, about five pesos' worth of bread, chocolate, sugar, a large pot of specially made tamales, and another of atole made with brown sugar. Everything is divided among the relatives of the girl. The wedding takes place about six months later, during which time the boy works for the girl's parents in the fields or at home. He eats with them but goes home to sleep. In addition, for every saint's fiesta, he has to give them three pesos' worth of meat.

On the eve of the wedding, there is a fiesta with dancing to a stringed instrument, beginning at the home of the godparents and continuing at the houses of the bride and groom. Early next morning, the bride is dressed at the home of the godparents. Then all go to church, where the couple are married, kneeling all during Mass with their heads covered by the same cloth. Afterwards, dancing starts again, going the round of the same houses. The party breaks up at the groom's house. Then the bridal couple go to their own house, which the groom has prepared in advance.

In the Chinantec village of Yolox, the boy's parents or a professional go-between ask for the bride. If the boy is accepted, he gives the parents of the girl about twenty quarts of brandy for themselves and relatives. A young steer is killed for the wedding fiesta and two meals are served to all the guests.

When the godparents escort the newlyweds from the church to the groom's house, his mother greets the bride with a little speech— "Welcome! This is your house. Now that you have married my son, you shall work with him all your life and your labors shall bear much fruit. Do not let the light of this house go out now or ever" (referring to having children).

The municipal authorities are also invited to the wedding dinner and the President counsels the young couple, who with their godparents stand while he speaks: "You shall love each other and be mutually helpful all your lives. From the moment that you are married, you the husband, have the obligation of respecting your wife's parents as if they were your own; likewise that of esteeming her sisters, brothers and relatives. The same I recommend to you, the bride. You shall both obey the authorities, the principal elders of the village and the members of the Honorable Municipality."

After that a cup of brandy and a cigarette are served to each one of the authorities and they are thanked formally. Then the bride, groom, and godparents dance a jarabe all by themselves.

Among the ancient Mexicans, especially the Aztecs, the wedding speeches were long and flowery. The counsels of the Mazatecs of Huautla Jiménez, spoken in the ancient tongue by one of the authorities, are reminiscent of the counsels of long ago.

"With the permission of all those present and complying with the request of the godparents, I shall say a few words to the bride and groom.

"Now that you are united in marriage, things are not the same as they were yesterday or the day before, because you have entered upon a new life. Marriage is not a game like those you played when children. The ceremony which has just taken place is eternal. You must live together and love and cherish one another until the end of your days."

To the husband: "If you truly loved and desired marriage, conduct yourself worthily. Now that you are a man, never forget the dignity and respect which you owe yourself. From now on, childish actions would be unbecoming. You have undertaken the responsibility of the material and spiritual maintenance of your wife. With sweetness and kindness explain to your wife her duties in the home. Respect yourself and your fellow beings. Treat your parents with reverence, likewise your relatives; in like manner, the parents and relatives of your wife; your friends, with courtesy and consideration.

"Treat the federal and state authorities with respect. Think profoundly about your work, and shape your future carefully. Comply religiously with the mandates of the authorities, and never oppose them. When they make a demand upon you, forget your own work.

"Don't get drunk, for one who drinks excessively seeks crime. Remember all that has been said to you, point by point, for now you are a man. Comport yourself well, because you do not know whether your life will be short or long. This I repeat three times and you must swear to me that you will comply with your obligations.

"The law has given you but one wife; be respectful to her. Educate your children, teach them to work. The good that you do and what you teach them will be their best heritage. In your old age you will reap the harvest of your teachings, but also you will be responsible for your children's faults.

"And you, noble woman," turning to the wife, "upon giving your heart to this man, are from this moment mistress of the new home; the one who will ordain and distribute everything. The duty of keeping careful watch over the product of your husband's labors should be a sacred one for you. Be faithful to the grave. Love and respect his parents as your own.

"It is you who are in charge of the education of your children. Teach them to respect their elders.

"It is not seemly that you go anywhere without the consent of your husband, for difficulties arise when a wife does as she pleases. Respect yourself and others will respect you. Obey the mandates of authority and no ill shall befall you.

"Thus you will both live happily together, respecting and cherishing one another, for which purpose God Himself put man and woman in this world. Take care of each other tenderly in sickness. Try to help your parents in all their needs. Love one another until the last handful of earth is thrown into your graves as a token of respect.

"Of these words and of your solemn promise to fulfill them, I name as witnesses all of the worthy and highly esteemed persons here gathered."

The Zapotecs, a large and progressive group, have most elaborate weddings when they marry in church, but often they merely have a chocolate-drinking party instead of a wedding, after the bride has been asked for and given.

In the Zapotec village of Mitla, the boy's parents send a professional go-between, called a huehuete, to the house of the girl to ask for her in formal speech. He takes cigarettes, flowers, and two candles for the household altar. The acceptance of the cigarettes augurs a favorable answer, but it is not seemly to accept the proposal too quickly, so the huehuete has to return three more times. After the acceptance, relatives and godparents are invited to drink corn gruel or chocolate. But it is more than a mere drinking party, for the groom has to furnish three turkeys with the necessary ingredients for the *mole*, ten pesos worth of white bread and ten of sponge cake, twenty-five pounds of chocolate, and a pot of tepache. The party is held on a Saturday night, and the following day the couple live together at either of the parents' houses or their own.

Frequently weddings take place after the couple have lived together and had children, so their purpose is purely ostentatious. They are costly affairs, especially in the villages near Oaxaca City. The bride, instead of wearing a regional costume, as is generally done, hires a bridal gown and veil; the Mass and the services of a real priest have to be paid for, in addition to which there is food for a large number of people, and music for one or several days. But the Zapotecs, being good business people, have invented the unique custom of having the guests contribute food, drinks, and smokes. As the natives believe in paying for everything, the gifts are entered in a book and are scrupulously returned in kind when the contributor has a wedding or any other important fiesta in his house. Thus the burden is made easier, and in addition there are gifts from the godparents and relatives to the bride and groom.

One Sunday in 1941, I attended a Zapotec wedding in the village of San Sebastián, near Oaxaca City. When I arrived at the house with the two Oaxaqueños who invited me, there was a group of women cooking out of doors in the patio. The household altar was adorned, and in the hut where it stood, a long table was set. There was great animation. We were received as cordially as if we were among the guests who had brought gifts.

The bride, seventeen years old, and the groom, nineteen, were a charming couple. She was wearing the hired white satin gown, veil, and artificial orange blossoms; he, a spick and span white cotton outfit with red sash, a new sombrero, and a red silk kerchief around his neck. Before leaving for the church, they knelt at the altar to receive the blessings of the groom's father and the godparents. After that we all marched to the church, with the band playing at the head of the group. As we entered the churchyard, firecrackers were set off.

There was no priest to meet us at the door; he was still at breakfast, so we had to wait. Finally the couple was married with the arras, wedding rings, and around their necks a chain instead of a cord for the Mass, all things being hired at the church. I was told later that the groom would wear the chain for several days.

After the church ceremony, we returned to the groom's house with the band playing. Again the bride and groom knelt at the altar to pray. Then a meal was served, the first dish being scrambled eggs with chicken livers, which were prepared in huge quantities in immense clay pots. There was also much chocolate and bread. The band played a special folk tune in the patio, as the groom took the first bite from his bride's bread and she from his. Afterwards they served turkey with *mole*, tortillas, other food, drinks, and cigarettes, but none of these for the bride and groom. Each guest was given a little bouquet.

When the meal was over, the dancing started in the patio. The bride danced first with the godfather, and the groom with the godmother. Then anyone who wanted to dance could. But they did not dance ballroom dances—just little jarabes or fandangos as they are called in Oaxaca, to gay folk tunes, the couples dancing in front and around one another but never touching.

Around four o'clock in the afternoon, the dancing was interrupted to permit the party to go to the bride's house for the gifts. Again we all marched through the streets with the band playing, and everyone turned out to look at us. The bride and groom and godparents entered first to kneel at the altar to pray, and more blessings were showered on the newlyweds. Then a painted chest filled with clothes, kitchen utensils, and agricultural implements was loaded on to a little burro and the party started back to the groom's house. Again the band played, but this time we stopped at every corner to dance a little fandango. Thus the entire village was taking part, either as guests at the homes or on the streets.

As the day wore on I became very friendly with the bride and groom, so that they were no longer shy with me. Finally, the groom asked me if I would not like to see their baby. I was surprised because they were so young. The child was already seven months old, a beautiful little boy, dressed in great finery for the wedding of his parents.

When my friends and I left the wedding it was quite late at night. Everyone was having a wonderful time and no one was able to tell us how long it was going to last. For me it was the most exotic, the gayest and loveliest wedding I had ever taken part in.

Tarascan Weddings

Although practically everywhere in Mexico it is the custom to ask for the bride, and to steal her is the exception, among the Tarascans of the highland villages of Michoacán—around Uruapan, the Cañada, Lake Pátzcuaro and the others—the rule is to steal the bride and the exception to ask for her.

In Cherán the favorite time for the theft is in broad daylight, on Sunday morning, when the girl is coming from church, accompanied by female relatives only. Although the girl has previously given her consent to being stolen, she makes a pretense at being outraged by screaming and struggling, as her companions run for the male relatives to rescue her. The boy's accomplices help him by blocking their way, but they must not use force. If the boy is caught before he has been able to reach the house of an uncle with the girl, which is generally where she is taken, he must not resist even though the pursuers beat him. When the theft is successful, as it usually is, the girl remains hidden and the union is consummated while arrangements are being made for the wedding.

In order to secure the consent of the girl's parents for the wedding, it is necessary to placate the irate father. The boy's parents, accompanied by some of their relatives and a professional marriage-maker to do the pleading, visit the home of the girl. Upon entering the house, all kneel, while the marriage-maker says a Catholic prayer in which he makes references to the marriage of Mary and Joseph as an example of the necessity of bringing about the one in question. Then he offers cigarettes to the girl's father. If he accepts them, it is a favorable sign; if not, it means that he is really angry or that he wants bigger favors. Sometimes the girl's father refuses to receive the peacemakers and leaves the house to hide where he cannot be found. But in the end, a father is obliged to give his consent for the sake of his daughter's future, as no boy will marry a girl who has been stolen by someone else.

Some of the weddings of Cherán and nearby villages are even more elaborate than those of the Zapotecs. A typical one of the well-to-do is as follows: Immediately after the girl's father gives his consent to the marriage, there is a drinking party for relatives and friends. Eight days later, there is a ceremony at which the relatives of the bride exchange tamales for bread with the relatives of the groom. On this occasion the bride is present for the first time since she has been stolen. This party, like the first, ends up in drunkenness.

After another week, the civil wedding takes place. It is attended by the godmothers of the groom, and close relatives, who all sign as witnesses. Often the mayor makes a little speech, counseling monogamy and good conduct.

On the eve of the religious wedding, the parents of the bride hire a band to go to the groom's house with gifts of clothing for him— several pairs of white cotton trousers, three shirts, a sombrero, a pair of shoes—the cost of which is divided among the bride's godparents and relatives. One of the party dresses the groom in his new clothes. The bride's sisters and cousins bring narrow, colored, homespun ribbons for the female members of the groom's household to wear in their hair. After the gifts have been presented, the band plays a regional *son*, dance tune, to which the groom is obliged to dance. Sometimes the visitors bring atole or something else to drink and the affair ends up in a party.

Early the next morning, the parents, godparents and close relatives of the groom go with a band to take gifts to the bride, who has returned to her home a few days before the wedding day. The gifts consist of three rebozos, a skirt and blouse, earrings, a sash, a pair of shoes, and beads, the cost of which is divided among them. The bride is then dressed, wearing all three rebozos, and goes to church with the group and musicians. The priest performs the ceremony in the usual manner, using a ring the groom has either brought or borrowed at the church and giving the bride the thirteen pieces of silver, which if furnished by the groom bring better luck. No chain is used here.

After the church ceremony, all go to the house of the bride, where she and all her relatives are left alone; the rest of the party go to the home of the groom. Within a short time, all return with the godparents to invite the bride and her relatives to the groom's house for breakfast. The godparents escort the bride. The breakfast consists only of a cup of chocolate and piece of bread, but it is very formal. The men sit on logs of wood in the patio, one log placed higher to serve as a table. At one end an image or picture of a saint is placed with a lighted candle, incense and flowers before it. Near the altar sit the godfathers and the marriage manager, who offers a prayer of thanks before the guests are served. The women sit apart, the godmothers on a petate in the center of the courtyard, the groom's godmother being distinguished by a ribbon tied in her hair.

After breakfast, the bride and her group return to her house. The band continues playing in the courtyard of the groom's house. Between ten and eleven o'clock, guests drop in and are served food, sitting apart from the relatives. Everyone is welcome because the greater the number of visitors, the more prestige for the wedding. In the meantime, the grandparents, brothers, sisters, and cousins of the groom hire another band to march through the streets, ultimately to eat at the home of one of the groom's uncles; the rest of the party eat at home.

After the dinner, the parents of the groom, their brothers and friends, each one carrying iris leaves, go for the bride. On the way, they stop at the house of her godparents. While the musicians serenade outside, the closer friends enter and surround the godparents, and the marriage-maker in a long informal speech asks their permission to take the bride. The godfather replies in the affirmative. Then all present shake hands with the godparents, making a movement as if to kiss the hand. The godparents then join the group which goes next to the house of the bride. As by that time a big crowd has joined the wedding party, here also only the close relatives enter, but this time with the musicians. Again the marriage manager asks permission to take the bride away. When it is granted, all start for the groom's house, taking with them the clothing that has been prepared. In the meantime more of the groom's relatives arrive, with their own musicians, to help carry the clothing, consisting of men's trousers and shirts, women's sashes, bags, and tortilla napkins.

In the courtyard of the groom's house, all are seated as during breakfast time. Guests continue to arrive. More ribbons and little sticks with elaborate adornments are put on the godmothers' heads. As the relatives of the groom come in, they give cigarettes to his father and godfather; and to the mother and godmother, five or ten centavos each. The money is placed on a china plate covered with a cloth. The recipient tips the plate, allowing the money to slip into her hand so that the amount cannot be seen by the others and then shakes the hand of the donor in thanks. When the wedding is a big one, the money

gifts sometimes amount to ten or more pesos. After all the close relatives on both sides have arrived, they all go to the kitchen where the
marriage manager performs a simple ceremony of polite assurances
and drinking together to cement the relationship of the compadrazgo
among them.

The next ceremony consists of the groom's father giving a piece of
bread, usually in the form of a crown, to each guest. Then follows
that of the gifts of clothing from the bride's relatives to those of the
groom; in return for which they receive large quantities of bread.
While all this is taking place, the musicians are playing regional folk
tunes and the guests are dancing. Sometimes two groups of persons
exchange gifts at the same time, each with their own musicians, playing different tunes. When the exchanges of gifts are over, bags and
napkins are hung around the neck and on the arms of the groom, and
he is made thus to dance two sones, or regional folkdances. Drinks
are served continuously. By the end of the day all the men are gloriously drunk and everyone has had a wonderful time.

The following day the groom's parents visit their son's godparents
of baptism and marriage to thank them for their services, and there is
more drinking in the homes of each couple. Meanwhile, the bride's
grandparents, brothers, sisters, and cousins of both sexes hire musicians and go to the home of the groom to wash all the dishes used on
the previous day, which is the obligation of the bride. However, there
is more drinking than dish washing. With this general drinking party
the wedding festivities are ended, the groom's father some three
hundred pesos poorer on their account. But he is content, for weddings are one of the few opportunities for the display of wealth and
social prestige. The weddings of the poorer families are much less
luxurious.

In the large, progressive town of Chilchota, not far from Cherán,
an amusing episode forms part of the wedding festivities. While dancing goes on in the house of the wedding godparents on the afternoon
of the wedding day, the newlyweds' godparents of baptism select
a party including musicians to go to the groom's house. They take
along a big jar of atole adorned with green branches, flowers, and
paper streamers; a basket of bread and bottles of brandy. Each one
of the party takes a turn at carrying the jar and the basket and dances
with it at every corner, while his companions circle around him.

Another group of relatives of the groom by marriage, called the
"cats," attempt to take away the jar of atole, striking with nettles
whoever happens to be carrying it until they get it away. Then they
take the jar to a store to "sell" it, asking for brandy and cigarettes in
payment. Another group of relatives of the groom, called the
"sisters," helps to defend the jar of atole. When it is stolen and sold,

they buy it back by paying for the goods given to the "cats." This little drama is hilariously repeated several times, the group with the jar and basket reaching their destination at sunset.

The wedding godparents have in the meantime strung a rope across the street to receive the group with the gifts with lighted pieces of pitch-pine as a rebuke for coming so late. Then they use the rope to hinder them from entering the house. But after the game is played for some time with shrieks of laughter, the party gets in somehow, either climbing over or under the rope.

Huejutla Weddings

In 1944, I spent Holy Week in the mountain town of Huejutla, Hidalgo. On the morning of Saturday of Glory, a goodly number of couples were married at the same time, very early in the morning. It was still dark when we crowded into the church.

The brides looked charming in their daily regional costumes, consisting of a full skirt and quexquemetl, but of finer weave and more elaborately embroidered for the occasion. Their adornments were silver earrings, strings of colorful glass beads, and various handwoven ribbons in the hair, their heads covered with a piece of cotton cloth folded into a square. Some of the brides wore veils, but even they wore the same kind of cloth under them, so it must have had some special significance. When I asked about it, I received the usual reply, "es costumbre," "it is the custom." I believed that they could give me no other, because they often do not know.

The grooms were dressed in new, ordinary, white unbleached cotton suits, with red silk handkerchiefs around the neck, and all of them had many red bandannas over each shoulder, which their friends had put on them for good luck. The brides wore more than one outfit, one over the other, as they believe that their luck increases in proportion to the number worn for the ceremony.

In the nearby village of Macuxtepetla, where many of the couples came from, the special wedding dish consists of tamales filled with white and black beans. The beans are believed to have the magical power of affecting the sex of the offspring of the couple, the two colors producing babies of both sexes.

The advice given to the groom is very practical, but poetically expressed; he is told not to wait to hear the song of the papán—a bird that sings very early in the morning—still lying on his petate, but to listen to it in the cornfield or in the woods with his machete in his hand.

The fiesta takes place in the home of the groom. When the wedding party arrives, it is received with music and firecrackers. An arch of green leaves and flowers frames the doorway, where a new petate is placed for the bride and groom to kneel on. First the godparents give each one a copita of brandy to drink. Then they throw wet flowers at them. Afterwards the godmother adorns the bride, and the godfather the groom, with flowers. They are in turn adorned by the bride and groom. Finally this pretty ceremony ends with the newlyweds putting flowers on one another. This adornment with flowers is called the tope, climax; while it is taking place the musicians play a folk dance, called "The Canary." After it is over, the couple go inside to sit near the altar, bashfully turning their backs to one another.

Next two huge clay cooking bowls are brought in with a whole turkey in each one. The godfather gives seven mouthfuls of turkey with tortilla to the bride; and the godmother, seven to the groom; then they exchange places and give each one seven more. Then the extra clothing is taken off the bride and if she is going to live in the groom's house, he takes her to the river to show her where she is going to do the washing; he also indicates the place where she is to grind the corn. If the couple are going to live in the bride's house, they go there together after the fiesta. That goes on throughout the night, ending up in the morning with the taking of turkey, tortillas, and tamales to the homes of the godparents. The following night the bride and groom sleep together on their new petate.

Yaqui Weddings

Weddings are also generally arranged by the parents among the Yaquis, but sometimes by the mutual consent of the young people. They are married in church by the maestro, who conducts the Catholic services. The bride wears a new dress of regional style, which is part of the trousseau the groom has provided for her. The godparents pay the wedding expenses. The bride's parents furnish the food for the feast, consisting of tamales and huacabaque, a beef stew.

On the wedding day, the bride, accompanied by her godparents and relatives, takes a bowl of tamales to the groom's house. When they arrive, they are received with firecrackers, the groom and all his relatives shooting them off. A new petate is placed near the cross in the courtyard; on this the gifts of food and other objects are placed by both sides and exchanges are made.

It is considered a good omen for the bride to bring tamales to the groom because the tamales are symbolic of money, and of the union between them. After the gifts are exchanged, the bride and groom kneel to pray and to listen to the counsels of their parents and god-parents. The young couple usually lives for some time with the boy's parents, where the bride is expected to help in the household tasks.

In the older marriage customs of the Yaquis, sometimes still observed, the bride wears two ribbons of different colors in her hair, one of them blue to indicate her virginity. She may also wear a piece of naca on a blue ribbon around her neck for the same purpose. After the wedding festivities, the couple go to their own house. Immediately upon arriving there, the bride goes to the nearest well or river to bring water; both drinking it from the same gourd constitutes the real marriage. The drinking of water in this way among the Yaquis always establishes a bond.

Huichol Weddings

The Huichols, always very strict in their ritual, are nevertheless lax in their social relations. Their young girls are very modest, but they are often seduced by drunken youths during fiestas and no one thinks the less of them on that account. Some marry the young men who have violated them, while others may become concubines of older men.

The custom of asking for the bride is often observed, but only in the case of virgins. The mutual agreement, followed by an exchange of presents between the two families, often constitutes the only marriage ceremony.

Among the Huichols of Jalisco, a shaman occasionally performs the ceremony for the very young and inexperienced. He sings the marriage myths of the gods, holding a gourd of sacred water in one hand, and flowers in the other. A plate of special food is prepared, containing tortillas, bananas, cheese and meat; the eating of it by the couple after the shaman has spat upon it, solemnizes the union.

While the singing goes on at night, the boy and girl have to lie on the same mat. When they have fallen asleep, the shaman joins their hands and spits on them. Then he sprinkles them lightly with the sacred water and scatters flowers over them. If the couple are willing to eat the food from the same plate when they have awakened, they are considered married. But if not, the services of the shaman are retained for several days longer. Usually after the boy and girl are left alone, excepting when food and intoxicating drinks are served them, they are willing to live together. If they continue to do so for a month, the shaman is given a present of a cow in addition to his fee of six pesos.

The Huichol boys and girls have more freedom to live their own lives than those of other tribes. Often a boy goes directly to a girl who has taken his fancy, without consulting parents or anyone else, and brings her a present of a squirrel, a fish, or any other object that he thinks may please her. If she likes him, she weaves a ribbon for him. After they have both agreed, they then ask the consent of their parents and get married.

In Nayarit, the marriage ceremony consists of the girl going for water in the night and the boy for wood. The next day, they fast and run deer. The girl's parents give the boy some clothes, a machete, and a deerskin in which to carry wood.

Among those of mature age, a woman may propose marriage to the man, but the young girls are more independent and the boys have to make the advances. Often neither one asks the consent of the parents. They have the opportunity to make arrangements at the feasts where violin and guitar are played for dancing. If the parents are very angry, they take the matter to the native court to be settled. The young couples separate easily, especially when either one has reason for jealousy, but many live together all their lives.

A Huichol man often takes two or three wives. The first one is called la reina, the queen. They join her family unit, building a separate hut to live in. When the husband wants to take another wife, he asks the consent of the first one and builds another hut nearby for the second; if a third one is to be added, the first two are consulted.

Seri Weddings

Among the Seris of Sonora, the man buys his bride, paying for her with goods, such as a canoe or fish. However, the price is not the only consideration; he must be pleasing not only to the girl but to her whole family. Every member of the girl's family receives a share of the gifts. If anyone of them refuses to accept his share, the marriage negotiations may be broken off and the boy loses all that the others have already accepted. After marriage, the husband is obliged to support all his wife's family, if necessary. But if the girl should prove unworthy, he has the right to send her back home.

The wedding festivities last a whole week, with dancing and singing to the accompaniment of the violin going on unceasingly. The ceremonial drink is tepache, fermented with potatoes, brown sugar, and water. The mother of the girl, according to custom, cries a great deal during the time. Only after the celebrations are over are the boy and girl permitted to sleep together.

Legal divorces are practically unknown among the folk, but sometimes the civil authorities are asked to intervene when separations are necessary. Desertions because of some other man or woman seldom happen, although extra-marital relations are frequent, especially among the men who have to observe long periods of abstinence during their wives' pregnancy and childbirth. There are groups in which flagrant adultery is severely punished, as among the Yaquis, where both culprits are whipped publicly.

Prostitution per se is practically non-existent, since all marry young and few men are ever without a woman. Yet in the larger places there are always some few loose girls and women, especially widows, who serve strangers and some of their own men. The compensation they receive ranges from a five-centavo cake of soap to about fifty centavos in cash, which is considered high.

On the whole, the sanctions of the village groups keep morality on a much higher standard than the laws do in the cities. Separations among the former take place only for good reasons. When they happen, an equitable settlement is made for the protection of the children. In the cities desertions are common among the poor. A man often has several children with a woman; then he deserts her with impunity and she has to support them with no help whatever from any source. The poor mothers, though, are very loyal, working night and day to support their children. One often sees them with infants, selling in the market places or on the streets.

Love Magic [1]

Love magic is little practiced, if at all, among the more primitive groups. But the more sophisticated folk, especially those living in and near cities, either employ sorcerers and witches or perform certain magical rites themselves to win back a lover or husband.

According to an unnamed seventeenth-century Spanish author, poetic prayers in magical terms were addressed by the Aztecs to Xochiquetzal, their goddess of love and flowers, to ask for help in matters of love. But today the women of the same race and others appeal to the saints.

In villages of the State of Morelos and others, it is believed that a woman who has been abandoned by her husband can force him to return by performing the following rite: She must lie stretched out on the floor with funerary candles lighted on both sides of her, as if she were dead. She must stay in that position until the candles have burned out, saying the prayers of the Christian Creed. When she comes to the last word of the prayers, she must repeat it three times, while pounding on the ground with both fists. Immediately afterwards, she must pronounce the name of the unfaithful one, uttering this invocation to someone in Rome—"Soul of Tulimeca, thou who art in Rome, I wish you to send me"—here pronouncing the name of the absent one—"repenting of all the grief that he has caused me by going away." In order to be effective, the rite must be repeated on three successive nights.

A widespread belief exists that if a woman will measure her sweetheart or husband with a ribbon while he is asleep, and keep his length rolled up with a scapular of St. Anthony from which it must not be separated for a moment, she can dominate her man. If the magic is to work, he must know nothing about it.

Another common belief is that if a man wears a dead hummingbird in a bag hanging from his neck, he will be sought after and loved by many women. This bird was considered sacred before the Conquest and its feathers were highly prized as adornments.

A Mexican philologist once asked a medicine woman in the village of Tepoztlán, Morelos, what he should do to make himself beloved by the girl he wanted. She answered him simply, "Love her!" He was surprised at her Ovidian counsel and pressed her for more tangible help. But she persisted—"If you wish her to love you, love her."

Some years later when I was being treated by the same woman for a feigned illness, I told her that my husband had left me, asking what I should do to get him back, and she was kinder to me. First she threw a piece of alum on some burning coals, and from the form it took she concluded that he had left me for another woman. Then she promised me that he would return because my rival was not so attractive as I. The next day, she brought me a bottle of medicine to take myself and some powders to throw into any liquid that my husband might drink.

Doña Refugio, a medicine woman in Mexico City, told me of an experience her daughter Juana had had with her ex-husband. While he was away from home, some friend wrote him things about Juana that made him jealous. He went to a Yaqui sorcerer and asked him to make her ill. The Yaqui made a rag doll to represent the wife, attaching to it a lock of her hair and a gold ring she had worn, loaned by the husband. Then he tortured the doll by sticking pins into it. At the same time, Juana began to feel frightful pains in various parts of her body. She also imagined herself bitten by snakes, buzzards, squirrels and other animals. But they all disappeared as soon as she confessed. Through a friend who was with the husband and wrote to Juana's mother, and through the magic she herself was performing, she knew that her daughter had become the victim of magic. Then it took her a whole year, with the aid of prayers, candles, and incense, to cure her daughter.

In the cities, where life is complicated and there is more infidelity than in the villages, one finds many love charms. Every vendor of herbs has them in various forms. Once I bought several from a woman in the Puebla City market. In one paper she gave me a dried hummingbird; in another, a stone, covered with what looked like gold dust, on top of which were some red and black beans, of both sexes, I was told. If I wanted just one man to love me, I was to wear them next to my heart; if more than one, in my stocking. In order to keep the magic alive in the stone, I was to wash it in wine every Tuesday and Friday, Wednesdays and Saturdays being the days for men. The woman did not touch the objects with her hands, but picked them up carefully from a box with a pair of tweezers.

Since then I have learned that the stone is the miraculous Imán. The publishing houses of religious and folk literature print little leaflets telling its history, how to treat it, and the prayers that should be addressed to it to bring good luck in everything, including love.

The Imán (magnetic) Stone is the one on which the body of Christ rested for three days after its descent from the cross. Godfrey of Bouillon discovered that it was miraculous when he led the first Crusade (1096–1100) to Palestine. He and his soldiers fought for a long time against the infidels outside the walls of Jerusalem. When everything seemed lost, Godfrey went to Christ's sepulchre, which had been discovered on the outskirts of the city, and humbly implored help of the Lord. As he was praying, a voice whispered to him, saying that he would be victorious if he carried away with him a piece of the stone upon which the sacred body of Christ rested, because it had magnetic properties. He did so and was able to conquer the Holy Land, as the voice predicted.

As long as Godfrey ruled the Holy Land, all went well because of his devotion to the sacred stone, but the kings who succeeded him paid no attention to it, so the Holy Land was lost to Christianity.

Many of the Crusaders were eye-witnesses of the miracles worked by the stone and propagated its devotion in the Christian world. It always grants what is asked of it with faith.

One of the little leaflets, entitled, "The Secret of the Virtuous Imán Stone," tells how to treat it.

You take the stone to church, light two candles to put near it, spill a little fine salt on it and put it in holy water, saying:

"Imán, yo te bautizo en nombre de Díos Padre, Díos Hijo; yo te bautizo, Imán, y serás para mi fortuna y suerte llamarás." ("Imán, I baptize you in the name of God the Father, God the Son; I baptize you, Imán, and you will be my fortune and will bring me good luck.")

Immediately afterwards, you kneel in the middle of the church and say an "Our Father." Then you go home and put the stone in a little red woolen bag, saying:

"Hermosa Piedra Imán, mineral y encantadora, que con la Samaritana anduviste, a quien hermosura, suerte y hombre diste." ("Beautiful, mineral and enchanting Imán Stone, who went about with the Samaritan, to whom you gave beauty, good luck and a man.")

"Te pongo oro, para mi tesoro," ("I put gold on you for my treasure,")

"Plata para mi casa," ("Silver for my house,")

"Cobre para el pobre," ("Copper for the poor man,")

"Coral, para que me quite la envidia y el mal," ("Coral, so that you remove from me envy and evil,")

"Trigo, para que Fulano o Fulana sea mi esposo o esposa, según lo que desea, se le pide." ("Wheat, so that"—here you mention the name of a man or woman you want—"be my wife or husband as the case may be.")

You must prepare all the objects mentioned above to put on the stone in their proper order.

On Fridays you bathe the stone in consecrated wine with this prayer:

"Hermosa Piedra Imán, mineral y encantadora, que con la Samaritana anduviste, a quien hermosura, suerte y hombre diste; a mi me darás suerte y fortuna." (This is the same as above, adding at the end—"and to me you will give good luck and wealth.")

Then you put the stone with everything on it in the little bag, and drink the wine.

There are other long prayers to the Imán Stone, to Santa Elena de la Cruz, who is miraculous in love; to the Blessed Crown, to the Lonely Soul of John the Miner, to the spirit of the person and to the Holy Spirit; and various are addressed to Holy Death, the shortest of which is:

"Muerte querida de mi corazón,
no me desampares con tu protección
y no me dejes a Fulano (here you mention the man's name)
de tal momento tranquilo,
moléstelo a cada momento,
mortifícalo, inquiétalo
para que siempre piense en mi."

"Beloved death of my heart,
do not leave me unprotected
and don't leave "John Doe" tranquil
for one moment—molest him, mortify
him, make him restless so that he
will always think of me."

All the other prayers are of this order—they beg that the person they want be given no peace until he is at the supplicant's side.

Not only the poor and humble seek love charms and magic. I know a woman who makes a good living performing magical love rites for well-to-do women in Mexico City. She told me that she had learned them from a Zapotec sorcerer of Oaxaca but that she only uses his ideas; that in reality she invents her own formulas, using candles, herbs, flowers, prayers—anything that is suited to the circumstances of the case under treatment.

MEDICINE AND MAGIC [1]

Medicine is still in a primitive state even among the most progressive of the folk. All of them have some practical knowledge concerning minor aliments and home remedies, but practically everything that is at all serious is attributed to supernatural causes or witchcraft. Common beliefs are that illness is caused by evil spirits in the air, evil winds, the evil eye, or black magic; hence it has to be diagnosed and cured magically.

The folk doctors are the curanderos, medicine men and women, among whom are witches and sorcerers. The curanderas, or women, predominate in the central states; and curanderos, men, in the remote ones. Shamans, pagan priests, also cure. They all learn their arts from others practicing them, but some also receive mandates directly from the gods, often in dreams. An elderly medicine woman told me that, when still in her teens, she dreamed she saw a procession of men and women, carrying very tall candles, entering the church. The next morning she found a little glass Christ at her head. Shortly afterwards she had another dream in which there was only air and the spirits whispered to her that she could cure.

Very few curanderos devote all their time to their profession. The majority make a living at normal village tasks. They are generally respected and well treated, receiving compensation in cash, food or drink. Occasionally, however, a witch or a sorcerer comes to a tragic end. When too many bad deeds are attributed to one of them, he or she may be killed without mercy.

The practices of the curers of today are a fusion of Mexican indigenous and European folk methods—massaging, bleeding, cupping, sucking, spitting, sweating, prayers and offerings to pagan gods and Christian saints, as well as to good and evil spirits. Practically all curers use magic, herbs, and mineral and other objects; many perform magical rites.

Before the Conquest, botany was one of the advanced sciences,

Thousands of plants and herbs were minutely and accurately classified for medical purposes. The present-day curers also have a vast
knowledge of herbal lore. In every large and small market of the
country there are stands with great varieties of medicinal herbs, roots,
sticks, twigs, wild flowers, minerals and all other objects used for
curative purposes; besides, men and women sell them from baskets on
the streets. Always the vendors know the names of everything, how
each object is to be prepared and its curative properties.

It was through an herb vendor in a large Mexico City market that
I became acquainted with Doña Refugio, a noted medicine woman,
and was able to see her give a treatment. The patient was a middle-
aged man, whose illness was believed to have been caused by a witch
employed by his neighbor with whom he had quarreled. He had been
treated in a free city clinic but he had no faith in the doctors, yet he
was certain that Doña Refugio could cure him. However, he had to
wait for several months before he could afford her treatments. When
I heard that he had sold his only warm shirt for a peso and was des-
perately trying to find some more money, I offered to come to the
rescue. The treatments were, indeed, expensive, not because of the
fees but because of what was needed for them.

The first treatment was given the patient out of doors, near Doña
Refugio's hut, with his family, a few curious neighbors and myself
present. The man, pale and thin, with stomach and legs swoolen, was
stretched on a petate. Then his body, badly in need of soap and water,
was rubbed with a fragrant mixture of yellow daisies, violets, poppies,
and blessed rosemary, all wet with alcohol. After the massage, the
throat of a black hen was cut, the blood poured into a dish and mixed
with grated pineapple, to which Jerez wine, sweetened with sugar
was added; a mugful was given the patient. He was told to take it
slowly and to commend himself to the Virgin of Guadalupe, for she
would surely cure him. Afterwards the hen was cooked and given
to the sick man to eat. The hen had to be black in order to drive out
the evil spirits. Similar treatments were repeated once a week for
some time and the last I heard was that the patient was recovering.
He would feel better, naturally, with some good food to eat.

One constantly hears of cases where faith is preferred to science,
and the fear of witchcraft persists with the many who live in large
cities in an apparently modernized way. On January 9, 1945, I read
in "El Excelsior," one of the important dailies of Mexico City, that a
school teacher of a poor district had made an accusation in the police
court against her neighbors, alleging that they were trying to kill her.
She stated that on the twenty-fifth and twenty-sixth of the past several
months, they had burned herbs and performed magical rites before an
idol, that these caused her serious physical and mental disturbances;

that when she informed them of her sufferings the man of that family said he would add a piece of topaz to the herbs to make her condition worse, which made her certain of their evil intentions.

A more exciting story appeared in the issue of the same paper of September 24, 1945, about a man turning into a ferocious dog and robbing chicken coops. This happened among the poor families living near the Pedregal, an area covered with lava rocks near Mexico City. The people said the dog was a nagual, a sorcerer who had turned into an animal in order to harm them. They told the reporter that they had beat the dog severely, and that when he ran off they saw him assume his human form, which was that of a man, wounded and bleeding, dragging himself to a neighboring hut. As a matter of fact, the man living there died a few days later from wounds he said he received from falling among the sharp lava rocks when he was coming home in the dark on that very night the neighbors beat up the nagual, but no one believed him.

The best way to learn about cures is to see them given and to take them. I have tried both methods. I was treated by Doña Juana, a very good curandera in the village of Tepoztlán, Morelos. She diagnosed my illness by "cleaning" my entire body with an egg, which she afterwards broke into a saucer. The form it assumed looked to her like a snake, which was a sure indication that I had been hit by the aguajque, their Aztec term for the spirits in the air. The treatment was a vigorous massage with a warm lotion of herbs and oil on two successive days. On the third, the cure was completed by a bath in the temazcal. This aboriginal sweatbath was so low that I had to crawl into it. Then while I baked and sweated on the hot wet floor, my curandera gave me the best scrubbing I had ever had, with a handful of maguey fibre and coarse soap. Afterwards she beat me all over with a branch of moist leaves. When I was dressed and ready to leave, she gave me the branch to throw into the stream I had to cross on the way back, and told me to pray to the Virgin that the aguajque leave my body. She explained that they are always thickest around streams and in the hills.

Doña Juana and others in the village with whom I talked about cures told me that when the aguajque are stubborn about leaving a body they have taken possession of, it is necessary to bribe them with gifts—a common practice everywhere. Here the patient orders a quantity of little toys made of dough and clay in the form of tiny dolls, toads, snakes and other reptiles. Along with these, they take a pair of candles, tamales, mole de pepita (meat, with a gravy made of pumpkin seeds), eggs, chiles, raisins, and other good things to eat. Everything is attractively arranged in baskets, which are decorated with crepe paper of brilliant hues because the spirits like bright colors. Then the curer takes the baskets to the place where the patient has been "hit," and begs the aguajque to leave the sick one in peace. The baskets are supposed to be left there for the spirits, but the skeptical say that the curer takes the food home to eat. In some places the offerings are buried.

There is ritual connected with even such a simple matter as taking a purgative. During one of my visits to Tepoztlán, I called on a native family. The woman hospitably invited me to eat with them, but she told me regretfully that they were having very little to eat because her son was "in physic." She had given him a dose of water of boiled Castilian roses. It was to be repeated for several days, during which time the whole family would thoughtfully abstain from eating foods, such as meat, that are difficult to digest. Without knowing it, they were performing magic.

During my first visit to Tehuantepec, Oaxaca, I was treated by Doña Patricia, a Zapotec curandera. She, too, cleaned me with an egg, but instead of breaking it as is the custom, she said she would bury it under the sands of the nearby river; that the cooling of the egg under the wet sands would cool the fever in my body so that she could better determine what ailed me. At that moment she thought I had tristeza, sadness, because I was so far away from home. However, the next day, when she called at my hotel to treat me, she said I was ill from espanto or fright, a common cause of illness.

Doña Patricia began my treatment by making crosses in the palms of my hand and up and down my arms. Then she massaged me with rosemary leaves soaked in anizado, a local alcholic drink, as she prayed aloud in meaningless words to her favorite saints and to the evil spirits of fright to leave my body:

> "Timorous body, why get frightened?
> Cowardly body, don't be afraid.
> Return Bartolomé to your house and to your stable,
> That you may pardon her.
> May she not die of childbirth,
> May she not die of fright,
> May she not die without confession.
> May that fright fall into the ocean,
> May it fall into the mountains,
> May it seize another unfortunate."

The muttering of the prayers and massaging almost sent me to sleep, but suddenly I was aroused by the need for self-protection. Doña Patricia had filled her mouth with anizado and was sprinkling me in Chinese-laundry fashion. With this my cure was completed.

I tried consulting a medicine man in Tehuantepec. He was not at ease with me, but it was interesting to see how he received his patients while I was waiting. He had a disagreeable personality and behaved more like a city quack than a village curer, lacking the kindliness and charm of Doña Patricia. However, both were respected and were making a living at their professions. Doña Patricia told me she often earned a peso a day—which was considered a great deal—and could have earned more, but she considered it dangerous for the patients if she went from one to another.

Later I made another attempt at being treated by a man. This time he was of the Otomí race, living near Pachuca, Hidalgo. He was a very nice person, middle-aged, but very shy. He also cleaned with an egg, but over all my clothes, and said some prayers silently, which was all.

Some treatments have some common sense, but others have no relation whatever to the illness. The most serious diseases among the highland tribes of Chiapas are diagnosed by pulse-taking, and are cured chiefly by the pulse-takers imbibing huge quantities of chicha, the regional brandy. They pray also, and occasionally some of them cook a fowl of which they and the patients eat. Here as elsewhere diseases are believed to be a punishment for breaking some law sanctioned by the group, or to be caused by incurring enmity or envy. When an individual belongs to a clan, as among the Tzeltals, he is made ill by a sorcerer of his own clan, as outsiders have no power over him.

In order to be able to inflict illness or other harm, the sorcerer of the Chiapas clans must have a nagual or supernatural animal. Those of the municipality of Oxchuc send their naguales out at night with instructions as to the victims and the diseases they are to inflict. When a sick person gets worse, he is often moved from his own house to another, in order to put the nagual off the track. On the other hand, the very sorcerer who has done the evil is often among those who come to cure the patient. His presence is welcomed because it is necessary to discover him and find out from him why he made a victim of the sick person; also the sorcerer must stop his witchcraft before the person can be cured.

When a child or adult gets sick and the ailment does not yield to prayers and home remedies, the family sends for several pulseadores or pulse-takers, as the curers of Oxchuc are called. In very serious cases as many as eight sometimes work together because the greater the number consulting the easier it is to find out who caused the illness, as the guilty one is more likely to be among them. They do not charge for their services, yet the amount spent on chicha would constitute a high fee anywhere—from ten to twenty pesos. But the drinking is a necessary part of the curing ritual.

The diagnosis consists of taking the pulse and drinking. Each pulseador takes the patient's pulse either of the left or right arm or of both. If it is weak, it is proof that the illness is due to witchcraft. Then follows the curing. First it is necessary to discover why the patient was made a victim of witchcraft—what sin or sins he has committed. Thus he must reveal all his hidden past, at least tell all that he has done or thought of importance during the last ten or more years of his life. Typical questions are—"Do you get along well with your spouse?" "Have you had illicit sexual relations?" "Have you quarreled with your in-laws?" "Have you revealed any family intimacies to your neighbors?" "Have you denied favors or services to relatives or friends?" "Have you complied with all your social duties?" "Have you invited to your fiestas all the persons who should attend them?" "Have you insulted or beaten some friend?" On occasion several or all the members of the family are questioned in order to form a more complete opinion as to the patient's guilt. If it is a child who is ill, the parents answer for him.

After the questioning is over, the pulse is taken again, the pulseador silently mentioning the names of the probable responsible sorcerers, including those present. If when a certain name is mentioned the pulse beats become stronger, it is an indication that the guilty one has been discovered. "The blood speaks," they say. "This is the way it has of accusing."

The pulse-takers do not always agree; they sometimes blame one another. Then passions are aroused because it is considered a disgrace to perform witchcraft. When the sorcerer named is not present, a commission is sent to bring him. The accused comes willingly to explain his acts and to defend himself. If he is not absolved by his colleagues, he must plead guilty and promise to suspend the witchcraft as soon as possible; he must also give reasons for having started it. The reasons are always based on faults in behavior, along the lines indicated by the above questions, committed either by the patient or by a member of his family. When the guilt is finally placed on the right person, he or she is "purified" with six or more lashes, which are intended to satisfy the offended ones. The whipping may be done by one of the pulseadores or a member of the family. No one is spared—old or young, male or female. After the lashes are applied, all part on friendly terms and the cure is completed, sometimes with death. The pulse-takers' sessions, accompanied by convivial drinking and arguments, sometimes last for several days. While they are going on, the patient is often completely neglected and dies from lack of attention.

In Cancuc, where the inhabitants are also organized into clans and speak the same language as those of Oxchuc, the beliefs concern-

ing illness and its causes are the same, but there are differences in
their manifestations. They call their pulse-takers by their Tzeital
name, picabal, and there are a few women among them, but only men
have naguales and perform witchcraft. Here they pray more, drink
less, and do not whip their sick ones for having brought on the revenge of sorcerers.

The Cancuqueros call the supernatural animals of the sorcerers
pále. Some describe them as tiny creatures, about ten inches tall,
"dressed like a priest who comes to baptize, in a long black robe, hat,
and shoes." Others say that they assume the forms of tigers, wild-
cats, lions, squirrels, sparrow hawks, buzzards, owls, lightning, wind,
and various others.

The pále do their evil at night, spoiling its beauty with the menace
of illness and death. The people avoid going out after dark and using
the names of members of their families for fear of being overheard
by the pále. They try to keep a fire burning in the hearth while they
are awake, or longer, because it makes the pále disappear.

There is a mero or chief pále, but he has to take orders from the
wispa (a corruption of the Spanish for bishop), who tells him which
houses he is to look into. Then he reports his observations and the
wispa, "comfortably seated in his own house," sends him out again
with instructions for all the pále. But there is still another higher
personage whose permission they must obtain to work evil—San
Juan, the patron saint of the village. So when a pále wishes to harm
a person on good terms with the saint, who prays to him and brings
him candles regularly, the saint will answer, "No, you cannot eat his
soul because he is my good son," or he may say "yes" immediately,
according to the circumstances. The pále who come over from
Oxchuc in the form of owls, also have to obtain San Juan's consent
to do their evil—he never gives it, but tells them to return where they
belong.

As soon as someone becomes ill, the pále takes his soul away to
imprison it in one of the ten caves belonging to the village. The
patient cannot be cured until his soul is returned, and the soul can
only be freed through prayers, which are addressed to San Juan, who
knows in which cave it is being held. The pále drags the soul from one
cave to another, and if it is not released before he gets it into the last
one, he then eats it and the patient dies. The bones of the soul are
eaten by his tiny white dog which always follows him.

After the picabales take the pulse, they immediately begin to pray.
They call it "talking at the cross to cure." They use candles, incense,
and three pine branches of varying lengths. They pray to Tat (for
tata, meaning Father) San Juan, their patron saint; to Tat Manuel,
who is God in Heaven, and to all the other saints they are aquainted

with. When the illness is very serious, prayers are said several times a day at regular hours—at six in the morning, noon, evening, and midnight. If the picabales fast, abstaining from salt and sex, it helps the patient. In some cases, especially when children lose their souls through fright, a hen is killed at the cross for a female patient, and a rooster for a male; all who are present eat a piece, including the sick one; the fowl is considered a reposition of the soul. The picabales are then given a half quart each of chicha.

The pále are said to have wives and mothers. They are tiny creatures, too, who dress in white and go about in the daytime. The mothers are believed to send the recurring diseases, such as malaria, dysentery, and influenza, which periodically take a heavy toll of lives.

The pále, who are always looking out for souls to eat, announce these epidemics by flying through the air and beating a tiny drum as the natives do when they announce a fiesta. Those who hear the drum do not become ill, but if one sees and speaks to the "mother of the sickness" he is immediately smitten. Nothing happens to the ladinos because the pále only know the natives.

There are other types of diseases, among them a bad conscience, which also cause death. This happens when one has stolen or killed his neighbor's animals and does not atone for his crime. The offended person waits for some time, and finally he goes to church to state his case to San Juan as to a judge, bringing him candles and incense. He pleads that he is an honest, hard-working man; that he has never forgotten to pray to his patron saint nor to bring him candles nor to fulfill all his religious obligations, concluding that he is certain San Juan will take all this into consideration and mete out just punishment to the evil doer. The guilty one, who has seen or been informed that his victim has appealed to San Juan for justice, is convinced that there is no way out. He goes home, gets into bed, and before three days are over, he dies.

Similar beliefs and practices exist among all the other groups of this region.

The beliefs of the Mayas with respect to the causes of illness are more poetic but not any more scientific. They also believe in witchcraft, but to a greater extent in punishment by offended gods, spirits, and the souls of dead parents. They, too, fear animals of evil omen and evil winds. The winds are the most difficult to avoid. The people try to keep themselves and their children out of them, but sometimes they take the form of little old men or frolicsome children, who throw pebbles at night and enter the house to rattle dishes and play other pranks, leaving all sorts of illness in their wake. These evil winds enter the body and are contagious. Persons susceptible to catching them from someone are those who are in a weakened or overheated condition. Thus a man returning from work or a long journey will refrain from touching his children or sitting near a woman in confinement or otherwise ill.

The Mayas also attribute minor ailments, such as toothache, headache, or intestinal disorders, to an unbalanced diet of "cold" and "hot" foods. Such disorders are treated with home remedies by some close relative, but when supernatural causes are suspected the services of a professional curer or more generally that of the h-men, their pagan priest, are sought.

In order to diagnose the illness, two methods of divination are employed—counting with grains of corn and crystal gazing. For divining with corn an indeterminate number of grains is taken from a pile of thirty and put into piles of four. If the results are an even number of piles and an even number of grains taken, then the response to the specific question is favorable; if the number of grains and the number of piles are both odd, the answer is negative; if one is even and the other odd, there is doubt.

Crystal gazing consists of looking into a bit of translucent glass, like a bottle stopper, which is considered sacred. The name for the crystal in Maya is zaztun, meaning "stone of light" or "clear stone." Before using the zaztun the h-men dips it into a bowl of balche rum "to cleanse it of evil winds" or "to awaken its power." Then in the reflected candle flame, called the lucero, he discovers the will of the gods and the cause of the illness. After that the case is treated with herbs and ritual and any of the methods already described, such as massaging, bleeding, etc., which the case requires.

Unless the evil winds leave the body of which they have taken possession, the patient will not recover. Prayers, spells, ritual washing and stroking are used to get the spirits to leave. While giving the treatment, the h-men will say, "break the wind, sweep away the wind, unwind the wind."

The Maya curers perform two special cleansing rites on patients sick from winds. One is santiguar, the Spanish for making the sign of the cross, which in this case means "to heal by blessing." For this, rum and several plants are used, the most efficacious being zipche. In Chan Kom the h-men performs this ceremony by drinking some rum first. Then he brushes the patient with the plants while praying to San Lázaro, San Roque and the Virgin Asunción to make the winds leave. Sometimes he also sprays around the sick man's hammock, or his head and eyes, with rum from his mouth. He brushes the hammock and posts with zipche. Afterwards he pretends to gather up the winds and throws them away together with the plants he has used. To prevent their return, he casts a little rum after them in a motion forming the sign of the cross. Finally all of the patient's clothes are changed.

The other rite is called kex in Maya, meaning exchange, and is in the nature of an offering of various foods to the winds for leaving or having left the patient, never to return. In Dzitas the requirements of one medicine woman for one of these ceremonies were two packages of cigarettes, a half bottle of rum, rue, one large and four small candles, a hen, a chicken, some pork, and tortillas. The ceremony was generally performed on Thursday at midnight, the woman first strangling a chicken over the patient's head and praying in Maya. Then she sprinkled him with rum, and drank a glass of it herself to ward off the evil winds. Immediately afterwards the chicken was buried in the bush with a glass of rum. If anyone were to dig up the hen and drink the rum, he would die. On the following day the offerings were enjoyed by the patient and his friends.

The Huichols also attribute disease to supernatural causes, such as displeasing the gods. It is caused by sorcerers, who employ black magic to place corn grains, stones, lizards and other such objects in the body of the victim. A diseased person, therefore, is considered in a state of ritual uncleanliness and can be cured only by being "cleansed." The shaman performs the "cleaning" by preparing the body with ceremonial spitting, using spittle or sacred water for the purpose. Then he brushes it with his plumes or motions of the hands. Finally he sucks out the object or animal causing the condition. The "unclean" may contaminate anyone who touches him, especially the shaman and his wife while the treatment is being given, so they protect themselves by ceremonial fasting from salt, he even abstaining from drinking. Some of the shamans sing the myths to help cure, while others simply cure, but all of them must have the ability to dream which god is punishing the patient, why, and what the sickness is.

The Tarahumaras have curing fiestas, with chanting and dancing, for people, animals, and fields.

Seri medicine men also sing while curing. In order to cure the pain caused by a thin white thread magically inserted into the body of the victim, visible to the healer only, he kneels in front of the patient, holding small branches of torote on which he spits every few minutes, intoning, "shoo, shoo, shoo" and singing.

The shaman curers of the Mazatecs of Oaxaca, who employ methods similar to those already described, use some unique ones. They eat several varieties of narcotic mushrooms, and while under their influence, sing, dance, and pray. "The mushrooms are perform-ing," they say, "not the shaman." A shaman must not eat more than six at one time, as otherwise he would go insane, and the patient would die.

The shaman in curing invokes not only the Christian saints and pagan deities but also the "masters" of the rocks, rivers, mountains, thunder, earth, stars, sun, moon, plants and a sort of mountain-dwell-ing dwarf. The shaman also makes a curing bundle, consisting of eggs, tiny guacamaya feathers, copal, cacao, and bark paper, which he buries in the house of the patient. Often six bundles are prepared, each one containing an egg, a few bits of copal, four or five cacao beans, and a small feather rolled in bark paper; brandy is sometimes added. These are buried in the patio, oriented east and west.

The explanation for the use of the objects is that the shaman's prayer is written on the bark paper with the feather; the egg repre-sents strength; the cacao, wealth; the copal is an essential ritualistic ingredient; the brandy, an offering to the spirits.

Divination with corn grains is common in southern Mexico, but the Mazatecs, Chinantecs, and Zapotecs also use chickens or turkeys. In Mitla, a chicken is killed over a cross drawn on the ground; if it dies with its head toward the east, the patient will recover.

Beliefs in witchcraft exist everywhere. The same witches and sorcerers inflict and cure illness, employing black magic for bad purposes, and white for good. All of them use common elements in different combinations—candles, incense, prayers, dolls to which an object of the victim is attached (which they torture), and others al-ready described. Most of them have the power to transform them-selves in some way, assuming animal and other forms. The following beliefs, fairly widespread among the Catholicized folk, exist in various Aztec villages near Mexico City, in the Texcoco region.

There are three kinds of witchcraft—red, white, and black. Red is for bewitching, white for healing, and black for death. Witches can enter houses as the air, if they are not protected by a cross. When they get power over persons, they come to suck their blood. They prefer hearts that are pure and open like flowers, bringing them sickness and sorrow. But they cannot enter a heart that has hair around it. For that reason hair is used in many of their potions and cures.

Witches can be prevented from entering a house by putting a cross formed of needles in the door or window, or under the pillow. A pair of open scissors placed in a crack of the door or at the head of the bed serves the same purpose. Careful persons always have a cross of blessed palm over the door, and another of salt under a baby's pillow before it is baptized. A good precaution is to place a mirror behind one's head; it looks like water, which the witches cannot cross. One should never follow a ball of light at night because it is a witch who will lead you to death by drowning or by some other means.

The witches usually meet and practice their evil arts on Wednesday and Friday nights, especially during the rainy season. Before leaving their homes, they stand over a pan of water and tie a rebozo around the waist, but leave their legs exposed; this gives them the power to fly. They are always quarreling among themselves, even when in the air. "They are evil people who sell their souls to the devil."

A common method employed for working black magic is to make a beeswax or rag doll to which some object belonging to the victim is attached, and then to torture it to make it suffer. There are other ways, too, in which something of the person to be injured can be used. A man in Guanajuato City told me of a case in which his cousin was involved. Both he and the overseer of the hacienda where he worked were heavy drinkers and quarreled a great deal. On one occasion his cousin went too far and the overseer sent him to jail. The injured man wanted revenge and his mother helped him by going to see a witch in Guanajuato. The witch told her to return to the hacienda and to watch the overseer, and when she saw him urinate out of doors, to bring her a bit of the earth he had wet. With this she performed some magical rites which she did not permit the mother to see, and shortly afterwards the man became very ill and died. First his legs swelled, and then the rest of his body, until he looked like a "monster." Although he had the best medical care, the witch was more powerful than the doctors.

In this region one way of diagnosing and divining is by using tallow candles. One is lighted and named for each person concerned, and as they burn down they inform, in the way they drip, concerning the condition of the person one wants to know about, even if he is not present. If they drip in a certain way, they say "las velas lloran," "the candles weep," which is an indication that a person is injured or seriously ill. Before curing a person for witchcraft, here as elsewhere, the curer must ask permission of the one who performed it, as otherwise he or she may be killed for interfering.

Some curers make the patient sit over a little clay censer with burning charcoal and then jump over it from one side to the other. Every time he jumps, the curer says, "May you be praised; may you be praised." After the sick one sweats from the heat and exercise, he is given a purge, which cleanses him completely from the witchcraft.

In the Sierra de Hidalgo, near Huejutla, the curers diagnose and divine with pieces of alum, as my Tepoztlán medicine woman did; they burn this afterwards on a little charcoal stove. The natives of that region, Aztec and Otomí, believe that the shadow, spirit or soul of a person remains in the place where something happens to cause the illness, and the cure consists of taking offerings there. After examining the patient the curer dreams what has to be done. If the patient is not very ill, the offering is only of tortillas, cigarettes, and brandy, but if he is seriously ill it is much more elaborate.

A special *tamal* (a large tamale) is made with which to clean the affected parts of the body, and the patient is taken to the place of the offering. Seven persons are given seven drinks of brandy, seven cigarettes, and seven pieces of the tamal, each one putting a part of what he has received in a clay jar, near which a piece of the sick person's clothing is placed. The curer then says, "You, masters of the seven airs and the earth, alleviate this child of God, make him well, take this illness and pain away from him. In return I bring you this humble offering of brandy, tobacco, candles, copal, and *tamal*. I bring you this fire so that you may show me the exact spot where he met this illness, whether it was on the road, on the river bank, or elsewhere." Then he prays to the saints, "La Magdalena" among them, ending with, "Help me with this patient, who supplicates and humiliates himself so much before you!"

Among other ever present dangers that are a menace to the peace of mind of the people is that of illness caused by the "evil eye," called ojo. Children are the chief victims but adults also suffer from it. Ojo may be caused by perfectly well-meaning persons who are unaware that they possess that power or who are in a certain physical state. In Chenahlo, a pregnant woman makes a child nervous by looking at it. In order to make it stop weeping, a cotton thread is tied around the right wrist and another around the left ankle.

The wearing of amulets by children and adults as a protection against the evil eye, as well as other diseases and dangers, is widespread. Those worn by Catholics, in the form of scapulars and medallions, are sold at every church, where the person can have them blessed for a small fee. The natives make their charms of seeds, bones, stones, shells, false deer-eyes, tiny gourds, shells.

The Mayas of Chan Kom believe that certain animals—domestic fowl, parrots, owls and others having fixed stares—also have the power to inflict ojo. Their amulets take the form of necklaces and bracelets. Among the objects with which they are strung are small oyster and snail shells, cross-shaped pieces of the prickly ash tree, and bones or deers' toe nails. A bone of the agouti's head is often included, which not only drives illness away but endows the child with the gift of being able to find sweet potato and other roots easily. These and other protective charms are against evil winds and other children's diseases as well as ojo.

When a Maya has inflicted diarrhea on a child by merely looking, he may cure it by taking the child's finger in his mouth or by rubbing a little of his saliva on its mouth or by giving it nine slight blows, saying, "Go away diarrhea," or by bathing the sick child in water in which he has bathed, or by giving the child a drink of water from which he himself has previously drunk.

The same belief that the one who has inflicted ojo can cure it through contact also exists among the Tarascans of Cherán, even though it may have been done unwittingly in admiring a clean and pretty child, for such children are especially susceptible. The person must take a piece of his own soiled clothing and "clean" the patient with it. Thus when a child shows symptoms of ojo—paleness and weepiness—the mother takes it to a street intersection and asks all who pass to "clean" it, in the hope of hitting upon the person who caused the sickness. The cleaning is done by passing something the person is wearing lightly over the child, while repeating cita kaka in Tarascan three or more times, which is an exhortation for the illness to go away. Sometimes a woman lifts the shirt of the child and makes a motion as if spitting over its heart.

It is also believed here that persons can inflict ojo in absence if they want to see one another very much, as in the case of lovers. The symptoms are sadness, lack of sleep, or—when sleeping—dreaming sorrowfully of the person who caused the sickness. If a cure is not affected, the patient may die of vomiting and fever.

Adults may be cured of ojo by having the entire body rubbed with the grease of pigeons, black cats, and dogs. Children may also be cured by being rubbed with these greases, one or two being used.

In Cherán, for adults, amulets against ojo are the religious ones; the amulets for children are deer-eyes, or little sacks filled with salt, lime, and black chile, hung on their necks.

The variations in the general beliefs as to the causes of illness and the practices in curing it are so numerous that it is impossible to go into them any more deeply here. However, I hope there are a sufficient number of examples to give an idea of the present status of folk medicine in Mexico. One wonders that so many patients ever recover and go on living. But that is probably because the weak do not survive childhood.

The worst feature in connection with the folk ideas of sickness and its cures is witchcraft. Whatever influence it may exercise as a social control, as for example in Chiapas and elsewhere, is greatly outweighed by the evil it causes as an impediment to the freedom of thought and action of the persons who believe in it.

The remedy for witchcraft, as for all other beliefs and practices that are obstacles to a happier life, is education. Until about twenty-five years ago medical treatment among the folk was completely in the hands of their own "doctors." A change took place when in the early twenties the first Revolutionary-Reconstruction Government established Salubridad, the Federal Health Department. Since then Salubridad has been opening clinics and hospitals in many places, in co-operation with state governments, and sending brigades of doctors and nurses to villages to vaccinate and to help in times of epidemics; also doctors and nurses form part of the personnel of higher federal rural education institutions and missions.

In 1939, the Medical School of the National University passed a law requiring students who had completed all their work to practice for eight months in some village or town without a doctor and to write a report on health conditions, before receiving a degree. Some of them have done excellent work, treating without charge those who cannot afford to pay, and making converts for scientific treatment.

The progressive folk are no longer afraid of doctors; they go to their offices and to free clinics. Even the more conservative ones now take patent medicines. I know from my own experiences and from those of ethnologists who have spent much time in field work, that in case of illness the most primitive of the natives will ask help of strangers in whom they have confidence. But usually their reactions to the medicines that produce immediately apparent results, such as aspirin, argyrol, and antiseptics for wounds, is to assimilate them into their system of therapeutics, attributing their efficacy to some supernatural qualities; in any case, they are unwilling to believe that the patient has been helped by simply using the medicine. But if the help extended to them were continuous and systematic, they would come to understand it in time.

What is needed for this sort of work, as much as a great expenditure of money on the part of federal and state governments, is a body of specially trained doctors and nurses. In order to be successful, it is absolutely necessary that they know the customs of the groups they are working with, understand the psychology of the primitive mind, and be equipped with a great fund of patience and understanding.

DEATH AND BURIAL [1]

Among the beliefs in connection with death and burial, as in all the others, are some staple elements, while others vary from village to village. The most important of the ancient beliefs still existing everywhere is that the personality continues after death in much the same way as before. This leads to the conclusion that the dead need the same things as the living, hence the widespread custom of burying with them their personal possessions and other objects. The belief also creates a constant awareness and fear of the dead, inducing relatives to perform all the proper ceremonies in order to keep them from returning to do harm.

LORD OF DEATH

Death, if not by accident, seldom comes as a surprise. It is generally announced by curers or birds of evil omen, the owl being an outstanding one. The natives accept death fatalistically and stoically, weeping and wailing only where it is a custom, as among the Zapotecs of Oaxaca; whereas the Mayas of Chan Kom refrain from showing grief in order not to delay the soul in leaving. Those of X-Cacal help the souls whose death agony is unduly prolonged after the prayers are said, by giving them twelve light lashes, administered by some member of the family; these lighten the burden of sin and thus hasten the departure of the soul.

Prayers are commonly considered the most efficacious means of speeding the soul on its way and keeping it from falling into the power of demons, supernatural animals, and beings. The more Catholicized natives try to get a priest to help the soul "to die well," the phrase in Spanish being, 'ayudar a bien morir." But as there are many churches without priests, the rezadores or maestros, who officiate in their stead, usually perform the last rites. The Mayas not only help the soul to reach Gloria with prayers, but make a hole in the thatch above the dying person's hammock so that it may leave the house more easily.

The news of death travels rapidly, either by word of mouth or the ringing of church bells. Immediately, relatives, compadres, and friends come with gifts of food, candles, drink, and often some cash for the funeral expenses. Then the women help prepare the food for the wake, while the men go to see about the burial.

In Mexico the dead are not embalmed, and burials take place twenty-four hours after death. Adults are laid out on the ground with something hard for a pillow, like a few bricks or a piece of concrete or tree trunk. There are usually lighted candles near the body, which is sometimes covered with flowers, and has the stamp of a saint on it. The corpse is occasionally laid on a cross of lime, and this lime is left on the floor during the novena or nine days of prayers following the burial, after which it is gathered up and buried in the grave. This is done in many villages near Mexico City as well as in other parts of the country. The Zapotecs of Oaxaca believe that lying on a lime cross shortens one's stay in purgatory. In the Mixtec village of Cuilapán, of the same state, the lime cross is outlined over finely ground charcoal on a background of sand about three feet square, on which little red stars, branches, and vases with flowers are formed with pulverized brick. This bed for the dead is reminiscent of the elaborate Navajo sand paintings, and the same technique of sprinkling the pigments from the hand is used.

The wakes are social affairs with food, drinks, and smokes. Sometimes a friend brings a guitar to play the dead man's favorite songs. Usually women do the mourning, while the men tell stories and get drunk.

The wakes for children are different. The custom of making them gay with music and dancing exists in all progressive, and in many of the primitive, villages, such as those of the Mixe in Oaxaca. This derives from the Catholic belief that young children are free from sin, and go straight to Heaven. When they die, therefore, one should rejoice and not mourn. The corpses of children are called angelitos, little angels, and are usually laid out in costumes similar to those worn by the favorite saints, with all the insignia. Little girls are often dressed like Virgins.

The dances are nearly always jarabes or sones, simple regional folk dances, intended to amuse the angelito. However, on occasion they are followed by couples dancing modern dances and embracing in the usual way. In the progressive Aztec serape-weaving village of San Miguel de Chiconcuac, Mexico, it is customary for three people to dance little jarabes to lively tunes throughout the night. One of the dancers is a man who makes himself tall by putting a high clay jar on his head, and short by stooping down; the other two are a man and woman, often the godparents of the dead child. At intervals the three stop to drink from the same bottle.

I once asked an intelligent Otomí student the reason for the hilarity at children's wakes. He thought for a while and answered, "You see, señorita, it is because they have not lived long enough to enjoy many fiestas." From the older people I learned of a general belief that if you treat the angelitos well, they will intercede for you in Heaven, where they have great influence because of their purity. In some parts of the State of San Luis Potosí, the corpse of an angelito is solicited by various small communities for wakes in its honor.

Children are generally buried in fancy coffins into which may be put food and toys, as among the Aztecs of Milpa Alta, Mexico. Here, too, if the child has been baptized, a small clay jar is included with which the little angel may water the flowers in heaven. A small cross of wax or palm is placed in the hands of the angelito, and usually a profusion of natural or artificial flowers is placed in and outside of the coffin, with a crown or wreath of either kind at its head.

Children are nearly always buried with a band playing gay tunes and the shooting off of firecrackers. I was once an uninvited guest at a funeral of a baby in Tepoztlán, Morelos. It took place on the Saturday of Holy Week. My notes read as follows, "About 4 P.M., I stopped to speak to a group of musicians seated near the church. They told me they were going to play at the funeral of a baby. Near the entrance stood a small box-shaped bier, covered with square pieces of pink and blue cloth; on top a small dark brown coffin, adorned with gilded fret designs; over that a canopy of red and purple bougainvillea blossoms, ending in a small cross. After the Rosario, the priest came out to pray at the open coffin and to sprinkle it with holy water. The angelito wore a pretty yellow dress with a crown of artificial flowers, and had a small cross of blessed palm in its hands. While the priest officiated, the bells began to toll the death knell. Then the procession started toward the cemetery, with the band leading.

"Two small boys carried the bier, followed by women and children carrying branches of flaming bougainvillea, clay censers, and jars of holy water. A mist of rain was falling, enveloping the mountains in a purple-blue haze. At the cemetery the musicians found shelter under a tree and continued playing. The coffin was placed in a deep grave with a skull upon it, and handfuls of dirt were thrown in by the nearest kin. After the grave was filled, the canopy of flowers was placed on it, with a tall branch at the head. A man passed around clay mugs of hot tequila and cigarettes, which were furnished by the godparents, who also paid the rest of the expenses. The men kept on drinking and the women were talking and laughing naturally, but not the mother; she was trying hard to hold back her tears. The friend who accompanied me, and I, kept in the background as much as possible, fearing to offend with our presence. But in the end, when all the men were quite tipsy, the eldest and drunkest of them all staggered up to us and said with great dignity, 'Thank you for accompanying us. We all come to this, and some time in some other part of the world, someone will do the same for you.' Then he invited my friend to show his good will by drinking with the rest of the men."

Adults, too, are often buried with music, consisting of funeral dirges or other tunes played in a like tempo. On one such occasion I heard Chopin's Funeral March played by a band of barefoot natives, and they did it quite well. The adult dead are usually dressed in their best clothes, with the rest of them rolled up and put under their heads in the coffin. Often their working tools and other possessions are buried with them, as well as food and other objects that will be mentioned later. The majority are buried in coffins, but many are merely rolled in petates, serapes, or just placed on boards in the grave.

The belief that the way to the next world is beset with difficulties is quite general. The dead often have to walk rough roads, along which they find troublesome animals. For that reason men are shod with new sandals with heavy fibre soles, made especially for the dead. From Tehuantepec, Oaxaca, it is necessary for them to traverse a road filled with thorns and brambles, and to cross a river sown with sharp stones. Without such sandals the dead could not even reach the river to moisten their lips.

The Otomís of the municipality of Huxquilucán, Mexico, believe that a goat hinders the dead from crossing the river, so they put hay in the coffin with which to bribe the animal. When a funeral procession has to cross a stream in that region, little boys run on ahead to throw stones at the imaginary goat, in order to get it out of the way. In Otzolotepec, another Otomí village of the same state, a piece of prickly-pear or maguey bark is put into the coffin for the dead to throw at a wild bull that tries to keep them from crossing the plain to reach purgatory. While the bull is busy trying to see if he can eat the maguey, the dead get by.

There is also a general belief that the dead have to cross a river and that a little dog swims them across. In Chiconcuac they say that the dead come to a river where they find a little white dog. If he has just finished bathing, he cannot take one across as he would get dirty, so he asks a little black dog to do it for him. When the dead reach the other side of the river, they find a man standing with an outstretched arm, pointing out the direction they are to take; his hand is burned black from the sun because he never lowers his arm. After a while they come to a closed gate, which is opened for them by a woman. On the inside is purgatory, where they are received by two men with red-hot irons. In this village they believe that the dead are conscious of all that is going on around them until they reach the steps of the church to receive the last rites, after which they are truly dead, but they continue being aware of those whom they have left behind. If relatives do not fulfill their dying wishes, they return at night, hide in the shadows of house walls or cactus fences to await the passing of the guilty ones and beat them up.

When an adult or child dies among the Totonacs of Vera Cruz, the water in which their feet are washed is kept for several days for household uses; in some villages near Coyutla they make chocolate with it. As the natives of that region are well off, they prepare turkey with *mole* and other good food for their wakes, and invite the entire village. The next day when the corpse is about to be taken out of the house, a member of the family stands on the threshold and throws corn grains out to the fowl so that they should not follow the dead one. Much liquor is served at the cemetery. After the grave is filled, it is covered with zempasuchitl, the yellow flowers of the dead since before the Conquest. For four days after the funeral, the house is neither cleaned nor swept. On the fourth day, a simple feast of tamales filled with meat is served with chocolate atole, and the barrendera, or the woman who is going to do the sweeping, is served a dozen tamales. Eight days later there is a sumptuous feast with which the first period of mourning is ended.

The Popolucas, also of Vera Cruz but speaking a different language, do not dress their dead but wrap them in a white cloth, leaving the head uncovered. They place in the hand of the corpse a whip woven of seven strands of white cotton, to be used on the dangerous animals who obstruct the way to the other world; seven is their mystic number. The body is carried to the cemetery on a stretcher made of sticks and poles, the procession being led by the singers of alabanzas, religious chants. The clothing of the dead person, tortillas, beans, water, and some coins are placed beside the body in the grave, the money being to pay for entering the hereafter. Before the grave is filled, the corpse is sprinkled with holy water and more alabanzas are sung. Then each one throws a handful of dirt into the grave in a motion forming a cross. After the earth is all put back, three lighted candles are put at the head with an iris bulb to indicate the location. Weeping is considered dangerous for the soul.

Rosarios, or evening prayers, are said for several weeks following the funeral. These are terminated with a special rosario, for which pigs are killed and much other food prepared to be served together with drinks throughout the night. At midnight musicians, alternating with the singers, begin to play a violin and jarana, a small stringed instrument. At two o'clock, chocolate—a beverage reserved for funerals here—is served to everyone. After that the music and singing continue, reaching a climax at about four o'clock. Then seven tamales are taken out of a pot which has been smoked with copal, and placed on an improvised altar in the house, on which are candles and pictures of Virgins. All the possessions of the deceased are then purified by smoking them with copal before the altar, which makes their destruction unnecessary.

After this ceremony, all the members of the immediate family take tamales, tortillas, water, and some clothing of the dead one, together with the jaw bone and cooked brains of one of the pigs killed for this fiesta, and all go to a secluded spot near a stream, where they throw everything into the bushes, excepting the copal which is placed on the ground. Each one steps over it seven times to become purified. When the family returns to the house, the music, singing and feasting are continued. In the morning the house is swept for the first time since the death. All refuse is thrown into the stream, after which everyone bathes. Thus end the funeral rites.

Following the funeral the progressive Mixes of Ayutla, Oaxaca, end the novena for the dead by praying at the grave on the ninth night. When the mourners return to the house, each one takes three drinks of mezcal, after which they breakfast on turkey or beef stew, tortillas, and coffee. Those who can afford it have music and dancing. The conservatives have similar rites, but also kill a turkey in the cave above the town. This is offered to the spirits together with baskets of tortillas, gourds of tepache, and many small pots which are first made useless by putting small holes in the bottoms or sides. The people here believe the souls go to heaven if prayers are said for them; otherwise, they go to the inferno, from whence they return to annoy their families. Some will not sleep in the house after a death because they are afraid; they believe the dead return to it, for they hear noises. After the novena, however, all is normal again. The drinking of the tepache during the novena seems to "lay" the ghost. Some mourners purify their houses and themselves after a death, with creosote or plants.

The Mixes also tell the well-known Mexican story about the

journey after death. The following version is from the village of Teputepec: "The dead travel eastward for three years to a lake across which they are carried by a black dog. There are white dogs, too, but they will not carry anyone across. For this reason, black dogs are not beaten; if one steals, it will be forgiven. After crossing the lake, the soul travels for three years more to the house of Jesus Christ. There is a man at the door who tells the soul to wait. It waits until the sun comes up. Then it is given a letter to return to this world. What it does in this world is not known. If an angelito dies, it goes to heaven."

The Mayas of Chan Kom believe that a good man goes to Gloria when he dies, a place high up behind the clouds, where St. Peter stands at the gates with the keys. The region of the angelitos, where the souls of little children go, is just outside of the gates. Adult souls have to pass through it in order to reach Gloria. If anyone of them has not been kind to children, the angelitos tell St. Peter and he will not admit them. The men who are received in Gloria are those who do not lie with women before marriage and are true to them afterwards; who do not beat their wives or children; who obey their parents; who do not expect others to share their belongings with them; who do not mistreat animals; who do not swear; who learn prayers every Saturday and Sunday; who pray and make the sign of the cross upon retiring at night.

The souls that have sinned go to Purgatory to be burned white, after which they are received in Gloria. The very bad souls go directly to hell, which is called metnal in Maya, and is beneath the earth. Sorcerers go there because they sell their souls to the devil in exchange for his teaching them his black arts; also the souls of those possessing any weird abilities, even such inoffensive ones as great skill in bullfighting and needlework, belong to the devil. Suicides go straight to metnal, so they are sometimes buried facing downward.

Various other punishments are meted out to sinful souls. Those who have sinned with their wives' sisters are transformed into the whirlwinds that fan the flames for the clearing of the cornfields. A person who leaves money without telling anyone about it, cannot go to Gloria until he has communicated the fact to someone on earth on some May 3, the Day of the Holy Cross. Those who die without paying their debts may have to go about in the form of a wild turkey or deer until their creditors meet and shoot them. Then after the creditors sell the meat and recover what is due them, the souls of the debtors are received in Gloria. Some sinful souls are changed into frogs that live enclosed in trees or rocks until they are released by some hand, when they are free to go to Gloria.

The Mayas also believe in reincarnation, because "God has not enough souls to keep forever repopulating the earth." After a long time, all souls are reborn.

Practically all the Mayas have similar beliefs. Those of X-Cacal say that the souls of the dead are not aware at once of their changed status, so they remain among their relatives for several days continuing their ordinary way of life. On the third day, the souls discover they are dead when they hear their names mentioned in the prayers for them. Then they weep bitterly and so loudly above their graves that the neighbors can hear them. Here the dead are not buried in coffins because coffins would hinder them, since they would only have to carry their coffins along every time they returned to earth for the Day of the Dead.

The Mayas of Quintana Roo prefer to bury their babies in the house and their adults outside but nearby. Some of them say, if they buried their dead in cemeteries, more of them would die; they also believe if they had doctors living among them, there would be more illness.

Only the Catholicized persons among the primitive northwestern tribes use cemeteries. The majority bury their dead in caves or near their houses. The Huichols bury them in the bushes and close the path with thorny branches so that the souls cannot find their way back.

The highland tribes of Chiapas also avoid using cemeteries as much as possible. Those of Cancuc bury their children in a corner of the house, and adults nearby, out or inside, when they can secure permission from the authorities. Here and elsewhere in the region the dead are buried in their best outfits, one put on over the other; the rest of their possessions are placed near the body. A man is covered with his woolen chamarra, and if he has held some political or religious office, his insignia are buried with him. After a funeral, the house is abandoned for three days, because the soul returns at night and attracts the pále. The souls of children do not come back because they are too young to have become accustomed to their home.

In Chenahlo an old woman washes a female corpse and an old man, a male. They are buried in brand new outfits and their old clothes are rolled and used for a pillow. The women are dressed as for a fiesta, with strings of beads around their necks, and rings on their fingers. The hair which has fallen out in combing, and the fingernails which they have cut off, are buried with them. If they are left behind, the soul has to return to look for them because "everything has to be returned complete to Jesucristo." A man is buried in new cotton clothes and is not covered with his wool chamarra, as wool is "hot and burns the soul." Here funerals may take place at dawn. When the corpse is taken up from the ground, a handful of chile is burned "to lift up the spirit." Then someone goes ahead of the bier, sprinkling water and calling to the soul to follow the body. Everyone throws three pieces of dirt into the grave, and all who help in the burial wash their hands well afterwards. The men drink much liquor.

City women are always wearing black, both because it is a favorite color with them and also because they are generally in mourning either for someone in the immediate family or for a close relative, like an aunt, uncle, even a cousin. The natives never wear black. Some of the Catholicized women sometimes sew something black on a garment after a death in the family, as among the Mayas; sometimes mothers and wives observe this custom for a year. Otherwise, mourning is expressed through ritual and ceremonies.

In one of the Mixe villages of Oaxaca, when a man dies, his widow sits in a corner of the hut for nine days with her rebozo drawn over her face, without looking at or speaking to anyone. On the ninth day she is given clean clothes, with which she runs directly to the river, stopping only three times to draw her breath; she speaks to no one on the way. Arrived at the river, she takes a complete bath. This kind of silent mourning is a sign of conjugal loyalty to the dead husband. After the bath, however, the tie between herself and her dead husband is broken. On the tenth day, her house is purified with burning chile seeds, and she is then free to communicate with the world as before. The bath is known as the liberating ablution.

Among the Tarahumaras three fiestas with food, drinks, music, and dances are given for a man during the year after his death, and four for a woman. After that it is believed that their souls have reached heaven safely and that the duty of the near relatives toward their dead is completed. During that period of mourning a widow must be careful not to drink too much at fiestas; she must not have relations with men nor remarry.

The Yaquis also have a ceremony which is necessary to end their mourning and to free them from the dead. As it costs several hundred pesos to perform it, it is customary for several families who have had deaths at about the same time, to co-operate. Even then, they sometimes have to wait longer than the required year to gather the necessary funds, during which time the period of mourning is continued by wearing a black cord around the neck.

I once witnessed one of these ceremonies at Lencho, a new Yaqui village near the other eight, around Wicam Switch, Sonora. Like the rest of the Yaqui villages, Lencho is situated on level ground with very little vegetation. An arbor was constructed outside of the village in open country. Inside was an altar with a small image of a Virgin on it, in a glass-enclosed niche. Also on the altar were the books in which the names of all the dead were written, both of children and of adults. The mourners were seated inside to preside over the ceremonies.

All the afternoon the Pascolas were dancing, this time without a deer, because there were not sufficient funds.

At sunset everyone ate, and afterwards the mourners placed on the ground in front of the cross a petate on which they sat to receive gifts of food and pots of coffee and atole brought them by their relatives and friends. As they approached with the gifts, firecrackers were shot off, and when the empty pots were returned, there were more firecrackers.

After the gifts were received, a procession came to bring a crucifix on a little black wooden platform and the tiny Virgin of Loreto, dressed like the Yaqui women, with many strings of brightly colored beads. The procession consisted of the tenanches, the women attendants of the female saints; the saints, carried under a canopy, which was followed by the godmothers, carrying lighted candles; the Matachine dancers; the fiesteros; the soldiers, the rest of the people. They went to a cross about two hundred feet from the arbor and connected with it by several arches, where they deposited the images on a petate. There all knelt to pray. In the meantime the Matachines, all dressed in white, with red adornments, made three turns around all the arches, dancing to the accompaniment of a drum and flute, playing out of tune purposely because that indicates mourning. When the procession started again, the Matachines danced to the music of violins, always facing the Virgin; the Pascolas and people followed. Then the procession stopped at the arbor where the images were deposited to witness the fiesta.

The mourners left the arbor with their petates and all knelt to pray while the fiesteros made turns around them waving their flags. The dancing then continued until morning. At midnight food and drinks were again served.

The following morning, the Matachines and Pascolas led the procession to return the Virgin and crucifix to the church. Again they stopped at the last cross to pray. There the maestro preached a little sermon and thanked everyone for taking part. As it happened to be Sunday morning, all went to attend church services. It was a weird, beautiful ceremony.

Even when the varying periods of mourning are over, the dead are never completely forgotten nor neglected. They return every year for All Souls and All Saints days, when a beautiful reception is given them. This will be described later.

RELIGIOUS FIESTAS

Religious fiestas are an ancient Mexican tradition. Before the Conquest they were for the pagan deities, and since then they have been for Christian saints. Yet even after over four centuries, the Catholic fiestas have some pagan elements and preserve some of the primitive color and beauty in dances, costumes, and decorations.

The fiesta-makers are the humble folk. A fiesta is their highest expression of community life. Everyone co-operates, giving unselfishly of his means and time. It is also their highest artistic expression because they bring to it the best they are able to create—dances, music, drama, costumes, fireworks, and all the ritual arts.

Because the folk believe the saints are human, they are at ease with them and their fiestas are natural, colorful, alive. They pray to the saints, but they also play, sing, and dance for them.

A fiesta is a time for paying mandas or promises for special favors. Many go on long, hard journeys to do so, but that is no reason for not having a good time. The pilgrims meet friends and acquaintances. There is more to eat and drink than usual. Men get gloriously drunk, and many women sufficiently so to forget some of their habitual reserve. It is an opportunity for making new acquaintances and becoming more intimate with old ones, for fun, courtship, and even for trade.

Among the big body of fiesta-makers are special committees of men who collect funds, look after the saints' robes, the church decorations, the ordering of fireworks, engaging of bands, and the supplying of food for musicians and dancers. They are called mayordomías and their members mayordomos. However, in a few states they have different names; as for example among the Yaquis, fiesteros, a word invented by the natives for persons who like fiestas too much. In Michoacán they are called cargueros or burden-bearers. The office is indeed a burden in work and expense, but few ever refuse it and some seek it because it means prestige.

Women either belong on these committees or help their husbands. In the northwest those who devote themselves to the care of the saints are called tenanches. Besides helping the men, there are certain things that only they can do. They prepare the food, look after the incense and dress the female saints. The mayordomos and their wives also wash the saints' clothes, which is a solemn occasion everywhere. In Chenalho and other villages of the highlands of Chiapas, they go to the river with music and incense. The clothes of the Virgin of Santa María, an Otomí village of Hidalgo, are washed with water from a holy spring, and the washing is the occasion for a fiesta. It takes place on the eighth of August and is called "El Lavatorio de la Virgen," The Washing of the Virgin.[1]

There are always fiestas somewhere in Mexico because every day is a saint's day, and the folk celebrate those of the patrons of their churches annually. It so happens that the dates of important saints' fiestas coincide with those that used to be celebrated for pagan deities before the Conquest, a fact which must have had special significance when they were still remembered by the natives.

There are various ways of announcing fiestas. In small villages they are announced by two native musicians. One plays a primitive flute and the other a drum, their music being heard for miles around during several days. Information about big fiestas is printed and posted on church doors long in advance. In the city and valley of Oaxaca, calendas—gay nocturnal parades with music, lanterns, figures of various kinds—are both an announcement and an invitation. In Tepoztlán, Morelos, a week before carnival time, the dancers go about the streets at night with a band, their faces blackened with charcoal ashes. They jump and act like clowns to remind the people of the gay time to come.

Fiestas to ordinary saints last from one to two days, while those for the very miraculous ones go on anywhere from one to two weeks. The latter are called ferias, or fairs, as they are attended by many pilgrims from far and wide and take on some of the characteristics of a commercial fair. At all fiestas there are many things for sale, such as amulets, candles, pictures of saints, silver ex-votos, food, drinks, pottery, toys, and generally some wearing apparel; but the markets connected with the ferias have more and a greater variety of things, as well as special eating booths, places for gambling, merry-go-rounds, Ferris wheels, tent shows, and often also races and bull-fights.

All fiestas begin at dawn with the ringing of church bells and the shooting off of firecrackers to announce the first Mass. Sometimes these are preceded with mañanitas, the traditional birthday songs, the texts adapted for the occasion. When there are groups of dancers, they always dance inside the church first for the saints and then continue outside in the atrium. There are various church services throughout the day, and the people either attend some one of them or just enter to pray. The rest of the time they are outside, working or enjoying themselves in the most natural manner.

When it is a feria, the pilgrims camp in the open near the church. Women cook, nurse their babies; men and women sell and buy; everyone eats and drinks; young people make love; some watch the dancers, others listen to the bands or vendors of songs; some play games, ride merry-go-rounds and Ferris wheels, or experience the wonders of tent shows.

No fiesta is complete without elaborate fireworks. Occasionally one of those amusing daylight fireworks castles is burned, but nearly always there is a fantastic castle for the last night. The people stand around in awed silence, watching each part as it lights into magic beauty and then dies out in a fantasy of light and color. Sometimes, as at Pátzcuaro, Michoacán, the castle is replaced by huge, picturesque balloons.

Fiestas were at their best when there were no competing amusements. They have degenerated rapidly since 1920, when the country entered into its present era of modernization. The rural schools have many entertainments, most of the larger towns have movie houses now, and in many villages either a storekeeper or a school has a radio with an amplifier for broadcasting programs to the people gathered on the plazas.

Paradoxically, the many splendid highways constructed during the last two decades, which are such a boon to the country, spoil fiestas more than anything else. They make it possible for city vendors to bring their cheap wares and amusements to many remote places. Also over these highways come the automobiles with their horrible loud-speakers to deafen the people with their announcements of patent medicines and other things, including the virtues of politicians. It is only in the villages difficult of approach that the fiestas are still unspoiled and often lovely. But all of them have some beautiful moments.

The Virgin of Guadalupe

In other countries the First Lady of the Land is generally the ruler's or President's wife; in Mexico she is the Virgin of Guadalupe. She is the most widely known and beloved of all Mexican santos.

There are, naturally, liberals and agnostics who do not count among the worshippers of the Virgin, but they are a minority. Some of them even protested publicly over all the ostentation displayed during her coronation in 1945.

The Virgin of Guadalupe was the first of the various miraculous apparitions on Mexican soil. Immediately after the Conquest, Fray Juan de Zumárraga, first Archbishop of Mexico, ordered the destruction of all important pagan deities and their shrines. The one having the widest cult near the capital was that of the Aztec goddess of Earth and Corn, Tonantzin (also virgin and little mother) whose shrine was on Tepeyac hill. The natives mourned her loss so deeply that the dark-skinned Virgin of Guadalupe was sent to take her place. In order that they might accept her with greater confidence, she appeared to one of their own humble sons.

Early on the Saturday morning of December 9, 1531, Juan Diego, a poor convert, was on his way to the Franciscan church at Tlaltelolco to receive Christian instruction. As he was crossing Tepeyac Hill on the way from his village, he heard heavenly music and a sweet voice calling his name. Soon he saw the Virgin, "radiant as the

TONANTZIN, GODDESS OF EARTH AND CORN

sun," her feet resting on the rocks, gleaming like precious jewels under them. She addressed him gently, calling him "my son," and said she wished him to tell the Bishop that she wanted a church on that spot—where the one for the Aztec goddess stood—so that she might be there near his people, to protect and to love them, "For," she added, "I am the Mother of all of you who dwell in this land."

Juan promised to obey her commands. He had difficulty in seeing the Bishop, who listened to him incredulously and told him to come again when he was less occupied. So Juan returned sadly to the hill, where the Virgin awaited him. He reported the results of his interview and begged her to find a worthier messenger. But she insisted that he was the one she wanted and told him he must try again.

The following day, Juan went again to Tlaltelolco. After the religious services, he succeeded in seeing the Bishop. Juan knelt at his feet, with tears in his eyes, begging to be believed. The Bishop was impressed by the fact that Juan's story was exactly the same as on the previous day, so he sent him away more gently, and told him not to return unless he could bring a token from the Virgin. After Juan left, the Bishop ordered some trustworthy members of his household to follow him. They were able to keep him in sight until he reached the hill, when he suddenly vanished and they could find no trace of him. They reported this to the Bishop, saying that Juan must have dreamed or made up the story, and suggested that he be punished for doing so. In the meantime, Juan was with the Virgin, telling her what the Bishop had said. She told him to come for the token the following day.

On Monday, the next day, Juan had to stay home on account of the illness of his uncle. The doctor who saw the uncle said there was no hope, so on Tuesday Juan was sent to Tlaltelolco for a priest to administer the last rites. Juan had been so worried over his uncle, that he forgot all about the Virgin until he reached the hill. Then, fearing he had incurred her displeasure and wanting to avoid a scolding, he took a round-about path. But the Virgin came to meet him. She spoke to him gently and told him not to worry; that his uncle was already well again. Then she said he must go to the place on the hill where he had first seen her, and pick some roses, which were to be the token for the Bishop. Juan obeyed, and was astonished to find beautiful Castilian roses among the rocks, where previously only cacti had grown. Then the Virgin told him to hide the roses in his tilma or cape and to take them to the Bishop.

The attendants at the Bishop's Palace asked Juan what he had in his tilma. He tried to keep them from seeing the roses, but finally had to show them if he wanted to be announced. When the servants saw the roses they were as surprised as Juan but when they tried to take one, the flowers seemed to be part of the tilma. They told the Bishop about it, who immediately realized that this was the token from the Virgin. Juan was admitted at once. He knelt and in reaching for the roses to hand to the Bishop, he let his tilma fall. At that moment there appeared upon it the image of the Virgin of Guadalupe. Then the Bishop fell upon his knees to pray for forgiveness for having doubted Juan the first time. Afterwards he took Juan's tilma and placed it over the altar in his chapel and asked Juan to point out the place where the Virgin wanted her church. Juan did so, spending another day away from his home. On Wednesday, when he returned, he found his uncle perfectly well.

The news of the miracle spread with lightning speed. A chapel was constructed in which the tilma with the image of the Virgin on it was hung. Converts were made by the thousands. Yet in spite of that, the personalities of the Virgin and Tonantzin were so confused in the minds of the natives that some of the leading missionaries were in favor of abolishing the shrine. But the Virgin was so miraculous that she succeeded in establishing herself.

In 1544 there was a terrible epidemic in the capital in which thousands of people died. The Virgin was brought to the city and her presence abated the pestilence. In 1629, there was a flood, and her presence caused the waters to subside. In 1754, a Papal Bull declared the Virgin of Guadalupe Patroness and Protectress of New Spain.

APPARITION OF THE VIRGIN OF GUADALUPE

During the Conquest and for a long time afterward, the Virgins took part in the battles with the natives on the side of the conquerors. When the images produced miracles, they received military degrees according to their merits, some as high as general.

The patriot Father Miguel Hidalgo y Costilla started the Revolution for Mexican Independence at his church in Dolores, Guanajuato, with the cry, "¡Viva La Virgen de Guadalupe y muera el mal gobierno!" "Long live the Virgin of Guadalupe and down with the bad government!" During the ten years of revolution her image was on the banners of the Insurgents and that of the Virgin of the Remedies, la Virgen de los Remedios, on those of the Royalists. This image, which was brought to Mexico by the conquerors, was very helpful to them in the conquest, so they called her La Conquistadora, The Conqueress.

When either side got a banner away from the other with the "enemy" Virgin on it, it was shot like a traitor. During the ten years of fighting, the people did not dare to have an image of the Virgin of Guadalupe in a niche outside for fear of being shot by the Royalists. But after the Insurgents won, their Virgin had more influence than ever. Now her image is seen everywhere—in churches, chapels, in niches on bridges and houses, even on liquor bottles; it is reproduced in paint, stone, metal, glass.

The Basilica of Guadalupe, situated at the foot of Tepeyac Hill, about three miles from the Mexico City Cathedral, is in the town of La Villa de Guadalupe Hidalgo. It is unimpressive architecturally, but of great human interest. On the hill stands an eighteenth-century chapel to mark the spot where Juan found the roses; below, about a block away from the big church, is La Capilla del Pocito, the Chapel of the Little Well. It is round and well proportioned, a lovely example of the Mudejar style of architecture, with its yellow-tiled dome shining like gold. Inside is the well of the Virgin, which opened under her feet during one of her appearances. Here come the healthy and the sick, the blind and the halt, to drink of its brackish waters from a little iron bucket. The sick pour it over their sores and take it home in bottles. It is said if a stranger drinks of this water, he will return to Mexico.

The shrine of the Virgin of Guadalupe is the holiest in Mexico, and it is the dream of every good Catholic to visit this Mecca, at least once in a lifetime. Many come at all times from far and near, but for the fiesta on December 12, the anniversary of her last appearance to Juan Diego, the crowds are immense. As there is very little space around the Basilica, the natives camp on the back streets, in the plazas, on vacant lots, and on the hillsides.

Formerly many pilgrims would crawl on their knees the distance of a mile or more from the edge of the city to the shrine, over the cobbled path along the fourteen stations of the cross, but since a railroad track has been laid there the handsomely carved landmarks are no longer used. Since then it has become a custom to go that same distance on foot along the tree-lined Calzada de Guadalupe. During the entire night of December 11 the wide sidewalk along this boulevard is filled with pedestrians, the young folks making a lark of it—singing, jesting, laughing.

Many a time I have seen the dawn at the Basilica on December 12, heard the mañanitas to the Virgin and seen the dancers perform reverently for the Virgin in the dimly lighted church. Afterwards I have followed them to the top of the hill to see them put up the three huge, freshly-painted crosses and dance around them, blow incense at them, and then offer it to the four cardinal points as in the days of the Aztec goddess. Then I have seen them dance for hours on a plaza at some distance away from the church, which has no atrium. But it was on the hill in the soft light of dawn that the dances were most beautiful.

In recent years, since the population of Mexico City and suburbs has increased by over a million, the attendance at the fiesta is so much greater that it takes a strong man to get into the church even early in the morning. But it is still best to go early, for by noon it is almost impossible to move around.

The town market is near the Basilica, where there are always outside booths, but for the big fiesta extra ones are set up and vendors spread their wares along the sidewalks of every street leading to the church and chapels. There is much pottery for sale and such curious objects as the long gourds for sucking the pulque from the maguey plants, many sweets, piles of sugar cane; gorditas de la Virgen, little fat corn cakes of the Virgin, wrapped in colored paper; rosaries of carved wood, glass, silver, red or black seeds; aluminum medallions stamped with the image of the Virgin; candles of all sizes and thickness, some of them curiously twisted and man-high; amulets of all kinds and silver ex-votos. There are also petrified deer-eyes on red woolen strings to be hung on children's necks as a protection against the evil eye, and so many other things that it is impossible to enumerate them all.

Many of these things are always sold there. Permanent features are the itinerant photographers with their fantastic back drops and accessories. A poor little girl may be photographed in a China Poblana costume which she could not possibly own; a little boy, in a charro suit on horseback; or a couple may be photographed, each one looking out of a plane window—magical moments fixed forever on paper and taken home to be looked at. Every Sunday the Villa is crowded with the city poor, who go there to visit the Virgin but also to amuse themselves.

On December 12, 1931, the annual fiesta was the four-hundredth anniversary celebration of the apparition of the Virgin. The crowds were larger than ever, and there were visiting church dignitaries from many foreign countries. But even bigger than this was the fiesta on October 12, 1945, in honor of the coronation of the Virgin as La Reina de la Sabiduría y de las Americas, The Queen of Wisdom and of the Americas. The services, attended by high church representatives from everywhere, lasted a week. Late every afternoon, some delegation—students, workers, charros and others—would meet at the pilgrims' path to walk from the edge of the city to the Basilica with lighted torches, singing alabanzas.

Before 1931, the domed ceiling of the Basilica was painted a sort of Copenhagen blue with golden stars, reminiscent of the Virgin's cloak, which had become softened by much candle and incense smoke. For the fourth centenary celebration it was renovated in white and gold, and a new fifty-thousand dollar organ was installed. Yet even after that it continued to be the church of the humble. The city elite attend on special occasions only. But the suffering poor are always there, from dawn until late in the day, with their gifts of candles, incense, flowers, centavitos. For centuries they have been praying and praying for the help that never seems to come to change their condition.

The Señor de Chalma

The next miraculous apparition was that of the Señor de Chalma, a life-sized Christ on a cross. It happened shortly after that of the Virgin of Guadalupe, with whom he has been sharing honors ever since. This time the miracle was granted to the Augustinians, who together with the members of the other orders, were envious of the divine favor granted the Franciscans through the appearance of the Virgin on the Tepeyac.

In 1533, Nicolas Perea and Sebastian Tolentino, two Augustinian friars, went to Ocuilán to proselytize the natives. The region was isolated from the capital by mountains and forests, dangerous with wild animals, and the Augustinians claimed it to their glory that they dared to do what the Franciscans and Dominicans feared to undertake.

After learning to speak Ocuilteco and making some converts, the friars found that their work was being obstructed by the worship of Otzocteotl, God of the Caves, a stone idol in the cave above the present sanctuary. Not only the Ocuiltecos, but the natives from the entire region, came to pray to him with the usual offerings of flowers, incense, and sometimes of palpitating human hearts, and they celebrated brilliant fiestas in his honor.

On one occasion when many people were gathered at the cave, Father Perea talked to them eloquently in their own language, exhorting them to give up their cruel idol for the loving Christian God. Many were moved by his appeal but all of them feared to abandon the god they knew for a strange one. The caciques asked for three days in which to consider the matter.

After the time had expired, the friars, accompanied by many of their converts, returned for their answer. They brought with them a huge wooden cross with which they hoped to be able to replace the idol, but there was no need for it. As they entered the cave, they found a miracle had taken place. The idol lay in pieces on the ground and in his place stood the crucifix of the Señor de Chalma! All vestiges of the "ugly" pagan cult had disappeared from the cave, which was now filled with flowers and holy fragrance.

The news of this miracle, like that of all the others, spread rapidly. The natives who came to see for themselves, were convinced and converted. For the time being nothing more was done than to make the entrance to the cave larger and to hang a picture of San Miguel over the altar. At first the shrine was called El Crucifixo de Chalma; then for a long time, San Miguel de las Cuevas.

From the very first the Señor de Chalma began performing miracles. He freed the region of fierce animals and dangerous reptiles; when the natives were in trouble or danger and appealed to him, he came to their rescue; he even influenced some couples living in sin to change their ways.

Among the constantly increasing number of pilgrims to the shrine, came a shoemaker from Jalapa, Vera Cruz. He was so impressed by what he saw that he decided to become a monk and remain in the service of the Señor de Chalma for the rest of his life. His devotion won for him the position of head of the order, under the name of Padre Fray Bartolomé de Jesús María. When he prayed in the cave, celestial music was heard, and when his grave was dug in front of the altar, the hard rocks opened easily at the first machete blow. Before his death at the end of the century, he had built the convent with its cloisters and cells for pilgrims.

As time went on it became evident that more space would be needed for the pilgrims who came in ever increasing numbers to pray to the Señor. The opinion of the more pious of the order was that the image should not be moved, but the more practical won out. In 1683 the big church was dedicated with solemn ceremonies and native dances. The Señor de Chalma was placed on the altar in a gilded glass case, where it still stands.

Some time in the past it became a custom for pilgrims from the same villages to go annually to fiestas at Chalma in groups, taking with them one of their images to visit the Señor and one or more of their groups of dancers to give him pleasure. In order to distribute the attendance more evenly, it occurred to one of the friars to assign the villages fixed annual dates. January 6 is for Aztec and Otomí villages from the State of Mexico; February 2, for Zapotecs from the Isthmus of Tehuantepec; the first Friday in Lent, for pilgrimages from the states of Morelos, Guerrero, Tlaxcala and Puebla; Pascua chica or the Pentecost, a movable date around the end of May or beginning of

June, for the folk from Mexico City and suburbs—the last two are
the most crowded and least comfortable time to attend, but they are
interesting fiestas because of the crowds; the smallest and nicest is
on January 6. Unassigned groups and thousands of individual pilgrims
attend all the fiestas, including the small ones for San Agustín, August 28; San Miguel, September 29; Holy Week, and Christmas.

The tiny village of Chalma, from which the Señor derives his name,
is situated in the deep Ocuila canyon, State of Mexico, surrounded by
mountains and caves. The turbulent Chalma River rushes through
the canyon, ending at the high cliffs, surrounding the sanctuary. The
climate is tropical and the vegetation, lush—orchids, coffee bushes,
bananas.

Although Chalma is only about a hundred miles distant from Mexico City and some of the roads leading there have been improved in
recent years, a part of the way still has to be made on foot or horseback. One can now go by car or bus as far as Ocuilán, via Tiangüi-
stengo; Malinalco, via Tenancingo; Ajusco, a road branching off the
Mexico City-Cuernavaca highway. The pilgrims from Mexico City
go in trucks to Ocuilán, which is the shortest road for them. I have
seen trucks so filled with them—women with babes in arms—that
they had to stand up all the five or more hours that it takes to reach
the place. But in spite of the improved methods of transportation, the
village pilgrims still go on foot, some of them walking days, a week or
even longer.

A pilgrimage usually starts out from the mayordomo's house before
dawn; there he entrusts the image to the care of the group. The entire village is awake to speed the pilgrims on their way with blessings
and gifts of food, as well as of money for alms and for the purchase
of blessed relics. Those who stay at home want to do something for
the pilgrims because they are going to make sacrifices for them too.
Many accompany them beyond the village limits and shoot off firecrackers as they take leave.

The group is organized in a certain order—women blowing incense go at the head, followed by the image on a litter or even on a
man's back in a niche, supported by a tumpline from the forehead;
musicians, and dancers who perform on the way; men, women and
children. If there are burros, they also fall in line—a very colorful
parade. When night overtakes them in the mountains, they make
bonfires to warm themselves and their food; some sleep wherever
they happen to be, while others try to reach some ranch or village.

As the pilgrims pass through villages on their way, they announce
their arrival by singing, ringing a little bell, and shooting off firecrackers or pedreros, metal containers with gunpowder, that make a
very loud noise. The inhabitants crowd around to kiss the image, to

offer food and money as the neighbors did at home. On their way back, the pilgrims stop in the same places, bringing with them blessed candles, ribbons, scapulars, rosaries, medallions, pictures of the saint in gay frames, and whatever else they may have been asked to buy for their friends, which may be typical for that special fiesta. If it be Holy Week, they bring maguey fibre cords and crowns with red spots, which symbolize the blood from the wounds of the Savior.

Chalma consists of one street with some thirty families living on it. There are a number of liquor and grocery stores but no hostelries in the place. Some houses rent space on the ground with petates to sleep on for as many as a room will hold.

When the pilgrims arrive at the church, they send someone to advise the priest, who comes to the entrance of the atrium to receive them. He blesses the group while his assistants asperge the image and group with holy water and blow incense. Then all enter the church, carrying their offerings of flowers or branches; place their image as close to the Señor de Chalma as possible; pray to him and go outside to find places to stay or camp.

For the big fiestas as many as from fifteen to twenty thousand people gather there. They quickly fill the pilgrims' cells of the convent, overflowing into the atrium and all the available space around the town and hillsides, where they cook, eat and sleep in the open. There are no sanitary facilities; the place becomes dirty and smelly, yet because of the beauty of the natural surroundings, the natives and their dances, the Chalma fiestas are among the most interesting.

Next in the order of things is to bathe in the sacred pool of the river, which refreshes and cures. Waters, which are good to drink, flow into it from a holy spring under the rock of the cave. The women usually bathe naked while the men try to keep their white calzones on, their bodies glistening in the sun like bronze. Children are also bathed. When the natives bathe, it means a thorough scrubbing of bodies and heads. Afterward, each adult washes her or his own clothes, the men even dragging their serapes into the water for a cleansing, so that everyone begins religious devotion perfectly cleansed.

The purifying bath was also a custom at Chalma before the apparition. For this reason and because of the pagan manner of worship of the natives, it has been said of this shrine as well as of that of the Virgin of Guadalupe that they go there to worship their idols rather than the Christian saints. This must have been true in the beginning when they still remembered the idols, but now all that remains for most of them is a confused idea of the images. One morning an elderly Otomí confided to me in the church that the real Señor de Chalma was buried under the altar in a subterranean crypt, and that the one on the cross was only a pilgrim. Indeed, I noticed later that everyone stops at the entrance to the crypt, enclosed with a heavy iron grille, and that some leave offerings. Many also visit the cave, some crawling up on their knees in the fulfillment of a vow. And when the fiesta of the Pentecost takes place, the conchero dancers dance in the cave and paint the crosses and dance around them, offering them incense in pagan fashion.

I have traveled nearly all the roads to Chalma, twice with pilgrims, and have found the one via Ocuilán the most interesting. I walked from there with the pilgrims down the ancient mountain trail that descends into the very atrium. It is beautiful with the mountains on one side and the gorge with the river tumbling through it on the other. As we chatted, they told me I must not repent of having come, no matter how tired I might be, because if I did, I would turn into a stone. Then the unsuspecting pilgrims kick you as they walk along, but you cannot be desencantado until you are kicked all the way to the sanctuary. If you commit sins of the flesh, it is even worse. The woman pointed out to me two large stones, in which she assured me the souls of a padrecito and his maid servant were imprisoned for having slept on the same petate, saying, "Pobrecitos, if they could but reach the Señor, he would pardon them."

On the way down there is a pool where one can bathe, and a sacred ahuehuete tree on which the pilgrims hang offerings—a wreath of flowers, a hat, a piece of child's clothing, anything that has some connection with the manda they are going to pay to the Señor.

The Chalma fiestas have the same rhythm as the others—church services, dances, various amusements, fireworks—but they are freer from commerce and amusements because of the difficulty of reaching the place.

On my first visit to Chalma, in January 1926, I went with a group of pilgrims and spent five days at the shrine with them. The two other foreigners with me were the only strangers at this fiesta. We bathed in the river—not in the sacred pool, however—and slept on mattresses on the floor in the convent; otherwise, we mixed with the people all the time and found them perfectly friendly. In the daytime there were all the usual activities, including dances and church services as well as confessions. I would often steal into the sacristy and watch the people crowd in to have something blessed, kiss the priest's hand, and leave a silver coin—I was told that many coffers were filled with money at such times.

Every night a mystery play was given by the same group from the Otomí village of Otzolotepec, Mexico; their scenery and acting were charming. Afterwards there would be fireworks, and sometimes the young people would get the musicians to play dance music for them, to which they danced in the cloisters where they slept.

I often wandered off by myself and never felt afraid. It was beautiful at night when only the outline of things could be seen in that strange little world into which so many human beings were crowded, all living in harmony. Even the drunks were gentle, sitting together, huddled under their serapes and singing or chatting in slightly raised, tipsy voices.

Before I left Chalma I had many friends among the pilgrims for I had become godmother to a legion of children. The ceremony consisted of buying a ribbon, medallion, or whatever the child wanted, going to church, kneeling, and putting it on his neck, while he crossed himself and prayed. Soon I was greeted everywhere as madrina.

Upon leaving Chalma, pilgrimages and individuals take leave of the Señor, walking out backwards as far as the gate in order not to turn their backs to him, and weepingly sing their good-byes. A well-known one is:

Señor De Chalma

Adiós, Cristo Milagroso;
Adiós, brillante lucero;
Adiós, santuario dichoso
Hasta el año venidero.

Good-bye, Miraculous Christ;
Good-bye, Shining Light;
Good-bye, Blessed Sanctuary
Until the coming year.

Another one is:

Adiós, Dotor (doctor) afable,
Salú (salud) del corazón;
Adiós, del alma encanto,
Dame tu bendición.

Good-bye, affable Doctor,
Health of the heart;
Good-bye, delight of the soul,
Give me your benediction.

Coro
Adiós, Señor de Chalma,
Divino bienhechor;
Adiós, padre amoroso;
Adiós, adiós, adiós.

Chorus
Good-bye, Señor de Chalma,
Divine Benefactor;
Good-bye, Beloved Father,
Good-bye, good-bye, good-bye.

Adiós, prenda exquisita,	Good-bye, Exquisite Jewel,
De altísima valor;	Of highest value;
Encanto de los cielos,	Delight of the Heavens,
Del hombre redentor.	Savior of men.

| Coro | Chorus |

The verses are endless, but all tender and reverent.[2]

The Virgin and the Fiesta of San Juan de Los Lagos

The feria at San Juan de Los Lagos, Jalisco, on February 2, is to the Virgin of Candlemas, or the Purification; in Spanish, La Virgen de la Candelaria. She is a small figure, made of a light vegetable paste, and is very miraculous. During an uprising of the Chichimecas of that region in 1542 against the Spaniards and their gods, the Virgin disappeared. After the natives were subdued again, the Virgin was found in a hut, badly battered and wearing an ordinary woman's dress. She immediately began performing miracles.

One of the great devotees of the little Virgin was Sra. Ana Lucia. Her husband was an actor in a circus, and one day when he was practicing one of his tricks, he sank a dagger into the throat of their little girl. They all, naturally, thought her dead, but the frantic mother appealed to the Virgin, taking the child with her. By simply being in her presence, the child revived and there was no sign left of the wound.

The father, in gratitude, took the image to Guadalajara to have it repaired. At the shop he visited he found two beautiful youths who offered to mend and retouch it. When he returned to pick it up, it was waiting for him in perfect condition, but the youths had disappeared without waiting to be paid for their work, so it is believed that they were angels.

During the years that followed, so many pilgrims came to visit the Virgin that in 1732 the first stone was laid for the present sanctuary. At the same time, the Viceroy authorized the fair, "permitting all goods to come to the plaza free of duty, in order to give commerce an opportunity to profit, and to avoid frauds." When the church was completed shortly afterwards, Carlos IV conceded an annual fair to San Juan de Los Lagos, which was to last fifteen days. Soon it became one of the most famous in the country. In addition to the folk arts and products of all the surrounding states, a unique feature of this fair was the sale of good horses, mules, and burros. This aspect of it no longer exists, although some animals are still sold there.

The Virgin and the fair are visited by people from all parts of the Republic. The town can now be reached via the Guadalajara-Pan-American Highway, but formerly one came to the Santa María railroad station and then went on foot or in old Fords over bumpy roads to San Juan. It was late one night on February 1 when I reached Santa María. Freight cars filled with pilgrims came at the same time. Soon we all started for San Juan, I in an old car, most of the pilgrims walking, with torches to relieve the darkness of the pitch-black night. When I remarked that I was sorry for their having to walk so far over such bad roads, a woman in the car said that she was sure none of them would complain, for if anyone repents of having come, he will be turned into a stone or an animal. She also said if anyone makes a promise to come to the feria a certain number of times and does not complete the visits before death, his soul will return each year until someone completes the number of journeys still owing.

The town is barren and unattractive but the feria is animated and colorful with dances and people. The inhabitants are proud of the feria and love their little Virgin, inventing nice tales about her. One of them is that she sometimes comes back to play marbles on the hills and makes them herself. The spot from which she takes the mud is now called el pocito de la virgen, "the little well of the Virgin."

Everyone who comes to the fiesta visits this little well, especially the sick who rub the mud from it on the sore and aching parts of their bodies. There are also those who make little mud cakes from it, stamped with the image of the Virgin, which they sell to all those who have faith.

In the mountain village of Copoya, near Tuxtla Gutiérrez, capital of the State of Chiapas, there are three images of the Candelaria—one large and two small. Every February they are brought down to Tuxtla, so that the Zoques who live there may honor them with fiestas. Sometimes a mayordomo who can afford it invites all three. He constructs a special altar for them in his house, decorates it with pine needles, flowers, and candles, and anyone who wishes may come to pray.

At the fiesta for them, which I attended, there was a dance of women. They called themselves inditas, although few of them wore regional dress. The altar was in the patio and they danced around it. The young girls who took part wore full, long red skirts, white embroidered blouses and elegant big charro hats, from which red silk kerchiefs fell to their shoulders. I was invited to join the dance, which I did, because one does not refuse such invitations. The steps were simple and I soon fell into the rhythm. Two elderly women carried bottles of comiteco, a regional sugar-cane brandy, and at intervals they passed them around for us to drink to the Virgins. Afterwards

a stew was served with plain tamales of white corn, baked in the oven.
Very few men were present and they included those who gave the
fiesta and the musicians—an old man who played a flute and two
young ones who played small drums.[3]

The Virgin and the Fiesta of Los Remedios

La Virgen de Los Remedios, the Virgin of the Remedies, is a foot-
high crude wooden figure holding an Infant Jesus, brought to Mexico

LA VIRGEN DE LOS REMEDIOS

by one of Cortés' men. After Cortés ordered the idols on the altar
of the great Aztec temple destroyed, this little madonna image was
the only one available to put in their place.

Later when the Spaniards were driven out from the Aztec capital
on the "Sad Night" of July 20, 1520, one of them rescued the image
to take along. On that night it disappeared but not without first hav-

ing helped the Christians to survive. Some said that the Virgin was last seen with Captain Alvarado when he made his miraculous jump over the bridge on the Tacuba Causeway-canal; others, that she was fighting, with St. James on a white horse, against the natives.

Twenty years later, when an old cacique was hunting on the hill where the sanctuary now stands, the Virgin appeared to him. She told him to look among the magueys for the lost image of Our Lady of the Remedies, but he could not find it until after her third visit. Then he took it home and built an altar for it. But the image disappeared from his home three times, the last one after having been locked in a chest with the cacique sleeping on the lid. Each time he found it on the same maguey.

The bewildered cacique then went to Tacuba to tell the priests there what had happened. They were happy to learn that the miraculous image had been found, and had no difficulty in interpreting the miracle—the Virgin wanted a more fitting abode than the hut of the cacique and indicated where it should stand by returning always to the same place.

Although the Virgin of Guadalupe was the Patroness of New Spain, the Spaniards preferred Our Lady of the Remedies. The clergy and nobility paid her homage by bringing her to the cathedral in magnificent processions, the Archbishop and Viceroy accompanying her a long distance on foot.

Our Lady of the Remedies was given the title of La Conquistadora by the Spaniards because she had been so helpful in the battles of the Conquest. During the Revolution for Mexican Independence, her image was on the banners of the Royalists against that of the Virgin of Guadalupe on those of the Insurgents. When at first it seemed as if the Spaniards were winning, they conferred the military degree of General on their Virgin in a splendid ceremony and dressed her in the uniform. But even though the Virgin of Guadalupe won and is first in the hearts of the people, they also love the "enemy" Virgin. The simple folk do not understand politics; they believe that she, too, pities and helps them.

The fiesta to the Virgin, September 1 to 8, is next in importance to that of the Virgin of Guadalupe. The sanctuary stands on a maguey-covered hill, on the edge of the village of San Bartolo, a few miles from Mexico City, in the opposite direction from that of the Basilica of Guadalupe. The church and convent are small, surrounded by a spacious atrium with fine old trees.

The fiesta goes on for a whole week but the 8th is the principal day. It begins with mañanitas at dawn, fireworks, church services. The conchero dancers set up the freshly painted crosses as in the other

fiestas, pray, blow incense, and dance around them. Later in the
morning the atrium is filled with their groups.

The hill, which is usually deserted, is filled with color and noise
because it is near enough to Mexico City for all the usual amusements
to come out. There are also eating booths, itinerant singers, many
vendors of holy relics and the folk arts.

Every now and then there is a hush in the crowd and attention is
focused on the stony path leading from the bottom of the hill to the
church. Some penitent, man or woman, is climbing up on his knees,
usually wearing a crown of thorns. The people look on with com-
miseration, and persons vie with one another in spreading a serape or
some garment on the ground in front of the suffering one to alleviate
the pain in his bruised knees. When there are many penitents coming up at the same time, a group of conchero dancers leads the way,
dancing and singing to give them courage:

Santísimo Sacramento	The Most Holy Sacrament
Se ve brillar,	Is seen shining,
Se ve brillar;	Is seen shining;
Ya vienen los pecadores.	The sinners are coming now.

Because this fiesta is not so popular as that for the Virgin of Guadalupe, December 12, and because of the landscape, it is much more
picturesque.[4]

In Cholula, Puebla, the municipality in which it is said there is a
church for every day of the year, there is also a picturesque fiesta
on September 8. An image of the Virgin of the Remedies stands in
a little chapel on top of the grass-covered Toltec pyramid to Quetzalcoatl. She is less popular than the one of Los Remedios near Mexico
City, and the fiesta is smaller but very charming.

The Virgin and the Fiesta of Zapopan

Another famous Virgin is that of Zapopan, Jalisco, whose fiesta is
celebrated on October 4 and 5. She is the Virgin of Conception, and
the fiesta is not on her day, but on the day when her visit to the Guadalajara churches ends. The image is tiny, measuring about ten inches in
height, and dark skinned. Because of her color, some believe that she
was made by the Tarascans of Pátzcuaro.

This Virgin first acquired fame in the battle between the Spaniards
and Chimalhuacanos, at Mixton. At the most terrible moment of the
fight, the Franciscan Friar Antonio Segovia, who had the confidence

of the natives, ascended the hill with the image of the Virgin in his hand. As soon as the natives saw her, they surrendered.

It is said that Father Segovia carried the image hanging from his neck for ten years, and that she always helped on his dangerous journeys. But in 1541, when many Chimalhuacanos settled in the village of Zapopan, he made them a present of the image. The church which now houses the Virgin has an elaborate plateresque seventeenth-century façade and fine towers, an attractive tile dome and a spacious atrium. Zapopan, about a half-hour's ride from Guadalajara, is very pleasant.

The little Virgin kept on helping with her miracles for which honors were conferred upon her. In 1734, she was made patrona de aguas, patroness of rains, by the civil and ecclesiastical councils, who then determined that she spend from June 13 to October 4 of every year visiting churches in Guadalajara, capital of Jalisco, and the second largest city in Mexico. The custom is observed to this day.

About a century later, September 15, 1821, a generalship was conferred on her. The ceremony took place in the Guadalajara cathedral, attended by high church dignitaries, military and civil authorities. She was dressed with the insignia of her high rank and presented with the gold cane of divine generals.

The Virgin is sent off on her annual visits to Guadalajara with a solemn Mass. While it is going on, the natives shoot off firecrackers from the towers and ring the bells. As she is taken away, they sing military and religious hymns, protesting loyalty to her in case of war. Some weep because they fear she may not return; the citified women dress in black.

The Virgin is taken to Guadalajara by a priest and attendants without any ostentation because of the law forbidding outdoor religious processions. But the faithful of Guadalajara know which church she will visit first, and there are thousands of them there to receive her. The church bells ring, there are fireworks and great rejoicing. Inside of the church the altar is loaded down with flowers, and hymns are sung.

There are many churches in Guadalajara, so that the Virgin can spend only from one to two or three days in each one, depending upon its importance, but she stays eight days in the cathedral and returns for one more before leaving the city. She receives the same warm welcome in each church and is never left alone day or night. The farewell at each church is characterized by great sadness. The people weep and sob as they beg the Virgin to return the following year and to grant them the privilege of being there to receive her.

Many, especially the sick, try to get the priest to stand the image briefly on their heads. This custom had its origin in 1721, when an epidemic took a big toll of the population of the city. One of its victims was the Bishop, who was at death's door, when the image of this Virgin was brought to his bedside. By merely touching his head with her robe he regained consciousness and health.

On the last day of the Virgin's stay in the city, all the religious congregations unite to take leave of her with double the amount of bell ringing and fireworks. The most eloquent of the priests is selected to preach the sermon in which the virtues of the Virgin are extolled and the faithful exhorted to greater devotion. Then a collection is made. The people thus emotionally prepared, give much more than they would otherwise. On the last day, too, the Virgin is visited by many religious organizations and individuals. The prayers and offerings of candles and flowers are greater and the leave-taking more passionate.

In 1942, I made a special trip to Guadalajara with a friend to see this fiesta. We tried to get some sleep at our hotel before setting out at midnight, but it was impossible. The place was alive with cars honking horns, and pedestrians talking and laughing. Through a Mexican friend I was able to find out which church the Virgin was leaving from—the church authorities try to keep it a secret in order to avoid the crowds. When we arrived there, the gates were locked but we were admitted.

The church was ablaze with light; the altar, heaped with flowers; prayers were said and hymns sung for about two hours. Then, while it was still dark, a priest and some men and women all in black took the image off the altar, amidst grief-stricken farewells, and drove off with her in a carriage drawn by two pairs of horses.

When they arrived at Zapopan, we were among the crowd that went out to meet the cortege. As they entered the town, the carriage was drawn by men instead of horses. The early morning light fell upon a sad-looking crowd of people—most of them were from the city and dressed in black—but the native dancers added a note of color and gayety as they danced in front of the carriage to give the Virgin pleasure.

After the Virgin is restored to her place on the altar amidst the joy expressed by the ringing of bells, by fireworks and hymns, the dancers take their places in the atrium and the fiesta falls into the rhythm of all the others. But this one is less colorful because there are too many city people, dressed in black.[5]

The foregoing saints and fiestas are nationally famous, but there are some of regional fame everywhere. The following are a few of the many, including the national religious holidays, as well as two civic ones which are uniquely celebrated.

January First

The New Year is a national holiday and is received by city Mexicans in much the same way as in the United States. Those who like to drink and dance go to cabarets, private parties or public dances or to restaurants. The religious attend the misa de gallo, midnight Mass of the cock, which is often followed by a supper at home.

To the natives the New Year in itself means nothing. However, there are often celebrations in villages on that day. In some the patron saint's fiesta falls on the New Year, while in most of them the newly elected officials take office on January 1, which is a motive for a fiesta with special food, drinks, music, and sometimes folk dances.

The New Year at Mitla, Oaxaca

The Zapotecs of Mitla, "The Town of Souls" and near-by villages go to the ruins on New Year's Eve as "to the middle of the world," bringing offerings of flowers, candles, and incense; they believe the souls dwell there, as the name indicates. Formerly, before it was forbidden by the Federal Department of Archaeological Monuments, they used to leave their gifts in the Palace, on a boulder behind the column of death. Some of those who go there tell weird tales of seeing dances in the courts of the ruins, performed by the souls of the ancients in all their splendor. They say if one seeing a tiny cock coming out of the buildings, should catch it and lock it up in a box at home, it will turn into gold.

There is also a fiesta here on New Year's Eve, at the Cruz de los Pedimientos, the Cross of the Petitions, which stands just outside of the town on a stone base. This is attended by outsiders as well as by the town folk, who spend the entire night there.

First they pray at the cross, kissing it and offering it flowers, candles, and incense, which they blow in the four directions in the sign of the cross. Then they make miniature reproductions of their wishes, over which they pray and watch.

The people believe so firmly in the magical power of suggestion that they make everything as realistic as possible. Houses are made of split cane, twigs for thatch or stones for tiles. Tethered horses, burros and cattle are represented by erect sticks; sheep, goats and pigs, by heaps of stones inside a circular corral formed of larger stones; a corn crib, by a little heap of stones near the house, surmounted by a cross of twigs. Cornfields are laid out with furrows and straws to represent the corn, with bags of soil as the grains; yellow

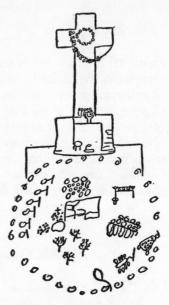

CROSS OF THE PETITIONS

berries suggest oranges, grapefruit, and lemons. Some families make completely hedged-in establishments, with farming implements, a yoke of oxen, other animals, and beehives, all cleverly portrayed with seeds, sticks, twigs, pieces of maguey or sugar cane. Families of means ask a mason to construct their "prayer" houses, and when they have sufficient money to build, hire him to do the actual work. Hundreds of such constructions are set up around the cross, forming a strange and picturesque ensemble.

The Zapotecs of the mountain villages who do not visit this nor the cross of petitions at Matatlán, make prayer offerings in the enchanted caves near their villages. Those of San Baltazar kill turkeys, of which parts are left for the cave spirits and parts cooked and eaten at home. In San Miguel the women make animals of dough to take to their sacred well in the hills above the village.[6]

January Sixth

Los Reyes Magos, the Epiphany, is a happy celebration for city children. January 6 and not Christmas is their present-receiving time. They write letters to the Magi, telling them what they want, and set their little shoes out on the balconies to receive their gifts. This day is celebrated even in homes which have adopted the Christmas tree and Santa Claus.

Native children have neither shoes nor balconies, but in some places they can afford special clay toys made for this holiday, sold cheaply in the markets. In places where the Reyes Magos are patrons, the annual fiesta is celebrated on January 6th. The kings are always represented by three young boys, wearing robes and crowns like those they have seen in pictures, who sit on thrones and receive homage. In Almoloya del Río, Mexico, a feature of the fiesta is a parade, which is led by the three boy kings on horseback.

A custom among city people on January 6 is to invite friends to eat roscas, round cakes with a hole in the middle, in which are baked a few inch-long porcelain kewpie dolls, representing the recently born Christ child. Whoever finds one of the dolls has to give a party.

January Seventeenth

This is the day of St. Anthony the Abbot. In many churches a ceremony of the blessing of animals takes place, which is often bizarre and picturesque. The people take their barnyard fowl, dogs, pigs, burros, oxen, and adorn them for the occasion, painting them gaily with vegetable dyes and putting flowers and streamers on them. They stand out in the atrium, where the priest blesses them.

February Second

On Candlemas Day there are purification services in the churches during which seeds and candles are blessed, and sometimes also animals. Wherever a Virgin of the Purification is patroness, there is a fiesta.

Carnivals

The date for carnivals is movable—sometime it falls in the last half of February or early in March.

The idea of the carnival as a last fling before Lent was introduced into Mexico by the Spaniards. It originated in Italy, but the meaning of the word in Italian, "good-bye to meat," extends to other pleasures including those of the flesh—

Miércoles de Ceniza	On Ash Wednesday
Se despiden los amantes	Lovers take leave of love
Y hasta el Sábado de Gloria	Until Saturday of Glory
Vuelven a lo que eran antes.	When they love again.

This verse, sung by the primitive Otomí carnival entertainers of Huixquilucan, expresses the Catholic command to abstain.

Carnival celebrations in Mexican cities are similar to those of other countries—hilarious and unrestrained merry-making at dances and on the streets. The outstanding ones at the present time, although they have lost much of their former brilliance, are those of Mazatlán, Vera Cruz, and Mérida.

The carnival festivities in Mexico City reached their climax about the middle of the nineteenth century and have died out since the 1910–20 Revolution. Attempts have been made at intervals to revive them, but without success.

The note of unique interest of city carnivals in Mexico is furnished by the groups of native male entertainers, called comparsas. They wear fancy costumes and masks, dance and sing on the streets or in the patios of the rich, who give them food, drinks, and money.

The village carnivals are more original and have preserved their vigor and color down to the present time. The natives like them because they afford an opportunity for good-humored play. In fact, they call them juegos de carnaval, carnival games. But they are more than mere games. Some contain serious dramatic and religious elements, together with those of burlesque and fun.

The most elaborate and brilliant of the village carnivals is that of Huejotzingo, Puebla. It dramatizes the capture and death of Agustín Lorenzo, a famous bandit, who with his men used to rob convoys between Mexico City and Vera Cruz and then hide in the near-by gorges or mountains. According to the carnival plot, he ran off with the beautiful young daughter of a rich hacendado, took her to one of his hideouts and was having a wedding celebration when the federal soldiers fell upon them.

The troops that take part in the carnival consist of some thousand men, formed into battalions, representing Mexican and foreign soldiers. Each group is under the command of a "general," responsible to the "general-in-chief." The following are the traditional battalions:

The Zapadores, or Sappers, rank the highest in this "army." Their uniforms are a blue shirt, red cotton or sateen trousers, white or colored apron-like tunics, sometimes one over the other; a tall rounded-off black hat, adorned with gilt or orange colored cords with a red, white and green cockade on the right side, and in front the Mexican shield with the eagle and the serpent; a pink mask with a heavy black beard.

The Apaches wear the most elegant and colorful of the uniforms —a vari-colored feathered kilt and headdress, adorned with small mirrors and shields; a pink, brown or magenta jersey shirt with stockings to match; strings of beads around the neck, and anklets of feathers and bells; a leather or painted wooden carcase on the back. The face is painted brown or a mask is worn, adorned with gilded or silvered circles or spirals. A black mustache is worn, and gilded or silvered rings in nose and ears. They carry long swords.

The Zacapoaxtlas from the Sierra de Puebla, who fought heroically against the French in the sixties, wear black shirts or tunics to the knees, with gilt fringe in front and back, embroidered in colored floral designs with beads and sequins; white cotton pantalets with lace at the bottom, or green and red stripes; black stockings, embroidered in colors over the instep and up the leg. Leather belt and small black cartridge box on the back; large felt or straw hat with huge bunches of red and green streamers on either side, and pink mask with a heavy black beard complete the costume. They carry guns.

The French Zuavos costume consists of blue cotton shirt, knee-length trousers; cap with vizor; a white silk kerchief falling from the head in back; knapsack with "Viva Francia" on it and a loaf of French bread on top; pink mask with an enormous black beard or mustache. Many have short-stemmed pipes in the mouth. They carry guns and swords.

The Serranos are the poor mountain people. They wear a black cotton tunic or small serape belted in at the waist; short white cotton trousers; small-brimmed battered felt or straw hat; long hair and face painted black or brown; bare legs and feet. They carry a bandolier to which a small stuffed animal is fastened at the back or side, a gourd and flat net bag in two parts between which are scraps of food. Their belts are inscribed with "De las Sierras," "from the mountains," or "Viva Zacapoaxtla!" Each one has a gun, machete, or bow and arrows. The Serranos are the clowns of the fiesta; they go about talking in Aztec and performing funny pranks.

The uniforms vary a little every time new ones are made. All of them are quite expensive, those of the Apaches costing as high as a hundred pesos or more. In addition, much is spent on gunpowder, fireworks, music. The merchants contribute toward the expense because the carnival attracts so many outsiders, but the greater part of the burden falls upon the actors, who are poor people. They must also spend time in rehearsing for months in advance.

The "Carnival Games" last for five days, but the principal one is on the Tuesday preceding Ash Wednesday. At eleven o'clock in the morning, the troops come marching in, headed by the general-in-chief on horseback, wearing a splendid uniform with a white plume on his hat. The bandits follow on horseback, led by Agustín Lorenzo. When they reach the plaza the parade disbands and each battalion with its own leader and musicians forms a group. After this the usually quiet plaza is filled with noise and color until late in the afternoon. The soldiers dance and shoot their rifles into the air or at the passing bandits, who pretend to rob the stores.

About noon, all the soldiers gather in front of the Municipal Palace, a two-story building. Lorenzo sends a letter to the girl he is going to steal, who is waiting to receive it near a second floor window. She is represented by a young man, wearing a white dress over his ordinary clothes, a white woman's hat, and heavy, black shoes. After reading the letter, "she" is apparently willing, for immediately afterwards she slides down a rope, falling upon the horse waiting below and gallops off with the bandits, pursued by all the troops. After giving them some chase, they leave them alone, fall into groups as before, and continue dancing, shooting, and robbing.

About three o'clock, in the afternoon, Lorenzo's wedding takes place in a hut constructed of branches to represent one of his hide-outs. A mock ceremony is performed by a make-believe priest. Then when everyone is dancing happily, the soldiers attack, burn the hut, free the bride, and "kill" Lorenzo.

The program ends the next day with music and fireworks on the plaza (Pls. 89, 91, 92, 93).

After I first saw this amazing carnival drama in 1928—I have seen it many times since—I returned to Huejotzingo to try to find out something about its history and the hero. Although I talked with the general-in-chief and several other participants, one an elderly man who had been a soldier for over twenty years, I was unable to secure any factual data. None of them knew when, how, why or by whom the carnival was first started, and they knew nothing more about Agustín Lorenzo than was in the play. Apparently all that matters to the actors is that the juegos be good, and in their opinion they are never better than when a few soldiers are actually killed in battle.

A similar carnival play is enacted in the nearby village of Santa Ana and at the Peñon, near Mexico City. These also end on Wednesday with music and fireworks, but they have in addition a mock funeral to bury Sadness and Bad Humor as they do in Spain.

In some places there is an octavo del carnaval, another celebration on the following Tuesday. Formerly the Huejotzingo army used to go to fight a sham battle with the soldiers of Santa Ana, but this is no longer done.

In recent years some new features have been added to the Huejotzingo carnival. At dawn all the forces fight against the French, who occupy the plaza, which is besieged and taken. The bride is said to be the beautiful daughter of the French Emperor Maximilian, instead of a rich hacendado. After she is stolen, she learns of the death of her father and changes her white bridal dress for a black one.

An interesting and amusing octavo del carnaval takes place in the Otomí village of Huixquilucan, Mexico, in the form of a battle over a long-existing feud between two of its barrios on account of the saints of their respective churches.

VIRGEN DE LA CANDELARIA

In the church of the barrio of San Juan is a humble little Virgen de la Candelaria. She wears a long simple pink dress, a white veil and crown. Her adornments are several strings of colored beads around the neck, and silver earrings like those worn by the native women. In one hand is a doll infant, and in the other a bouquet of paper flowers tied with a ribbon.

In the church of the barrio of San Martín is a small man-sized image of St. Martin on horseback. He is elegantly dressed in a chamois riding suit with a bullet belt and pistol, silver spurs, a cloth cape, and a handsomely embroidered charro sombrero. The people of the barrio adore him. Every year they give him a splendid new hat and often a new suit. But they feel that even with his fine clothes he must be lonely so they have invented a little love affair for him. It has become common gossip that every night he rides over to the church of San Juan, and while San Jacinto holds his horse outside, visits with the Virgin.

ST. MARTIN

The people of the barrio of San Juan also love their little Virgin and resent any aspersions against her reputation. They indignantly deny that their Virgin would receive a man in the night, even though he were a saint.

On Tuesday, el octavo del carnaval, the last event, late in the afternoon, is the battle between the two barrios, the friends of each side helping and the rest of the inhabitants looking on. By that time spirits are high on both sides from the good pulque made in the village, and the results have been so serious that of late years the village police are always on hand. To avoid personal clashes the combatants are requested to put up barriers of boards about thirty feet high, leaving a short space between the barriers. Both sides use as missiles various kinds of firecrackers, bad eggs, egg shells filled with paint, and in the end, sticks and stones.

During the battle someone will come to the barrier and dance a doll on a stick to ridicule the Virgin. Then those of San Juan become infuriated and retaliate by holding up a male doll on a little mule, yelling, "Here's your San Martín." Both dolls are blown to pieces with fireworks bombs. The insults become offensive and spicy. "Now San Martín will take away your Candelaria because he is cold." The others answer, "We aren't afraid of that thief, that one without shame, that bandit." The retort is, "He may be a thief but he isn't a gossip like your San Juan."

San Juan, the patron of the church and barrio bearing his name, is a handsomely stuffed santo, wearing a lambskin which scarcely reaches his waist line; his chest, arms and legs are bare, so those of San Martín yell insultingly, "San Juan, chiche pelada," "St. John, naked teats."

In this way the battle goes on for about two hours, until the authorities force both sides to retire. It is never known which side wins because both claim victory. But there are always some wounded, and sometimes corpses to prove that the fight was a good one.

At one time this feud was so bitter that the inhabitants of both barrios were mortal enemies, not only during carnivals, but at all times. But in recent years the rancors are dying out, as is the bitterness of the battle.[7]

In Zaachila, a village near Oaxaca City, the carnival also takes the form of a battle. Here it is between devils and priests, the devils winning.

This carnival is a very popular one and is attended by people from the city and neighboring villages. Food and drinks are sold from booths adorned with festoons of colored paper cut into attractive designs and perforated with geometrical figures and flowers. The usually quiet plaza, shaded by magnificent ash and wild fig trees, becomes magically alive with sound and color.

The costumes and masks are extraordinarily imaginative. A green devil may be covered with brilliant bits of china paper, so that his costume is reminiscent of those of the ancient warriors. The devils present a kaleidoscope of bright solid colors which shine and alternate with the black cassocks of the priests and their white masks, pointed black hoods and enormous rosaries.

The devils fight with long canes, at one end of which are standards of perfect geometrical forms, painted in bright colors and adorned with shells. They jump and dance about as they attack the priests, who defend themselves with whips, sticks, and lances. The fights become heated, the combatants hurling insults at each other in Zapotec. They continue until after dark, affording a beautiful spectacle of bright colors dancing in the dim torch lights and shadows of the night.

CARNIVAL DEVIL

At intervals the devils make prisoners of some of the priests, whom they take into the presence of the head devil to be tried publicly, with the spectators joyously applauding the sentences.

The Huichol carnival at Tuxpan, Jalisco, revolves around the singing of the Christian myths, the bull dance and the burlesque on Mexican treasure hunters. All three aspects are integrated in a most natural fashion, affording either reverence or fun. It lasts for nine days, taking place at the Casa Real, the temple reserved for Catholic ritual, and there are ceremonies daily in the houses of both the civil and religious officials. The special food for this fiesta is pinole, corn meal, mixed with honey and formed into "beads," which are pleasing to the palate as well as to the eye.

During the first night the shaman sings the pagan myths on the porch of the Casa Real; from then on the Christian myths are sung inside by three old kawiteros, the guardians of the banners. Each one is attended by a youth, who holds over him a flag, consisting of a ten-foot reed pole to which is attached a bandana with ribbons and a bunch of parrot feathers on the extreme end. Two pairs of bulls' horns with a piece of the frontal bone are put on the altar, on one of which lighted candles are placed. The officials' wives and tenanches, young women who are assistants to the mayordomos, keep the candles lighted and the incense burning, put the necessary number of bowls of pinole on the altar, and prepare the food.

Every night there is devotion in the Casa Real, followed by processions to the officials' houses, where all three aspects of the carnival are repeated at their altars and in their patios.

The bull is represented by a youth accompanied by a substitute and attended by a waquero, a corruption of the Spanish word vaquero, or herdsman. He must begin fasting a month before the carnival, denying himself meat, salt, and sex. If he does not observe his fast rigorously, he will be unable to play his part well. The bull, according to the Christian myth, is a descendant of the deer-snake of Nakawé, Grandmother Growth; thus he is both pagan and Christian. He, therefore, performs pagan antics outside and roars inside during the Catholic ceremonies.

The first bull dance is performed in front of the Casa Real. The dancers form a circle around the bull-boy, who goes up to each one in turn to chase him into the center, roaring behind him and making a gesture of hooking his buttocks with the horns. In the center the bull-boy and his prey make several side springs in opposite directions, the bull roaring and the other yelling from feigned pain. After this play goes on for some time, the bull-boy, roaring furiously, begins digging his horns into the dirt and rolling in it, as the dancers try to madden him still more by throwing dirt on him. Then he arises, still roaring, and leads the others in a brief jumping dance; all jump as high as they can, bringing their heels up under them. After this, the bull-boy rolls on the ground as before.

Next the dancers join hands to form a corral around the bull, who walks in the four directions, the ring moving with him. Then he tries to break out of the ring; he rushes in unexpectedly here and there, jumping high into the air and falling down on someone's shoulders. After he succeeds in getting out, the dance starts all over again, to the delight of the spectators.

Besides the bull dance, there is an army of young men, commanded

by a general, captain, and lieutenant, who mock the Mexican treasure hunters. The general, an older, serious man, directs his soldiers
with a cow horn, uses reed tubes for field glasses, and scribbles on
paper to communicate with the saints. The soldiers cleverly carve
sabres, pistols and rifles from wood, and ride sticks for steeds. As
they are unacquainted with horses, they treat them as they do their
burros, insulting and beating them as they jump, kicking and pretending to be thrown off, shouting and howling with laughter. This
burlesque alternates with the bull dance. When all gather at the
Casa Real before retiring at midnight, the soldiers march seriously
down to the river to water their "horses" before shutting them up
for the night in the jail.

The highlight of the burlesque is the treasure hunt. The Mexicans
arrest all the Huichol officials, tying ropes around their necks and
threatening them with hanging if they will not reveal the hiding place
of the treasure. The officials maintain they know nothing about it
but when they see that the soldiers are about to hit upon the treasure
with their reed field glasses, they point out the place where it is
hidden. The soldiers then release the officials, but retain the topiles
to help them find more treasures, which consist of broken pieces of
pottery, buried during the previous carnival. However, they serve
as barter for tortillas, salt, and chile.

Soon after the carnival starts, the Mexican liquor vendors appear
on the scene, bringing with them musicians who are hired by the
Huichols to play folk tunes on harp and violin, to which they dance
late into the night. All this adds to the gaiety of the festivities but does
not disrupt the ritual.

Toward the end of the week there is a pretty ceremony with the
pinole "beads." They are strung on eighteen-inch-long fibre strings,
fastened to sticks and carried to the Casa Real. There the officials
put them on the people's heads in the form of crowns, and hang them
around their necks. They also adorn the pictures of the saints and
ceremonial canes with them. Then everyone thus adorned forms a
procession to visit the officials' houses.

At one of their homes a young bull is sacrificed with much ceremony. The women put flowers and blow incense on its horns, and
there is music of violin and guitar as it is being killed. The officials'
canes are anointed with the first blood, and the kawiteros' banners
are offered blood as they are lowered over the bull in his death throes.
The bull-boy, squatting at the head of the dying animal, wets his
hand in the fresh blood and smears it on his own face. When the
slain bull is removed, he rolls in the blood-stained dirt, rubbing it on
his clothes. The soldiers also smear blood on their faces and baptize
their sabres by sticking them into the wound. Then the pictures of

the saints, that have been witnessing this ceremony, are moved into the house, and the soldiers with faces and sabres smeared in blood mount their "steeds" and engage in a good-humored sham battle, feigning great ferocity. After this, the bull dance is performed again.

Later all go in procession to the house of the mayordomo of Santo Cristo to perform a simple but charming ceremony as commanded in the Christian myths. It is to commemorate the rain caused to fall by Grandmother Growth to refresh the saints during the first carnival, who in the beginning walked with Santo Cristo in the flesh. The rain is represented by tossing the pinole "beads" into the air.

Most of the fun is furnished by the bull-boys. When they dance in the patios of the officials' houses, they take the host and his wife or wives into their circle, pretending to make prisoners of them. If there is an infant, he too is taken in, as they believe that rough play is good for him. The waquero leads the bull across the patio several times; each time they meet the host and his wife, who throws a handful of dirt into the bull's face to make him angry, and he stoops over roaring, to dig his horns into the dirt. After this he starts the jumping dance and, roaring louder than ever, follows the couple around. In the end he chases the women into the house and to frighten them still more, thrusts his horns through the grass over the door as they scurry in.

Later the host and his wife return alone to the patio for rougher play. Everyone jumps and shouts, "toro, toro, toro,ˣ "bull, bull, bull." The host has a bottle of liquor, which he pretends to throw into the air as he jumps. In the end he does throw it and the soldiers rush to catch it. The soldier who jumps the highest gets the bottle, which he gives to the bull-boy, who runs into the house with it to offer it to the saints in the pictures. Afterwards he returns and gives the bottle to the "general," who pours the contents into a large container, from which the soldiers drink from time to time.

On carnival Tuesday, the last day, everyone gathers at the Casa Real. The civil officials give thanks and drinks to the mayordomos, who in turn thank the *fiscal*, the Christian official, who sits in state as each one takes his hand as if to kiss it, in the way they have seen Catholics do with priests, and the *fiscal* returns the gesture. There is so much emotion expressed in the thanksgiving that some are moved to tears.

On Ash Wednesday only the officials remain to parade the images, after which they put ashes on one another's forehead—the ashes gathered from the burnt candle-wicks, which must be removed carefully by children with scissors, as commanded in the Christian myths. Lent is observed by fasting until noon on Wednesdays and Fridays.[8]

The village carnivals in the highlands of Chiapas, like those of the Huichols, are a fusion of ritual and burlesque and are only next in importance to the fiestas of patron saints. The one of Chenahlo is among the most elaborate, although it is similar to the others of the region.

The carnival takes place during the last five days of their aboriginal calendar, which almost coincides with the Christian dates. All the expense involved is borne by four Pasiones, who are the hosts of the entire village. It gives them great prestige and they solicit the honor a year in advance. Their relatives help, contributing wood, corn, and liquor, but the cash expenditures amount to hundreds of pesos. Often the Pasiones get so deeply in debt that it is necessary for them to work on coffee fincas for years to pay off.

Before the carnival the Pasiones celebrate a novena of nine weeks instead of nine days of prayers. Every three weeks they come from their parajes to the village church to pray, during which time they must fast from meat, salt, and the pleasures of the flesh. A week before the carnival begins, they must maintain strict continence. During the novena the families and relatives of the Pasiones are careful not to annoy them, because if they are upset over anything it will rain. If it should rain in spite of their devotions, they show anger by jumping three times in front of the saint; then from the threshold of the church, they spit outward three mouthfuls of salt water. They fear the people will not believe they have complied with their religious duties and will blame them for the bad weather.

Besides the Pasiones there are two captains who organize the races and give brandy to the authorities; a medidor de trago, one who measures the drinks; a woman who distributes the food equitably; a man who makes and sets off the fireworks. The instruments are a harp, violin, guitar, a maraca or long gourd rattle with a deer bone handle, and two clay jars, the openings covered with leather, which are played with both hands like a drum, and sound like one. The latter are used only for carnivals.

The groups that act in the carnival are colorful and gay. There are six icales or Negroes, whose faces are painted black; they wear citified trousers, shoes, straw or felt hats or caps. There are others, their bodies painted with ochre and white circles, carrying branches; some are dressed in women's regional fiesta clothes; they mock all the serious ceremonies; among them is a couple who act as husband and wife, all of them introducing a humorous and malicious note which delights everyone. Another group, called tzacales, enemies of the "Negroes," wear brilliant red costumes, consisting of short red trousers trimmed with gold, and frock coats. The suits of the Pasiones and captains are the same in style and color, but the Pasiones wear in addition long black capes, red and white turbans, felt sombreros over them, and leather sandals.

Throughout the carnival days the civil authorities sit on benches in the portal of the cabildo, where the Pasiones come to invite them with great dignity to witness all the acts and to be guests of honor at their banquets. The Pasiones take this opportunity to explain the significance of everything and to assure them that they have performed their religious duties. An assistant always accompanies them, bringing a big gourd of atole and several bottles of trago, or liquor, which are passed from one to the other. When the bottles are empty, the man who has served the drinks kneels to ask pardon because there is no more.

On the first day of the carnival the ceremony of taking the oath of the Pasiones is performed in the house of each one. He and his wife kneel on petates and kiss the cross of the red and white standards offered them by the regidores, as incense is being blown and firecrackers shot off. While this is going on, the group of mockers is mimicking everything that takes place. When the Pasión and his wife lie face downward on their petates and the regidores wave the big banners over them three times; the pair playing the part of husband and wife also lie down, the man atop the woman, pretending to make love. The authorities and all the others present maintain a serious, respectful attitude, only smiling a little now and then. When the rites are finished, drinks are served and all chatter gaily. Then all go to the house of the next Pasión, where everything is repeated. But each time there is more joking because of the additional drinks.

On the eve of the horse races, the captains go to church to pray that there be no accidents; their wives, accompanied by their relatives, pray before the image of the Nazarene.

The next morning the Pasiones pretend to be fighting a duel with long lances adorned with colored ribbons. They run to meet one another, holding their lances high and beating them one against the other several times.

The captains with their aids visit the cabildo, where each one makes a speech to the authorities, saying more or less—"Now I am finishing my term of office; next year there will be another captain in my place who will do better than I have. Everything has ended well for me and my family. I do not look upon the carnival merely as pleasure for my body but also for my spirit—this holy, colorful fiesta has gladdened my heart because I have fulfilled my obligations with God. . . ." Then the four Pasiones come to invite the authorities to the formal meals that take place in each of their four houses, one after the other.

The authorities are seated in the order of their rank around the table. The old Governor stands to bless the meal three times, making the sign of the cross. The Pasión does not eat with his guests, but is on his feet all the time to see that they are properly served. "The host offers the repast so must not partake of it." Everything served is accepted but not eaten. Each guest brings his own or some one else's child, who holds a vessel to receive the food to be taken home later, as among the Zapotecs of Oaxaca. There is a bottle with a little tin funnel for the drinks that one cannot imbibe. Cigarettes and small cigars are also served. After the meal is finished a member of the family collects six centavos from each guest, as a symbol of paying. While everyone is eating, the group of "Negroes" and fun-makers are present, mocking, joking, telling off-color stories, and making everyone laugh. The same happens in the house of each of the four Pasiones.

The horse races, which take place late in the afternoon, are a brilliant spectacle—the riders with their gay costumes, their sticks held high, and their black and white capes flying in the air. They are also very exciting because the riders compete in pulling out feathers from live turkeys, which have been tied to ropes strung across the street in front of the church, each one trying to pluck the greatest number as he rushes past. Later the "Negroes" cut off the heads of the turkeys with their machetes, and they are cooked in front of the cabildo and divided into small pieces for the mockers.

On the afternoons of the third and fourth days, there are fantastic races with a "bull" constructed of twigs, about one and a half meters long by one wide, covered with a petate, with a cow's horns and tail. A man puts the frame on his head, which rests on a woolen cloth, and guides it with his hands.

This bull does not attack the people but is pursued by them, some trying to capture him with a lasso. Some of the men dress in vaquero or herdsman's suits, like those of a country charro; carry guns and try to shoot him. All the groups in costume, musicians and everyone else in the village are there to take part in the fun, all shouting, "toro, toro, toro. . . ." After everyone is exhausted from running and yelling the race is over and drinks are served.

On the nights of the third and fourth days, when everyone is indoors and the village is dark and silent, a sex comedy in pantomime takes place in the houses of the four outgoing and incoming Pasiones and captains. The actors are three "Negroes" and three others, one of them disguised as a woman. The latter enter the first house and lie down on one petate in the middle of the room, covering up with another. A little later, three "Negroes" come along, one of them pretending to be master of the other two, who are his dogs. They knock at the door but are not admitted. Then the master orders his two dogs to climb up the walls, where they can squeeze through an opening and let themselves down from the beams on the inside to open the door. When all are inside, they begin looking for the three others, pretending not to be able to find them. They ask the people of the house where they are, but receive no reply. Finally, they begin scratching at the petates and lift them up. Those under them feign to be sound asleep. Then the "Negroes" fall upon them and mimic the sexual act with the "woman" and the two men. Afterwards one of them gets up and taking a gourdful of water, throws three mouthfuls of it over the others so that their souls may return to their bodies, for they believe they have been lost through the efforts of love-making. Then all of them get up to offer and partake of drinks with the family amidst much joking and laughter. The same pantomime is enacted in each of the other houses.

The important event on the fourth day is the banquet served by the outgoing Pasiones to the incoming ones. Each incoming Pasión and his wife sit on small chairs in front of the outgoing couple. While the food and drinks are being served, the outgoing Pasión tells the incoming one all that he has done for the fiesta, how much it cost, whom he named for the various offices, the prayers said and speeches made. At the same time his wife instructs the other woman. This goes on until two o'clock in the morning when everyone retires to rest, after putting out the fires and gathering up the dishes.

The fifth and last day is one of leave-taking, the people returning to their homes in the parajes.

During the five carnival days there is but one religious procession with the Nazarene in the church, on the third day, but the sacred banners are reverently taken out for every ceremony, including the banquets and races.

In many instances the reasons and origins for customs have long been forgotten. Even though all the acts in this carnival cannot be explained, there is no doubt that most of them have religious significance, including the sexual pantomime. Sex, children, the need for food, and fertility—all are related. There is also the belief in sympathetic magic.[9]

Lent

Lent begins on Ash Wednesday with services in the churches, during which the priests mark crosses with ashes on the foreheads of those who attend. Where there are no priests, the maestros who perform the Catholic services make the crosses, in some places using ashes from burnt candle wicks and pieces of palms, as among the Huichols and Mayas respectively.

Although Lent is a season of feasting and abstinence, many fiestas take place, especially on Fridays, the principal fast day. It seems paradoxical but there is a practical reason for it. It is still the dry season, the weather is good and the people are free from agricultural tasks.

When small fiestas fall on week days, they are generally celebrated on the following Sunday, especially where the men are busy in the fields or at other tasks. But the big important ones, those with ferias, come off on schedule when they are due. Of the latter within reach of Mexico City the following are the most outstanding during Lent.

On Ash Wednesday a big fiesta takes place to the Señor del Sacromonte, the Lord of the Holy Mount. The Sacromonte is a few minutes' walk from the plaza of Amecameca, an interesting old Aztec town, lying in a fertile valley at the feet of the volcanoes Popocatépetl and Ixtaccíhuatl. It is a popular feria, attended by thousands of Aztecs and Otomís from the surrounding villages. Both the people and the market, which extends along all the streets leading to the Mount, are very interesting.

The life-size, reclining image of the Señor lies in a glass coffin, housed in a small chapel on the Mount, constructed over the cave in which dwelt Fray Martín de Valencia, one of the first Franciscan missionaries to come to Mexico. The stone steps leading to the top, carved out of the hillside, are lined with stately trees and the fourteen stations of the cross. Many pilgrims make their way up on their knees, stopping to pray at each one of the crosses. Everyone who comes to visit the chapel also goes to visit the crypt where the Franciscan lies. Near it is a holy well into which they throw offerings of flowers, after rubbing parts of their aching bodies with them. Near the chapel stands one of those ancient ahuehuete trees, a sacred tree of petitions, on which are also hung offerings symbolical of new prayers or those already granted, such as an old hat, a piece of clothing, some strands of hair (Pl. 21). When there are services at night, the processions are especially beautiful; sometimes they are accompanied by groups of dancers.

On the very summit of the Holy Mount, whence the views of valley and volcanoes are stupendous, stands a small chapel to the Virgin of Guadalupe, with huge canvases of all her apparitions. The old caretaker told me that it was constructed there because the Virgin stopped on that very spot on her way to the Villa before appearing to Juan Diego. At first they only put up a grass hut, which burned down. But after the Virgin became famous, the clergy and people of the town asked her to return to them. She did not refuse, but permitted herself to be taken on a man's back to be carried to

Amecameca. However, the burden became so heavy that he could not bear it, which was a sign that the Lord wanted her to stay where she was. After that the chapel was built for her, and every December 12 a fiesta is celebrated in her honor.

The Señor del Sacromonte is naturally very miraculous. The old man said he often disappears in the night to say Mass in Rome. Amecameca cannot be destroyed while he is there. Every time the town was attacked during the various revolutions, some disaster fell upon the troops. He also saved it from destruction by the great forest fires of 1886 by sending a heavy rain storm to extinguish them. Benito Hernández, a scoffer, who said, "Why does not the Señor put the fires out if he is so powerful," became ill and died suddenly.

On the fourth Friday of Lent a big and interesting fiesta and feria is held in Tepalcingo, Morelos. The Señor de Tepalcingo is very miraculous and is visited by pilgrims from his own state as well as by those from the neighboring states of Mexico, Guerrero, and Puebla. As the village can be reached by train and bus, merchants from all those states and vendors of folk arts come there, and the market is huge. Specialties are the lacquer objects from Olinalá, Guerrero, and painted fibre bags from villages in the State of Mexico; the craftsmen will paint any design you select while you wait.

The eighteenth-century church has a handsome façade, sculptured all over with figures, fruit, flowers, and an Aztec sun and moon. The atrium is shaded by fine old trees, forming a good stage for the dancers. One also finds there vendors of herbs and love charms, who use a red-crested woodpecker as a sign.

There are many amusements, including cantinas and dance halls, where men may have city girls as partners.

The biggest fiesta at Taxco, Guerrero, the most famous tourist town, is for the Señor de la Santa Vera Cruz, which also takes place on the fourth Friday. As the place is popular with Mexicans as well as with foreigners, many city people come to the fiesta. In recent years, there are greater crowds, more noise, and less dance groups and the religious mystery play is no longer performed. However, the place is exceedingly picturesque, there are many handicrafts for sale, and the fireworks castles are still very beautiful.

On the last Friday in Lent, el viernes de Dolores, or the Friday of the Virgin of the Sorrows, the traditional fiesta of Santa Anita used to take place on the Viga Canal, just outside of Mexico City. It derived its name from the village, but in the old days it was called el paseo de la Viga, the promenade of the Viga, and was attended by all social classes, including the Spanish nobility.[10]

After 1920 it became the fiesta of the popular classes only, but as it was also the day of the charros, they continued turning out for the paseo in great numbers on spirited horses. They were always dressed in gala costume and many were accompanied by China Poblanas on horseback.

It was also a favorite fiesta of artists, writers, and their friends, who would come very early in the morning to breakfast on tamales and atole, the girls wearing lovely wreaths of red poppies. The banks of the canal were filled with vendors of flowers, fruit and immense radishes, balloons, and confetti. In the village there were all sorts of amusements, the adults eating, drinking, gambling, and dancing until late at night.

Recently, however, the canal dried up, and with it the spirit of the fiesta.

Holy Week

Mexico being a Catholic country, Semana Santa, or Holy Week, is celebrated by the entire nation. Educational institutions have vacations, and all commerce is closed on Thursday and Friday. For-

merly no one did any work in the villages all week long, but that is changing now.

Holy week begins on Palm Sunday with the blessing of palms in all the churches. But this ceremony is more picturesque in the villages. The natives come to church, spick and span in their fiesta clothes, each member of the family carrying something to be blessed—attractively woven palms, stuck with flowers, bouquets, or just branches. In some places they give one the impression of a walking garden.

In addition to the blessing of the palms at Cherán, Michoacán, there is a unique custom of taking picturesquely adorned crosses to church on Palm Sunday, by a young unmarried couple from each barrio.

Some time before Holy Week, the collector, an official of the cabildo, invites a boy from each of the four barrios, with the consent of his father, to bring fresh palm leaves for the church from the hot country.

Before starting on the trip each boy invites a girl, usually his sweetheart, to help him adorn the cross. He gives her about fifty liters of ordinary corn, five of black corn, and brown sugar. The girls grind the white corn for pinole, and mix it with the brown sugar. They make large balls of the pinole, which they wrap in corn husks and paint with attractive designs with vari-colored aniline dyes. The black corn is also ground, but is made into gorditas, small thick cakes.

After his return, each boy gives his girl a wooden cross about five feet in height. The pinole balls are fastened to the arms and upright piece, together with many attractive fibre bags and napkins for wrapping tortillas. The girl's parents give her one bag and one napkin; the rest are gifts from her relatives, sometimes as many as twenty of each. At the top and at the ends of the arms are green palm leaves.

On Palm Sunday the boy carries the cross and the girl a pole about two yards long, on which every kind of fruit is hung, including a bunch of bananas and sometimes also a watermelon, all provided by the boy. Or the girl may carry the watermelon with some honeycombs on her back. Often the burden is almost more than she can bear, but it is a matter of pride and competition. The girl who has the largest and best decorated pinole balls, the greatest number of bags and napkins, and carries the heaviest load of fruit wins the most praise for her barrio.

In the afternoon of Palm Sunday, the four young couples, carrying their crosses and poles, with the relatives on both sides who have given them presents—accompanied by friends and the musicians whom the four boys have hired—go to some point on the edge of the town; afterward they march to the church where they remain a few moments. Then the couples return to their respective homes with their own group, and everything on the cross and pole is divided among them.

The Passion is always dramatized. Before the Reform Laws of 1857 forbidding outdoor religious manifestations, the Holy Week processions used to go out into the streets. Now the city churches have them inside, and in the villages they go out into the atriums only.

After Palm Sunday, nothing happens until Thursday (in some churches they have the service of the Tenebrae on Wednesday night) when the Last Supper and the arrest of Christ take place. Friday is full of events—in the morning the sentence and procession of the three falls; in the afternoon, the crucifixion, the descent from the cross, and various processions. At nine o'clock on Saturday morning the Mass of Glory occurs, followed by the fun with the Judases, and all is over. Nothing unusual happens on Easter Sunday and the custom of showing off new hats does not exist.

The churches are beautifully decorated for Holy Week with green growing things and golden fruit, but the altars and saints are covered during the days of mourning; the bells are silenced, matracas or wooden rattles being used to announce services.

The blessing of the fire and water on Saturday morning in the villages is often a charming ceremony. In Huejutla, a leading town in the mountains of Hidalgo, young girls go to church at six o'clock in the morning with lovely primitive clay jars of water, adorned with flowers around the rim, they themselves also lovely in their embroidered huipils. They line up on each side of the long walk leading to the door, and after the priest has blessed them, saunter off gracefully with their jars on their heads.

Formerly the entire story of the Passion was so realistically dramatized that it is said a living Christ was nailed to the cross in some villages. But now in most places only some of the scenes are enacted and the presentations vary.

One of the most beautiful folk dramas I have seen in Mexico was the Passion at Tzintzuntzan. This poor village of some few thousand souls was at one time the magnificent capital of the Tarascan kings. It is situated on the edge of Lake Pátzcuaro, and when I first went there, could be reached only by boat or horseback. The church, convent, and chapel are old, with a spacious atrium, picturesque with ancient cedars and olive trees, planted over four centuries ago by the Franciscans—probably for the very purpose of providing a proper setting for this drama. It is perfect!

I arrived at Tzintzuntzan early Thursday morning of Holy Week in a canoe with two Tarascans who paddled me over from the island of Janitzio. A letter of introduction from the Bishop of Michoacán secured for me an invitation to stay in the priest's house. His household made me feel at home and he invited me to witness all the ceremonies. Visitors from neighboring villages filled the place, but I was the only stranger. They were intrigued by my being there alone, but were perfectly friendly. Some of them asked me qustions about the distant land I came from, while others thought I was a friend of the President of Mexico and sent him messages—utterly naive and charming.

When I landed in the village, I noticed that many houses were being vigorously swept, which seems to be a custom in some villages on that day. Later in the morning, young boys on horses without saddles, Pharisees acting as spies, rode around the town in search of Christ, stopping at every cross to blow their whistles derisively. They wore short white suits, blue sashes, flaming red hoods covering the face with holes for the eyes, and long pink cotton stockings without shoes. At the atrium, platforms were being constructed for the play. Women were selling food, and men were having their hair cut under the trees by itinerant barbers.

In the afternoon all the actors came out in costume. The mob (or Pharisees and Roman soldiers) wore short cambric or sateen trousers, capes, and original hats with paper plumes. A few among them could afford dignified cloth suits with silver buttons and real feathers on military hats. But the cheaper costumes were more exotic and colorful—violent blues, pinks, yellows and reds—startling against the background of those fine old trees.

The centurion, slender and erect on his horse, with spear in hand, was most strikingly attired in a long white voile, tight-fitting gown with a deep pleated flounce, spreading over his horse's back and falling over his heavy black shoes. The waist was trimmed with red coral beads and pearls. A red girdle, a pointed white hat with a tall feather, and a mask completed the costume.

In the evening the Last Supper was served out of doors near the convent. The twelve apostles were humble elderly men, wearing the usual white cotton suits, but they were waited on by a rich man, whose superior social standing permitted cloth trousers, a fine white shirt and a ribbon with a feather stuck in it around his forehead. The food was ample. After the supper in the church, the priest solemnly but vigorously scrubbed the right foot of each apostle and kissed it.

The first spoken scene of the play took place later under the trees in the moonlight. The Church Doctors sat with great dignity on a wooden platform, wearing white suits and flowing capes; soft low turbans encircled their dark brows. A Pharisee began, "Hear, oh hear, ye wise Doctors, what Jesus, son of Nazareth, says of the priests and Pharisees of Jerusalem. . . ." Then followed a list of startling accusations, cries of the mob for justice, and the selling of Christ by Judas.

The whole text of the drama, following the Biblical narrative in substance, was for the most part rendered with such dramatic aplomb of voice and gesture as many a professional actor might have envied.

At some distance from the tribunals, in the deep shadows of the olive trees, stood a platform with a life-sized image of Christ on it. Here the next scene—the most dramatic of all—was enacted, when Judas in black, dangling his long money bag, ascended the platform to imprint the false kiss. A wave of indignation passed through the multitude. Then the soldiers followed Judas to make a captive of Christ, throwing a rope around the image. From a nearby pulpit rose the voice of the priest, giving a passionate account of the scene as it happened centuries ago.

In the next scene, a living Christ appeared. He was pushed roughly before the judges, slapped by Malcus, and insulted by the terrible Annas, a handsome young Tarascan with splendid voice and great dramatic ability. Then Christ was pulled over to the tribunal of Pontius Pilate, followed by the jeering mob of Pharisees and soldiers. Nicodemus argued for justice, while Caiaphas, supported by the mob, argued for condemnation. It all ended with the order for imprisonment, and the last act took place in the church with the imprisonment of an image of Christ, which was put into a cell with iron bars.

On Friday morning the bright sunshine fell upon a scene in the atrium that gave no hint of tragedy. The actors were all there in their gay costumes, many women in bright red woolen skirts and elaborately embroidered blouses; men in white, some wearing serapes with red designs. But everyone was serious, and the weird plaintive music of flute and drum lent a note of sadness.

About eleven o'clock the trial began. Again a living Christ—tall, graceful, in a blue satin cape—stood before the judges. He was dragged from one tribunal to another. All the historical characters were present, each one speaking his part—Pontius Pilate, Flavius, Nicodemus, and the rest. The mob of Pharisees and soldiers called for the gallows. At last a great silence fell upon the multitude. Pontius Pilate was actually washing his hands in a basin and paraphrasing the famous utterance:

"I take Heaven as my witness that I am innocent of the death of this just one. May the wrath of Heaven fall upon his hangmen. Amen."

Immediately after the sentence was announced, the "procession of the Three Falls" took place. An image of Christ with a huge wooden cross on his shoulder was on a platform borne by men; on another the image of the Virgin Mother, dressed in black with a gold crown, was carried by women. Actors and spectators followed reverently, forming a striking mass of color. The priest's pulpit was moved, and after each fall, he told the story. At the second fall, the image of the Virgin was brought up close to that of her Son for the kiss. At this point, Barabbas, unkempt, ragged, with one foot shod and the other bare, dragging his chains, came into evidence with his clowning to lend a light note.

After the last fall the procession reached the chapel where the crucifixion was to take place, and a crown of golden thorns was placed on Christ's brow. Then he was nailed to the cross with two huge gilded nails between two images, also on crosses, representing the thieves. Deep silence prevailed during these acts, broken only by mournful drum beats.

Late in the afternoon came the descent from the cross. Joseph and Nicodemus in long white robes, caps, and colored belts, climbed upon the ladder and with some assistance from below took down the image. At this moment the women burst into loud and bitter weeping, sobbing as if their hearts would break. The Sermon of the Seven Words, which seemed endless, was then given, the flitting candlelight revealing sad and tear-stained faces. When it was over, the procession of the Santo Entierro—Christ in a magnificent coffin—set out.

First came the Cristo de las Cañitas, a small seated image in red surrounded by branches; then a large image of Christ, also in red, the one that had been imprisoned. Following these on platforms were the Virgin Mother and the three Marías dressed in black with silver crowns and wings. Next the Santo Entierro in his old Colonial coffin with projecting silver candlesticks. The centurion followed close to the coffin, his white costume replaced by a black one. It was moonlight, but the people carried candles and sorrowfully sang alabanzas.

At midnight the sad procession of the Virgin Mother took place. She alone in black on a litter carried by women and followed by others in black, with lighted candles, moved slowly, silently over the "trail of blood." In Yalalag they say she is looking for her son whom "she has not seen since morning."

Holy Week is also a time when persons pay their mandas or promises for favors received from some of the Christ images or from Heaven. On Friday morning I saw a father, mother, and child, wearing crowns of thorns, crawl on their knees the entire rough path from the entrance of the atrium to the church. But the self-inflicted torture of the penitentes was even worse. There were several of them that morning, with naked torsos, a white piece of cloth folded around the lower limbs, a hood covering the face and with ankles grilled, hopping around the atrium in the hot sun, asking for alms for the fiesta. The grills cut into their flesh and mangled it.

At night other penitentes came out just before midnight. They were dressed like those in the morning, but instead of grills they carried immense unhewn wooden crosses. They ran from one cross to another in the atrium and village. At each one a friend would hold the cross while the penitente prayed and smote himself with his disciplinas, little pieces of leather with metal at the ends to draw blood. One of the penitentes, a young man with a strong well-formed body, returned laughing from his circuit of torture. This was his seventh and last year; he had promised this to the image of the Señor del Rescate, the Lord of Rescue here in the church, for helping a member of his family to recover from a serious illness. To me the penitentes were a painful sight, but the people of the villages looked at them unmoved, as if it were some sort of an endurance test. To them it was merely another aspect of the their centuries-long scourgings.

On reaching the atrium Saturday morning, I found women sitting at the graves marked with little wooden crosses. They had brought offerings of food in baskets, covered with new daintily embroidered napkins, flowers, and candles which they lighted and put on the graves. This is usually done on All Souls Day but to these mourners the Mass of Glory seemed an appropriate time, for they sat there until it was over.

When the bells burst out joyously at nine o'clock to announce the Mass of Glory, Judas attempted to enter the church. The Pharisees and soldiers drove him away, giving him a merry chase. After the people came out of the church, the mob went after Judas again and pretended to hang him from a tree, after which they carried him away "dead."

This Judas and others around the Lake were given the powers of policemen from Wednesday until Saturday of Holy Week. Mule drivers returning from long trips feared them because they would not permit them to complete their journey home. They arrested and fined mischievous boys or men who sometimes pretended they were committing some misdemeanor in fun, knowing that the fines would go to the church. The Judas role is unique in this region; elsewhere the Judases are usually huge papier-maché figures, strung with fireworks and shot off immediately after the Mass of Glory.

After this Passion Play, I realized what excellent teachers the first Spanish missionaries were; they had all our modern ideas of teaching plus the zeal to put them into practice. The Mexican natives know much about church history but practically nothing about that of their country. And they learn it in play and pageant, singing and dancing.

Tzintzuntzan is now connected with the outside world by a paved road, branching off the Mexico City-Guadalajara highway. The people have changed in these years, but the Passion Play is enacted much as when I saw it in 1925. From all I have read about the Passion Play at Oberammergau, this one, it seems to me, must be more beautiful—it is so spontaneous, so colorful, a genuine expression of native dramatic and spiritual impulses.

I have recently learned that the penitentes at Tzintzuntzan are now looked upon as ghosts by some of the people and considered "figuratively and literally dead." When one passes a penitente, it is necessary to bow the head; otherwise the dead spirit will prevent the person from passing. If a penitente dies before he has completed the number of years of penance he has promised, he must return each year until they are fulfilled.[11]

There are no societies of penitentes in Mexico like those in the Southwest of the United States. They are simply individuals who promise to inflict that form of punishment on themselves for so many

A PENITENTE

years in return for a favor, but doing it this way during Holy Week is a custom limited to very few villages. The only ones I know of besides Tzintzuntzan are some in Guerrero. I have seen them in Noxtepec and Taxco. There they wear black skirts and hoods; their torsos and feet are bare and they carry huge bundles of organ cacti fastened together with rope, which are laid across the nape of the neck and tied to the wrists. In order to support them, they must keep their arms extended at shoulder level. Those in Taxco hold a lighted candle in each hand, which adds to the torture by burning the flesh. They come out Thursday night for the arrest, on Friday morning for the sentence and procession of the Three Falls, and again late in the afternoon for that of the Santo Entierro after the crucifixion, staying out each time anywhere from one to two hours or more. Sometimes their hands are black from lack of circulation, and wounds are visible where the thorns have cut into the flesh.

I met one of the penitentes in Taxco. He was a young man in his late twenties, who dressed in modern clothes; he sang, played the guitar and was quite up-to-date. He told me that he expected to go on being a penitente for the rest of his life, because when bandits were about to attack him in the mountains, he promised it and was saved.

The most spectacular of all the Passion Plays that I know of takes place in Ixtapalapa, a village on the Viga Canal, near Mexico City. It is situated at the foot of El Cerro de la Estrella, the Hill of the Star, where the Aztecs used to light their new fires at the beginning of each cycle of fifty-two years. The present inhabitants are their descendants, inheriting their love of ostentation.

The play is held in the atriums of the parish church and the older, smaller church, as well as on the streets. One year I stayed in the village from Holy Thursday morning until Saturday afternoon to see it all.

It was the same story yet it was presented very differently from the one at Tzintzuntzan. The Last Supper was served in a sacred grotto behind the parish church, the priest wearing purple vestments, and the disciples long cotton robes of solid colors in yellow, red, and purple; all wore yellow flowered crowns.

Later at night all the actors, excepting the Pharisees, met and went searching for Christ. Their robes, rented for the occasion in Mexico City, were very elegant. The costumes consisted of short trousers, velvet capes trimmed with gold, and hats with feathers. The kings and judges wore heavy black beards to lend dignity. All rode good horses with handsome mountings, their heads and tails adorned with artificial roses. On foot came the Nazarenes, a group of old men in long purple robes and yellow crowns. Here, too, a man was impersonating Judas, wearing a long rose-colored messaline robe, bloused at the waist, with two bands of Valenciennes lace at the bottom; a cape of the same color, sandals and black stockings. He carried his money in a maguey fibre bag. The spy, fantastically dressed, also came on foot, carrying a lantern and leading a white dog with a collar adorned with artificial flowers.

The procession disappeared for a long time in the dark village streets. Then the chirimía and drum announced that Christ had been found. The image had been placed in someone's orchard. Then followed the accusations and imprisonment in the small church.

Here, too, on Friday morning, a living Christ was brought before the judges, and the acting was excellent. Herodius made a passionate speech to Christ, shaking a finger in his face. After the sentence. there was great excitement as the heralds rode up and down the atrium on horseback, announcing it loudly.

For the crucifixion a mount is built on the street near the parish church, banked with jasper and olive branches to give it an appearance of rocks among shrubbery. Village maidens with very long hair represent the Virgins in the processions. But during the day the city crowds make it impossible to see all the acting. On Saturday morning Judas is chased as in Tzintzuntzan but the fireworks Judas figures are also shot off.

A widespread custom on Saturday after the Mass of Glory is to lift children by the ears to make them grow. In some places they pull their ears and beat them on the buttocks with branches so that they may obey their parents and the Lord. When children misbehave, their parents often threaten, "Just you wait; you'll get your Glory for this." Adults pull one another's ears in fun and say, "Here's your Glory, Judas." Some people beat their fruit trees to make them produce well.

In remote, primitive villages, where there are no resident priests, the Passion is much less historical but very interesting.

The Tzeltales of Oxchuc, Chiapas, grind corn on Holy Thursday for the chicha which they will imbibe the rest of the week. The apostles are elderly, respected men, four from each of the four barrios; they are served a noon meal at the church, consisting of snails from the river, wild honey, tortillas and chayote roots, atole—no meat nor liquor. After eating, they spend the rest of the day praying at the church.

Friday at dawn, the church is adorned with fresh pine needles and the funeral coffin with Tatic Maestro, an image of Christ, in it, is left open. All morning, on each side of it sit eight apostles looking very sad. All this time they cannot eat anything, but a little comforting drink is permitted them. At noon the coffin is closed and put back in its usual place with great solemnity. No ordinary work can be done on this day because it is believed that all nature is converted into the body of Christ—if one were to plant something, His body would be wounded every time the planting stick made a hole for the seed; if one were to cut wood, every blow of the ax or machete would bruise His flesh.

On Saturday morning the "little resurrection" is celebrated by shooting off firecrackers as a sign of rejoicing because Christ has risen and gone to Heaven. The "big resurrection" is on Sunday because Tatic Maestro is in Heaven and completely recovered. The apostles are in church again wearing floral crowns.

It is believed here that Tatic Maestro was killed by very bad men, called juros, who have all died out since that time; that he was sent by God to settle all the quarrels among men on earth, so it is strange that he should have been killed.

Sútash, a rag doll, representing the soul of the Jew who ate the soul of Tatic Maestro, is kept in the belfry from Thursday until Saturday morning when the resurrection takes place. Then it is taken to jail as punishment. On Sunday, Sútash is released from jail and burned in a big bonfire in front of the cabildo amidst mockery and laughter for his failure.

In the parajes, where there are no churches, the celebrations consist of drinking much chicha and not working. Those who do not work on these holy days will be given big fiestas in Heaven, while the others who have disobeyed this command will spend their days after death in work and sickness.[12]

An important Holy Week event among the Mayas of X-Cacal is the blessing of the palms with which crosses are made to put behind the door to keep out the devil and evil spirits. On Thursday and Friday the altars are kept covered with curtains of leaves and branches as a sort of protection, in memory of the persecution of Jesucristo. On Thursday during the Mass in the main church and oratories, seven gourd bowls of atole are placed on the altar. Friday, during the hour of the crucifixion, prayers are said, and this time seven gourd bowls of zaca instead of atole are placed on the altars, because that was the refreshing drink which alleviated the fatigues of Jesucristo in the woods. The women show they are in mourning by wearing their huipils wrong side out and leaving off their jewelry.

The most important of the events, however, is that of lighting the new fires. At midnight on Friday all the fires in the domestic hearths are extinguished. All the married men gather at the church at four o'clock on Saturday morning. The new fire is lighted with two pieces of wood in the ancient manner, the chief beginning and other men continuing the rotating of the same stick, which fits into perforations of another to ignite the wooden shavings at the point of friction. A candle is lighted from the first little flame and taken to the altar, where a Low Mass is said. But most of the men remain around the virgin fire to blow on it. As soon as it blazes, they light their own fire wood. While some of the men are lighting their wood, others are shooting off their guns in the air to "kill the Jews, who at the moment of the resurrection were trying to prevent Jesus Christ from rising to heaven." Some of these Mayas believe that the first flames of the new fire are the spirit of Jesus Christ returning to life; others, that the fire-kindling ceremony commemorates Jesus' ascent to heaven over a long and cold road, along which he had to stop occasionally to light a fire for warmth.

When the men return to their homes, they rekindle in their hearths the fires which are carefully kept lighted until the next year.[13]

Before ending the Holy Week descriptions, it is necessary to add something about those of the Yaquis because they are so exciting. One year I saw them in Tlaxcala, where a Yaqui regiment with many families was stationed. Their representation was similar to those in their villages in Sonora, excepting that their services were held in an arbor which (together with the crosses) was set up especially for the fiestas.

The principal actors were the Chapayecas, meaning "long nose" in Cahita, who played the part of the Pharisees. They wore checked blankets over their ordinary suits, caught at the waist with leather belts from which nails of deer were suspended on pieces of leather. Around their ankles were strings of tenavari, dried cocoons filled with tiny pebbles, which together with the deer nails made a peculiar rhythm. Their masks were of goatskin, painted, with big ears, and long noses, and some had beards. Over them were caps. In their right hands they carried painted wooden machetes and in the left, short pointed wooden lances.

The Chapayecas, like the Judas in Tzintzuntzan, had police power, but for a much longer time; their activities began on Ash Wednesday and lasted until Saturday of Holy Week. As they passed houses, they took anything of value they could lay hands on, and then the owners were obliged to give alms for the church in order to redeem the confiscated objects.

The masks of the Chapayecas are a symbol of their power; they can do nothing without them on. When putting on or taking off a mask, the Chapayecas must lie down on the ground and make the sign of the cross. Each has a medallion of a blessed rosary in his mouth to keep from spitting or talking while wearing the mask. When it is necessary for them to communicate with one another they do so by beating their machetes against their lances to call attention, and by making signs; but if they must speak they lie down near one another, remove their masks, cross themselves, and whisper. If they do not observe these rites, their souls will be lost after death and will wander about forever.

Some of the Chapayecas serve for life; others only for three years. Each one has a godmother, who goes with him to church, where the initiation ceremony consists of prayers, chants, and music of flute and drum. Every Friday afternoon during Lent they come out in procession.

On Palm Sunday the palms were sent to be blessed at the parish church and then distributed among the soldiers and their families. On Monday, Tuesday, and Wednesday afternoon processions took place, led by Pilate on horseback. Wednesday at midnight the men went to church for the ceremony of the tinieblas or Tenebrae. There were fifteen lighted candles. During the chants, all were blown out but the largest one, called María, which was placed behind the altar. Then in the dark the men beat each other with whips. Some of those whose parents were dead invited padrinos to represent them in beating the sons for any offenses they may have committed. The number of lashes is always uneven—threes, fives, sevens, nines or more.

On Thursday there were more processions, and the angels appeared —little girls in white, with gilded crowns and flowers on their heads. The apostles wore short white tunics and crowns, but there was no supper because it rained. However, the traditional menu of the Last Supper consists of twelve meatless dishes, which are passed from hand to hand from the kitchen to the apostles.

An olive orchard was improvised and the Chapayecas approached it three times to ask for Christ, walking to the rhythm of their machetes and lances. The last time, his guardian turned him over because they explained that he was an impostor. In their Sonora villages some old man plays the part of Christ on Thursday, but here it was an image, which was blindfolded and brought to church with a rope around its neck. The angels and singers gathered around it to pray and chant, while the Chapayecas watched outside.

The next morning during the procession of the three falls, when Christ and the Virgin met to kiss, they were showered with petals and confetti. Then they formed two groups, the men going with Christ and the women and angels with the Virgin. At three o'clock in the afternoon, a small ivory crucifix was placed on the altar to symbolize the crucifixion. The Chapayecas who were watching outside, entered, each one to give the crucifix a blow with his machete, while those outside pretended to be doing the same by beating their machetes and lances together. Then the crucifix was taken down and placed in a small white, satin-lined coffin. Meanwhile the Chapayecas were making a show of great glee over the crucifixion.

The procession of the Santo Entierro was very impressive with many dressed in black with black veils. The crosses were thrown down and covered with laurel branches and there were more processions afterwards, during which the plaintive music of flute and drum was heard. But from midnight until morning the Chapayecas danced gaily with dolls to the music of violin and guitar.

On Saturday morning the Deer and Matachine dance groups appeared in costume accompanied by their musicians, and everyone else wore his best outfit.

In front of the arbor-church a serape was spread over a petate on which the women threw flowers and confetti while the Chapayecas made indecent gestures over it. It seemed to symbolize Christ's open tomb. Then they tried three times to enter the church for the Mass of Glory, each attempt being frustrated by the angels. Finally when the singing was over and the curtains were drawn aside, the Chapayecas fled. At this moment bells rang, fire crackers exploded, the musicians began to play loudly, and the dancers to dance vigorously. Women threw flowers and confetti into the air in their overflowing joy.

In the meantime the Chapayecas had fallen on the ground and taken off their insignia. Their godmothers, recognizing them by the color of their ribbons, covered their heads with blankets and led them to church for the blessing of the maestro who pardoned and absolved them. After that the godmothers gave them new shirts and shoes to put on. Then the Chapayecas formed a circle and gave thanks to the Lord for having passed the week without accidents, and to their godmothers for their kindnesses.

When all this was over, another procession formed to take an image of Christ to the arbor constructed for the dancers. There it was placed on an altar from which he could watch the dancing, which went on for the rest of the day and night. Several of the army officers who came with the Yaqui general sat on a long bench, while the public stood around.

During the outburst of joy that followed the Mass of Glory, I noticed a man send a messenger with a letter. I asked what it was about and was told that it was to inform the Mother of God that her Son was alive again and in Heaven.[14]

May Third

May 3 is the day of the Holy Cross. Mountain, roadside and village crosses are adorned with flowers, and there are many fiestas to miraculous crosses all over the country

There is a fiesta on that day at Amatlán, a charming Aztec village, near Córdoba, Vera Cruz, where the women still wear lovely long huipils and coral chains strung with old pieces of money.

On the Cerrito, a little hill, near Ixtlahuaca, a fiesta takes place which attracts Otomí pilgrims from all the surrounding villages. I went there once with a group of them, walking almost all the day over the hills. There were groups with their saints, carrying candles and flowers in their beautifully embroidered ayates; their musicians played and dancers danced as we walked along, and the time passed quickly. That night in the church a timid Otomí boy asked me if I were a padrecito, a "little priest." As I wore a dark coat, soft hat, and glasses, I must have looked like one to him. My friends and I found a spot to sleep, out of doors, on a sloping hillside, where it was so crowded that I remember being kept from sliding down by my feet resting on someone's head farther down.

In the villages of the highlands of Chiapas, the natives decorate their crosses with pine needles and flowers. There are fiestas in many of them but not always on May 3. In Chenahlo, where they still use their aboriginal calendar, this fiesta was celebrated in 1944 on April 30. The people began to prepare for it in February, bringing wood from the hills. On the eighth of April, the mayordomos and their wives went to the river to wash the clothes of the Holy Cross of the small chapel, called the Ermita. The musicians went first, and then a boy with the clothes rolled in a new petate. He carried it on his back supported by a mecapal or tumpline from the forehead. Behind him were two women blowing incense, followed by the two mayordomos. The clothes were turned over to the new officials on the thirtieth.

At one o'clock in the afternoon, all the civil authorities with the two mayordomos of the Holy Cross came with three new crosses to take the place of the old ones, coming by the church first. They were accompanied by musicians, playing a harp, guitar and drum. The crosses were dressed in new clothes, kerchiefs and ribbons. The outgoing and incoming alféreces danced in between the benches that stood between the three crosses, dancing three times until they reached the small chairs on which were seated the Municipal President and Governor. Then they returned, backwards, dancing three times. Then they danced three times around the benches. That afternoon the entire village came to the Ermita to eat and drink.[15]

Also on the day of the Holy Cross, the patron of masons, new crosses are set up on every building job, and decorated with flowers and colored streamers. The bigger the job, the more elaborate the cross. At noon, all work is stopped; the men get around the cross, take copitas of tequila, mezcal or any other liquor, and shoot off firecrackers. Since 1941 much building has been going on in Mexico City and the noise of fireworks at noon of May 3 is deafening.

May Fifth

May 5 is the anniversary of the victorious battle over the French in 1862, after Mexico stopped paying indemnities to Spain, England

and France. The Mexican army under General Ignacio Zaragoza repulsed the French with heavy losses during three attacks at Puebla. The victory in itself was not so important as its moral significance, because it symbolized the defeat of the French Intervention. Five years later, in 1867, the French were driven out of Mexico and on June 19 of that year Maximilian was executed.

Since that memorable fifth of May, the city of Puebla has been called Puebla la heroica and on that date the Ministry of War stages a sham battle there to commemorate the event.

While that military battle goes on, a different one takes place at the Peñon, an old Aztec village, a couple of miles away from the center of Mexico City. This one is more than a mere fight; it is a folk play in which the antecedents that led to the battle are also represented. The actors are the men who live in the village, now incorporated into Mexico City. The scene is the village plaza and the nearby peñon, big rock, from which the place derives its name—an excellent substitute for the Puebla forts. Situated on the dusty, windswept plain that was once the bed of Lake Texcoco, the place furnishes a splendid theatrical environment for this sort of performance. There is plenty of room, too, for the audience to follow the actors and to take part in the fight when swept away by the reality and excitement of it.

The performance is called la Batalla de Cinco de Mayo, "The Battle of the fifth of May." It was first given in some villages in Puebla and then in San Juan Aragón, Mexico. Some of the Peñon people saw it there, liked it and have been putting it on since 1920 or thereabouts.

The long text follows historical events quite closely, and the cast consists of soldiers, officials, and music. Naturally, there are some anachronisms, especially in the costumes, which are fantastic.

General Zaragoza is the chief of the Mexican army. A respected citizen is chosen for the part. He rides a magnificent horse and wears an elegant charro suit. From the back of his hat hangs a "sun-cloth," embroidered with "Viva Mexico! Gral. I. Zaragoza." From his belt dangles a military sword. Usually the general contributes more money than anyone else. The one who filled the office when I first saw the play told me that he had had to sell some of his cows and pigs in order to raise it. Aside from the costumes, the music and gunpowder cost hundreds of pesos, and the majority of actors are poor.

Among the other generals is Porfirio Díaz, who wears an ancient uniform, lavishly embroidered, hung with many medals, and a hat with plume. He must have a mustache, which is sometimes made with ocote smoke. General Negrete's uniform is similar but with less medals. General Berriozabal, in either a military or charro suit, is recognized by his name on the cloth. General Manuel Doblado wears a diplomat's dress coat and military trousers, a trimmed cap; he has a small gala sword. General Prim dresses like the other Mexican generals but he has a Spanish flag across his chest from which dangle numerous medals on yellow and red ribbons. Marshal Dunlop wears a combination military and marine uniform—a blue coat profusely embroidered with gold. Count Saligny is characterized by a combination military and diplomatic suit, a dress coat with a small gala sword, binoculars and pipe which he never abandons even in battle. Marshal Lorencez wears an ancient gala uniform, sun cloth, falling down his back, embroidered with ¡Viva Francia! Gral. Lorencez! The natives call him General Lorenzo because it is easier for them to pronounce.

The Indian Lucas is head of the native forces from the Sierra de Puebla, called los Zacapoaxtlas. He wears a cotton uniform, consisting of a short cotón or serape, hanging from the shoulders over his shirt, which is belted in at the waist with a piece of maguey fibre cord; pants are rolled up to the knees and over them are chamois trousers, called tapabalazos, "cover against bullets," buttoned on the sides from hips to waistline. He carries a fibre bag on his back on which rests a little crate of sticks, filled with tortillas, cheese, vegetables, and roasted meats. His military arms are a short wide machete sheathed in a crude leather case, large pistols of the sixties, and short old muskets. Face, arms, and legs are blackened.

The suits of the Zacapoaxtlas are exactly like those of their general but they do not carry pistols, and their rifles are of the old Remington-50 type. Among them are "women"—men dressed in women's clothes— to represent the soldaderas, or women soldiers, who follow their men to cook for them and help them; also some little boys to give their squadron greater reality. The women look like the men, excepting that they wear skirts and more feminine hats, trimmed with flowers. Their faces are blackened; and each carries on his back a doll to represent a baby, and a small basket with food and water. They take part in the fighting, using the same type of rifle as the men.

The rest of the Mexican troops are the Chinacos, composed of the liberal soldiers in characteristic uniforms, consisting of red blouses, wide chamois trousers, open on the outside from the knee down, showing white breeches with high boots, wide sombreros. Instead of using lances like those of the real Chinacos, which would be dangerous in single combat, they have machetes and short rifles. On their hats and pennants are red badges. They are divided into cavalry and infantry. There is also a considerable group of common soldiers, wearing uniforms of all periods. And last come the armed citizens, in their every-day suits but with leggings and Texas sombreros. They carry old rifles and pop guns and look exactly like the classical revolutionaries. Their cavalry uses horses of the most diverse types and statures.

The French Zuavos are attired in appropriate uniforms—balloon red or blue trousers, white canvas leggings, small blue sack coats, blue or red fez from which hangs the white sun-cloth with "¡Viva Francia!" inscribed on it; canvas knapsack with a long loaf of French bread on top and roast chicken inside. Their officers use swords but the soldiers carry the Remington rifles. Fighting with the French army is a small group of conservative Mexican soldiers in charro suits, wearing the same white cloths as the French.

The play begins, at eleven o'clock in the morning, with a parade of all the forces led by the generals, bands, and native musicians. This is called the convite in Spanish, meaning an invitation to attend. After the order to break ranks, the soldiers go to eat in small groups, and then starts the game of stealing food, ammunition and arms from enemies.

At three o'clock, all the forces meet on the plaza, where they form a wide circle. The positions taken are symbolical of those in the battle of 1862. Before the serious business of the afternoon begins, a little comedy takes place to amuse the audience. It consists of clipping the heads of the "wild" Zacapoaxtlas, who have come down from the mountains with long hair. Those who represent them pantomime fear of the scissors and weep over the loss of their hair.

In the meantime, the stage is being set in Chinese fashion. A man brings on a table, puts a bottle of water and glass on it, and writing materials; he places chairs around it. Then all attention is focused on the diplomats who take their seats around the table to present their claims before the Juárez Government for injuries to persons and property during the so-called Three Year War. The actors speak in loud voices with expressive gestures so that what they say may be heard by the public standing outside of the circle. They repeat verbatim long sections of the real treaties, and each diplomat tries to speak in the manner of the country he is representing. General Doblado speaks to General Prim in noble Spanish verse in a high voice, and Prim answers with a long poem, the conclusion of which is marked by a volley of musketry. Dunlop in turn recites a long poem on England as defender of her own and foreign rights, the end of which is marked by another volley. General Doblado answers in verse. Then the discussions become heated. The English and Spanish representatives, after being made to see the injustice of their claims by General Doblado, solemnly declare that they will withdraw them and leave the country with their forces. France alone declares war!

The Mexican diplomat sends an envoy with France's declaration of war to Zaragoza, who reads it, tears it up angrily, and tramples on the pieces. Next he mounts his horse, harangues his soldiers to prepare for battle; hoists his flag. A volley marks the end of his discourse. Chief Lucas addresses his soldiers in Aztec, who punctuate his speech with volleys. One of their "women" also urges them passionately to defend their country.

Saligny, Prim, and Dunlop now become officers of the French army, the last two by changing their colors.

The battle is on! The Mexican army takes possession of the hill, but the Zacapoaxtlas remain on the plaza, dancing on a high wooden platform enclosed with branches, called el castillo, the castle. Their music, played on the ancient type of flute and huehuetl drum, sounds very primitive.

The French army, in a sweeping circle, rushes to assault the hill. As they begin to climb, a Chinaco shouts loudly, "Stop! Who's there?" Lorencez replies, "Long live France!" The Mexican shouts in answer, "Right about face! Long live Mexico!"

After this there is continuous action and noise of rifle and cannon, loaded with powder only. The French attack the "forts" three times and are repulsed. Excitement is high! Generals and cavalry rush back and forth, changing positions. There are shouted dialogues, either real or invented on the spur of the moment. The war bugles sound military blusters and orders, such as "Fire!" "Enemy at the front; enemy at the right." "Advance the cavalry!" The impression of a real battle is very vivid.

The fight on the hill goes on for some hours. Then the Mexican army initiates an attack that sends the French down to the village. General Díaz is at the front, dealing the French blows with the blunt side of his machete. In the meantime the Zacapoaxtlas try to surround the French, who take possession of the "castle" abandoned by them, but the Mexican soldiers come to the rescue and drive the French out.

When a soldier's powder gives out, he is considered dead and must retire from the field of battle. The possession of a cannon is very important, as the most rudely attacked is the artillery. A stolen cannon is considered a trophy of glory.

The battle continues around the plaza with great intensity. There is hand-to-hand fighting; spectators intervene in defense of the Mexicans, beating the enemy with their fists and sometimes throwing dirt in their faces. Meanwhile the heads of both armies fight on horseback in personal encounters, attacking with machetes, glorying in their skill in fencing and riding.

The fighting continues until nightfall, when Zaragoza and Lorencez meet face to face. They both fight courageously but the Mexican wins. The bands play military marches; the bugles proclaim victory! The Mexican flag waves high, while the French is lowered. General Zaragoza makes a speech to the people in a loud voice and reads the report sent by the real Zaragoza to President Juárez: "The arms of the Republic have been covered with glory. The French soldiers behaved with courage and their generals blunderingly." At the end the bands play the national anthem and the people shout "vivas" to Mexico.

By this time night has fallen. The vendors light up their stands. Everyone is tired and excited. But all is not over yet. The dead must be buried. All those on both sides that are considered dead are placed on canvas cots or wooden stretchers or in coffins, and a funeral procession is formed, which leaves the plaza led by bands playing funeral marches; trumpets are heard and the hoarse beat of the huehuetl. The procession is lost in the darkness, broken by dim torch lights.

I first witnessed this folk battle in 1930 and have seen it many times since. The last time I was there was in 1945, an interval of some years. The only change I found was in the stage. Since Mexico City has incorporated the Peñon, a soldiers' barracks and a big schoolhouse have been constructed near the plaza, destroying its vastness. Apparently the authorities are encouraging this performance because the act of the treaties took place in the school yard; some of the teachers and a few soldiers from the barracks attended. Everything seemed to be done in the same old way. But there was one innovation. The Zacapoaxtla chief made his Aztec speech through a microphone, with flourishes and gestures as if speaking directly to his soldiers.[16]

Corpus Christi

Corpus Christi falls on a movable date, sometimes at the end of May and sometimes after the middle of June. There are services in all the churches, and many fiestas in private homes for all those whose name saint is Manuel. Around the markets, plazas, and the cathedral in Mexico City, tiny mules are sold. They are made of sticks and corn husks, adorned with flowers and loaded with sweets. Some city mothers dress their little boys like the native men. They carry on their backs little crates made of sticks—filled with anything that one is likely to take to the markets—with tiny pots hanging outside. Little girls are dressed in China Poblana or other regional costumes of native women. They attend the services of the cathedral wearing them (Pl. 74).

Annual village festivals also take place. One of the most beautiful in the country is that at Papantla, Vera Cruz. The people are of the

Totonac race; they cultivate vanilla and are well-to-do, so they can afford nice clothes for themselves and expensive costumes for their dancers. Both men and women dress in white, the women wearing quexquemetl. They are clean and attractive.

The special feature of this fiesta is the Volador or Flying Pole Dance, which is done more beautifully there than anywhere else (See dances in Part III). There are in addition three other dance groups—the Quetzales with their gorgeous feathered headdresses, the Negritos and Moros, all in elegant costumes.

Formerly one had to go part of the way to Papantla on horseback but now it can be reached by car over a paved highway from Mexico City, via Pachuca, Hidalgo, in less than a day. What effect this will have on the fiesta remains to be seen.

The Corpus Christi fiestas in Tarascan villages of Michoacán are charming and unique. They take the form of mock markets in which

A MINIATURE REPRODUCTION SOLD AT A CORPUS CHRISTI FIESTA

everyone sells miniature reproductions of what he works at, for make-believe money. There are also church services, music, food and drinks.

The Corpus Christi fiesta at Cherán lasts from Monday to Saturday, the main events taking place on Wednesday, Thursday, and Friday, when the mock market is held.

An especially interesting feature of this fiesta is the part played by the panaleros or honey-gatherers. About two weeks before it begins, they take two images of their patron saint, San Anselmo, musicians, food, and liquor, and go to the Ranchería of Cosumpa, where they camp in the woods. They return a few days before the fiesta with honeycombs, which are put into nets and hung on frames made of poles forming a "V." During the fiesta they are paraded around and then sold. The panaleros also climb a greased pole, at the top of which are cigarettes, handkerchiefs and other objects. The first man to reach them receives them as his reward.

At the market each one exhibits the kind of goods he has to sell or the occupation he follows—house builders make shingles, saw planks, and make miniature houses. Restaurant keepers set up small tables and serve tiny portions of food in tiny dishes; even tortillas are reduced to a few inches in diameter. After the persons have eaten, they ask "How much?" and are told some fantastic amount, which they pay with a piece of chewing gum, candy, or any small object. Weavers offer tiny blankets and belts for sale; farmers exhibit seeds of what they grow; arrieros, mule drivers, the goods they transport. Atole is made on the plaza, a man grinding the corn instead of a woman. Bakers make inch-size breads, which are used for money.

At about two o'clock on market days, all the exhibitors form a procession to carry their goods around the plaza. To attract attention, they emit peculiar high-pitched nasal cries, such as are never used otherwise, uttering Tarascan words which mean "Come quickly everyone! Look at it! Buy it!" Then the mock trade is carried on with mock money until seven o'clock in the evening, after which there are public amusements.

The Corpus Christi fiesta at Tzintzuntzan is altogether different. The personages who make it picturesque are the arrieros with their animals, the huacaleros or crate-carriers, and the yunteros or plowboys with their plows drawn by pairs of oxen. On the day of the fiesta they meet at Ojo de Agua, just outside of the town, with their musicians, and at one o'clock march into the atrium. First in line are the horses, mules, and burros of the arrieros, loaded with bags of sand to represent merchandise. Then follow the plows drawn by the oxen, with the share of the plow hooked over the yoke and the beam dragging as when they plow the fields. The heads, horns, and yokes are adorned with corn cobs in pairs, tied with husks. Some of the oxen also have vari-colored china paper adornments and most of them have small wheat cakes hung on the horns and backs, many in animal forms. Last come the little huacaleros, children from four to eight years old, each with a tiny crate on his back, filled with a great variety of objects—herbs, flowers, young calabash plants, roots, fruit, tiny petates, fans, tin horns and rattles, pails, clay toys, and bottles of colored waters supposed to be medicines.

Each group usually has its own band. When they are inside of the atrium, the arrieros unload their animals and begin to prepare their food; the yunteros start plowing the piece of ground set aside for them. A boy and woman follow the plows and make a pretense at planting. As the women of Tzintzuntzan do not do that kind of work, it is intended as a burlesque of their neighbors who do. The little huacaleros take off their crates and dance. Those who furnish the most merriment are the arrieros burlesquing the work of women.

There are church services in the afternoon and just before the Rosario, fruit, wheat cakes and pots are thrown from the church porch for anyone to catch who can. This is great fun for both adults and children.

The octavo of this fiesta, eight days later, is celebrated by the more primitive natives from the villages of Ichupio and Ojo de Agua. It seems to be a ceremony to insure good crops for the coming year because it centers around the cornfield. They adorn their oxen with gorditas or little fat corn cakes, bougainvillea flowers, and corn; they also plow in the atrium. Their musicians play more primitive sounding repetitive tunes.

They set up a miniature cornfield with growing things. The velador or watchman wears an overcoat, a wooden mask, an old straw hat, and boots, and carries a musket; no doubt a travesty on a mayordomo, a Spanish overseer. In the field are a stuffed opossum and a fox, with which the watchman performs a little comedy. He loads his musket with blanks, pouring powder from a horn into a bamboo measure, then into the barrel, and rams the wad into it. He stalks about the cornfield with his loaded musket until, as if by accident, he discovers the animals. Then he kneels, shoots, shouts, and runs, holding up the stuffed animals for everyone to see. The little boys shout with glee.

Another masked figure in the cornfield, of large stature, carrying a cane of authority, represents the owner. A man dressed in woman's clothes, his face covered with the rebozo, plays the part of the wife. About a dozen young girls of various ages follow the wife and dance around her to music. This, too, is a travesty.

There is also a mock market as in Cherán but with very few things—vegetables, small petates, fire-fans, fish, corn, gorditas. Exorbitant prices are asked for things. The women vendors get up from time to time to form a ring and dance, into which they try to draw spectators, practically all natives, to dance with them. They say things in Tarascan and shriek with laughter, probably making fun of the people of Tzintzuntzan, who consider themselves superior.

After the church services in the afternoon, the whole program is performed anew. Things are also thrown from the church steps. This time there is a man with a big dried fish, which he swings around as if to throw it into the crowd; then he lets it drop gently from his hand right in front of him. At this there is much shouting and laughing.

Here, too, the market tax collector is burlesqued by someone going around with a slip of paper with fifty centavos written on it, collecting five centavos' worth of produce from the vendors.[17]

Every other village has some peculiar feature in the Corpus Christi fiestas, depending upon its products and interests.

Fiestas in June

A clue to fiesta dates is to find out the name of the patron saint of the place, which is generally included in the fiesta name. For example, in the village of San Juan Teotihuacán, the annual fiesta should be on the twenty-fourth, which is the day of San Juan, or St. John the Baptist. But when it falls on a week day, it is likely to be postponed for the following Sunday. However, there are many celebrations on June 24.

It is the custom everywhere to organize midnight swimming parties on the twenty-third. In Mexico City, and other cities, groups of youngsters often go to a public bathhouse; take musical instruments, throw flowers in the pool to swim among, dive, and race. After they are tired, they have food, usually consisting of tamales with coffee or atole. Sometimes they even dance. Wherever there are rivers, the parties are held out-of-doors.

Around the bathhouses where such parties are a tradition, as they used to be in the old Alberca Pane of Mexico City, one finds native women sitting outside, selling coffee, tamales, bread, flowers, little mules of sticks and corn husks, and toys.

In the villages everyone bathes in the streams, but mostly in the daytime, and no one is afraid of evil spirits because San Juan has chased them all away. Even the saints are bathed, especially where San Juan is patron, as among the Coras of San Juan Carapán, Nayarit.

Girls usually ask some male relative to cut the ends of their hair with a machete on that day to make it grow; it will grow even better if the chopping is done on the threshold.

"San Juan llora," St. John weeps, say the old folks, as it often rains on his day, "but they are good tears."

Fiestas in July

The day of the Virgen del Carmen, Virgin of Mt. Carmel, is on the sixteenth. In Villa Obregón, a suburb of Mexico City, a fiesta in her honor is always celebrated on the Sunday following that date. There are groups of dancers and it is not too crowded.

A popular saint, after whom many places are named and to whom many fiestas are offered on the twenty-fifth, is Santiago, or St. James. He is always portrayed sitting on a white horse. In the Santiago dances, showing him winning victories over the heathen, the dancer representing him has a small wooden horse's head in front and a rump behind to make it seem as if he were riding (Pl. 68).

Fiestas for Santa Ana are on the twenty-sixth. There are various villages named after her—two in the State of Puebla, which are not difficult to reach.

Fiestas in August

The big day in August is the fifteenth, that of the Virgin of the Assumption. Wherever there is a village called Santa María—there are many—there is usually a fiesta; also in other villages.
The annual fiesta in the Aztec village of Milpa Alta, near Mexico City, takes place on the fifteenth. It is small but very pleasant.
The fiesta at Santa María Tonantzintla, Puebla, is especially attractive because of the beautiful church there.

Fiestas in September

The eighth is the day of La Virgen de Los Remedios, the Virgin of the Remedies. The most important of the fiestas in her honor is given near Mexico City and has already been described.

The Mexican Independence celebrations, September 16, have some unique features. In Mexico City, Avenida Madero—the principal street leading to the Zócalo—is closed to traffic early on the night of the fifteenth. From then until midnight it is filled with gay pedestrians, who frighten you by blowing horns or throwing confetti into your face. But no one minds it because it is part of the fun.
On the Zócalo and elsewhere in the city, all important federal

buildings and the Monument to Independence are lit up with numerous rows of red, white, and green electric lights. Sections of the
Paseo de la Reforma are strung with them.

At eleven o'clock the Zócalo is jammed with thousands of people.
Here the President of the Republic stands on the balcony of the
National Palace reserved for him, where he gives the grito, the call.
This is referred to as El Grito de Dolores, the call to arms, of Father
Hidalgo, who started the flame of the Mexican Revolution for Inde-
pendence in 1810, from his church in Dolores, Guanajuato, with:
"Long live the Virgin of Guadalupe! Down with the bad govern-
ment!" The present-day grito is: "Mexicans, long live our heroes!
Long live our independence! Long live Mexico!"

Above that balcony hangs a small, very old bell, which is said
to be the one from the church at Dolores. The President pulls a
rope attached to it, which is a signal for an outburst of rejoicing.
The air is filled with the clamor of church bells. Factory whistles and
automobile horns join in the noise. And the huge fireworks pieces
set up on the Zócalo begin to weave beautiful patterns in the clear,
deep blue skies.

The following day there is a mammoth military parade reviewed
by the President, the Secretary of War, and other high officials, from
the Palace balcony. There are ceremonies at the Monument to Independence and at the graves of heroes.

In the rest of the capitals of the country, the governors do the
honors on the night of the fifteenth. Early in the evening there is
a band concert and promenade—a serenata or paseo—on the main
plaza where the state palace stands. After the grito by the governor,
beautiful fireworks pieces are burned, which sometimes take the form
of revolutionary heroes. In other cities, towns, and villages the municipal president officiates and there is also a serenata followed by
fireworks. In rural schools there are fiestas on the sixteenth, attended
by the municipal authorities. The students put on programs with
songs, dances, and recitations.

In the cities there are military parades, but in many small villages
only the people and school children march in an informal way.
They usually select a boy, who dresses like a priest, to represent
Hidalgo, and a young girl to be a queen, or the Patria, the fatherland. In a village of Oaxaca I saw Hidalgo and the queen driving
around in an old carriage, whereas in San José Vista Hermosa, Morelos, the young Patria in white rode horseback on a side saddle, while
Hidalgo walked. He was accompanied by a Chinaco, an insurgent,
dressed in a charro suit, carrying a Spanish flag to show that it was
all forgiven. Thus popular fancy creates its own little historical
fictions.

On the twenty-ninth, many fiestas are offered to San Miguel, St. Michael. The one at San Miguel Allende, a lovely small colonial city in Guanajuato, is a big and interesting one. It is attended by many groups of Conchero dancers from everywhere in the state.

San Miguel is patron of charros, so there are always jaripeos or rodeos on his day.

Fiestas in October

One of the most beloved of all the saints is San Francisco de Asís. His day is on the fourth and there are many fiestas offered him, big and small. One of the most beautiful of them takes place in the picturesque Aztec village of Cuetzalén, in the mountains of the State of Puebla, just at the point where one drops into the hot country. Here the women are attractive in their regional costumes and exotic way of doing their hair, and the dance costumes are gorgeously colorful (Pl. 159).

To reach the place one must go either by train or over a bad country automobile road to Zacapoaxtla, whence it takes almost a day on horseback or on foot. However, it may be possible to go all the way by automobile within the near future.

The Day of the Dead

The Mexicans, fatalists that they are, accept death uncomplainingly but also bravely. They fraternize, play, and joke with death even while they weep. In their blood is the spirit of adventure of their conquerors, many of whose traits are so admirably typified by Tirso de Molina in his "Burlador de Sevilla," "The Mocker of Sevilla" or the famous Don Juan. Also in them is the blood of their ancestors, who met death of their own volition for the sake of their gods.

A typical attitude of the common man and soldier is to be found in one of the most popular songs of the Social Revolution of 1910–20, entitled "Valentina." The lover comes to see Valentina; he is in danger but his last words are:

"Si me han de matar mañana,   "If I must be killed tomorrow,
Que me maten de una vez."   Let them kill me today."

El Día de los Muertos, The Day of the Dead, November 2, is a national holiday. For days before and after, death is everywhere present. He leers invitingly from bakery windows, where there are special panes de muertos or the bread of the dead in animal and human forms; from candy shops, in skulls with bright tinsel eyes. In the markets are sold special candlesticks and censers and beautiful candles of all sizes and shades; amusing toys for children—little coffins from which a skeleton jumps when a string is pulled; funeral processions with priests carrying a coffin, their bodies and hats made of shiny black and colored paper, and heads made of chick-peas;

PANES DE MUERTOS OR THE BREAD OF THE DEAD

miniature altars with ofrendas or food offerings for the dead on them; dancing skeletons on sticks with clay faces and feet; also many inexpensive papier-maché masks. Among other things, one can also buy there skeleton necktie pins with weird shining eyes, dangling ribs and fleshless thigh bones. Young girls present them to their lovers.

Other amusing features of the Day of the Dead in cities are the verses called calaveras, printed on broadsides and sold on the streets and in the market places for a few centavos apiece. They are satirical and mocking, addressed to well-known persons in public life and groups, such as the policemen, who are referred to as tecolotes or owls. There are times when no one is spared, not even the priests, of whom fun is made good-naturedly but with the tongue in the cheek. The following verses are from the religious calaveras that came out in 1925, when the priests refused to officiate because the government insisted that they register like ordinary citizens:

Pobrecitos padrecitos,	Poor little priests,
¿Qué harán para trabajar	What work can they do now,
Si su única profesión	Since their only profession
Era de predicar	Was that of preaching
Nuestra Santa religión?	Our holy religion?
Pues yo no sé, pero sí	Well I don't know; anyway,
Los compadezco de veras;	I pity them truly,
Aunque para mantenerse	Although to maintain themselves
Tienen algo y mucho más,	They have something and more . . .
Pero, ¡ya son calaveras!	But now they are calaveras!

The first meaning of calavera in Spanish is skull, but it has others, such as dare-devil, scapegrace, and dead-one, which is slang. So many of the last verses end with, ya son calaveras, "now they're dead ones."

A CALAVERA

Cemeteries are visited all day long. In the cities, the well-to-do who can afford graves in first-class sections, take flowers to them and return home. But the poorer people who visit graves in the lower class parts of the cemetery—in the Dolores of Mexico City there are as many as six, the last where the poor are buried free—take flowers, candles, perhaps a toy for a child. Priests are there with their attendants to serve those who wish to pay for responsories or to have a grave blessed. Outside of the cemeteries are vendors of candles, flowers, food, sweets, drinks. Many stay around, making a social event of the occasion. Formerly the people would picnic at the graves, bringing music with them, but there was so much drunkenness that it is no longer permitted.

For the evening there are the usual amusements but many go to see "Don Juan Tenorio," which is traditional at this time. The play is presented for about a week in first and second class theaters as well as in tent shows, announced in newspapers and on billboards with skulls and cross bones. It is not Tirso de Molina's masterpiece but a version by José Zorrilla, in which the end is spoiled by a repentant Don Juan, taken to heaven by a group of angels. The people adore this. Don Juan is a favorite character in Mexico as well as in Spain; many educated Mexicans are able to quote reams about him by heart.

The people who preserve the customs, whether in cities, towns or villages, expect visits from their dead and receive them as honored guests. They prepare ofrendas or altars of food for them, always trying to serve the dishes of which they were fondest in life. They believe that the dead partake of the food in spirit, and the living eat it afterward.

The ofrendas are usually attractively arranged. Sometimes they are put on the floor on a new petate, but more often on the table with the household saint, covered with an especially nice cloth or one of those china paper covers perforated with lovely designs. They are always adorned with flowers, in most places with zempasuchitl, a kind of marigold which is the traditional flower of the dead. In addition to the dishes of food and fruit, there is incense and a candle for each dead soul, usually adorned in some way. Some of them are of rich yellow or black beeswax.

All Saints Day, November 1, is for the angelitos or little children. They do not have special ofrendas but candles, some special dish of food, or a toy, are added to those of the adults. They are generally expected at night and parents often shoot off firecrackers outside to attract their attention to the house, so that they will be sure to find it. In some villages of Vera Cruz and Puebla the people trace a path with petals of zempasuchitl from the house to the cemetery or to the street.

All Saints Day is also the day for the adults' souls, but they may come any time on the night of the thirty-first of October. On that evening, it is customary for men and boys to go from house to house to sing alabanzas to the dead at the ofrendas. After they have finished, they are given drinks and something from that which is prepared for the souls. All the candles are lighted and the name of the one for whom each candle is intended is called. The following day the village folk visit the cemeteries as they do in the cities.

The foregoing is, more or less, what happens in Catholicized communities, but great differences exist among the more pagan groups.

The Zapotecs of Oaxaca all believe that the dead souls reside in tombs of the archaeological zone in Mitla, and that they come from there to visit them on the first and second of November. Those of Yalalag celebrate a novena, which terminates on those dates. Every night they pray in the church, where there is a catafalque around which are flowers and candles. At quite a late hour, all the men, women, and children in the church form a procession which goes around the atrium and then to the cemetery. In it are musicians, those who set off fireworks, the images of San Juan and the Virgen del Carmen. Everyone carries candles, which have been used previously, furnished by the mayordomos. On the way to and from the cemetery there are stops to give the people an opportunity to kneel and pray.

At the cemetery the images are placed near the entrance, where the prayers started on the way are finished. Then the man who has led them speaks in Zapotec with great emotion to the souls, expressing the gratitude of their relatives for the favors received, and the love and esteem they feel for them. The speaker makes it clear that they are being honored as they deserve to be, and begs them to pardon everything and to continue their help.

If the harvests have been good the ofrendas are very elaborate; otherwise, not. They must correspond in quality and quantity to the gifts received during the year. When good crops are obtained the living never receive any credit for the work they put into them; the success is always attributed to the vigilance of the dead relatives and their intercession with God and the saints. But some years the people sin so much that not even the souls can help them.

On the morning of November 1 the angelitos arrive. They leave early in the afternoon, when the adult souls come. To the ofrendas for the adults are added a few things for the children—small breads in animal forms, a few toys used by them in life. In good years the food for adults is very rich, consisting of special bread, made with eggs, in human forms; *moles*, sweets of calabash, fruit of the season both regional and imported. The table on which everything is placed is adorned with arches of reeds or sugar cane and zempasuchitl, on which are hung fruit, dried fish, and colored glasses filled with sweetened water. The more primitive families have simpler foods—chicharrón or pork crackling, much bread, cider, orange leaves. Glasses of liquor are added for the men. All have candles. Some families remember in their ofrendas persons who are not related, if they have lived with them, and some take them to where their ancestors used to live; for they believe that the souls for whom no candles are lit weep and grieve until they join those who receive them. The souls only take from the food their agreeable smells and tastes, carrying them off mounted on the wings of grasshoppers; for that reason the people in Yalalag do not eat the food of the ofrendas but set other food aside for themselves.

Those who are away from home try to return before the first of November, in order not to run the risk of meeting any of the souls on the lonely roads. The people comport themselves seriously and keep their children from being boisterous, admonishing them not to take food from the ofrendas in order not to incur the displeasure of the souls. Many make an effort not to sleep during the nights the souls are in the town, in order not to fall a prey to those who carry away the sleepy heads. Others go to the cantinas to enjoy themselves, drinking and gambling at the tables set up for the occasion.

The program in and outside of the cemetery is similar to that in most places—visits to the graves, responsories for the dead which, "like the dew, refresh and alleviate them." Some even weep at the graves, but on the whole there is a festive spirit, especially outside, where the people have a good time.

On the night of the second and the following day, the priest and musicians go through the village, saying responsories and Salve Reginas, with or without music—according to what the people are willing to spend. They are said in and outside of the houses for the purpose of making sure that no souls are lurking about, for some lose their way and others are reluctant to return; with these prayers they must leave and not perturb their relatives.[18]

The Tzeltales of Oxchuc, Chiapas, believe that the souls have a thirteen-day vacation on earth. During the first days nothing is offered them because they are busy looking for food for themselves in their old haunts. On October 25, the living begin to celebrate what they call "la fiesta de las santas ánimas," "the fiesta of the holy souls."

The graves near the huts are cleaned, and adorned with pine needles and yellow wild flowers, called tusus. About ten o'clock in the morning the ofrendas are put on them, consisting of one dish with cooked meat, another with beans, tortillas, salt, chile, sweet oranges cut in halves; a bottle of brandy for the men; incense and a candle.

After everything is arranged on the grave, the offering takes place. The one who speaks weeps bitterly, telling the soul how much it is missed and expressing the hope that it may enjoy the food as in life. The ceremony ends when the lighted candle and incense have burned out, which takes about a half hour. As the one performing it recalls certain epochs in the life of the deceased, the weeping becomes louder and the grief more profound. The grandparents and parents of the husband are remembered first—sometimes those of the wife are buried elsewhere—the children come last. The ofrendas are not all offered on the same day, so that one hears lamentations for several days after the twenty-fifth. The men also weep, but are less emotional than the women; most of them are soon drunk.

A few days after the twenty-fifth, the souls begin to leave. Not all of them go at the same time, because some are too drunk to travel. People say they hear noises around the graves at night that demonstrate the souls are celebrating by themselves.[19]

The Mayas of Yucatán believe that the souls who do not go to metnal or hell, have a week's vacation on earth, beginning on October 31. In the X-Cacal group of villages in Quintana Roo, the angelitos arrive in the morning of the first day. They are served a breakfast of "new atole" made of green corn, and boiled new corn on the cob. The offerings take place in the church and family oratories with appropriate prayers. More food is served for the afternoon meal—cooked fowl, sweet squash, new atole, chocolate, crackers, and other delicacies. Relatives invite one another and friends for both ceremonies, who partake of the food, so that there is a festive atmosphere of visiting. At night a candle is lighted on each little grave to help the angelitos find their way back.

The adults arrive on the following day and receive similar offerings, with the additional courtesy of having their graves cleaned and decorated with the hacacikin flowers. The afternoon offerings are in the houses, where the family cross, a lighted candle, and the food are placed on an improvised altar. At this time the main dish consists of stuffed pork or fowl. Visits and gifts of food are exchanged as on the previous day. Candles are not lighted on the graves of adults because they are old enough to be able to find their way back in the dark.

On both days a part of the food is hung in a gourd at the entrance to the house for the souls who have no one to remember them.

During the rest of the week only the very pious say prayers and make small offerings to the dead. But on November 7 the angelitos, and on the eighth the adults, are taken leave of with the same prayers and offerings of food with which they have been received.[20]

In the Maya village of Chan Kom the angelitos come at midnight of October 30; the next day they are entertained at breakfast and dinner, as are the adults on the following day, the offerings accompanied by suitable prayers taking place in houses. Relatives and friends are also invited. The tables on which the ofrendas are placed are decorated with flowers and silk blossoms, the latter known as the flowers of San Juan or San Diego. They are also fastened over the doors as a symbol of welcome. Here, too, the souls who have no one to care for them are remembered with a gourd of chocolate, a piece of bread, and a lighted candle set in the doorway. Only hens are cooked for the afternoon meal, as roosters would crow and frighten the souls away. Care is taken to divide the portions evenly in an even number of gourd vessels. One of the gourds is filled with water and flowers for the hand-washing of the dead, who, like the living, dip their hands into one before and after eating. Black beeswax candles are customary for the adults.

During the week between the ceremonies of the first two days and the last, the graves are emptied of the bones that have been in them for three years. Because of the shallow soil of Yucatán, it is necessary thus to make room for new burials, but this practice is followed elsewhere, especially in city cemeteries unless a longer time is specified and paid for.

The ritual connected with the removal of the bones is similar to that of a wake. A few men go to the cemetery. Upon opening the grave, a little holy water is sprinkled into it and the bones are blessed. After they are taken out of the grave, they are put on a new piece of cloth, cleansed, and put into a box on another cloth, where they receive another aspersion of holy water. The box is then closed and taken to the shelter in the cemetery where an "Our Father" is said over it. Then it is taken home, where it is set under the table which contains the ofrenda. The Maestro Cantor says the same prayers as at a wake. Afterwards a table of food is offered to him, and another to everyone else.

At night, chocolate is set on the table, more prayers are said and the name of the person whose bones are in the box is called. After the chocolate has been served, the box is once more sprinkled with holy water, returned to the cemetery and left there in the shelter. During this ceremony, the people do not refrain from expressing grief, because the soul is now safely out of this world and cannot be affected.[21]

The most exotic and beautiful of the ceremonies for the dead takes place in the Tarascan island village of Janitzio on Lake Pátzcuaro. Here, as elsewhere, ofrendas are set up and decorated. Early in the evening of the first of November, contrary to custom, women and children go to sleep; the head of the house stays up to receive the groups of singers. Everything is perfectly quiet in the village until just before midnight, when the women get up to dress themselves and their children in their fiesta clothes. Soon one sees shadows with

soft lights climbing the hill to the cemetery, which is in the churchyard above the houses.

Each woman takes with her a basket of food, covered with an attractively embroidered napkin; an arch adorned with zempasuchitl
and strung with bread in animal forms; and candles for all the dead
of the family. They put everything on the grave and light their
candles, after which they and their children sit around it for the rest
of the night, giving warmth and companionship to their dead. They
look lovely sitting there in the golden candle-light. Before dawn so
many candles are lit that it is possible to take pictures (Pl. 85).

Inside the church is a catafalque, with flowers and candles, for the
dead who have no relatives and for those who are no longer in their
graves. The women who remember them form a group in or outside
of the church door, with their baskets or lacquer bowls of food and
candles. Some of these natives believe that after three years nothing
is left of the personality of the soul; that it becomes part of the great
whole.

The men and grown up boys are apart from the women, standing
or sitting near the big wall, wrapped in serapes because the night is
cold. From time to time they sing alabanzas and pass the bottles.
When the first rays of dawn appear, the women open their baskets
and make offerings of their food to the heavens, to the souls, and to
persons. In none of the other lake villages do the people go to the
cemeteries in this way, but all observe the fiesta in the traditional
manner.

A food delicacy for the ofrendas is wild duck. Just before the Day
of the Dead there is a duck hunt on the lake, in which many villages
take part. There are numerous canoes. They close in on the ducks
gradually in ever-narrowing circles. Then as the frightened birds try
to fly away, the men harpoon them with spears thrown with great
skill. There is much yelling and excitement.

December

December is a very festive month. In Pátzcuaro, the fiesta on the
eighth to la Virgen de la Salud, our Mother of Health, is very picturesque. The plazas and streets are filled with natives from far and
near. Some come with their handicrafts and spread them along the
sidewalks. Those who come in canoes from around the lake are especially attractive in their regional dress. On the eve of the eighth,
the monigotes come out—boys in funny white suits and masks, on
stilts—and furnish much fun for the youngsters. There is great animation on the streets, especially at the little tables where women serve

hot cinnamon water with or without charanda; there is also great activity around the cantinas.

On the eighth, there are church services and occasionally some dances. At night several huge, painted balloons are sent up into the

A MONIGOTE

heavens; they look like ships in the dark with just one light. Afterwards big fireworks pieces are burned.

On the twelfth there are many fiestas to the Virgin of Guadalupe. In the city of Guadalajara there is a verbena to the Virgin at the Sanctuary of Guadalupe, which lasts a week. In the daytime the people come to worship, and in the evenings to eat and have a good time.

A charming fiesta takes place at Guadalupita, Mexico, a small village of weavers. The people are cleanly dressed in their best, and there are several groups of dancers, among them that of the arrieros or drivers of pack trains.

And there are many other fiestas because everywhere there is a

Guadalupe church or chapel. These fiestas have been described previously.

In Oaxaca City the fiesta to la Virgen de la Soledad, the Virgin of the Lonely, on the eighteenth, is one of the loveliest of all those celebrated in cities. She is the Patroness of the State, and the natives come to visit her from all its mountains and valleys, with gifts and sorrow-laden hearts. She is also the Patroness of the sailors, who have presented her with marvelous pearls for her crown.

For several nights previous to and on the eighteenth, there are

calendas. These are religious processions from the various barrios, men, women, and children taking part. They carry Japanese lanterns on poles, candles, and some very beautiful figures of birds, a boat or some other objects wrought of flowers, leaves, or colored paper.

On the streets around the church are many eating booths, the specialty being bonuelos—big crisp pancakes, fried in lard and eaten with syrup. After one eats them, it is the custom to break the plate on which they have been served.

There are usually no dances but in Teotitlan del Valle, a serape-weaving village in the valley, the plume dance is performed in honor of the Virgin.

On the night of the eighteenth, the fiesta ends with a fantastically beautiful fireworks castle.

On the night of the twenty-third, also in Oaxaca City, the unique and charming fiesta of the Radishes takes place. Around the two plazas, which are close together, people sell big radishes cut out into many imaginative forms—men riding animals, some phallic figures, all different so that the variety is endless. There are also lovely birds made of seeds, and dried fish. People promenade about, buy things, eat bonuelos, and break their plates as on the eighteenth. As it is near Christmas time, and posadas are taking place every night, everyone is in a gay holiday mood.

Posadas—Christmas Celebrations

Christmas is a happy time for citified people everywhere. The celebrations begin on the sixteenth and end on Christmas Eve. They are called posadas, or lodgings, because they commemorate the journey of Mary and Joseph to Bethlehem and their nightly search for a place to stay.

About a week before the sixteenth, the markets are alive with all the little Biblical clay figures and others for the mangers, toys, and plenty of good things to eat—candies, nuts, candied fruit. However, the piñatas are the most coveted objects for the posadas. They are clay jars of various sizes, covered with fantastic papier-maché figures —a bird, an animal, a plane, a symbolical cradle—filled with sweets and toys; at least one is broken every night.

Posadas are never a one-family affair. Relatives and friends co-operate and they are generally given in a different house every night, adults and children taking part. As soon as it is dark, a procession is formed, out of doors, led by two children carrying a small litter, decorated with pine twigs, on which are clay figurines of Mary riding a burro, with Joseph and the angel following. All carry lighted candles and sing litanies. After they have finished singing them, they stop at the closed door of the house to ask in song for lodging. The man of the house also answers in song, telling them to go away; that everyone is asleep; if they will not leave at once he will beat them. But when he is convinced of the importance of the travelers, the doors are opened wide and they are admitted amidst great rejoicing.

Upon entering the house, all kneel in front of the manger to pray and sing. After that is over, everyone, but especially the children, ask in humorous verses for sweets, mentioning the name of the hostess and telling her not to be stingy. Refreshments are served. Sometimes they are followed by social dancing. Then comes the anxiously awaited moment for the breaking of the piñata. A child or adult is

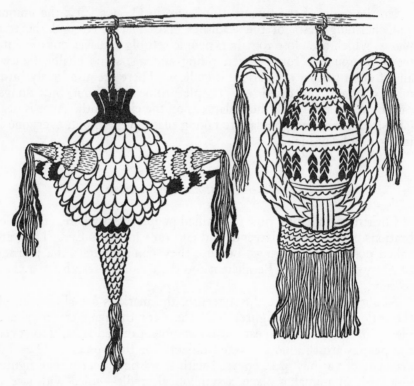

PIÑATAS

blindfolded, given a stick, turned around, and sent off in the wrong direction beating the air wildly, as two persons hold the piñata on a rope, carefully out of reach. After this fun goes on for a while, someone is permitted to break it, and there is a wild scramble for the contents. Often posadas are given without any of the ritual but never without piñatas.

The poor also enjoy posadas. Those who live in vecindades, the city tenements, co-operate and have one every night, with the processions, refreshments, dancing, and piñatas. Knowing from experience how hospitable the poor can be, I have on several occasions gone with a friend to their neighborhoods, taking a bag of sweets or a piñata, lingered at a door where a posada was taking place in the patio, and been invited in. The simple spirit of fun prevailing at those which I attended was perfectly charming.

The posadas during the eight nights before Christmas Eve vary only in refreshments and piñatas, but on the ninth night the journey is ended and the birth takes place, which is celebrated in song:

Blow the whistles
And play the tambourines,
For there is coming to earth
The King of the Heavens.

Let us render homage of
Unequaled affection
To the exalted Mary,
To Joseph and the Son.

A half hour before midnight nine Ave Marias are said, and everyone sings:

Oh beautiful Holy Mary,
Full of glory and sweetness,
The desired night has arrived
Of your confinement, Virgin Pure.

At some posadas little children are dressed as shepherds who stand at both sides of the manger. Nearby is a table with an image of Christ, the holy pilgrims, and a baby doll to represent the Infant Jesus. The godparents take it, and passing between the shepherds, put it on the manger. Then all kneel and sing it to sleep with the A La Rorro Niño.

In the cities there is a midnight Mass or misa de gallo, after which there are fireworks, the blowing of little whistles, and the ringing of bells. In some city churches a piñata is broken after the misa de gallo. Then most people go home to a supper. The traditional dishes are a revoltijo, a dish of prickly-pear, shrimps, rosemary, chile, and potatoes; bean soup; a mixed fruit salad with nuts, and beets to give it color. But those who can afford it have much more.

In the city of Querétaro there is a Christmas Eve parade in which

Biblical scenes are represented on floats. The year I saw it, a band came first, followed by monigotes, or boys walking on stilts under huge grotesquely painted cardboard figures, and persons representing the holy pilgrims on burros; then the floats. It was very picturesque and gay. People came long distances to see it. Such parades take place in Celaya, Guanajuato; Quiroga, Michoacán, and perhaps elsewhere.

The natives do not celebrate Christmas in their huts, but often posadas are given in village churches, especially where there is a resident priest. Little boys and girls take part in the dances of the shepherds, and dance in the church to the music of violin and the rhythm they make by stomping their sticks. Sometimes a pastorela is given in the atrium, representing the announcement to the shepherds of the birth of Christ. Often the dance groups of the village take part in entertaining the new-born Infant, as in Cuetzalén, Puebla.

After the Infant is sung to sleep, whether at home or in church, He is not taken up until January 6. Then the godparents give a party, and those who find the dolls in the rosca give other parties.

Christmas in Mexico is not a present-giving time but an occasion for ritual and fun. Some families, especially in Mexico and other cities, have adopted the foreign Christmas tree and Santa Claus, but most children prefer the posadas; some have both. Presents to children are given on January 6 and are brought by the Magi, to whom children write letters as to Santa Claus.

The posadas, being connected with the Catholic religion, are, naturally, of Spanish origin but they have acquired many Mexican traits, like the procession to ask for lodging and the use of the piñata, which in Spain is broken only on the Sunday following Ash Wednesday. On the other hand, the Mexican clay Biblical figures have become popular in Madrid at Christmas time. There they have the white cotton trousers and sombreros of the natives, while here they prefer those in elegant robes but in order to make them familiar they put a sombrero on their backs (Pl. 46).[22]

The twenty-eighth of December, the day of Los Santos Inocentes or the Day of the Holy Innocents, is Mexico's April Fools' Day. A favorite trick is to ask someone seriously for a loan of something— money or some object—and to return immediately a silly toy with a note:

Inocente palomita,	Innocent little dove,
Que te dejaste engañar,	You have let yourself be fooled,
Sabiendo que en este día	Knowing that on this day
Nada se debe prestar.	You should lend nothing.

Sometimes one says the verse without even taking the loan.

Another favorite trick to play on one's friends is to invite them to supper or tea and to serve some pastry filled with cotton, or almond paste filled with flour. This is called making an "innocent" of one.

There are thousands of fiestas. Many can be located by remembering to associate their dates with those of the patron saints of the parish and barrio churches. Their form is likely to remain for a long time more or less as described here, but their content is constantly changing—more rapidly in some communities than in others. But nevertheless changes are taking place everywhere.

Peyote Pilgrimages and Fiestas

The peyote plants are small cacti that live for months after being uprooted. The eating of them immediately allays hunger, thirst, fatigue; it produces color visions; the trees dance, yet one does not get

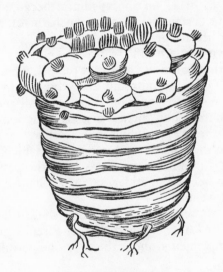

PEYOTE PLANT

dizzy even when walking along a precipice. Peyote has great curative powers; it brings luck, long life; it is a sort of protecting genius, a demi-god.

Some peyote eaters become exalted under the narcotic influence of the plant. A man may suddenly jump up from his seat, talk loudly, wave his arms about as if wanting to fly, then sit down again. On the whole, however, the majority are happy, the only after effects being a feeling of great depression.

The two tribes for whom peyote is most sacred are the Huichols and Tarahumaras. They live hundreds of miles apart; speak different tongues; have no contact, yet they call the variety of the plant they worship by the same name—hikuli, which we refer to as peyote. It is the *Lophophara Wiliamsii*, about two inches in diameter. As peyote does not grow in the regions in which these tribes live, they go on long, hard pilgrimages to secure it.

The Huichols have a corn-deer-peyote complex. They believe that the peyote were deer at one time and that the deer were corn. Corn is necessary for life, and both deer and peyote are necessary for producing good corn crops. So after the harvests are in, some time in October or November, the Huichols' thoughts turn toward Peyote-land, far away in the northern state of San Luis Potosí. The journey, which is made on foot, takes forty-three days, with only five for the gathering of the plants. Delegations of peyote-seekers are sent from the principal temples. Sometimes it is difficult to secure a sufficient number of men to make up an expedition because of the hardships involved, but the certain rewards in the form of rain, good crops, health, and long life are great incentives.

Eight to twelve men are sufficient to make up a pilgrimage. Before leaving, the pilgrims bathe and go to the temple, where they sleep with their wives. Early in the morning everything is in readiness. Some of the men wear squirrel tails on their hats; all must have tobacco gourds which confer upon them a priestly function. Before leaving, all pray around the fire, to which five tortillas are sacrificed. Then the men sprinkle their heads with a deer tail which has been dipped into herb water. In taking leave of his wife, the peyote-seeker places his right hand on her left shoulder, saying, "Good-bye; we shall meet here again." All weep.

Four captains are selected, two walking ahead of, and two behind, the single file. The leader is called "Father Fire," whom he represents. He carries the implements, and is the only one permitted to strike fire on the journey.

During the entire forty-three days, there is a man who stays in the temple to watch over the pilgrims by following them with his thoughts day by day. He has a fibre string with forty-three knots in it. The leader on the trip has a similar one; both untie a knot each day. As the peyote-seekers always camp in the same places, there is constant telepathic communication between them and the watchman. Upon their return, each pilgrim puts the calendar string twice across his back, once around each foot, once around his body, then down to each knee. This ceremony takes place in the temple, the man who has watched at home doing the same with his string. Then both strings are burned.

The wives help their husbands in their search for peyote by observing the same restrictions at home as the pilgrims do from the time they leave home until after they have returned and have been freed by the peyote fiesta, which may be some months later. They may not bathe, and they wash only on certain occasions with holy water from Peyote-land. They must not run nor walk quickly; they must fast much, and observe strict continence. Should the women break any of these laws, they may become ill and jeopardize the success of the peyote hunt; any woman breaking the last law is in danger of receiving a good beating from her husband.

The peyote-seekers and their wives must also be purified from all past sins by the god of fire, for whom the plants are as a drinking gourd. On the afternoon of the fourth day, the wives gather in the temple to confess their sexual indiscretions to Grandfather Fire. They must not omit even one, so before coming they recall all their past love life and tie as many knots in a palm leaf string as they have had lovers. As each one takes her turn before the fire, she mentions aloud a name for every knot. Then she throws the string into the fire. The consumption of the string by the flames of the god means that her sins are forgiven, and she is thus purified. Such confessions cause no hard feelings because the important thing is to secure peyote.

The men also make knots in a string as they recall their past loves on the way. When they camp at La Puerta de Cerda, they first "talk to the five winds" and deliver their "roll-call" to the leader to burn. After this the peyote-seekers are looked upon as gods, the four leaders eating nothing more than stray pieces of peyote that they find on the way during the remaining five days of their journey.

At the next camping place the ceremony of the distribution of the tobacco is performed. It begins in the afternoon with the placing of ceremonial arrows toward the four directions of the world. Then all sit around a fire until long after midnight. The leader puts a ball of native tobacco, called macuchi, on the ground; and touches it lightly with his plumes as he prays aloud. Then he wraps small portions in corn husks in tamale form and gives one to each man, who puts it into a separate gourd tied to his quiver. This act symbolizes the birth of tobacco, and those who have received the sacred little parcels must guard them carefully, and while they are on their persons, keep themselves apart from the rest of mankind. Now no man can leave his place in line without permission. When he does, he hands his tobacco gourd to the one behind him to guard. The march is not resumed until he returns. It is only after the men have put their precious little gourds on a bed of grass for the night that they may walk about freely. Upon their return home, one of the conditions for their living with their wives again at home is the returning of the tobacco gourds to Grandfather Fire by burning them at the peyote feast. Thus they remain in the temple with their sacred tobacco because a woman may not touch the tobacco nor the gourds in which it is kept.

If anyone should affront the peyote-seekers while on the road by walking in front of them, he will become ill. Should a Mexican horseman pass them, the horse and rider would drop to the ground in punishment for incurring the anger of the sacred tobacco and the arrow of the god of fire.

The Huichols meet many of their deities in the form of mountains, stones, and springs as they walk along, because once upon a time they, too, came to seek peyote. But they became too tired to return, so they remained there.

The dreams of the men on the road take on special importance, as in them it is decided who shall make the fires at the peyote feasts and who is to sacrifice the cattle in the ceremonies for rain.

Upon reaching their destination and unloading the mules, the men fall in line; each one prepares his bow as if to shoot, pointing it toward the six regions of the world—first toward the sun, in the east, then to the right and left sides; backwards, upwards, downwards, without letting the arrow fly. Later they hunt the peyote as if they were deer because they first appeared as deer.

The leader then indicates a high mesa as the principal altar and tells the men that the deer are there. Only he is able to see them. The four captains lead the advancing men with their bows drawn. When anyone of them sees a peyote, he shoots toward it but is careful not to hit it; it must be taken alive. One arrow is sent to its right and another to its left, crossing each other above the plant. Each man shoots at five plants without stopping to pick up either the plant or the arrows. When all reach the place where the leader saw the deer, they make a ceremonial circuit. Meanwhile the deer assume the shape of a whirlwind, only to disappear, leaving in their wake two peyotes —one is toward the north, the other toward the south.

Here is where the peyote-seekers leave their best offerings—beautiful votive bowls, arrows, back-shields, paper flowers, coins, glass beads—as prayers for health, addressing them to the five winds of the world. They also beg of the peyote, who at one time were people as well as deer, not to make them insane. After this they march back to pick up their peyote plants which they eat with great delight. Now all of them see the deer. Later, offerings are left at the sacred springs of this region.

The men gather plants for three more days, using their knives with care so as not to injure them. They proceed as when they are running the deer—the first day is for Grandfather Fire, the second for Great Grandfather Deer Tail, the third for all the gods.

On the fifth day they start for home, each man first placing his peyote in front of him to ask it for luck on the way. All make a ceremonial circuit around the fire before leaving. Now the men will sleep facing toward the west, which is the direction in which they are going. Most of the plants are carried on the men's backs, which is the ancient way of transporting them.

The food the men take with them is never sufficient to complete their return journey. Often there is nowhere to buy any, so they live on the fresh peyote plants. When they are about five days distant from home, people from their region meet them with fresh tortillas. They find the peyote-seekers tired and emaciated, but happy at having fulfilled their duty toward their gods. But before returning to their temple, they must still run for deer for the peyote feast in the pine forests on the way.

When they finally arrive at the temple, they are given a ceremonious welcome. Men and women paint their faces with the yellow root from the peyote country with symbols of the gods and designs that express prayers for rain, luck in hunting deer, good crops, health or any other wish in their hearts (Pl. 1). Some of the women may wear flowers in their hair, but all of them keep strictly apart from the men, who have in the temple their own fire from which no one else may take a light. The shaman and peyote-seekers sing all night long about the gods who long ago had gone to look for peyote—Great Grandfather Deer Tail, the Morning Star and others. During this first night those who have broken the laws confess their sins. The sinners are usually the women, who have stayed at home in comfort, and the husband is the one to mete out the punishment.

At sunrise all wash their paint off in water brought from the peyote country, and come out to greet the rising sun with clean faces. All make reverences to Father Sun, the leaders blowing him incense. Using flowers as cups, they sprinkle the peyote-land water in the four directions, and pray for long life and luck in the deer hunt (Pl. 14).

Among the Huichols of Jalisco, the last of the peyote fiestas is in connection with the corn parching ceremony at the time the fields are being cleared for the spring planting. This takes place in every ranchería, given by the families living there for themselves and for the outsiders who have helped with the work. Finally, there is one communal fiesta at the temple at Ratontita sometime in May, lasting two days.

Most of the first day is devoted to the preparation of the food and drinks. Late in the afternoon, the shaman, with an assistant on each side of him, sits with his back to the fire. He begins to chant in a low voice, his aids repeating the phrases. In front of them is an improvised altar, consisting of a piece of sackcloth on the ground, with four deer-tail plumes standing along the outer edge. As the singing gains in volume, the young men who are to lead the dance come out from the temple. They carry handsomely carved ceremonial reed canes in one hand and deer-tail plumes in the other, and wear shaman's plumes over each ear. They approach the singers, take up their chant, and do a slow trotting step around the fire. They repeat this several times, stopping after each one at another altar on the ground to rest on their canes, keeping time with their feet to the singing. Later, other men join the dance informally, until all are dancing in single file. They are soon stomping. At intervals they take some backward steps, swing in circles; raise and lower their heads, bending from the waist. Soon they are shouting and laughing from sheer good spirits. Suddenly they stop, marking time until the singers begin a new phrase. It is taken up by the leaders, and the dance starts again, slowly. After a while it gains in momentum with more stomping, individual dancers swinging and turning as they make a circuit around the fire. At the end there are hurrahs in Huichol, and another pause until the singers start a new tune. Sometimes they sing in falsetto and then go into a lively tune as if to invoke the gods to join them. It is said that this dance is a dramatization of the popping of the corn as it is being parched.

At dawn, women join the dance to greet the rising sun. The singers are now facing east. On their altar are two candles to light the sun on his arrival. The shaman, singing loudly, stands up to beckon to the sun. His song is repeated by his assistants and taken up by the leaders of the dance. Everyone is dancing around the patio with great abandon. Most of the faces are beautifully painted. As it is orchid time, many wear the flowers—the men in their hats and the women in their hair.

At about seven o'clock in the morning, some dozen men stand around the fire with cups of tesgüino, their ritual corn beer. Behind each one is a woman holding a lighted candle. They pray for a while and throw the drink into the fire. Thus it is consecrated and distributed all morning long in the temple, while the dancing goes on outside.

At about one o'clock, a procession takes place to symbolize the freedom of the couples to resume their marital relations, interrupted by the peyote pilgrimage. The men and women to take part gather with shaman's plumes, god-bowls, corn pouches, candles and other ceremonial paraphernalia. The men form one line, each holding to the girdle of the one in front; the women another, each taking hold of the quexquemetl of the other. The shaman stands up singing and on a new phrase, they follow the dancers around in a circle and stop. The men all take their hats off. Four assistants bring in bowls of water from the sacred caves at Santa Catarina, with which they sprinkle the heads of all adults and children, using orchids for the purpose. Then they sprinkle everything in the god-houses. With this the people are free to abandon their abstinence.

Then, after twenty hours of singing, the shaman, his aids, and the leaders of the dance are finally able to wet their throats. They are served cups of ritual beer, which they offer to the four directions before drinking. Afterwards tamales, elongated tortillas, and more beer are brought them, which they share with their wives. In the end they are given sacred water for the ritual washing of their faces and hands; this also they offer first to the four points. The rest of the afternoon and night the people are free to do as they please. Some spend it in social dancing and drinking; others, too exhausted to do anything else, sleep.

Deer are plentiful in this region. As they are caught, the men cut them up into pieces, which they string and hang on trees in the sun to keep for the fiesta. The next morning, pots of strings of deer meat, with dust and all, are cooking. In the meantime a procession is formed of one member of each family carrying several ears of corn in a pouch, their contribution for the parching; it is led by the singers. The procession enters the temple to make a ceremonial circuit of the fire, and another one is made around the fire in the patio. Then, with an offering gesture toward the fire, each one lays his corn on the altar in the center of the circle, where it is shelled by two men.

Later, all are seated in a circle in the patio on all available seats and logs. The comisario, or head official of the place, is handed a bowl of moistened bread with a few elongated tortillas; he goes around the circle, giving each one a bite of the bread from a tortilla which serves as a spoon.

Afterwards, the comisario puts a bowl of sacred water with the orchids, a bowl of corn beer, and another of shelled corn on the altar in the center of the circle. He takes a woman by the wrist and leads her into the circle, giving her some shaman's plumes to stick in her hair, for she is to parch the corn. The shaman arises, and taking on his back the comal on which the corn is to be parched, offers it to the four points; then it is put on the fire for the parching. The comisario then gives the three bowls he has put on the altar to the three singers, who go around the circle with him as he sprinkles the heads of every-one present from the one containing the sacred water, giving each person a sip of it from the orchids. Thus everyone is consecrated with the same water as the corn, and brought into relation with the gods. Then women go around the circle with corn beer, giving each one a drink from tiny gourds. In the meantime the parching of the corn goes on to the music of violin and guitar. Many get up to dance, some of the men holding a tiny infant on shoulders or back.

After the parching is finished, the venison is taken off the strings, and bowls of it are served in broth. The cleaned bones are thrown into the fire as an offering. With the passing around of the parched corn, the ceremony is completed and the fiesta comes to an end. Some of the people stay around for a day or two longer to drink and carouse.

In the corn parching ceremonies it is customary to "tame" Grandfather Fire. Two young children, a boy and girl representing the gods, with some adults, make a ceremonial circuit of the fire, followed by all the men, carrying tiny tamales. Then all stand in a close circle around the fire, praying and chanting for some minutes, after which they throw their tamales into the fire, believing that they turn into peyotes. This is done so that the fire may burn the brush on the mountain sides for the cornfields without doing damage to huts or animals.

Some of the Huichols say that there is a sex distinction among the peyote plants; these they use as charms, the man carrying the female and the woman the male. For love, the peyote must be bathed in the ritual corn beer; for good luck, in liquor and sun. It must be danced and sung to, and dressed in a little red silk dress. It is necessary to keep the plant whole and to carry it always under the heart or near the right knee.

A piece of peyote boiled or chewed and put into a drink or food will cause the person who takes it to fall madly in love. Anyone who is much in love, whether or not he has been given peyote, is said to be empeyotado.

One can get rid of an enemy by touching his hand with peyote hairs or by throwing the hairs over the shoulder in the direction in which the enemy is walking.

Tuesdays and Fridays at twelve o'clock are the best times to perform these ceremonies.

The peyote cult among the Tarahumaras is less extensive and not so elaborate as that of the Huichols, but very important nevertheless. The Tarahumaras believe the plants possess human attributes, the power to cure, to purify, and to bring luck.

When Tata Dios went to heaven, he left peyote behind as a remedy and talisman for the Tarahumaras. The plant has four faces and sees everything; it is very powerful.

It is related that one day the Bear and the Peyote met in a cave. The Bear said to Peyote, "Let us fight and let us smoke over there." So they smoked and fought and Peyote was the stronger of the two. He knocked the Bear down and all the wind went out of him. But the Bear wanted to fight and smoke once more. They did, and again Peyote knocked him down. Then the Bear sat on a stone and wept. After that he went away and never returned.

Catholicized Tarahumaras make the sign of the cross when they approach a peyote, greeting it as if it were a person. Some say that the greatest peyote is the brother of Tata Dios, so they call him uncle. But he is not so great as Father Sun, even though he may sit near him.

The peyote plants are believed to be very modest. In order not to shock them by the immodest things they could not avoid seeing if they were kept in the house, they are put away in a jar or basket in a separate store house. Before they are taken out for use, an offering of meat and tesgüino must be made them. If this were neglected, the plants would eat the man's soul. If mice were to nibble at the peyotes or if they were bruised in any way while stored, the owner might go insane for not taking better care of them. Should anyone steal peyote, he would certainly go crazy. In order to be cured, the plants must be returned to the original owner, an ox sacrificed, and a fiesta given to make peace with God and the people.

The peyote plants are sometimes dressed in pieces of blankets and offered cigarettes. Only the shamans know how to handle them properly; they wash their hands carefully or use sticks to pick them up. A boy must never touch the plants, and a woman only when she is helping the shaman to grind them.

For external application the plant is either chewed or moistened in the mouth. It is good for snake bites, rheumatic pains, burns and wounds of any kind. When ground and mixed with water, it becomes an intoxicating drink, but its effects are different from those produced by drinking liquor. While they last one is exhilarated and happy; when they wear off, depression and sadness set in.

In recent years the peyote-seekers are generally from the region of Nararachic. The pilgrimage consists of about ten men with a peyote shaman as leader. They find their plants in the State of Chihuahua, taking about a month to bring them back. They may attend to business on the trip in Chihuahua City and do not observe all the restrictions of the Huichols.

When they are on the ground, however, they are serious and respectful, eating only pinole with water. In order to pick the plants, all the men are permitted to touch them. They must handle them with great care so as not to injure the roots, for that would not only prevent the plants from growing again but also offend them.

The peyote seekers set up a cross in the field, and the first plants they pick are placed near it; the second batch is eaten by the men. After that they are too drunk to do anything but sleep. They spend two more days in picking the plants, which they put into separate bags for transportation, so that they will not fight when they are being carried by the men on their backs.

The plants apparently like to be picked, because they sing beautifully to attract the attention of the peyote-seekers and say, "I want to go to your country so that you may sing your songs to me." Sometimes they even sing as they are being carried.

When the peyote-seekers are returning, the people meet them with music. Then they make a fiesta in their honor, for which an animal is sacrificed. While it is taking place, the fresh plants are piled up under the cross and sprinkled with tesgüino, for they, too, want to drink. If their thirst were not satisfied, they would return to their own country. The dances go on throughout the night and there is much food and drink.

The Tarahumara peyote fiestas are generally for the purpose of curing, and they are expensive. They require the sacrifice of a cow, much food and drink. The dutuburi is danced on a patio with three crosses, and sometimes the matachines in front of another cross. But there is a special patio for the peyote dance. On it is one cross for the jar with the peyote and another for God. Upon entering this patio, the men remove their hats and cross themselves; they cannot leave it without permission. There is a hole in the ground for spitting and cigarette butts. A big fire is kept lighted, around which the dancers circle all night. The shaman receives a quarter of the beef and food for his services.

Early in the evening everyone drinks some of the ground peyote with water and a little of the ritual corn beer, which keeps them in a tipsy state all night long. A hole is made in the ground and marked with a cross, as a container for peyote; it is covered with a bowl or gourd, upon which the end of a notched stick is placed to be scraped by another, producing a peculiar resonance. The wood for these sticks is brought back by the peyote-seekers one at a time. Only a shaman may own them; should a layman keep one, he would die.

In the morning the dancing ceases, the tesgüino is dedicated; the people eat and drink, then the curing ceremony is performed. The most usual way is to mark crosses on the patient's body with a cross' dipped in tesgüino as the shaman sings and rasps. Then the rasping stick is scraped three times over the head of the sick. Afterwards the shaman faces the sun and moves his notched stick three times above and below the one for rasping. The peyote which the sick have eaten have been singing to them, while the dance was going on, and giving them courage. In the end everyone drinks liquor with water, and washes hands and face.

Around Gauchochic the curing ceremony in the morning is more elaborate. At dawn the shaman who has been rasping for the dance gives three raps as a signal that it is over. The people gather around the cross at the eastern end of the patio. The shaman arises with his rasping implements, followed by a boy with a gourd of sacred water, and confers a blessing on everyone present. Then he solemnly dips his rasping stick into the water and touches the middle and ends of the notched stick with the wet end. He daubs the head of the sick person with it three times. He rests the end of the notched stick against the man's head and rasps three long strokes, throwing his hand far out into the air after each one. After this he turns to the sun and holding out his implements, makes a strong rasp from end to end, passing his hand out far from the stick toward the rising sun.

By performing the last act three times, the shaman sends the peyote home. They had arrived a short time before on pretty green doves to partake of the food and drink of the Tarahumaras. The greatest of the peyotes eats with the shaman, for the shaman alone is able to see the peyotes. Their presence at the fiesta frees the people from the danger of sorcery.

After the great peyote has given his blessing, he rolls himself into a ball and flies back home in the company of an owl who is also returning at this time.[23]

CHILDREN'S GAMES

The native children of primitive communities of today are undoubtedly playing the same games as those played by their ancestors before the Conquest. They are either taught them by their elders or are imitations of the elders' sports and pastimes. Whatever the children need to play with they usually make themselves. As a rule there are no commercial toys available in those regions; if there were, their parents could not afford to buy them. So the children learn early to create their own play world and to take advantage of what their environment has to offer. They show great ingenuity.

For example—Tarahumara boys—whose parents raise cattle, carve hoofs of horses, burros, sheep and other animals on the ends of sticks with which they jump along to make tracks on the soft earth. They also carve animal heads from branches, with small twigs for horns, using those of the bull for bullfighting as they see their parents do. From pine twigs they make traps for animals, canoes, corrals with tiny animals, toy plows, wagons, and horses.

The little Tarahumara girls play at housekeeping and make mud tortillas as all the others in the country do, but they are especially clever at making charming dolls of plants and sticks, and dressing them with flowers and weeds.

Both the boys and girls enjoy imitating their elders' drinking feasts, so they pretend to serve corn beer to their dolls in cup-shaped stems of acorns until they get them gloriously drunk and make them behave as their parents do on such occassions.

Some of the Maya boys make pellet guns of plants, whistles of cane, trumpets of palm leaves, sling shots of rubber or sisal fibre; they extract a liquid from shoots of pomolche for soap bubbles to blow through a can tube.

Boys and girls a few years old are given fruit pits to play with; little girls make necklaces of flowers; boys improvise rattles of dried pomegranates or anything else that serves the purpose, and often their fathers teach them to dance to their rhythms.

Boys everywhere play at marbles, bullfighting, and lassoing bulls. They fly kites, and spin tops, which the poor make themselves even in Mexico City. Here, too, the games of boys living in the poor neighborhoods whose parents have come from villages are influenced by their beliefs. One of them is called, "enchanting." There are two bands—the enchanters and those to be enchanted. The latter have a space allotted to them in which they are immune, but when they leave it and are caught by one of the enchanters, they are obliged to stand still as if bewitched, until one of their own side touches them. The aim of the game is to have all of the enchanters bewitch the other side. They also play at jumping the burro or donkey. The boy representing the burro has to get down on all fours while the others jump over him; the one who falls first has to take his place. During the apricot season the boys play a game called huesitos, or little bones, with the stones of that fruit. A hole is dug in the ground just big enough to hold one stone. The boys take turns at throwing their stones at it from a certain distance. The one whose stone falls into the hole, wins all the stones around it.

City boys also play at being gendarmes and thieves (cops and robbers), the former trying to arrest the latter. In this game they are often influenced by characters in the movies. They also play with tin or clay soldiers, but the village boys, especially where there are barracks, are the soldiers themselves. They organize in military fashion with commanding officers, drill, and fight battles, using sticks for arms. Sometimes little girls play the part of soldaderas in this game—the women soldiers who follow their men to battle to cook for them and nurse them. They have their make-believe encampments and reproduce all the reality with which they are familiar and which appeals so much to the child's imagination.

Little girls everywhere play at housekeeping and dressing themselves like adults and their dolls like children. Those who have the means have at their disposition the marvelous world of Mexican toys —clay animals, figures, dolls, tiny utensils, musical instruments—in which everything that adults use is reproduced in miniature. Often the parents of the poor help their children by carving things for them. There are some very marvelously expressive wooden dolls made in the State of Guerrero and elsewhere. Potters make clay toys for them. But most things they make for themselves, as we have already seen.

The rural schools have greatly influenced children's games in recent years, particularly those of boys, with whom volley ball and basketball are popular. I once saw a basketball game in the mountains of San Luis Potosí. It was played in the schoolyard on a hilltop, surrounded by tropical trees which hid the huts of the small settlements around it. The boys, about fourteen years old, slender and lithe, yelled excitedly and shouted commands in the Huasteca tongue.[1]

In Yolox, Oaxaca, the prettiest girls of the village become madrinas or godmothers of the boys on the basketball teams, presenting the winners with beautifully hand-embroidered ribbons. Thus these games become part of the ethnography of the village.

City mothers or nurses play with babies' fingers as ours do. The following two verses are counterparts of our "This little pig went to market. . . ."

El niño chiquito y bonito,	The little pretty child,
El señor de los anillos,	The master of the rings,
El tonto y loco,	The foolish and crazy one,
El lame cazuelas,	The one that cleans the bowls,
El mate piojos.	The one that kills lice.

Este se robó un güebo (huevo),	This one stole an egg,
Este lo puso a asar,	This one fried it,
Este le echó la sal,	This one put salt on it,
Este le comió,	This one ate it,
Y este viejo perro lo fué a chismear.	And this old dog went and tattled.

Taking hold of the baby's hand, the mother will run her fingers up and down its palm, saying:

Andaba la hormiguita	The little ant went about
Juntando su leña.	Gathering its firewood.

Le coge un aguacerito.	It is caught in a shower.
¡Que corre pa' su casita!	Run for your little house!
Se metió en su covachita.	It got into the ant-hill.

Playing with a baby's foot, the mother waves it around and says:

Cuando me voy en casa tio Peña,	When I go to Uncle Peña's,
Con la patita le hago la seña.	I signal to him with this little foot.

When bathing a baby, the mother or nurse will say, as she throws water over it:

Cruz de mayo, si te hace daño,	Cross of May, if this harms you,
Jamás te baño;	I shall never bathe you;
Cruz de abril, si provecho,	Cross of April, if good,
Todo el día te echo.	I shall do this all day long.

An adult often teases a young child by starting a story, which is repeated without end:

Este era una vez un gato	Once upon a time there was a cat
Con su colita de trapo	With a little rag tail
Y sus ojos al revés.	And eyes wrong side out.
¿Quieres que te lo cuente otra vez?	Do you want me to tell it again?

¿Quieres que te cuente el cuento	Do you wish me to tell the tale
De la buena pipa?	Of the good pipe?

The child says "yes." The person repeats the same thing until the child becomes vexed and says, "¿No te digo que sí?" "Did I not say yes?" The adult answers, "¿No te digo que no?" "Do I not say no?" and so it goes on.

Another charming verse for playing with a child's finger is:

Cinco pollitos tiene mi tía,	Five little chickens has my aunt,
Uno le canta y otro le pia;	One sings to her and another chirps;
Tres le tocan la chirimía.	Three play the flute for her.

When children are old enough to play by themselves, they are taught the game of the little frogs: They form a circle squatting and say:

Al agua ranitas	To the water, little frogs,
Al agua ya	Now to the water,
Cua cuá, cua cuá, cua cuá.	Cua cua, cua cua, cua cua.
Salten ranitas,	Jump little frogs,

Salten así,
Cua cuá, cua cuá, cua cuá.

Jump like this. (They imitate the jumping of the frogs and repeat the cua cua.)

There are many more delightful play rhymes for little children, but we must now turn to those for the older ones.[2]

There are innumerable counting out rhymes and jingles. A version of our Eenie, meenie, minie, mo . . . is:

Ini, ini, maini, mo,
Que cheleque palestó,

Que jingale, lestingó,
Ini, ini, aini, mo.

The words mean nothing, so there is no translation possible. Others like it, are:

De tin marín,
Dedo pingüé,
Cúcara, mácara,
Títere fue.

De una de dola,
De tela canela,
Zumbaca tabaca,
De bire birón,
Cuéntalas bién
Que las once son.

(The last two lines are: "Count them well, it is eleven o'clock.)

Many of the counting out rhymes are of Spanish origin, but the following two are purely Mexican:

Al subir una montaña
Una pulga me picó;
La cogí de las narices
Y se me escapó.
Botín, botero y salió.
Rosa, clavel y botón.

Upon climbing a mountain
A flea bit me;
I caught it by the nose
And it escaped me.
Botín, Botero, and off it went.
Rose, carnation, and bud.

A, e, i, o, u, arbolito de pirú,
Díme cuantos años tienes tu.

A, e, i, o, u, little tree of pirue,
Tell me how old are you.

(The one whom the tu hits has to say how old he is, and then the counter has to go on until the number is finished.)

A popular Spanish rhyme of which the Mexican version is:

Mañana domingo
Se casa Benito
Con un pajarito.
¿Quién es la madrina?
Doña Catalina.
¿Quién es el padrino?
Don Juan Botijón.

Tomorrow Sunday
Benito marries
A little bird.
Who is the godmother?
Doña Catalina.
Who is the godfather?
Don Juan Botijón.

The Spanish original verses are not so polite as may be seen by the following example:

Mañana es domingo,	Tomorrow is Sunday,
Es día de respingo.	The day of rest.
Se casa Benito	Benito will marry
Con una pajarito.	A little bird.
¿Quién es la madrina?	Who's the godmother?
Doña Catalina.	Doña Catalina.
¿Quién es el padrino?	Who's the godfather?
Don Juan Rivera.	Don Juan de Rivera.
¡Mal haya su culo	The deuce take his behind
Que tanto lo menea!	That he wiggles so much!

Another favorite counting rhyme is:

Pin-uno, pin-dos, pin-tres,	Pin-one, pin-two, pin-three,
Pin-cuatro, pin-cinco, pin-seis,	Pin-four, pin-five, pin-six,
Pin-siete, Pinocho.	Pin-seven, pin-eight—Pinocchio.
(In Spanish, the long-nosed Pi-	
nocchio, whom the children	
love.)[3]	

Among the traditional children's games to music, the following are among the most popular:

El Florón (The Large Flower)

The children provide themselves with some pebbles, which one hides in his hand; all the others clench their fists and form a circle around one who gets down on all fours to represent a piano. All strike him on his back with their clenched fists, singing:

El florón está en las manos,	The big flower's in his hands,
En las manos del señor;	In the hands of the señor;
Y él que no me lo adivine	And he who doesn't guess in which,
Se le parte el corazón.	May lightning strike his heart.

When the verse is finished, "the piano" stands up and asks,

> Flower, flower,
> Who's got the flower?

All the children extend their clenched fists. The child in whose fist the pebbles are discovered pays a forfeit by becoming the piano.

The Florón and other running games are played by children from about five to seven years old. Up to the age of nine or ten, they are fond of religious games like the following:

Santo Domingo (Saint Dominic)

This is played by girls; they form a circle and are directed by a leader, who sings:

Santo Domingo	Saint Dominic,
De la buena, buena vida;	Of the good, good life;
Hacen así, así, así,	This, this is the way
Las lavanderas . . .	The washer women do it . . .

The leader imitates the movements of washing, ironing, grinding corn, or whatever she sings about. Those who make a mistake in the movements are out.

The following are played by children from ten up, when they are already beginning to be sex conscious.

Mata-rili-rili-rón

Boys form one line and girls another, facing each other; they advance alternately an equal number of steps and sing:

Amo-a-to, mata-rili-rili-rón (repeat)

One line chooses someone from the opposite and all sing:

¿Qué oficio le pondremos?	What trade shall we give him?
Mata-rili-rili-rón.	Mata-rili-rili-rón. (repeat)

The line which has chosen, decides on the trade and sings:

Le pondremos zapatero,	We shall make you a shoemaker,
Mata-rili-rili-rón.	Mata-rili-rili-rón. (repeat)

When the companions of the one chosen are satisfied that he is to be a shoemaker, they all sing:

Ese oficio sí le gusta,	Indeed he likes his trade,
Mata-rili-rili-rón.	Mata-rili-rili-rón. (repeat)

But if they sing no instead of sí, then the trade can be changed as many times as necessary until one is hit upon which they like. Then both sides sing:

Celebremos todos juntos,	We'll celebrate all together,
Comeremos chicharrón.	We shall eat crackling.

A version of this game is to give boys a trade and girls the name of a flower. When they do that, they sing "¿Qué nombre le pondremos?" instead of "¿Qué oficio. . . . ?"

La Viudita (The Little Widow)

Girls form a circle around the "little widow," who sings:

Yo soy la viudita	I'm the little widow
De Santa Isabel,	From Santa Isabel;
Me quiero casar	I want to marry
Y no hallo con quién.	But cannot find anyone.
El mozo del cura	The priest's servant
Me mandó un papel	Sent me a note
Y yo le mandé otro	And I sent him another
De Santa Isabel.	From Santa Isabel.

Mi madre lo supo;	My mother found it out;
¡Qué palos me dió!	What a beating she gave me.
¡Malhaya sea el hombre	The devil take the man
Que me enamoró!	Who made love to me!
Pasé por su casa	I went to his house
Y él estaba llorando;	And found him crying;
Con un pañuelito	With his handkerchief
Se estaba secando.	His eyes he was drying.
Me gusta el cigarro,	I like cigarettes;
Me gusta el tabaco,	I like tobacco,
Pero más me gustan	But I like better
Los ojos del gato.	The eyes of the cat.
Me gusta la leche,	I like milk,
Me gusta el café,	I like coffee,
Pero más me gustan	But I like better
Los ojos de usté. (sic)	Your eyes.

When the song is finished, the circle breaks up and the little widow chases the girls until she finds one to take her place.

Doña Blanca (The White Lady)

The children form a circle holding hands. In the center is a girl, Doña Blanca; outside, a boy who is Jicotillo, the hornet. All sing:

Doña Blanca está cubierta	The White Lady is covered
Con pilares de oro y plata;	With pillars of gold and silver;
Romperemos un pilar	Let us break down a pillar
Para ver a Doña Blanca.	To see the White Lady.

Then the circle moves to the right and Doña Blanca sings:

¿Quién es ese Jicotillo	Who is that Jicotillo
Que anda rondando mi casa?	Hovering around my house?

Jicotillo answers:

Yo soy ese, yo soy ese	I am that one, I am that one
Que anda en pos de Doña Blanca.	Who is after Doña Blanca.

The pillars are broken with the children letting go of each other's hands. Jicotillo runs after Doña Blanca until he catches her. Then the whole thing starts over again.

Amadrus Señores

The children form a circle; one stays outside. They run around and sing:

Amadrus, señores,
Vengo de La Habana,
De cortar madroños
Para Doña Juana.

Amadrus, señores,
I come from Havana,
Where I cut madrones
For Doña Juana.

When the verse is finished, they stop, let go of hands, and do everything indicated in the next verse:

La mano derecha;
Y después la izquierda;
Y después de lado;
Y después costado;
Una media vuelta
Con su reverencia.
Tin, tan, llaman a la puerta,
Tin, tan, yo no quiero abrir,
Tin, tan, que vienen por tí.

First the right hand,
And the left;
And to the side;
And afterwards down;
A half turn
With a bow.
Tin, tan, someone is knocking,
Tin, tan, I don't want to open,
Tin, tan, they have come for you.

The children make any motions they wish and after they have finished singing they all run because the one who remains outside tries to catch one to take his place.

Naranja Dulce, Limón Partido (Sweet Orange, Divided Lemon)

The children form a circle with one in the center. All sing:

Naranja dulce, limón partido,   Sweet orange, divided lemon,
Dáme un abrazo que yo te pido,   Give me an embrace, I beg you;
Si fueran falsos mis juramentos,   If my vows were false
En otros tiempos se olvidarán.   In time they will be forgotten.
Toca la marcha, mi pecho llora;   Play the march, my heart weeps;
Adiós, Señora, yo ya me voy.   Good-bye, Señora, I go now.

When the verse is finished, the one in the center approaches someone
in the circle to comply with the request in the song, and they exchange
places. A version to the same music:

Naranja dulce, limón partido,   Sweet orange, divided lemon,
Díle a María que no se acueste.   Tell Mary not to lie down.
María, María, ya se acostó;   Mary, Mary, she did lie down;
Vino la muerte y se la llevó.   Death came and carried her off.

La Pájara Pinta (The Spotted Bird)

The children form a circle with the spotted bird in the center;
they move around slowly, singing:

Estaba la pájara pinta   The spotted bird was
A la sombra del verde limón.   In the shadow of the green lemon
Con el pico picaba la rama.   tree.

Con la cola movía la flor.
¡Ay! sí, ¡ay! no, ¿Cuándo
vendrá mi amor?

With its beak it picked the
branch,
With its tail it moved the flower.
Ah, yes! Ah, no! When will my
love come?

When the song is finished, the spotted bird chooses one of the circle
and sings:

Me arrodillo a los pies de mi
amante;
Me levanto fiel y constante,
Dame una mano, dame la otra,
Dame un besito de tu linda boca.

I kneel at the feet of my beloved;
I arise faithful and constant,
Give me your hand, give me the
other,
Give me a kiss from your pretty
mouth.

This game is played by girls. The spotted bird does all required by
the song, and the one whom she has chosen takes her place in the
center.

A La Víbora (To the Snake)

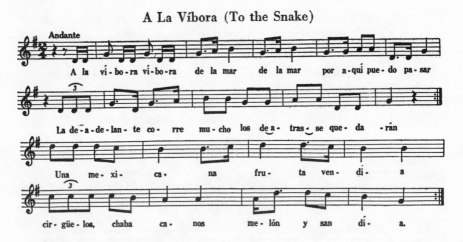

A la vi-bo-ra ví-bo-ra de la mar de la mar por a-quí pue-do pa-sar

La de-a-de-lan-te co-rre mu-cho los de a-tras se que-da-rán

Una me-xi-ca-na fru-ta ven-di-a

cir-güe-los, chaba ca-nos me-lón y san di-a.

The two tallest children form an arch with their hands high over
the heads and remain in this position throughout the game. One of
them is a melon; the other a watermelon. The rest of the group form
a line, according to height, each one holding on to the waist of the
other in front. As they move forward toward the arch, they sing:

A la víbora,
De la mar, de la mar
Por aquí puede pasar.
La de adelante corre mucho

To the serpent, the serpent
Of the sea, of the sea,
Here it can pass by.
The one in front runs fast

La de atrás se quedará . . .   The one in back will remain
Trás, trás, trás, trás . . .   Behind, behind, behind, behind
    . . .

Una mexicana   A Mexican girl
Que fruta vendía—   Who was selling fruit—
Ciruelas, chabacanos,   Prunes, apricots,
Melón y sandía . . .   Musk and watermelons,
Trás, trás, trás, trás . . .   Behind, behind, behind, behind
    . . .

Manzanita de oro   Little golden apple,
Déjame pasar   Let me pass
Con todos mis hijos   With all my children
Menos él de atrás . . .   Excepting the one behind,
Trás, trás, trás, trás . . .   Behind, behind, behind, behind
    . . .

At this moment all pass under the arch and the Melons lower their arms to catch the last one. The one caught is asked, "Whom do you want to go with, Musk or Watermelon?" According to their choice they form a line.[4]

The foregoing does not by any means exhaust the repertoire of games. There are many more with and without music—all imaginative and the tunes melodious. All are interesting in that they reveal the character and tastes of the children.

"Matarililirilirón" and "A La Víbora" are great favorites. Adults often sing them when recalling their school days.

The games described here, and others still popular in city schools, were played as long ago as the eighties. Since about 1935 they have been taught in rural schools. In recent years, however, boys have devoted their recess time to athletic games.

ADULT GAMES AND SPORTS

The pre-Conquest races, especially the Mayas and Aztecs about whom most has been written, were fond of games. The players had great agility and strength, and the people had strong gambling instincts. But their games like their arts were dominated by religion.

Their three outstanding games were: (1) tlachtli, a ball game; (2) patolli, a game of chance similar to the old-fashioned parchesi; (3) the flying pole, which is now considered a dance and will be described in Part Three.

Tlachtli was probably the most important of the three, since it was played in well-constructed courts in the temples. One in a very good state of preservation is to be found in Chichén Itzá, Yucatán. There are others in the Maya area, and another was recently uncovered at Xochicalco, Morelos.

The tlachtli courts were enclosed and laid out in the form of an

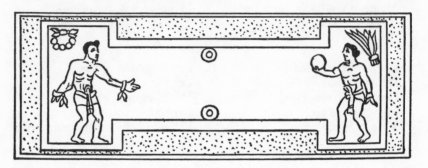

THE GAME OF TLACHTLI

"H," being twice as long as wide. The game was between two contending parties with a varying number of players. It consisted of sending a small, solid rubber ball with the elbow, thigh or hip from one side to the other without permitting it to rebound more than once. The ball was so hard that the thighs of the men had to be protected with a sort of hard leather apron. They were not permitted to touch the ball with hands or feet. At the end of the line that divided the court in half, two stone rings were imbedded in the wall. The side that passed the ball through the ring first won automatically, without taking into account any previous fouls, as the manner of handling the ball, and its size in relation to that of the ring made it a very difficult feat.

Tlachtli was a favorite both among the Mayas and Aztecs. According to Tezozomoc, one of the early Aztec chroniclers, the game was a representation of the movements of the stars, which were never hidden in the Valley of Mexico. As to the Mayas, their "Popul Vuh," the sacred Maya-Quiché book, relates that their two mythical heroes played tlachtli for the destiny of humanity against the infernal deities.

The Aztecs played patolli on a board in the form of a cross. In each of the arms was marked a double line of little houses, the player having to cover fifty-two houses from the starting point until returning to it. The luck of the game was decided with dice for which beans were used, hence the name of the game—patolli are beans in Aztec. This game also seems to have had an astronomical-religious significance because the cycle of the Aztecs consisted of fifty-two years, so that the numbers on the board may have been taken from the image of the sun passing through the fifty-two houses of the cycle.

The deity of patolli was Macuilxochitl, Five Flower, god of flowers; the deity of all the games, as well as of wine, was Ome Tochtli, Two Rabbit.

THE GAME OF PATOLLI

When professional patolli players were about to throw their first five dice, they invoked Macuilxochitl in a loud voice. Then they warmed their dice in the way players do now, threw them, and jumped to see how they fell. The players also prayed in their houses before games, offering food and incense to their god.

Gamblers and gambling were looked down upon but they existed. Betting was very heavy on all games. There were men who bet their clothes and their jewels, even pledged their women and themselves as slaves.

Since the ancient temples were destroyed, tlachtli is no longer played. However, in villages of the states of Nayarit and Sinaloa, a ball game is played by mestizos, which is reminiscent of that game.

This game, called hulama, is played with a good-sized hard rubber ball, weighing about seven pounds. The players are barefoot and naked excepting for a breechclout and a chimal or ten-inch wide belt, lined on the inside with soft leather and laced with leather thongs, which they draw so tight that it makes them feel "light."

Hulama is played on a long and narrow court, its limits marked with stones or bricks, with one at the center of either side to indicate the central, transverse lines. The number of players varies from one to several, a team consisting of from two to five men. When there are five, one of each team is stationed at the center, the remaining ones strung out behind in order to cover their side of the court. The golpeador or striker stands at the back.

Each team has its own juez, judge or umpire. He starts the game by throwing the ball into the court. The nearest player throws it to the opposing team; from there it is returned either at full volley or on the bounce, and it must be received either on the hip or thigh within four-fingers' distance of the knee. Disputes in this connection can often be settled by an examination of the welts on the body.

Points are scored when either side does not receive the ball at the required places on the body and does not return it to the other court. The ball need not be returned on the first bounce. Sometimes players leap into the air for a high ball or fall to the ground for a low one. The rules are not complicated but the game is difficult and dangerous, especially when the big hard ball hits vulnerable parts of the body.

A team may be organized by an individual who sometimes is the umpire but who is always considered the dueño or owner because he feeds the players and supervises their practice. The players may eat normally, excepting on the first day of the game, when their diet is restricted to liquids, usually milk. If the game lasts more than one day, solid food is permitted. They are expected to abstain from pleasures and sex, and to bathe directly after the game. The organizer receives no compensation except the attendant prestige and winnings from bets. Heavy betting, in which women participate, accompanies the game. But the losing team receives nothing but puros golpes, just blows.

This game has no religious content but it is generally played on Sundays, the Saturday of Holy Week, and during the fiestas in honor of St. John, St. Peter, and St. James. While archaeologists have as yet found no connection between tlachtli and hulama, a relationship is implied in that both are played in a corridor-like court with a solid rubber ball, which is struck only with the hip and thigh, and both are accompanied by lavish betting.

A game which seems to be an offshoot of hulama exists among the Cahitas of the north. It is played with a small rubber ball, batted against the right forearm, which is protected by a guard. If the ball touches any other part of the body, it is considered a foul.

Patolli was being played some fifteen years ago—and probably still is—among the Totonacs and Aztecs in the Sierra de Puebla.

However, instead of beans they used pieces of cleft reeds on which they made certain marks for the concave part.[1]

The Tarahumaras play a game similar to patolli, which they call *quince*, or fifteen. They use four short sticks of equal length, inscribed with marks for indicating their value, which serve the same purpose as dice but are thrown differently and counted in accordance with the way they fall. The one who passes first through the figures outlined by small holes wins. *Quince* is a popular game because it is complicated and accompanied by heavy betting. A man may go on playing it for days if he can afford it. He may lose everything he owns but he does draw the line at his wife and children. Gambling debts are paid scrupulously.

Another game requiring holes in the ground, called cuatro, or four, is also played by the Tarahumaras. In this one two players throw disks, made of old pot sherds or stones which are ground into shape, from three to four inches in diameter and one thick. The holes, just large enough to admit the disks, may be from twenty to one hundred feet apart. Two men play on each side. A disk that falls into the hole counts four points; one near it, one point. The game is played up to ten points or over.

The Tarahumaras are good at sports and like gambling. They have great endurance and enjoy the fun and competition of games. But of all their many games, they are fondest of foot-racing, which may also be considered a gambling game because of the attendant extravagant betting.

All the natives living in mountainous regions are good at running but it is not a sport with them as with the Tarahumaras, who are outstanding long-distance runners. Some of them have been known to run over a hundred miles without stopping, taking nothing more than pinole and water. They catch deer by running after them for days until they tire them out. The root of the name Tarahumara refers to foot running.

In 1926, three Tarahumaras gave the "civilized world" their first demonstration of their ability to run. Three of them were brought to Mexico City from the mountains of Chihuahua and were taken to Pachuca, Hidalgo, where the governor gave them letters of greeting to the head of the Federal District in Mexico City. At 3:05 A.M. on Sunday morning of November 7, they started running from the State Palace in Pachuca, followed by a Red Cross ambulance with doctors and nurses, anthropologists, and newspaper men. A huge crowd awaited them in the stadium of Mexico City and many of us went to meet them quite a distance out. One of the men dropped out after running fifty-six kilometers because of an old lesion in his knee;

otherwise the doctors found him perfectly all right. The remaining two runners arrived at the stadium at 12:42 P.M., having made a distance of 100 kilometers or sixty-two miles in nine hours and thirty-seven minutes, with thirty minutes out for pinole, water and other necessities. They were in perfect condition upon their arrival and continued running around the stadium track.

The public was amazed at the prowess of the runners and even more so when the papers reported that there were better ones at home. One of them was called "The Tiger of the Sierra"; he had run for three consecutive days that same year, near Norogachic, Chihuahua, covering a distance of 300 kilometers, or 186 miles, of mountainous country.

The Tarahumaras do not measure their running time in long races by the clock, but by the evolution of the heavenly bodies. For an approximate twelve-hour race, they say from sun to moon; if it continues, then it is from sun to moon to sun to moon, and so on.

Two years after the run from Pachuca, four Tarahumaras were brought to Mexico City for the National Marathon trial races for the Olympic games that were to take place in Amsterdam that year. They had been selected from thirty-five who had been tried out in their own region in the mountains of Chihuahua and had made the twenty-six-mile Marathon in two hours, forty-nine minutes over broken ground. It had been difficult to get them together for the tryouts, as many would run away to hide when they saw the white men approaching their villages.

In the Mexico City trials, the four Tarahumaras easily won the first four places against thirty contestants from other sections of the country. After much persuasion José Torres and Aurelio Terrozas, two of the four winners, were induced to join the Mexican contingent for Amsterdam. The task of convincing them was especially difficult, as it had to be done through an interpreter. They feared they would not be safe on the wide river that took "seven suns and seven moons to cross."

The Tarahumaras, like all the other indigenous races still existing in Mexico, do not lose their dignity in the presence of the white man and his civilization. José and Aurelio very soon behaved as if they were accustomed to beds and other modern conveniences. In New York they were taken around to see the sights; they were impressed but said they did not like the city, because "the streets were like their ravines, the sun never hitting the bottoms."

Everyone on the ship was interested in José and Aurelio, the girls especially, for they were good-looking, well-built young men. In the daytime they would train and study Spanish, which their University companions were teaching them, but at night they would watch the dancers. One night Aurelio surprised their head coach, by telling him shyly that he would like to dance. Their monosyllabic conversation was somewhat as follows:

"Jefe, I want to dance."

"Yes, Aurelio, with whom?"

"Girl," he answered with an expressive look.

"Which girl?"

"Blue girl," pointing to a blonde across the room in a blue evening dress.

When Aurelio was presented to the blue girl, she accepted his invitation with delight. Aurelio was so perfectly at ease and danced so well that the other couples left them the floor, forming a circle to watch and applaud.

José and Aurelio lost the first places in the twenty-five mile race at Amsterdam by three minutes, the winner having made it in two hours, thirty-six minutes and some seconds. Their comment was, "Too short; too short!" [2]

Upon their return to Mexico City, José and Aurelio were asked what they wanted to take back with them to the mountains. After discussing the matter, according to native custom, they asked for iron plows; they had noticed in their travels that the iron ones cut deeper and turn the soil over better than the wooden plows. They also asked for oxen to pull the iron plow since it was too heavy for a man. When they were told they could have the plow and oxen and asked what else they wanted, their eyes danced with joy. José wanted a guitar and Aurelio a violin.

The Tarahumaras do not have to train for their races. They are always running somewhere, either between their widely scattered corn patches, or to look for a warm cave in which to spend the winter, or on some errand. Wherever there are gatherings of men, they organize races spontaneously. However, for the big races they make various preparations, and practice with a massive, wooden ball which they kick as they run.

The runners are careful not to be made the victims of black magic, at the same time employing magical devices for their own success. Sometimes a manager, who may be a shaman, goes to a burial cave with two balls to be used in the race. He takes out a bone from the right leg of the skeleton, the tibia whenever possible. Putting it on the ground, he places before it a jar of tesgüino and some dishes of food. On each side of the vessels he places one of the balls; in front, a cross. The offering is to the dead person, so that he may help by weakening the opponents of the one making it. Human bones are sometimes buried along the race course, where the men of the opposing team will have to run over them, for it is believed that they produce fatigue. The man burying the bones is careful not to touch them with his fingers, lest they dry up.

Sometimes herbs are thrown into the air to weaken opponents, or some outsider may sell the Tarahumaras an expensive white powder for the purpose. However, the evil effects of anything used may be offset with counter-remedies, so in the end either side, without knowing it, has to win the race by actual running.

A shaman is always employed to prepare the runners. He rubs them with herbs and smooth stones to give strength, and makes passes over them to ward off sorcery, and the day before the races he performs a curing ceremony. He puts the water the runners will drink on a blanket under a cross; food, remedies, and various magical objects and a lighted candle at each side. The herbs are tied up in bags, as otherwise they would break away because they are so strong. The runners bring their balls and form a semi-circle around the cross. Then the shaman standing in front of them sings songs about the tail of the gray fox and others, as he blows incense over them. He also warns them not to accept food or drink from anyone but their relatives as a precaution against witchcraft. Afterwards the runners drink three times of the water and strengthening remedies, and their head runner leads them in a ceremonial circuit around the cross, going around as many times as there are circuits in the race they are to run. When the ceremony is ended, the shaman questions each one as to whether he has kept to his diet, eating only deer, rabbit, rat, turkey or chaparralcock meats, which are considered good for winning a race. The men are also questioned as to whether they have abstained from sex. That night they all sleep together around the cross to see that nothing under it is touched. As a precaution against danger while they are asleep, an old man sleeps with them because the old see even in their sleep.

The losing side always attributes to the winning foul means, such as witchcraft or having put injurious herbs into the drinking water. Sometimes a head runner becomes nervous and feigns illness, or someone from the opposing team offers him a bribe of an animal and the race may not come off, but generally it takes place as scheduled.

There are no race tracks but the managers of both sides decide on the terrain and number of miles, which may be run in circuits or back and forth, the course being indicated on trees with crosses or other marks.

The big races are always between two localities, and as many as two hundred men, women, and children gather to bet and follow the fortunes of the runners. As cash has little value to the Tarahumaras, they bet pieces of clothing, houses, land, cattle; the poorest risking their only serapes. The wagers, amounting to thousands of pesos, are left with the managers. As soon as the excitement of the betting is over, everyone is ready to give undivided attention to the race.

The runners, wrapped in their blankets like the rest of the men, mingle with the people, but they take nothing but pinole and tepid water, and in the morning their legs are rubbed with warm water.

Near the starting point a number of stones, corresponding to the number of circuits to be run, are placed, and one is removed after each circuit. Both sides appoint men to observe that all the rules are followed. Pregnant women are kept out of the gathering, as a runner may become heavy by merely rubbing against their blankets. Also, drunks are shunned.

When everything is ready, the gobernador exhorts both sides not to cheat and not to touch the ball with their hands, else they will go to hell. Then the signal is given. The men throw off their blankets. One man from each side throws the ball as far as he can, and all start after it. Another ball is always at hand, should the first one get lost.

The opposing sides are distinguished by headbands of different colors. The runners sometimes paint their faces and legs with white chalk and for speed adorn themselves with bird feathers, those of the macaw and peacock being preferred; they also wear deer-hoof rattles tied on a strip of leather for the same reason, as well as for the purpose of keeping themselves awake with the noise of the rattling.

The men run steadily mile after mile, followed by their friends who urge them on and tell them where the ball is so that there is no time lost in looking for it. The women of the racers hold out gourds of pinole and warm water for them for rapid refreshment, and throw water over their shoulders.

When night falls, the audience scattered along the heights near the race course keep bonfires burning while the friends accompanying the runners carry resinous pine torches. As the circuits are of many miles, the silence and darkness are broken only every few hours with the passing of the racers. Some of them have to drop out. Then the excitement increases. In the end only one or two may be left. The winner receives nothing but praise, which is sweet to him when it comes from certain women. However, the winners of bets make presents to him and to his father.

Sometimes old men's races take place before the strenuous ones of the young. These receive much attention. Women also run races; their distances are shorter and their speed is less, but the betting and excitement are great. The women do not kick the ball with their toes but toss it with a two-pronged stick. Sometimes, instead of a ball, they use rings made of yucca leaves which they throw with a curved stick. They run in their ordinary long skirts, lifting them to cross a creek or waterhole.[3]

There are numerous other regional games and sports of various types, some of them variations of patolli or *quince* or versions of golf and hockey. The Yaquis of Sonora play one called palillo, in which they use a stick similar to a golf club. Five or eight form a team. Both sides decide on the number of players and the distance between them, usually twenty or thirty meters. The opposing teams begin to play at the same time at each end. The side whose ball first reaches the goal in the middle, wins.

The Tarascans of the highlands of Michoacán have their own version of *quince* and play a game similar to hockey. The Tarascan name for this game is uaukuni and it is played from December to carnival time, when the men have most free time. There are two teams of unspecified numbers. A ball is made of rags or cord, the latter wound around a white substance secreted by the green worms of the madrone tree. The game, beginning at a street intersection, is played around a block of the town. The two teams line up at the starting point, each player holding a stick. A man from each team stands in the middle of the intersection. As the ball is thrown into the air by one of them, every player tries to knock it toward his own side. The team that takes the ball all around the block to where it was first thrown, wins.

The Spanish Jai-alai game, called frontón in Mexico, was a popular public spectacle in Mexico City until betting was forbidden in 1934. However, it is still played everywhere by many of the well-to-do in their own private courts.

Those who play frontón professionally throw the ball against a wall with a curved wicket basket, extending the hand into a leather glove attached to the handle. But the country folk simply throw the ball with bare hands against any convenient wall. This game is similar to our handball. When played well the game is both graceful and exciting.

Cock fights were introduced by the Spaniards and patronized by high society all during the Colonial period, as well as for a long time afterward. As recently as twenty years ago, cock fights were still a social event in Taxco, Guerrero. Both the people and the cocks were dressed up for the fights.

Since the ban on gambling in the Federal District, cock fights are no longer held publicly, but they still take place elsewhere in the country, especially during fiestas.

An old game of chance, still fairly popular, is la lotería or lottery. It began to be played in Mexico in the last half of the eighteenth century—at first only in high social circles but later by all classes.

THE GAME OF JAI-ALAI

At most village fairs, on Saturdays and holidays wherever the people gather to amuse themselves, there is generally a lottery game going on. This is quite like our Bingo game. There are men who make a business of it and transport the necessary equpiment from place to place. It consists of a booth with two long wooden boards used as tables and benches. In the middle are a table or shelves for the display of the prizes and room for one or two persons to move about. Anyone who wishes to play sits down at the table, pays five or ten centavos or whatever the charge is, and is given a card with corn seeds or beans with which to mark the places.

The Mexican version of the game consists of having pictures instead of numbers on the cards. These usually are painted by folk artists. Some of them are conventional, such as a key, a ladder, dice, an animal or a type like "Uncle Ferruco in the Alameda." The man who calls off the names always says something first in prose or rhyme to indicate what it is, as for example:

Those of St. Peter—The Keys!
It is best not to shake them—The dice!
How you stretch—The giraffe!

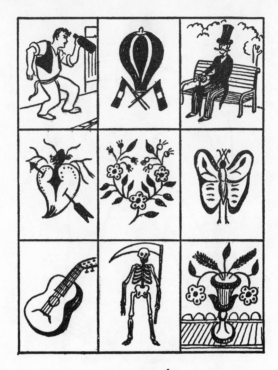

LA LOTERÍA

The scorpion of Durango neither sucks nor goes to the fandango—The
    scorpion!
Oh, how ugly you are, godmother—Death!
Where pretty girls look at themselves—The mirror!

It is this manner of calling off the pictures that makes the game
amusing; it can even be exciting when a clever man is doing it, en-
livening his cries with comments and jokes of double meaning, inventing plays on words and making allusions to well-known persons.

There are regional versions of the pictures on the cards and the
cries describing them. In Oaxaca they use poetic verses, inspired by
love, jealousy, or malice, but always gay and amusing:

"Don Ferruco es un catrín   Don Ferruco is a dude,
Que viste de sobretodo   Who wears an overcoat.
Y al dar la vuelta en la esquina   Upon turning a corner
Se fue de hocico en el lodo.   His snoot hit the mud.

        ¡El Ferruco!   —The youth

El Barco va navegando
Y en medio las tres Marías;
Ya no es tu amor como era antes
Que encantado me tenía;
Ahora es como el comerciante
Que viene cada ocho días—

¡El Barco!

Soy el diablo y he llegado
Aunque no me pueden ver;
No vengo pidiendo fiado
Ni tampoco de comer.

¡El diablo!

De lo verde del nopal
Lo que me gusta es la vena;
No hay bocado tan sabroso
Como la mujer ajena,
Que aunque se come sin sal
A todas horas es buena.

¡El nopal!

Ya viene la luna hermosa
Rodeada de campanitas.
¡Qué dichosas son las madres
Que tienen hijas bonitas!
Que las encomienden a Dios
Y a mi las ánimas benditas . . .

¡La luna!

The boat goes on sailing;
In the middle the three Marys.
Your love is not as before
When it had me enchanted;
Now it is like the merchant
Who comes every eight days.

—The boat!

I'm the devil and I'm here
Although you hate me;
I don't come asking credit
Nor anything to eat.

—The devil!

Of the green prickly-pear
I like best the veins;
There is no morsel so savory
As someone else's wife,
Which although eaten without
   salt,
Is always good.

—The nopal!

The beautiful moon is coming
Surrounded by little bells.
How fortunate are the mothers
Who have pretty daughters!
May they commend them to God,
The blessed souls, and to me!

—The moon!

There are innumerable such verses, which seem to have no connection with the picture, but the people like them because they express something they want to hear.[4]

CHARREADAS AND BULLFIGHTING

The two outstanding national sports are horseback riding and bullfighting. Both were introduced by the Spaniards immediately after the Conquest.

Originally, the Spaniards got their horses and learned to ride from the Arabs; in Mexico the Spanish horses, their equipment, riding costumes, and feats were adapted to their new environment. Now the Arabian-Spanish elements are fused into a Mexican figure and sport— the dashing, picturesque charro and his brilliant charreadas, riding stunts.

When the natives first saw the Spaniards on horseback, they thought the man and animal to be of one piece and that they were supernatural beings. But later when they were able to kill them in battle, they became aware of the true nature of the horse.

Seven years after the Conquest, 1528, the Spaniards who had settled in the country, received an order from their rulers, instructing them to raise horses but to take care that the Mexicans should not ride them. For horses were useful in battle, as well as for ostentation. However, on the large cattle-raising estates, the Spaniards found it necessary to employ native vaqueros or herdsmen, and also to permit them to handle and ride their horses. Thus they soon learned to catch and to train wild horses, and became excellent riders.

The horses were so highly valued that when there was insufficient iron for shoeing them, Cortés ordered that silver be used. Soon the Mexican horses began to take on different characteristics from the Spanish. A Spaniard writing about them in 1554, said they were ". . . excellent, agile, tireless and more beautiful than the Spanish horses. . . ."

The Spaniards from the very beginning of their sojourn in Mexico made fortunes in mining and from their immense estates. For their own pleasure and to impress the people they were exploiting, they lavished their wealth on horses, carriages, dress, showing off at bullfights, in riding games, promenades, and processions. In 1623, Felipe IV sent an order forbidding such scandalous public displays. But no one paid any attention to it because the governing group were among the guilty.

At about this time a new social class arose—the mestizo rancheros, ranchers or small landholders. As their chief amusement was riding, they took pride in owning good horses and in riding them well. It was they who modified the Arabian-Spanish saddle to suit the Mexican topography, adding the pommel and changing other details.

The rancheros had plenty of money and nothing to spend it on in the country, so they adorned their horses' harnesses with silver, and wore suits of rich materials with much embroidery. Some of them so loaded themselves down with adornments, that the people of good taste began calling them charros, which means "loud," "flashy." But the peasants of Salamanca, whose costume was the basis of that worn by the rancheros, are also called charros. Hence the name may have originated in either or both ways.

The rancheros were the first real representatives of the new Mexican race of Spanish-indigenous blood; they were very patriotic and played a leading part in the Revolution for Mexican Independence. They were also the first genuine charros.

The present charro costume is the same as the one evolved and worn in the nineteenth century. It consists of long, tightly-fitted trousers, covering the riding shoes, with straight pockets; many are adorned

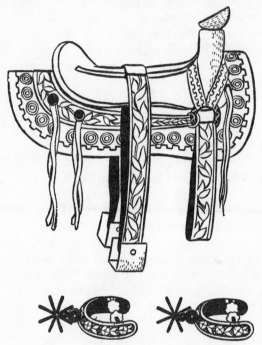

A CHARRO'S SADDLE AND SPURS

with two rows of silver buttons in the form of horses' heads on the outside seam. The guabavera or shirt, is full with long straight sleeves; it is made either of heavy homespun cotton cloth or finer materials, such as linen—the color of the guaba—some are discreetly embroidered. They are worn either inside the belt or with long ends tied in front. The classical tie is of the same weave and design as the rebozo, but is often of silk, tied in a flowing bow. A short cloth jacket, sometimes homespun, is worn on all gala occasions, generally embroidered or trimmed with braid.

The charro sombrero is either of felt or heavily woven palm, with a high crown and wide brim, sometimes rolled either in front or back or both, as in Jalisco. It is sometimes embroidered or appliquéd, and worn with a toquilla or a band of some kind, often of handwoven horsehair.

The charros wear handsome wide leather belts, carved, appliquéd, or embroidered with heavy white, silver or golden thread. They have places for cartridges and a holster for a pistol, without which a charro never rides. Some have an inner lining for money. The charros' shoes are made of fine leather in one piece, tightly fitted and pointed.

To complete his costume, the charro wears a serape folded and thrown over the right shoulder, or strapped to the saddle.

The suits of the ranchero charros are of good strong homespun materials, with very little adornment.

The charros have good harness—some of the saddles are handsomely carved, the bridles and stirrups adorned with silver. Some of the spurs are very handsomely engraved and adorned with gold as well as with silver.

There are three classes of charros: (1) the gentleman charro of the cities and country; (2) the professional charro, for whom a new field has been recently opened in the movies; (3) the vaquero charro or herdsman, who takes care of and trains the horses.

The first and second classes have their own organizations. That of the first is called La Asociación Nacional de Charros, of which there are about thirty-five groups in the country.

The vaquero charros are the descendants of the natives who began inventing charreadas immediately after the Conquest. They used to catch the wild horses, lassoing them with ropes by the tail and legs, then train them for their masters. From this class come most of the professionals; also the cowboys, for when Texas was annexed to the United States, the Mexican vaqueros became cowboys.

The women riders are called charras, those of the cities wearing the China Poblana costume. This consists of a long full green flannel skirt with a red yoke, trimmed with sequins; a white embroidered shirt worn inside the skirt; a folded rebozo over the shoulders, crossed in front; red ribbon bows in the hair; red or green slippers. But the charras modify it by wearing a man's sombrero and over the shoulder a serape instead of the rebozo. The country charras wear their usual regional dress. All of them use a sidesaddle but many are splendid riders. A few are able to compete with the men in their most daring stunts, even to bullfighting on horseback.

A formal jaripeo or rodeo is always attended by many China Poblanas—some of them charras and others merely wearing the costume. After the lassoing and other stunts on the program are finished, the band strikes up a Jarabe Tapatío, the national folkdance. A charro and a China Poblana perform it, he spinning a rope throughout the entire dance.

Aside from the jaripeos, the charros always take part in fiestas, performing stunts which they call juegos or games. One which used to be popular in Colonial times is still played by the rancheros with very little variation. It is called carrera de cintas, a ribbon race, or correr las argollas, to run the rings.

A wire is strung across the track between two posts at half the length of it. The ribbons are hooked to it, each one wound around a reel at the end of which a small ring is attached. The hook comes off

CORRER LAS ARGOLLAS
RUNNING THE RINGS

easily, provided the rider can get the point of his machete or a stick through the ring as he rushes past at full speed—not an easy stunt.

It is customary to invite the most attractive girls of the place to act as godmothers or queens. They contribute the ribbons that are on the rings and that serve as prizes for the winners.

On the day of the race they sit together in a box, looking their prettiest. The charros are also at their best for the occasion. They take turns. When one of them succeeds in getting a ring off, he holds it up high to show that he got it off legitimately, the ribbon floating gaily in the air. The people shout and applaud; the band plays Dianas, the Spanish piece of applause. He approaches the queen's box and hands his trophy to the judge who tells him to whom the ribbon belongs. Then he takes his hat off with a sweeping gesture and kneels at her feet to receive the ribbon. It often happens, as if by coincidence, that the girl is the one of his heart's desire. The truth of the matter is that the judge, usually an old charro, has whispered a little secret in his ear, so that he knew which ring to try to make.

The ranchero charros play other games which are not so beautiful nor romantic as the carrera de cintas but are very exciting. A popular one is correr el gallo, run the cock. One of the riders takes a cock in his hand and extending his arm, rushes off at full speed; the others chase after him to try to take it away. The successful one receives a prize. A dove is sometimes used for the same purpose, and the riders try to take it away as they rush to meet the charro holding it. Sometimes roosters or hens are buried in the ground up to their necks and the charros try to pick them up as they gallop past; they also hang up roosters like the rings and try to pluck their feathers.

The great mass of charros are Catholics and the majority are superstitious. They harness their horses from the left side and trace a cross on the animal's back with the saddle, and cross themselves before beginning a dangerous feat. Some put certain herb plasters on their temples, believing that they make the horses lighter. A charro who leaves his hat on a bed will have bad luck.

The charros also believe that they have better luck with horses of certain colors. The alazán-tostado—a golden brown—is very popular. Another favorite is the tordillo-carbonero—a color in which the spots look like charcoal stains. A black horse must have white spots; otherwise, he will become unmanageable or blind when affected by a full moon. There are sayings about the colors: "Caballo alazán-tostado, primero muerto que cansado," "the alazán-tostado dies before he tires." "Caballo moro, ni de oro," "a wine-colored horse, not even of gold."

The country charros use the typical Mexican horses—short, broad, with thin legs, that climb mountain sides like goats and from which they can get bulls by the tail more easily; taller ones are used for lassoing other animals.

These horses are very intelligent. They learn to enter a cantina and to drink with their masters, to dance to music with them; they become acquainted with their habits—the roads they take, so that they do not lose their way when their riders fall asleep; the houses they visit. The last trait sometimes gets the charros into trouble, especially when a jealous woman is on their trail.

Certain regions of the country are noted for their good charros, those from the highlands of Jalisco being outstanding. In September from the sixteenth to the twenty-sixth, they hold a fair in La Unión de San Antonio. The best charros of the region meet there and perform formidable competitive feats.

Since about 1935, the fourteenth of September has been the Day of the Charros. They celebrate it with a picturesque parade and jaripeos. Formerly it used to be on Friday of the Virgin of the Sorrows, the last one in Lent, when they would turn out with their charras to parade along the Viga Canal.

The charros usually take part in parades on national holidays, especially in the cities. They are always given a place at the head of the line, where they lend a note of color and gaiety. When an important personage like the President visits the provinces, the ranchero charros turn out en masse to welcome him, presenting a spectacle of vigor and dash.

The charros are very much admired. They are the Mexican "he-men"—muy hombres.[1]

Bullfighting was introduced immediately after the Conquest and is still popular. It has not only appealed to the Mexicans as a spectacle, but has influenced their ethnography. The passes with the cape are imitated in various folk dances, and everywhere men and boys play at bullfighting.

For over a century there were no regular bullfight seasons. The first fight was put on August 13, 1529, the day of San Hipólito, to celebrate the taking of the Aztec capital in 1521. Afterwards bullfights became a feature of all celebrations, religious and profane— the canonization of a saint, the arrival of a new Viceroy, the birthdays of the Spanish monarchs and princes, the queen giving birth to a child, the coronation of a king, a peace treaty between Spain and some other country, the news that a shipment of gold and silver sent from Mexico had reached Spain safely, and finally to raise funds for charitable institutions and the royal treasury.

During that same period the art of bullfighting was in a state of evolution. The first bullfighters wore beautiful costumes and were quick at avoiding horn-thrusts, but they were not well prepared to defend themselves. Many were hurt and killed.

Until about the middle of the nineteenth century, bullfighting was generally combined with other attractions. Features of the first fights were juegos or games on horseback. One was juego de cañas —two groups of riders attacked one another with cañas, sugar-cane stalks, defending themselves with shields. In another the attacks were with alcancías—hollow clay balls, about the size of an orange, filled with powder, ashes, or flowers. Both games were dangerous and exciting. A third game is the one still played by the charros, but there were no ribbons on the rings and they were picked off with lances; the name, too, was different—the Spaniards used the word sortijas for rings instead of argollas. There was always music, too. In the beginning native musicians were employed, who played flutes, trumpets and drums.

The first bullfights were attended by Spaniards only, among them the nobility with their ladies, and the Archbishop, all dressed in great gala. As there was no ring, the fights took place near the main plaza so that they could be watched from the balconies of the Viceroy's Palace, where refreshments were served.

In time the bullfights became popular with the Mexicans, and all social classes began to attend them. Then boxes and seats were constructed. Also more features of entertainment were added. There were spectacular representations of the battles between the Moors and Christians; races between hares and greyhounds who pursued their prey relentlessly; cock fights. A bullfighter would dress like an inmate of the insane asylum; he would get the bull to go for him and disappear into a pipe. Funny cartoon figures on reed frames, loaded with lead, were put into the ring. When the bulls attacked them, they would topple over but immediately return to a standing position. Tightrope walkers and buffoons, in costume, fought the bulls, jumping over them and playing tricks. A Monte Parnaso, or greased pole, was put up for the common people, with good pieces of cloth, birds of rich plumage, fowl, and animals as prizes. The fights were held mornings, afternoons, and nights, with wonderful fireworks, sometimes lasting several days for important events. From twenty to thirty or more bulls were killed on these occasions. The meat was given to charitable institutions. Bullfighting was so popular that bulls were run and killed between the acts of comedies in the patio of the Coliseo.

About the middle of the seventeenth century, a place called el Volador was conditioned for a bullring; it derived its name from the juego del volador, the flying pole game, which the Aztecs used to play there.

In the last half of the eighteenth century, bullfighting was becoming conventionalized into an art. Professional bullfighters had come from Spain, and the Mexicans were acquiring great skill. Some fought on horseback and others on foot. There were some few women among them. At that time, too, the bullfights were put on as spectacles in themselves, and there were seasons.

The most important bullfights held outside of Mexico City were those to celebrate the coronation of Carlos IV, in 1790. They were the most brilliant ever held in the capital and the provinces tried to emulate them. In some the natives took part, playing their music and performing gorgeous indigenous dances. In Tehuantepec there were twenty-seven groups, one in which ten youths wore tilmas of gold and silver cloth and crowns set with fine pearls, precious stones, and rich plumes.

The style of the costume of the modern torero or matador, the bullfighter, is the same as in the days of Goya, over one hundred years ago. It consists of short, skin-tight trousers, a fine white linen shirt, a handsome hand-embroidered jacket, pink stockings, black ballet shoes, and a montera or pointed black hat. The coleta or braid of false hair is worn as part of the costume as well as to protect the base of the skull. A short cape is carried over the arm for the entry. The suit, called traje de luz, is made of very heavy silk and padded; it weighs eighteen pounds and is made for protection as well as for show. The first ones were homemade; some of them still are, but

TORERO OR MATADOR

the stars order theirs from Spain at exorbitant prices. The peones or helpers of the toreros wear the cast-offs of their masters, who sport new ones often.

The ritual rigorously followed in the fight is as ancient as the style of the costumes. First the man representing the Spanish alguacil or constable—dressed in black suit, short cape, hat with a plume—enters the ring on a spirited horse. He approaches the box of the autoridades or judges, takes his hat off to ask permission for the fight to begin. The judge waves a white handkerchief in assent. The rider then backs his horse out of the ring and returns leading the paseo de las cuadrillas, the promenade of the crews. The toreros walk abreast, each followed by his own cuadrilla of two or three peones and two picadores on horseback. Last come the ring attendants, called mono-sabios, or wise monkeys, in white suits with red caps and sashes. They drive the mules that remove the slain bulls. As soon as the parade disbands all leave the ring. The bugle sounds and the bull is admitted.

PICADOR AND MONOSABIO

As the bull rushes in, he is incited by helpers from opposite sides of the ring to give the torero the opportunity to judge his speed and method of attack. Then the torero begins a series of graceful passes with his big red and yellow cape, the first of which are called Veronicas after the woman who washed Christ's face. They always end with a downward sweep over the bull's face.

Next enter the picadores in heavily padded suits to protect them from the bull's horns. The horses are covered with a peto or padded blanket for the same purpose. When the bull attacks the horse, the picador pushes him off by planting the pic—a long pole with a short barb—in the heavy shoulder muscle. Each bull has to charge the horses three times, and each torero in turn takes him away with a series of passes called *quites*. It is in these that the toreros do their fanciest cape work, each one trying to excel the other in the beauty and daring of his passes, some of them becoming classics and bearing the names of their inventors.

If a bull is unsound or cowardly or refuses to fight, the crowd demands that he be taken out and another substituted. This fault is usually obvious as soon as he enters the ring and he must be taken out before he charges a horse. To remove the bull from the ring, trained oxen are brought in who surround him and lead him out.

After the *quites* are finished the bugle sounds for the banderilleros to come to place the banderillas—short gaily adorned sticks with a small hook at one end that pierces the skin and hangs on. The banderillero incites the bull to make him charge in his direction, as he leaps into the air as if on wings, leaving a pair of banderillas in the thick shoulder muscle to the left of the center. There are toreros who place their own with great skill and beautiful movements.

After three pairs of banderillas have been placed in the thick shoulder muscle left of center, as close together as possible, the bugle announces the faena or kill—the last and most dramatic phase of the fight. The torero usually dedicates the bull to some important personage, throwing him his montera. Occasionally he honors all the spectators, in which case he throws his hat into the middle of the ring. Then he enters the ring alone, holding a light sword in his right hand covered with the muleta, the small blood-red cape. The passes with the muleta to dominate the bull are the most difficult and dangerous. The torero is always close to the horns of the animal, and if he is good, he stands solidly on his feet. He may even kneel.

When the torero is ready for the kill, his sword is exchanged for a heavy steel one. He incites the bull with it in his right hand, making the sign of the cross over his left, holding the muleta close to the ground to make the bull lower his head. Then as the bull charges, the torero leaps to meet him, his body poised between the horns for the thrust which sends the sword into the small area between the shoulder blades and the heart. When the plunge is made in the right place, the bull falls down and a helper gives him the descabello or *coup de grâce* with a small dagger. All is over in fifteen minutes.

The whole event lasts two hours, with six bulls and three toreros, each torero killing a bull in order of seniority. Sometimes there is a mano a mano, a hand-to-hand, between two star toreros, with three bulls for each one. In the competitions for the golden and silver ears there is only one bull for each torero.

Only Mexico City can support two long bullfight seasons. In the summer the novilleros who are preparing to become toreros fight with young bulls, their fights being called novilladas. Those of the toreros are corridas. They begin in October and end at Easter time. Both take place Sunday afternoons at four o'clock—the one function that never fails to begin on time, because the audience is always eagerly watching the clock. Before the fight and between bulls a band plays the gay pasos dobles, the favorite being "La Macarena."

Mexico City now has the new modern Plaza Mexico with fifty thousand seats. They are divided into Sol y Sombra, Sun and Shade, the former being half the price. A corrida with around thirty thousand spectators is not unusual. Among them may be found the highest officials of the Republic as well as bootblacks, women, and children. The aficionados, or professional fans, have formed two groups—porra and contra porra. They sit in Sol on opposite sides of the ring, each having their own favorite toreros, and furnish a lot of fun with their heckling.

Practically the whole audience are fans. Bullfighting is in their blood, and they grow wild with excitement when the torero is excellent, fluttering white handkerchiefs as a sign that they want the judge to reward him with an ear and sometimes also the tail and both ears. But when a torero is clumsy and shows fear, no matter how popular he may be, the fans hurl insults and cushions at him. When all the fighters and bulls have been bad, they start bonfires on the stairs as a sign of protest.

A bullfight is a brilliant and exciting spectacle with elements of beauty similar to those of a classical ballet. However, many persons, especially foreigners, cannot enjoy them because they are sorry for the bull. The aficionados protest that bulls for the ring have a much better and freer life than those for the slaughter house; that when they are angry and fighting they do not feel the short-lived pain inflicted on them during the fifteen minutes of the fight; that often they wound a torero—sometimes mortally, so the fight is not all one sided.

Toreros have to go through long years of training, some of them beginning as youngsters. They fight first as novilleros in the off-season fights, during which time they secure the protection of a torero as padrino. When the novillero is about to take his alternative, or kill his first bull, as a full-fledged torero, the ceremony consists of his padrino's giving him an embrace and handing him his sword and muleta.

The life of a torero in the ring depends on his success, health, and other circumstances. If all is favorable, it may last for twenty years. When he is ready to retire, the despedida or leave-taking ceremony takes place, which is always fraught with emotion. Friends bring flowers, wreaths with "Adiós" and his name on them, bouquets, confetti, a live cock or doves. And all the time the torero is killing his last bull, the band plays "Las Golondrinas," the traditional farewell song. At the end, someone close to the torero cuts off his coleta.

There are several cattle-raising ranches in the State of Mexico that specialize in breeding and training bulls for the ring. They are well cared for, and each one has a name, which appears in the ring together with that of the hacienda they come from. Some haciendas are specially noted for good bulls.

The toreros, whose work is dangerous to the point of death, are very religious and superstitious. They always pray before entering the ring, either at home or in the chapel at the ring, to La Macarena, who is their protectress. Before starting anything in the ring, they cross themselves, and some receive applause with a rosary in their hands. Often toreros make a point of visiting the grave of a beloved person the morning of the corrida and are careful to blow out themselves the veladora or light they have left on the altar before going to the ring. When a torero is fighting away from home, his parents keep a special light for him on the household altar.

Toreros, like charros, believe that some animals are luckier than others. When they are dressing for the fight, they will not have certain persons around who are supposed to be unlucky; they will say, "Put that one out; he has ashes." Women are also kept away at such times and must not put on any of the garments to be worn in the corrida. Leaving the montera on the bed is unlucky. Thirteen toreros or bulls in a ring is bad luck, as is anything that suggests death—the advertisement of a funeral agency in the ring, the sight of a skull or skeleton, to fight on a date on which a companion has been killed, meeting a cross-eyed person. Toreros do not like fighting on rainy or windy afternoons because the rain chills the spirits of the spectators and the wind makes the fighting difficult.

In many village fiestas the tradition of having bulls is still preserved. They are run, ridden, lassoed, made passes at, but not killed. However, in some places they have real bullfights in which a few of the old tricks are played to entertain the people.

Sometimes a man will represent the old tancredo figures of cartoons by standing perfectly still in the ring. As the bull only sees moving objects, he does not attack him. Such a person may wear a black robe with white lines painted to make the figure look like a skeleton. Then the people say the bull does not touch him because he respects death.

Another trick is called la suerte de la rosa. A torero carries a paper rose on a little hook, holding it behind his back until the bull is close to him, when he hangs it on his forehead. La suerte de la garocha consists of jumping over the bull with the help of a garocha or goading stick, which affords the bull a good opportunity for a horn-thrust. In la manola the torero lies on his back, with his feet in the air, supporting a clay jar filled either with lime, plaster, flowers, doves or confetti. When the bull attacks, the jar is broken and the contents fly at him, as the torero turns a somersault, landing on his feet. Some stick oranges on the bull's horns or put in a banderilla with their teeth.

Sometimes a torero comes from Portugal to perform in the Mexico

City ring on horseback. Recently, Conchita Citrón, a good-looking young girl, born in Uruguay, now living in Peru, has fought there on horseback, though killing the bull on foot. She was a sensation, especially as a rider.

When the Spanish colony of Mexico City have their annual cor-

LA SUERTE DE LA GAROCHA
JUMPING OVER THE BULL

rida on September 8, called the Covadonga, there is a parade of "queens"—pretty girls in elegant Spanish mantillas. They ride around the ring in automobiles before the fight starts, and sit together in a box. It is always a gay affair, a little reminiscent of colonial times.

When the Mexico City Stadium was constructed in 1923, one of its purposes was to offer counter attractions to bullfighting. Athletics and outdoor sports are practiced much more now than at that time, but bullfighting is still very popular.[2]

PLATES

1. A Huichol from Las Juntas, Nayarit, adorned for the peyote ceremony. His face is painted with the yellow root brought from Zacatecas, where a pilgrimage is made every year to bring back the peyote.

3. A singing shaman with his ceremonial chair and primitive drum, always decorated for fiestas. The Huichol songs to the pagan gods are always sung to the accompaniment of a drum. *El Aire, Nayarit.*

2. A Cora in "The Dance of the Bows." The costumes are colorful and the dance rhythmic, with bows, rattles, and strings of bamboo around the skirts. *San Pablo, Nayarit.*

4. A Huichol shaman in his ceremonial costume — plumes, hairband, cape, bags, bracelets. No other Indian men in Mexico dress so extravagantly. *Huilotita, Jalisco.*

5. Huichol participants in a squash fiesta. The shaman has his plumes, and a boy is carrying the horns of a bull that was sacrificed at dawn. *El Limón, Nayarit.*

6. The Cora Dance of the Palms. The dancers' headdresses are adorned with flowers and tropical feathers, the white cotton on their tips being a prayer for rain. *Jesús María, Nayarit.*

8. A Huichol family camping on the Chapalagana River near Huaynamota, Nayarit. The rope chains worn by the young mother are of fine blue and white beads. Babies are carried on the hip.

7. One of the campers of the group on the Chapalagana River. The Huichols use the bow and arrow exclusively in hunting deer and other game, and are excellent marksmen.

9. A morning dance after a night of singing. *Huilotita, Jalisco.*

10. A Huichol mother and children. *Huilotita, Jalisco.*

11. Playing and singing is a favorite Huichol pastime. *Tuxpan, Jalisco.*

12. A Huichol house on stilts. *Near Tuxpan, Jalisco.*

13. Preparing the Huichol ceremonial corn beer. *El Limón, Nayarit.*

14. An offering to the rising sun. Fiesta, *Huilotita, Jalisco.*

15.   The mitote, a primitive musical instrument of the Coras in Nayarit.

16.   A Cora Indian altar. *Village of San Juan Corapan, Nayarit.*

18. A young Huichol girl of Huilotita, showing how water is carried in the double gourds. The forms of these gourds are used in various stylized designs on woolen handwoven belts worn by the men.

17. Huichol women of Huilotita with the pictures of the saints lent them from the church at Tuxpan, Nayarit, for their fiesta. It was given to implore the help of the gods to cure their sick.

19. A Huichol making "god-eyes" for the prayers of his family. They are formed with colored crewel on bamboo frames and symbolize the eyes of the gods invoked in prayer. *La Mesa, Nayarit.*

20. One of the pascolas of the Deer Dance of the Mayo village of Masiaca, Sonora. He wears a mask to dance to the music of flute and drum, and takes it off when dancing to violins and harp. Rattles, bells, and strings of dried cocoons add to the rhythm.

21. One of the old ahuehuete or sabine trees. This one is believed to be sacred, and the natives bring offerings to it—crosses with flowers, cigarettes, candles, and other objects. There are many such trees in the Republic. *Sahuaral, Sonora.*

22. A Yaqui pascola. The Yaquis and Mayos are neighbors in the State of Sonora, and their Deer Dance is the same.

23. A deer-dancer of the Yaqui regiment at Tlaxcala. He also dances to drum and flute. The three men sing in falsetto to the accompaniment of scrapers.

24. Tarahumara Indian.

25. A Tarahumara couple from the Sierra of Chihuahua, showing their typical dress. The men usually wear homespun wool blankets of dark natural wool colors.

26. Seri medicine men who have been praying all night long to cure a patient, with their little wooden images, which they believe are endowed with supernatural power.

28. A Seri woman wearing a cloth on her head, and beads. Only women paint their faces, each having her favorite design, which she executes with great artistry. Favorite colors are red, white, blue, and ochre. *Desemboque.*

27. A Seri musician with his unique one-stringed violin, showing oriental influence in its shape. The Seris are a music-loving people. Men, women, boys, and girls all sing.

30. Seri Indian of Bahía. A married woman paints her face in green.

29. Seri Indian of Bahía. A girl uses black paint on her face.

31. A Seri woman. The women wear simple cotton dresses, sometimes of plain brilliant colors, and paint their faces. They are generally tall and slender.
Desemboque, Sonora.

32. A Tehuana wearing her huipil of white lace, used to cover the head for church especially. Most of the women of the region wear them instead of rebozos.

33. One of the old-time charro hats of Tehuantepec, Oaxaca. In some regions of this state, the men wear felt instead of straw hats. Usually they are black with high pointed crowns and narrow rolled brims.

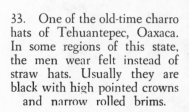

35. Mixtec women from Pinotepa Nacional, Oaxaca, visiting the regional State Fair, at Oaxaca City. They often cover their heads with their huipils and show their handwoven wool skirts with crosswise stripes in reds.

34. Women from Zacatepec of the Mixteca Baja, Oaxaca, also visiting the fair. Their huipils are of fine white cotton with interwoven and embroidered adornments in red and the skirts of dark homespun wool.

37. A Zapotec woman from the Valley of Oaxaca. She wears a full dark wool homespun skirt, an embroidered shirt, and a long white wool scarf.

36. A Zapotec woman from the village of Yalalag, Oaxaca, in her holiday huipil, wearing a white rebozo on her head in a unique style.

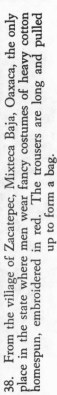

39. A group of Triques from San Andrés Chicahuaxtla, Oaxaca, visiting the State Fair in the Capital. The woman's huipil is of fine white cotton adorned with red, and her skirt of dark homespun wool.

38. From the village of Zacatepec, Mixteca Baja, Oaxaca, the only place in the state where men wear fancy costumes of heavy cotton homespun, embroidered in red. The trousers are long and pulled up to form a bag.

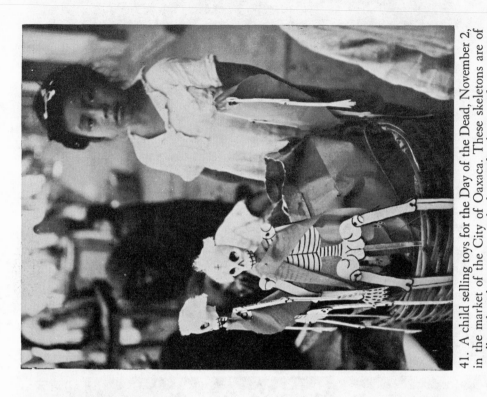

41. A child selling toys for the Day of the Dead, November 2, in the market of the City of Oaxaca. These skeletons are of cardboard with strings attached to make them perform capers.

40. An Aztec girl of the Villa de Guadalupe, posing in a costume worn by the Chinantecs of Valle Nacional, Oaxaca. The huipils here are generally of dark red or purple wool, always richly embroidered.

42. Women from Tehuantepec at the State Fair in Oaxaca City. Their gourd bowls
are filled with toys and sweets and fruit to throw to the public, a typical performance
in their home fiestas.

44. Couple from Choapan, northern Zapotec country, Oaxaca. The girl's costume is simple, but her silver cross and medallions are extraordinary.

43. A Zapotec woman from the village of Santo Tomás, near Oaxaca City, showing a typical costume and petate belt under a red sash.

46. A detail of a very old and elaborate nacimiento or manger. The figures are of clay and the construction of cardboard. A great variety of clay figures is made for Christmas everywhere. *Oaxaca City.*

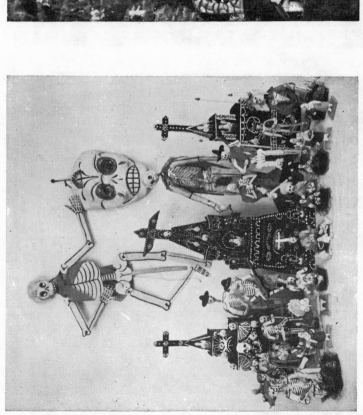

45. A group of toys for the Day of the Dead, November 2, from the Oaxaca City market. They are made of cardboard and painted in black and white. The death motif is found even in candies for this fiesta.

48. A corner of the market in a mountain village. It is held on the plaza, beautifully shaded by Indian laurels. All transactions are in the Zapotec language. *Yalalag, Oaxaca.*

47. Mixe women selling fruit, vegetables and food at the Mogoñé railroad station, Isthmus of Tehuantepec. This is the custom at all Mexican railroad stations, which makes a train trip an interesting adventure.

49. A figure in the Dance of the Conquest, Cuilapan, Oaxaca, taken in Mexico City.

50. A folk dance by men and women from Yalalag, Oaxaca, at a fiesta near Mexico City. Note coiffure of women.

51.   The Dance of the Gardeners of Cuilapan. The dancers are men in red silk dresses.
Oaxaca State Fair.

52.   The clown from the Dance of the Conquest, of Teotitlan del Valle.
Oaxaca State Fair.

53. Dance of the pachecos or herdsmen from the Mixteca. *Oaxaca State Fair*.

54. The Dance of San Marcos from near Villa Alta, Sierra, de Juárez, Oaxaca, at the State Fair, with gay costumes and steps.

55. Typical folk dances on an outdoor stage for the big festival of the Guelaguetza, on El Fortín Hill near Oaxaca City. Guelaguetza means presents in Zapotec, and the fiesta is given to honor important guests.

56. A humorous dance called los huehuenches, from Villa Alta. The dancers play at bullfighting with a papier-maché bull.
Oaxaca State Fair.

57. The Dance of the Tigers from San Marcos, District of Villa Alta. The tigers are little boys, their costumes painted to resemble the tigers' skin. The aim of the dance is to catch the tigers, which the men do with ropes. *Oaxaca State Fair*.

58. A Marriage Dance by Mixtec girls from Santa Caterina Estetla. At one stage in the dance the girls carry the bride on their shoulders. They were a charming group, including the men. *Oaxaca State Fair*.

60. An Aztec girl from Cuetzalán, Puebla, dressed in adult style like her mother, and with her hair done in the same manner.

59. An Aztec girl in a typical costume of the Tehuacán region, State of Puebla. The blouse and skirt are of white cotton cloth.

61. A sophisticated Otomí girl from the State of Mexico wearing one of the handsome black handwoven wool shawls from Hueyapan, Puebla. The embroidery is in brilliant colors.

63. Man from the State of Mexico, wearing one of the small serapes of homespun natural wool colors, typical of the region.

62. A corner of the Toluca market, one of the largest and most interesting markets in the Republic.

64. Two native boys of the Valley of Toluca, State of Mexico, wearing palm-leaf raincoats. They are rain-proof, and are used by men also.

65. Masked dancers from Zacatlán de las Manzanas in the Sierra de Puebla, where the Dance of the Flying Pole also takes place.

66. Pilgrims on the way to the spring fiesta at Chalma, Mexico. The Señor de Chalma is very miraculous, and the devout come from far and wide. One man is carrying a fireworks piece to be burned in his honor.

67. Fiesta in honor of the Señor del Sacromonte, or the Holy Mount, at Amecameca, Mexico, during the first week in Lent, which lasts for several days.

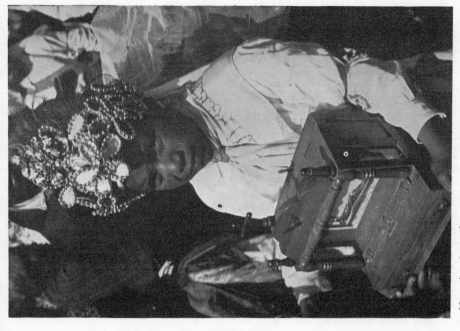

69. An Aztec boy carrying a small image of the Señor del Sacromonte in the procession during the fiesta at Amecameca, first week in Lent.

68. The dance of the santiagos of the Sierra de Puebla, representing the battle of St. James against the heathen. St. James carries the horse.

71. The headdress of one of the acatlaxqui dancers. It consists of a paper cone with brilliant china paper ribbons flowing from the point.

70. Acatlaxqui or reed-throwing dancers of Santa Caterina, Hidalgo. La Marinquilla is represented by a boy in girl's dress.

72. The acatlaxqui dance, with the reeds thrown out and the Marinquilla on the platform.

74. Children are dressed in this fashion, the girls in china poblana costume, for services in the Mexico City Cathedral.

73. Rosita, an officer in a group of conchero dancers of the Federal District. It is the only dance in which adult women may take part.

75. Conchero dancers of the Federal District.

76. A bridal party. The reed mat which serves for a bed is being carried as a symbol of union. *Tuxpan, Jalisco.*

77. A dance of Moors and Christians from Iguala, Guerrero. This state is noted for its excellent and expressive masks.

78. The dance of the tla-cololeros from Chilpancingo, Guerrero; carriers of food to workers in the mines and fields. Costumes are of **burlap.**

79. An Aztec pottery maker. This pottery is unglazed, with a cream-colored background, adorned with primitive designs in dark brown or black.

Zumpango, Guerrero.

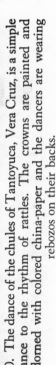

81. A musician of Tantoyuca, a village in the Huasteca mountains of the state of Vera Cruz. He plays the teponaxtli, an Aztec style drum of which there are pre-Conquest examples in the museums.

80. The dance of the chules of Tantoyuca, Vera Cruz, is a simple dance to the rhythm of rattles. The crowns are painted and adorned with colored china-paper and the dancers are wearing rebozos on their backs.

83. A figure of the hunters' dance. To the music of a small teponaxtli. In the background are three clowns, one of them in woman's clothes. Their masks are modern, while the dancers' are primitive. *Tantoyuca.*

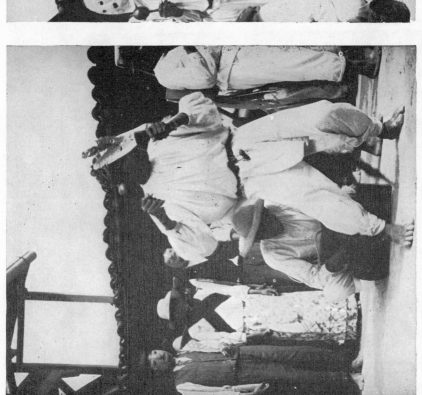

82. A hunters' dance. The dancers wear their ordinary suits, with unique colored paper caps and streamers hanging down their backs. They use gourd rattles and "palms", with feathers. *Tantoyuca.*

84. Participants in the dance of los negritos (little Negroes) of Nahautzín,
Michoacán. They wear black lacquered masks and vari-colored ribbons.

85. The cemetery on the island of Janitzio, Lake Pátzcuaro, Michoacán, after midnight on All Saints' Day.

86. Los viejitos of Michoacán.

87. Carnival. Mexican soldiers in the representation of the battle against the French. *Mexico City*.

88. Los chinelos, a carnival dance. *Tepoztlán, Morelos*.

89. The group of orientals of the Huejotzingo carnival. They are a formidable-looking lot with their black beards and dresses.

90. The headdress of a chinelo at Tepoztlán, Morelos. No two headdresses are alike, but all are fantastic and colorful. The dancers wear long loose satin gowns of different colors over their suits.

91. A soldier of the French regiment taking part in the carnival battle against the bandit Agustín Lorenzo at Huejotzingo, Puebla. Over a thousand men take part, each regiment wearing different costumes.

92. Soldiers of the Apaches at the Huejotzingo
carnival. Their feathered headdresses and skirts are of
bright colors, and each mask is different. The scene is
a riot of color, noise, and music.

93. The bride riding around with the bandits before the wedding. They ride about
the villages pretending to rob the stores.

94. Los paragueros (the men with the umbrellas), a humorous and satirical carnival
dance. *Santa Ana Chautempan, Tlaxcala.*

95. A typical middle-class dining room in the Popular Art Museum at Pátzcuaro, Michoacán, furnished with native handicrafts.

96. A kitchen in the Popular Art Museum at Pátzcuaro. The table, chairs, and dish rack are made by native carpenters, and are typical.

97. The interior of a hut in Guerrero. The picture was taken in the morning unexpectedly, and the room was clean and in order.

98. A corncrib of the State of Morelos, the walls covered with mud plaster. Many are larger and of better materials, but not more attractive.

99. A house in the State of Guerrero, suited to the tropical heat. Some houses are of adobe, which keeps the heat out.

100. Interior of a weaver's hut in Milpa Alta, State of Mexico, showing the type of loom and wheel introduced by the Spaniards.

101. Weaving woolen cloth for a skirt on the horizontal pre-Conquest type of loom, called *telar de otate*.

Ranch near Zitácuaro, Michoacán.

102. A native mason wearing a serape made in Santa Ana Chautempan, Tlaxcala.
It is finely woven; blue background with black and white designs.

103. Upper serape by Mayos of Sonora. Lower serapes by Aztecs of San Miguel de Chiconcuac.

104. Handiwork in weaving and embroidery by Tarascan women.
Nahuatzín, Michoacán.

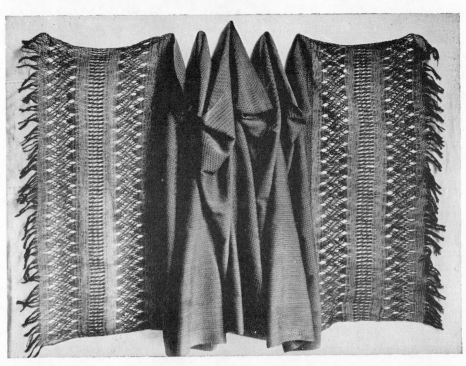

105. A blue-gray rebozo of very fine thread from the famous rebozo-weaving town
of Tenancingo, Mexico.

106. Sombreros everywhere! Innumerable styles; primitive ones most interesting.

107. A variety of interesting sandals for sale, but the salesman is asleep!

108. Beautiful green glazed pottery adorned in relief with stylized animals, flowers, and leaves. *Patamba, Michoacán.*

109. Two lovely old tecomates of unglazed clay, made and decorated by the famous Tarascan potter Amado R. Galván. *Tonalá, Jalisco.*

110. Old gourd bowls. Each color in the design is rubbed in separately with the palm of the hand. *Uruapan, Michoacán.*

111. Some of the black unglazed toys from Coyotepec, Oaxaca, many with whistles.

112. A painted pig from Tlaquepaque, with unique decoration.

113. Some of the delightful clay animals from Tlaquepaque, Jalisco.

114. Primitive unglazed pottery from the State of Guerrero. Cream background with a variety of stylized designs in human, animal, and bird forms.

115. Two Mexican Talavera jars, the covered and uncovered types, made in the City of Puebla. Designs are blue on white.

116. Two types of black glazed censers, made in Puebla and also in the State of Mexico, especially for the Day of the Dead, November 2.

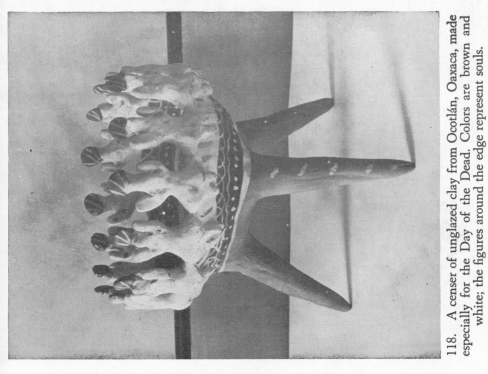

118. A censer of unglazed clay from Ocotlán, Oaxaca, made especially for the Day of the Dead. Colors are brown and white; the figures around the edge represent souls.

117. An elaborate censer of unglazed clay, painted in red, green, and blue, forming a beautiful composition. *Puebla.*

119. Black and green glazed pottery with censers for the Day of the Dead,
November 2. *Patamba, Michoacán.*

120. Hand-hammered copper objects from Santa Clara del Cobre, Michoacán.
Copper is mined there in primitive fashion.

121. Old lacquer trays from Pátzcuaro, Michoacán, forming part of the collection of the Popular Art Museum in that city.

122. Primitive wooden sculptures made in Nahuatzín, Michoacán, where expressive masks are also made.

123. Marionettes representing characters in a religious play, sometimes given at church festivals.

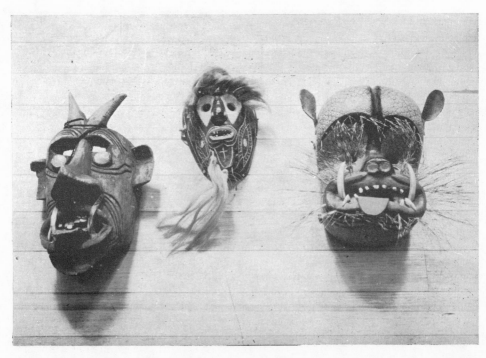

124. Masks from the State of Guerrero, where primitive dances are performed with a great variety of animal masks.

Milagro que hizo el Sto Niño de Atocha a Jesus Garamillo estando en la Mina de Sn José de
Gracia trabajando con otros Señores, sin salir por el agua que reventó del Crusero Biejo, estando
todo el noches se en comendo con todo Corazon y salieron sanos y por tan potentoso
milagro dedica este retablo recuerdo en 23 de ... 1897

125.   A votive offering to the saint who averted an accident in a mine in Guanajuato.
Painted on tin.

En el mes de Julio del año 1838, D. Mariana Carrasco, Enfermó peligrosamente de
una maligna fiebre nerviosa que por momentos aumentaba su gravedad; en ese estado su
familia llena de confianza invocó con el fervorosamente à la Milagrosa Imajen del
Señor de la SALUD, y en breves dias el enfermo cobro la salud.

126.   A votive offering painted in oil on canvas in gratitude to the saint that cured
the sick one.

127. Paintings on a pulquería by art students of Frida Kahlo Rivera. *Coyoacán, Federal District.*

128. Popular marionettes — kings of death and hell — made of scraps by a poor old woman of Mexico City to sell on the streets.

129. A procession bringing offerings to the church in X-Cacal, where the people pray to both pagan gods and Christian saints.

130. Maya leaders of the X-Cacal group of Quintana Roo, one military and one spiritual.

131. Two Maya women who, like others, resemble the sculptures on Maya ruins.

132. A Maya woman of Yucatán, who is a descendant of the historical Xius and is called "Princess Xiu." Her huipil is of the ordinary type.

133. A Maya woman from the X-Cacal group, in holiday huipil and jewels.

135. A Lacandón drinking from a water gourd.

134. A Lacandón medicine man working magic in a cave.

136. A Tzotzil of Zinacantán, near Las Casas, Chiapas. Both men and women of
this village are fine physical types, slender and elegant.

137. Chamula, a village near Las Casas, Chiapas, where the Chamulas from the parajes attend church and celebrate fiestas.

138. A Chamula woman from the village near Las Casas. Her huipil and skirt are of heavy black home-spun and the tassel of red silk.

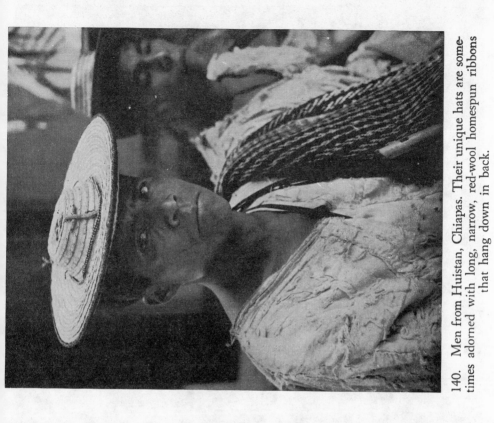

139. Tzeltzales from Tenajapa, Chiapas. They wear short white cotton suits under their serapes, some of them beautifully embroidered.

140. Men from Huistan, Chiapas. Their unique hats are sometimes adorned with long, narrow, red-wool homespun ribbons that hang down in back.

141. Three Tzeltzal musicians from Tenajapa. These three instruments are the usual ones of this region; they are of home manufacture.

142. Zoque dancers of Tuxtla Gutiérrez, who dance to the music of several small drums and a flute. Their trousers are of red bandannas, and their hats are adorned with peacock feathers.

144. A white dress from Chiahuatlán, State of Vera Cruz, with full skirt and elaborately embroidered blouse.

143. Two Totonac women in primitive style dress of modern materials. *Papantla, Vera Cruz.*

145. Two Totonac girls of Papantla wearing their holiday **huipils**.

146. Showing how the pole for the Flying Pole Dance is being dragged into Papantla. A new pole is set up each year, and it takes weeks to find and bring one in.

148. All the dancers on the pole at Pahuatlán, with one dancing in the center. Each one dances in turn and does homage to the four winds.

147. Climbing the pole at Pahuatlán. The ropes or cables are always carefully fastened.

149.   The Flying Pole Dance at Pahuatlán, State of Puebla. Here there are six
dancers, and their costumes are different from the Papantla.

151. The clown of the dance of the Moors and Christians of Papantla, wearing a wooden mask.

150. The captain of the voladores at Papantla, who is also the musician, and often plays while turning corner.

152. A view of the Pahuatlán flyers immediately after taking off from the pole. *Pahuatlán, Puebla.*

153. The platform, twenty-three inches in diameter, on which the flyers dance, and the frame on which they sit high in the clouds. *Pahuatlán, Puebla.*

154.   A ceremony of voladores or flyers before climbing the pole. *Villa Juárez, Puebla.*

155. The entire group of Moors and Christians of Papantla, the Moors with half moons.

156. A Moor of the Dance of Moors and Christians, Papantla, Vera Cruz. Their costumes are very elegant, the cape of black velvet, the crown adorned with colored paper.

157. A Christian captain of the Dance of Moors and Christians at Papantla. His coat is of black velvet, his headdress of ribbons of colored china paper.

158. The dancers of los negritos (the little Negroes) dancing down the steps near the church at Papantla. Their suits are of black velvet.

159. A fiesta at Cuetzalán, where the quetzales are dancing. The fiestas here are very beautiful, with the Aztec women in their white quexquemetl over shoulders and head, their hair in rolls with purple crewel.

160. The dance of the quetzales — brilliantly hued tropical birds with **long graceful** tails. Their headdresses are of brilliant colors, forming a dazzling **ensemble**.
Cuetzalán, Puebla.

161.   The Dance of the Huaves at the fiesta of Corpus Christi at Papantla, Vera Cruz.
Their costumes are red, and the headpieces are of feathers in beautiful colors. This
group is from the Sierra de Puebla.

162.   Musicians from Alvarado, Vera Cruz, where the music and dances are very gay.

163. Placing the banderillas in the bull's shoulder muscle.

164. A pass with the muleta during a bullfight.

165. A parade before a bullfight in Mexico City, showing the picadores, matadores, and toreros.

166. Portion of a parade at Rancho del Charro, Mexico City. A charro fiesta and exhibition is held here every Sunday. The charro in the foreground is wearing the typical costume with tightly-fitted trousers and embroidered jacket.

167. Market day in Taxco. Every Sunday the Indians come from their mountain villages to sell their produce. Taxco is well known for its silver products.

168. Ranchero jarabe from Jalisco.

PART THREE

MUSIC–VERSE–DANCE

MUSIC—VERSE—DANCE

Mexico has a wealth of folk music and dances, part of them an ancient heritage. But whereas among the pre-Spanish races they were chiefly forms of prayer, now they are also for pleasure. Therefore, there are many secular as well as religious songs and dances.

Singing and dancing were important arts before the Conquest. The Aztecs had their cuicacuilli, houses of song, near their temples, where teachers lived who devoted themselves exclusively to instructing the young to play, sing, and dance. Boys and girls from the ages of twelve years on had to attend, and were punished if they failed to do so.

In the Aztec capital the classes began just before sunset. The boys were brought to school by elderly men and the girls by elderly women. They were assigned to separate rooms, but met in the patio to dance. Generally those of the same barrio danced together, taking hold of hands to form a circle with the teachers and musicians in the middle. Then they would sing and dance happily for hours. Often, in spite of the chaperons, promises of love were whispered, which were kept when the children were old enough to marry.

The god of music and dances was Macuilxochitl, "Five Flower"; also known as Xochipilli, "He who gives the flowers." The fiesta in his honor, on a movable date, was called xochilhuitl, the fiesta of the flowers. For four days before it took place the people fasted, and if husbands and wives slept together, they would be afflicted with a serious disease. On the day of the fiesta a man was dressed in the adornments of this god, as if he were his image. With him the worshippers sang, danced, and played the teponaxtli. At noon many quail were beheaded, their blood was spilled before the god, and the people offered him blood from their ears and tongues, pierced with maguey needles. Various offerings were made in the form of food—toasted corn, tamales, arrows, and figures of corn dough.

In the cuicacuilli and the palaces of rulers and nobles, composers of music, verses, and dances were employed. These arts were necessary for every religious and secular fiesta, as well as for magical rites. They serve the same purposes at the present time, but there

MACUILXOCHITL OR XOCHIPILLI
GOD OF FLOWERS

are no longer special schools for teaching them; the young learn
from their elders. As to verses, they are composed by those who sing
or by professional poets who speak the language of the people.

MUSIC [1]

In order to learn something about pre-Spanish music, it is necessary
to turn to that of the Aztecs as an example, because more is known
about their arts than about those of any of the other races.

Aztec musical instruments consisted of drums, flutes, conch shells,
whistles, clay and gourd rattles, bells and shell tinklers. Music, like
everything else in their lives, revolved around and served religion.
Its main purpose was to influence the gods in their favor and to impress men through the magic of powerful sound. It was a forceful,
vigorously rhythmic music—the expression of a virile warrior race.
Their percussion instruments, therefore, were the most important.
They worshipped their teponaxtli drums as gods, with fiestas and
offerings.

While the great body of Aztec music was composed to express group religious sentiment, it also meant much to individuals. When they went alone on long trips, they always carried an instrument to while away the lonely hours, and there were times when they played and sang for the pure joy of it. How much music really meant to them is exemplified in the following story of the slave, who lived like a king for a year, paying for it with his life. When the time came to die, he carried his flutes with him to the last moment.

TEXCATLIPOCA, THE MEXICAN JUPITER

During the annual fiesta in honor of the god Texcatlipoca, the Mexican Jupiter, a youth was always sacrificed. He was chosen from their war captives for his physical perfection and valor. He was put in charge of the priests of this god, who taught him the arts of a nobleman, among them those of elegant speech, singing, and the playing of clay flutes. He was dressed richly with the adornments of Texcatlipoca, wore his hair down to his waist, and always carried flowers. When he went among the people, he was accompanied by a retinue. He greeted everyone graciously and all prostrated themselves before him because they knew he was the incarnation of Texcatlipoca.

Twenty days before his death, four beautiful maidens were sent to him, with whom he held "carnal conversations." At the same time his hair was cut in the style of a captain's and his costume was changed for a more gala one.

Five days before his death, fiestas and banquets were given him, attended by the principal men. When the day arrived for the sacrifice, only the priests accompanied him to the temple. He ascended the stairs to the sacrificial altar alone. On each step he broke one of his flutes—symbols of his greatness and his happiest hours.

A sufficient number of ancient drums, flutes and other instruments have been excavated so that musicians have been able to draw conclusions about the kind of music they produced. The flutes obeyed one system, ruled by the natural relations of the octave—the fifth and fourth.

What indigenous music might have evolved into is impossible to say, since its development was interrupted by the Conquest. That which exists at the present time is sufficient to give one some idea of its strength and beauty but it cannot represent all of it. Unfortunately, the ancient system of writing was inadequate for music, and the Spaniards did not think it worth while, apparently, to write any of it down. But the natives are still playing replicas of all their original instruments, and even the European ones they make and play have a primitive sound.

The pagan groups are more musical than the intermediate Catholicized ones because music, together with singing and dancing, still plays an important role in their religious and magical rites. It is the language their gods understand best.

The most musical of all the primitive groups are the Seris of Sonora. They have the Orpheus idea of the creation of music, attributing it to their medicine men. An interesting myth exists about Nacho Morales, who is still alive and is looked upon as a "son of God."

When Nacho was a boy, he used to go to the hills to look for food. One day he met a woman carrying a basket filled with various kinds of fruit. She was wearing a long, full skirt and a blouse with long sleeves; her feet were small and bare. She surprised Nacho by handing him the basket and asking if he did not recognize her. Nacho said he did not, so she continued, "I am your Mother. I watch you from the skies and know everything you do." Nacho had naturally never seen the woman before because she was "God in disguise." She was very kind to him and taught him to sing many songs. Then she told him to return to his people.

After that encounter, Nacho stayed in bed a whole year without seeing anyone but the person who brought him his food. The Seris were happy over the miracle because they believed a new prophet had been revealed to them. They feasted merrily all that year, playing, singing, and dancing. The women painted their faces, adorned their hair with flowers, and all drank tepache.

When Nacho came out from his seclusion, he gathered all the tribe around him and said, "Observe me well, for I am going to sing all the songs God has taught me. Listen that you may learn!"

Soon all the tribe were singing the songs, and sometimes they could see Nacho flying at night with a knife stuck in his chest. Every generation has a medicine man who is a song-maker and semi-god.

The Seris have fewer religious and war songs now, since they no longer celebrate fiestas nor fight wars, but their medicine men sing to cure and for other magical rites. Hunters and fishermen sing for luck. All the people—men, women, and children—are always singing; they have songs about love, the sun, the moon, the stars; for matrons, young girls, and babies. They all sing the tribal songs but many sing their own personal ones, which they themselves have invented and no one else sings.

The Seri songs are composed on simple, primitive principles, yet they are among the most melodic in Mexico. Most of them are sung as solos, without musical accompaniment. The people have good voices, the men, sweet tenors. Those of the women are harsher, although they sometimes sing in falsetto and have wide ranges. They all sing with great feeling, expressing delicacy and pathos with tears in their eyes.

Their musical instruments are rattles, wooden rasps, and a peculiar, one-stringed violin (Pl. 27).

The Huichols come next to the Seris as singers, but they have more religious music. Men, women, and children sing the chants during pagan ceremonies, led by the shaman and two assistants, who are selected from the best singers in the community. Aside from that they play and sing secular music all the time. Some of their songs in their own language are on such modern subjects as trains and planes. Women and girls sing them, too, but only in the privacy of their homes.

The Huichols accompany their pagan chants with a primitive huehuetl drum (Pl. 3), and play the music for their Christian ceremonies on crude, tiny, homemade violins and guitars. They, strangely enough, are one of the few tribes without flutes.

Whenever one meets some Huichols away from home, one of them is certain to have a violin along and another a guitar. They are a gay, pleasure-loving people, never without music (Pl. 11).

Music also plays an important part in the lives of the Coras, but with them it is chiefly religious. They have special chants for their pagan ceremonies and secular songs in their own language.

Practically all the men know how to play and to make reed flutes, and they make new ones every year during Holy Week. Their other instruments are drums, violins, triangles, and mitotes.

The mitote is their sacred instrument and is played only for the pagan corn rites. The players are generally old medicine men. One from the village of San Francisco, Nayarit, said that the mitotes are made by God in heaven and sent to earth; that he knew how to play at birth because God had taught him. But his father and grandfather had been mitote players. The fathers teach their sons music, as all the other arts (Pl. 15).

The Yaquis of Sonora have interesting primitive music and instruments for their deer dance. A flute and drum are played by the same musician, while others play wooden rasps, and one an Aztec type of water drum. The latter is formed by placing a half gourd on the surface of the water in a large clay container. The musician holds the gourd in position with his left hand, striking it with his right on the concave side with a stick which is covered with corn husks to deaden the sound of the wood. This produces a lovely resonant sound. The dancers carry gourd rattles, wear cocoon rattlers, and three old men sing the words in falsetto. The rhythm of the ensemble is thrilling.

The Mayos, neighbors of the Yaquis and of the same language group, have the same deer-dance music and instruments (Pls. 22, 23). The Seris, Tarahumaras and other groups use wooden rasps and rattles for their deer dances, but none have the water drums.

The most musical of the primitive races of the highlands of Chiapas are the Tzotzils. And of this race, the Chamulas who are the most progressive and aggressive are also the most musical. The musical instruments of the region consist of drums, flutes, harps, and guitars, but the Chamulas of the village of Chamula near Las Casas also have an accordion and small crude violins with only two strings. Their guitars have twelve strings, which produce a rich flowing sound like that of water. Almost every house has one, for the young men often play and sing secular songs. They make their own instruments and sell them to other villages, as they do many other objects.

These Chamulas, like the Tzotzils of Chenalho, also have the bajbín or jar-drums, played only during carnivals, which they venerate as the Aztecs did their teponaxtlis. Between carnivals, the two guardians of the drums keep them on a table in one of their houses, where they are worshipped and offered incense at regular intervals of either one or two weeks.

The day before the carnival, the guardians give the drums a drink of chicha, their ceremonial brandy, wash them and change their cords. Before doing this they dance around the table on which the drums stand. While one of them dances with a chilón on his head—a tiger

skin with cascabeles—the other waves a large banner in the four
sacred directions; then they change places. Afterwards a woman
brings in hot water with camomile plants for the washing, and while

SACRED POTTERY DRUM FROM CHIAPAS

it goes on, fireworks are shot off. On the fourth day of the carnival,
there is a dance near the church door to the music of the bajbín, the
dancers wearing the chilón.

All the rest of the groups in the country have various kinds of
drums, flutes and occasionally an unusual instrument. The Chinantecs,
for example, have the musical bows, and on the Isthmus of Tehuantepec turtle shells are played with a pair of deer horns, as before the
Conquest.

It is not only in the remote regions that one hears natives playing
primitive music on the ancient type of instruments, but everywhere
else. There are those of Aztec descent in villages around the famous
archaeological zone of Teotihuacán, near Mexico City, who can imitate animals on their reed flutes, the noises of coyotes when stealing
chickens, the birds.

In 1945, during the fiesta of St. Michael in the village of Chiconcuac, also near Mexico City, I heard primitive music played in the
church by three indigenous musicians on a huehuetl drum and flutes.
They had come down from their mountain village, invited by the
mayordomos, and were taking part in the high mass, together with
the organist, choir, and a brass band.

Everywhere, too, one finds natives playing in stringed orchestras and in brass bands. Usually one member of the group can read music; the rest learn to play by ear and do it well. Men and boys of all ages play in bands and other musical groups. Often boys of twelve or thirteen play brass instruments almost as big as themselves. Their fathers are musicians, so they learn to play at an early age.

A TURTLE SHELL INSTRUMENT, PLAYED WITH A PAIR OF DEER HORNS

The bands are always picturesque in their regional outfits and sometimes startle one by playing such foreign music as pieces from the Italian operas or a Strauss waltz. They play everything sincerely, with much feeling, but usually change the rhythms so that the most familiar music sounds strange. Both bands and orchestras are at their best in Mexican music, especially with their regional tunes.

The State of Oaxaca probably has more native bands than any other and certainly better ones. The village government furnishes the instruments, and the musicians practice and play without compensation, in exchange for which they are exempt from other communal work. They usually give one concert a week at night on the village plaza, play on national and religious holidays, for dances, and for funerals. One Holy Week I heard the Yalalag village band play in church on Thursday night, after the "arrest" of Christ. They were playing music that they themselves had composed for the psalms, which sounded so modern that at moments one was reminded of Stravinsky.

The Oaxaca bands also play for the entertainment of honored guests. A friend of mine once made one of these bands very happy by visiting their village. The entire band was in jail for not practicing. When he appeared, the musicians had to be released.

Native bands are less numerous elsewhere, but one finds them everywhere. In and around the Federal District, they are somewhat commercial. The musicians purchase their own instruments, hence receive a small fee for playing at home, and a bigger one when they are invited to play for fiestas in other villages. On such occasions all bands are fêted by the mayordomos.

There are regions in which mestizo folk music predominates and the musicians are also mestizos. The most outstanding for this type of musical production is Jalisco. It was there that the mariachis originated, which are also popular in Colima and Nayarit.

The mariachis are strolling folk orchestras. Originally, they were composed of stringed instruments only—guitar, guitarron or large guitar, violin, and the tiny vibuela. In recent years cornets have been added. The groups vary in numbers from three to a dozen.

In the smaller places, they stroll around the main plaza and stop to play for anyone who will pay. In Guadalajara, a very large city, they are to be found around the old, well-known markets, where the people go to hear them or to hire them to play for fiestas and serenades.

In the early thirties, a few mariachis came to Mexico City. They did well, so others followed. Their rallying-ground there at night is the Plaza Garibaldi. They play and sing on radio programs and in movies, and have made recordings for various companies.

Unfortunately, this popularity is degenerating the type of music the mariachis play. The tourists and city people ask for the pieces that are the fad at the moment. Many of the younger generation are no longer learning the old pieces. In most instances, to hear genuine folk music, one has to know what to ask them to play.

No one seems to be able to explain why these orchestras are called mariachis but there is a nice little hypothesis about it. Maximilian was very fond of these folk orchestras, so during his reign they were often employed to play at fiestas in the homes of the French court. Some of these occasions were weddings, hence the Mexicans began calling them mariachis, a corruption of the French *mariage*.

However they may have acquired the name, they are known everywhere by it. They have not only become popular but also professional, for they are among the few folk music groups that live by their music. Their voices are seldom good but they play well. They always begin a song with what they call a sinfonía, a gay little tune, having no relation to the melody. Between verses, the tune of the song is repeated. Occasionally one finds a rustic Bach among them.

The Tarascans of Michoacán have much mestizo music, and lovely songs in their own language. The sones of Vera Cruz are famous for their gaiety and verve, as a result of the mixture of indigenous, Negro, and Spanish blood. All along the Huastecas, from the border to the

Gulf States, the huapangos are popular, gay dance songs. The Sandunga and Llorona of the Isthmus of Tehuantepec are nationally
popular.

Folk music exists everywhere in Mexico. It has persisted and gone
through practically the same evolution as the plastic arts. Immediately after the Conquest, the Spaniards employed native musicians
because they had none of their own. Later they did not need them,
so ignored them. Now folk music and musicians are appreciated more
than ever, but a change is taking place of which the end is not clearly
in sight.

In pre-Spanish times, as now, only men and boys played musical
instruments, but the boys and girls learned to sing and dance together,
and continued doing so throughout their lives. After the Conquest,
only boys received musical instruction for a short time in the first
Catholic schools, the most famous being the one established by Fray
Pedro de Gante at Texcoco in 1527. Many became good musicians
even without knowing the language of their instructors. They were
also skillful in making copies of the European instruments. In a short
time there were a sufficient number of competent musicians, so that
every church could be supplied with choirs and orchestras. However,
such education conflicted with the interests of the Spanish exploiters;
they felt the natives were spending too much time in schools, and some
of the clergy supported them. Then boys were not permitted to attend the schools. Thus they had to be closed and the work of the
good friars came to an early end.

The musical education of the natives, nevertheless, continued, but
it was no longer religious. The Spanish merchants found they could
sell more liquor by teaching the people to sing and play guitars.
Mendieta in his "Historia Eclesiástica Indiana" laments that everywhere men and women who were prudent and abstinent under their
own institutions, gave themselves up to drinking and playing the
guitar, encouraged by the leniency of the laws and badly advised by
the get-rich-quick opportunists who were coming from Spain in
great numbers, and devoting themselves to flooding Nueva España
with intoxicating drinks.

As time went on women sang less. With the exception of the Seri
and Huichol women and girls, they sang chiefly in church. One
never hears a woman singing at her work. When she is putting her
infant to sleep, she may sing a religious song quietly, as if afraid to
raise her voice. Men also sing less than they used to, although more
than women. Only a few in each village sing the secular songs, and
never when they are sober. The people seldom sang after the Conquest because only those who are free and happy sing.

Since the 1910–20 Revolution conditions have been changing in this respect. The folk are still poor and still exploited, but they feel freer. The rural schools are teaching the children to sing, so that this generation sings more. They need no longer fear to raise their voices or to sing their songs, because folk music is now popular everywhere.

City people are singing folk songs more than ever before, and clever composers of popular songs have made hits by using folk themes and melodies. Folk songs are favorites of movie and radio audiences. Folk songs and dances are always a part of the floor shows of high class cabarets. Modern Mexican composers have written orchestral music based on folk themes, and primitive songs have been arranged for city school children.

One way of knowing a people is to listen to their songs. The Mexican folk do not have especially good voices but they sing because they have something to say. As one singer expressed it:

> I sing that I may be heard,
> Not because my voice is good;
> I sing to make known my laments
> In my own land and in others.

In their music the people express the entire gamut of their emotions. For this reason their songs are rich and varied.

Songs

There are great quantities and many varieties of songs. They fall into several classes and a sufficient number are published here to illustrate all of them.

I. Primitive Songs. These exist in both the pentatonic and modern scales. Of the pre-Spanish ones only about a hundred odd have been written down but, alas, without music. They are very beautiful poetically and much richer in imagery and content than any that are sung at the present time.

II. Religious Songs. These are in Spanish and consist of hymns, responses, alabados, and alabanzas, or songs of praise; also those of the coloquios and pastorelas, the medieval mystery plays, seldom given any more. The songs of praise composed by the natives to the saints are especially delicate and tender.

III. Corridos or Ballads. The Mexican corrido is the offspring of the Spanish *romance*. The first ones composed in Mexico were Spanish in content and form. But as they became popular, they took on a Mexican character. Then the Spanish octosyllabic verses were changed to quatrains, which were more pleasing to Mexican esthetic sensitivity.

The music of the corridos is simply a repetition of the same musical phrases, but the words are always exciting. They tell of the adventures of heroes and bandits, of revolutions, of catastrophic accidents, of love tragedies, of what happens to disobedient sons. They reveal the true character of the people and express all their sentiments—stoicism, pathos, humor, mockery. Sometimes the first verse begins with "I am going to sing you a ballad about. . . ." and ends with an apology for not having composed better verses, but more generally in the less sophisticated corridos the singer takes leave with a stock verse, which he adapts to the content.

The production of corridos has been continuous and prolific. As soon as something of general human interest happens, the large publishing houses of folk literature have their poets write verses for a corrido about it. Then it is illustrated, published on colored sheets and sent out for sale at a few centavos a piece. The vendors take them to fiestas and markets in cities and villages throughout the Republic. The folk singers learn them quickly, but as they cannot read, they sometimes change words, add or leave out a verse. Thus the corrido becomes their own and takes on a local character. Some corridos are composed locally and never printed.

The corridos about politics and current events are soon forgotten, but they have served an important social function in bringing news to the folk that they did not receive through other sources, especially before the days of the radio.

Corridos like "La Güera Chabela," "Lucio" and others that appeal to the emotions live on and on and are sung everywhere. They have no logic but much pathos, naïvely and tenderly expressed. The people love to listen to them because they are about themselves; they can understand and feel them.

IV. Revolutionary Songs. Those that are popular at the present time—"Adelita," "La Valentina," "La Cucaracha"—date from the 1910–20 Social Revolution. But they have very little connection with it, excepting that they were sung by the soldiers. During the Revolution, when the troop trains, crowded to the roof-tops, left the stations, the soldiers used to sing these songs as they fired off their guns. They also sang them at all other opportunities, especially at night around camp fires, where guitars were never lacking.

V. Dance Songs. All the music for secular folk dances is in the form of songs, called sones, jarabes, and huapangos, the latter having a very marked rhythm. The tunes are light and gay; the verses picaresque and tender.

VI. Love Songs. There are two kinds of love songs: the simple, vigorous type including the rancheras, and the sentimental city type which have outlived their ephemeral popularity. All are composed by men, but the he-man does not like to wear his heart on his sleeve, so he blames the woman, puts on a bravado air, and consoles himself with, "There are more fish in the sea." The city songs are of the kind people in the United States are accustomed to hearing, excepting that they are generally more romantic and melodious.

There are love songs for special occasions; "Las Mañanitas" for birthday serenading in the wee hours of the morning and others for gallos. The gallos are the serenades of young men, who either are or aspire to become lovers of the girls they sing to. Gallo is the Spanish for cock. As the serenades take place at the hour the cocks begin to crow, shortly after midnight, they are called gallos. The girl serenaded sometimes peeks through the window but she must not turn on the light nor let herself be seen. So formerly it was the custom for the lover who organized the gallo to leave a little clay cock-bank with his card in the slot on the window ledge.

There are traditional songs for the gallos, sung to the accompaniment of a guitar. The one to begin with is "Si Estás Dormida," "If you are asleep, my love, awake and listen to the voice of the one who loves you. . ." The last song is generally one of leave-taking.

Usually gallos are organized by several friends, who practice the songs together and then sing them at the homes of their respective girls. Those who cannot themselves sing, hire singers or a mariachi. A rich man in Guadalajara once created a sensation by hiring the entire Russian Cossack Chorus, giving concerts there, to serenade his love. He also had a number of mariachis. As the gallo took place at the hour when the natives were taking their produce to the market on burros, they also joined the group. Such a gallo has never been heard of before nor after!

There is still another kind of music which does not fall into any of the above classes. Among the primitive tribes it takes the form of playing the drum to call people together and to send out messages that are far-reaching and often complicated. Sometimes a conch-shell is used for the same purpose, or a man may lend his voice. In the cities vendors sing their wares as they walk the streets. Their songs, called pregones or proclamations, are usually in rhyme and sometimes humorous even though not always musical. In some of the neighborhoods of modern Mexico City, organ-grinders still add a tinge of nostalgia to the twilight hours.

Mexican folk music is always sung to the accompaniment of a guitar or other stringed instruments. But as most persons using this book will be more familiar with the piano, a few songs, intended for a new edition of the "Cancionero Mexicano" (Frances Toor, 1931), are published here with accompaniments. These serve for both piano and guitar. They are and should be very simple, and can be simplified even more. Anyone can arrange them very easily to suit his own taste.

DANCES

"Whosoever knoweth the power of the dance, dwelleth in God," sang the Persian poet Rumi. The ancient Mexicans used the dance and performed it to perfection.

The Aztecs believed that to win favors from the gods it was necessary to make sacrifices, to sing and to dance to them. They danced for them on their feast days and on all other occasions when it was necessary to be in their good graces, such as for luck in marriage, birth, curing, hunting, rain, good harvests, victory in war. They, like other primitive tribes, shared the Chinese belief that song and dance keep the world in motion and predispose nature in favor of man.

DANCERS AND MUSICIANS

The Aztecs danced from childhood on. Men, women, and children danced separately and together. During fiestas for the most important of their deities, as many as a thousand or more persons sang and danced together in the temple patios. When the groups were large, they formed circles. The first ones near the musicians were composed of the elderly men of authority; then there was a little space with more circles of men and women of lesser degree; then another space and the outside circles of the youths. The guides were selected from the best dancers.

Shrill whistles informed the public that the dance was about to begin. Then the music began slowly and quietly, gradually increasing in volume and speed. First the leaders started dancing and chanting. After a while the others joined with voice and body, singing and moving every limb in perfect unison, never losing a beat. The movements of the inner circles were slower, but all danced with equal grace and harmony.

Each song was repeated several times. The first one, in a low key and slow tempo, lasted the longest. When that was finished there was an interval of rest, after which the musicians and leaders would start another in a higher key with a livelier theme. Sometimes very small children danced and sang with their parents, enriching the chorus with their shrill young voices. During the intermissions, the people were entertained by buffoons, who mimicked others in their way of dressing and dancing, or disguised themselves as animals. When some of the dancers tired, there were always others to take their places.

Not only did the nobles dance but also the king and priests. All dressed elaborately for the dances, the men wearing their finest mantles and the women their huipils, with inwoven designs of gorgeous feathers; their richest adornments of gold, precious stones, and plumes. For some dances they carried plumage and rattles in their hands; for others, flowers. The women were beautiful, with garlands on their heads or flowers in their long loose hair. Sometimes the dances required splendid headdresses and masks. It is difficult to imagine the grandeur and beauty of those brilliant throngs, moving and singing —a symphony of sound and color, producing ecstasy to hypnotize gods and men.

A very beautiful dance was performed in honor of Hutzilopochtli, the god of war. The dancers adorned themselves with roses, and made an arbor of them in his temple, in which sat a woman representing Xochiquetzalli, the goddess of beauty, love, and flowers. Nearby were artificial trees, filled with fragrant roses. While the dance was going on, little boys dressed as birds and butterflies, adorned with brilliant plumes, climbed the trees and jumped from branch to branch, sipping the dew of the flowers.

Then men in the adornment of the gods came out from the temple and pointed their cervantanas as if to kill the birds. At this moment Xochiquetzalli came out, led the men into her rose-house, seated them near her, and accorded them the respect and honor due the gods they

DANCE OF LAS PASTORAS

represented. She gave them roses and wafted incense about them for their pleasure and solace.

The dances in private temples and the homes of the rich were composed of less dancers, who formed two lines, swaying and executing various steps and figures. Sometimes both sides stood still, while one or two of the dancers performed special steps in the middle, as is still done in some dances.

There were frivolous dances in which young men sang songs of love and flattery. In one of them, resembling the saraband, gay youths and "immodest" women moved their bodies and made grimaces as if they were being tickled or had the itch.

In another dance of this kind, some of the dancers painted themselves black, some white, others green, their heads and feet adorned with feathers. The women danced in the middle, all the dancers carrying cups and making motions as if drinking from them, and feigning drunkenness.

Soldiers of high rank were permitted to dance in public with women of questionable character as a reward for their valor. They would invite any girl or girls that appealed to them and spend an entire afternoon in their company, dancing with them, paying them compliments and giving them presents. These women painted their lips and cheeks, wore feathers in their hair and jewels around their necks.

XOCHIQUETZALLI, THE GODDESS OF BEAUTY, LOVE, AND FLOWERS

In other dances men exhibited humor and great skill. In one dance of buffoons a jester was introduced who pretended not to understand what his master was saying, repeating and changing the meaning of his words. Or one of them would lie down on his back and "dance" a thick log, about eight feet long, tossing it into the air and catching it again with his feet. Then with both feet he would make it turn with a man astride at each end.

Another dance which the young men often performed consisted of one of them dancing with another standing on his shoulders, accompanying some of the movements, while a third one danced on the head of the second.

Some of the Spaniards were so astonished at these displays of skill, strength, and agility that they said they could not be achieved without the intervention of the devil, but the early chroniclers—mostly priests—frankly admired these performances of the natives and their beautiful dances.[1]

CERVANTANA

This strength, agility, and grace still persist in the games and dances of the natives. Even the mestizo folk show greater ability and endurance in sports and dances than city people.

Ritual Dances

There are numerous ritual dances at the present time, some with Christian themes, but all are danced with faith, ability, and grace, as before the Conquest.

The friars encouraged dancing, since through the dance they were able to dramatize what they wished to teach. The natives were permitted to continue some of their own dances, and for a long time all of them were performed on a magnificent scale. They began to decline about the end of the nineteenth century and much more rapidly after

AN ANCIENT AZTEC DANCE

1910. Yet in spite of the changes there are still some very beautiful dances, a few of them preserving the ancient color. But the dancers no longer sing as they dance, excepting among the Huichols who follow the old forms.

The ritual dances, as will be seen, have nothing religious about them excepting their intention. They are danced for the saints during their feasts and for various other rites. Those that are pre-Spanish in origin or that have aboriginal characteristics are the most beautiful. Of that type, three are outstanding:

I. The Flying-Pole Dance

Los voladores or the flying pole dance is the most thrilling and beautiful of all. It is centuries old, having existed among various of the Middle American tribes. The Aztecs performed it for about a century after the Conquest on the same plaza they had set aside for it near their Great Temple. In the seventeenth century the Spaniards turned the place into a bullring and called it El Volador.

Some of the early writers called the volador a game and others a dance, but it is the same in either case. The natives brought a tall, strong, straight tree trunk from the woods; set it up in the middle of

EL VOLADOR
THE FLYING POLE

a plaza; fitted the top with a small cap-like revolving platform and frame. Ropes were wound around for the flyers and a ladder of a strong vine was formed around the pole. Four flyers and a musician climbed to the top. After a ceremony performed by the musician on the tiny platform, the flyers who were sitting on the frame, tied the ends of the ropes around their waists, threw themselves into space and, as the ropes unwound, flew like birds around the pole to the ground. Sometimes an extra man would come down jumping from rope to rope without being tied.

The point of the game or dance was to secure a pole sufficiently

high so that the flyers could make thirteen revolutions around it before reaching the ground, which represented their cycle of fifty-two
years, divided into four epochs of thirteen each. The flyers were
dressed as eagles or as macaws—the beautiful birds dedicated to the
sun—or as other birds.

Today the flying pole dance is performed by Huastecas, Otomís,
Mexicans, and Totonacs, from the Huastecas in San Luis Potosí to the
lowlands of Vera Cruz, as it was in pre-Spanish times but with some
differences in details. The ancient symbolism seems to be forgotten
or is unknown to the majority of flyers, yet in most cases there are
four flyers who make the thirteen revolutions around the pole.

Among the Huastecas of San Luis Potosí, the volador is referred
to as la danza del gavilán because the dancers dress to represent the
gavilanes or sparrow-hawks. All the men of the village en masse,
headed by the authorities, go to the woods to find a suitable tree. Before cutting it down, a prayer is offered to the Pulic-Minlab, the all
powerful god of the trees, promising that the massive trunk will be
used only for the dance. Then after spilling a little brandy where the
tree is to be cut, the captain of the dancers strikes the first blow. After
the trunk is ready to be moved, the men carry it, full weight, not
dragging nor letting it touch the ground. A crowd follows and disputes for the honor of sharing the burden.

On the village plaza a deep hole is dug in which the pole is to be
set up. But first a live hen is put into it, which thus sacrificed, will
furnish food for the pole to give it sufficient strength to support the
flyers. They must fast before flying and the authorities examine
everything carefully before they are permitted to go up.

The flyers wear on their heads a crest of feathers, held by a ribbon
tied under the chin, and feathers on their backs to simulate the wings
of the gavilanes. The captain wears a red shirt and trousers with a
white diagonal band. All are barefoot.

The five men climb up to the top; four sit on the frame, and after
the captain has danced on the small platform, playing his flute and
drum, they tie the ropes around themselves and fly down. Just as the
flyers are about to land on their feet, the captain slides down one of
the ropes, reaching the ground at the same time as the fliers, without
having stopped playing his instruments. This feat excites great admiration and applause.

The customs in connection with the volador, like all others, differ
in every region as well as in every village. The Otomís of the mountain village of Pahuatlán, Hidalgo, think it more elegant to have six
flyers than five. They apparently know that the traditional number
is four, as one of the older men said, "In the old days there were al-

ways four voladores, because we are really the four sacred birds that fly with the four winds to the cardinal points."

Here the pole is also brought from the woods with ceremony, but it is used for about three years, which is as long as is considered reliable. Before it is set up, an offering of food is placed at the bottom of the deep hole—tamales, tortillas, a cooked or live hen, brandy, cigarettes—whatever they think will give the pole pleasure and make it stronger for the flyers.

One of the six flyers of Pahuatlán dresses as a woman to represent Malinche, Cortés' mistress, his skirts making his acting so much more difficult. The rest wear red suits with two bandannas crossed in the back, vaguely reminiscent of the wings of the pre-Spanish birds. Five carry rattles, and the sixth one carries a flute and small drum and plays both at the same time.

Each flyer, excepting the musician, dances on the tiny, twenty-four-inch platform. In turn, he faces all the four winds, devoting a few minutes of dancing to each. With each turn, the tune changes slightly. Malinche, who seems to be considered of greater importance than the others, performs a more intricate dance to four different melodies, at the end of which "she" leans forward at a dangerous angle to enfold every dancer in turn in a large bandanna.

After the dancing is finished, the flyers tie the ropes around their waists and jump into space with a piercing shriek. As they fly in ever-widening circles, the music of flute and drum keeps increasing in tempo and intensity until the flyers land gracefully on their feet.

The flyers here are the same year after year. In 1936, the captain was sixty-three years old and had been flying for thirty-five years. They seem not to be subject to any restrictions, for some of them drink to bolster up their courage when they are about to fly. There have been serious accidents on account of drunkenness not only here but in other villages of the region, so that in some of them the authorities have forbidden the dance (Pls. 147, 148, 152, 153, 154).

The Totonacs of Papantla, Vera Cruz, have only four flyers and a musician, who is also the captain. The flyers are generally young, unmarried youths, who promise to fly for seven years in return for some favor already, or yet to be, received through the intercession of a saint. The boys are not supposed to have sweethearts, and thus to keep their thoughts pure and their bodies strong for their offering. Before flying they must observe a diet free from strong condiments and abstain from liquor and women.

The volador in Papantla is performed every year during the fiesta of Corpus Christi, and each time a new pole is set up. A week or so before the fiesta, which is on a movable date, a large group of men go with the flyers to look for the pole, cutting their way through the jungle forests with their machetes, indifferent to the dangers of reptiles, heat, and fatigue. When they reach their destination, they select a meeting place and disperse to look for the tallest, straightest, slenderest, strongest, and most beautiful tree that is farthest away from where women live. Sometimes they find it quickly, because before leaving they have consulted a sorcerer or have invited one to come along. "God wanted the dance, so He told the sorcerers the kind of tree to use and where to find it," often in dreams.

After finding the tree, the groups dance around it and beg its pardon for cutting it down. Then before cutting the branches off, the men give it a drink of tepache and spill a little on the ground after the first twenty blows to make it forget its pain. And some of them sing, play, and dance until it falls. The cutting off of the branches, the felling and transportation of the trunk are done with the greatest care so that there will be no scars on the tree when it is put up. Whenever it is necessary to stop to rest on the way in, the men sprinkle the trunk with brandy in the middle and at the ends.

A messenger informs the people at home when the party is to arrive, and many men go outside of the town, to meet them at a place called La Garita. When they reach the plaza, more people are there to welcome them. Church bells ring, rockets burst, and the band plays. Then all are given a festal meal at the home of the mayordomo, but before going there, the flyers go to church to pray. Afterwards the tree is also fed, for the hole in which it is to stand is blessed with holy water and in it is placed an offering of food, drinks, and smokes so that it may be content and not claim the life of a flyer.

On the morning of Corpus Christi, the flyers, who are called tocotines, arrive on the plaza, dancing in single file, with their captain playing and dancing at their head. They wear red suits, short trousers and tight jackets; pointed hats with a bunch of feathers on top and ribbons hanging down behind; heavy black or brown shoes. First they dance in front of the main church entrance. From there they dance all the way to the pole, without breaking their line, marking figures to the rhythm of the music. At the pole, the musician dances away from his companions, who form couples, facing each other. Then they weave a dancing chain, one going to the right backwards, the other, left forwards, but always taking care not to turn their backs to the pole. Each movement is repeated three times and the entire dance, seven times around the pole.

After this dance is finished, the flyers climb the pole one after another to their places on the frame, where they arrange the ropes for the flight. The captain climbs up last and sits on the tiny platform, facing east, with his feet placed so that the ropes pass over his insteps.

TOCOTIN DANCER OF PAPANTLA

First the musician greets the east with his tune, which he repeats as he bends his body back until it forms an arc, playing all the time with greater intensity until he returns to a sitting posture. He then repeats the melody seven times. After that he renders the same homage to the west, north, and south. He then hands his cap to the flyer to whose right sits the one with another flute and drum, who rubs the cap on the instruments as a sign of approbation. When he has it on his head again, he stands up facing the east, and makes seven turns on the minute platform. As he turns, he marks synchronously with both feet in jumps about ten inches high the rhythm of the melody he is playing. Sometimes, while standing on one foot, he makes ballet steps with the other in the air as he marks his beautifully embroidered rhythm. In changing from one foot to the other, he often makes two turns instead of one, so that each cardinal point receives fourteen instead of seven turns.

When the musician is again seated, he hands his flute to the same flyer, at his right, who receives it as if it were sacred, and expresses veneration for it by rubbing it against the frame and ropes as far as he is able to reach. After returning the flute, all prepare to fly. Upon hearing the first notes of the melody, they let their bodies fall gently backwards. The ropes begin to unwind; they twist their feet around them, and with heads down, arms extended, fly around the pole in circles.

The captain remains on top, playing. The other musician plays the same melody as he flies. When both have played the tune seven times, the flyers change positions, flexing their abdomens and leaning backwards. They remain thus until the new tune is played seven times, after which they return to their former position. When only two revolutions are lacking to reach the ground, the flyers turn a somersault and land lightly on their feet. They do not free themselves from their ropes until their captain joins them. Then all take leave of the pole by dancing around it.[2]

This fiesta lasts about five days. When the weather is good, the volador is performed both in the morning and afternoon. One must see it to appreciate the wonder and beauty of it—the breathless white throng, the bird men against a blue sky and a white church tower (Pls. 146, 150).

II. Conchero Dances

The conchero dancers are the most extraordinary from the point of view of numbers, organization, and practices. There are, perhaps, some fifty thousand of them in the states of Guanajuato, Queretaro, Tlaxcala, Hidalgo, and the Federal District. They are organized in military fashion; accept women into their ranks who may become officials; adore the Holy Cross and four winds at the same time. Among them are curers, witches, and sorcerers.

Even though the concheros are all related and their dances are similar, there are always some differences. The following descriptions pertain to those of the Federal District, where there are about four thousand.

Each group, of anywhere from fifty to a hundred concheros, is called a mesa or table, referring to the altar around which it is organized. Sometimes the mesa stands in a little separate oratory, but mostly it is part of the furnishings where the family eat and sleep. It is covered with a beautifully embroidered cloth, and on it are the saints of their devotion, an image of a soul in purgatory, glasses with artificial and fresh flowers, censers and other adornments. Each mesa is named after some saint.

CONCHERO DANCER

All the concheros are "soldiers of the Conquest." They are also concheros or those of the shells, because most of the instruments they play are made with the shell-like covering of the armadillo. They call themselves Chichimecas, too, since the dances originated among that tribe shortly after the Conquest. Today the concheros are trying to imitate the old way of dressing and to keep alive their traditions.

The officials of a mesa are the first and second captains; sergeant of the mesa and field sergeant; men and women standard bearers; two Malinches and a devil. Then come first, second, third, and all the rest of the concheros, according to their merits as dancers. All the officials and mesas are under the command of the Captain General of the Conquest of the Great Tenochtitlán, who presides over the Mesa General.

The first captain teaches his soldiers their obligations and dance steps; he is assisted by the second captain, his substitute. The sergeant of the mesa has to see that the altar is always taken care of and that everyone behaves in an orderly, respectful manner around it.

A DEVIL OF THE CONCHERO DANCE

The field sergeant is responsible for the conduct of the soldiers when they are on the road and dancing—no one can leave the circle without permission. The standard-bearers must always be with their banners when they are taken away from the mesa; the Malinches must keep the censers supplied with incense and have them ready to light; the cane-bearer must always be in the center of the circle when the dance is going on. The Devil clears the way for the dancers, amuses the spectators, and keeps them from crowding.

A person joins a mesa for various reasons—it may be a tradition in the family; on account of a promise to a saint for past or future favors; or simply because the idea appeals to him. He applies to the first captain of the mesa. If there is nothing against the applicant, the captain informs him what the rules and regulations are, and tells him that he must be prepared to obey them and to make sacrifices—to spend money, to suffer fatigue and loss of sleep; that he must bring offerings for the mesa every time he attends.

All the officials and concheros are present at the initiation ceremony. The new member comes with an offering of flowers and candles. First he swears allegiance to the banners, promising to be a faithful soldier. Then he is covered with them, and must remain in a kneeling position at the altar for an hour and a half. While he kneels, the captain rubs him with flowers, rosemary, pirú branches, and candles. The new conchero meanwhile holds flowers and lighted candles in both hands. Afterwards everyone wafts incense toward him and gives him the traditional Mexican embrace of good will. When the man has gotten to his feet again, he thanks everyone and promises to fulfill all his obligations as a soldier of Christ and of the Conquest.

Some of their obligations are to treat everyone with respect and consideration; to help one another in case of sickness or death; in everything necessary, even to raising funds for the afflicted family. Any conchero, male or female, disobeying these or any of the other rules or regulations is subject to the punishment decreed by the superior officers, which in serious cases may be a certain number of lashes. When any of the concheros have quarreled, they make up their differences before fiestas, and always help each other on their trips.

The concheros meet regularly and frequently to practice their dances and for ceremonies. They always bring flowers and candles for the altar, and one of them performs the duties of a priest. He begins by lighting five tallow candles, which he makes stick to a brick with the drippings from the sixth one; then he blows a series of smoke crosses in the air with the censer. The service starts by the singing of warrior hymns, with verses like the following:

Vamos, humildes soldados,	Let us go, humble soldiers,
Vamos a hacer ejercicio (a danzar)	Let us make exercises (dance)
Para que en el día del Juicio,	So that on the Day of Judgment,
Estemos bién preparados.	We shall be well prepared.

Sigan su bandera y también su pabellón,	Follow your banner; also your standard;
Que esta es la conquista	That is the conquest
De la Santa Religión.	Of the Holy Religion.

The concheros dance regularly at numerous fiestas. But since they worship the four winds or cardinal points, their most important ones are those at the sanctuaries situated in the four directions in relation to Mexico City—La Villa de Guadalupe, Chalma, Los Remedios, and Amecameca. Chalma is the most distant, and takes from one to two weeks of their working time.

The night before the concheros leave for a fiesta, they pray and sing alabanzas until midnight. Then four officials are assigned to decorate the Santa Suchitl—a wooden chalice, adorned with flowers to form a rose, probably in memory of the cala suchitl that gave shade to the miraculous cross of the Cerro of Sangremal. The act is accompanied with chants to the strumming of the conchas. After it is completed, the suchitl is placed at the foot of the altar, blown with incense in the four directions, and everyone makes reverences to it, kneeling and asperging himself.

Before leaving the oratory, the dancers kneel to pray to the saints as well as to the souls of the departed captains of the Conquest for permission and for help in fulfilling their obligations, as their captain blows little crosses with incense around the image of the souls in purgatory. Then he gives the order to march and begins marking the steps of the road in four-quarter time. The concheros form two columns; at the head of the right one is the first captain; at the left, the second captain, followed by those next in rank, with the female standard-bearer in the middle. Only the Devil may go by himself as he pleases.

The conchero costumes have a very primitive flavor. All wear headdresses adorned with long, waving, colored feathers, mirrors and beads; sometimes strings of beads fall over the face. They all look alike, yet each one is a little different, which is also true of the dress even in the same groups. The women use the same kind of head-dresses as the men, but wear their usual style dresses in brighter colors, their hair hanging loose. The men wear wigs of long hair, because the Chichimecas wore theirs long.

The style of the dress of the concheros is changing. In the twenties most of the men wore gay ballet-dancer skirts trimmed with beads, cotton shirts, long colored stockings, heavy leather sandals, with a small bag adorned with shells hanging at the waist. In recent years many of the groups wear brown chamois-skin suits, adorned with beads and leather fringe, feathered crowns as usual, and bright silk kerchiefs. In some groups all the men wear elegant long satin capes of different colors with only a breechclout underneath in the pre-Spanish style.

The standards, bound with ribbons of different colors, have the images of the saints of the four frontiers in the corners; sometimes they, too, are adorned with beads. They also bear the names of the captain of the mesa, the ensign who carries it, and the date and place of the installation of the mesa.

Before a fiesta the concheros renew the big green crosses that are the landmarks wherever they dance. They gather around the cross, blow incense at it and to the four winds; take it off the pedestal, leaving a cross of flowers in its place. After they paint the cross, they spend the night around it, praying, singing alabanzas, dancing and shooting off rockets; then they take it to church to hear Mass. At dawn on the day of the fiesta, they put the cross back in its place, with alabanzas, incense, dances, and firecrackers.

After the crosses are set up, the dancer groups go to church to pray and dance and to ask permission for the dances in the atrium. They sing their alabanzas to the saint whose day is being celebrated, and dance backwards out of the church, so as not to turn their backs to the altar. But before entering the church, they make the figure of the cross or form four columns in the directions of the four winds, to invoke the four frontiers—La Villa de Guadalupe, Chalma, Los Remedios, and Amecameca—to ask their permission. When they come out from the church to dance, they again greet the four winds.

The concheros of each group form a circle as in ancient times, but instead of singing as they dance, they play their stringed instruments. The majority play conchas, strung and tuned like a guitar; a few have mandolins or even banjos. The dance is initiated by the leader, who calls out in a clear strong voice, "He is God," at the same time making the sign of the cross with the right foot and then with the left, which is called the sign of the dance. As he yells, he arches his body backwards, lifting his instrument as if it were a bow, reminiscent of the way the Chichimecas used to shoot their arrows when they danced and yelled. Then all the others follow the captain.

The dance steps are varied, consisting of nimble springs, raising the knees and contracting the legs, dancing on one foot while marking a cross with the other in the air; crossing the feet and rocking from side to side; jumping into the air with both feet and landing on the toes like a rooster; making genuflections. They perform all their figures with lightness and grace, but end them with a vigorous stamping on the ground in the aboriginal manner.

The dance and music begin slowly, increasing in speed and volume until they reach a climax and suddenly stop; then begin again with new steps to different melodies. The concheros form fascinating ensembles of sound and color.

Before leaving the fiesta, the concheros take leave of the four winds in the atrium, first entering the church to render thanks and to take leave of the saint. Then they return to their mesa, there also to give thanks, and finally to their homes. They are very tired after one of these excursions, as they sleep very little. Aside from their vigil over the cross, they arise at dawn to help with their alabanzas and dances, the penitents who are crawling to the church on their knees; and they dance practically all day long, with just a few hours off in the middle of the day for food and rest.

The conchero dances and the devotion of the cross or the four winds seem to have originated in connection with one of those early miracles that were so instrumental in subduing the natives.

During the last bloody battle fought between the Christians and the pagan Chichimecas, on the hill near the present City of Querétaro, July 25, 1531, both sides agreed in advance not to use arms. But they used fists, feet, and teeth. When the fighting was at its worst, there appeared a shining cross, suspended in the air above the field of battle, and at its side the image of St. James, whose day it was. The Christians had invoked his aid to detain the sun, as night was coming on and the fighting was bitter.

Upon beholding this marvel, the pagans calmed down. They wept and promised to accept the light of the Gospel. Afterwards they asked that a cross be erected as a landmark on the battlefield that should last "forever and ever," and that the place be called "Sangremal," in memory of the blood spilled there by both sides.

The following day the Catholics set up a pine cross on the hill, at which a Mass was said. But the newly converted Chichimecas were not satisfied with the cross; they hid it and insisted on being given one of permanent materials. The Catholics gave them one of stone but that did not please them either because it was small and unattractive. So Don Nicolás de San Luis, the Cacique in charge of the Spanish forces, ordered Don Juan de la Cruz to go out to find better stones for a larger cross and to bring it back at once, for he feared the discontented Chichimecas.

After walking half a league, praying all the time to the Lord and the Holy Virgin for help in his hard task, Juan de la Cruz came upon a quarry of beautiful shining stones of three colors—red, white, and purple. Delighted, he set to work at once, and within twenty-four hours he finished carving a handsome cross, ten feet high. He immediately sent word to the Caciques and meanwhile sought a shady spot for the cross, which he found under a "rose, called a calalosuchil," probably the reason for the suchitls of the concheros.

Don Nicolás was overjoyed at the good news. He ordered the drummers and buglers to call the Catholic soldiers and officers, who together with some of the milder Chichimecas set out to bring the cross.

When they saw the cross, they were amazed at its beauty. As they knelt in prayer around it, a fragrant odor filled the air, and a beautiful white cloud, held by four angels, hovered over it to furnish shade. Afterwards they picked up the cross to carry it back, which although large and of stone, was as light as straw on their backs. And a fragrant odor followed the cross.

The Chichimecas received the cross with great rejoicing, dancing, skirmishing, yelling, and shooting arrows into the air as it was set upon its foundation. When Mass was said, both Catholics and pagans took part, beating their breasts at the same time.

After the services were over, the Chichimecas examined the cross from top to bottom; they sent for their chief who did likewise. As he was looking at it, he saw four angels putting palms and crowns of the most beautiful roses on the arms of the cross, while a lovely blue cloud was making shade for them. So the chief was filled with joy and said aloud, "This is the cross that shall serve as a landmark; that shall last forever and ever; the cross forever and ever; this is the cross we want."

For a whole week afterwards the natives celebrated, kissing the cross, shooting arrows, dancing, and yelling with contentment.

The concheros of the Federal District present a very interesting phenomenon. They are workers, some of them in the skilled trades, who in appearance seem no longer to belong to the classes living in a primitive state. Yet they are good concheros! They mention the Chichimecas and the Hill of Sangremal; when they go to dance for the Virgin of Guadalupe, they remember Tonantzin; when they go to Chalma, they dance in the cave, recalling the idol who some of them believe was Huitzilopochtli.

When the Chichimecas first began their dances and the cult of the cross, it may have been to cover up their pagan beliefs and practices. Today it is difficult to know what the concheros actually believe, even though their ceremonies and dances are predominantly pagan. They undoubtedly make sacrifices to keep the dances alive as much from a desire to escape briefly from a sorry existence as because of any beliefs.[3]

The same must be true of all the thousands of concheros outside of the Federal District. For all of them, when they change from their overalls into their beautiful dance costumes, are transformed into personages. They move in an aura of glory, absolutely absorbed in their parts, yet conscious of the respect and admiration of the multitudes (Pl. 73).

III. Yaqui Pascolas

The Yaqui pascolas constitute the third notable group of Mexican dances. The Deer Dance around which all the pantomime revolves is undoubtedly of pre-Spanish origin. At one time it must have been danced for luck in hunting, but now it is always performed together

YAQUI DEER DANCER

with the pascolas at all religious fiestas and ceremonies. The manner of performing the dance must also have changed, but even as it is, the choreography and music are beautiful.

The deer always dances with two, three, or four pascolas, from whom the dances derive their name. His torso and feet are bare; a stuffed deer's head is fitted on his head over a white cloth, drawn tightly above his eyes, the ends falling backwards; the head is held by a leather strap tied under the chin; a string of beads with a medallion hangs around his neck. From the waist to his knees he wears kilts formed of a rebozo or a piece of white cloth, held with a leather belt from which hang deer claws. Around his legs are strings of ténabari, dried cocoons filled with gravel, and he carries a large gourd rattle in each hand.

The pascolas also dance with bare torsos and feet. Their heads, too, are bare, with a knot of hair standing up tied with a ribbon, called a "candle." A small wooden mask with grotesque features, shaggy eyebrows and beard, is tied to the head so that it can be moved easily. Their trousers are formed from a checked blanket, and from their leather belts hang brass or copper bells. They wear the same kind of necklaces and strings of cocoons as the deer, but their rattles are of wood, hollowed out above the handle to admit some metal disks.

The pascolas and the deer dancer have their own governor, whom they obey implicitly, never doing anything without his permission. He watches over them like a hawk before and during fiestas, his greatest concern being to keep them sober.

The pascolas are always danced in an enramada—a thatched arbor with open sides. There are one or more crosses near-by and sometimes an altar at one side. The fiesta is opened by the pascolas. When a saint is being feted, the image is there to witness the dance. Then the pascolas' governor leads them, with his cane of authority, to the altar where they kneel to ask permission to begin. Afterwards the oldest one of them enters the arbor with his mask on and is led around by the governor three times in counter-clockwise circuits. The pascola then takes the stick and puts it into the holes of the harp, talking to it and naming all the animals of the woods. In the end he says, "Now with the favor of God, we are going to dance," and goes out to shoot off three firecrackers at the cross to announce the beginning. When the fiesta is over, each pascola dances a few steps in front of each musician in leave-taking. They all go again to pray to the saint and to ask pardon for any offenses they have given during the dancing.

The first dances are by the pascolas to the music of harp and violin. One dances after another, with his mask pushed off his face and the rattle stuck in his belt. They dance close to the musician, with body slightly stooped, arms hanging at the sides and knees bent a little, at times performing steps that resemble the European clog, at others the Spanish zapateado, but always stamping the ground twice with the same foot and alternating. Every dancer introduces variations—he may drag one toe around in a semicircle, while hopping on the other; extend the heel and drag it back; skip, jump up and down on both feet, strike heel against ankle—as if in competition. As they move, the rustling sound of the cocoons affords a pleasant accompaniment to the music.

While waiting to dance, the pascolas amuse the spectators, for

they are also clowns. They make jokes, take liberties in making sa-
lacious references to the female relatives of the men around them, including the wives. But nothing they say or do is resented, even their
obscene stories and movements. The people answer back all talking
Cahita and everyone laughs good naturedly, saying "Ah well, that
is why they are pascolas."

When the last of the pascolas finishes his dance, the three old
musicians, their hats adorned with flowers, are seated on the ground
near the drummer with the flute—one with his water-drum, the others
with their rasps—ready to receive the deer. He enters, stepping
lightly, looking about him cautiously, imitating perfectly the posture
and movements of the real animal. The music, syncopated and irregular, reveals his restlessness. When he is convinced there is no enemy
around, he becomes tranquil, pretends to nibble at grass, to drink
from a stream by playing with the gourd-drum water, his feet dancing
all the time. The music then repeats a quiet rhythm several times as
the three old men sing in falsetto the lovely, simple songs, which
translated freely from Cahita are: (1) "This is the ténabari (butterfly
cocoon) that is caught in the tree and when the wind blows it
moves." (2) "Botóboli Segui" ("the flower of the dark tree"), "This
is the flower of the dark tree that blossoms in the month of August
when the rain falls." This mood changes with the melody of the
coyote, the deer's great enemy. The deer shows fear; he dances
wildly. The music and the dancing become intensely exciting (Pls. 20,
22, 23).

The pascolas enact with the deer little dramas which the Yaquis
call juegos or games. A favorite one is the killing of the deer by the
coyotes. The pascolas represent the coyotes, pursuing the deer until
they trap and kill him. Then they take his "carcass" on their shoulders
to the man giving the fiesta or to the person in charge of it, who is
obliged to purchase it, the price being bottles of liquor. There are
other juegos in which the pascolas are tigers, buzzards, or any other
animals that annoy deer. They also play a humorous game of enchantment in which no one is killed.

The deer dance of the wilder Yaquis in the Bactete Sierra is danced
around a bonfire and over its flames, while the singers sing:

Vámonos, vámonos a bailar	Come on, let us dance
A la hoguera de Satanás;	At Satan's bonfire,
A ver que fin tenemos,	To see what happens,
A ver si no nos quemamos.	To see if we get burned.
Y antes que nos vayamos,	But before going,
Vamos a persignarnos,	Let us cross ourselves
En nombre de Díos.	In the name of God.
¿Qué fin hemos de tener?	What can happen to us then?

The pascolas begin to learn their dances as children, but they have to wait a long time for the opportunity to replace their elders. Most of them dance until long past middle age. Yet in spite of their years and heavy, powerful bodies, they are amazingly light of foot and playful. They can imitate every animal to perfection and dance twenty-four hours at a time with little time out for rest.

When an adult who has not learned the art of the pascola dancers and musicians wants to become one of them, he can do so by going through the test of the magic cave in the red mountain near the upper river. When he comes to the cave, he is received by a snake into whose mouth he must enter, and is ejected into the interior from the anus. Then he finds himself in a large room among many snakes and other animals. The benches in this room are made of snakes. On the walls hang all the wearing apparel and musical instruments of the pascolas.

The man must continue walking to the end of the cave, fearlessly and without looking back. There he meets the king of all the snakes, which winds itself around his body and then licks his face all over with his tongue. If he is not frightened, the snake frees him and leads him to the objects on the wall, from which he may choose according to what he wishes to become—a pascola, a deer-dancer or a musician. As soon as he has selected his equipment, he becomes an expert in any one of those arts. Then he takes leave of the animals, who say "good-bye" to him, and he may leave the cave at once. But those who are afraid never return. As punishment for their cowardice, they are transformed into animals.

This cave also contains equipment for charros, and a man may become one in the same way.[4]

Yaqui Coyote and Matachine Dances

These two dances, although less complicated and less beautiful than the Deer Dance, play an important part in the ceremonial organization of the Yaquis.

The *Coyote* is danced by three men dressed in ordinary clothes but with a coyote skin hanging from the forehead down the back and a crest of eagle or hawk feathers rising from the headband in front. They carry in the left hand a hunting bow, which they beat with a reed cane that has several lengthwise incisions to make it more flexible and sonorous. They dance to the music of a drum, performing a slow, stamping step in a crouching position with bent knees, toward the musician. When the drum beats become irregular, the *coyotes* dance backwards. When they are about ten feet away from the drum,

YAQUI COYOTE DANCER

the beats become regular again and they return with quicker steps, straightening their bodies and moving their heads in the manner of a coyote. This is the only figure of the dance and is repeated for hours.

The drummer, generally an old man, wears a special headband for the occasion. He sings in a low voice into a hole in the side of the drum, which he holds upright in his hand and beats with a round stick, the head of it covered with cloth. One of the various songs for the dance in Cahita, is "Crow, crow, outside, outside, he comes, not playing, playing."

The insignia of the war captains and other officials is also a coyote skin, falling from the front of the head down their backs, held with a red band adorned with pearl buttons or shells, from which rises a tall parrot feather. At the fiestas of the saints whom the soldiers consider their patrons—the Virgin of Guadalupe, Santa Isabel, the Holy Cross—the captains and soldiers participate in the *coyote* dance, each one dancing it three times.

Whenever the *coyote* dance is performed, the civil officials of the villages sit on a bench with their staffs of authority and watch them. A corporal in a feathered headdress hands out cigarettes to the spectators during pauses in the dances.

At dawn, when a fiesta is about to end and the *coyotes* have danced all night long, three plates of meat are placed between the dancers and the drum, which each man while dancing picks up with his teeth and brings to the drum.

The *coyote* dance is performed upon the death of all soldiers, village chiefs, and Matachine dancers, as well as at fiestas.

The Matachines are a society of dancers who call themselves the "Soldiers of the Virgin" and are a part of the church organization,

YAQUI MATACHINE DANCER

the head of the church being usually selected from among them. The group is directed by a chief with two assistants. There is a chief dancer, called a monarca, who also has two assistants. The membership is for life and consists of persons who because of illness have made a vow to join. Parents sometimes pledge their little boys when they are ill, and they begin to dance as soon as they are old enough to do so. Those who become too old to dance instruct the young ones.

The dancers wear white shirts with red ribbons interlaced across the chest, a small crown of colored flowers over a red bandanna, carry a wooden rattle in the right hand and in the left a three-pronged wand adorned with feathers. The monarcas of some of the villages wear black velvet over-trousers, open on the outer side from the thigh down.

The Matachines dance in two lines, with an assistant monarca at the head and the chief one in the middle, forming a variety of simple steps and figures. The music is furnished by two violinists, who answer each other in an interesting manner, which the dancers accompany with their rattles.

Besides dancing at fiestas, the Matachines dance at the funerals of all their members and those of their close relatives, and at the church every Sunday, taking part in the procession to the cross.

In some of the villages, the Matachines perform a ribbon dance around a pole at sunrise. At Bacun, six dancers in two opposite lines with the monarca in the center, wind the ribbons as they dance around the pole; in Corcorit, three on each side wind the ribbons, while another group of six with three on each side braid the ribbons without winding them around the pole.[5]

Mayo Dances

The Mayos, neighbors of the Yaquis and speaking the same language, have the same dances. Their costumes are the same, excepting that the pascolas and deer-dancers wear jersey shirts; their procedure is also similar but with some differences in customs (Pl. 20).

The musical instruments are of the same kind as those of the Yaquis but the melodies and verses differ. Two of the songs the old musicians sing for the deer, freely translated from the Cahita, are: (1) "Go step, little brother, now the sun is rising, traveling beneath the sun, throwing flowers on the way while dancing with all your heart." (2) "Deer, deer, coyote is hunting you. Place yourself in the water. No harm will he do you."

Mayo men may also learn to be pascolas and musicians if they are not afraid of wild beasts. The pascola dancers are "part of the religion of the woods," so some believe they can learn better there. If one becomes frightened, he will soon die. Both dancers and musicians are said to have dealings with the devil. Yet they are subject to witchcraft. When they are victims of either witches or sorcerers, they have pains in their legs. As a protection they wear a charm of wild chile or chiltipin, which they also eat during fiestas.

The Mayos no longer have the coyote dance, but their Matachine organization and dances are similar to those of the Yaquis. However, their dancers do not perform the ribbon dance, but two others. One is the mó-el or bird dance. The dancers form a circle and dance around jumping vigorously, while the monarca dances with a little boy seated on the back of his neck, representing the bird. The mó-els, small birds with gray, white, and black bars, are thick around Easter time and eat wheat and vegetables. The dance is probably a pantomime for driving them away or for placating them.

The other is the "sleepy" dance, which is combined with the regular figures of the matachine dances. After performing one of the main ones, the musicians suddenly stop and the dancers fall on the ground, facing the altar, pillowing their heads on their arms, feigning sleep. After a pause the music begins softly, slowly, but gradually increasing its volume and tempo. The monarca is the first to awaken. He raises his head and glances around him and returns to his sleeping posture. After repeating this three times, he leaps to his feet and begins to dance; all the others follow. The same thing is repeated several times during the course of a dance. These dances like the Yaqui ribbon dance are performed early in the morning, in the villages of San Ignacio and Navajoa.[6]

Tarahumara Dances

The simple primitive dances of the Taranumaras are still vehicles for all their prayers. There used to be the rutuburi and yumari, but now both are combined in the dutuburi, which is danced at all fiestas, on all ceremonial occasions, as well as for curing the sick and dispatching the dead. All Tarahumaras have dance patios near their huts and are constantly giving small and big tesgüinadas—dancing, drinking, and praying parties. To make the prayers effective, an animal must be sacrificed and his blood offered to Father Sun, who commanded the people to dance.

Men and women take part in the dutuburi but dance separately. The women line up to the right of the chanter, each one holding the left hand of the one in front with her right hand, and perform a skipping step which begins with the left foot and ends on the right in a slight hop and stamp. They dance back and forth and form an arc, while the men walk forward and backward with the chanter. The chanter repeats a simple refrain to the steady shaking of his rattle, continuing his singing even when the dancers stop to rest for long intervals during the night.

This dance is always performed out of doors, so that Father Sun and Mother Moon may witness it, and near three crosses, because the dancing and singing is directed to them as well. Another small cross is placed at the edge or just outside of the patio when the dutuburi is being danced to ward off sickness. When food is placed on the altar, a small vessel of it is put near the cross with the formula, "Sickness is going to eat; after eating it will go away."

The peyote dance is also simple but a little different. About ten men and women take part in it. The women are led into the dance patio by the two assistant chanters, the men following. Then all dance around a fire to a tune played on a violin and guitar, at intervals slapping their mouths and shouting.

TARAHUMARA MATACHINE DANCER

The Tarahumaras also have pascola and Matachine dances, which they had adopted at some time in the past, and always perform at Catholic fiestas. The pascolas wear the same rattling tenábari and jingling belts and do clogging steps like those of the Yaquis, but there the resemblance ends. On Friday of Holy Week at Samachique one lone pascola, accompanied by two little boys, enters the church to dance in the four directions and then continues to the music of a violin and guitar in the convent patio, where he is given food and tesgüino. Later another pascola may join him. The pascolas also dance for the dead.

The Matachines dance in greater numbers and seem to be more important, their organization and costumes differing in the various villages. Those of Samachique dress more elaborately than others. They wear a red cloth cape with a blue or white lining, reaching to the knees, over an ordinary white cotton shirt; two pairs of trousers, the red outer ones cut so at the knees that the white pair shows bagging; a belt from which hang red bandannas in front and back; long colored stockings and real shoes of any kind available. The crowns made of thin wood or bark and the arch formed of curved sticks are covered with colored paper, mirrors and other shining things, and fitted on the head over a red bandanna tied under the chin. In the right hand they carry a rattle and in the left an adorned wooden wand.

The dance formation and steps are similar to those of the Yaquis. They also have a monarca, who stands in front between the two lines and indicates all the movements with his wand, and all the dancers beat the rhythm as they form their figures to the music of violin and guitar.

The Tarahumara Matachines are not organized like the Yaqui, but in Samachique each dancer is in charge of a chapeón, who stands to one side of him, marking the rhythm of the dance and shouting the changes in figures in falsetto. The leader of the chapeones wears a wooden mask on the back of his head, painted in white lines, with false white hair and beard. This man holds a position of respect in the community; he often dedicates the tesgüino at fiestas and sits with the judges when they are trying offenders.

There seems to be no explanation as to why these men are called chapeones, unless there is some remote relation between them and the capeos, Spaniards who used to fight bulls without weapons at certain fiestas. In New Mexico there are chapeones under different names, who pantomime bullfighting in the Matachine dances.

The name matachín is also of Spanish origin. In ancient times it was applied to gay masqueraders, wearing masks and long vari-colored robes, who danced and made merry, dealing blows with wooden swords and bladders filled with air. But those are a far cry from the Matachines of today in their ritual dances.[7]

Huichol Dance of Nayarit

We have already seen the riutal dances of the Huichols of Jalisco; those of Nayarit are similar. All of them are more like the pre-Spanish dances than most others. They revolve around the singing shaman with his drum and assistant chanters; men and women dance in circles or lines with leaders, who take up the songs of the shaman as in ancient times. Every dance has different songs and ritual, but the manner of dancing is similar.

In Cerro del Roble, Nayarit, the dance for most occasions is done by men and women around a fire. First the shaman sprinkles the flames with tesgüino, after which he begins his chant as he lifts his hands to the heavens in a gesture of invocation or offering. After dancing for a while, all go to the god-house, which has only two walls and a roof of brilliant feathers of birds killed by hunters, where they dance to the four winds. Then they return to dance around the fire again until the dance comes to an end.

The same dance is performed before a hunt for luck, and afterwards to render thanks. The first animal killed at the fire is dedicated to the gods. Those who have had luck dance with some part of the animals they have killed. When they bring back snakes, the meat is offered to the gods and the skins put on the temple roof, together with the bird plumage and tails. The following year they are used as adornments on hats.

When this dance is for a dead person, adult or child, the dancers cover themselves with blankets as a sign of mourning. Strings are tied to the corpse for each member of the family present. These the dancers cut while dancing, to symbolize the separation.

The same dance is performed as part of a marriage ceremony, which lasts for twenty-four hours. While the fiesta goes on with dancing, eating, and drinking, the boy and girl sit together naked under a sheet, without food or drink. This is done so that they will become accustomed to one another.

Cora Dances

The Coras, neighbors of the Huichols in the Sierra of Nayarit, have altogether different dances. One of the most popular is los maromeros, the acrobats, reminiscent of the pre-Spanish ones. The dancers wear their ordinary white cotton suits, but adorn their hats with ribbons and carry big crude bastones or canes; the one of el viejo, their leader, being thicker than the others and supplied with metal disks. All of them have hanging from the shoulder one of those colorful cross-stitched Cora bags. They dance and perform their acrobatic feats to the music of a small drum and flute played by the same musician—another indication that the dance is primitive.

The maromeros of Jesus María—the largest place in Coraland and the only one that has a Catholic church—dance inside of it for the fiesta of San Miguel, September 29. The first maromero does a solo dance. When el viejo calls out something, he dances slowly with gestures in the four directions. Then he puts one end of the bastón down and holding the other end at an angle, he continues to dance and swings under it, repeating this difficult feat until he reaches the altar.

Another attractive dance at this fiesta is that of las palmas, the palms, which is done in many villages. It consists of about ten young men, wearing their usual white suits with red bandannas hanging down in front from under their shirts. Their crowns are adorned with flowers and tall blue huaraca feathers, tipped with down, representing prayers for rain. From the headdress is suspended a fine net of blue beads with some white, falling over the face to about the middle of the chest. In one hand the dancers carry a painted tin rattle and in the other a fan-shaped bamboo palm, adorned with artificial blue and yellow flowers. They also have hanging from the shoulder those bright bags on pretty handwoven ribbons with little balls of colored wool at the ends (Pl. 6).

The leader, who at the same time is the clown of this group, also is called viejo, meaning "old man," but he is not necessarily old. He wears a wooden mask with a horsehair mustache, a cocoa fibre cap and a bag, and he carries a whip. There is a little girl representing Malinche in ordinary adult clothes, but wearing the same headgear as the dancers.

The dancers perform elaborate figures to the music of violin and flute, a characteristic step being to spread the feet apart and bend backwards. At intervals Malinche performs a solo dance with one of the men.

The music for both dances is very beautiful. One of the maromeros plays a lovely, complicated melody to San Miguel, which sounds as if he were talking to him.[9]

Other Cora dances will be mentioned later, as they are not peculiar to their culture.

The Dances of the Bows and Rattles

These dances are popular in many of the northwestern states—from Nayarit and Jalisco, to Zacatecas and Coahuila. There are regional differences but they follow a general pattern.

The costumes are of bright colors, red being preferred. They consist of tunics, embroidered with sequins or beads in bird or other designs; short skirts with three or more rows of reeds a few inches long, tipped with colored wool; colored stockings, and sandals. All wear crowns, adorned with mirrors and beads, with tall feathers of various kinds—peacock, turkey, eagle, or any other. The dancers all carry painted tin rattles, and in some groups also bows made of wood, with an arrow attached for the purpose of producing rhythm when drawn.

The leaders are elected periodically from the most popular dancers of the groups. In Nayarit they are called los viejos, and in Jalisco, los mayordomos or morenos. They also play the part of clowns, so they dress in old torn clothes, wear grotesque masks, carry a stuffed animal or doll and whips, with which to amuse and frighten. They mimic and play pranks on the dancers, amuse the spectators with grimaces and surprising actions—such as feigning to kiss a woman—and jokes.

Their more serious functions as leaders are to teach the dances and to see that they are well executed; to make all arrangements and provisions for food and lodging when they dance away from home; to see that the dancers keep well, sober, and in order.

The groups from around Guadalajara, Jalisco, elect a new mayordomo every year and often ask the old one to stay on if he has been very popular. In this way they may have several at the same time, together with a curandero, or medicine man, to keep everyone well. When they take office the dancers form a circle with the mayordomos and curandero in the middle. With their right hands on their hearts, they say, "By the ashes of our ancestors and of our mayordomos, I swear to be faithful to our customs." All promise to work together for the good name of the group and village.

They dance to various sones played on a violin and some other stringed instrument or on a crude kind of wooden drum, called a tepenaje, with two openings, one having a deeper tone than the other. When the introduction is played, the dancers shake their rattles and turn in their places, while the mayordomos yell, jump, snap their whips, and raise their stuffed animals in bold gestures. This is finished with the dancers facing each other in two lines, then performing a variety of steps and figures. In one of them, they dance in the four directions, forming a cross, at the end of which the mayordomo calls, and all bend in a kneeling gesture in homage. In another figure, the mayordomo dances between the lines with the Malinche—who is represented in every group either by a young girl or a man in woman's clothes—all the men dancing at the same time. Then Malinche dances with the first dancer of each line to the foot of it, leaving him there and returning for the next one until she has danced with all of them. Meanwhile the mayordomo dances around by himself, acting the clown. The dance then ends with the same music and figure with which it began.

Some of the Cora groups around Jesus María are called los arcos but one of them is known as los matachines. In this one there are two viejos who wear ludicrous masks with long fibre hair and carry whips. One of them has a stuffed monkey and the other a little gourd filled with ashes with which he tries to mark crosses on the women, saying "It may do you good and cannot harm you." Then the viejos get together, chat, and tell off-color jokes. They dance by themselves and with Malinche and make everyone laugh.

The dancers dress like all the others elsewhere, but have in addition to their bows and rattles, deer-skin covered quivers for small wooden arrows which they do not use but carry in memory of their ancestors. They perform various figures to sones played on a violin alone, some of them with animal names, like "The Snake," "The Deer," "The Mule," which they accompany with rattles and bows. Occasionally they dance a *son* to the rhythm of their bows only; or when there is other music, at a signal from a viejo, all pull their bows together in unison. It is a very dynamic dance.[10]

No one seems to know how these dances originated. The dancers themselves say they are very old. In and near cities, the groups are composed of the same class of men as the concheros, so it is possible that they are an offshoot of the ancient Chichimeca dances.

The Sonajero and Paixtle Dances of Jalisco

The sonajeros or rattlers, especially the group from the Aztec town of Tuxpan, is one of the most exciting of dances. It is composed of youths who are organized into a closed society of about thirty members, carefully selected by a committee. They wear their usual white cotton suits with red sashes, their shirts trimmed with rows of red, pink, blue, green, and yellow ribbons in front and back, and colorful embroideries; also, a red colzonera, or over-trousers, and a pointed black cloth apron in front and back, adorned with yellow and green ribbons. The cuffs of the trousers are red and about six inches wide.

The name is derived from sonaja, rattle, which each dancer carries. However, they are not of the ordinary kind but are made of a thick stick with handles at both ends, between which are four groups of metal plates. These are shaken hard by the dancers to the music of a little drum and a very shrill, high-pitched flute. About fifteen dance at one time in single file, forming many interesting figures of a variety

THE DANCE OF THE SONAJEROS OR RATTLERS

of vigorous steps, stamped with such enthusiasm that when performed in the Palace of Fine Arts in Mexico City, they have never failed to bring the house down. Several other villages of that region have the same dance.

A most interesting dance from Tuxpan and neighboring villages is that of the paixtles, or moss-covered ones, who represent sorcerers. It probably originated in pre-Spanish days as a magical dance, but is now danced at Catholic church fiestas. The dancers are covered with a cape formed of paixtle—the Aztec word for moss—from head to foot. They wear either wooden or paper masks with human features, and cover their heads and faces with a large kerchief. Each one carries a shepherd's staff, carved with an animal's head, around the neck of which hangs a string of cascabels, with which the dancer strikes the ground as he walks or dances. The costumes are so unwieldy that the dancers can perform only the simplest of steps. They form two lines and move in a most dignified fashion to sones played on a violin, marking the rhythm with their staffs. At intervals they emit in their

A DANCER OF THE PAIXTLE OR MOSS-COVERED ONE

masks hoarse cries, which sound like those made by mysterious animals.[11]

A very popular dance in the State of Jalisco, in addition to those already described, is that of The Conquest, which will come under the
next heading.

La Conquista—Los Moros—Los Santiagos
(The Conquest—The Moors—The St. Jameses)

The above dances are the oldest, most important, and most widespread of those with Christian themes.

La Conquista

This represents the tragedy of the Conquest, which ends happily
in the dance, because Moctezuma and the other heathens become

"Christians." The characters, which are historical, always include Malinche, the native woman who became interpreter and mistress of Cortés. This dance is performed on saints' day fiestas in many places along the West Coast, from Nayarit to Chiapas, but is most popular in the states of Jalisco and Oaxaca; in the latter it is often referred to as "The Dance of the Plumes," La Danza de las Plumas.

The costumes, texts and music of all the groups near Oaxaca City are similar, but the most famous is that of Cuilapan. Their narrative is an old one, written in longhand, which follows historical events more closely than some of the others. Moctezuma and his men wear beautiful costumes of bright rich materials, silk shirts and kerchiefs, and very huge headdresses of brilliantly colored feathers, adorned with mirrors and beads. They carry rattles and perform light, graceful figures to music furnished by a band. In contrast, Cortés and his men are young boys, dressed in unattractive blue soldier suits and caps. Often the dance is performed without the Spaniards. Malinche is represented by a little girl, wearing an ordinary dress but a fancy headdress. She does a solo dance with Moctezuma and seems to be his companion rather than Cortés' (Pls. 49, 52).

The dancers of La Conquista in Jalisco wear robes and skirts of good materials, their headdresses resembling those of the concheros. Their texts are full of anachronisms but charming. In the one from the Hacienda de Camichines, there are various post-Conquest characters. It opens with a Negro informing the Monarca, who is Moctezuma, that he and an Indian saw a big squadron coming of "very decent people in glittering suits, in houses of sticks by water . . . horrible men, taller than a pine tree. . . ."

When Cortés and his men arrive on the scene, messengers are sent back and forth between him and Moctezuma, who say some very amusing lines. In this dance the Spaniards are very good, religious people, who do not want heathens' gold; they are only interested in saving their souls. Finally Malinche, Moctezuma, Chimal, and the Kings of Tlaxcala, Cempoala, Xochimilco, and Tonalla are converted and freed. The King of Tlaxcala, who tried to sell charcoal to Cortés, alludes to the soldiers of Mohammed and the Sultans in his last speech; Cortés mentions the fights between Republicans and Conservatives, Federalists and Centralists, and once Cortés is referred to as a tejano, a Texan.[12]

Los Moros

Los moros y cristianos, the Moors and Christians—referred to simply as los moros—were introduced immediately after the Con-

quest in the form of sham battles on horseback. The Spaniards themselves took part in them at bullfights and other fiestas. Later they
were performed on a grand scale at religious fiestas only, all social
classes taking part. Since 1910, they have been reduced to groups of
about a dozen, more or less, composed of humble folk.

An example of one of the elaborate dramas of "The Moors," which
took place until just before the Revolution of 1910, was the one of
the City of Zacatecas, on June 24, to celebrate the fiesta of St. John
the Baptist. It was called Las Morismas, meaning a multitude of
Moors. About a thousand men were recruited for the forces of both
sides. The officers were generally retired soldiers, who made the men
maneuver daily to bugle and drum. Preference for the important
roles—the Moorish king, the Moor Muza, Don Juan of Austria, the
Catholic monarchs Ferdinand and Isabella, the odalisques—were given
to retired actors, who memorized their parts in verse.

The costumes were highly picturesque and full of anachronisms.
As each one had to supply his own, there were military suits of every
epoch and quality, but the Moors could always be distinguished by
their turbans. The leading personages, however, dressed in character,
while Don Juan of Austria always managed a suit of an Insurgent general, a large sombrero and a pair of Frederick boots.

The battles lasted for three days around the small Bracho Chapel,
dedicated to St. John. Two camps were set up—one for the Christians and another for the Moorish kings, their harems, and their soldiers. The encounters began at sunrise with constant marching and
discharge of firearms, which were loaded with powder and plugs.
The variety of arms ran from small cannon, bronze mortars, flint-
lock pistols, rifles, swords, lances, and machetes to hatchets of every
epoch. Everything was done with great military precision.

On the second day the Moors were the victors. After long speeches
in verse, they cut off the head of St. John and carried it bleeding on
the point of a lance, surrounded by banners, and presented it with
military pomp to the Sultan, who sat up high in a box, called a "castle,"
surrounded by his harem. On the third day, the last, the Christians won, taking the Moors' castle amidst great clamor and discharge
of firearms. Then they cut off the head of the Moorish king; also
carried it bleeding on a lance offering it first to Ferdinand and Isabella
and then to St. John in the chapel. That night a display of fireworks
ended the fiesta.

Los Moros is one of the most widespread of the ritual dances at
the present time, especially popular around the Federal District and
in the central states. The costumes and performances vary greatly in
quality. Some dancers wear cheap cotton suits, while others wear
costumes of good materials, but the acting is often better among the

poorly dressed. The suits consist of short trousers and capes, red or black; the Christians wear vizors and crosses; the Moors, crowns with half moons. The monarchs generally wear superior costumes and masks in order to represent their parts better. There is always a clown wearing a devil's mask (Pl. 77).

There are long, supposedly historical texts, which the actors learn by heart and say well. Whenever they speak, they walk up and down, "So that the throngs may know there is something going on." They fight with machetes, to music furnished by stringed instruments, dance, and march. When it is all over, the dancers sometimes carry away the dead on their shoulders to solemn music. In some villages the soldiers appear on horseback, and each side has a wooden platform for the monarchs.

The Moros of Michoacán are different from all the others. There are only four of them, elegantly dressed, who take part in Catholic fiestas. They wear velvet capes and over-trousers, slashed at the sides, profusely trimmed with sequins, gilt braid and fringe. Their crowns are tall, adorned with colored paper, mirrors, feathers, and shining beads, some with a kerchief falling from them to cover the face partially. All wear shoes with spurs, to which are attached metal disks instead of rowels. The Moros from around Lake Pátzcuaro adorn their costumes with silver fish. For the fiesta of St. Francis, October 4, in Iguatzio, they appear on horseback at the church, dismount, pray, dance. Then they mount again and ride through the streets, followed by a throng. They stop to dance wherever they are invited or are likely to be treated to food, drinks and cigarettes—often at stores. Their steps are simple, performed to pleasing sones played on stringed instruments, with much clashing of spurs. They always dance at the house of the carguero, who furnishes the festal meal, as well as at the priest's house.

This custom of dancing everywhere is not widespread. Generally the ritual dances are performed only at the church (Pls. 77, 151, 155, 156, 157).

Los Santiagos

Los Santiagos, or the dance of St. James, fighting the heathen on his white horse, is also popular and widespread. The procedure and costumes are similar to those of the Moors—short trousers, capes, and the same style hats. St. James has parts of a small white wooden horse tied to his waist so that it looks as if he were riding it; he is dressed better than the soldiers and he carries a lance. Like the Moors, those taking part act, dance, and fight, the Christians winning and making the heathen ruler accept Christianity.

The Santiago dances in the remote villages are more interesting and colorful than those of the central ones. In that of the Aztecs of Cuetzalán, Sierra de Puebla, Santiago el Caballero wears his horse on a painted wooden belt. The suits are colorful, the "pilots" and soldiers wearing masks, but not St. James. They fight and dance to music of flute and drum (Pl. 68).

Here the horse is believed to be endowed with life and is venerated. The newly elected Santiago receives the horse from the outgoing one, and has to take care of him until the next fiesta the following year. He keeps him either on the household altar or in a small box-like stable, made especially for the purpose. Santiago obligates himself to feed the horse a bowl of corn and another of water every day. If he does not do this faithfully, the horse may run away to another village, which will be very bad.

In the Cora village of San Juan Peyután, Sierra de Nayarit, during the fiesta on January 1, a group of Moors come out on horseback, in ordinary clothes, carrying wooden lances pointed with tin. All day long they ride up and down one street, pursuing a St. James, also on horseback, wearing a red cape adorned with gilt paper, and a white cloth cap. He carries a lance and fights the heathen soldiers valiantly. However, in the end they make him prisoner, contrary to the Catholic intention of the dance.[14]

In a very old Santiago text, still used in the village of Tepetlaostoc, Morelos, the characters are Santiago, Ambassador, First Cain, Second Cain, Pilatos, Sabario, and twelve soldiers.

It begins with a march and a dance, after which follow speeches. Santiago sends an Ambassador to Pilatos with a long written ultimatum—if he does not accept Christianity, he will annihilate him and his armies. He makes a long speech, saying in part:

> Here we must convert
> That nation of Turks;
> Here to abandon the errors
> Of that prophet, that Maoma (Mohammed)
> That false traitorous God
> Whom they blindly adore . . .

The Ambassador takes leave in long speeches to Santiago and the Cains. Santiago blesses him:

> May that God of armies
> Who loves and cares for us so much,
> Bless you eternally
> And keep you from misfortune.

In Jerusalem the conversations between the Christian Ambassador, General Sabario, and Pilatos are not pleasant. Pilatos, upon reading Santiago's message and talking with the Ambassador, breaks out angrily:

> Silence, wretched Christian,
> You talk of things you know not,
> For my God has all the human race at his feet.

The Ambassador returns to Santiago to inform him that Pilatos and Sabario will not surrender. In the meantime Pilatos orders Sabario to prepare his soldiers so that they will not be taken unawares. He harangues the soldiers, who answer him in chorus:

> Viva our general!
> Death to every Christian!

Then each of the twelve soldiers makes a separate speech. Both sides are ready for battle. Santiago prays:

> Sacred God omnipotent,
> Divine Jesus, I adore thee.
> Give me a bit of courage
> To overcome this Moor.

Santiago appears and Sabario says to him:

> Do you know, great coward,
> That I was born immortal . . .
> I am a thunderbolt embracing
> The voice of this agitation.

As Sabario takes leave of Pilatos and is approaching the battlefield, he prays:

> Let the wrath of my burning resolve
> Give off flame
> Leaving Christianity
> In dust and ashes . . .

When he sees the battlefield, he makes a long speech in which he bemoans his fate, because his ramparts are destroyed and his army vanquished; a part of it follows:

> O Maoma, how can you forget
> Your faithful Africans?
> On whom shall I call now?
> I find no one . . .

> I shall seize my dagger
> And open my heart.
> Open, O earth, and bury me!
> Mountains, wilderness, crags,
> Bitter waters of the sea,
> Help to bring me death.
> Throw yourselves on this place,
> Detach yourselves from the empyrean.
> Morning and evening stars
> Fall upon the earth
> To bring an end to Sabario . . .
>   To Santiago
> I am General Sabario,
> Who when I go into action,
> If daylight fails me,
> I make the sun stand still . . .

He still threatens that he will bring Santiago dead or alive into the presence of his Majesty.

After many more speeches, Pilatos, seeing that Maoma has failed him, accepts Christianity.

Sabario makes the last speech. At the beginning he is dying but in the end he says:

> Because I feel regret
> That I am going to leave
> This delightful pleasure
> As a humble companion.
> But by next year I will return
> If God allows me to come back.[15]

This text is interrupted often by dances and the clashes of machetes. Whoever wrote it seems to have preferred the character of General Sabario to all the others, because he presented him as the bravest of all and gave him the best lines to say. The dancers themselves are not worried about who's who nor chronological or factual accuracy; all they care about is that their costumes be showy and their dancing good. Subconsciously they prefer the pagans. An interesting example is the Dances of the Conquest in Oaxaca, in which the conquered Moctezuma and his men shine, and the conqueror Cortés and his men are so unattractive that no one notices them.

Quetzales and Acatlaxquis

The quetzal dances are performed in villages of the lowlands of Vera Cruz and the Sierras of Puebla and Hidalgo; the acatlaxquis in Hidalgo only. Both are primitive and beautiful.

The Quetzales

The Quetzales seems to have been inspired by the handsome tropical bird of that name, whose plumes were so highly prized by the ancient Mexicans. The costumes are of vivid colors, red predominating, consisting of three-quarter length or short trousers; white or colored shirt, embroidered or trimmed with ribbons, sometimes crossed at the neck with red bandannas or silk kerchiefs that fall over the shoulders; long colored stockings and sandals; a cape of the same or contrasting color, also with fringed and shining embellishments. Then all this color is crowned by a most extraordinary headdress. It is composed of a huge wheel, over five feet in diameter, with colored paper or silk ribbons interlaced through a network of slender reeds with a border of lovely feathers. This brilliant wheel, justly called a "splendor," is attached to a conical cap on the head of the dancer, held by a ribbon or kerchief tied under the chin. The point of connection of the two is covered by a cross or some other adornment, and some dancers have the head of the quetzal outlined in front of the cap (Pls. 159, 160).

The dance in itself is simple—a few figures to different melodies played on a little drum and flute, the dancers marking the rhythm with their rattles. There are in a group about a dozen or more dancers, who form two facing files and move with poise and dignity. Each figure begins with reverences to the right and left, then the dancers do simple steps, changing places, forming a cross and a snake chain to the tune of the "Little Snake." In some few villages the last figure is done with four dancers rotating on a wheel—a fascinating whirl of color.

The costumes and the dance of the quetzales follow a general pattern throughout the region, excepting for variations in colors and adornments. The names also vary. In Papantla the group wearing the quetzal costume is called guaguas, and in Cuetzalán, voladores; in both places they no longer use the wheel (Pls. 160, 161).[16]

The Acatlaxquis

The acatlaxqui, or dance of the reed-throwers, is performed by Otomís in the municipality of Pahuatlán, Hidalgo. The young dancers wear their everyday white cotton suits, with short red, knee-length over-trousers; two red bandannas tied crosswise over one shoulder and under the other, a third serving as a loin cloth, and cone-shaped paper caps with streamers attached to the points.

Each dancer has under his arm his acatlaxque, formed of one strong reed (about a yard long) and attached to it a dozen or more slender reeds, all adorned with brilliant feathers. These slender reeds are attached to each other in such a way that when the dancer casts them out, they slide out one from the other to form a huge arch (Pl. 72).

The dance revolves around a little girl, called la Maringuilla—probably referring to Malinche—whose part is played by a boy in a long white dress, holding a gourd in which is a painted wooden snake. It begins inside the church, where the dancers in two rows perform intricate steps to the music of a flute and drum. In the atrium they dance first in one long row, back and forth, in front of the entrance; then form a circle around the little Maringuilla, near whom a man stands, wriggling the snake above her head. Later she is lifted on to a small wooden platform, the dance going on in a circle around her. At a given moment the dancers stop and fling their acatlaxqui into the air to form a dome over the dancing Maringuilla, repeating the action several times gracefully, as church bells ring and skyrockets burst around them—a rousing climax (Pls. 70, 71, 72).[17]

Los Negritos

Los negritos, or the Negro dances, exist in various of the states along the coasts to which the Spaniards brought Negro slaves. Those of Puebla and Vera Cruz are similar in the way that their other dances are, the costumes varying a great deal with the economic circumstances of the groups.

The negritos of Papantla, Vera Cruz are among the most interesting. The dancers wear black velvet trousers and little jackets over white shirts, richly embroidered in color; wide-brimmed hats, turned up in front and adorned with ribbons, mirrors, and feathers. In 1945 when I last saw this dance, there were ten men, representing field workers, and a foreman similarly clad; two clowns in old torn coats and trousers and battered hats, their faces painted with black lines, dots and little snakes; a white adult Maringuilla, whose part was enacted by a man in woman's dress, wearing a rose-colored mask. He carried a whip in one hand and in the other a gourd vessel in which a small, live snake was carefully tied with handkerchiefs (Pl. 158).

The Maringuilla with the snake is part of all the negrito dances and others of this region. In some of the groups, the dance motif is to kill the evil instinct in woman, which the snake symbolizes, but in Papantla it was the danger to workers in the jungle forests of the surrounding country.

The musicians, who never wear costume, play a series of gay sones on violins, a big guitar, and sometimes a harp, marked by vigorous rhytnm, requiring lively steps. The dancers form various figures—sometimes they advance and recede in single file as when walking through the woods; in other figures they form a circle around the woman.

Toward the end of the dance there is a pause and the foreman sings, imitating the priests' chanting:

Cuídense de ese animal	Beware of that animal
Que no los vaya a picar,	Lest he bite you;
Ese maldito animal	That accursed animal
Que no deje trabajar.	That doesn't let you work.

Ese maldito animal,	That wicked animal,
Sus colmillos de alfiler,	With fangs like pins;
Su lengua de Barabas,	His tongue like Barabbas',
Sus ojos de Lucifer.	His eyes like Lucifer's.

After the workers repeat the verses, the dance is renewed; Maringuilla lets the head of the snake out and one of the workers pretends to be bitten. He falls to the ground complaining of the pain. The dancers take him to the center of the circle. There he is treated magically, the sorcerer invoking the four winds to cure him. They bandage the spot where the bite is supposed to be, and the patient makes his will. But the sorcerer saves him and the dance continues.

In the meantime the clowns dance as they please by themselves and among the spectators; they also feign having received snake bites; are convulsed with pain, dying, but the sorcerer pays no attention. Then they jump to their feet, jumping, yelling, and joking with the spectators.

The dance ends with the snake escaping from Maringuilla, and all the dancers killing it. In this part the rhythm of the dance is accelerated—the dancers yell and jump, yet in harmony with the music. In the end they sing of the danger this wicked animal represents, which some of them say is the treachery of woman personified by Malinche, the woman who helped Cortés conquer Mexico.

In some of the negrito groups of the Sierra de Puebla, the dance ends with the dancers weaving and unweaving ribbons around a pole.[18]

The negritos of Michoacán are a complete contrast to those of Puebla and Vera Cruz. They dress like catrines or in citified clothes; wear black masks with Europeanized features, from the top of which many wide colored silk ribbons hang almost to the ground (Pl. 84).

Those of Cheran wear as many as twenty-four ribbons because they are an indication of wealth. They suspend earrings from the mask and use strings of beads. Their performance takes place at Christmas time and consists of singing and reciting verses to the Christ Child. The two persons reciting the major part of the relato are la letra and el segundo, each one heading a file at the end of which are little girls. After certain songs and verses, they form complicated figures which they walk rather than dance. They repeat their performances during several days at the church, the government house, at the homes of the priest and the carguero, the man who organizes the dance and teaches it.[19]

Los Viejitos

Michoacán has many other dances besides the negritos, the most unusual and interesting being that of los viejitos, the little old men. The dancers are usually youths, who begin by acting like decrepit

DANCERS OF LOS VIEJITOS OR THE LITTLE OLD MEN

old men; then they do a series of virile zapateados to gay sones played on a tiny stringed instrument, the jarana.

The viejitos of the villages around Lake Pátzcuaro wear white cotton suits—long flaring trousers, embroidered at the bottom, a tunic with a red sash tied at the side, and strong shoes; a wide-brimmed, low-crowned hat, with colored ribbons crossed from the point and falling over the brim; silk kerchief around the neck and a white jorongo with colored stripes. The masks are of a light wood, carved and painted with old faces, some sad and others smiling, with fibre hair, and some also with beards. Each dancer carries a strong staff with an animal's head carved at the handle.

The musician directs the dancers, who sometimes dance together and singly, each trying to outdo the other in steps and clowning. One of their serious figures is called "The cross of the four stars," in which the dancers form files, one pointing in each direction.

Some of the mountain groups are rougher in their clowning, pushing each other around but never losing a measure of the dance. In Petamba there are sometimes as many as forty viejitos taking part, one of them a Maringuilla in fine city clothes and a mask of a pretty white face. The dancers form two files and each one dances with the woman; then they form a circle around her; then in pairs they make a reverence to her and dance a *son*. When all have finished, the dancing continues in two files to a variety of jarabes or any other dance tunes. When the dancers want to change the *son*, they shout and pause to make a circle around Maringuilla, after which the music starts again. The costumes here are similar to those of the lake villages, except that the dancers wear kerchiefs over their heads instead of hats.[20]

The viejitos is danced on secular occasions but chiefly during religious fiestas. How old the dance is no one knows, but there was such a dance before the Conquest. "There was another dance of viejos, danced with masks of old men and humpbacked; it lacked grace but was gay and very funny," wrote Durán.

Dances of Oaxaca

La Conquista, the most ostentatious of the Oaxaca dances, has already been described, but there are many others. Some are illustrated here and will be described briefly, since space does not permit more.

Los Jardineros, or "The Gardeners," popular in the villages of the Valley, is a charming burlesque of court life. The king heads a file of courtiers wearing short trousers and blouses of vivid silks, and the queen with her ladies-in-waiting form another, represented by men in silk dresses, trimmed with lace and beads. All wear masks with smirking expressions, and carry wreaths of flowers arched over the heads. They dance to social dance music—polkas, mazurkas, waltzes —played on stringed instruments, lightly, gracefully, mimicking courtly manners (Pl. 51).

The Pachecos, or "Cowboys," from the Mixteca, is a jolly rhythmic dance. They wear leather suits, trimmed with fur along the legs; straw sombreros; shoes with spurs. One of them represents a bull, and two clown in women's clothes (Pl. 53).

The dance of San Marcos, from the village of the same name in the Sierra near Villa Alta, is another battle between Christians and non-Christians. There is a Christian king in black, with long black hair; a blond Jewish king in a red costume with long light hair, and a little boy representing San Marcos. The young, gaily attired soldiers dance and fight rhythmically with wooden daggers, tipped with tin, to music played on flute and drum. Their clown wears a tiger-skin suit and mask (Pl. 54).

In the village of Santa Catarina Estetla the girls do a wedding dance. At one stage of it, they carry the bride on their shoulders, as if taking her away, and the groom and his friends follow dancing. Some of the dancers carry little bread dolls, symbolizing the progeny (Pl. 58).

The Huehuenches is a colorful humorous dance from Villa Alta, in which the dancers in bright costumes, hats adorned with feathers and mirrors, dance lightly and gaily (Pl. 56).

The dance of the Tigers from the Villa Alta region is performed by little boys, their suits painted to resemble tiger's skin, whom adult men try to catch with ropes (Pl. 57).

The zanco dance of the same region, of which there is no illustration, consists of youths dressed as girls, moving about on stilts in perfect rhythm to music, as was done before the Conquest with great perfection.[21]

Huasteca Dances

The Huasteca dances of the Sierra of San Luis Potosí, are simple but very interesting. Besides the Flying Pole dance, previously described, there are various others, some connected with the hunting of animals.

One of their unique dances is that of la Malinche, in which a youth in woman's dress represents the woman who became Cortés' interpreter and mistress. She dances to a regional folk tune in movements that reveal remorse and shame for having followed the conqueror and thus earned the eternal reproach of her people.

Another one of their unusual dances is that in which men and women dance around a teponaxtli drum, at intervals making reverences to it.[22] (Pls. 80, 81, 82, 83).

Dances of Guerrero

Guerrero is famous for its animal and other dances in which good masks are used. It is the only state in which I have seen the Dance of the Three Powers, representing the struggle between the devil and an angel over the soul.

The group that I saw was from the mountain village of Pocotitlán. They had a text and the characters were Christ, the Virgin, Angel, Soul, Body, World, Flesh, Understanding, Will, Memory, Lucifer, Devil, Sin, Death, and viejos who enacted the clowns. Angel wore a pair of small wings; Soul, a crown of artificial orange blossoms and veil; Death, a white mask and a white cotton suit with black stripes to give it the appearance of a skeleton. He also carried a black and white hatchet. Lucifer and Sin, who danced with Death, both wore black and white trousers and capes, and each had a stuffed, red-crested serpent coiled around his neck. The dancers performed intricate steps and figures to the music of a violin in and outside of the church and said their parts like actors. In the end there was a realistic struggle for Soul. Finally Sin was burned as Soul soared to heaven.

The tiger dance, which at one time must have been performed for luck in hunting, is now a long comedy with a Master, for whom the tiger is to be caught. The personages, besides the Master, are the mayordomo, several men who are owners of dogs, guns, and rope; five old retainers; two medicine men; two dogs; two deer; four ospreys, dark brown, hawk-like birds; a tiger, and a man dressed as an old woman. The birds and tiger were little boys, whose costumes and headdresses were made to represent their respective roles—the tiger in a suit of cloth like a tiger's skin; the deer in one-piece gray suits with deer's head and antlers, and the vultures in black.

The dance begins with a series of figures composed of swift steps to lively sones, during which the tiger annoys the dancers by tickling their faces with his detached tail. Then there is conversation about how to capture the tiger—the text is partly in Aztec—and all set out to hunt him, the rewards being fixed in advance by the mayordomo. Some of the hunters return wounded, and there are funny remarks at the expense of the doctors. The dance ends with the bringing in of the tiger, whose skin is to be used for riding breeches for the Master. His measure is taken, and then there follows a dance of leave-taking in the atrium and the church.

The tlacololeros is an interesting and unique agricultural dance, performed in Chilpancingo and surrounding villages. The name is derived from the Aztec tlacolol, "to prepare the land for cultivation."

The dancers, representing the men burning the bush and cleaning the corn-patch, wear burlap tunics, leather pants, thick boots that reach above the knees, laced at the sides; big interesting masks and very wide-brimmed sombreros with conical crowns. They are directed by a "captain" and dance to violin music, marking the rhythm with their whips with which they hit each other on their padded left' arms to imitate the crackling of the fire as it burns the trees.

The Chilpancingo group has a text with one scene in which perra, a she-dog called la maravilla or the marvel, goes after the tiger that is harming the cornfields. At one stage of the dance the fires go out. While trying to find out whose fault it is, they go about whipping one another as if to start the fire again. Their whips are combined with chains, reproducing the bursting flames to the rhythm of the music. Some of their masks are quite extraordinary.[23]

Dances of Yucatán

This state also has a variety of interesting dances. The Xtoles have been described in connection with carnivals; the Jaranas will be included under folk dances; and here are two which are from Dzitas.

On the eve of the fiesta for Santa Inez, the dance of The Sacrifice of the Turkeys takes place. There are thirteen dancers, wearing turkey feathers on their heads, each one with one of the birds hanging by its feet under the left arm. The dancers form a circle in the center of the plaza around the musicians, who play primitive melodies on flute and drum. As they dance, they wring the necks of the turkeys. At midnight, the music stops; each dancer places his turkey on the ground in front of him for the leader to investigate. If one of them is found alive, the dancer lowers his head in shame and the bird is beaten against it until it is dead. After this the dance starts again and is transformed into a frantic pulling out of feathers—the air is filled with them as the people jump and yell.

The following morning the dance of the kub-pol or the offering of the pig's head takes place. The dancers carry roasted pigs' heads in iron skillets, adorned with colored paper flags, and dolls, each with a little round white bread in its mouth. Other dancers carry complicated cylindrical frames, covered with flowers and lacy paper ornaments, which are called ramilletes. They all dance together to the music of a small orchestra, one with a pig alternating with one with a wreath. When the dancing is finished they all go inside of the church to offer the heads to Santa Inez.

A similar dance takes place on the Island of Cozumel, near Quintana Roo. Here a woman carries a roasted pig's head on an enormous tray adorned with pretty colored paper flags, packages of cigarettes, candies, cakes. Men and women dance in pairs, the woman with the tray alone in the center. At the end of the dance, the woman hands the tray to another one, who is thus obligated to furnish the head the coming year. Then everyone eats what is on the tray, smokes the cigarettes and drinks.[24]

Dances of Chiapas

The dances of the primitive highland tribes, as we have already seen, are very simple—with rattles, stringed instruments, or flute and drum. When the women dance, they do so apart from the men and at home ceremonies.

Even the more sophisticated Zoques, who live in and around Tuxtla Gutiérrez, have simple dances. In Chiapa de Corzo one is performed on January 20, called parachicos. Young men come out on horseback, wearing masks with gray Oaxaca serapes flying from their shoulders, and go for the little ones as the name indicates.

In Tuxtla, the state capital, there are various saints' fiestas at which the Zoques dance. The most interesting one is performed for St. Michael, September 29. In it are six men—three Lucifers and three angels, all wearing masks, with as many others as wish to join in clowns' costumes with devils' masks. The first angel, representing St. Michael, has a scale in one hand and a sword in the other; the second and third angels also carry swords, with flowers instead of scales. The Lucifers carry short staffs in one hand and a wooden hand in the other. The steps are simple, to the music of stringed instruments. In the end, one Lucifer is seated on a chair to which are fastened bunches of fireworks. When they are set off, he jumps off, furnishing laughs for the spectators.

For the fiesta of San Roque, August 23 to 25, four men dance, wearing dark coats with white kerchiefs at the neck, over-trousers of bandannas, and hats trimmed with tall peacock feathers (Pl. 142). The music is furnished by a flute and drum.[25]

The Ribbon Dances

Las Danzas de Los Listones, or the Ribbon Dances, exist in Yucatán, Campeche, and in other regions. They are like our maypole dances in that they consist of winding and unwinding ribbons around a pole and undoubtedly originated as fertility dances long before the Conquest. However, this dance now is performed during religious fiestas and usually by men. When it constitutes one of the figures of another dance, as with the Yaqui Matachines and the Puebla negritos, the same costumes are worn; when it is given as a separate dance, then there are special ones, and half the dancers dress as women.

In Ixmiquilpan, Hidalgo, the men wear short suits of vivid colors, trimmed with spangles; wide-brimmed palm hats, turned up in front and caught with colored feathers, adorned with a mirror and the image of a saint; those who represent women are dressed in the regional costumes—the chinquete and quexquemetl with many strings of colored beads—a wig of long hair, the top of the head covered with a square piece of embroidered cloth, held by a ribbon.

Fastened to the top of the pole is a ribbon of different color for each dancer, who holds the other end in his hand. Then, dancing around the pole all together, in a simple sort of two-step to whatever music is customary, the dancers interlace the ribbons around it, forming a beautiful colored hood for the top. Afterward they dance in the opposite direction to unwind.[26]

Dances of the Federal District and Surrounding Country

We have already seen that the dances of the Concheros and Moros are the most popular in the Federal District and environs. But there is another with a religious military theme which has also captivated the folk imagination—Los Doce Pares de Francia, Charlemagne with his warriors or "twelve peers." The costumes of the dancers are always colorful, and in some groups of rich materials, imitating those of that "period."

The legend of the dance texts revolves around the Moorish king stealing Charlemagne's daughter and his recapturing her; she is generally represented by a little girl. In the village of San Miguel de Ajusco, the young daughter by some miracle becomes the Virgin of Guadalupe and is taken to France with great pomp after the victory over the Moors.

This dance is also performed in the State of Puebla and elsewhere.

Los Arrieros

Los Arrieros, Mule-Drivers Dances, are performed in many of the villages of the Valley of Toluca, a short distance from Mexico City. They are entertaining and among the most interesting. The men appear in white suits, wearing red bandannas around the neck, their hats adorned with flowers or ribbons. They have a few burros to carry their utensils; they usually set up camp and the men make tortillas, cook, and do all the tasks usually performed by women. As they work, they tell funny stories about what happens to them on their trips, or talk about their merchandise and about other adventures. They bring their own musicians and dance. After having prayed and taken leave of the saint, they continue to dance while harnessing their animals. and then they are ready to leave.

There is one group, however, that attends the fiesta at Tenancingo, December 8, that follows a different procedure. They are organized to do penance because of promises to saints. This group does not pre-- pare food but brings it in bags. The dancers dress in the usual way, wearing heavy sandals with nails in the soles for the purpose of producing a rhythmic noise to accompany the music of violins and guitars. They carry whips either of crude leather or knotted rope; dance in a straight line, back and forth, as if walking the roads, with sufficient distance apart so that the one behind can whip the one in front. When they turn back, the one who received the lashes gives them. In order to diminish the force of the blows the dancers hang their sacks on their backs, but even so they sometimes draw blood.

The dramatic moments are when the dancers stop to sing alabanzas to the Virgin; everyone present joins in the singing, the men removing their hats, and all pray together. The public does this to help the arrieros comply with their penance. It is a most impressive ceremony with hundreds of people taking part.[27]

Space does not permit me to go on with this description of ritual dances. I have presented the most important ones and a sufficient number of others so that one can form an idea of the creative genius of the folk in their dances and costumes. But there are many more, no one knows how many, since no one has listed them all.

Certain general observations can be made about all of the ritual dances. They are performed chiefly by men, principally for the saints during their fiestas, but are also a part of various ceremonials, Christian and pagan. The dancers expect something in return for their sacrifices from the saints or pagan deities, for themselves, their families and communities. They always dance first in the church at fiestas, and ask permission from the saint to go on dancing in the atrium. Before leaving for their homes, they take leave inside the church with prayers and dances, never turning their backs to the altar. They try to make their costumes as beautiful as possible and to dance well to please the saints and the public.

Folk Dances

There are secular dances everywhere, but they are not danced to
the same extent by all the folk. Among the very primitive groups,
women and young girls do not dance them, even though some may
take part in ritual dances.

The basis of practically all the folk dances are the jarabes or sones,
names by which both the dances and tunes are designated, most of
them being songs. Jarabe means a syrup or sweet drink in Spanish, but
various dances introduced by the Spaniards in the form of zapateados
were called jarabes. In fact, one called jarabe gatuna and another
pan de jarabe, or sweet bread, were brought to the notice of the Inquisition, accused of being indecent. The literal meaning of *son* is "an
agreeable sound." The dance songs began being called sones about
the middle of the eighteenth century.

Jarabe Tapatío

The Jarabe Tapatío is the Mexican national folk dance. It is a
stylized form of the old folk jarabes, and developed around 1920 in
Guadalajara, Jalisco. Tapatío is applied to anything from that state,
hence the name which distinguishes it from all the other jarabes.

The Jarabe Tapatío is internationally known. It is often danced in
the United States by Mexicans and Americans who have learned it in
Mexico at the Summer School of the National University and elsewhere. Such famous dancers as Pavlova and La Argentina learned
and danced it during their visits to Mexico.

This jarabe consists of nine gay, captivating melodies and dance
figures, the dancers meeting and moving around each other but always some distance apart. They dance with heel and toe, beating a
strong rhythm to the music. The entire dance takes about ten minutes. At the end comes "The Dove," during which the man follows
his partner as she dances around the broad brim of his sombrero. As
she stoops to pick it up, he passes his right leg over her. They finish
by facing the audience, dancing back and forth to the "Diana," the
man's arm around the girl. The girls wear the China Poblana costume
and the men that of the charro.

The Jarabe Tapatío is danced in theaters, cabarets, at secular fiestas,
rodeos—actually no program is complete without it. It always
awakens a joyous response with handclapping for the "Diana." If
there are many young men in the audience, they whistle and yell. It is
irresistibly gay, beating its rhythm into the very blood.

When this jarabe is danced by rancheros, especially those of Jalisco, it is even gayer and more fiery. Often they dance it spontaneously, but when they plan for it, a wooden platform is placed over an excavated area or over buried jars to produce resonance. The music is furnished by mariachis and singers. The dance sometimes lasts for hours, with the dancers improvising verses and steps.

Some students of the Jarabe Tapatío attribute to it a pre-Spanish origin because of the courtship element in the figure of "The Dove" —an imitation of the way doves, as well as other animals, follow one another in their courting—but that is just a hypothesis. There is nothing primitive about the dance, particularly as performed by city people.

The folk jarabes and sones are much simpler and are danced differently. When a man and woman dance together, they never touch one another. The woman always dances slowly, modestly, with downcast eyes, lifting her skirts slightly but never flirtatiously, seldom looking at her partner. The man dances faster, doing a greater variety of steps, but always holding himself stiff above the waist. The dancers are light and graceful, the men showing their native ability in controlling their muscles by dancing with a glass of water on top of their heads without throwing it off, or in tying and untying a knot in a sash or kerchief with the feet. No special costumes are worn in these dances.

There are various formalized folk jarabes. El Jarabe de la Botella, The Jarabe of the Bottle, is popular in Jalisco because of its humor and because of the skill required in dancing it. The couple dance for a while; then they both take a drink from the same bottle of tequila, stand it on the floor, and take turns in dancing over it. As each one dances, the musicians sing, telling him or her not to spill the contents. If one of them does, it will have to be replaced by a full bottle.

The Morismo, or Knife Dance, is also danced to jarabes. Two men or a man and woman may dance it, the men making two machetes meet under each leg to the rhythm of the music—a dangerous but gay dance. The name comes from the fact that the Spaniards, who introduced the dance, learned it from the Moors. This dance is performed in Jalisco, Nayarit, and perhaps elsewhere.

When jarabes are danced at funerals of young children and at weddings, they assume a ceremonial character. In Chicomcuac, Mexico, the dancing at a wedding begins with a jarabe. The parents of the bride dance with plates of food in their hands, others with jars of pulque on their heads, one person with a basket of tortillas and another with a live turkey—the tortillas and turkey being gifts of thanks for the bride. In Oaxaca weddings, the jarabes and sones are called fandangos.[28]

The folk dances of every region are different as a result of climate and the character of the people. The following are nationally known.

Huapangos

The folk dance next in popularity, but not in beauty of melodies and songs, to the Jarabe Tapatío, is the huapango. It is danced all along the Huastecas, from the State of Taumalipas to Vera Cruz.

HUAPANGO DANCERS FROM VERA CRUZ

The huapango is a rhythmic dance, performed on a platform or a wooden floor, when possible, by men and women in files facing each other. The steps are simple—heel and toe, beating once with the heel and twice with the toe—but often the men introduce complicated zapateados. The music consists of a series of sones, called huapangos, played on violins, guitars, and jaranas, the latter like a ukelele; in some regions harps are added. The rhythm is marked by bringing down the fist or open hand on the strings of the guitars for the last note of each measure. Together with the beat of the feet, it is very gay. Although the music and steps are European, the dance may be related to some of the pre-Spanish mitotes, also danced on a platform. The name is Aztec, derived from "cuah-panco-cuaitl," the first meaning "log" or "wood"; "ipan," "on or over," and "co," "place."

At one time huapangos were danced by the higher social classes; now, although they are still the custom among the well-to-do ranchers of the State of Tamaulipas, they are chiefly danced by the mestizo folk living in the old tradition. When a huapango is taking place on a Tamaulipas ranch, it is the custom for friends to dash in on spirited horses, break the strings of the harp and gallop off. The offenders are pursued; if caught, they have to pay for the next huapango.

Huapangos are often held during religious fiestas and holidays, but always away from the church; often at household fiestas, especially weddings.

In the Huastecas of San Luis Potosí, the wedding huapangos last as long as the means of the parents permit. The first one is danced in the room where the altar stands. The bride and groom, both with downcast eyes, lead the couples in forming a circle. Each dancer carries a small jar of incense in his right hand and flowers in the left. The only others besides the dancers are the musicians, playing the wedding huapango, entitled "Xochipitzahua," the verses of which are sung from the outside. At the end of the dance the purity of the bride is symbolized by putting the incense and flowers on the altar. This huapango is often the last one at which the bride dances, as in most villages it is considered improper for married women to dance.

In many places the huapangos constitute the weekly Saturday night dances, often organized by merchants for business reasons. They are announced by shooting off sky-rockets, and the men come to them from the fields, with their machetes, smelling of hay. There are permanent platforms with thatched roofs, and sometimes a special one for the best dancers. When the music starts, the men step up to the girls with whom they wish to dance, raise their hats in silence, turn around, and the girls follow them to form the files.

The dance goes on endlessly, but the musicians change the tunes and the singers improvise new verses; some of them are humorous ones about mothers-in-law or some of the outstanding spectators. Once when I was visiting a huapango in the mountains of the State of Hidalgo, I heard my name sung and correctly pronounced. The friend who had invited me had given my name to the singers and musicians, and they made up some verses about my visit there.

Occasionally two rivals begin a challenge in song. The less favored suitor may direct insults against the girl, the other defending her, while she dances with downcast eyes, apparently oblivious of what is going on. Such quarrels may become so heated that the contestants leave the platform to settle them with their machetes. No one interferes, and the victor gets the girl.

In some places it is permissible for a man to take away another's partner by putting his hat on her head. If she is not pleased, her companion may remove it—a hint that the other is not wanted. This custom is one of the various ways of demonstrating a girl's popularity.

Certain sones or huapangos are played for definite purposes—"El Caimán" and "La Bamba" when a dancer is balancing a bottle or glass on his head, or tying and untying a sash with his feet. When such feats are about to take place, they are announced and all the other dancers step to one side to watch and applaud. "El Torito" is a sign for the men to take out their handkerchiefs to play at bullfighting with their partners. "Los Panaderos" is played as a hint that the musicians want to rest, as well as a suggestion to the men to invite the girls for refreshments. The words say that "It's a great obligation of those who are dancing to give their partners cake and wine." Most of the men walk away as usual, without supplying cake and wine, which is not taken as an offense. Some huapangos go on for days, but they are never dull.[29]

Jaranas

The folk dance of Yucatán is the jarana. The dance, the music, and the function derive their name from the ukelele-like instrument, called a jarana, but the word only means "noisy diversion." The steps are zapateados and the music consists of gay sones without words, played on jaranas, brass instruments, and drums, to which are sometimes added the Cuban güiros, or gourds.

The couples, in their usual fiesta clothes, dance facing one another, the man with his hands behind his back and the girl raising her skirts slightly. At intervals they pass one another with arms curved upwards, snapping their fingers in Spanish fashion. When the Torito is played, the couples play at bullfighting as they dance. During the dance, the musicians frequently stop playing and someone shouts, "bomba!"—a signal for the man to say a compliment to his partner, in verse, sometimes improvised on the spur of the moment.

A popular bomba is:

Me gusta mucho tus ojos,	I love your eyes
Me gusta mucho tu cara;	I love your face;

Y si nu fueras casada,	And if you weren't married,
Otro gallo me cantara . . . Ah!	It would be another story . . . Ah!
	(Lit. Another cock would sing to me. . . .)

A man may compliment a girl with whom he is not dancing by putting his hat on her head, and there is much play in getting it back. When the owner is a public functionary, he may buy it back with a present of money. This custom, of course, prevails only in progressive, citified communities, where the girls dance more gaily and coquettishly.

The village jaranas are different; they are vital in the life of the community, having a ritual as well as a social function. They are danced during novenas, or nine days of praying, as offerings to saints, and at religious fiestas. When a jarana is being organized, the municipal president or mayordomo invites the girls to come and dance. They do not know with whom until they are facing their partners. But they welcome such opportunities, since these dances are the chief opportunities to meet boys, and the results are many unions.

During the annual religious fiesta in Chan Kom and other villages of the region, the jaranas are associated with the bullfights. The young men who dance in them and go out to bring in the bulls for the fight, are called vaqueros, herdsmen; the girls, because they dance with the boys' hats on at the first jarana, vaqueras, the female counterpart; and the dance is called a vaquería instead of a jarana. These vaquerías always end with the "Torito," in which the girl bullfighter tries to make the "bull" dancing opposite her lose his balance or step off the platform.

Generally four vaquerías are given during a fiesta, each sponsored by a man known as the cargador. Two men—the nohoch mayol and his assistant, the chan mayol—Maya titles—manage them. They direct the musicians, lead the dancers on to the floor, and perform other services. After the last vaquería, the night before the bullfight, they invite two h-mens to make the offerings of zaca, the ritual corn gruel, to the Yuntzilob or the supernatural beings that guard the village, and to X-Juan-Thul, the guardian of the cattle, who also helps the vaqueros to dominate the wild steer. At the same time they pray to the balams to be present to protect the dancers from the evil winds.

The vaqueros spend the rest of the night with their mayoles in visiting the houses of the cargadores, where they are treated to drinks and cigarettes. They are warned by the h-mens not to sleep because the Yuntzilob are present, and especially not with their wives. They keep the ropes for the bulls with them, so that spending the night in this way is referred to in Maya, as "giving the night to the lasso; twisting it so thick that it will not break on account of the bulls."

After the bullfight, there is a short jarana, without a sponsor, called "half a night," when the girls again wear hats. After it is over, the dancers go to the house of the nohoch mayol, where the back-beating ceremony takes place. Each vaquera is taken to a table on which are rum, cigarettes, and zipche leaves, where the chan mayol beats her on the back with a rope twist of three large handkerchiefs. Then she passes to the two *h-mens*—one gives her a drink of rum, while the other strokes her head with the zipche leaves in a clockwise, and then in the opposite, direction. Then the other takes a little rum in his mouth and blows some on her head. Both *h-mens* pray to expel the evil winds, which are feared because the vaqueras have danced so long and slept so little. If this were not done, when the vaqueras married, their children would die.[30]

Canacuas

Canacuas, meaning "crowns" in Tarascan, is a folk dance of the city, and surrounding villages, of Uruapan, Michoacán. It is apparently of pre-Conquest origin, as it is mentioned in one of the early chronicles of the state in connection with weddings. "On the following day, a ceremony of a wholly intimate nature took place in the Nuptial abode. Youths and maidens assembled, the former with garlands of flowers on their heads, the latter carrying beautiful bouquets, and after offering the newly-married couple gifts of objects useful for the new family, they took part in a dance. Afterward, a figure of a child, made of dough, was passed from hand to hand, with the singing of allusive songs. The fiesta was called 'canacuas' and still exists in various towns of Michoacán."

There are similarities in the present-day canacuas. Only young, unmarried girls (who are in the charge of an elderly, respected man, called a carguero) take part in them. During the dance, however, el indito, a young man, joins the girls to chat and dance a jarabe with one of them. The canacuas are still performed at weddings and other secular fiestas, but chiefly to honor important guests in the community.

The girls who take part are of the progressive mestizo folk, who dress in modern clothes; but for the dance they are called güaris, after the Tarascan women, whose costume they wear—wide pleated skirt, gaily embroidered shirt, rebozo crossed in front, attractive aprons, strings of colorful beads, bright ribbons in the hair. Each one carries one of those painted gourd bowls, called xicapexli, filled with flowers, fruit, and lacquered and clay toys.

DANCERS OF THE CANACUAS OR CROWNS

The guest in whose honor the canacuas is given sits at a small table at the head of the two files which the dancers form. The little orchestra of stringed instruments, including a harp, is at one side. The spectators fill the patio or garden.

The songs are sentimental and melodious, with a mixture of Spanish and Tarascan words, the latter having lost practically all meaning. The first one is a greeting, which the güaris sing swaying back and forth—"Good evening, good evening, our very dear friend; we are coming to sing to you and to visit you, too."

Next an emotional offering song—"Tata niñito, good father, little friend, good father" . . . mentioning the name of the person. . . . This is followed by a dance movement with the swaying of the bowls and skirts, and one of the most beautiful of all the Tarascan melodies —"La Flor de Canela," "The cinnamon flower"—"At the cinnamon flower I sigh because it reminds me of you."

The fourth song is again addressed to Tata niñito, the good little father; this the girls sing, formed in three lines—the first one seated on the ground, the second kneeling, the third standing.

In the following number the indito and compadrito, the good little friend, appears. He is dressed in white, with a sombrero and sandals, a serape over his shoulder. He carries a live hen or turkey. He is welcomed gaily with a song that sounds like childish patter. Then all sit down on the ground and he and one of the güaris sing in dialogue:

SHE: Indian man, why are you sad, ha, ha?
HE: Indian girl, for a good time.
SHE: Indian man, come with me, ha, ha.
HE: To sing a song.
THEN TOGETHER:
  To my friend whom I love best
  To sing a song to him.
  I bring you nothing more
  Than a plate of turkey.
  And so with humility
  I now leave it with you,
  Offering you a sigh
  From our hearts.
SHE: Indian man, how does one dance, ha, ha?
HE: Indian girl, this is the way.

Then begins a jarabe in which one or many may shine. They dance the "jarabe of the bottle," but it is empty, with a piece of silver money on the stopper, which must not be knocked off; and the "jarabe of the knot," tying and untying a knot with the feet. The couples dance with abandon, and those who are not dancing are clapping enthusiastically.

This outburst of gaiety is followed by a sad, sentimental love plaint, "The Flower of the Changunga"—addressing the flower of the changunga, the sweet orange blossom, the purple banana. This is sung by the güari with the best voice, while the rest of them in chorus comment, "Ay, what a thing is love."

This sad song of unrequited love is followed by "La Patera," with a happier theme, after which the offerings are made to the guest. Each güari approaches the table where the guest is seated and with a pretty obeisance empties the contents of her bowl on it. When the turn of the leading güari comes, she goes through the measures of a pretty dance before him, holding in her hand an apázaca flower adorned with corn leaves. As she dances, she holds it out to the visitor, but when he makes a motion to receive it, she quickly withdraws.

She repeats this several times, in the end keeping her apázaca. Some say the flower symbolizes the purity of the güari.

After this the dancers pay their respects to all the guests according to their stations. Then follows the solemn moment of the "petition." It is a tradition that whatever the güaris ask of the honored guest, he must grant; otherwise he will lose prestige.[31]

The Sandunga

Although the Sandunga is of the limited area of Tehuantepec, it is one of the best known of the regional dances, as well known as the

SANDUNGA DANCERS FROM TEHUANTEPEC

popular Tehuanas who dance it. It is purely secular, performed at home fiestas, and forms part of the regular social dance programs.

The music is sentimental, beautifully romantic, with Italian influence. It is played on a marimba, accompanied by stringed and brass instruments. There are verses to it, which are not always sung. Some of them are literary, while others are popular, like the following:

La Sandunga

An-te no-che fui a tu ca-sa..... Mu-chos gol-pes di-al can-da-do tu
no-sir-ves pa-ra amo-res..... tie-nes el sue-ño pe-sa-do
Ay— San-dun-ga San-dun-ga ma-má por Dios
San-dun-ga no seas in-gra-ta——— ma-má de mi co-ra-zon.

Antenoche fui a tu casa	Last night I passed your house,
Muchos golpes dí al candado	Many knocks I gave at your door;
Tu no sirves para amores;	You're no good for love;
Tienes el sueño pesado.	Your sleep is too heavy.

Chorus

Ay, Sandunga, Sandunga mama,	Ay Sandunga, Sandunga mamma,
por Dios,	oh God,
Sandunga, no seas ingrata,	Sandunga, don't be ungrateful,
Mamá de mi corazón.	Woman of my heart.

Perdóname, mamacita,	Forgive me, little sweetheart,
Lo sinvergüenza que he sido;	That I have been so daring
Si tu no fueras la hermosa,	If you were not so beautiful,
Yo no fuera el atrevido.	I would not be so bold.

Chorus

Por vida de ese lunar	I vow by that little mole
Que tienes en tu pechito,	That you have on your breast,
Mira, no le pagues mal	Look, don't treat me badly;
Al pobre de tu negrito.	I'm your poor little Negro.

Chorus

(Another version of the chorus is:)

Ay, Sandunga,	Ay, Sandunga,
Sandunga mama, por Dios	Sandunga mamma, I vow (by
Sandunga, tu eres Tehuana.	God)
Cielo de mi corazón!	Sandunga, you're a Tehuana,
	Heaven of my heart.

(Tehuana is what the women of Tehuantepec are called.)

The Tehuanas in their vivid dress, fantastic gold chains and earrings, do a simple waltz step, moving gracefully and haughtily, without deigning to look at their partners, who dance around them in a variety of quick zapateado figures.

Various legends have been invented about the origin of the Sandunga. One of them is a sad one about a young boy who was studying in Oaxaca City, about five days on horseback from Tehuantepec. He was informed that his mother was dying, hurried to her bedside but arrived too late. In his anguish, he began a plaint from which originated the melody and words. Another is that it developed out of the singing and dancing of a group of friends who came to console a lovelorn maiden.

A recent Oaxaqueño investigator asserts that the Sandunga music is a popular *son* of Tehuantepec by an unknown composer, of about the middle of the nineteenth century. It probably received its name, to which the steps and verses were composed, much later. The translation of sandunga in the Spanish dictionary is—"gracefulness, elegance, winsomeness, allurement, fascination"—adjectives which may well be applied both to the Tehuanas and the music.[32]

Sones of Vera Cruz

The sones of Vera Cruz are famous for their gaiety. They are danced by couples, without touching, to the music of a harp, violin, and guitar, and one or two male singers, who never take their hats off. The musicians and dancers are mestizos of native, Spanish, and Negro blood, the mixture producing an unusually exuberant type. The girls wear their customary fiesta dresses—long cotton skirts with ruffles, a blouse, a kerchief around the shoulders and crossed in front, always of vivid colors; strings of bright beads, earrings, and bows of colored ribbons in their hair. The men wear their usual white cotton suits, with some color in the form of a sash or red silk kerchief. The girls, lifting their skirts a little at the sides, keep up in their zapateados, with the men who dance with their hands behind their backs, without moving the upper part of the body.

The best dancers of these sones are from Alvarado and Tlacotalpan, many of whom have found their way to the City of Vera Cruz and Mexico City. They were especially popular during the presidential campaign of Licenciado Miguel Alemán, a native of their state, when "La Bamba," one of the gayest of their sones was sung and played everywhere. It was a favorite number in floor shows of the most fashionable cabarets.

There are many other regional folk dances, like the Chilenas from the coast of Guerrero and Oaxaca, to pleasing sones which are practically unknown. But many—the jarabes, huapangos, the sones veracruzanos, the Sandunga—may be seen in Mexico City, in stylized versions for the stage, or at fiestas. The Sandunga and Chiapanecas of Chiapas are taught for school fiestas.

Just as it is impossible to describe all the ritual dances in this section, so with the secular. No one has listed these either, and they are different in every region and village. Many are danced in the form of cuadrillas, similar in figure to our square dances, yet completely different. The varieties are as numerous as the places in which they are danced. It may be said of all of them, in general, that the music is gay, the costumes colorful, the dancing good.

Modern social dances have been penetrating into the most unexpected places. As long ago as 1928, I saw a number of married Chinantec couples of a variety of ages dancing a one-step, played by a brass band. Both the music and dancing were a far cry from a city one-step. This happened in a Chinantec village in the Sierra de Juárez—San Pedro Yolox—where few of the inhabitants could speak Spanish. This is not typical, but social dancing is becoming more widespread among the folk.

SONGS AND DANCE MUSIC

PRIMITIVE SONGS

Los Xtoles

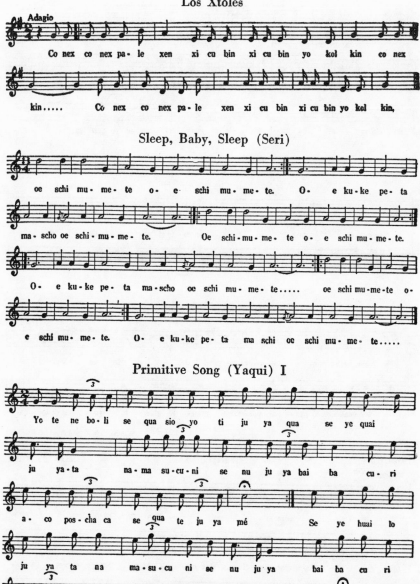

Adagio

Co nex co nex pa - le xen xi cu bin xi cu bin yo kol kin co nex

kin..... Co nex co nex pa - le xen xi cu bin xi cu bin yo kol kin,

Sleep, Baby, Sleep (Seri)

oe schi mu - me - te o - e schi mu - me - te. O - e ku ke pe - ta

ma - scho oe schi - mu - me - te. Oe schi - mu - me - te o - e schi mu - me - te.

O - e ku - ke pe - ta ma - scho oe schi mu - me - te..... oe schi mu - me - te o -

e schi mu - me - te. O - e ku - ke pe - ta ma schi oc schi mu - me - te.....

Primitive Song (Yaqui) I

Yo te ne bo - li se qua sio yo ti ju ya qua se ye quai

ju ya - ta na - ma su - cu - ni se nu ju ya bai ba cu - ri

a - co pos - cha ca se qua te ju ya mé Se ye huai lo

ju yn ta na ma - su - cu ni se nu ju ya bai ba cu ri

a - co pos - cha ca se qua - te ju ya me ———

377

Primitive Song (Yaqui) II

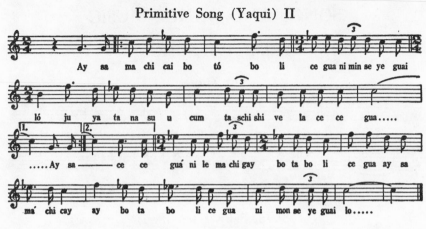

Ay sa ma chi cai bo tó bo li ce gua ni min se ye guai

ló ju ya ta na su u cum ta schi shi ve la ce ce gua.....

.....Ay sa ——— ce ce guá ni le ma chi gay bo ta bo li ce gua ay sa

.ma' chi cay ay bo ta bo li ce gua ni mon se ye guai lo.....

Primitive Song (Yaqui) III

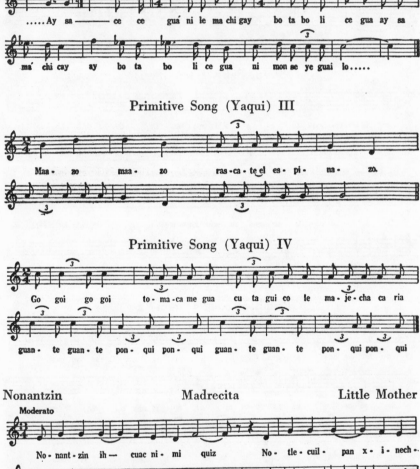

Maa - zo   maa - zo   ras-ca-te el es - pi - na - zo.

Primitive Song (Yaqui) IV

Go goi go goi to - ma -ca me gua cu ta gui co le ma - je -cha ca ria

guan - te guan - te pon - qui pon - qui guan - te guan - te pon - qui pon - qui

Nonantzin   Madrecita   Little Mother

Moderato

No - nant - zin ih - cuac ni - mi quiz No - tle - cuil - pan x - i - nech -

to - ca   Huan cuac tiaz ti..... Tlax cal - chi - huaz   Om - pa no -pom - pa xi -

cho - ca   Huan cuac tiaz ti - Tlax cal - chi - huaz   Om - pa -no -pom -pa xi - cho - ca.

RELIGIOUS SONGS

Religious Songs of Praise

Alabado

Author unknown. Collection, Concha Michel.
Men of the Pacific Coast regions sing this alabado when they are about
to grind sugar cane or at the wake of a man who has been killed in an
accident or in a fight.

Gracias te doy, gran Señor,
Y alabo tu gran poder.
Pués con el alma en el cuerpo
Me dejaste amanecer.
Pues con el alma, etc.

Thanks I give to thee, Great Lord,
And praise your great power.
For with my soul in my body
You have permitted me to arise.
 (Repeat the last two lines)

Por el rastro de la sangre
Que Jesu Cristo derrama,
Caminó la Virgen pura
Toda una triste mañana.
Caminó, etc.

Over the trail of blood
That Jesus Christ spilt
The pure Virgin walked (Repeat
 these last two lines)
A whole sad morning.

¿Señora, no vió pasar
Al hijo de mis entrañas?
Si, Señora, si pasó
Tres Horas antes del alba.
Si, Señora, etc.

Madam, did you not see pass by,
The Son of my heart?
Yes, Señora, yes he passed
Three hours before dawn.
Yes señora, etc.

Una cruz lleva en los hombros
De madera muy pesada,
Una túnica morada
Que hasta el suelo le llegaba.
Una túnica, etc.

He carried a cross on his shoulders
Of very heavy wood.
He wore a purple tunic
That reached to the ground.
He wore, etc.

La Virgen oyendo esto
Cayó al suelo desmayada,
San Juan, como buen sobrino
Luego vino a levantarla.
San Juan, etc.

La sangre que derramó
Cayó en un cáliz sagrado,
El hombre que la bebiera
Será bien aventurado.
El hombre, etc.

Viste de luto la Virgen
Que ha muerto su bién amado,
Y le dan noticia al pueblo
Que ha muerto por su pecado.
Y le dan noticia, etc.

Lloraban las tres Marías
Al ver que el pecho manaba,
Virgen pura, Magdalena,
Y la otra Marta su hermana.
Virgen pura, etc.

El sol se vistió de luto,
La luna se enterneció,
Las piedras vertieron sangre
Cuando Jesus expiró.
Las piedras, etc.

Santísimo Sacramento,
Que seas por siempre alabado,
Por las ánimas benditas
Y las que estén en pecado.
Por las ánimas, etc.

The Virgin hearing this
Fell to the ground in a faint,
St. John, like a good nephew,
Then came to lift her up.
St. John, etc.

The blood that he spilt
Fell into a chalice,
The man who will drink it
Will be very fortunate.
The man, etc.

The Virgin is dressed in mourning,
Her well beloved is dead,
And the news is proclaimed to the
  people
That He died for their sins.
And the, etc.

The three Virgins wept
To see that he suckled,
Virgin pure, Magdalene,
And the other, Martha, her sister.
Virgin pure, etc.

The sun dressed in mourning,
The moon was moved to pity,
The stones bled
When Jesus expired.
The stones bled, etc.

Most Holy Sacrament,
May you ever be praised
By the blessed souls
And by those in sin.
By the blessed souls, etc.

Alabanza a la Virgen

A song of greeting to the Virgin on her fiesta day. (Col. C. Michel)

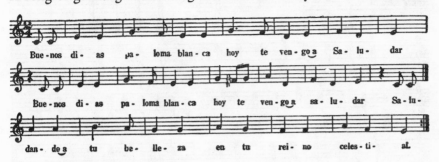

Bue - nos di - as pa - loma blan - ca hoy te ven - go a Sa - lu - dar

Bue - nos di - as pa - loma blan - ca hoy te ven - go a sa - lu - dar Sa - lu -

dan - de a tu be - lle - za en tu rei - no celes - ti - al.

Buenos dias paloma blanca
Hoy te vengo a saludar,
Saludando a tu belleza
En tu reino celestial.

Eres guía del marinero
Eres estrella del mar,
En la tierra y en el cielo
Yo te vengo a saludar.

Good morning, white dove,
Today I come to greet thee,
Greeting thy beauty
In your celestial reign.

You are the guide of the sailor,
You are the star of the sea;
On earth and in heaven,
I come to greet thee.

Alabanza I (Yaqui)

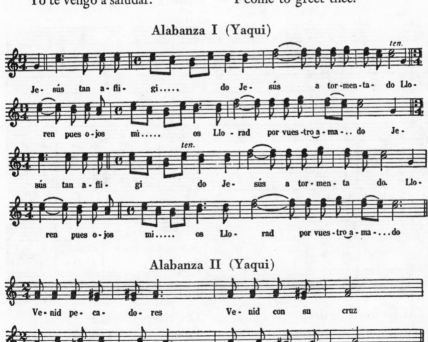

ten.

Je - sús tan a - fli - gi..... do Je - sús a tor - men - ta - do Llo -

ren pues o - jos mi..... os Llo - rad por vues - tro a - ma - .. do Je -

ten.

sús tan a - fli - gi do Je - sús a tor - men - ta do. Llo -

ren pues o - jos mi..... os Llo - rad por vues - tro a - ma - .... do

Alabanza II (Yaqui)

Ve - nid pe - ca - do - res Ve - nid con su cruz

a - do - rar la san - gre y - dul - ce Je - sús

Alabanza III (Yaqui)

SONGS FROM A RELIGIOUS MYSTERY PLAY

Canto De Luzbel

Acaba sueño de dar
Alivio a tanto tormento
No aflijas mi pensamiento . . .
Déjame ya descansar.

Oh, Sleep, give me
Relief for my tortures!
Afflict not my thoughts . . .
Let me rest in peace.

Canto De Eva

Pajarillos tiernos
que cantais al alba,
árboles vestidos
de verde esmeralda

Tender little birds
That sing at dawn,
Trees dressed up
In emerald green.

Al Trabajo Convida

Al trabajo convida,
pastores, este día;
la aurora con su encanto
y el alba con su risa.

To work this day
invites you, shepherds;
The dawn with its enchantment
And day-break with its smile.

En Este Nuevo Dia

tri - i - bu - ta - a - a - mos; oh, Dios om - ni - i - po - te - e - en -
te y Se - ñor de lo cre - a - a - do, oh Dios om -
ni - i - po - te - e - en - te y Se - ñor de lo cre - a - a - do.

En este nuevo día
gracias te tributamos;
Oh, Dios Omnipotente
y Señor de lo creado.

On this new day,
Thanks we give Thee,
Oh, Omnipotent God
And Lord of Creation.

Montes Primorosos

Mon - tes pri - mo - ro - sos que al-bo-rean su cum - bre Del sol al vis - lum - bre
na - ce el más her - mo - so. Mon - tes pri - mo - ro - sos que al - bo - rean su
cum - bre del sol al vis - lum - bre na - ce el mas her - mo - so

Montes primorosos
que alborean su cumbre
del sol al vislumbre
nace el más hermoso.
Montes primorosos
que alborean su cumbre
del sol al vislumbre
nace el más hermoso.

Marvelous mountains,
Whose summits are lighted
By the sun as it awakens
When it is most beautiful.
Marvelous mountains
Whose summits are lighted
By the sun as it awakens
When it is most beautiful.

Sal Arcangel

Lento

Sal, Ar- can- gel, con tu tro- va- dor pa- ra
que veas en él su sem- bla- an- te; sal, te rue- go si- quie- ra un
ins- tan- te a cal- mar de mi pe- cho el do- lor. Sal te
rue- go, ve- ras los ful- go- o- res de las pu- u- ras le- ja- a- nas es-
tre- e- llas; te di- ré mis fer- vien- tes que- re- e- llas de la lu- na su pá- li- da luz.

Sal, Arcángel, con tu trovador
para que veas en él su semblante;

Come out, Archangel, with your
    minstrel!
So that you may see in him your
    likeness;

sal, te ruego, siquiera un instante,
a calmar de mi pecho el dolor.

Sal, te ruego, verás los fulgores
de las puras lejanas estrellas;
te diré mis fervientes querellas
de la luna su pálida luz.

Come, I implore thee, but for an instant
To calm the pain in my heart.

Come out. I beg thee, you'll see the splendor
Of the pure and distant stars;
I shall tell thee my fervent plaints,
In the moon's pale light.

Marchemos Cantando

Marchemos cantando	Let us march singing,
marchemos cantando	Let us march singing,
con gozo y fervor	With joy and fervor
para ir saludando	To go to greet
las glorias de Dios!	the Glories of God!

Bendito el instante
que nos anunció
tan santo prodigio,
bendito sea Dios!

Blessed be the moment
That announced to us
Such a holy portent
Blessed be God!

Estrella Brillante

Estrella brillante,
luz del peregrino,
estrella, ilumina
hoy este camino
Alabado sea, alabado sea,
alabado, caminante.
Alabado sea, alabado sea,
el Señor que hizo estrella
tan brillante.

Brilliant star,
Pilgrim's light,
Oh, star, illuminate
Today, this road.
Praised be, praised be,
Praised be, pilgrim.
Praised be, praised be
The Lord who made a star
So brilliant.

Canto De Gila

Ya los gallos cantan
y el demonio llora,
porque ya nació
el Rey de la Gloria!

Now the roosters crow
And the devil weeps,
Because already is born
The King of Glory!

Todos Los Pastores

Todos los pastores
vamos a Belén
a adorar al niño
y a María también.

All of us shepherds,
To Belem let us go,
To adore the Infant
And Mary also.

CHRISTMAS MUSIC

Pedida De La Posada (Asking for Lodging)

Andante

En nom-bre del cie——e-lo os pi-do po-sa——da pu-es no pue-de an-dar——mi es-po-sa a-ma——da a qui no es me-son——si-gan a-de-lan—te yo no pue-do a-brir——ne sea al-gun tu-nan.——te.

San Jose	St. Joseph
En nombre del cielo	In the name of Heaven
Os pido posada,	I beg you for lodging,
Pues no puede andar	For she cannot walk
Mi esposa amada.	My beloved wife.
Casero	Man of the house
Aqui no es meson;	This is not an inn
Sigan adelante.	So keep going;
Yo no puedo abrir;	I cannot open;
No sea algun tunante.	You may be bad people.
S. J.	St. J.
No seas inhumano;	Don't be inhuman;
Tennos caridad.	Have mercy on us.
Que el Dios de los cielos	The God of the heavens
Te lo premiara.	Will reward you for it.
C.	C.
Ya se pueden ir	Better go on
Y no molestar.	And don't molest us.
Porque si me enfado	For if I become angry,
Los voy a apalear.	I shall beat you up.

S. J.
Venimos rendidos
Desde Nazareth.
Yo soy carpintero
De nombre Jose.

C.
No me importa el nombre;
Dejenme dormir,
Pues que ya les digo
Que no hemos de abrir.

S. J.
Posada te pido,
Amado casero,
Por solo una noche,
La Reina del Cielo.

C.
Pues si es una reina
Quien lo solicita,
Como es que de noche
Anda tan solita?

S. J.
Mi esposa es María
Es Reina del Cielo,
Y madre va a ser
Del Divino Verbo.

C.
Eres tu Jose?
Tu esposa es María?
Entren, perigrinos,
No los conocia.

S. J.
Dios pague, señores,
Vuestra caridad,
Y asi os colme el cielo
De felicidad.

C.
Dichosa la casa
Que abriga este dia
A la Virgen pura,
La hermosa María.

S. J.
Dichosa esta casa
Que nos da posada;
Dios siempre le de
Su dicha sagrada.

St. J.
We are worn out
Coming from Nazareth.
I'm a carpenter
My name is Joseph.

C.
Your name doesn't matter;
Let me sleep,
For I am telling you
We shall not open.

St. J.
Lodging is asked of you
Dear man,
For just one night
By the Queen of Heaven.

C.
Well, if it's a queen
Who solicits it,
Why is it that at night
Does she travel so alone.

St. J.
My wife is Mary,
She's the Queen of Heaven
And is going to be the mother
Of the Divine Word.

C.
Are you Joseph?
Your wife is Mary?
Enter, pilgrims,
I did not know you.

St. J.
May God pay, señores,
Your kindness,
And thus the Heavens heap
Happiness upon you.

C.
Fortunate the house
That shelters this day
The pure Virgin,
The beautiful Mary.

St. J.
Fortunate this house
That gives us shelter;
May God always give it
Its sacred happiness.

C.
Posada os damos
Con mucha alegria,
Entra, Jose justo,
Entra con María.

C.
Lodging I give you
With much joy;
Enter, just Joseph,
Enter with Mary.

The preceding verses are sung by the groups in and outside of the
house but when the doors are opened all sing together:

A - bran - se las puer - tas rom - pan - se los vo - los que vie - ne a posar el Rey de los
cie - los que vie - ne a po - sar el Rey de los cie - los.

Abranse las puertas,
Rompanse los velos;
Que viene a posar
El Rey de los Cielos.

Let the doors fly open!
Let the veils be broken!
For here comes to rest
The King of the Heavens.

Entrad pues, esposos,
Con satisfaccion,
Que os damos posada
Con el corazón.

Enter then, spouses,
With satisfaction,
For we're giving you lodging
With our hearts.

Entren, santos perigrinos,
Reciban este rincon,
No de este pobre morada
Sino de mi corazón.

Enter, holy pilgrims,
Receive this corner,
Not of this poor dwelling
But of my heart.

Esta noche es de alegria,
De gusto y de regozijo,
Porque hospedamos aqui
A la Madre de Dios Hijo.

This night is of joy,
Of pleasure and of rejoicing,
Because we are lodging here
The Mother of God, the Son.

Fin Del Rezo (End of the Prayer)

Allegro

Al - mas a - man - tes tier - nas las que sa - ben sen - tir
ve - nid a - cá ve - nid ve - nid a - cá ve - nid

Almas amantes, tiernas,	Souls, loving and tender,
Las que saben sentir,	Those that know how to feel,
Venid acá, venid.	Come here, come!
La jumentilla humilde	The humble little beast
Inclina la cerviz	Bends its neck
Y dobla la rodilla	And doubles its knee
Para poder subir.	In order to climb.
El bendito José,	The blessed Joseph
Lleno de amor asi	Filled with love thus
A su querida esposa	To his beloved wife
Le comenzó a decir:	Commenced to speak:
Oh, Reina de lo creado,	Oh, Queen of all created,
Tu merecías venir,	You were worthy of coming
O en alas de querube	Or on the wings of cherub
O en trono de zafir.	Or on a sapphire throne.

Al Quebrar La Piñata I

Hora y fuego, que buena piñata!	Time and fire, (Gee) what a good pinata!
Se mece con gusto,	It swings with pleasure
Colgada de la reata.	Hanging from the rope.
Luego a darle seguido.	Then keep on hitting it
A ver quien la rompa	To see who breaks it
Con garbo y con tino.	With style and tact.

Ay que bueno el sentido
Que tiene por dentro.
Ay que bueno el sentido
Que tiene por dentro.

Si la pego yo recio o quedito,
Se mueve y se escape
Y me hace guajito.
Y de risa se mueve, caramba!
Ay, olla, que zumba.
¡Que viva piñata!

Oh how good the content
That it has within.
How good is the content
That it has within.

If I hit it hard or softly,
It moves and escapes me
And makes a fool of me.
And it moves from laughing.
Oh, pot, there crack.
Long live the pinata!

Al Quebrar La Piñata II

Andale, Pepe, no pierdas el tino
Que de la distancia pierde el camino.
Con los ojitos vendidos y en las
  manos un baston.
Se hace la ollita pedazos sin com-
  pasion.

Dale, dale, dale, no pierdas el tino,
Que de la distancia se pierde el
  camino.

Come on, Pepe, don't lose your
  touch,
Which from the distance misses the
  direction.
With your eyes blindfolded and a
  stick in your hands
Break the jar to pieces without com-
  passion.

Hit it, hit it, hit it, don't lose your
  touch,
Which from a distance misses the
  direction.

Al Quebrar La Piñata III

En las no - ches de po - sa - das la pi - ña - ta_es

lo me - dar la ri - ña mas re - mil - ' ga - da

Se al - boro - ta con ar - dor

Da - le da - le da - le no pier - das el ti - no que de la dis - tan - cia se pier - de el cami - no.

En las noches de posada
La piñata, es lo mejor;
La niña más remilgada
Se alborota con ardor.

Dale, dale, dale,
No pierdas el tino,
Que de la distancia
Se pierde el camino.

Of the Christmas fiestas
The pinata is the best;
The quietest girl
Becomes hotly excited.

Hit it, hit it, hit it;
Don't lose your touch
Which from a distance
Misses the direction.

Para Pedir Los Juguetes (To Ask for the Toys)

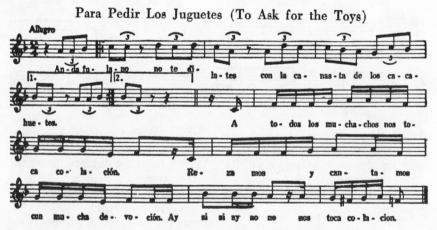

An - da fu - la - no no te di - la - tes con la ca - nas - ta de los ca - ca -

hue - tes. A to - dos los mu - cha - chos nos to -

ca co - la - ción. Re - za mos y can - ta - mos

con mu - cha de - vo - ción. Ay si si ny no ne nos toca co - la - cion.

Anda, Fulana, no te dilates (Fulana
    stands for any name)
Con la canasta de los cacahuetes.

Andale, Tina, no seas coditos, (sic)
Con la charola de los jugetitos.

Come, Fulana, do not delay
With the basket of the peanuts.

Come along, Tina, don't be stingy
With the tray of toys.

A todos los muchachos nos toca colación,
Rezamos y cantamos con mucha devoción.
Ay sí, sí; ay no, no; Nos toca colación.

Numerous other verses are sung, and then

All us children deserve goodies;
We pray and sing with great devotion.
Ay yes, yes; ay no, no; we deserve goodies.

Despedida De La Posada (Taking Leave of the Posada)

Muy agradecidos de aqui nos marchamos;
Al cielo rogamos premie nuestra acción.
Quiera Dios divino que al dejar el suelo
Disfruteis del cielo la hermosa mansión.

Repeat

Very grateful we go from here;
We pray to heaven to reward our action.
May the divine God grant upon leaving this earth
We may enjoy the beautiful mansion of Heaven.

Ave Marias

Estrella de rendición peregrina imaculada,
Yo te doy mi corazón para que tengáis posada,
Humildes peregrinos, Jesús, María y José,
Humildes peregrinos, Jesús, María y José,
El alma os doy, con ella el corazón tambien.

Oh, peregrina a graciada;
Oh dulcísima María.
Os ofrezco el alma mia,
Para que tengáis posada.

Handsome, immaculate star of rendition,
I give you my heart so that you may have shelter,
Humble pilgrims, Jesus, Mary, and Joseph.
The soul I give you, also, with the heart.

Oh, gracious pilgrim,
Oh, sweetest Mary,
I offer you my soul
So that you may have shelter.

CORRIDOS (BALLADS)

(An 18th century ballad, composed in Mexico City. Recorded by
Graciela Amador)

Romance de Román Castillo

¿Dónde vas, Román Castillo?
¿Dónde vas? ¡Pobre de tí! (repeat
    two lines)
Ya no busques más querellas,
Por nuestra damas de aquí. (repeat
    two lines)

Where are you going, Román Cas-
tillo?
Where are you going, poor man?
    (repeat the two lines)
Don't look for any more quarrels
On account of our ladies here. (re-
    peat two lines)

Ya está herido tu caballo;	Your horse is wounded,
Ya está roto tu espadín.	Your spade is broken,
Tus hazañas son extrañas,	Your feats are strange
Y tu amor no tiene fin. (repeat four lines)	And your love has no end. (repeat the four lines)
Antenoche me dijeron	Night before last I was told
Que pasaste por aquí. (repeat two lines)	You came here. (repeat two lines)
Que tocaste trece veces	That you knocked thirteen times
y el cancel querías abrir. (repeat two lines)	And wanted to force the screen. (repeat two lines)
Que mis criados, espantados,	That my frightened servants
Por nada querían abrir,	Would not open for anything;
Y que entonces tú gritaste:	That you shouted,
"¡Abran o van a morir!" (repeat four lines)	"Open or you will die!" (repeat four lines)
¡Ten piedad, Román Castillo!	Have mercy, Román Castillo!
¡Ten piedad, pobre de mí! (repeat two lines)	Have mercy, poor me! (repeat two lines)
Si persiste en tu vida,	If you persist in your ways,
de dolor voy a morir . . . (repeat two lines)	I shall die of sorrow. (repeat two lines)
Tu eres noble, eres bravo,	You are noble, you are brave,
Hombre de gran corazón;	A man of good heart;
Pero que tu amor no manche	But may your love not stain
Nunca mi reputación. (repeat four lines)	Ever my reputation. (repeat four lines)

La Güera Chabela
(Corrido from Jalisco. Recorded by Graciela Amador)

An - da - ba Je - sus Ca - de - nas pa - sián - do- se en un fan -

dan - go di - cién -do- le a sus a - mi- gos: e - sa güe - ra yo la man - do.

Andaba Jesús Cadenas	Jesús Cadenas was out
pasiandose en un fandango	Enjoying himself in a fandango,
diciéndole a sus amigos:	Telling all his friends,
"esa güera yo la mando."	"I'm boss of that blond."
Les decía Jesús Cadenas:	Jesús Cadenas said to them,
"ese güera yo la mando,	"I'm boss of that blond.
les daré satisfacción,	I'll give you satisfaction,
no se anden equivocando."	Don't fool yourselves."
Decía su comadre Antonia:	Her godmother said,
"Chabela, no andes bailando	"Chabela, don't go dancing;
que ahí anda Jesús Cadenas	Here is Jesus Cadenas,
que nomás te anda tantiando."	Trying you out."
"¡Ay!," le contestó Chabela	"Ay," Chabela answered her,
soltando juerte risada,	Laughing loudly,
"no tenga miedo, comadre,	"I'm not afraid, godmother,
ya conozco mi güeyada."	I know my man."
Pero este Jesús Cadenas,	But this Jesús Cadenas,
como era hombre de sus brazos,	As he was a man of action,
echó mano a su pistola	Put his hand on his pistol
para darle de balazos.	To fill her with bullets.
Decía su comadre Antonia:	Said her godmother Antonia,
"Compadre, pase pa' dentro	"Come inside, compadre,
a tomarse una cerveza,	To take a beer
que se le borre ese intento."	So as to forget your intent."
No quiso corresponder	He did not answer
por ninguna distinción;	For any consideration;
cuatro balazos le dió	Four bullets he gave her
del lado del corazón.	On the side of her heart.
Decía la güera Chabela	Said the blond Chabela,
agarrándose el vestido:	Taking hold of her dress,
"pongan cuidado, muchachas,	"Pay attention, girls,
dónde me pegó ese tiro."	Where that bullet entered."
Decía la güera Chabela	Said the blond Chabela,
apretándose las manos:	Pressing her hands together,
"ya no se apuren, muchachas,	"Don't worry any more, girls,
que allí vienen mis hermanos."	There come my brothers."
Salió su papá de adentro	Her father came outside,
con las lágrimas rodando:	His tears flowing,

"¿Que, tienes, güera Chabela,
por qué te vienes quejando?"

"What is wrong, blond Chabela,
Why are you complaining?"

"¡Ay!"—le contestó Chabela—,
"sólo Dios sabrá hasta cuándo
esto me habrá sucedido
por andarlos mancornando."

"Ay," Chabela answered him,
"Only God knew how soon
This would happen to me
For going about flirting."

Su pobre madre lloraba,
lloraba muy afligida:
"¿Quién ha sido ese malvado
que te ha quitado la vida?"

Her poor mother wept,
Wept, very afflicted,
"Who was this wicked one
That has taken your life?"

Decía la güera Chabela,
cuando se estaba muriendo:
"Pongan cuidado, muchachas,
miren cómo van viviendo."

Said the blond Chabela
When she was dying,
"Be careful, girls;
Watch how you live."

Ya con esta me despido,
con la flor de la cirgüela,
y aquí se acaba el corrido
de Cadenas y Chabela.

Now with this I take leave,
With the flower of the cirgüela,[1]
Here ends the corrido
Of Cadenas and Chabela.

Corrido de Lucío

(From the State of Michoacán. An example type)

A las on - ce de la no - che es - ta - ba Lu - cio ce - nan - do cuan -do lle -
gan sus a - mi - gos y lo in - vi - tan al fan -dan - go

A las once de la noche
estaba Lucio cenando,
cuando llegan sus amigos
y lo invitan al fandango.

At eleven o'clock at night
Lucio was eating supper,
When his friends came
And invited him to the fandango.

Su madre se lo decía,
que a ese fandango no juera;
los consejos de una madre,
no se llevan como quera.

His mother told him
Not to go to that fandango;
The advice of a mother
Cannot be taken lightly.

[1] Cirgüela is a corruption of ciruela, the Spanish for prune.

Lo sacaron a la orilla por ver si sabía jugar; tres puñaladas le dieron al pie de un verde nopal.	They took him aside To see if he knew how to play; They gave him three stabs At the foot of the green nopal.
	(Here repeat chorus)
Su hermano de compasión, la pistola le brindó; "Ora para que la quero, si ya la hora pasó."	His brother out of pity Offered him his pistol. "Now, what do I want it for, It is too late?"
Madre mía de Guadalupe, de la Villa de Jerez, dame licencia, Señora, de levantarme otra vez.	Mother mine of Guadalupe, From the Villa of Jerez, Give me leave, Señora, To get up again.
Su pobre madre lloraba, paseándose en los portales; "¿Cómo queres levantarte, si son heridas mortales?"	His poor mother wept, Pacing in the entrance "How can you want to get up; These wounds are mortal."
	(Chorus)
Santo Niñito de Atocha, de la Villa de Jerez, dame licencia, Niñito, de levantarme otra vez.	Holy Child of Atocha, From the Villa of Jerez, Give me leave, little one, To get up again.
Vuela, vuela, palomita, avisa a toda la gente, que no sigan el ejemplo del hijo desobediente.	Fly, fly, little dove, Tell all the people, Not to follow the example, Of the disobedient son.

Note: This same corrido is sung with different verses in other parts of the country.

Corrido de Cananea
(About an experience with an American sheriff. State of Sonora.)

Voy a dar un pormenor
de lo que a mí me ha pasado,
que me han agarrado preso,
siendo un gallo tan jugado.

I am going to give an account
Of what happened to me;
How they made me a prisoner
Being such a wise guy.
(Siendo un gallo tan jugado; liter-
ally, being a cock who has fought
or been played so much.)

Me fuí para el Agua Prieta
a ver quién me conocía;
y a las once de la noche
me aprehendió la policía.

I went to Agua Prieta
To see who knew me;
At eleven o'clock at night
The police arrested me.

Me aprehendieron los gendarmes,
al estilo americano:
como era hombre de delito
todos con pistola en mano.

I was arrested by the police
In American style,
As if I were a criminal,
All with pistol in hand.

Me enviaron a Cananea
atravesando la sierra,
no me les pude pintar
por no conocer la tierra.

They sent me to Cananea,
Crossing the Sierra,
I could not run away,[1]
Not knowing the country.

Al llegar a Cananea,
allí perdí la esperanza,
porque allí fuí consignado
a un juez de primera instancia.

Upon arriving at Cananea
I lost hope there,
Because I was consigned
To the first judge.

A otro día por la mañana
nos raparon la cabeza
porque me iba a visitar
el administrador de mesa.

The next morning
They shaved our heads
Because I was to be visited
By the administrator.

[1] Slang for I could not play.

Me sacaron un recibo
de la casa del congreso,
donde preguntaba el juez:
"¿Sabe usted por qué está preso?"

Yo le contesté muy serio,
poniéndome muy formal,
"no me han de formar un templo,
ni un palacio de cristal."

La cárcel de Cananea
se edificó en una mesa
y en ella fuí procesado
por causa de mi torpeza.

De tres amigos que tengo
ninguno me quiere hablar,
comenzando por el chango,
y leoncito y el caimán.

Despedida no la doy
porque no la traigo aquí,
se la dejo al Santo Niño
y al Señor de Mayumi.

Ya con esta me despido
por las hojas de un granado,
aquí se acabó el corrido
de este gallo bien jugado.

They made me give a receipt
Of the House of Congress,
Where the judge asked,
"Do you know why you're in prison?"

I answered him seriously,
Putting on a formal manner,
"I don't expect a temple,
Nor a crystal palace."

The prison of Cananea
Was built on a hill
And in it I was tried
Because of my stupidity.

Of three friends I have
Not one will speak to me,
Beginning with the monkey,
The little lion and the alligator.

I cannot show my discharge;
I do not have it here;
I'll leave it to the Infant Jesus
And the Señor of Mayumi.

Now with this I take leave
With the leaves of the *granado*
Here ends the corrido
Of the wise guy.
(the gallo tan jugado)

Corrido de Rivera
(A strong man from the North, State of Coahuila)

En e-se ca-ñón de tu-la un dia-blo se a-pa-re ció

con to-dos queria pe-lear-se no-más con Ri-ve-ra no.

En ese cañón de Tula
un diablo se apareció,
con todos quería pelearse,
no más con Rivera no.

En dicho cañón de Tula
una boda se rugía,
no más lo supo Rivera,
las noches las hizo día.

Estaban en dicha boda
cuando Rivera llegó,
les atravesó el caballo
y a la novia se llevó.

La madre de atribulada
cien pesos le prometió
porque le dejara su hija;
Rivera dijo que no.

Llegaron los del resguardo
cuando Rivera salió,
los otros eran cien hombres,
Rivera solo y su amor.

Salieron de los portales
con rumbo hacia Ticubeta,
todos iban a caballo,
Rivera en su "bicicleta."

Salieron de Ticubeta
con rumbo hacia Ticumán,
cómo se quedaría el novio
abriendo las de caimán.

Esos pobres del resguardo
no pudieron alcanzar
a Rivera con la novia,
con la que se iba a casar.

In this Cañon of Tula,
A Devil appeared.
He wanted to fight everyone,
Only not with Rivera.

In this Cañon of Tula
A wedding was to take place.
As soon as Rivera knew it,
He turned night into day.

The wedding was taking place
When Rivera arrived;
He put his horse in the way
And carried off the bride.

The mother of the afflicted one
Promised him a hundred pesos
For him to leave her daughter.
Rivera said, "no."

The guards arrived
When Rivera left;
They were a hundred men,
Rivera alone with his love.

They left the portales
In the direction of Ticubeta;
All were on horseback,
Rivera on his bicycle.

They left Ticubeta
In the direction of Ticumán,
The groom must have had his
Mouth open like an alligator.

The poor men left behind
Could not catch up
With Rivera and the bride
Whom he was going to marry.

The last verse is the same as the
first.

La Maquinita (The Little Train)
(A Parody)

Aquí yo he venido
porque ya he llegado
y vengo muy descansado,
cantando canciones
me paso la vida
un poco más divertida.

Fué en el año de cuarenta
antes del cincuenta y cuatro
cuando murió tanta gente
entre Tula y Guanajuato.
El tren que corría
sobre la ancha vía,
de pronto se fué a estrellar
contra un aeroplano
que estaba en el llano
volando sin descansar.

Quedó el maquinista
con las tripas fuera,
mirando pal aviador
que ya sin cabeza
buscaba el sombrero
para librarse del sol.
Los pocos supervivientes
los contemplaban llorando
y la máquina seguía
pita, pita y caminando.

Here I have come
Because I've already arrived
And I come very rested,
Singing songs
I spend my days
A little more pleasantly.

It was in the year forty,
Before that of fifty-four,
When so many people died
Between Tula and Guanajuato.
The train that was running
Over the standard tracks,
Suddenly went and crashed
Against an airplane
That was on the plain,
Flying without resting.

The engineer was left
With his guts outside,
Looking for the aviator,
Who already without a head
Was looking for a hat
To free himself from the sun.
The few survivors
Looked at them weeping
And the train went on
Puff, puff, on we go.

El güen fogonero
también quedó muerto
debajo del chapopote
y hasta el garrotero,
sin brazos ni cuerpo,
se agarraba del garrote.
Buscando al agente
de publicaciones
lo encontraron moribundo;
ye el pobre gritando
"¡Cervezas heladas!"
se fué para el otro mundo.
Todo esto nos sucedia
sin saber cómo ni cuándo,
y la máquina seguia
pita, pita y caminando.

Llegó la Cruz Blanca,
llegó la Cruz Roja,
a auxiliar a los heridos,
y alli se encontraron
que todos los muertos
de miedo ya habían corrido.
Estos cadáveres
salieron huyendo
en tan críticos instantes;
ha habido dijunto
que lo han encontrado
cuatro leguas adelante.
En una zanja los muertos
solos se fueron echando,
y la máquina seguía
pita, pita y caminando.

Y yo ya no quero
seguir esta historia
para no cansar a ustedes;
rueguen por aquellos
que allí se murieron,
hombres, niños y mujeres.
Al recordar tanto muerto
todos están vacilando
porque la máquina sigue
pita, pita y caminando.

The good fireman
Was also dead
Under the coal
And even the brakeman,
Without arm and body,
Was holding on to the brake;
Looking for the agent
Of publications,
They found him dying;
The poor devil calling,
"Cold beer!"
Went to the next world.
All this was happening to us
Without knowing how nor when,
And the train went on,
Puff, puff, on we go.

The White Cross arrived,
The Red Cross arrived,
To help all the wounded,
And there they found
That all the dead
Had run away from fright.
Those corpses
Went out fleeing
In such critical moments;
There were corpses found
Four leagues ahead.
In a ditch the dead
Only threw themselves,
And the train went on
Puff, puff, on we go.

And I no longer wish
To continue this story
So as not to tire you;
Pray for those
Who died there,
Men, children, and women.
Upon recalling so many dead,
All are having fun,
Because the train goes on
Puff, puff, on we go.

El Venadito

From San Luis Potosí

This corrido is full of double meaning, quite impossible to translate truly.

Note: The musical form of this song and of El Conejo is like the ballad though the text, of "versitos" or disconnected verses, is not.

Soy un po-bre ve-na-di-to que ha-bi-ta en la se-rra-ni-a   Soy un ni-a   Co-mo no soy tan man-si-to no ba-jo al a-gua de di-a de no-che po-co a po-qui-to y en tus bra-zos vi-da mi-a

Soy un pobre venadito,	I'm a poor little deer
que habita en la serranía.	Who lives in the mountains.
Soy un pobre venadito	I'm a poor little deer
que habita en la serranía.	Who lives in the mountains.
Como no soy tan mansito,	As I'm not so gentle,
no bajo al agua de día,	I don't go down to drink by day,
de noche, poco a poquito,	By night, little by little,
y en tus brazos, vida mía.	And in your arms, my love.
Me subí al cerro más alto,	I climbed the highest hill
para devisar los planes.	To make out the planes.
Donde riscan aguilillas	Where big eagles fly,
No mandan los gavilanes,	Don't send sparrow-hawks,
ni las naguas amarillas,	Nor yellow skirts,
aunque se pongan olanes.	Even with white flounces.
Quisiera ser perla fina	I wish I were a fine pearl
de tus lucidos aretes,	In your shining earrings,
pa' morderte la orejita	To bite your little ear
y besarte los cachetes.	And kiss your nice cheeks.
Quien te manda a ser bonita,	Who told you to be so pretty
que hasta a mí me comprometes.	That you compromise even me.
Tengo un nicho de cristal,	I have a niche of crystal
hecho con mis propias manos,	Made with my own hands,
para colocarte a tí,	In which to place you
si seguimos como vamos;	If we continue as we are.
pero si me pagas mal,	But if you're bad with me,
pobre nicho, lo quebramos.	Poor niche, we shall break it.

Voy a hacer una barata	I'm going to make an auction
y una gran realización;	And a great clearance sale:
las viejitas a cuartilla,	The little old ones at a quarter,
las muchachas a tostón,	The girls at four bits;
los yernos a seis centavos	The son-in-laws at six cents
y las suegras de pilón.	And the mother-in-laws thrown in.
Entré al jardín de Cupido	I entered the garden of Cupid
a cortar de sus rosales,	To cut from his rosebushes.
y allí mi chata me puso	And there my little one
el maíz a veinte reales	Gave me corn for a dime
y me dijo que no fiaba	And told me she did not trust
ni prestaba los costales.	Nor loan the bags.
Ya con esta me despido;	Now with this I take leave
pero pronto doy la vuelta.	But soon I shall return.
No más que libre Dios	Only may God free me
de una niña mosca muerta,	From a dead-fly girl,
de esas de: "¡Ay, no, no, por Dios!"	One of those—"No, no, for God's sake!"
y hasta salen a la puerta.	And they even come to the door.

El Conejo (The Rabbit)

(A love song from the State of Mexico. Recorded by Rufino Tamayo)

Mi a-mor es co-mo el co-ne-jo sen-ti-do co-mo el ve-na-do
mi a-mor no co-me za-ca-te vie-jo ni tam-po-co muy tri-lla-do
co-me za-ca-ti-to ver-de de la pun-ta se-re-na-do

Mi amor es como el conejo,	My love is like the rabbit,
Sentido como el vanado.	Sensitive as the deer. (repeat)
No come zacate viejo	It does not eat old hay
Ni tampoco muy trillado,	Nor when it is very thrashed;
Come zacatito verde	It eats tender green hay
De la punta serenado.	From the bottom of the hill.
Pavo Rial, que eres correo	Royal turkey, who art the mailman,
Y que vas a Rial del Oro.	And goest to the Rial de Oro. (repeat)

Si te preguntan qué hago,
Pavo Rial, diles que lloro
Lagrimitas de mi sangre
Por una mujer que adoro.

Soy como el pájaro verde
Que en la sombra me detengo.
La palabra que me diste
En el corazón la tengo,
Ya que no me la cumpliste
A que me la cumplas vengo.

Cuando pase por tu casa,
Hermosa prenda querida,
Si te despierto cantando,
Vuélvete a quedar dormida,
Que yo paso por tu casa
Dándole gusto a la vida.

If they ask you what I am doing,
Royal turkey, tell them I'm weeping
Little tears of my blood
For a woman that I adore.

I'm like the green bird
That stops in the shade. (repeat)
The promise you gave me
I have in my heart;
Now that you did not keep it,
I come to make you fulfill it.

When I come to your house,
My beautiful jewel, (repeat)
If I awake you singing,
Go to sleep again;
For I come to your house
To give you pleasure in life.

REVOLUTIONARY SONGS

La Valentina

A Revolutionary Song from Chihuahua

Una pasión me domina,
es la que me ha hecho venir,
Valentina, Valentina,
yo te quisiera decir:

    Dicen que por tus amores
un mal me van a seguir,
no le hace que sean el diablo,
yo también me sé morir.

    Si porque bebo tequila,
mañana bebo jerez,
si porque me ves borracho,
mañana ya no me ves;

    Valentina, Valentina,
rendido estoy a tus pies,
si me han de matar mañana,
que me maten de una vez.

I am dominated by passion,
Which is what has made me come;
Valentina, Valentina,
I wish to tell you.

They say because of your love,
Some evil will follow me.
I don't care if it's the devil,
I also know how to die.

If it's because I drink tequila,
Tomorrow I shall drink Jerez;
If it's because you see me drunk,
Tomorrow you will not see me.

Valentina, Valentina,
I prostrate myself at your feet
If they are going to kill me to-
    morrow
Let them kill me right now.

Adelita

The most beloved of all the revolutionary songs, sung by everybody
everywhere. From the State of Durango. Recorded by Carmen
Mendizabal.

En lo al-to de u-na a-brup-ta se-rra-ni..... a don-de es-ta-ba ya cam-

pa-do un re-gi-mien- to u-na jo-ven que va-lien-te los se- guí

a por-que es-ta-ba e-na-mo-ra-da de un sar- gen- to. Po-pu- lar en-tre la

tro-pa e-ra A-de- li- ta la mu-jer por el sar-gen-to i-do la- tra-

da por-que a más de ser-va-lien-te e-ra bo- ni- ta y has-ta el mis-mo co-ro-

nel la res-pe-ta-ba..... y se cuen-ta que de-cí-a él cuan- la que-rí-a

Si A-de- li- ta se fue- ra con o- tro le se-gui-rí-a las

En lo alto de una abrupta serranía
donde estaba y acampado un regimi-
    ento,
una joven que valiente los seguía
porque estaba enamorada de un sar-
    gento.

Popular entre la tropa era Adelita,
la mujer por el sargento idolatrada
porque a más de ser valiente era
    bonita
y hasta el mismo coronel la respe-
    taba.

Y se cuenta que decía él cuánto
    la quería:

Si Adelita se fuera con otro
le seguiría las huellas sin cesar,
si por mar en un buque de guerra,
si por tierra en un tren militar.

Si Adelita ha de ser mi esposa,
si Adelita ha de ser mi mujer,
Adelita, Adelita del alma,
Adelita de mi corazón.

Si Adelita quisiera ser mi esposa,
si Adelita fuera mi mujer,
le compraría un vestido de seda,
para llevarla a bailar al cuartel.

On the heights of an abrupt ridge,
Where a regiment was camping.
A valiant young girl followed it
Because she was in love with a ser-
    geant.*

Favorite among the troops was Ade-
    lita,
The woman idolized by the ser-
    geant,
Because besides being brave she was
    pretty,
And even the Colonel respected her.

And it is related that he said how
much he loved her:

If Adelita were to go with another,
He would follow her tracks without
    rest;
If by sea, in a war boat,
If by land, in a military train.

Yes, Adelita must be my wife,
Yes, Adelita must be my woman.
Adelita, Adelita of my soul,
Adelita of my heart.

If Adelita wished to be my wife,
If Adelita were my woman,
I would buy her a silk dress,
To take her to dance at the barracks.

* I have been told by men who fought with Villa that Adelita actually existed. Some
girls of good families became soldaderas of their own accord, while others were
carried off by officers.

Adelita, por Dios te lo ruego,
calma el fuego de esta mi pasión,
porque te amo y te quiero rendido
y por tí sufre mi fiel corazón.

Si Adelita se fuera con otro
le seguiría la huella sin cesar,
si por mar, en un buque de guerra,
si por tierra, en tren militar.

Toca el clarín de campaña a la
    guerra,
sale el valiente guerrero a pelear,
correrán los arroyos de sangre,
¡Que gobierne un tirano jamás!

Y si acaso yo muero en campaña
y mi cuerpo en la sierra va a quedar,
Adelita, por Dios te lo ruego,
con tus ojos me vas a llorar.

Adelita, for God's sake I beg you
To calm the fire of this my passion,
Because I adore you and love you
    devotedly
And for you my faithful heart suf-
    fers.

Here the first verse is repeated,
    which is the refrain.

The bugle of battle plays to war,
The brave knight leaves to fight,
Streams of blood shall flow,
Let no tyrant ever govern! **

And if perchance I die in battle
And my body remains in the sierra,
Adelita, for God's sake I beg you,
To weep for me with your eyes.

** This is the only verse I have ever found in any of the revolutionary songs that
referred to the aims of the revolution.

La Cucaracha

A Revolutionary Song from Chihuahua

This song begins with the chorus, which is sung after each of the
following verses. The number of verses is endless as each singer makes
up new ones and there are certain regional verses.

La cu-ca-ra-cha la cu-ca-ra-cha ya no pue-de ca-mi-nar por-que no
tie-ne por-que le fal-ta ma-ri-hua-na que fu-mar— la cu-ca-
ra-cha ya mu-rió la cu-ca-ra-cha ya la lle-van a en-te-rrar
en-tre cua-tro zo-pi-lo-tes y un ra-tón de sa-cris-tan

Coro:

La cucaracha, la cucaracha,
ya no puede caminar;
porque no tiene, porque le falta
marihuana que fumar.

Ya murió la cucaracha,
ya la llevan a enterrar,
entre cuatro zopilotes
y un ratón de sacristán.

Con las barbas de Carranza,
voy a hacer una toquilla,
pa' ponérsela al sombrero
de su padre Pancho Villa.

Un panadero fué a misa,
no encontrando qué rezar,
le pidió a la Virgen pura,
marihuana pa' fumar.

Una cosa me da risa:
Pancho Villa sin camisa;
ya se van los carrancistas
porque vienen los villistas.

Para sarapes, Saltillo;
Chihuahua para soldados;
para mujeres, Jalisco;
para amar, toditos lados.

Chorus

The cockroach, the cockroach
Can no longer walk,
Because it hasn't, because it hasn't
Marihuana to smoke.

The cockroach is now dead
And is taken to be buried
Between four buzzards
And a rat of a Sacristan.

With the whiskers of Carranza,
I'm going to make a hat band,
To put it on the sombrero
Of his father Pancho Villa.[1]

A baker went to mass,
Not finding anything to pray for,
He asked the pure Virgin
For Marihuana to smoke.

One thing makes me laugh,
Pancho Villa in his shirt;
Now the Carranzistas are leaving
Because the Villistas are coming.

For sarapes, Saltillo; [2]
Chihuahua, for soldiers;
For women, Jalisco;
For love, everywhere.

La Jesusita
A Revolutionary Song from San Luis Potosí

[1] Father is used in slang as the one who is the boss.
[2] All these states are famous for the subjects mentioned.

Vamos al baile y verás qué bonito,
donde se alumbran con veinte lin-
ternas,
donde se bailan las danzas modernas,
donde se baila de mucho vacilón.

Let's go to the dance and you'll see
how lovely,
Where it is illuminated with twenty
lanterns,
Where they dance the modern
dances,
Where they dance with great abandon.

Refrán:
Y quiéreme, Jesusita,
y quiéreme por favor,
y mira que soy tu amante
y seguro servidor.

Chorus
And love me, Jesusita,
And love me, please,
And look I am your lover,
And your humble servant.

Vamos al baile y verás qué bonito,
donde se alumbran con veinte lin-
ternas,
donde las niñas enseñan las piernas,
donde se baile de mucho vacilón.

Let's go to the dance and you'll see
how lovely,
Where it is illuminated with twenty
lanterns.
Where the girls show their legs,
Where they dance with great
whoopee.

De Las Torres De Puebla (The Towers of Puebla)

(Dating from the French Intervention, middle of the Nineteenth
Century) *From Romance y Corrido by Vicente T. Mendoza*

¿Dónde están esas torres de Puebla?
¿Dónde están esos templos dorados?
¿Dónde están esos vasos sagrados?
Con la guerra todo se acabó.

Where are those towers of Puebla?
Where are those golden temples?
Where are those sacred chalices?
With the war all is gone.

Entre escombros gemían los heridos
que lucharon con tanto valor,
y las madres decían a sus hijos:
—¡Vamos pues a morir con honor!—

The wounded sigh amidst the ruins,
Who fought with such valor
And the mothers said to their sons,
Let us then die with honor!

Estribillo:
Pa' los fuertes de Loreto
comenzaron a tirar
esas tropas de franceses
que gritaban sin cesar;
a los nuestros les decían:
—¿Qu'és de las piezas de pan?
—¡Aguárdenlas, que *ai* les van!
¡Pom . . . !—

Refrain
Toward the Forts of Loreto
They began to shoot
Those troops of Frenchmen
Who yelled without stopping
And they said to our soldiers:
What about those pieces of bread?
Keep them, there they go, pom. . !

¿Dónde estás Zaragoza valiente?
¿Dónde está tu lucido escuadrón?
A luchar por la Patria ha marchado
a luchar y a morir con honor.

Where are you, brave Zaragoza?
Where is your brilliant squadron?
It has marched off to fight for the Fatherland,
To fight and to die with honor.

Entre escombros gemían los heridos,
etc.

Refrain (Second and Third Verses)

Si mi suerte es morir en campaña,
defendiendo mi patria y mi honor,
mexicanos, adornen mi tumba
con la enseña de mi pabellón.

If my fate is to die in battle
Defending my Fatherland and honor,
Mexicans, decorate my grave
With the colors of my flag.

Entre escombros gemían los heridos,
etc.

Refrain (Second and Third Verses)

El soldado del norte es muy pobre,
su vestido una tosca mezclilla;
su divisa una blusa amarilla,
pero nunca su patria vendió.

The soldier from the North is very poor
His suit is of rough drill,
His badge a yellow blouse
But he has never sold out his Fatherland.

Entre escombros gemían los heridos,
etc.

Repeat all the first part.

DANCE SONGS

Sones (Sons)

El Palo Verde (The Green Stick)

A *Son* from the State of Nayarit. (Recorded by Concha Michel)

Señora, su palo verde, ya se le estaba secando
y anoche se lo regué y hoy le amaneció floreando.

Señora, your green stick was already drying;
Last night I watered it and this morning it was blooming.

A mí no me ande con esas cosas,	Don't say such things to me,
diablo de viejo tan imprudente	You old imprudent devil,
que aunque me mire con estas trazas	Although you see me like this,
yo siempre he sido mujer decente.	I've always been a decent woman.
Una guacamaya pinta espiaba que amaneciera	A spotted guaycamaya was awaiting the dawn
para darse un agarrón con un pájaro cualquera.	To grapple with any old bird.
A mí no me ande con esas cosas	Don't say such things to me,
diablo de viejo tan atrevido,	You old imprudent devil,
que siempre he sido mujer decente	I've always been a decent woman
y hasta en ausencia de mi marido.	Even in the absence of my husband.
Ya se cayeron las peras del árbol que las tenía	The pears have fallen from the tree that had them,
así te cayites, tú, y en mis brazos, ¡vida mía!	Thus you fell into my arms, my darling.
Y a mí no me ande con esas cosas	Don't say those things to me,
diablo de viejo tan ordinario	You ornery old devil,
siempre creyendo que uno lo quere	Always believing that one loves you
considerándose el necesario.	Considering yourself indispensable.

Camino Real de Colima (The Royal Road to Colima)
A *Son* from the State of Colima. (Recorded by Concha Michel)

en e - se ca - mi - no re - al los tra - ba - jos que pa - sé en e - se

ca - mi - no re - al

Camino real de Colima	Royal road to Colima,
no me quisiera acordar	I should not like to recall
los trabajos que pasé	The troubles I had
en ese camino real.	On that royal road.

Camino real de Colima.
Royal Road to Colima.

Tomo la pluma en la mano
para escribir y firmar
los trabajos que pasé
en ese camino real.

I take the pen in my hand
To write you and to sign
The troubles I had
On that royal road.

Tomo la pluma en la mano.
I take the pen in my hand.

La golondrina en el viento
platica con el avión,
le cuenta los sentimientos
que abriga su corazón.

The swallow in the wind
Chats with the plane;
He tells him the sentiments
His heart cherishes.

La golondrina en el viento.
The swallow in the wind.

Camino real de Colima
dicen que yo no lo sé
y en compañía de mi chata
de rodillas lo andaré
y en compañía de mi chata
hasta en sueños lo andaré,

Royal Road to Colima,
They say I don't know it,
With my little one
I would walk it on my knees.
With my little one
I could make it in my dreams.

Camino real de Colima.
Royal Road to Colima.

La Vaquilla (The Little Cow)
A *Son* from the State of Nayarit

Le dirás a la vaquilla,	Tell the little cow,
Le dirás a la vaquilla,	Tell the little cow,
Que no se ande ladereando,	Not to go climbing hillsides,
Que no se ande ladereando,	Not to go climbing hillsides.
Que un becerro trai al pié	She has a calf at her feet
Y otro que se le anda hijando;	And she is breeding another.
Que un becerro trai al pié	She has a calf at her feet
Y otro que se le anda hijando.	And she is breeding another.
Le dirás a la vaquilla,	Tell the little cow
Que no se ande ladereando,	Not to go climbing hillsides,
Que un becerro trai al pié	She has a calf at her feet
Y otro que se le anda hijando.	And she is breeding another.
Le dirás a la vaquilla, (repeat)	Tell the little cow (repeat)
Que se baje pa'l camino, (repeat)	To come down to the road (repeat)
Para darle mamantones,	To give some pulls (To suckle)
A ese becerro bramino.	To that noisy yearling (roaring little bull)
Le dirás a la vaquilla. (repeat above three lines)	Tell the little cow. (repeat above three lines)

Le dirás a la vaquilla,
Que se baje pa'l estero
Para darle mamantones
A ese becerro grupero.

La vaquilla tuvo cuates, (repeat)
El día primero del mes, (repeat)
Uno le mama al derecho
Y otro le mama al revés. (repeat the
two lines)

La vaquilla tuvo cuates, (repeat)
Y uno de ellos está sordo, (repeat)
Mientras uno está durmiendo,
L'otro está mamando gordo.
    (repeat the two lines)

The little cow had twins (repeat)
The first day of the month (repeat)
One suckles on the right side,
The other upside down. (repeat
    the two lines)

The little cow had twins (repeat)
And one of them is deaf; (repeat)
While one is sleeping,
The other suckles much. (repeat
    above two lines)

El Tecolote (The Owl)

Tecolote, ¿qué haces hay
Sentado en esa pared?
Tecolote, ¿qué haces hay
Sentado en esa pared?
Esperando a mi tecolota,
Esperando a mi fiel esposa;
Esperando a mi tecolota,
Que me traiga de comer.
Te cu ru cú.
Te cu ru cú.

Tecolote, what are you doing there,
Seated on that wall?
Tecolote, what are you doing there,
Seated on that wall?
I'm waiting for my Tecolota,
Waiting for my faithful wife;
I'm waiting for my Tecolota,
Who brings me something to eat.
Te cu ru cú,
Te cu ru cú.

Tecolote de Guadiana,
Pájaro madrugador,
¿Quién tuviera tus alitas,
¡Quién tuviera tus alitas,
Quién tuviera tus alitas
Para ir a ver a mi amor,
Para ir a ver a mi amor!
Te cu ru cú.
Te cu ru cú.

Tecolote from Guadiana,
Early-rising bird,
Would that I had your little wings,
Would that I had your little wings,
Would that I had your little wings,
To go to see my love,
To go to see my love!
Te cu ru cú,
Te cu ru cú.

Pobrecito tecolote,
Ya se cansa de llorar;
Si yo fuera tecolote,
No me ocuparía en volar;
Me estaría en mi nidito,
Me estaría en mi nidito,
Me estaría en mi nidito
Acabándome de criar,
Acabándome de criar.
Te cu ru cú.
Te cu ru cú.

Poor little Tecolote,
He is already tired of weeping.
If I were a tecolote,
I would not bother about flying,
I would remain in my little nest,
I would remain in my little nest,
Just finishing breeding,
Just finishing breeding.
Te cu ru cú,
Te cu ru cú.

La Chachalaca (The name of a bird)
From Guerrero Collection, Concha Michel

Andaba la chachalaca pasiandose en San Miguel,
Andaba la chachalaca pasiandose en San Miguel;
Es que estaba enamorada de dona Concha Michel,
Es que estaba enamorada de dona Concha Michel.

The chachalaca was having a good time in San Miguel,
The chachalaca was having a good time in San Miguel.
That was because it was in love with Concha Michel,
That was because it was in love with Concha Michel.

Andaba la chachalaca con una patita chueca,
Andaba la chachalaca con una patita chueca;
Es que estaba enamorada de don Antonio Güereca,
Es que estaba enamorada de don Antonio Güereca.

The chachalaca was going about with a twisted foot,
The chachalaca was going about with a twisted foot.
That was because it was in love with Don Antonio Güereca,
That was because it was in love with Don Antonio Güereca.

Note: The words are chosen to rhyme with the name of the person mentioned. In the second part, it is not possible in English.

Jarabes

Jarabe Tapatío

El Jarabe De La Botella (The Jarabe of the Bottle)

(The Jarabe is danced by a couple, each taking a turn at dancing over a bottle of liquor, while the other sings a warning not to throw it over, because if any of the liquid is spilled it will have to be filled again.)

Jalisco. Recorded by Concha Michel

An-da- le co— ma-dre- bái la—la bo-te- lla que-si me la

ti- ra— me la vuel- ve lle- na Se pu-so la nu- be

ca yó la tor -men- ta se ya se can-sa- ron pór que no -se sien- tan

Andale, compadre, baila la botella
Que si me la tumba, me la vuelve
  llena.
Andale, compadre, sígala bailando
Que si me la tira, me la va llenando.

Come on, compadre, dance the bottle. (The man dances the bottle)
If you throw it over, you will return it full.
Come on, compadre, keep on dancing it;
If you spill it, you will refill it.

Andale, comadre, baila la botella,
Que si me la tira me la vuelve llena,
Andale, comadre, sígala bailando,
Que si me la tira, me la va llenando.

Come on, compadre, dance the
  bottle. (The woman dances the
  bottle)
If you throw it over, you will return
  it full;
Come on, compadre, keep on dancing it,
If you spill it, you will refill it.

(These verses are repeated until the
  dancers tire, then they both sing)

Se puso la nube, cayó la tormenta;
Si ya se cansaron, como no se sien-
  tan.

The cloud is dissolved; the storm is
  over;
If you are tired, why don't you sit
  down.

Huapangos

Xochipitzahua

Xo-chi-pit-za-hu-a del al-ma mi-a que an-te la vir-gen me

das tu-a mor y en-tre las flo-res de la a-le-gri-a

pue-do de-cir-te que e-res mia. Lle-ga ya la luz del di-a

a-lum-bran-do nues-tro ho-gar to-do to-do en

mi con-fi-a di-jo. Dios y es cri-to es tú.

Xochipitzahua del alma mía
que ante la virgen me das tu amor
y entre las flores de la alegría
puedo decirte que eres mía.

Llega ya la luz del día
alumbrando nuestro hogar . . .
todo, todo en mi confía,
dijo Dios y escrito está.

Xochipitzahua of my soul,
before the Virgin give me your love
and among the flowers of joy
I can say you are mine.

The light of day is now breaking
lighting up our home . . .
all, all confide in me,
said God, and so it is written.

Los Panaderos (The Bakers)

Es de los que bailan
grande obligación;
es de los que bailan
grande obligación
darle a su pareja
vino y polvorón;
darle a su pareja
vino y polvorón.

Of those who dance it's
a great obligation;
of those who dance it's
a great obligation
to give to their partners
wine and cake;
to give to their partners
wine and cake.

Cielito Lindo (Lovely Little Heaven)

De domingo en domingo	Only on Sundays
te veo la cara,	I see your face,
cuando vas a misa,	when you go to mass
por la mañana.	in the morning.

Ay, ay, ay,	Ay, ay, ay . . .
ay! yo quisiera	ay! I wish
que toda la semana,	every day of the week,
Cielito Lindo,	Cielito Lindo,
domingo fuera.	were Sunday.

El Caimán (The Alligator)

Si el Caimán quieres bailar	If you wish to dance the Alligator
para lucir con destreza	to show off with mastery
tu habilidad y admirar,	your nimbleness and marvel,
lleva el paso con firmeza,	keep your step firm
y mal no habrás de quedar.	and you'll not fail.

Amor como el que hay en mí
no tiene el mundo memoria;
si tu me amaras así,
los angeles de la gloria
celos tuvieran de mí.

Al mismo Dios ha admirado
las virtudes que te dió;
de ti se había enamorado:
al saber que te amo yo,
con gusto se ha retirado.

Ausente de mí tu estarás
pero no de mi memoria;
esto, así lo asentarás,
y para ti es una gloria:
"ausente te quiero más."

Love such as I feel
has never existed in the world;
if you loved me thus,
the angels of Glory
would be jealous of me.

God himself has been admired
for the virtues he gave you;
they have fallen in love with you;
but knowing I loved you,
have stepped aside with pleasure.

You may be absent from me
but not from my memory;
this you will affirm,
and for you it's glory,
"when absent I love you more."

Yaqui Dances

Juego del Venado y El Coyote (The Deer and the Coyote)

Primitive Deer Dance

La Paloma (Pascola)

D.C.

Concheros

To the Conquering Souls

¡Viva Jesús! ¡Viva María! ¡Vivan las animas conquistadoras de los cuatro vientos!

Long live Jesus! Long live Mary! Long live the conquering souls of the four winds!

To the Virgin of Guadalupe

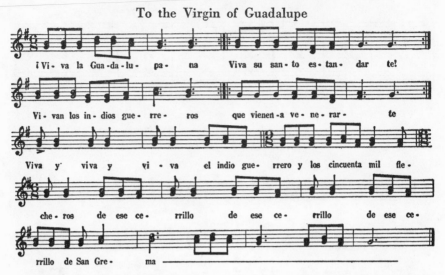

¡Vi- va la Gua-da-lu- pa- na Viva su san-to es-tan- dar te!

Vi- van los in- dios gue- rre- ros que vienen-a ve- ne- rar- te

Viva y' viva y vi- va el indio gue- rrero y los cincuenta mil fle-

che- ros de ese ce- rrillo de ese ce- rrillo de ese ce-

rrillo de San Gre- ma

¡Viva la Guadalupana! ¡Viva su santo estandarte! ¡Vivan los indios guerreros que vienen a venerarte! ¡Viva y viva y viva el indio guerrero y los cincuenta mil flecheros de ese cerrillo, de ese cerrillo, de ese cerrillo de San Gremal.

Long live the Virgin of Guadalupe! Long live her holy standard! Long live the Indians and the fifty thousand bowmen of that little hill, of that little hill, of that little hill of San Gremal.

To the Virgin Mary

Lento

Re- ci- be Mari-a las flo- res re- ci- be Ma- ria las flo- res que son

tan pu-ras y be- llas que son tan pu- ras y be- llas con sus

fra- gan-tes o- lo- res con sus fra- gan-tes o- lo- res, mis o-

ra- cio- nes con e- llas mis o- ra- cio-nes con e- llas.

Recibe, María, las flores, recibe, María, las flores que son tan puras y bellas, que son tan puras y bellas con sus fragantes olores, con sus fragantes olores, mis oraciones con ellas, mis oraciones con ellas.

Mary, receive the flowers; Mary, receive the flowers that are so pure and beautiful and with them my prayers, and with them my prayers.

Two Concheros (*Son*)

Conchero (*Son*)

Conchero (*Son*)

To the Señor De Sacromonte

A ño de mil qui-nien-tos trein-ta y nue-ve del pa- sa- do cuan-

do fuist-te a- pa-re- ci- do mi Je- sús Sa- cra- men- ta-do.

Año de mil quinientos, treinta y
nueve del pasado, cuando fuiste
aparecido, mi Jesus Sacramentado.

In the year one thousand, five hundred and thirty-nine of the past,
was when you appeared to us, my
transubstantiated Jesus.

Señor De Chalma

Oh Santo Señor de Chalma, el Santo
lo más mejor, solo te faltan las
alas pa (sic) ser la madre de Dios!
Oh Santo Señor de Chalma, el
santo lo más mejor. No Más te
falten las almas pa (sic) ser la
madre de Dios.

Holy Señor de Chalma, the best
Saint of all. You only lack wings
to be the Mother of God! (Repeat.)

Conchero

Mexicanos, salid presurosos, defendiendo a nuestra nación, reboli-
endo (sic) banderas triunfantes,
defendiendo nuestra religión.

Mexicans, come quickly! Defend
our nation, waving triumphant
banners and defending our religion.

The Troops of the Saviour

Las tro-pas del sal-va-do-or mar-chen a pa-so ve-loz

Si-gan con cre-ci-do a-mo-r y a las ban-deras de Dios.

¡Las tropas del Salvador, marchen a paso veloz! Sigan con crecido amor y a las banderas de Diós.

The troops of the Saviour, march in quick time! Follow with greater love the banners of God.

Conchero

Cuan-do nues-tra A-me-ri-ca fué con-quis ta-da de to-dos los ha-bi-

tan-tes nin-gu-no vi-do na-da a-llá en la gran en la gran te-noch-ti-tlán.

Cuando nuestra America fue conquistada de todos los habitantes, ninguno vido (sic) nada alla en la gran Tenochtitlan.

When our America was conquered from all the inhabitants, no one saw anything there of the great Tenochtitlan.

Canacuas

Canacuas (Introduction)

Buenas tardes Buenas tardes se-no-ri-to ve-

ni-mos a can-tar y tam-bien a vi-si-tar bue-nas

Buenas tardes, buenas tardes, senorito, venimos a cantar y tambien a visitar buenas.

Good afternoon, good afternoon, young man, we have come to sing and to visit.

Tata ninito, tata ninito, cananeran
las quique de pi cunque de quanda
cua mejor cate ma jum bo que sha
rit que no gue yuacha se vas tu.
La la ra la la la la ra la la la la cual le
se sera buen de la linda violeta.

Hush-a-bye, baby . . . (The rest is
crooning.)

Flor de Canela (Cinnamon Flower)

Flor de canela suspiro porque me
acuerdo de ti.

pa cuan pa cuan pa cuan pa en cu
no nu ri cu rin ya ca ya guache
cha za pi ri ti scha porque si no
cuando qui cha pi tin pingun cu-
erda paran gastia.

Cinnamon flower, I sigh because I
remember thee, etc.

Other Dances

Dance of the Moors and the Christians

Tiger Dance

La Danza De Las Plumas (Oaxaca)

Dutuburi (Tarahumara)

Pascola (Tarahumara)

Pascola (Tarahumara)

LOVE SONGS

Las Ilusiones (The Illusions)
(Jalisco) Collection of Concha Michel

Las i-lu-sio-nes lle-van al hom-bre... lle-van al hom-bre a la perdi-ción o-ja-lá y nun-ca lo hu-bie-ras he-cho y un sen-ti-mien-to en mi co-ra-zón.

Las ilusiones llevan al hombre
Llevan al hombre a la perdición,
Ojala y nunca lo hubieras hecho
Y un sentimiento en mi corazón.

The illusions lead man,
They lead man to perdition,
Oh, that you had never done it,
Left a pain in my heart.

Te quiero mucho, pero me acuerdo
Que amaste a otro hombre y antes
    que a mi,
Ojala y nunca lo hubieras hecho
Jurar en vano y por ser a mi.

I love you much but I remember
That you loved another man before
    me,
Oh, that you had never done it
Vow in vain and to me.

Me Abandonas (You Abandon Me)
(A love song from Jalisco) Recorded by Concha Michel

Me a-ban-do-nas me des-pre-cias por-que quie-res pe-ro nunca me ver-ás llo-rar por-que al ca-bo en el mun-do hay mas a-mo-res co-mo te quí-se tam-bién te sé ol-vi-

dar   Si al - gún   di - a   pa - sa - ras por mi   ca - ba - ña no ol - vi - des

nun - ca   que   yo tu_a - man - te   fui   por - que_al

ca - bo   en el   mun - do hay más   a - mo - res   co - mo te

qui -   se   tam - bién te_a -bo - rre - ci

Me abandonas . . .	You abandon me,
Me desprecias porque quieres;	You despise me because you wish to,
Pero nunca me verás llorar,	But you'll never see me weep
Porque al cabo en el mundo hay más amores;	Because anyway there are more women in the world;
Como te quise, también te sé olvidar.	As I loved you, I can also forget you.
Si algún día,	If some day,
Pasaras por mi cabaña	You should come to my cabin,
No olvides nunca	Do not forget ever
Que yo tu amante fuí . . .	That I was your lover.
Porque al cabo en el mundo hay más amores;	Because anyway, there are more loves in the world.
Como te quise, también te aborrecí.	As I loved you, I can also hate you.

Lo Que Digo (What I Say)
Collection of Concha Michel

Andantino Energico

Lo que di - go   de hoy   en diá,   lo que di - go   lo sos - ten - go

yo no   ven - go   a ver si   pue - do si - no   por que pue - do ven - go

Lo que digo de hoy en día,	What I say now today,
Lo que digo, lo sostengo:	What I say, I mean.
Yo no vengo a ver si puedo,	I don't come to see if I can
Sino porque puedo vengo.	But because I can I come.

A las once de la noche	At eleven o'clock at night
Allá te espero en el kiosco,	I'll wait for you near the bandstand
Pa sepas que te quero	So you'll know that I love you
Y el miedo no lo conozco.	And fear, I do not know it.

Hay Un Ser (There Is Someone)

(An old love song from Michoacán. Recorded by Graciela Amador)

Hay un ser que es el Dios de mi vida,	There's someone who's the god of my life,
Cuyo nombre mi pecho enternece;	Whose name softens my heart; (makes my heart tender)
Si dormido, en mi sueño aparece,	When asleep, he appears in my dreams,
Si despierto, me mata el dolor.	When awake, he kills me with pain (the pain kills me).

Yo lo quiero con amor de fuego,	I love him with love of fire (with burning love)
La pasión en mi pecho se abrasa;	The passion in my heart is consuming.
Y jamás perderé la esperanza	And never shall I love the hope
de volvernos los dos a mirar.	That we two shall meet again.

La Paloma Azul (The Blue Dove)

(An old city love song from Jalisco. Recorded by Graciela Amador)

De tus encantos, celestial Paloma Azul,
Al verte el dulce ruiseñor se enamoró.
Déjalo triste y apasionado,
Mientras tú, amante, lloras por él.

Si alguno pasa y te jura amor,
Que te quería te prometió;
Paloma blanca, dile que no,
Que me has jurado eterno amor.

¡Ay, Paloma Azul! . . .

Yo te suplico que no vuelvas a querer
A otro tirano que se burle de tu amor.
Déjalo triste y apasionado,
Mientras tú, amante, lloras por él.

Of your charms, heavenly Blue Dove,
Upon seeing you the sweet nightingale fell in love.
Leave him sad and passionate,
While you, lover, weep for him.

If someone comes and swears love to you,
That he loved you and promised you.
Blue Dove, tell him no;
That you have sworn me eternal love.

Ay, Blue Dove. . . . !

I implore you not to love again
Another tyrant who will mock your love.
Leave him sad and passionate
While, you sweetheart, weep for him.

La Llorona (The Weeper)

From Tehuantepec, Oaxaca Collection, Concha Michel

La pe - na y lo que no es pena ay llo - ro - na to - do es pe - na pa - ra mí.

Ayer llo - ra - ba por ver - te ay llo - ro - na y hoy llo - ro por - que te vi

Ay   de   mi llo - ro - na llo - ro - na llo - ro - na de a - zul 'e -

les - te.   Aun - que la vi - da me ues - te llo - ro - na no de - ja - ré de que - rer - te.

La pena y lo que no es pena, ay llorona,	Pain and what is not pain, alas llorona,
Todo es pena para mí;	All is pain for me;
Ayer lloraba por verte, ay llorona,	Yesterday I wept to see you, alas llorona,
Y hoy lloro porque te ví.	And today I weep because I saw you.
Salías del templo un día, ay llorona,	You came out of church one day, alas llorona,
Cuando al pasar yo te ví.	When in passing I saw you.
Hermosa huipil con blondas llevabas	So beautiful a huipil with lace you wore
Que la Virgen te creí.	That I thought you were the Virgin.
Me subí al pino más alto, ay llorona,	I climbed up the highest pine, alas llorona,
A ver si te divisaba.	To see if I could get a glimpse of you.
Como el pino era tierno, ay llorona,	As the pine was tender, alas llorona,
Al verme llorar, lloraba.	On seeing me weep, it wept.
Cada vez que entra la noche, ay llorona,	Every day when night falls, alas llorona,
Me pongo a pensar y digo:	I begin to think and I say:
De que me sirve la cama, ay llorona,	What good is my bed, alas llorona,
Si tu no duermes conmigo.	If you're not sleeping with me.
Ay de mi, llorona, llorona,	Ah poor me, llorona, llorona,
Llorona de azul turquí,	Llorona of deep blue,

Ayer lloraba por verte, ay llorona, Y hoy lloro porque te ví.	Yesterday I wept to see you, alas llorona, And today I weep because I saw you.
De la mar vino una carta, ay llorona, Que me mandó la sirena, Y en la carta me decía, ay llorona, Quien tiene amor tiene pena.	From the sea came a letter, alas llorona, Which the siren sent to me, And in the letter she told me, alas llorona, He who loves, suffers pain.
La pena y lo que no es pena, ay llorona, Todo es pena para mí. Ayer lloraba por verte, ay llorona, Y hoy lloro porque te ví.	Pain and what is not pain, alas llorona, All is pain for me. Yesterday I wept to see you, alas llorona, And today I weep because I saw you.
Ay de mi, llorona, llorona, llorona de azul celeste, Aunque la vida me cueste, ay llorona, No dejaré de quererte.	Ah poor me, llorona, llorona, Llorona of celestial blue, Although it may cost me my life, alas llorona, I shall never cease to love you.

Barca de Plata (The Silver Boat)
(Recorded in Jalisco by Concha Michel)

Barca de plata, que silenciosa
De vieja orilla te alejas ya.
Azules ondas, blancas espumas. . .
¿A dónde, a dónde, barca de plata
Te llevarán?

Boat of silver, how silently
From the old shore you glide away.
Blue waves, white foam. . .
Where to, where to, boat of silver
Will they take you. . . ?

Gaviotas blancas, blancos pañuelos
A despedirte volando van.
En otros mares, barca de plata
Qué nuevas almas encontraras?

White sea gulls, white handker-
chiefs,
Upon taking leave you go flying.
In other seas, silver boat,
What new souls will you find?

La Flor de Changunga (Flower of the Changunga)

Ay, flor de changunga, ay que na
san jun de dulce, ay que platano
mor-
rado Ay, que es lo ama Ay, scho lin
ta ta ce lo so
ay, sho lin na na ce lo so
ay que triste sinto muerto

Oh, Changunga flower, oh, how
sweet the orange blossom
Oh, how purple the banana
Oh, what a thing is love,
How sad is death (lit., how sad I
feel dead).

Ay que lo que es amor
y sing ama suena na cutz ana·chan
  esin bono
Hue cana Ay qu es lo que es amor.
  El guna ro se pe no por andar con
  la guitarra

Guitarra To no es pe-dir a buscar
  va le mas que con de nana
Ay yo soy la pa tera que viene a so
  gar el patoco
Si do que ayer fui a guaras.

SERENADES

Las Mañanitas

A birthday song, sung at dawn. Jalisco. Col. Concha Michel

El día en que tu naciste
Nacieron todas las flores.
El día en que tu naciste
Cantaron los ruiseñores.

The day when you were born
Were born all the flowers.
The day when you were born
The nightingales sang.

Ya viene amaneciendo,
Ya la luz del día nos vió
Despierta, amiga mía,
Mira que ya amaneció

Now the dawn is coming,
Now the light of day has seen us
Awake, my friend, (my beloved)
Look, it has dawned.

Quisiera ser solecito
Para entrar por tu ventana
Y darte los buenos días
Acostadito en tu cama.

I wish I were a sunbeam
To be able to enter your window
And say good morning to you
Lying in your bed.

Por la luna doy un peso,
Por el sol doy un tostón,
Por mi amiga Marianita (or what-
ever the name of the girl may be).
La vida y el corazón.

De las estrellas del cielo
Quisiera bajarte dos,
Una para saludarte
Y otra pa (sic) decirte adiós.

For the moon I'd give a peso
For the sun I'd give a half;
For my friend, Marianita, (or any
other name)
My life and my heart.

Of the stars from the heavens
I should like to take down two—
One with which to greet you
And another to say good-bye.

Las Mañanitas Del Rey David

The National Birthday Serenade at Dawn

Estas son las mañanitas,
Que cantaba el rey David,
Y a las muchachas bonitas
Se las cantaba así:

These are the Mañanitas,
That King David sang
And to the pretty girls
He sang them thus:

Despierta, mi bién despierta,
Mira, que ya amaneció;
Ya los pajaritos cantan,
Ya la luna se metió.

Que bonitas mañanitas,
Parece que va a llover.
Así estaba la mañana,
Cuando te empecé a querer.

Si el sereno de la esquina
Me quisiera hacer favor
de apagar su linternita
Mientras que pase mi amor.

Y ahora, sí, señor sereno,
Le agradezco su favor,
Y encienda su linternita,
Que ya mi amor ya pasó.

Awake, my love, awake,
Look, it is already dawn;
The birds are singing
And the moon has gone in.

What a lovely morning,
It looks as if it will rain.
The morning was the same
When I began to love you.

If the watchman of the corner
Wished to do me the favor,
He would put out his little lantern
While my love passes by.

And now, yes, Mr. Watchman,
I thank you for your favor,
You may light your little lantern
For my love has passed by.

Si Estas Dormida (If You're Asleep)
Collection of Concha Michel

gir - te un a - diós por - que hoy me voy Per - dó - na -

me si te o - fen - den mis ca - ri - cias Per - dó - na -

me si te o - fen - den mis can - ta - res Yo lo que quie-ro si-ces

co - ro - nar - te de a - za - hares ya di - ri -

gir - te un a - diós por - que hoy me voy

Si estás dormida, mi negra, ya no duermas,
Oye la voz de aquel que de veras te ama.
Si estás despierta asómate a la ventana
Para dirigirte un adios porque hoy me voy.

Perdóname si te ofenden mis caricias,
Perdóname si te ofenden mis cantares.

If you're asleep, my negra, sleep no more
Listen to the voice of your true love;
If you're awake, look out of your window
To say good-bye because today I'm leaving.

Pardon me if my caresses offend you;
Pardon me if my songs offend you.

Yo lo que quero (sic) es coronarte de azahares,	What I wish is to crown you with orange blossoms
Y a dirigirte un adiós porque hoy me voy.	And to say good-bye because today I'm leaving.

MISCELLANEOUS

Cradle Song

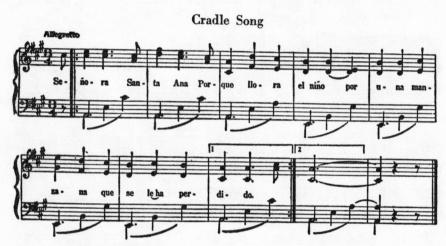

Señora Santa Ana, ¿por qué llora el niño? —Por una manzana que se le ha perdido.	Mrs. Saint Anne, Why does the baby cry? —For an apple That he has lost.
—Si llora por una, yo le daré dos, para que se duerma como el Niño Dios.	If he's crying for one, I'll give him two, So that he'll sleep Like the Infant Jesus.
Señora Santa Ana, toca su jarana, señor San Joaquín, toca su violín.	Mrs. Saint Anne, Play your jarana, Mister San Joaquin, Play your violin.
Este niño lindo, se quiere dormir, tiéndele la cama en el toronjil.	This lovely baby Wishes to sleep, Make his bed In the grape-fruit tree.

Cradle Song

Duér-mete ni-no duer-me-te soli-to que cuando des-pier-tes te da-ré-el atoli-to.

El Rorro

A la ru-ru ni-ño· a la ru-ru-ru

duér-me-se mi ni-ño du-ér-ma-se ya.

El Rorro (Christmas Cradle Song)

A la ru-ru-ru ni-ño chi-qui-to du-er-me-se

ya..... mi Je-su-si-to..... del e-le-fan-te ha-sta el mos-

qui-to guar-den si-len ci-o no ha-gan ruido a la ru-

ru-ru ni-ño chi-qui-to duér-me-se ya.... mi Je-su-si-to.

A la rururu, nino chiquito,
Duermese ya, mi Jesusito.
Del elefante hasta el mosquito,
Guarden silencio, no hagan ruido.

A la rururu, nino chiquito,
Duermese ya, mi Jesusito.

A la rururu, little boy,
Go to sleep, my little Jesus.
From the elephant to the mosquito,
Keep quiet, don't make a sound.

A la rururu, etc.

Vendor's Song

A Pregón (An Announcement or Selling Song)

Vengan pués a regalarse
Con el ante de turrón.
Tiene almibar y canela
Y es de un gusto seductor.

Vengan a comprar el ante
De almendra, de anis y de azahar
A cuatro por medio
Y a dos por un real.

Come then to feast
With the nougat,
It has sugar syrup and cinnamon
And is of an enticing flavor.

Come and buy the nougat,
Of almonds, anise, and orange-blos-
som,
At four for a half
and two for a quarter.

La Rana

Equivalent to The House That Jack Built
From Romance y Corrido by Vicente T. Mendoza

Estaba la rana cantando debajo del
   agua,
cuando la araña se puso a cantar,
vino la mosca y la hizo callar.

The frog was singing under the
   water,
When the spider began to sing,
Came the fly and made her shut up.

Callaba la mosca a la rana
que estaba cantando debajo del agua;
cuando la mosca se puso a cantar,
vino la araña y la hizo callar.

The fly made the frog shut up,
who was singing under the water;
When the fly began to sing,
Came the spider and made her shut
   up.

Callaba la araña a la mosca, la mosca
   a la rana
que estaba cantando debajo del
   agua;
cuando la araña se puso a cantar,
vino el ratón y la hizo callar.

The spider shut the fly up, the fly
   the frog
Singing under the water;
When the spider began to sing
Came the mouse and shut it up.

And so on, a sort of House That Jack Built.
In the last verse all are there:

Callaba el hombre al cuchillo, el
   chuchillo al toro, el toro al agua,
el agua al fuego, el fuego al palo, el
   palo al perro,
el perro al gato, el gato al ratón, el
   ratón a la araña,
la araña a la mosca, la mosca a la
   rana
que estaba cantando debajo del agua;
cuando el hombre se puso a cantar,
vino su suegra y lo hizo callar.

The man shut the knife up, the
   knife the bull, the bull the water,
The water the fire, the fire the
   stick, the stick the dog,
The dog the cat, the cat the mouse,
   the mouse the spider,
The spider the fly, the fly the frog
That was singing under the water:
When the man began to sing
Came his mother-in-law and made
   him shut up.

PART FOUR

MYTHS–TALES–MISCELLANEA

MYTHS–TALES–MISCELLANEA

Before the Conquest, when the system of writing was not sufficiently developed to record historical events, the oral accounts about the gods and their great deeds constituted the history of the people. Some of these, to which Catholic and modern elements have been added, are still "history" to the primitive folk.

Much of the pre-Spanish customs and lore was recorded by Spaniards in the sixteenth century and later. The most notable work of that early period is that of Fray Bernardino de Sahagún on the Aztecs in "La Historia General de las Cosas de Nueva España." He availed himself of the help of various intelligent natives who had learned to read and write in the Texcoco Seminary. They wrote their texts in Aztec and illustrated them in the pictographic form of the codices, which are works of art. This splendid work exists in Spanish in several volumes, the first part of which was published in English by Fisk University.

Fray Diego de Landa did the same for the Mayas in "Las Relaciones de las Cosas de Yucatán," but on a much smaller scale.

Besides these major works, there are those of Durán, Las Casas, Torquemada, Mendieta, the letters of Cortés, and those of the minor chroniclers like Cervantes de Zalazar and Burgoa, who wrote on special regions. On the events of the Conquest, there is the brilliant and dramatic account of Bernal Diaz del Castillo, one of Cortés' soldiers—stranger and more thrilling than any fiction.

Among the books by famous travelers in Mexico, the most human, interesting and informative accounts of the people are to be found in the works by John Stephens in his "Incidents of Travel in Central America, Chiapas and Yucatan" and "Incidents of Travel in Yucatan." "Unknown Mexico" by Carl Lumholz, and other of his writings similarly present a sympathetic and authentic picture of Northern Mexico. There are also many excellent books on archaeology and ethnography by Mexicans, Frenchmen, Germans, and North Americans, several of whom have made studies of villages and regions during the last twenty years.

There is, however, no one book devoted specifically and solely to folk literature. Because of their importance, myths, legends, and stories from various regions have been recorded sporadically here and there. Ballads and songs have also received much attention for the same reason, as well as for the pleasure they give.

There are many texts of religious plays, called coloquios and pastorelas; also there are texts of the Passion and dances. Some of them are in possession of the groups performing them, written in longhand, while others are published in pamphlet form by the popular printing houses, who also publish ballads and songs. But the texts are not used in their original form, the same ones differing from group to group. I once heard a native dictating a Passion play he was teaching in his village. He was combining two printed texts and making changes according to his own ideas of the fitness of things. Once he changed an epithet applied to Christ because it was too grosero, insulting.

Many sayings and riddles have been recorded and published by Mexicans, especially sayings, but few have been translated from the indigenous languages. The natives also have formalized greetings, which are really blessings. And very expressive curses and insults enliven their daily conversation.

The Spanish argot is also rich in abuse, some of it in sign language and whistles. Then there are the cries of street vendors, some of them poetic, as well as humorous; the names on pulquerías, cantinas, stores, and trucks; nicknames and epithets.

The texts of plays and dances are too long to reproduce completely, but an idea of what they are like has been given in connection with fiestas and dances. I shall, therefore, devote this section to the more interesting myths, legends, and stories. I shall also include names, slang, riddles, and sayings. The latter are practically neglected by investigators; at least, they do not appear in their published works.

AZTEC AND MAYA MYTHS AND BELIEFS ABOUT CREATION

The Aztec and Maya myths and beliefs about creation are similar, as are their gods and religions. Both races believed that the gods made several attempts at creation before the present world came into being, and that corn is the flesh and blood of mankind.

Aztec Beliefs

The Aztecs represented their world in various forms. In one it was a great disc, surrounded by water. The water was said to be "divine" or "the water of heaven" because it touched the sky at the horizon. From across those waters came the people in canoes or on the backs of huge turtles. The dead, too, had to be carried over them by dogs, as they had no boats.

Another representation of the world was in the form of a cipactli, or a mythical crocodile, set down in the middle of the waters by the gods, after they had created fire, sun, the gods of the lower regions, the heavens, and the water with its deities. The irregularities of the earth's surfaces are accounted for by the scaly prominences on the animal's back.

The earth was also represented in the form of a tlatchli, ball-game, the court extending from north to south with rings, placed at the eastern and western sides, through which the sun had to pass daily.

Over the earth were the heavens, and below, the infernos. The last of them was the dwelling place of the dead, "The place from where no news comes; the place eternally forgotten, with no roads leading out, where we must all go and where the doors are lefthanded."

In the highest heaven dwelt the Procreators, the Engenderers of all that exists. They were the masculine and feminine creative principle, whose names indicate dual origin—Ometecutli, "Two-lord," and Omecihuatl, "Two-lady." They are also called "The Lord and Lady of our flesh and food," and are represented with symbols of fertility because they are the Engenderers; also, with ears of corn because they are the Lords of life and food.

The Four Directions

A fundamental idea of the Aztec religion was to group all beings according to the four cardinal points and the central direction (or upwards); thus the numbers four and five were important to them.

The first four children of the divine couple symbolize the four directions. Their colors are red for the east, black for the north, blue for the south, white for the west; the white preserved in the primitive myth may have awaited a white Tezcatlipoca.

In this we find the origin of the veneration of the cardinal points by all the primitive Mexicans of the past and by those of the present, which may also account for their ready acceptance of the cross, the ends of which point in the four directions.

The Creations and the Legend of the Four Suns

There were four suns, each marking a world epoch and terminating in a cataclysm. The first was destroyed by tigers, the second by a hurricane, the third by fire, the fourth by a deluge.

The stories vary. Here is one of the interpretations.

According to this account, the deities responsible for the creation of the various suns and their destructions were Quetzalcoatl, the benevolent god who founded agriculture, industry, and the arts; and the black Tezcatlipoca, the omnipotent, multiform and ubiquitous god of the night, patron of evil and sorcerers. It was the wars between these two gods, the struggle between good and evil, that made mankind victims.

Tezcatlipoca, when god of the night, disguised himself as a tiger whose spotted skin resembled the sky replete with stars. Then he transformed himself into the sun to light the world. For the epoch of this first sun the gods created a race of giants. They lived like nomads, who neither tilled the soil nor planted, but ate wild things, like acorns, roots, and fruit.

In the heavenly constellations Tezcatlipoca was the great bear, the form of which to the Mexicans appeared to be that of the ocelotl or tiger. When his enemy Quetzalcoatl struck him down into the waters with a staff, he assumed the form of a tiger. In the darkness that followed, the tiger devoured the giants. This sun is known by the calendrical name of the day on which it occurred as "Four Ocelot."

Quetzalcoatl, as god of the wind, then became the second sun. He ruled until one day Tezcatlipoca reached out his tiger's paw and pulled him down to earth. His fall caused a great hurricane, which uprooted all growing things and destroyed man. A few that survived became monkeys. This happened on the day called "Four Wind."

The Procreators then banished the two quarreling sun deities from the sky and made Tlaloc, god of rain and heavenly fire, the third sun. But Quetzalcoatl caused a rain of fire to devastate the earth. Those who did not perish were transformed into birds. This catastrophe took place on "Four Rain."

Quetzalcoatl then made Chalchiutlicue, "She of the jade-green skirts," the fourth sun. This epoch ended with a deluge, believed to have been sent by Tezcatlipoca. The survivors became fish.

The Creation of the Historical Sun

The flood had so submerged the earth that it could not appear again until Quetzalcoatl and Tezcatlipoca lifted from it the water-laden sky. But the sun had been destroyed and there was no light.

All the gods assembled in Teotihuacán to do penance so that they might have light. Two offered to sacrifice themselves—Tecuhcizté-catl was rich and powerful; Ránahuantzin was poor and ill. The rich one made gifts of precious things to the Father of the gods, while the poor one gave moss and maguey thorns wet with his blood.

During four days the two gods fasted and made sacrifices in preparation. On the fifth day a brazier heaped with burning coals was prepared in which the gods were to be purified so that they might illuminate the world. The turn of the rich god to jump into it came first. He made three attempts, each time stopping short of the brim. But the poor god closed his eyes and leaped straight into the heart of the fire. A great flame shot up from which he emerged as the sun. Then the rich god, shamed by this example, hurled himself into the dying flames and was slowly consumed; from these a brilliantly shining moon appeared. The gods, angered at the moon's audacity, threw a rabbit at it, which explains the dark spots on its face, and why the Mexicans see a rabbit instead of a man in the moon.

The sun continued shedding its radiant light but it stood still. When the gods in their perplexity inquired as to the reasons, they learned that the sun wanted more sacrifices—the rest of the gods who were the stars. So they all fell before the tyrant. The last one to disappear before its first rays was Xolotl, the twin brother of the beautiful Venus. Venus had tried to save herself by throwing an arrow at the sun, but the sun simply caught it in a shaft of light and killed the daring Venus.

This fifth sun, called "Four Movement," is destined to terminate by earthquakes. The Aztecs expected the end with every eclipse, in every tremor of the earth, in a great plague, or when each fifty-two-year cycle terminated. This creation was considered the perfect one and the human beings in it were situated in the center of the country. The rest of the tribes living toward the four cardinal points were inferior, talked different languages, and had different customs.

A legend, which seems to have been influenced by Biblical teachings but recorded by the early chroniclers, relates that a couple saved themselves from the deluge by taking refuge in a cave and their descendants are the present generations of men. Their names were Nota, "Our Father," and Nona, "Our Mother."

An authentic creation legend is the one in which Quetzalcoatl is the Creator. He descends into the lower regions to obtain from the gods of the Kingdom of the Dead the bones of men and women who had previously perished. When the bones are given to him, he falls down and breaks them to pieces. He takes them to Tamoanchan, "the place of birth," the mythical source of the tribes. There he gives them to one of the goddesses to grind on a stone. The pulp is then sprinkled with the blood from the male organs of several gods willing to make the sacrifice. This is the masa from which men were created, receiving the name of los amasados con sangre, kneaded with blood; or los creados de ceniza, created with ashes.

THE CORN GOD

After man was fashioned it was necessary to provide him with food. The ants knew where it was and took it to Tamoanchan. The gods masticated it and placed it on the lips of the recently formed men, as a mother does on those of her infant. Thus they were nourished and grew.

Quetzalcoatl wanted to take all men to the Cerro de los Mantenimientos, "The Hill of Provisions," but he lacked strength. He, therefore, sought the co-operation of Thunderbolt, so that he would cleave the earth and scatter the food. But the rain gods heard of his intention and carried off all the food. For this reason humanity must turn to them in order to obtain sustenance.

Another version is that Quetzalcoatl discovered corn, which was concealed in the mountain of Tonacatépetl. All the gods were searching for it, but only the ants knew the way. Quetzalcoatl transformed himself into a black ant, and a red ant showed him how to find the place. But the mountain was too heavy for him to lift alone, so Xolotl split it open. Later the corn was stolen by Tlaloc, the rain god, in whose possession it has remained ever since.

Corn, as the prime food representing sustenance in general, is ruled by the young Xochipilli, son of the sun and moon. Food had its origin in the highest heaven, the seat of the Engenderers, the region in which the sun is to be found at half its course in the zenith. On this account, the fiesta to Xochipilli is celebrated at midday.

Food is always connected with orgy and sin; that is why the sun becomes ill and feeble and wants to die after having reached the highest point in his march through the skies, sinking out of sight in the west, to be purified in the undying flames. After this bath, he is able to reappear in the east the next morning, renewed and resplendent.

The sun is accompanied during the morning hours by the souls of the dead warriors; the rest of the time to the point of setting, by the souls of the women who die in childbirth and become the goddesses Cihuapipiltin. When the warriors complete their mission, they turn into humming birds or butterflies and entertain themselves by sipping the honey from the flowers. On the other hand, the women turn into malevolent ghosts, "who haunt the crossroads."

The warriors were anxious to secure even a hair from a woman who had died in childbirth, as it was considered a most valuable amulet— "It paralyzed the march of the enemy."

Another belief was that if a thief knocked with the arm of a Cihuapipiltin at the door of the house he wished to rob, the persons within would instantly fall asleep.

Epilepsy was attributed to having met one of the Cihuapipiltin.[1]

Maya-Quiché Creation Myth:
Excerpts from the Popol Vuh

In the beginning everything was in suspense and silence. Only the heavens and waters existed. There were no human beings, animals, birds, or fish. There were no valleys, ravines, or hills. The surface of the earth was still invisible. But the gods stood out dazzling in clarity against the darkness of the night. And they possessed great sentiments.

The gods conferred and came to a happy agreement. The waters were to remain; they were to irrigate the earth, which was to appear in the form of a plate. Light was to be born in the heavens and on earth, so that food might be planted for the people, who were to express their gratitude for its appearance to the Creators.

THE GOD OF SUN   THE GOD OF FIRE

The formation of the earth was magical, strange, and marvelous. At first the space was filled with clouds and fog; then the mountains began to appear in the waters; cypresses and pines for the woods, coasts and valleys. Then the gods created the inhabitants for those places.

Afterwards the Creators talked about their creatures with great satisfaction, designating homes for the animals and the birds. "You, wild beasts of the fields, shall drink from the rivers, sleep in ravines; your bodies shall rest on grass and you shall cohabit and procreate among the banana plants and the bushes; you shall walk on four feet and serve to carry burdens," they were told. "You birds will be in the branches as we are in our houses; there you shall fecundate and multiply." Then they all selected their haunts and shelters; the birds began building their nests.

While everything was being arranged for the birds and beasts, the world was still in silence. Afterwards the gods said to them, "Shout, howl, chirp; speak to one another; understand one another; don't remain silent. Separate into groups according to your kind and ways. Then say our names, so that we may be honored in heaven, since we are your father and mother."

But they could not speak like rational beings; they only made gestures and sounds; they cackled, bellowed, and chirped without showing any signs of possessing a language.

When the Creators saw that their creatures did not pronounce their names nor recognize them, they were very sad. And they told the creatures that they would be replaced by others because they could not speak; they could not invoke and adore them. "You shall only serve to obey, and your flesh shall be crushed and eaten. That shall be your destiny."

The animals and the birds wanted to recover their preponderance, and tried in a new way to express their adoration. But as the gods were unable to understand them, they did not give them any help. So their fate remained as decreed by the gods; they were to be sacrificed, killed and eaten by the "intelligent" people.

The Procreators and Engenderers consulted once more and made a second attempt at forming creatures who would be impressed with their greatness. They fashioned them of wet clay, but they soon knew that they were not going to be successful. They dissolved, forming a heap of mire in which could be seen a neck, a very wide mouth, vacant, staring eyes, and no head. They could talk, but they felt nothing. Because of their constitution, they could not remain in water; they melted immediately; they had no consistency.

The Creators said to the creatures of clay, "Struggle to procreate and multiply but only until the new beings come." They soon fell to pieces, thus undoing the work of their Shapers.

Again the gods consulted and asked one another, "What shall we do to form people who shall see, understand, and invoke us?" And they asked for a new day of creation. They chose one from among them to obtain the presence of the grandmother of the sun, the grandmother of light, as they were told to do by the Creators. Then all met to discuss the kind of people to create, who should adore them as superior beings.

The magician of the grains of corn succeeded in making descend toward them the adoration of the sun, who said that an old woman should be their mother—the same one who was the mother of the magician, and grandmother of the sun and of the Revealer.

They talked and expressed opinions until just before sunrise, and they said to the Heart of Heaven, the greatest one of them, Kukamutz, "It is good to form wooden dolls that shall talk and converse like people on the face of the earth." Immediately the wooden dolls were constructed to resemble people, and they talked; these were to be the people to exist on the earth.

The wooden people established relationships; they gave birth to sons and daughters, who were also wooden. But they had no hearts

THE GOD OF NIGHT   THE GOD OF LIFE

nor feelings; they did not know that they were children of the Creator and Revealer. They only moved about like strange beings in a void, without aim or destiny.

As they were unable to comprehend the Heart of Heaven, they soon fell into misfortune; they were just frauds with mouths for eating. They talked, but their faces were shriveled; they had no feet nor hands nor blood in their veins, nor intestines in which to hold their food, nor limbs for defending themselves; and their cheeks and fingers were so dry that they could not be distinguished from their flesh. Thus they could not understand the Creators, who were mother and father of those who breathe and have hearts. So they were condemned to disappear by death.

The Heart of Heaven ordered the earth to be filled with water. A great flood came to destroy the wooden puppets. It came in the form of thick, heavy rain directly from the sky; the avengers also came to mangle their bones and crack their muscles, because they did not feel nor talk in the presence of their Maker.

Then came all the creatures who had served the puppets, and their household utensils, to accuse them. The animals said, "Much have you made some of us suffer; others you ate. Now your flesh shall be eaten." And the grinding stones added, "It is your fault that our faces are worn. Every day, morning and night, you were grinding—

¡joli! ¡joli! ¡juqui! ¡juqui! We had to submit then, but now we shall prove our strength."

The dogs cried out, "How many times did we go hungry on your account? We observed you from a distance with fear, standing before you while you ate. You drove us away with sticks. Thus you treated us. Why should we not kill you now? You should have had a presentiment of what was coming. Now we are here to tear you to pieces. Now you shall feel the sharpness of the bones in our mouths, for we shall bite you." Thus they spoke when they were face to face with their enemies.

The small pots also rose up, "You made us suffer, burning and smoking our mouths and faces, for you always had us cooking on the fire, torturing us. Now we shall put you to boil."

The puppets ran in pairs like the ears of corn, behind one another. They climbed the houses, but when they reached the roofs they fell; they tried climbing the trees, which gave way beneath their weight; they wanted to find shelter in the caves, but these repulsed them.

MAYA GODS

Thus the people of wood were destroyed, ruined. Because of their confusion, they fell to pieces one against the other. All that remained as proof of their existence was the apes that live in the woods.

Then the earth was in darkness. A resin-like rain fell night and day.

Again the gods met to discuss the formation of a new world, new people. "Dawn is approaching and we should have our work finished; we should consecrate the food that is to maintain our 'intelligent' children, deifying the existence of the people on the face of the earth," they said. Then they sent their prayers into the night and dispersed, well pleased.

From Pazil and Cayali, the places whence come all good things, came the yellow and white ears of corn. The animals that brought the information about them were the fox, the coyote, the parrot and the crow. These four told the gods about the white and yellow corn which was to form the flesh and blood of the new people, and they showed them the way to Pazil.

The gods rejoiced over finding corn, the cacao, fruits and honey. There were also trees and plants growing there for food and beverages.

Immediately they began to plan how to form our first ancestors. The flesh and muscles were made of the products of the yellow and white corn. Only four were made of this food. They had no father nor mother; they were simply called men. They were not born of woman, but were children created by the gods. Their creation was the supernatural and marvelous work of the Creators, who endowed them with the presence and likeness of people. Then these men talked and reasoned, they saw and felt, walked and touched. They were perfect of face and of handsome appearance. They saw and understood what was in the heavens and on the earth.

The new people were questioned by two of the gods. "What do you think of the senses that you have received? Do you not see and know that your language is as good as your way of walking? Then open your eyes, let your glances penetrate, and see as far as you can, even into the mountains and the coasts. Whatever you behold, as far as your eyes can see, you will possess it all," they said.

After they had seen everything under the heavens, they showed their gratitude to their Creators, giving them thanks two and three times. "You have given us our existence, our mouths, and our faces. We speak, hear, feel, move, walk, and possess the perception to distinguish that which is near and far from us. Because of this we can see the big and the little that exists in heaven and on earth. Thanks to you then, our Makers, for having given us life. You are our grandparents, our ancestors."

The gods were not pleased; their children knew and saw too much. So they took counsel once more and decided to limit their vision and understanding, for "would not each one in his wisdom want to come to know and do as much as we have made them comprehend, seeing everything!"

So the Creators veiled the eyes of man, covering them as one's breath covers a mirror. Their eyes became clouded and they could only see what was near. And their eyes were the same then as now.

Then women were formed, to be companions for these men. He who sees all, fulfilled their wishes. It was in a sort of dream that they received, by their word, women full of beauty. When the men saw them, their hearts were filled with joy, because they would no longer be alone, they would have mates.

These first men and their companions were the ancestors of our big and small tribes; they were the source of our origin—of the Maya-Quichés and their descendants.[2]

Thus the gods of both the Aztecs and Mayas, through trial and error, discovered that the human beings whose devotion they sought had to be made and sustained with corn, their sacred food.

Present-day Myths, Legends, and Tales

Of the above, many have been recorded in connection with ethnological village studies, and some separately, but there is no collection of various regions, nor have many been analyzed or classified. However, they follow the usual pattern—some are purely aboriginal or purely Spanish, but the majority are a fusion of both, with either one or the other predominating. It is safe to affirm that those dealing with mythical heroes, bandits, animals and customs are indigenous, even though mixed with and influenced by foreign ideas; also that all imported ones have acquired Mexican characteristics. And all widespread tales have localisms.

Most of the folk do not make the customary literary distinctions of myths, legends, and tales, but call them all "cuentos," stories or tales, whereas some also use the terms "leyendas" and "historias." All of them, by whatever name they are called, serve three important functions—to keep alive ancient events and traditions; to furnish examples or to rationalize and sanction conduct; and to amuse. Often they overlap, but all of them in all their forms reveal much of the character, beliefs, and customs of the people.

Stories are told everywhere both in the native tongues and in Spanish, depending upon which is more commonly used. They are a more common pastime in warm climes, where the people sit around out-of-doors at night with nothing to do, as well as among men away from home, when they gather around a campfire at night. But they are not easy to collect, for often those who know the best ones cannot speak Spanish or are shy about telling them. But in most villages there are outstanding storytellers, who can be induced to relate them.

I am including here as many different types as possible. Although the number must of necessity be limited, it is perhaps a greater variety than can be found in any other publication.

Maya Creation Myths and Beliefs

Recorded by Alfonso Villa R. in Quintana Roo

God created a number of human couples, giving each the racial characteristics of the group to which it was to belong. For example, he formed a Chinese, a Negro, and a Maya couple, and granted each one the portion of the earth in which they were to reproduce their kind and establish their rule.

At the time of the creation each couple received the characteristic and distinctive qualities which were to determine the destiny of their group. Thus, some men are ugly and occupy an inferior station, while others are good looking and are in a privileged position.

It is easy to see that the men most favored by God are those tall, blond, strong men who live an easy life and are known as Americans, whereas the Negroes and Chinese are poor and always subordinate.

The notions about the favoritism shown by God to the whites are based on the Maya natives' contacts with the neighboring colony of British Honduras, where marked social distinctions exist between the several groups living there. But the natives do not consider themselves as badly off as the Negroes or Chinese, although they do not believe themselves too highly favored by God. They think their personal appearance is inferior to that of the whites and that it is their destiny to live in the bush, where they must endure poverty and the hardships of "making milpa" or preparing their cornfields. They refer to themselves as "men of the bush" or "poor men," explaining that this is their destiny and that they cannot aspire to the white man's manner of living.

The following Biblical version of the creation also exists there, but is not taken too seriously.

The first human couple, created by God for the purpose of placing in their care an apple called "The Prince," were Adam and Eve. At first they faithfully complied with their obligation, although Eve was eager to eat the fruit and tempted Adam by telling him that it had a delicious smell. At the end of three days they could no longer resist the temptation and ate the apple. Shortly afterwards the couple noted with surprise that in the process of digestion the apple was causing changes in their bodies. One piece of the apple stuck in Adam's throat, becoming the little bone which is easily seen in the throats of men only, and his male organs grew from another. With Eve it was different—one part of the apple formed her breasts, and another her female organs. Thus transformed, the two began to wonder about the possible use for their new organs. Upon discovering it, they fell into sin and since then humanity has been multiplied through procreation.

Heavenly Bodies and Eclipses

The heavenly bodies which receive most attention from the natives are the sun and the moon. The former is called Father Sun and the latter Mother Moon. However, neither of these heavenly bodies is an object of religious beliefs or practices. . . . Other pairs of objects are also denoted as "father and mother." For example, it is believed that the nearby lake of Chichankanab (the little sea) is the "mother" and the sea (kanab) is the "father." They say if the waters of these two bodies were ever to join, a great flood would result; merely throwing into one of these bodies of water a bottle of liquid taken from the other would be enough to cause the deluge.

The explanation given for the setting of the sun and the moon is that when they arrive in the west, they enter a subterranean passage through which they pass to the point from which they started.

Eclipses are believed to occur when certain "very bad animals" try to eat the sun or the moon. Thus eclipses are called "the biting of the sun" or the "biting of the moon." A few expressed the idea that the "bad animal" is the ant known as xulab. According to one version, the eclipse occurs because the sun or moon is covered by a great colony of ants. According to another version, the sun or moon is attacked by a monster similar to the queen of the xulab. The belief attributing eclipses to ants of this family seems to be of pre-Hispanic origin.

Eclipses are greatly feared because it is believed that a total eclipse of the sun or moon would cause all the domestic instruments to be transformed into living creatures who would kill their masters, revenging themselves. This, we have seen, happened in the third creation of the Popol Vuh.[3]

Dreams as Omens

The above are important among all natives. The following, recorded in the Maya village of Chan Kom by Robert Redfield and Alfonso Villa, are examples of the form they may take.

Dreams are omens of the future, usually of misfortune or calamity. To dream of many pigs or of many cats, is a sign that there will be fighting or other misfortunes. To dream of zapotes, or of the small banana, is a sign that one is going to be sad. To dream of happy, laughing people is a sign of good things to come; but to dream of weeping people is a sign of misfortune ahead. To dream of darkness is a bad sign; while of light, a good sign. When an *h-men* is treating for sickness, he often inquires into the dreams of his patient to make the prognosis. If the sick man dreams of light, he is advised that he will get well. Tomatoes in a dream mean the lighted candles of a coming wake; guns mean the same candles not yet lighted. In an instance observed, when the patient dreamed of guns, the *h-men* gave the case up as hopeless. To dream of burning houses or milpas indicates a coming fever. Snakes mean the ropes of a coffin, or lashes that one is going to receive. To dream of red things is bad; it means blood. Doña Cef dreamt three times that she saw her husband dancing with a red handkerchief around his neck; two weeks later he was killed by machete blows in the neck. It is said that it is not uncommon to dream that the sky is falling; several dreamed this before the school fell. If one dreams he is digging sweet potatoes, it means he will help at a burial. To dream of the loss of a hat or other personal property means that one is to lose a member of his family by death. If one dreams he loses a small tooth, some child is going to die; loss of a molar means that an adult will die. To dream one is being married is the worst of possible dreams; that surely means one's death. If the old people dream this, they begin to give away their things and compose themselves for the end. To dream one is naked is a sign of one's coming illness. To dream of vultures, or black bulls, or horses is a sign of a coming funeral. To dream of full granaries is a sign one is to have good health. It is also good to dream of young maize plants. To dream of much corn in the house is a sign of wealth coming.[4]

The Story of the Creation

Recorded by Margaret Park Redfield in the Maya Town of Dzitas

Jesucristo made a very beautiful garden. And he put an old man named San José to watch the garden. But Jesucristo gave him the name of Adam. Now one day Adam saw two turtle-doves cooing together. And he felt lonesome, all by himself watching the garden. The next morning he woke up and saw a girl by his side. So he began to ask, "Where did you come from?" "They sent me here," she answered. Jesucristo had given his blessing to the rib of a dog and from this the female Eve was made. At this time both Adam and Eve were saints; they lived together as brother and sister and did not sin.

Every day San José (or Adam) went to Jesucristo to tell him how the garden was getting on. Jesucristo had given him a little book, and all he had to do was to read it and his dinner would be ready. So he left Eve watching the garden and reading the book. After a while she saw a man called Judio. "Let us eat apples," said Judio. "No, I will not till Adam comes back," said Eve. But Judio went ahead and took down some apples ("apples like those sold in the city, very delicious ones") and even though Eve would not eat them, he put a piece in her mouth and rubbed it all around her—but she did not eat it. Then Adam came and said, "Who got down some apples? Did you, Eve?" "No, I didn't," she replied. "The man did, but I didn't eat any." The next morning when she woke up, Adam saw that Eve's breasts and all her other sexual organs had appeared. And she was ashamed for the first time.

After a while Saint Michael came to ask Adam why he had not come that morning to make his report to God. He knocked at the door and said, "God sent me to ask you why you didn't make your report this morning." Then Eve was ashamed and she went and hid behind the door. So Saint Michael went back and told God that something had happened to the girl. And Eve took Adam's guayabera (man's shirt) and put it around her like trousers. Adam went up to see Jesucristo, and Jesucristo asked him, "What has happened?" When Jesucristo heard what had happened, he said, "Now that you have eaten what you shouldn't eat, I am going to give you a flock of goats, your little book, and some clothes, and send you out into the world." So Adam and Eve went out into the world, but on the road they met the Devil (or Judio) and he stole the book and the goats. Then Adam went back to Jesucristo and told him what had happened. "Now," said Jesucristo, "as you don't watch out for your things, you will have to work for what you eat." And he gave Adam another book and put his blessing upon it, but this book was full of witchcraft and insulting language, and that is how things began in the world.

Really, one should not insult anyone, because we are all children of the same parents; Jesucristo is our father and the Virgin Mary is our mother.

Now Adam and Eve began to have children, and they had three sons named Melchior, Gaspar, and Balthasar. Adam began to take much anís (rum) and to get very drunk. One day Melchior found him lying on the road drunk, and he said to himself, "Look, papa has fallen down. He ought to be ashamed of himself. I am going to paint his face with charcoal so that when he wakes up he will be ashamed." So he began painting up his face. Then Gaspar came by, and he said, "Not that way. This way." And he began blacking up his father's face still more. When they had gone on, there came Balthasar, the youngest (thup). He said, "Who has done this to my papa?" and he began wiping his father's face with his handkerchief. His father woke up and he said, "Papa, what has happened to you?" "Who did this thing to me, my son?" "Who knows, papa?"

Adam went home and sat down to eat. Then he called to Melchior and Gaspar and asked them if they had blacked his face. "No, papa," they both answered. Then all the boys went to bathe in the sea. Melchior went in first. When he came out he was black all over. This was because of what he had done to his father. Jesucristo cast his blessing ("made the magic") and brought it about. Then Gaspar went in, and when he came out he was medium dark. Last of all Balthasar came out, and he was white, white as could be, with green eyes. Then Adam said, "You said you did not do this, but here is a sign that you did." Then Jesucristo put his blessing on them and Melchior, Gaspar and Balthasar became saints, the Holy Kings of Tizimin—for it is known that they first appeared in the sea. (They are the three images of that place.)

But from this time on there began to spring forth Christians of three sorts, Negroes or Cubans like Melchior, Indians like Gaspar, and, like the youngest one, Balthasar, the vecinos (mixed blood inhabitants with Spanish patronymics) and the Americans. Both the Negroes and the Indians have to work hard for a living, but the vecinos can get along with just a pen, nothing but studying, like you, Doña Margarita.[5]

TWO LACANDON CREATION MYTHS

1. Recorded by Howard Cline in Chiapas

In the beginning there were two brothers, Sukuyum and Nohotsakyum, and they are the main gods. Sukuyum is older and maybe more powerful. These two lived in the sky in a house, but Sukuyum wanted a house for himself. He ordered his younger brother to make him a house, but would not help him make it because he did not want to. Nohotsakyum made a round ball like masa for making tortillas. That is our world and the house of Sukuyum, who lives in the middle of it. Where he lives there is much fire, and he orders earthquakes and volcanos. Evil persons who kill other people and who lie and steal go down where he lives after they die. He burns them and punishes them by running hot irons up their penises. Nohotsakyum made the world and everything in it. First he made the land and then the water, and when he had finished he put in it all the things people would need. First he had to make the sun to have some light so he could work, and then came the moon and the stars. Of the things that grow he made them in this order: maize, bananas, garlic, beans, and cane. After that, there was no special order, because he made plants and vines and trees, but he made rice before he made fruit.

When the earth was all ready, he made men. He made them by peoples. First came the Kalsia, which is to say, people of the monkey; then came Koho-ka, people of the peccary; then Ka-puk, or people of the tiger; and then Chan-ka, or people of the pheasant. This is how he made people. He made them out of clay—men, women, and children—giving them eyes, a nose, all other parts, then he put the clay on the fire where he was cooking tortillas. The clay got hard from the fire, and the people lived. After they had life, he gave each people a place on earth to live. He had to make clay babies and children of all sizes so that there would be someone to be people on earth after the first adults died.

When he finished making men, he made animals in the same way. He made them in this order: tiger, snakes, monkey, howling ape, peccary, mountain deer, pheasant, wild turkey, and then the other birds and animals in no order.

Nohotsakyum and his wife Nainohotsakyum and all the good dead people and santos of various kinds live in the sky where there is land, with roads, and trees like here, but no animals and no chickens. When the world comes to an end by being eaten up by the big jaguar, everyone will go up there and live like Nohotsakyum, who works in his corn patch, smokes cigars, and eats tortillas and beans.

Another rather long and complicated Lacandon creation myth recorded by Howard Cline has the following charming ending:

Metzabok is a santo who lives in a cave on a lake named after him. He makes rain by burning copal, and the smoke turns into rain clouds. Then, by waving the tail of a big macaw which he has, the santo makes wind which brings the rain. When the wind comes then there is rain. Inside the macaw's tail are dead caribes or Lacandons who now help the santo. They have rocks which they strike together, and that is the noise of thunder. When the rocks strike together, there are sparks. That is lightning. Sometimes after rain the tail of the macaw stays a little while in the sky. It is very pretty. That is the rainbow. Metzabok cares for all waters and rivers. He orders the alligators not to bite people who are going to the houses of the gods. At his house on the lake are all the souls of the caribes who have died. When the end of the world comes, they will go up above and cannot be killed again.

In the beginning Metzabok showed the caribes how to make arrows, and now the rocks for arrows come from his house. The santos become very angry when anyone touches the rocks of their houses, and will send a big snake to kill people like that, but Metzabok allows it if he gets paid. Qaq, the santo of fire, looks after arrows when they are shot so they will not be lost.

Some of the other santos are Itzamaku who makes hail; he lives in a very large house near Guineo. Kayom is santo of music, and he always comes dancing and whistling, for he is a very happy santo. Bohr is the santo who takes care of balche. If he is angry, the balche will not ferment. There are many santos—who knows how many?[6]

TWO STORIES RECORDED IN MAYA AND TRANSLATED INTO SPANISH

By Alfredo Barrera Vazquez

1. How the Basilisk Obtained His Crest

From Quintana Roo

The basilisks belong to the lizard family, the males being characterized by erectile crests on their heads and backs. "The *Basiliscus Americanus* reaches the length of a yard; its color is green and brown while its crest is reddish. This beautiful strictly herbivorous creature is rather common amidst the luxuriant vegetation on the banks of rivers and streams of the Atlantic hot lands of Mexico and Guatemala. . . ."

ENCYCLOPAEDIA BRITANNICA

One day the Lord of the Woods called together all the animals that could run and said to them, "Come here, my children; I wish to explain something to you."

When all were in his presence, he led them to a savanna and said to them, "I have assembled you to tell you that I wish to see which one of you is capable of winning a race to the big Pich that stands to one side of the road. The winner will receive a prize. I have had a bench placed there for the one who arrives first to sit on."

The Big Fox spoke first in answer to the Lord of the Woods, "My Señor, how can you think it possible that anyone of us can win a race with Big Deer? You surely know that he is much more rapid than we are. Why, he runs like a whirlwind. We shall all remain behind. We haven't sufficient power in our legs to outrun him, not even to arrive at the same time."

The rabbit added his opinion, "What Big Fox says is true." "Yes, yes," all the others assented in chorus. Even the serpents who run like lightning across the skies, said, "It is true, Our Señor; none of us have the capacity for winning a race with Big Deer in it."

But a young Basilisk slipped down from the branches of a Katsin to the feet of the Lord of the Woods and said to him, "Señor, what is the prize you offer?"

BASILISK

"If you win," he replied, "I shall put a sombrero on your head, so that everybody will know that you have won a race with the Deer."

All the other animals laughed when they saw the poor little Basilisk talking to the Lord of the Woods. "What does he think?" they asked. "He must be insane, that little devil of a Basilisk."

He heard what they said and turned upon them, shouting, "Shut up, you devils! You're afraid of the Deer, but I'm not. I'll show you all what stuff I'm made of. I'm little, yes; that's how you see me. Nevertheless, we shall see if I cannot make myself worthy of a sombrero."

"Look at him, look at him," all the other animals said together.

"Yes, look at him!" exclaimed the Lord of the Woods. "You all shut up! Come, Big Deer, stand here; you next to him, little Basilisk."

The Basilisk obeyed, saying, "Only one thing I ask." "Speak!" he was told. "What I wish is simply this—that you make everyone shut his eyes while we start off."

The Lord of the Woods agreed, "Very well, little Basilisk," and addressing the others, "When I count to three, all of you close your eyes. He who does not obey, shall be punished. Have you all heard?" Then he began, "One, two, three," and the race began.

When the other animals opened their eyes, all they saw was a cloud of dust on the road. Not even the Lord of the Woods was there. He had left by air to arrive first to see who won.

When Big Deer had run some distance, he thought, "Why am I hurrying so? The poor little Basilisk surely must be buried in the dust I stirred up with my claws at the start. Poor little thing!"

When Deer arrived at the Pich, trotting contentedly, the Lord of the Woods received him smilingly. Deer looked at the bench and made a quick movement as if to sit down on it. But before he touched it, the voice of the Basilisk caused him to jump; "Look out, or you will crush me, Big Deer. Go away, for I got here before you did."

Deer, turning around to look at the bench, remained speechless; he only trembled. Then, ashamed of himself, he walked away, thinking, "How did the little Basilisk do it? He must have a devil in his body!"

By this time the other animals had arrived and saw what had happened. The Lord of the Woods approached the little Basilisk and said to him, "Very good! You are an intelligent little fellow. Here's your prize."

Only the Lord of the Woods knew that the little Basilisk was able to seat himself on the bench before Big Deer because he had arrived on the tail of the Deer.

11. The Three Brothers and the Toad

Also from Quintana Roo, but nearer to Mérida

A rich farmer, who had three sons, noticed that his cornfield was being devoured by some animal. He proposed to kill him, but did not even succeed in seeing what he was like.

In view of his failure, he told his sons that he was disposed to leave all his wealth to whichever one of them would bring him the animal, dead or alive, that was causing his ruin.

The youngest was the first to promise his father that he would bring him the destroyer of the cornfield, but he was told that his elder brothers would be given the opportunity first, in turn. The brothers mocked at his promise, saying that a boy like him, without brains and judgment, could not expect to fulfill it.

The first born then asked for a horse, a fine gun, and some good food, and set out for the cornfield on a night with a full moon. About halfway out, he came across a toad singing loudly at the edge of a cenote (underground well). As he was tired, he stopped his horse, dismounted, tied it to a tree, and approached the cenote, saying to the toad, "It's easy to see that you aren't tired, noisy one; that's why you're in a mood for singing."

The toad answered, "If you'll take me with you, I shall tell you who is eating your cornfield." "What do you know, little toad?" the boy answered, and without more ado, he caught it up and threw it into the water. Then he mounted his horse and went on his way.

Upon reaching the cornfield, he saw signs of recent destruction, but not the destroyer. Although he watched all night long, the thief did not return on this occasion. At dawn he was tired and angry; he blasphemed as never before and returned home.

His father asked his eldest son what he had seen in the cornfield. He answered that he only saw the damage caused by that accursed animal thief, but that he had not been able to catch sight of the thief, even though he had not closed his eyes all night long.

Then said the old farmer, "You have lost, my son; you cannot be my heir."

Next it was the turn of the second son to try. His father asked him what he wanted to take along. He answered that all he wanted was a gun and a bag with something to eat, and left.

Halfway out, he also found the toad singing near the cenote, and said to it, "Shut up, little toad! I wish to sleep at the edge of this cenote and you will take care of me."

The toad replied, "If you will take me with you, I shall make you a gift of something with which you will be able to catch whoever is eating your cornfield." "I don't need your help," answered the boy, and went to sleep.

In revenge the toad stole his posol (corn meal). When he awoke and saw what the toad had done, he grabbed it by one foot, threw it into the cenote and marched off to the cornfield.

When he arrived there, he saw a big bird with showy feathers rising from the corn plants. He lifted his gun rapidly and shot, but all he brought down were some of the feathers; his aim to kill had failed. Nevertheless, he was pleased, thinking that he could deceive his father and brothers by making them believe that the plumes were proof he had shot the bird.

He hurried home and said to his father and brothers, smiling with satisfaction, "I've killed the thief of our cornfield. Here are some of its feathers. I'm the heir!"

But Benjamin, the youngest of them, said, "I'm not satisfied, because you only bring the plumes and not what wore them. I shall go for the whole bird and bring it back."

He then asked for a gun and a bag with some food, and marched off in the direction of the cornfield.

When he reached the cenote, he, too, found the toad, to which he spoke thus, "Little toad, I shall give you my food if you will tell me who is robbing our cornfield and how I can catch the thief. Moreover, I shall take you with me always, wherever I may go."

The toad was very pleased at hearing the boy speak thus, and answered, "I'm very happy, my boy, and am only sorry that your brothers would not listen to me and that they treated me badly, because things will not go well for them. On the other hand, everything will turn out happily for you." And added, "In the depths of this cenote lies a little stone which will grant you whatever you ask for right here and now."

The boy was delighted at hearing this. "If I asked for a beautiful wife, would it grant me that?"

"Oh, not only will the little stone give you a beautiful wife, but also a large and handsome house for you both to be happy in," the little toad answered.

Then the boy made his wish—that he might soon have the happiness of finding a lovely wife and a handsome, palatial house, and of being able to bring the destroyer of their cornfield into the presence of his father and brothers.

The little toad assured him that his wish would be granted and told him that next he must go to the cornfield to catch the ravager. Then both ate of the boy's food and started off.

Shortly after having arrived at the field, they saw a big handsome bird come flying in and stop not far away from them. The boy with his gun ready to discharge, advanced cautiously and was about to pull the trigger, when he saw it raise its head and heard a sweet voice, saying, "Don't shoot me, young man, because you may be killing the mistress of your heart."

The boy, too astonished to answer, let his arm fall, and grew pale. The bird then came toward him, speaking again, "Although I appear to be a bird, I'm just a girl to whom a wicked witch gave this form, because I would not marry her son, who is as bad as his mother."

The boy, recalling what he had asked of the little stone of the cenote, which the little toad told him would surely be granted, understood that the bride he had asked for was being given to him in that form, and drawing upon his heart for strength, exclaimed, "Oh, if what you say is true, then come with me and my companion. I shall take you to my house and turn you into a woman again. Then I shall ask to marry you, and give you a large, handsome house in which we two shall live happily."

The bird agreed and went with him and the toad to his house. When he arrived his father and two brothers were speechless with surprise at seeing him in the company of a rare bird and the toad, and even more so when they heard him say, "I bring you the entire bird, not only some feathers. It was she who ate the corn, but she is neither bird nor to blame for looking like one. She is really a beautiful girl, transformed into a bird with brilliant plumage by a witch who hated her because she would not marry her son. She will soon be a woman again because I have the promise of the little stone in the cenote to give me a beautiful wife, and she is the one."

Having spoken thus, he added, "With your help, little toad, let her be a woman once more and let the promise that we have a large and handsome house be fulfilled."

The toad sang and the bird disappeared, a beautiful girl appearing in her place, who thanked her saviors and accepted the boy's proposal to become his wife.

As soon as it was light the following day, they all contemplated with amazement the handsome, palatial dwelling that had miraculously appeared. After they were married, the little toad lived with them and sang, always recalling the day when he met the kind boy.

The envious brothers wished to do harm to the house but failed. So, filled with shame, they fled, leaving the victors rich and happy.'

TZELTAL STORIES

Recorded by Anne Chapman in Chiapas

I. A Story of the Underworld

What Happens to a Wife Whose Husband Does Not Beat Her

Men as well as women go to the underworld when they die. Those who have not been very bad return to live again on earth after a short stay, while those who have been wicked remain below a long time, or until they have received their full punishment. But sooner or later everyone comes back to live on earth. One does not know how he will look the second time, nor where he will live, nor who will be his parents. The only thing that is known is that a man will be a man and a woman a woman; also that those who live to an old age the first time will do so again the second time—and the same is true of those who die young.

"But now I'm going to tell you something so that you may see how the underworld is," said Antonio Gómez Ichilick, a native of Oxchuc, Chiapas.

An Indian's wife died and he became very sad. He wept much, saying, "Where are you? You, my wife, who prepared my food, who took care of me, where are you?" He became sadder as the days passed, as he had to go from house to house among his neighbors to ask for a few tortillas and a little pozol (corn gruel).

One night he went to his wife's grave and throwing himself upon it, began to weep and talk to her, "Where are you? Why did you leave me so alone?" He was still weeping when suddenly there appeared before him a human figure—it may have been God—who knows? He was dressed like a Ladino (a citified man), in cloth trousers and a new shirt.

He asked the man, "Why are you weeping so much? What is the matter?" At first the man was too surprised to answer but finally he said, "My wife has died and I'm weeping because I am very lonely and want to see her." Upon hearing this the Ladino answered, "So you want to see your wife. Very well, I shall take you to her. Now close your eyes and don't open them until I tell you to." A moment later he said, "Open them."

The man opened his eyes and saw that he was below the earth, in the presence of the Lord of Death. The Ladino who had brought him had disappeared. The Lord said to him, "If you wish to see your wife, go on until you reach a river. There on its banks you will find a horse; bring it to me."

The man obeyed and went looking for the river, which he found without any difficulty, but he saw no horse, only women washing their hair and clothes. He looked and looked, but found no horse. Then he returned to the Lord of Death and told him that he had not seen any horse, just women.

Then the Lord of Death said to him, "Go to the river again and ask each one of the women if she is a horse. The woman who says she is a horse will be your wife; when you ask her the question, she will be transformed into one. Tie the horse well and bring him to me."

The man returned to the river, and just as the Lord of Death had said, he found the woman who admitted being a horse; who upon his asking the question, was immediately turned into one. He tied the ribbon his wife was wearing in her hair around the horse's neck. Upon feeling the ribbon around her neck, the horse said to him, "Don't tie me so tight; you are hurting my neck." So he took off the ribbon and tied her with the cotton girdle he was wearing. And thus he led her into the presence of the Lord of Death.

Upon passing a well within which a big fire was burning, near which there was a heap of bones, his wife, or rather the horse, explained to her husband that she had to go to the river daily to wash and to look for wood; she was converted into a woman to wash herself and into a horse to carry the wood. But upon reaching the well with her wood, she became nothing but bones.

"Every day the Lord of Death throws me into the fire to punish me," she went on. "He leaves me in the fire until I'm changed into ashes, and when I say that I have suffered sufficiently for one day, he takes my ashes and makes a woman of me again. This punishment is very severe and I have to suffer it all because you did not beat me when we lived there above on the earth."

Then the wife led her husband to her hut, for all those below have huts like ours up here. She gave him some food, but only yellow corn and red beans. Down there they cannot eat white corn because it is the brains of man, nor black corn because it is our burned flesh, nor black beans because they are the pupils of our eyes.

Upon finishing their food, the wife said to him, "I'm going to sleep on the wooden bed, but you will have to sleep near the fire, for you already know that we cannot sleep together nor do as we did before when we lived on earth." The husband lay down near the fire, as his wife had said, but in a little while he had a desire to sleep with her as they used to. He moved closer to her but upon touching her he felt no flesh, only bones. The following day his wife scolded him, "Why did you touch me? You behaved very badly. Now I will be punished more, when I was already reducing the amount of punishment against me."

We do not know how many days the man stayed down there with his wife, because we cannot tell whether there are just days or just nights down there, for it is certain that it must be different.

One day or night, whichever it may have been, the woman said to her husband, "You will die in fifteen days after returning to the earth. If you had not come here, you would have lived a long life, for it is written that you should not die until you are old. But now that you have seen how it is down here, you will die within fifteen days." He answered, "That is all right; I don't care. I don't want to live up there any longer."

When the man was prepared to return to earth, the same Ladino who had brought him down, appeared and said to him, "Close your eyes as you did the other time and don't open them until I tell you to."

Upon opening his eyes, he found himself back on earth once more. At the end of fifteen days he died and went down below.

When drunk, the men of that region, as elsewhere, beat their wives. When sober, they are ashamed of themselves and rationalize their actions by saying, "If I don't beat you here, the Lord of Death will punish you much harder." F. T.

II. The Wicked Christ

"If it were not for this wicked Santo Cristo, all would be well with us and we would be living contentedly," said a Tzeltal of Oxchuc, Chiapas. This man was not different from the rest of his community, and had the same beliefs. He explained his statement.

God, yes, he is good, but that Cristo is very bad. But our patron saint, he of Oxchuc, well, he is as good as God himself. Our patron is Santo Tomás and he is the best of all the saints around here—better than San Juan of Cancuc, better than San Alonso of Tenejapa, and even better than San Miguel of Mitontique. These four saints are brothers because the four are sons of God and live in a cave or in a chencal, as we call it in our language. It is situated alongside of the road above here, which goes from San Cristóbal to Tenejapa.

All our people know that Santo Tomás is the best of all the saints, so they come to pray, to burn incense, candles and firecrackers to him on the day of his fiesta. Every year many come from far away—from Comitán and Simojovel. Yes, when their corn is growing and it has not rained sufficiently, they come to the fiesta of Santo Tomás to beg him for rain. They bring candles, incense, and firecrackers because they know our saint is very good for starting the rains to make the corn grow. Many come, as many as four hundred. They come singing and playing their guitars, harps and flutes. They come from Tenango, Pachjan, San Martín, Kuchun, Huistan, and from many other villages.

All the saints like having incense, candles, and firecrackers burned for them because the smoke from them rises to heaven and there God and the saints receive it as a gift. Moreover, the saints have to take all the incense, candles, and firecrackers of the fiesta up there to God. They have to pass through the gate of heaven. For this reason each saint has a mule to carry those things for him. Santo Tomás has a very big and strong mule. As we give him a great deal, he needs a sturdy one to be able to carry it all to the gate of heaven. On the other hand, San Juan, San Alonso and San Miguel—as they are not so good as our saint, the people of those villages only give them tiny yellow candles that cost five or ten centavos each. For this reason they have only very small mules, about the size of a dog. Thus Santo Tomás is very different from his three brothers.

After his fiesta Santo Tomás puts all the incense, all the candles—which are of pure wax at one peso each—and all the firecrackers on his mule and starts out toward heaven. Upon arriving at the gate, he knocks with a big stick. But as the doorkeeper does not deign to hear, Santo Tomás has to keep on beating at it. Then he takes his good staff and knocks with such force that the man is obliged to open. Once inside, he takes all his presents and offers them to God. But when the other saints arrive at the gate of heaven with their little mules and tiny, cheap candles, they knock and knock without the guardian paying any attention to them. As they are not so strong as Santo Tomás they cannot oblige him to open for them. The truth is that God is not interested in receiving their tiny yellow candles.

Now I'm going to tell you something that my little grandfather related to me, so that you may see how good is our Santo Tomás and how bad Santo Cristo.

Many, very many years ago, men and women only lived to about thirteen or fourteen years of age. They grew up in two or three weeks and were already old when they reached that age. Those people fought a great deal among themselves; they were always killing one another. Much blood was spilt and the foul smell of it reached heaven and annoyed God very much.

God was already much displeased over it, and Santo Cristo began advising him that all the men and women should be killed once and for all, so that they should not continue fighting and infesting heaven with the smell of their blood. God then gave Santo Cristo permission to kill all the people. As this one is a very bad person, he was delighted. With his big cape made of reeds, Cristo fulfilled his mission, making torrents of water flow from the reeds. Thus all the earth was flooded, as if it were one great ocean. Naturally, all the people died. Nothing was left, only water.

But as God is good, he gave life again to all the men and women and, of course, that made Cristo sad. Soon he began to beg God for permission to kill all the people again. When Santo Tomás learned of the plot of Santo Cristo he warned God that what he proposed was very bad. He convinced Him that it would be much better to let the poor people live out their lives instead of only thirteen or fourteen years. God agreed with Santo Tomás, but he did not know how to tell Cristo that he would not permit him to drown the people as before, especially since Cristo was so determined to do it. Finally Santo Tomás and God decided to make a fiesta for Cristo and get him drunk on chicha (their fermented ritual drink), as it would be easier to convince him in that state.

The following day all the saints and their wives gathered. They sat down in a circle to drink chicha and to chat, as we do when we have a fiesta. But Cristo did not want to participate and remained outside, looking on. He would not drink any chicha, for he said, "I, no; I'm not going to drink your chicha because then I shall get drunk and shall not be able to drown all the people of the earth tomorrow with my stream of water."

Cristo resisted all temptation in spite of the fact that God Himself, Santo Tomás, and his wife, Santa María, explained all the merits of the drink with respect to taste, fragrance, and quality. Cristo paid no attention to them, maintaining himself firm in his plans. But Santo Tomás did not lose hope. He knew that in some way he had to make Santo Cristo drunk, so that he would be unable to carry out his evil intentions. He pondered until finally he found a solution. He made movements like little circles with his right index finger on his other hand and a little cup of aguardiente or brandy appeared in the palm of his hand. Until then no one had ever tasted that drink. Santo Tomás invented it to be able to make Cristo drunk. As it tastes much better than chicha, not even Cristo could resist it.

Now Santo Tomás, armed with his little cup of brandy, returned to Cristo's side and offered it to him. At first he refused but little by little Santo Tomás broke his resistance by making him smell it and describing it. "Very well, I shall take a little drink but just one, only to taste it," said Cristo. As is natural, after the first drink, he wanted more and more. He continued drinking until very late at night when he was so full and so drunk that he could not drink another drop. Santo Tomás and God also drank much aguardiente but they never get drunk.

When Cristo awoke the next morning he had a terrible hangover. He looked around him and did not know where he was until he recalled the fiesta of the previous night, but now there was no one around. All the saints had returned to their huts, leaving Cristo alone on the ground. Then he looked down at himself and jumped up in surprise because he saw that he was naked. The night before his companions had undressed him and he was so drunk that he was not even aware of it. Now upon finding himself naked, he began to run in search of the saints to ask them where they had hidden his clothes.

Santo Cristo was not so much worried about the loss of his clothes as of his cape of reeds, which he needed to throw over the earth the water with which to put an end to the lives of the people. By simply shaking the cape torrents of water burst forth from every reed. For this reason Cristo went about looking for it with great anxiety. He asked everyone of the saints where they had hidden his cape but not one of them answered him. Cristo became desperate; he did not know what to do. Finally, Santo Tomás said to him, "I'm going to tell you where your cape is but even then you will not be able to find it. Last night we tore it to pieces and threw the reeds away over all the hills of the earth." Because of this there are so many waterholes on the hills, for everywhere that a piece of Cristo's cape fell, a waterhole appeared.

Upon hearing this, Cristo began to complain bitterly. "Ah," he said, "now I cannot drown the people because I haven't even a cape." Instead of paying any attention to his complaints, all the saints jumped on him and tied him to a post. They tied him well, so that he could never escape, because they knew if he succeeded in untying himself from the post and escaping, then he would again insist on killing all the people. After tying him they took him far away, very far, way beyond where the sun sets, and there they left him tied to the post, so that he should never return to do harm.

Some years ago a tremor of the earth was felt, as if someone were shaking it. Then all the saints went to the west where they had left Cristo tied to the post, for they knew that he was trying to escape by breaking his ropes and that because of this the earth shook. Fortunately, Santo Tomás arrived in time to tie him up again with even stronger ropes. They say that roots have sprouted from under the post to hold him more securely. Still the earth continues shaking. Whenever that happens we know that Cristo is trying to free himself from the post.

We have already seen that the natives of this region have a very simple, human conception of God and the saints. This story confirms it. They behave exactly like human beings, having fiestas and getting drunk. **F. T.**

La Mazorquita Que Habla
The Little Ear of Corn that Speaks

From Anne Chapman's Diary
In the Colonia Agraria Coronado, Municipio de Huistan, Chiapas
January 28, 1945

María and I have become very good friends. She is a girl of great spirit. I have spent many hours listening to her tell about her life, her struggles against all that seems unjust to her. These have taken the form of quarrels with her female neighbors, with authorities of the Colonia or the Municipality, and with the merchants who try to rob her.

María had lived in the City of Tapachula, the commercial center of the coffee zone, where she had a store. She invested several thousand pesos and its success was assured. She confided that had she not left her business, she would now be a rich storekeeper instead of a poor peasant, married to an índio, who in addition to that, was a drunk, lazy, and worst of all, a fool, for he permitted himself to be easily deceived. Had he not married her, he would not have even one coffee plant, much less a decent hut, thirty chickens, two pigs and a store. "But in spite of all this," she would say to me, "I love him! God only knows why."

Once when she had been absent from her home for two years, she received the news that her mother was dying. But upon returning to Tapachula, she saw it was a trick of the family to get her to come back. She did not get angry. She was content to have returned, and she lived with her family until her sister died. Then she grieved so much over her loss, that her parents decided to send her to a nearby village to visit an aunt. While there she met Teodocio, her husband. It was five years now since they had come to live in this Colonia to cultivate a "little coffee patch."

María says she does not want any children because they are too much work. She is very restless, physically as well as mentally. She is always in action—singing, dancing, jumping, weeping, laughing. She accepts new things with enthusiasm. She speaks much of the German Evangelists who are in the region, saying, "I love to listen to them talk in their language; it is so strange, so pretty; I should like to learn it."

She was first to establish a store here; now there are three. She dresses in citified clothes, like the ladinos, wearing gay flowered cotton dresses; ribbons in her braids which she winds around her head with a bow on top; and always high-heeled shoes. She is the only woman in the Colonia who knows how to read and write. She is self-confident and says, "I'm not afraid of anybody; I know I can earn my living anywhere because I'm intelligent."

That night we began to chat as usual, she standing up, her voice raised to a high pitch, gesticulating excitedly as she related the story of the mazorquita that talked.

Two years ago in September, I was making bread when suddenly I felt an earthquake. I had never experienced such a strong one before in all my life. The house shook from one side to the other. The women who were with me began to weep and yell. I said to them, "Shut up; it is the same to die here inside as there outside." I grabbed a little girl who was beside me with one arm and the bread tray with the other and started to pray. During the following fifteen days there were other, smaller quakes—as many as three or four in one day.

A few days after the first big quake, news came from the Colonia El Litrero that while it was taking place there, a mazorquita began to talk, saying, "No one takes care of me nor do they like me. The people sweep me around the floor; they throw me to the animals; all despise me, I, who am the mother of mankind, because of whom they are alive. I feed everyone with my breasts but no one worships nor cares for me. All prefer coffee to me because it brings them money. But I, who am their mother, am neglected. For this reason there will come seven days of hunger." Seven days meant seven years. The holy mother of all, the Saint of Corn, had become angry with all of us because we did not treat her well.

When this news reached our Colonia, there was great excitement among the people. Some said it was not true; that it was pure magic;

that a mazorquita could not speak. There was much discussion and although the majority did not believe it, I did. I, of course, believed it because I know that God is all-powerful and that he can do everything, and that only because of the Mother of Corn can we live.

All of us who believed in the mazorquita, about twenty-five, got together and decided to make a pilgrimage to visit it. We were to be away for eight days. Each one took much food, only of corn, like tortillas and pozol, in little bags and each one carried a blanket. In this way we set out to fulfill the promises we had made to the Holy Corn and to pray to the mazorquita. It was all very nice; we were all fond of one another and we went along happily. Not everyone from the Colonia went because some did not believe in the mazorquita and others had animals to take care of and still others had no money. Teodocio and I spent ten pesos. Besides the food of pure corn, we each took along censers with copal, candles and one of the nicest little ears of corn we could find. We set out contentedly.

We spent the first night out on a coffee finca. The next day, while we were resting on a hill, a man with a goat came by and asked us, "And what are you doing here? Where are you going?" We told him we were on our way to "pay" promises and to pray to the mazorquita that talked. Then he said to us, "You cannot go to El Litrero because the little girl who found the mazorquita and all her family are in jail, and the presidente of Motonzintla threatens to lock up everyone who comes to worship it."

What could we do then? We did not want to return to the Colonia without seeing the mazorquita. But how? How were we going to worship it when the authorities were putting everyone in jail? We decided to go and see what happened. Upon reaching the next village, the people said to us, "Don't worry; another mazorquita that speaks appeared in the village of Santo Domingo; another little girl found it in the corn-crib. You can go there to make your promises good, but look out for the authorities—you know. . . ." We were all glad to hear this and set out in the direction of Santo Domingo, which was not far away.

We walked much and reached a cornfield, a very beautiful one with very high green plants, but very green. As we passed through it, I noticed a little house and approached it to ask about the mazorquita. No one was inside but it was certain that people had been there recently, praying and worshipping because all the floor was spotted with candle "tears" and much China paper hung from the ceiling, the kind used for fiestas. There were also withered flowers all over the altar.

Then we noticed another little house farther on. We sent three of our men to ask about the mazorquita. When they returned, they told us that they were not permitted to enter the house and that they could not ask them anything because they were natives who could not speak Spanish. Then I said to Doña Chabelita, "You go, you know their language well; find out what they have to say." When she came back, she told us they were going to permit us to enter their hut because we had come such a long distance to venerate the mazorquita; but that we could not see it because it was hidden from the authorities, for they feared that they would put them all in jail. We were not afraid of going to jail; what we wanted was to keep our word and to pray to the Holy Corn.

When we entered the hut, we found the natives with their heads covered and weeping and praying. We sat down on the floor with them in front of the little altar. Then they indicated that each one of us should put the little ear of corn he had brought on the altar, which was just a little table, decorated with China paper, candles, and flowers. We did as they wanted us to.

Suddenly a little girl came running in from the woods and put the mazorquita that talked on the table in the midst of our little ones. Then the mazorquita began to move a little. Everyone was very quiet and attentive. The mazorquita spoke, "You who have come to visit me, I shall take into account. Until now everyone has treated me badly; they have swept me around on the ground and thrown me to the animals. They care much more for coffee than for me. Because of this there will be seven years of hunger. But now that I see many are making me promises, there will be only three years of hunger instead of seven. While you are doing penance and praying, you cannot take even one sip of coffee, only pure pozol; you cannot drink any liquor either." And then it stopped talking. We all burned our candles and incense for the mazorquita and prayed much. Then the little girl grabbed it and returned running to the woods to hide from the authorities.

Later we heard that they had put all these natives in jail, for the authorities said that it was pure fraud; that they had said they found a little mazorquita only to make money; they said they charged from five to ten pesos each person who came to worship it. It was all lies for they did not charge us anything. We, of our own free will, gave one or two pesos each to the owner of the house, but they did not ask us even one centavo. Then we heard that another talking mazorquita had appeared in the village of Monte Flor during an earthquake. The mazorquitas always appear during earthquakes; that is their way of announcing themselves.

As we could stay only a very short time with the mazorquita, and we had nothing left to do, we started on our way home. We had to take secret paths to avoid the authorities, who were looking for all of us. When we were within two leagues of our own Colonia, we sat down to think what to do. We were not expected until two days later. We decided to send two of the boys running home to ask the advice of a friend, who was the most Catholic of all the women there and would know what we should do. The rest of us remained where we were, resting and eating until the boys returned. They told us the Señora had said we should continue on our way and when near the Colonia, to shoot off a sky-rocket. We did that and all the people came out to greet us. They had set up arches adorned with palms in our honor at the entrance. They embraced us and carried our bags for us. When we arrived at the church, they were already playing the marimba and victrola. We went directly to the altar where we left our corn. Also the woman who is the professional reciter of prayers of the Colonia came to receive us and was praying all the time. That day she did not charge for her prayers as usual. Everybody accompanied us to the church—everybody, men, women, children and even the old folks.

We spent much time dancing in front of the church, but only zapateados and not in couples, for that was what the mazorquita commanded us to do. It also commanded us not to drink liquor, but some of the men got drunk anyway, especially my Teodocio. But there was nothing one could do—the emotion was so great!

The next fifteen days were spent in dancing at each of the houses of the companions who went on the pilgrimage. During all that time we did not drink any coffee; we only took pozol or corn gruel, sweetened with honey, and ate tortillas. After that the people returned to their former way of living, drinking liquor and coffee.

But since then they have planted corn and every year they make a fiesta at harvest time to the Holy Corn, whereas before the mazorquita appeared to talk to us, no one did anything like that. Many persons began sowing the seeds from the corn they had taken on the pilgrimage. Mine fell to pieces from having taken so much care of it.

My Teodocio had a swelling on his body as punishment for having taken liquor. Doña Toña's feet swelled because she had said some bad words on the way, and others had pimples or little boils. Everyone had something wrong for having done something to displease the mazorquita. A little boy was lost a whole night on the way because he had said he did not believe in the mazorquita. Thus everyone was ill with something, excepting myself. I was the only one well and happy all the time.

When one goes to "pay" a promise or to pray, one must not think of a sweetheart nor of anything else like that. Once two sweethearts from Oaxaca went to visit the Sanctuary of the Señor de Esquipulas in Guatemala to "pay" a promise. When not far away from the place, they sat down to rest and the youth began to play his guitar and to sing to his girl. And the moment he felt a desire to embrace her, he turned into stone. One can see the stones there, one in the form of a young man playing a guitar and another with his arms outstretched as if about to take his sweetheart into them.

When a sick person cannot be cured by the doctors, he makes a promise to a Virgin or a Christ to go to visit her or him, and if he is cured he must keep it. Thus when we heard of the talking mazorquita, we made a promise to go where it was because we know our lives depend on the Holy Corn; that we cannot live without it; that she is our Mother. She herself said to us, "When God makes the world come to an end, I shall be there to help you. I shall die with you."

María affirmed that the mazorquita had told the truth in prophesying hunger. "Isn't it true that corn is scarce and expensive now? And on the coast it is very small. There is hunger!" she said.[8]

This interesting story reminds us of the "talking boxes" of the highlands of the same state. The time was propitious for mazorquitas to talk, since the cultivation of corn was neglected in favor of coffee, which paid better during the war. But apparently these authorities were more active than the others and cut the little business in the bud. F. T.

THE ZAPOTEC LEGEND OF TANGU YUH
Juchitán, Tehuantepec

Taken from the Poetic Version by Nazario Chacón Pineda

Among the toys made especially for the New Year, stands out the little clay figure of the goddess Tangu Yuh. Her dress is like that of the Zapotecas of the place—the huipil always red, although the color of her string of beads and skirt with a simple floral design and snow-white flounce may vary. Her braids form a crown simulating the thorns of Christ; her eyes are black and her lips are as red as a watermelon. Her glance, always fixed in one direction, is far-reaching; the position of her arms invites an embrace.

In the days when the goddess appeared, long, long ago, the people of Juchitán (Xavicende in Zapotec) lived happily together. They were like brothers, but not as now when brothers kill one another. They helped each other in everything, from the celebration of their fiestas to the construction of their houses—a custom which we have inherited from our ancestors.

Then as now, the village was divided into three parts—north, center, and south. Now as then, the women of the northern end weave objects of palm, and embroider, while the men are famous hunters of iguanas, deer, and wild boar; those of the center devote themselves to business, and those of the south work in clay. They are industrious potters, makers of toys, artists.

One New Year's morning at dawn, a voice from heaven was heard amidst celestial music and flashes of lightning, announcing that a goddess wanted to visit the gayest and happiest of all the villages existing on earth. At the same time the horizon was filled with mythical beings with long trumpets heralding the news to all the gods. Then the dawns of all the ages gathered and heaven donned its spring robe.

The goddess appeared but no one could describe her. She was most beautiful! Magically beautiful!

The people from the north of the village, who came there first, were astonished to see that the goddess wore a dress like those their own women wear for fiestas. Suddenly their faces acquired a formidable expression, especially those of the men, for they heard the goddess of the men of the clouds speaking to them in their own language.

Meanwhile the news reached every house. Those who lived toward the south suspected that something extraordinary was happening from the aspect of the heavens. When they heard what it was, they became jubilant, playing their drums, flutes, and tortoise shells.

"There come the men from below, with music!" said those of the center of the town. But by the time they reached the scene of the apparition, the goddess had already returned to the kingdom inhabited by the men of the clouds. The god of thunder announced her arrival to the land of the first inhabitants of the universe, who had fallen to earth from a cloud, singing sweet songs like birds. Their feathers were painted all the colors of the tropics.

When those of the south joined those of the north, they plied them with questions about the goddess. What was she like? How were her eyes? Her hands? Her hair? And they named her Tangu Yuh. goddess of the earth.

The answers they received did not satisfy them. They lamented in song:

> Goddess of the earth; goddess of the earth,
> What would I not give to have seen your eyes?
> What would I not give to have seen your eyes?
> Goddess of the earth!

They returned to their houses disconsolate, and translated their mood into song and dance.

Those of the north also composed a song:

> Celestial goddess, celestial goddess,
> You appeared with the dawn
> On a morning in florescence
> When the flower opens its petals.

Time passed and the people no longer talked of the goddess of the men of the clouds. But one New Year's morning, without anyone expecting it, a voice arose from the center of the village—"Tangu Yuh! Tangu Yuh!"

And the echo of the voice reached all corners of heaven and earth. It reached all ears like divine music. Then all the people from above, below and the center gathered and it was a day of fiesta, of music, of dancing.

Since then Tangu Yuh appears every New Year. And those of the south who model her figure from clay, know that each year the Tangu Yuh that comes from their hands is nearer to perfection. And the old folks say when they achieve perfection, Tangu Yuh will visit them again. Then the people will see and know her.[9]

THE HUNGRY PEASANT, GOD, AND DEATH

From the State of Zacatecas
Recorded by F. T.

Not far from the City of Zacatecas there lived a poor peasant, whose harvest was never sufficient to keep hunger away from himself, his wife and children. Every year his harvests grew worse, his family more numerous. Thus as time passed, the man had less and less to eat for himself, since he sacrificed a part of his own rations on behalf of his wife and children.

One day, tired of so much privation, the peasant stole a chicken with the determination to go far away, very far, to eat it, where no one could see him and expect him to share it. He took a pot and climbed up the most broken side of a nearby mountain. Upon finding a suitable spot, he made a fire, cleaned his chicken, and put it to cook with herbs.

When it was ready, he took the pot off the fire and waited impatiently for it to cool off. As he was about to eat it, he saw a man coming along one of the paths in his direction. The peasant hurriedly hid the pot in the bushes and said to himself, "Curse the luck! Not even here in the mountains is one permitted to eat in peace."

At this moment the stranger approached and greeted, "Good morning, friend!" "May God grant you a good morning," he answered.

"What are you doing here, friend?"

"Well, nothing, Señor, just resting. And, Your Grace, where are you going?"

"Oh, I was just passing by and stopped to see if you could give me something to eat."

"No, Señor, I haven't anything."

"How's that, when you have a fire burning?"

"Oh, this little fire; that's just for warming myself."

"Don't tell me that. Haven't you a pot hidden in the bushes? Even from here I can smell the cooked hen."

"Well yes, Señor, I have some chicken but I shall not give you any; I would not even give any to my own children. I came way up here because for once in my life I wanted to eat my fill. I shall certainly not share my food with you."

"Come friend; don't be unkind. Give me just a little of it!"

"No, Señor, I shall not give you any. In my whole life I have not been able to satisfy my hunger, not even for one day."

"Yes, you will give me some. You refuse because you don't know who I am."

"I shall not give you anything, no matter who you are, I shall not give you anything!"

"Yes, you will as soon as I tell you who I am."

"Well then, who are you?"

"I am God, your Lord."

"Uh, hm, now less than ever shall I share my food with you. You are very bad to the poor. You only give to those whom you like. To some you give haciendas, palaces, trains, carriages, horses; to others, like me, nothing. You have never even given me enough to eat. So I shall not give you any chicken."

God continued arguing with him, but the man would not even give Him a mouthful of broth, so He went His way.

When the peasant was about to eat his chicken, another stranger came along; this one was very thin and pale.

"Good morning, friend!" he said. "Haven't you anything there you can give me to eat?"

"No, Señor, nothing."

"Come, don't be a bad fellow! Give me a little piece of that chicken you're hiding."

"No, Señor, I shall not give you any."

"Oh yes, you will. You refuse me now because you don't know who I am."

"Who can you be? God, Our Lord Himself, just left and not even to Him would I give anything, less to you."

"But you will, when you know who I am."

"All right; tell me then who you are."

"I am Death!"

"You were right. To you I shall give some chicken, because you are just. You, yes, you take away the fat and thin ones, old and young, poor and rich. You make no distinctions nor show any favoritism. To you, yes, I shall give some of my chicken!" [10]

YAQUI TALES AND STORIES

Recorded by Ralph L. Beals

The First People

They say that Cristo Adán made an orchard with many fruits. He left a man and a woman to take care of it. They were naked and the woman had the body of a girl without breasts. They ate the fruits of the orchard, whatever they could find. Cristo prohibited one fruit, the apple, the big one of the Sierra. I can't remember the name of the man and woman. Right away they ate the apple. The woman ate the apple first. "How good this fruit is," she said, "try it." The man bit it and said, "Truly it is good."

The owner, Cristo Adán, came back to the orchard, shouting. These two took fig leaves and made breechclouts. They hid apart from each other and turned their heads away from Cristo when he arrived because they were ashamed. The woman's breasts had begun to come, too. Said Cristo Adán, "You ate the fruit I told you to care for. Now, you are going to have a family."

He gave them a house and some clothes and put them out of the orchard. From them came all the people.

I think this conversation (story) came from before the time of the king (that is, before Spanish times).

The Giant Harvest

A man began to sow. The corn grew and at harvest time it was so big and the ears were so high from the ground, it needed a ladder of three steps to reach them. He made a big pile of the corn and hunted a cart to carry it to his house. After working for a month, he had carried only half of it home. One ear filled his cart.

One day he left his mules in the field to graze. They ate a hole in the squash and went inside to continue eating. The man came and hunted all day to find them. When he found them they were still eating inside the squash. He drove them out with a whip.

Later, on the same ground, he planted onions. They grew so big, he had to cut them in half to get them in his cart. There were twelve arrobas, twenty-five pounds, in one onion.

This story is a local version of the Spanish wonder stories; my Mexican friends occasionally tell similar ones as tall stories. F. T.

Yomomúli

Before, there was a tribe from whom the Yaqui are descended. They knew nothing of God, but among them was a great pole, three spans in diameter, with one end in the earth, the other in heaven. It vibrated as though talking.

At that time all spoke one language, but only Queen Yomomúli could understand the pole. She interpreted that it spoke of a God who made the earth for human beings to live upon. The pole said that the time of the Conquest would come and all would have to be baptized. Many people were angry; only a few said they would receive the benediction. The others said it was not true, that only Yomomúli wished it.

So Yomomúli burned down the stick with a powerful cigarette, rolled up the river under her arm like a carpet, and went away. Those who had not wanted to receive benediction sank into the earth.[11]

The Coyote and the Fox

This story was told to me by a middle-aged Yaqui man, at Vicam Switch, Sonora. The mention of fiesteros, fiestamakers, and the shooting off of firecrackers, are localisms. Otherwise such stories are common in Mexico.

Once upon a time a coyote and a fox were walking together and they came to a lagoon in which the moon was reflected, and the coyote said to the fox, "Brother, what do you see in this tank?"

"It's a cheese, brother," answered the fox. "Let's take it out."

"How can we take it out, when the cheese is in the water?" answered the coyote.

"Well, by drinking the water," said the fox.

Then the coyote said to the fox, "We should never finish then. It would be better if I dived to get it out." Then the coyote threw himself into the water and as he could not go down, he came out again and said to the fox, "Brother, I cannot dive. You would have to tie a stone on to me for me to be able to take it (the cheese) out."

Then the fox said to him, "Yes, it would be better to tie a stone to you so that you could go straight to the bottom."

The coyote then went to the bottom and died and never came out.

But the coyote had a brother, who seeing that he did not return, asked the fox about his brother and the fox said, "Well, there he remained in the water because of trying to get a cheese out and he never came out."

Then the coyote said to the fox, "Well he's gone and will never come back." And they agreed to go on together.

After walking for a long time, they arrived at a place filled with reeds, and the fox in order to get rid of the coyote, said to him, "Brother, you stay here because we are going to have a fiesta in this capital. I'm going to bring the fiesteros and many hens for you to eat. When you hear the noise of fireworks, you begin to dance, and tie something over your eyes. You will not be able to see as there will be so much smoke from the powder."

Then the fox went behind the reeds and set them on fire and when they were burning, they crackled like firecrackers. Then it gave the coyote pleasure to hear the crackling and he said to himself, "Now let brother fox come and bring the hens. I'm going to eat a lot!"

But he did not come and there was nothing more than the noise of the fireworks, which was coming closer. Then the fire reached him. He came jumping out as best he could and he went to look for his brother fox and he found him leaning against and supporting a thick, high wall. "Now without fail, I shall eat you," the coyote said to him.

"No, brother," said the fox, "don't eat me. Look, I'm holding up the sky so that it will not fall down upon us, because if I let it go it will kill us. Stay here in my place so that I can go and bring you the hens." And the coyote stayed to support the wall so that the sky would not fall down.

Seeing that his brother fox did not return, the coyote let go of the wall and went to look for the fox, whom he found inside of a cage. "What are you doing here, brother fox?"

"Well, you see, brother; they have put me in here because they are going to bring me the hens. If you wish to remain here, open the door so that you can come inside and you shall eat the hens for me."

They were already boiling water in a pot to scald the fox. When the coyote saw that they were bringing pots of hot water to throw on him, he said, "Now they are bringing the hens. I'm going to fill myself full!"

When the people saw the coyote instead of the fox, they threw the water anyway, but the fox was free and he ran away.[12]

The Huichol Deluge Legend

This legend, recorded by Carl Lumholz almost fifty years ago, is still related and little arks are still made for votive offerings.

A Huichol was felling trees to clear a field for planting. Every morning he found that the trees he had cut down on the previous day had grown up again. He worried over this and grew tired of working. On the fifth day he came to try once more, determined to find the cause of the disturbance. Soon there rose from the ground in the middle of the clearing an old woman with a staff in her hand. She was Great-grandmother Nakawé, the goddess of earth, who causes vegetation to spring forth from the nether world. But the man did not know her. With her staff she pointed toward the south, north, west, and east, above and below; and all the trees which the young man had cut down immediately stood up again. Then he understood how it happened that his clearing was always covered with trees.

Annoyed, he exclaimed, "Is it you who are undoing my work all the time?" "Yes," she said, "because I want to talk to you." Then she told him that he was working in vain. "A great flood is coming," she said. "It is not more than five days off. There will come a wind, very bitter, and as sharp as chile, which will make you cough. Make a box from the salate tree, as long as your body, and fit it with a good cover. Take with you five grains of corn of each color, and five beans of each color; also take the fire and the five squash-stems to feed it, and take with you a black bitch."

The man did as the woman told him. On the fifth day he had the box ready and placed in it the things she had told him to take. Then he entered with the black bitch, and the old woman put the cover on, and caulked every crack with glue, asking the man to indicate wherever there was an opening. Then when the rains came she seated herself on the top of the box with a macao perched on her shoulder. The box rode on the waters for one year toward the south, for another year toward the north, during the third year toward the west, and in the fourth year toward the east. In the fifth year it rose upward, and all the time the world was filled with water. The next year the flood began to subside, and the box settled on a mountain near Santa Catarina, where it may still be seen.

Then the man took off the cover and saw that all the world was still covered with water. But the macaos and the parrots made valleys with their beaks, and as the waters began to run off, the birds separated them into five seas. Then the land began to dry, and trees and grass sprang forth.

The old woman became wind, but the man resumed clearing his field, as before the deluge. He lived with the bitch in a cave, and in the daytime, while he was in the field, she remained at home. Every afternoon on coming home, he found tortillas ready for him, and he was curious to know who made them. After five days had passed, he hid himself behind the bushes near the cave to watch. He saw the bitch take off her skin and hang it up. Then he noticed that she was a woman, who knelt down by the metate to grind corn. He stealthily approached from behind and quickly caught the skin and threw it into the fire.

"Now you have burned my tunic!" she cried and began to whine like a dog. He bathed her head with water mixed with ground corn that she had prepared, and she felt refreshed, and from that time on she remained a woman. They had a large family and their sons and daughters married. So the world was peopled and the inhabitants lived in caves.

In the Cora version of the same myth, the man is ordered to take along with the other things, the woodpecker, sandpiper, and parrot. He embarked in the middle of the night, when the flood began. As soon as the water had subsided he waited five days and then sent out the sandpiper, in order to see if it was possible to walk on the ground. "Ee-wee-wee!" said the bird when he came back, from which the man understood that the earth was still too wet. He waited five days longer and then sent the woodpecker to see if the trees were hard and dry. The woodpecker thrust his beak deep into the tree and moved his head from side to side to observe the effect. Only with difficulty could he draw out his beak again, as the wood was still very soft. He had to use so much force that he lost his balance and fell to the ground. "Chu-ee, chu-ee!" he exclaimed when he returned.

The man waited again for five days and once more sent out the spotted sandpiper. This time his legs did not sink deep into the mud but he could jump around as he was wont to do, so he reported that now the earth was right again. Then the man came out of the ark, stepping very carefully, and saw that the land was dry and all on a level.

TWO HUICHOL TALES FROM THE SIERRA OF NAYARIT

Recorded by Donald Cordry

1. Why the Hikuli Is So Far Away

(In this story hikuli or peyote is identified with maize or corn.)

Once there was a boy named Ucá, who lived with his mother, Ucaratsi. They had no corn; there was none at all. So the mother said to Ucá, "Go to the men who live nearby and who eat all day long, and get corn."

So the boy went to the Señores and said, "Good-day, good-day! Can you lend me some corn?" But they were not really men, only Sarú or arriero (mule-driver) ants that were very bad. They said, "Take these things—pine chips, grass and ashes, and go to the woman who lives over there and she will give you corn for them."

But Ucá said, "I don't know the way," and the Sarú answered, "We will take you." On the way the boy fell asleep and the Sarú took his eyes away. But he thought in his sleep that the paloma cantadora (singing dove) came and sat on a branch above his head and he said, "I don't know where to go." So the paloma flew up, up high in the air, and said, "Over there is a big house."

Soon Ucá could see a little; the paloma cantadora arranged it. So he went to the house and it was big and white inside and outside, and in it was a woman with her daughters and they were all corn, and all different colors like the corn. The woman said to the first, "Will you go with this boy to his house?" and she said, "No, because they will step on me and I will have to make tortillas and carry water." So the woman said to the second girl, "Will you go with this boy to his house?" and she answered as her sister had. And the mother said the same to the third, and she said she would go.

Then the woman, whose name was Tarawimi, said to Ucá, "You must never make her work in the fields or carry water or make tortillas or carry heavy things."

Five days later the boy had his eyes back and he could see well. So they went to his house and made an altar and put little gourds adorned with beads on it and arrows, and when they looked there sat the girl, Icú, and all around everywhere there was corn and they toasted it all day and were content.

One day the woman, Ucaratsi, said to the girl, "Go carry water," and Ucá said, "No, she can't; her mother said so."

The next day when he was in the field, his mother told the girl to grind corn on the metate. And as she ground the corn, her tears fell, and blood, much blood came from her hands. And she said, "I'm going," so she left.

And when the girl was gone, there was no more corn in the boy's cornfield—none, none, none; none any place, in no house.

Then the girl and her mother and her sisters went far, far away to the Real de Catorce and there they were hikuli. They live there now but they are corn. And we go there many days for hikuli, for it is the corn. And you must always take care of the corn, never step on it, but take care of it.

II. Why the Sun Is So High In the Heavens

In the early times the sun was very near the earth. One day there were many children and one of them said, "Here comes the sun," and another one said, "That isn't the name; I'll name it." He remembered what the turkey said in the mountains and named it "Shoé-pi-tou-tou-tou," and for this reason the Huichols call it "tou."

The sun was sad because it was lonely, and that is why it stayed near the earth. But the sun was so hot that people were burning up. So the boy said, "I'll go up with you, Tou, if you will go up higher in the sky." So the sun went up farther and said, "Is this all right?" But the people said, "No, go up farther still." Five times this was repeated, and each time the sun went up higher in the sky, and the boy went with the sun, and the last time the people said, "The sun is now in the right place."

So this was best for the sun because he had a companion; for the people too, because it was not too hot now on earth.

This is why there are people in the sun and why, too, the Huichols have a god in the sun. Often now the Huichols sacrifice a turkey to the sun, and when it is killed they throw the blood upwards to the sun.[13]

THE ORIGIN OF PEYOTE

Recorded by Nabor Hurtado

When the Huichols of Santa Catarina, Sierra de Nayarit, go on a peyote pilgrimage, they sing every day on the way to their gods and to Titihuitehuame, the musician, the name meaning "bird man." Their chant is in the form of a ballad of which the first verses relate the story of the Prince Jiculi, who became peyote.

A young prince called Jiculi went hunting for deer one day and in the forest he was surrounded by a group of witches who wanted to harm him. With cunning they captured him, and tying his hands and feet, put him into a cage.

The prince was trying in vain to break his bonds, when a plumed lion approached his cage and invited him to pull out one of his beautiful polychrome feathers. But the prince refused to do so in spite of the insistence of the lion, who was really a sorcerer trying to tempt him. If the prince had taken the feather, a great misfortune would have fallen upon him. Roaring with anger, the sorcerer withdrew. At this moment all of the tiyuitehua, singing birds, began to whistle, calling the animals of the forest to come to the rescue of the captive prince. Some mice gnawed the bonds that subjected his hands and feet, while others destroyed the bars of the cage.

Upon being freed, the prince began to flee, but the witches pursued him. The gods permitted him to become a deer so that he might run more swiftly. But the bad witches, transformed into fierce dogs, were gaining on him. And when they were about to surround him— when it seemed that the pack of hounds were about to devour the deer—he disappeared, transformed into a tiny knob-like cactus buried in the earth, which is none other than the peyote.

Thus the gods mocked the witches, and the prince, who was always good to his people, never again took the human form but continues living as the peyote, which does so much good for his people.[14]

TWO ZOQUE SERPENT TALES

Recorded by Donald Cordry in Tuxtla Gutiérrez, Chiapas

1. The Moyó

The Moyó are the thunderbolts that live in caves in the mountains. They are very old but look like little boys of about ten years of age. They carry whips which are really serpents.

Once there was a little boy who was returning from his cornfield. Some one called to him. When he looked up, he saw a Moyó sitting in a tree, who said to him, "Give me my whip!" He asked the little boy to do that for him because he could not fly away without the whip and it is forbidden for a Moyó to touch the ground, so he could not get it himself.

The little boy looked, but instead of a whip he saw a big snake. He was very much frightened and told the Moyó, "That is not a whip; that is a serpent." The Moyó replied, "That is my whip," and he begged and supplicated, "If you will give me the whip, I will clean your field. I shall clean it very well, only don't go there tomorrow, because I will be working."

The little boy procured a long stick, carefully put it under the serpent, and lifted it up to the Moyó. When the Moyó took it in his hand, he disappeared so quickly that the little boy did not know what had happened. When the boy returned to his field, he found that the Moyó had cleaned it thoroughly for him.

II. The Tsahuatsan

The Tsahuatsan is a huge serpent with seven heads that lives in the mountain tops. It does not have a fixed abode, but is driven from place to place by the Moyó or thunderbolts with their serpent whips. When it is in the air, it travels with big clouds and makes a whishing sound. Wherever it falls down, a lake is formed. It usually travels back and forth from Mactumatsá to the Sumidero. When the Moyó drive the Tsahuatsan, a big storm arises.[15]

THE ORIGIN OF MAIZE

Recorded by George M. Foster among the Popolucas of Vera Cruz

Once upon a time there was an old couple who had never had any children. Daily the woman went to the stream to carry water. One day when she went to the stream, she saw in the water an egg. When she returned to her husband she said, "I encountered good fortune." Her husband replied, "What is it?" "An egg," said the old woman. "Come with me to take it out." They went and they arrived. The egg was shown to the old man and he was astonished. He saw it swimming down there. "How are we going to get it out?" he asked. "I am going to take it out with a fish net," said the old woman. She began to try, but was not able to reach it. She did not realize that the egg was on a large rock over the pool in the stream and that what she saw was the reflection. Then the old man looked around and he saw then that the egg was above the rock. "You have been deceived," he said to his wife. "I encountered good fortune," she said. Then the old man climbed up and got the egg. Together they returned with it. "I am going to take care of it," said the woman, and she put it in with her clothing.

After seven days they heard a child cry, and looking in the clothing they found a tiny child with hair golden and soft like the silk of maize. "What did I tell you?" said the old woman. "I encountered good fortune." "We will raise him as our own," replied the old man. Then the boy grew, and after seven days he was already large, and could talk and walk. Then the old woman said, "Ai, my son, go and fetch water." When he arrived at the stream, he was made fun of. Little minnows said, "You are only a little egg taken out of the water with a fish net." "Don't make fun of me," said the boy. He returned home and told his little old grandmother and said, "They made a great deal of fun of me, the minnows." "Don't think anything of it," replied the old woman. "But it makes me very angry that they say that I am an egg taken out of the water with a fish net," said the boy.

The next day, his little old grandmother said to him, "Go and fetch water." "I am not going," said the boy, "because the minnows make fun of me." But he was sent. "You go," said the old woman. When he arrived at the water, they commenced to make fun of him. They said, "You are a little egg taken out of the water with a fish net." When he returned home he said to the old woman, "Make a fishhook for me. I am going to teach them a lesson for making fun of me." The next time he went to the water he took his fishhook. He arrived where the minnows were and said to them, "Now I am going to teach you a lesson for making fun of me." He commenced to take them out and put them in a sombrero. Then he returned with them to the house. "Didn't I tell you," he said to the old woman, "that I was going to take them out of the water?" The old woman said, "Ai, you, son. Why do you jest! You will have to put them back." Again he returned with them to the water, but before putting them back he warned them against making fun of him, and told them that from that time they would be sought by the rest of mankind to be eaten.

Then he returned to where the old woman was. One day he went to the cornfield with his foster-parents, and upon arriving there, the thrushes began to shout, "You are a little egg. You are a little egg." "The thrushes are mocking me," he said to the old woman. "Don't let it worry you," she replied. "I don't like to be mocked," said the boy. "Grandfather, make me a bow and arrow." His grandfather did not know that he wanted to shoot thrushes. The boy did not know that the thrush was indeed the chicken of his old grandmother. Then he killed a great many thrushes and the old woman appeared at the place where he killed them. She commenced to scold him, saying, "Now, you will have to revive these thrushes." The boy replied, "I killed them because they mocked me." Then he commenced to revive them, and said to them, "Never mock me," and he threw them up into a tree.

The boy did many other things he was not supposed to do. The old woman said "You do many bad things. You do not listen. Many times you are told not to do something which you immediately do again." Later she said to her husband, "We will have to eat our son. We will eat him. Now we will tell him to climb to the tapanco. Then when night comes we will drink his blood." The boy went up to sleep but he knew they were going to kill him. Up above he talked with a bat. "When my little old grandfather climbs up, cut his throat." Then he went up to the ridge of the roof. When the hour arrived the old woman said, "Our son sleeps." "He sleeps," said the old man. Then he went up to where he thought the boy was, but the boy was outside on the ridge of the roof. The bat came down and cut the throat of the old man. The old woman heard many drops of blood falling, tasted it, and said, "The blood of our son does not taste good." Then she said to the old man, "Why don't you talk? You have the best part (the flesh) and I am down here drinking something that is no good. Don't be stingy. Bring him down so that we can eat him together. The two of us raised him together, and it's not right that you should eat him alone." Then she saw that the old man didn't speak. She went to look and found him dead. It was his blood that she was drinking. And the old woman was very much annoyed because her husband had been killed. "Ai, you, son, why did you kill your little old grandfather? Now I am going to eat you." The boy went far away, but she followed him. He looked behind and saw his grandmother who called out, "Stop, let's talk things over."

"Let me alone," said the boy, "for I am very strong and able to destroy you. I am the one who is going to give food to all mankind." But since the old woman continued to follow him he climbed a tree in the middle of a savanna beside the shore, and from there he saw that the ground all around him was burning. "Don't eat me, for if you try to do it you will be burned." The old woman did not know that she was going to be burned. While she looked, the boy escaped through the flames which were drawing near. Then she looked and saw that the boy was not there, and she commenced to cry in a loud voice, "Ai, son, why are you going to burn me?" The boy went away and the old woman remained there in the enchanted place, for such it was, where she was burned to death.

Free of all danger, the boy went on his way. On arriving at the shore of the ocean he began to beat on his drum. Hurricane heard him and said "Who knows who is drumming there?" He sent a man to find out, saying, "Go and ask the name of the one who is drumming there." When the man came to the boy, he said, "I have come to see you. Tell me your name." The boy replied, "I am he who sprouts at the knees. I am he who flowers. This is what you shall say." The man returned to Hurricane and said, "He did not tell me his name."

"Return to him," said Hurricane. "Tell him that he must tell you his name." The man returned and said to the boy, "I came to ask you your name. You must tell me because Hurricane wishes to know." Then the boy replied, "Very well. My name is Homshuk. Tell him that I am the one who is shelled, and the one who is eaten." The man returned to Hurricane and reported, "He told me that his name is Homshuk, that it is he who sprouts at the knees and gives fruit." Hurricane answered, "He didn't tell you his real name. He is a nagual."

Then the boy spoke to a tarantula. "Build me a house," he said, "because it is going to rain very hard. Hurricane is going to send a heavy rainstorm and I will need protection." The tarantula did as requested. That night the rain poured down in torrents, but in the morning when Hurricane's men came, the boy was still on the shore, drumming. He had not been harmed. Hurricane said, "He is a nagual."

Then a tortoise came to Homshuk and asked, "What are you doing, uncle?" Homshuk said, "Well, here I am, uncle, drumming. I want to cross the ocean, and if you are a good fellow you will take me." Said the tortoise, "I will take you." "You are not going to deceive me?" asked Homshuk. "I am not going to deceive you," replied the tortoise. "Run along and and try and see if you are able to swim well," said Homshuk, and the tortoise showed that he was a good swimmer. "I am going to climb up on your back," said Homshuk. After he had swum only a short distance the tortoise shouted, "Ai, uncle, my chest is being broken." Said Homshuk, "Didn't I tell you that you were not big enough to bear my weight?" And then he came back to the shore. This type of tortoise has since been known as pecho quebrado (broken chest). Presently another much larger tortoise arrived and it asked, "What are you doing, uncle?" Homshuk replied, "Well, here I am drumming. If you are a good fellow you will carry me to the other side of the ocean. If you do this I will give you colors such as none other of your species has." "Well, if you do that," said the tortoise, "I will carry you." Immediately the boy painted the tortoise, then climbed on his shell, and was carried across the ocean to where Hurricane was. Ever since, this type of tortoise has been brightly colored.

"What are you looking for?" said Hurricane, and ordered him taken prisoner. In the land of Hurricane there were different kinds of jails: one in which there were hungry tigers, another in which there were many famished serpents, and still another in which there were arrows in constant flight. Then Homshuk was ordered placed in the jail where there were serpents. "You are a nagual," Hurricane said. "Here you are going to be eaten." But in the morning when they appeared, he was seated on a serpent. He had not been eaten. And the other serpents had disappeared, for Homshuk had said to them when he was locked up, "You shouldn't harm me, for I am a strong man, and it is essential that I live in order to give food to mankind. Moreover, you are supposed to live in the forests and the mountains."

The next night he was placed in the jail with the tigers, and he told them the same thing that he had told the serpents, keeping only the largest to serve as his chair. When Hurricane saw what had happened, he said, "This time we are going to put you where there are arrows," and he was put there so that he would die. Homshuk said to the arrows, "Don't harm me. You are to aid in the defense of man, and to help in the hunting." Then they all fell to the ground and he gathered them in a bundle, on which he sat. On the following day Hurricane saw that the boy was not dead, and he said, "That is a nagual." Then he pondered, and finally said, "We won't be able to kill him this way, but since he is a nagual, he can't continue to live amongst us." "I am not a nagual," replied Homshuk. "I am a good fellow and will be the source of food for all mankind. You should not try to kill me."

"We will have a competition, and if you win, you can live here. If you lose, you must die." "And what is this competition?" asked the boy. "Well, it's a question of who can throw a stone from here to the other side of the ocean," explained Hurricane. "Well, I don't know how to throw," said the boy. "But before trying I would like to get my own stones." So the boy went into the woods and called out for the Woodpecker and said to him, "I am in danger. If you don't aid me Hurricane will kill me." "What do you want of me?" asked Woodpecker. "Well, I want you to go to the other side of the ocean, and when I throw a stone you must begin to peck on a tree so that Hurricane will believe it is the sound of my stones against the tree." The boy returned. "You were very slow," said Hurricane. "Moreover, it appears that you didn't bring any stones." The boy threw the first stone, and after a little time they heard from far off, "tra-tra-tra," (which was only the sound produced by the bird). "Do you hear?" asked the boy. "My stone arrived on the other side, and with so much force that it goes bouncing from one tree to another. Now it's your turn." Hurricane threw his rock with all his strength, but when after several hours they heard no noise, he was declared vanquished.

But Hurricane was not able to get the idea of killing the boy out of his head, and after talking it over with his people he ordered a gigantic hammock placed between two large trees on the shore of the ocean. This done he said to the boy, "Are you staying here or are you crossing the ocean? My family and I are going to the other side.

If you care to come, it is very easy to cross with this hammock." The boy knew the intentions of Hurricane, but he knew he was safe, so he said, "Very well, I'll go with you." "Then climb into the hammock," said Hurricane, and he commenced to swing it until it was going as fast as possible and swung far out over the ocean. Believing that Homshuk had fallen into the ocean, Hurricane stopped the hammock, and out jumped the boy.

"Yes," he said. "It's really a very good way to cross the ocean, for I arrived half way over. I didn't go to the other side because I didn't know where you were planning to go. Therefore, it will be better if you go first and then I will follow." "Very well, all of us will go first," said the people of Hurricane, and they climbed into the hammock after him. Meanwhile Homshuk called to a Tuza (gopher) and said, "Señor Tuza, I want you to cut the roots of these trees very rapidly," and Tuza went off to do his task. "Ready?" asked Homshuk. "Yes," they all replied, and he began to swing the hammock. When it reached its greatest swing, Tuza cut the last root, and the hammock and trees fell in the ocean. All of the people were killed, but Hurricane alone miraculously managed to escape, though with a fractured leg, since he had fallen from a great height. Upon arriving at the shore, he begged, "Give me pardon. Now I know who you are." "Well, what are you going to offer me?" asked the boy. "When you are dry," replied Hurricane, "I can water your head." And since during the months of June and July there was not enough water for Homshuk to grow, he agreed to this. And since that time, Hurricane has watered the milpas during these months so that man can have maize to eat.

SERPENT BELIEFS AND STORIES

The serpent figured prominently in the highest of the pre-Conquest civilizations. One finds serpent motifs in the sculptures of idols and on monuments from Yucatán to the Central Plateau. They were used for the purpose of impressing the people with their gods as well as for decoration. Huitzilipochtli, the Aztec War God, wore a girdle of gold snakes in one of his representations, while the statue of his mother, Coatlicue, is a composition of vicious snakes.

Serpent beliefs still persist in all the primitive and isolated groups with which we are already acquainted, from the Mayas to the most northern ones. A very common belief is about a supernatural horned serpent, chiefly connected with springs, floods, torrential rains, and indirectly also with crops. The Yaquis and Mayos of Sonora believe horned water serpents live in mountain springs, for which reason they never go dry. When the serpents leave them, they go to the sea, causing floods which are necessary to their crops.

But when the floods become dangerous, then the water serpent must be stopped. This is done by Suawaka, a fat, naked dwarf, about a yard in height. He shoots the water serpent, thus ending the floods or the too-heavy rains. The thunder is the twanging of his bow string—according to the more sophisticated Mayos, the sound of his rifle—and the rainbow in the sky is his bow. Suawaka is also called Juan by the Mayos, who make it clear that he has no connection with San Juan.

The Mayos have Christianized their serpent beliefs a little. They say the water serpents are condemned souls which live in the ocean for a hundred years after they leave the springs, where they constantly increase in size. When the hundred years have expired, they are pardoned by God. Some of the Mayos say that formerly illegitimate children were thrown into the springs to the water serpent.

The Yaquis and the Mayos call the water serpent bakot in Cahita. They say it is black and has horns like those of a mountain goat. Some of the Yaquis confuse it with the serpent of a Spanish folktale about a king who was forced to feed his daughters to a serpent. The serpent appears in the form of the intense local cyclonic rainstorms or "waterspouts."

The Yaquis believe that men can become pascola dancers, musicians, and vaqueros or cowboys by going to a cave guarded by a serpent, through whose mouth they have to pass to enter it. Afterwards they have to go through tests of being licked by serpents who wind themselves around them. If they show fear, they are transformed into animals; if they are brave, the snake congratulates them and they are set free as experts in whichever art they have chosen.

There are serpent beliefs among practically all the Oaxaca tribes. The Mixe around Zempaltepec also believe in a horned water serpent that lives in the springs and is associated with heavy rains and floods. It has two horns, like those of a deer, each with seven points, with a back marked with red and green stripes interwoven like a petate. (There are small snakes with those markings in that region.) The men fear to swim in those pools because the water serpent will hold them under the water.

The Mixe of Tepuztepec make offerings, at the serpent springs, of tamales and tepache; also of the blood of turkeys and hens when they gather the first ears of corn. Double ears of corn saved from the previous harvest, and seeds of everything that has been planted, are left at the springs when a man prays for good crops, saying, "Give us corn, beans, squash," and whatever else he may wish to plant.

The Zapotecs in the mountains near Villa Alta believe the waterspout to be a water serpent which is destroyed by lightning. Both the water serpent and lightning are forms which may be assumed by their wizards and priest "advocates."

There is no doubt that the serpent beliefs are ancient, particularly when they are connected with rain and crops, since one of the manifestations of Quetzalcoatl, an important agricultural deity, is in the form of a plumed serpent.[16]

THE LEGEND OF AGUSTIN LORENZO

Recorded by William P. Spratling

We have already met Agustín Lorenzo in the role of the bandit hero of the carnival drama at Huejotzingo.

Mr. Spratling, whose home has been in Taxco for a long time, had heard about Agustín Lorenzo from Pancho, a native of Tlamacuzapa, the tiny village in the wilds of the State of Guerrero, where the bandit was born. One day Mr. Spratling decided to visit it in order to hear the entire story. There he met Don Huisache, one of the patriarchs who could speak Spanish as well as Mexicano, who told him the following tale. F. T.

Our little Agustín was born just above this house. He was still much under fifteen years old when he was carrying the daily gorditas to his grandfather. This little grandfather of his was a peon on the hacienda of Zapacualco, down in Tierra Caliente. The five leagues there and five leagues back he walked alone every day, every day.

One day he arrived there to find his little grandfather bruised and bleeding outside the hacienda gates. The Señor Mayordomo had had him whipped. Resentment and a deep pain moved in the breast of Agustín Lorenzo. He said that he was a man now and that he was going to take his grandfather home on his back. But the grandfather would not let him, saying that it was better that he stay and work. But not so Agustín. He finally said that the little grandfather could stay if he liked but that he, for his part, must dedicate himself to settling accounts.

That day on the long trail back to Tlamacuzapa, Agustín Lorenzo found a little snake. It was dead, cut in two among the sharp rocks on the path. And Agustín Lorenzo sat down and wept for it. He took the little snake in his hands and spoke to it. And then he took leaves of palm, the cojollo, and split them and wove a little casing, a sort of little serpent of palm. It was like those toys from Tlamacuzapa which you find of a Sunday in the market. He slipped it over the wounded parts of the animal. And he caressed the snake, and the little animal came alive and he finally left him, moving off into the under-brush.

Eight days later when Agustín was passing the same spot, he found a fine old man on a black mule. "Sweet Child, where do you go?" he said. "I must talk with you." And Agustín said, "What, then?"

The old man said it was about his work for which he owed him. "But," said Agustín, "I have not worked yet." "But was it not you who revived the life of a little snake a week ago?" And Agustín said, "Well, yes, Señor." "Well then," said the old man, "that was my son, and I owe you his life." "I ask nothing for that," said the boy.

But the old man said he could have anything that might please him. "Then," said Agustín, "let it be revenge, for that is what I desire more than money . . . and if I only had a horse!" "I will give you a horse," said the old man, "and you must only do as I say."

They had been walking through the forest when suddenly there appeared the palace of the old man. The palace was as fine, said old Huisache, as the hardware store in Iguala, with shining aluminum pans and victrola records and beautiful machetes of all descriptions in the windows.

The old man went into the palace and came out with five silver pesos, which he placed in the hands of Agustín Lorenzo. "With this money you must buy twenty reales worth of pulque, a little pano-chita (brown sugar) to put in the pulque, and petates of palm leaves. With the petates you must cover well the walls of your house so that no one may see in. For there you must keep and care for the horse." And then he embraced him and told him that in a week he would be a man; that for the moment he must go home and prepare his house and buy the pulque for the horse; that in three days time he should come back and he would give him a horse.

When Agustín went back three days later, there was the old man, and he gave him a horse the size of a cat. "Take this horse," he said, "beneath your blouse and let no one see him. Take him to your house and guard him well, but remember to feed him only pulque with panochita. In four days you will be a man and the horse will be fit to carry you."

And then the old man gave him a saddle of snake skin, all trimmed with silver, and a quirt of a coral snake, and trappings of zilcuate, another kind of snake. And he said, "Prepare yourself. Take this pencil; it is mine and knows well how to write. With it you must write a letter to the mayordomo, who beat your little grand-father. With this pencil you will need neither pen nor ink nor schooling."

And so it was. The horse in one week became a great white mare, and Agustín saddled her, and he wrote a letter to the mayordomo, and then he mounted the white horse and he rode down to the gates of the hacienda.

"Who are you?" said the mayordomo. "It doesn't matter," said Agustín Lorenzo, "here is a letter." "You will have to wait until I have eaten," said the mayordomo. "But no," said Agustin Lorenzo, "you cannot play thus with me; take the letter." And the mayordomo took it and began to open it; and when he was opening it Agustín, with one mighty cut of his quirt, opened his face. And the mayordomo fell down dead.

Then the federals who were in the hacienda wanted to shoot Agustín Lorenzo, but the balls did not enter, and his white mare was off the ground in two great leaps and was flying through pure air.

They sent to tell the government and the government moved itself. There were two thousand men and they pursued him into these mountains. But not one of the federals returned. And Agustín got his men together and they took a vast load of silver away from the government at Iguala. And later they took much more and they stored it safely in the caves of the canyon of Tepetlapa.

Then Agustín Lorenzo gathered all the old men of Tlamacuzapa and he explained to them that the silver was for their people and that he put the silver in their care; that they should never touch it until there was great need.

("And, señor," said Don Huisache, "we have never had to even touch it! Seven men, carrying the silver steadily for seven years would not be able to take it all out; but still we must guard the secret.")

There were years and years and years when the federals sought to vanquish Agustín Lorenzo. It was a constant war and the government was constantly in the wrong. Agustín Lorenzo's was a charmed life. The states of Puebla, Oaxaca, Morelos, Mexico, and Michoacán were the scenes of innumerable exploits. Guerrero was his own land, and Tlamacuzapa, his house.

The charm never failed. He came and went as he pleased. If he was alone, with the federals closing in on him, he would reshoe his horses with the shoes backwards, so that when he was going they thought he was coming. He had caves from one side of the country to the other. His caves communicated from Tlamacuzapa to Iguala, and from Huitztac to Teloloapan. And now there is no one who even knows the entrances!

Some say that at last he was betrayed; that the government paid a poor devil to join the forces of Agustín Lorenzo and then to stab him. But no one here believes that, because he is not dead. Too many of us here in Tlamacuzapa have heard the hoofs of his horse in the night.

And certainly Agustín Lorenzo was never betrayed by the poor. He loved the poor and he defended them all his life.

What the federals really did was to send a girl, and certain it was that they paid her well. They dressed her with much silk, like those women of the capital. She was blonde, something Agustín Lorenzo had never known. And she went and offered herself to Agustín Lorenzo, saying she hoped to please him. And so he took her with him to a little hut he had in the mountains, a little house of adobe with a roof of palm. And he locked the door. And then they were both pleased enough. And Agustín slept. And while he slept, this girl unlocked the door and went out, and then they locked the door from the other side. The federals were on all sides of the house, and they set fire to it. And then while they waited for him to burn to death, Agustín Lorenzo came through the burning roof in one leap and with his machete killed three thousand federals before they could manage to tie him.

They took him to Mexico and there in one of the palaces of the government they took the lead out of his body. And there were seven quarts of lead of bala-de-onza which they took out. But Agustín Lorenzo still lived and his horse was there waiting for him in the patio, and he leaped from the window of the hospital on to the horse's back and his horse flew off with him. . . . Sí Señor.

After a pause Don Huisache goes on to add, as though it might have occurred to me to doubt his words, that the seven quarts of lead which were taken from his body were used to make a big cross, the same great crucifix which they have there in the church at San Juan de Dios. "But," I remarked, "the cross I saw there was of gold, not lead." "That, of course, is true," said Don Huisache. "It was turned gold while I was still a boy. Agustín Lorenzo himself did that." [17]

LEGENDS ABOUT PANCHO VILLA

Recorded by José Montes de Oca

The folk love strong, daring men, so they invent beautiful legends and ballads about their bandits, celebrating their prowess and goodness of heart. Pancho Villa has much in common with Agustín Lorenzo, but he was a greater personage; he belongs to the world as well as to the people. During the Social Revolution of 1910–20 he became internationally known. He is, perhaps, the most famous guerrilla of the Americas.

Pancho was the illegitimate son of a rich hacendado in the Municipality of San Juan del Río, Durango. His father would not acknowledge him, so his mother gave him to a peasant, whom he called abuelo, grandfather. As a boy he worked in the fields, roamed the hills, and learned about animals and men. He attended school only eight days of his life.

Doroteo Arango, which was Pancho's name during the first twenty years of his life, began to gamble and steal at an early age, but did not drink. He was physically strong, fearless, cruel, and fond of women. Once he was caught by the police and sentenced to death for robbery. An influential person interceded for him, and he was freed on condition that he join the government soldiers in quelling an uprising of natives in Los Mochis. It did not take him long to distinguish himself for valor and to attract a group of his own kind of men who were willing to serve him. During that time, Francisco Villa, one of the bravest soldiers of the group, was killed. Someone jokingly suggested that his memory be kept alive by one of them taking his name. Doroteo immediately adopted it for himself and punished anyone for calling him anything else. A woman was impaled for doing so, and one man was burned alive.

Villa began as a simple soldier in the ranks of the Maderistas in 1910 and continued fighting on the side of the people. Later he became Chief of the Division of the North. He did not surround himself by a staff, but with a group of daredevils, called los Dorados, willing to follow him blindly and to face death every moment. After he gained fame and prestige, some of the finest and most cultured of the Mexican revolutionaries joined his ranks, among them General Felipe Ángeles, and they all admired him as a leader. When General Álvaro Obregón became President in 1920, Villa surrendered to his government.

When the general sent by Obregón wanted to treat with him in private, Villa said he had no secrets from his people. Thus the rendition pact was signed out of doors in the middle of the street, and Villa said to his men, "From now on I do not wish to kill any more of my brothers. I want to be an honorable man and to serve my country in another form. Come, boys, let us go to Canutillo to till the soil." And Villa would not accept the offer of General Martinez to be taken in a special train to the hacienda the Federal Government had given him. In 1923, he was assassinated there. No one knows by whom, but there were rumors that the Government did not trust him completely.

For the people Pancho Villa goes on living. They never tire of telling stories about that burly, swaggering man, who always wore a wide-brimmed sombrero and a belt full of cartridges and pistols. He was kind to the poor, always willing to listen to them and give them money, but he never forgave treason and often killed just for the sport of it. On one occasion he sat down at a table with five pistols on it and offered freedom to a group of prisoners if they could scale a wall before he shot them. The pistols kept functioning one after another and not one man escaped. A favorite game of his and his Dorados was to throw a loaded pistol into the air over a cantina table surrounded by men, to see whom the bullet would hit.

It is said that Villa's hatred for the landowners began when he learned that one of them had violated his sister. Villa persecuted him and made him marry her. At the happiest and gayest moment of the wedding feast, he ordered the bridegroom to measure his length and to dig a ditch into which he would fit. The bride knew what was going to happen, wept and begged, but her husband was not spared.

To the simple folk Pancho Villa was a supernatural being, an avenging god, both good and evil, and they find an explanation for his being as he was in the following legend.

Villa Sells His Soul to the Devil

North of San Juan del Río, in front of the Rancho Menores de Abajo, there is a natural eminence in the form of a coffer, where the young men of the region go when they begin an active life, and the legend is that they return completely transformed. The reason is, the old women assure us, that the interior of that hill is occupied by wizards, witches, sorcerers, and the devil himself, and they promise their souls to the devil at death in return for the power they most desire, which they receive by imbibing a powerful fusion of a marvelous herb. It is because of this that this part of the country boasts of the best gamblers, the most daring horsemen, fortunate lovers, invincible fighters, and the most prosperous merchants.

Villa also entered the entrails of this hill and made a pact with the devil. What he wanted for the rest of his life in exchange for his soul was to be brave and to be able to dominate people. Those who saw him say that when he returned to his hut he was completely changed —his glance had acquired the sharpness of an eagle, his strength was enormous, his cunning incomparable, and his power over men unique. All the young men obeyed him, and his influence over them was such that they became his slaves.

One of his intimate friends related what happened in the depths of the hill. There were many deformed animals living in caverns strung with precious stones and walled with purest gold. The heat from an intense fire filled every crevice. The devil was accompanied by military men, popes, cardinals, kings, gay women, wise men, and groups of individuals belonging to every race, who sang and laughed madly. Villa was not frightened by this strange spectacle, and was able to free himself from the dogs of seven colors and the spotted goats that tried to detain him. He was perfectly calm when making his pact with Satan, and was granted his wish. He was applauded, and when he left the place, his soul was weeping in a dark corner.

After that time Pancho Villa venerated the Hill of the Coffer. In order to be able to enter the Castle that is within its heights, one must not wear a rosary nor any other relic of a saint, nor think of God. It is necessary to blaspheme, curse, and become a renegade of the Holy Trinity.

Villa's Horse Lucifer

Lino Maturino, who lived in San Juan del Río and became a Villista, had a marvelous horse, the devil himself, the people said. He could smell an enemy and would awaken the soldiers with his snout, at the same time bringing them their saddles and arms. In battles he would dodge the bullets, look for safe places for the protection of his master, avoid ambush, and perform miracles in escaping in the face of defeat.

In the temporary encampments, he would hunt for chickens, steal eggs, round up the horses, and push open the doors of the huts of the women who made the tortillas and provided food.

When a certain Carrancista officer heard about the stupendous qualities of the horse, he tried to secure it for himself, sending a message to the owner that he would give him any horse he wanted in exchange and fifty pesos in cash. But his messenger failed to induce the owner to part with it. When he died, the devil-horse went to another Villista, who made a present of it to Pancho Villa. And that was the horse that Villa preferred to ride ever after.

Villa was always generous with his men. When he was in a good humor and felt like talking, he would gather around him those he liked best, and give them advice, "Always consider yourselves great; never permit anyone to humiliate you. When you are provoked, defend yourselves. Fight for justice and be men!" [18]

Emiliano Zapata Lives

Emiliano Zapata, the peasant Caudillo of Morelos, also became famous in the Revolution of 1910–20 for his fight for "Land and

Liberty." His soldiers were recruited mostly from among the peones of the haciendas of the State, and together they fought a war of vengeance against their owners whom they never forgave for the bad treatment they had received. They left practically every big estate in ruins.

Zapata had similar qualities to those of both Agustín Lorenzo and Villa. Like the former he loved ostentation, and like the latter he was illiterate and cruel. But although he was stern and pitiless, he succeeded in winning the devotion of all the humble people of the region, men, women and children.

On April 10, 1919, Zapata was betrayed and killed by the ex-federal Colonel Jesús Guajardo, who made him believe that he was coming over to his side with his men. When they arrived at Zapata's camp at San Juan Chinameca, he came out to welcome and review the new adherents, and they shot him.

Many of the folk who loved Zapata and believed he was going to be their liberator, do not believe he is dead. They say he is only asleep and will return one day to save his people; that often in the night they hear his horse's hoofs as he gallops through the villages, over the mountains or through the ravines, and some have even seen him on his favorite white horse El Relámpago, "Lightning." One old Zapatista soldadera said he will appear to those who did not betray him and that he will not kill the traitors but simply spit in their faces.[19]

LEGENDS OF THE TEPOZTECATL

Recorded in Tepoztlán, Morelos

On the highest one of the cliffs surrounding the village of Tepoztlán stands the pyramid dedicated to Ome Tochtli, or the Tepoztecatl, by which name it is known and from which the place derives its name. The structure itself is a small one, but because of its situation, it dominates the countryside, affording stupendous views.

At the foot of the hill of the pyramid, about two hundred feet below, lies the village, a lovely garden spot, with streams flowing around its edges, and fruit trees and flowers around every hut. The descendants of the builders of the temple, the Tlahuica, still live there, a simple agricultural folk, preserving the language and customs of their ancestors.

According to the early chronicles, the Tepoztecatl was the most prominent of the four hundred pulque gods, also connected with agriculture, for whom the Tlahuica had great veneration.

In one legend the Tepoztecatl is mentioned as having helped to develop the pulque as it is known today, which was invented by a woman and a man when the Aztecs were still in the caves of Tamoan-chan. Mayuel, the woman, scraped the magueys and extracted the juice and the man, Pantecatl, found the roots necessary for fermenting it. Mayuel became the goddess of the plants and was the mother of the pulque gods.

Red and black predominate in the colors with which the Tepozte-catl is painted, and one of his insignia is a copper hatchet. In the text describing the figure in the "Codice de Florencia," it says that when a Tepozteco died of drunkenness, all the rest of the men of the village took part in a big fiesta with copper hatchets in their hands.

According to the early Christian chroniclers and the codices, the Tepoztecatl was very ugly and a god of drunkards, but to the people of Tepoztlán, he is a hero, brave, strong and good, who defended the village from its enemies single-handed. The legends about him relate that he was born of a virgin, and he is confused with the son of the Virgin Patroness of the village.

Their fiestas are celebrated on the same day, the eighth of September, but that of the Tepozteco is held completely away from the church. A high wooden platform is set up on the plaza, called "The Castle," to represent the temple on the hill, and one of the older men of the place plays the part of the Tepoztecatl, dressed with his adornments. The chiefs of Cuernavaca and Yautepec and of other nearby villages approach the castle in the night on horseback to attack the Tepoztecatl. There is a simple dialogue in Nahuatl in which he speaks of himself as the Son of the Virgin Mary. After he has driven his enemies away, he does a sort of victory dance to the music of the Teponaxtli drum and flute, the instruments of the legend.

A similar but a much more dramatic representation is given privately atop the hill on the pyramid, and on occasions fowl are sacrificed, so his pagan origin is not forgotten. At one time when the village was suffering from a long period of drought, the Virgin, with the Tepozte-catl in her arms, appeared to one of the most active of the women of the church in a dream and told her if the people would give her a new robe and the Tepoztecatl a fiesta on the cliff opposite to the one of the pyramid, it would rain. The robe was furnished, and, taking advantage of the absence of the priest, the Tepoztecans climbed the hill with food and music and offerings for the Tepoztecatl. It rained.

1. Related By a Young Tepoztecan Peasant

There were three princesses. Those three princesses were cared for by a little old woman. Every day they used to go to bathe in a spring.

One day they found there a little clay doll, and one of them through curiosity picked it up. It disappeared from her hands, and a little later that same day she gave birth to a boy.

In order not to dishonor the mother and the old man, they thought of killing the boy. They threw him into a maguey so that its thorns might kill him. When they returned after a while to see what had happened they found him alive. So they threw him onto an anthill and went away. They came back later and found that the ants, instead of biting the baby, were adorning him with the little flowers growing around them. The princesses then threw him into a spring, expecting him to drown. But their third attempt failed, for again they found the child alive and unharmed. Finally they abandoned him.

Just then an old man came along and saw the abandoned child. What he did with a good conscience was to pick him up and adopt him. With that family he grew up a very intelligent boy. The old man seeing that the boy was enthusiastic about everything, first made him a little bow and arrow. Whenever the boy went out hunting with it, he was sure to bring home some bird; his shots never failed. When the child noticed that others were wearing sandals, he obliged his grandfather to make him a pair. He cut them out from a rabbit skin. The old folks were very fond of the boy. They rejoiced that so small a child was able to maintain them.

Thus time passed, but their happiness was soon disturbed. Not far away there lived a giant whose name was Xochicalcatl, whose custom it was to eat old people. He had seen the old couple who were bringing up the boy, and it was the turn of the old man to be eaten. How sad they were! The boy comforted the old man in his sweet childish way, "Do not fear, dear little grandfather. I shall go in your place." But he only answered sadly, "No, my son, you are too young and cannot satisfy his hunger. I am old anyway and it is fitting that I should die."

The boy followed his whim. Before the time came for them to take away the old man, he went out into the country and said, "I shall pass through this hill in order to see if I can pass through the giant's belly." And, indeed, he was able to pass easily from one side through to the other of that hill, called Cuicuizacatlán. Then the boy went home contented.

When the time came for the old grandfather to leave, the boy told him to hide; that afterwards they would take him instead; that he should be watching in the direction of Cuernavaca. A cloud would appear in the heavens as a sign for him. If it remained white, it would mean that his son was still alive; if it turned black, he would already be dead. With these hopes, he took leave of his grandfather.

Just then came the troops of the giant. They could not find the old man, so took the boy. As they were leaving the house, he grabbed his bag and went with them. On the way he kept on gathering little pieces of glass of which there were many on the road.

Finally they brought the boy into the presence of the big giant, who, gesticulating, said to him, "You will not satisfy me for a mouthful." Every time an old man came, it was customary to throw him into a vessel of boiling water in order to be able to eat him. But as the boy was small and tender, he snatched him as he was and threw him into his mouth.

The boy did not permit the giant to chew him, but went straight into his stomach. Once there, he began to carry out his evil intentions. He took the pieces of glass which he had in his bag and began cutting the giant's intestines. When the giant felt the pain, he said, "I'm still hungry. My stomach is burning. He does not satisfy me. It is necessary to bring me someone else, but at once!"

The soldiers went to carry out his orders. Every moment the giant felt his pain increasing. He fell into a faint and finally died.

In a little while the boy came out of the giant's stomach. When the soldiers returned they found the giant already a corpse with his stomach open. They permitted the victim they were bringing to escape and went in pursuit of the boy who had gone in the direction of Cuernavaca.

The grandfather was constantly watching to see if his son was still alive. He kept looking at the cloud which the boy told him about at parting, and it remained white as when it first appeared, the sign that his little boy was still alive.

In Cuernavaca the boy came upon a little feast. He heard the sound of the war drum called the teponaxtli and the flute called the chirimía. He was greatly attracted by the music and went to see what the instruments were like. He approached the boys who were playing and asked them to let him play, but they refused. The boy, however, was so enchanted with the instruments that he ordered a storm to throw sand into their eyes. Taking advantage of their being blinded, he grabbed the drum and chirimía and went off with them. When they were able to open their eyes again, they heard the drum sounding in the distance and at once began pursuing the boy. When he saw that they were near, he urinated and thus formed the gorge which now crosses Cuernavaca. This gave him time to get farther away.

Then the boy came to another fiesta, where he saw many gentlemen at a banquet table. As he was very hungry and knew that they were accustomed to eat tamales and green *mole* at these feasts, he wanted to enter to see if they would give him some. Upon seeing the boy in rags, they drove him away. He left, but stimulated by his hunger he began thinking that they might admit him to the banquet if he were well dressed, so he went to borrow a suit. When he returned to the gathering in a good suit, they received him with pleasure. After eating he left without thanking them. They deserved no thanks for admitting a rich boy and refusing a poor one.

Later the boy took possession of the highest hills surrounding Tepoztlán. Meanwhile, his pursuers from many villages kept on his trail and finally gathered below to fight him. In the end the Tepoztecal triumphed because of having taken possession of his hill, from which they could not get him down. They became disgusted and left him alone.

This Tepoztecal, who was the greatest Cacique of Tepoztlán and whom everybody obeyed, had no faith in the Christian doctrine. At that time they venerated an idol called Ome Tochtli. As the Tepozteco was the strongest of all his companions, he was sent on a commission to Mexico City. While there, he was captured and baptized so that he might believe in God. He returned to his village with a new faith, and became attached to the Virgin of the Nativity, patroness of Tepoztlán, whose fiesta is celebrated on the eighth of September.

As the Tepozteco became widely known, they sent for him again from Mexico City, when they were building the cathedral. The most expert of the engineers believed that he could help them place the bells and the stone to close the cupola. The Tepozteco, being distrustful and fearing that they were going to do something else to him, did not wish to go.

Finally he went because they sent a commission to urge him. He was received with honors by the wealthiest people of Mexico City. Afterwards they told him what it was all about. He did not wish to compromise himself, but the wealthy finally convinced him. They offered him much money at interest, but he did not care for money. What he told them was this, "I shall accept on one condition; that you furnish me some pigeons."

The rich said yes; that he could ask for whatever he wished. Then the Tepozteco promised them that everything would be arranged the following day, at two o'clock in the afternoon. They asked him if he needed people to help, but he answered that he could do it all by himself. All those wealthy people were filled with admiration and curiosity to see how he was going to lift up such heavy bells.

The rich immediately put carpenters to work at building high platforms for the people who wished to look on. They were all careful to arrive well ahead of time. At twelve o'clock they saw nothing; at one, nothing. Finally it was two o'clock and the Tepozteco still made no move. At that moment a strong wind arose. The people could scarcely stand it. Then they heard the sonorous bells.

The wind soon died down and the people were able to see that the Tepozteco had the bells and stone in their places. He himself was ringing the bells. No one had realized how it all happened, but upon seeing such a surprising sight, the people gave him gratefully, without any further delay, the box of pigeons he had asked for.

Back again with the prize he had received, the Tepozteco ordered several of the older men of his party to bury the box in the center of the village. The old men wanted to see what was inside before burying it. They could not overcome their curiosity and thought to open the box without doing it any harm. But all the doves with strong wings immediately flew away, and only those still unable to fly remained.

The doves that came out of the box dispersed far and wide. They were the greatest riches that could be found in the world. Each dove flew to a different village.

Our legends say that had it not been for the curiosity of those old men, the strong doves would still be enclosed in the box in Tepoztlán, and all the treasures of the state would be ours. But as only those that were unable to fly remained, the Tepoztecos are now among the poorest of peoples.

Long afterward the ruins of the pyramid were discovered. In order not to lose everything, the people began to clear away the debris. One night the caretaker, who worked there so enthusiastically, was staying at the temple all alone. The Tepozteco appeared to him and told him this was his house, asking who had given him permission to work there. The frightened man answered, "The people who command me said that I must clear away the rubbish." So the Tepozteco told him that he could go on with the work, but only on condition that he would always take care of the monument.

II. Related By the Man Who Was the Village School Teacher— a Native Tepoztecan

At the north of the village of Tepoztlán, in a house called Pocho-titla (Aztec; place where cotton abounds), there is a fountain to which I am going to refer.

In that house there lived a couple who had a young and very beautiful daughter. After she was born her mother had a strange dream. She dreamed that her daughter would not marry, yet she would have a son. Because of this, the girl was always watched and was never seen on the street.

In the center of the house was a fountain, always full of crystalline water, coming from a nearby place called Axitla.

The girl reached the age of seventeen very well. The dream had not been fulfilled and her parents rejoiced. But one day when the maiden had finished bathing and was sitting on the edge of the fountain looking at herself, she distractedly let slip a precious ring which she never took off. The ring fell from her hand into the water. The princess became frightened because she believed it signified some misfortune. She wept sorrowfully. Soon a fish lifted its head above the waters and presented her with the ring, which she accepted joyfully.

Shortly afterwards her parents noted that she was with child. They were indignant, but assured of her innocence, they said nothing and awaited results.

One morning when the wind was sweeping furiously through the gardens, a boy was born. The parents, ashamed, wrapped him in some clothes, and ran to deposit him on a hill, returning the following day to see if the child had died. They found him asleep, with the ants busy putting honey on his lips. They took the boy away and the father prepared a small wooden box, in which he placed him. Then he put it into a stream, believing that its weight would cause it to sink. But, it kept on floating.

In the neighborhood lived an old couple who had no children. The old man went out to look for wood. As he walked along the stream, he saw the box and pulled it out. He opened the box and seeing an infant inside, took him home to his wife, who received him with great joy.

The boy grew rapidly and was very precocious. He managed the bow and arrow skillfully; made his own arrows and hunted with great success. One day while the old folks were conversing beneath a tree, a bird alighted on a branch. The boy, pointing, asked his adopted father if he wished him to bring it down. Upon his answering in the affirmative, he did it with just one arrow. Meat was never lacking, for the boy provided sufficient birds, rabbits, or deer.

The old folks loved the boy dearly. When he was a little late in returning from his roamings, they became very anxious.

At that time, according to the tales our grandparents tell, there lived an ogre called Xochicalcatl, whose only mission was to devour old people. The old man was telling his wife that his day had come; that that night the emissaries of Xochicalcatl were coming to take him away in the company of other old men. She sighed as she listened to his parting words. The boy, who was apparently distracted playing with his arrows, quickly stood up. He faced the old man whom he called coltzin, "grandfather," and said, "You shall not go with his people; I shall go in your place." "But you are very small, they will not admit you." "Leave it to me, I shall arrange it."

The boy talked so much that he succeeded in convincing the old man, just as he knew how to convince the emissaries with whom he went away. On the way he stopped constantly, observing the places he passed, and naming them to suit his taste. Thus the first place at which he rested he called Cuicuizcattlán, (Aztec, for "place where there are swift-pacing horses").

After having walked a long time, they arrived at the home of Xochicalcatl, who, according to tradition, lived in Xochicalco. The servants had prepared the fire, upon which they put an enormous kettle in which the old men were to be cooked. When the boy's turn came, Xochicalcatl grew very indignant, rebuking his emissaries for having brought him such a small boy. As the ogre was still hungry, he resolved to eat the youngster raw.

The boy had secretly provided himself with pieces of obsidian, which he kept in his hands. The ogre opened his big mouth and swallowed him. When he reached the ogre's stomach, he took his pieces of obsidian and began cutting the tissues, causing the ogre such pain that he died.

Now men die of old age, because there is no longer any ogre to eat them.

In a third one of the Tepozteco legends I recorded in the village, related to me by two young men, the beginning is very different.

It is said that there once lived a maiden, who was called "The Princess." She was beautiful, with curling lashes, and beloved by everyone.

Once she was told that there were lovely caves at the bottom of the Hill of Light, the Hill of the Air, the Hill of the Moon, the Hill of the Little Hand, and especially the Hill of the Treasure, in which was to be found the largest and loveliest cave. She set out immediately. She went to see them. As soon as she stepped into the interior of the cave, she found a little idol, which she hid in her bosom so that no one might see it. Then the Princess left, smiling contentedly.

As soon as she returned to the house, she hid the idol in a box, where she left it. Some months passed and she began to feel ill. Her family became alarmed. They asked one another how she could have become ill, since she had never known a man. . . .

Time passed and she gave birth to a fat and pretty boy, whom they named Child of the Air, because he had become contaminated by the "Airs" that played with the Princess. . . .

The rest of the story, although told with different details, is the same as the first one.

In a fourth version of the legend, told to me by a serape-weaver of the village of Chicomcuac, Mexico, the Tepoztecatl was found by an old couple in the woods, but nothing was said of how he was born. It contains the detail about a dragon, who ate old people and lived in the village of Tepoztlán; also the story about the hanging of the bells in the Cathedral.

The legend of the Tepoztecatl is not limited to the village of Tepoztlán, but is related in many places of the states of Morelos and Mexico.

In Chan Kom and other villages of that region of Yucatán, a version of the ancient legend of the Dwarf of Uxmal is told about the boy Ez, who was born of an egg with qualities similar to those of the Tepoztecatl. At the age of two months, he could walk, talk, and play a guitar. At that time the King of Chichén had a beast who ate little children. While Ez was little, he hid from the soldiers who came for him to deliver him to the serpent. But when he felt strong enough he gave himself up and told his "Ma" Chich, who loved him very much not to worry. He hid a piece of glass under his tongue and after the serpent swallowed him, he cut its liver, heart, and belly, and jumped out. When the King heard of what Ez had done, he had several contests with him. In the last one they were to hit each other's heads with the hard cucoyol fruit. Ez cracked the king's skull, and ruled in his place.[20]

STORIES FROM TEPOZTLAN, MORELOS

Recorded by Pablo Gonzáles Casanova

1. The Maiden and the Beast

Once upon a time there was a merchant who had three very pretty young daughters. Every time he went out on business he asked them what they wanted him to bring them, and always each one asked for a very pretty dress. Once the youngest did not want him to bring her a dress, only a flower. Then the man went to attend to his business. Night overtook him on his way back, and then he saw a little light shining in the distance. He went toward it, and when he reached the house, he called out a greeting. As no one answered, he entered a stable, in which he saw much feed for horses.

He became sleepy and looked for a place to lie down, saying, "If someone were to come, I would pay for what my horse has eaten." He was about to lie down on the ground when he spied an open door. He entered through it into a room in which there was much food, and began to eat. As soon as he had finished, he thought again of going to sleep and then saw another open door. He walked through it and saw a very nice bed. Then he asked himself, "What is happening to me?"

He undressed at once and put all his clothes on a chair. Then he lay down and slept tranquilly. The next morning when he awoke, he looked for his old clothes but they were no longer there. On the other hand, he saw that there was a very fine suit in their place. He got up and put on the new suit. When he was ready to leave, he saw a table set; he sat down to eat, finished eating and still did not see anyone. He began to talk, "Now I am going and I give many thanks!"

When he was leaving, he saw many flowers planted outside and remembered that he had to take one to his daughter. Then he said, "I am going to cut me a flower." As soon as he had cut it, he saw a wild beast that began to threaten him, saying "Now I am going to eat you." Then the merchant said, "Don't eat me. Look, I cut that flower only because my daughter told me to bring her one."

The beast said to him, "I shall not eat you if you will bring me your daughter. In three days you must be here. If you are not here in three days, I shall go to look for you and eat you."

The merchant left, arriving at his house very sad. The youngest of the girls asked him, "What is the matter with you? Are you in pain? Have you lost something? Tell me."

He answered, "My child, I did not wish to tell it to you: Look, I entered a house": and he commenced to tell her all that happened, saying at last, "You told me to bring you a flower; I cut it and the wild beast became furious and told me that if I did not bring you to him, he would come to eat me."

Then the maiden said to him, "Let us go so that he may devour us together." They went and arrived at the house but they did not see the beast. They spent several days there and her papa said to her, "Now I'm going to leave you; I am going to see your sisters."

He left her alone, and every day her dress was changed for her and she did not know who changed it. When many days had passed, she began to hear someone saying, "Beautiful maiden, I want to sleep with you."

The voice seemed to come from below the wooden door. The maiden began to worry and wished to see her father and sisters. One morning she arose very early and saw that there was a letter in which the beast told her to go to her house to see her sisters and her papa, and it also said that at the head of her bed was a little stick. "If you wish to go, bite that little stick and immediately it will take you to your house; in this way also you will return in three days. If you do not return in three days you will find me dead."

And in truth, scarcely had she bitten that little stick, when she immediately saw her papa and sisters. Afterwards her sisters would not let her go back when the three days were up, and when she returned the beast had already died. Then the maiden began to weep and to caress its face, saying, "Why did you die, kind beast?" As she spoke, she fell asleep and she dreamed then that the beast said to her: "Cut a flower and sprinkle my face with the water the flower contains."

Then she awoke, went to cut the flower and sprinkled his face. At once that beast got up brusquely, and he was transformed into a handsome youth, and they were married.

ll. The Boy Horticulturist

Once upon a time a Señora had a son. When he was born he cried much, he did not want to nurse, he only cried. His mother began to examine him to see what could be the matter, but she found nothing.

Then his mamma ordered some atole blanco, white flour gruel, prepared for him. What she ordered was immediately done. While they were preparing what the child was to take to pacify him, he was crying much, and the Señora mother was restless. As soon as the white atole was cooked, the servant ran to take it to the baby. They began petting him to make him take it but he did not want it; they thought he wanted it sweetened. "Let it be sweetened," and it was sweetened. But even then he would not take it.

The servant said, "I shall go to look for atole made from corn." It was prepared, but he would not take that either. And as he kept on crying harder all the time, the mother feared that the child might die, and she ordered the servant, "Go to call the curandera, the medicine woman; let her come to see the baby who is crying so much and does not want to eat anything."

The woman went out to look for the curandera to come to see and to cure the child, who had who knows what that made him cry so much. She arrived at the house of the curandera, greeted, entered and said, "I am tired already. We live very far from here." "Where do you live?" "I live in the house of a Señora whose name is Doña Lagartija (lizard) and she ordered me to go to beg you to come to treat her son who is sick. If you will come, it must be at once." "Wait for me; we shall go together. I shall only prepare what is necessary." She put all the medicinal herbs in her basket and they left.

They came to the house of the Señora Lagartija, and as soon as the curandera saw how the sick child was, she asked them, "What do you give him to eat?" "He does not want to take anything; he only cries." She felt of his stomach; it was very shrunken, and then she said, "Bring a little pulque." And as soon as she began giving it to him, he was contented.

The curandera had seen before that the baby had a maguey painted in blood on his stomach, which meant that he should be raised on pulque. "While he is growing, give him what I have told you; when he reaches the age of seven, then we shall change his food. In the meantime we shall cure him."

She began to cure him. She sucked the blood over his stomach, she smoked him with hypericum, palm, incense, and many other medicinal herbs; she smeared his stomach with the blood of a cock, with which the maguey that was painted there would be wiped out; then she smoked it and thus he did not cry any more.

From the time he was treated, he did not cry again. He was always quiet. When he was given his pulque once, it was not necessary to give it to him again; he went to sleep and they did not give him more to drink until the next day.

When he was seven years old, that curandera went to see him again and smoked him again with cedar, incense, and white incense. When she finished, she waited a while and examined his body once more, and she found various kinds of fruit on his back, and she said to his mother, "Look, Señora, at what appears here; they are many little fruits which indicate that he should be sustained with fruit, and here in the right hand, he has an ear of corn, and in the left, look, he has a calabash plant with a calabash, which means he will be a worker when he is big. Now feed him with fruit only; go and pick the best there is in the ravine, where the Aires (the spirits of the air) promenade; that is the kind he should eat."

And thus they raised the child on fruit. Then the curandera said, "Now I am going to cure him." She sucked his little hands and his back. Three days went by, she boiled some roses of Castille, zempasuchitl, wild tea. When she had boiled all this with cedar, she left it for three days in a cave of the ravine and lit candles day and night. In nine days she washed his back with that perfumed water which the Aires had blessed. As soon as he was bathed by the curandera, all the fruit he had painted on his back disappeared, and since then he has been called el niño horticultor, "The child horticulturist."

There was not one field nor one plot of ground that did not have fruit trees, and it was said that it was he who planted them everywhere; that without him there would be no fruit trees.

Man blessed of the Aires, wherever he went everyone greeted him with humility.[21]

The Coyote and the Tlacuache

This story was told to me in Tepoztlán, Morelos. The tlacuache
(Aztec) seems to belong to the common opossum type, ranging from the
Central United States to Brazil. F. T.

One day a coyote was standing as if supporting a hill, and while he
was in that position, a tlacuache came along. He said to him, "What
are you doing there, good friend?"

Replied the coyote, "I'm bolstering up this hill because it is falling.
Don't you want to help me?" Said the tlacuache, "With much pleasure."

"Good! Wait for me then. I shall go and look for something for
us to eat, and you stay here holding the hill. Don't let go because it
will fall down upon you." The coyote took leave and went away.

TLACUACHE

He stayed away a long time and as the tlacuache was already tired,
he said, "I'm going to let go; I don't care if it does fall. I'm hungry
and I'm going to eat." He let go and ran away.

After running a long distance, he stopped to look and saw that the
hill was still standing. He became angry and said, "I'm going to look
for him (the coyote) and kill him so that he can never deceive me
again." And he went.

Upon coming close to a tree, he saw the coyote and said to him,
"You have deceived me, telling me that the hill was going to fall and
you were supporting it. And then you left me there, excusing your-

self that you were going to bring something to eat. As you did not return, I let go of the hill and it did not fall. And now you are going to pay for this."

Replied the coyote, "It was not I who deceived you. It must have been the coyote that passed by here running. So don't be angry with me. Look, you'd better come and eat some chirimoyas."

"But, I cannot climb. Throw me one!"

The coyote threw him a ripe one and the tlacuache ate it.

"It's very good; throw me another."

This time the coyote threw him a hard one and it stuck in his throat and the coyote ran away. The tlacuache was lying there helpless until some ants came along and took the chirimoya away. Then he went after the coyote once more.

This time he found the coyote eating tunas (prickly-pears) and said to him, "Why did you throw me that hard chirimoya?" Said the coyote, "It was not I; I've just got here. Look, don't get angry. Better come and eat some tunas."

Said the tlacuache, "But I cannot climb; throw me one!" The coyote threw him one from which he had taken off the prickles so that the tlacuache could eat it without any trouble. Afterwards, when the coyote was going to throw him another, he said to him, "Open your mouth so that you may catch it."

But he threw the tlacuache one with prickles, and it stuck in his throat. The coyote ran away and the tlacuache could not even cry out because of the prickles.

Again some ants came along and took out the prickles for him. Then the tlacuache went in search of the coyote, but he never saw him again.

STORIES OF THE BANDIT PEDRO DE URDEMALES

Pedro de Urdemales is undoubtedly the same personage as Juan de Urdimales, who appeared in the popular literature of Mexico at about the middle of the 19th century. The last installment of a story about Juan was published in the "Sexto Calendario de Juan de Urdimales," in 1860, which had been running in previous issues, following the astronomical data corresponding to each year.

This Juan de Urdimales lived during Mexico's Revolution for Independence, 1810–21, but fought on the side of the Spaniards. He was a wicked bandit, a bad friend, a traitor, an audacious, greedy leader of highwaymen, who always returned evil for good.

In the Sexto Calendario there is a page with small lithographic illustrations of some of Juan's deeds. In one he appears killing an entire family who had saved him from the police; in another he is enlisting with the

Spanish General José Calleja, who was pursuing the great Mexican hero, Father José María Morelos y Pavón; a third one shows him killing women and children belonging to the men in favor of Mexican Independence.

Finally Juan turned traitor to companion bandits, under the leadership of Pedro el Negro (Peter the Black), who later stabbed Juan to death in the woods of Ajusco.[22]

It is very probable that Juan de Urdimales never existed but was invented to symbolize all evil in men. The name itself suggests that, since urdir means to warp or to contrive and mal, evil.

Stories of the evil deeds of Urdimales live to this day. The man who told me those that follow was a native of Aztec descent from the village of Tlalmanalco, Mexico; he was about fifty years old, and illiterate.

Once Pedro met a group of arrieros (mule or burro drivers) in the mountains. As the pass was very narrow and it was already dark, they decided to camp where they were. They unloaded and invited Pedro to stay with them. Before going to sleep, they decided to put Pedro in a bag and throw him into the river. But Pedro was alert. When the arrieros were all snoring, he cut the bag open and put in his place their whips, machetes, and other belongings, and went away. The arrieros awoke very early in the morning and threw the bag into the river, saying "Good-bye, Pedro de Urdemales!" From a distance came the answer, "Good-bye to your whips and machetes!"

One time Pedro went to a hacienda to ask for work. The owner told him the only job he could give him was to take care of the pigs. One day when Pedro was out with the pigs, a merchant passed by and asked him, "Will you sell me some pigs?" He answered, "Well yes, but without the ears and tails."

Pedro pocketed the money and stuck the ears and tails of the pigs he had sold in a swamp. Then he went to see the owner and said to him, "Look, patron, some of the pigs are lost because they have sunk into the mud." The owner went with Pedro to try to pull them out of the mud by the tails, and got stuck himself. Meanwhile Pedro ran away.

Another time Pedro went to a priest's house to ask for work. The priest told him he only needed a stable boy to take care of the horses and he accepted. Pedro painted the white horses in various colors and sold them to a ranchero.

He took some of the pieces of the money he got for the horses and stuck them on to a little tree near the roadside. A Spaniard came along and asked him what he had there. Pedro answered that he had a little tree that grew money, and the Spaniard said, "Sell it to me." They agreed upon a price and Pedro went away. The Spaniard waited and waited for the tree to give him more money, but it never did.

One day Pedro was going to eat some of the little yellow jocote fruits, and was scratching the dirt off from them, when a Spaniard came by and asked him what he had. Pedro answered him in his native tongue and the Spaniard understood him to say something about a mine and pieces of gold. The man bought the jocotes from Pedro, who went away, and the Spaniard is still scratching them for gold.

Later Pedro returned to the ranch where he had sold the priest's horses. He found that the stable boy had washed off their paint. He stole them, painted them again, and went and sold them to their former owner. The horses looked dirty and the priest ordered them washed. As the paint came off, he discovered that he had bought the horses that were stolen from him. But Pedro was already far away.

Thus Pedro continued with his tricks until who knows where he may have died.

STORIES OF THE WICKED WOMAN

Stories of the wicked woman are told everywhere in Mexico under different names. Those most frequently used are La Llorona, the wailing woman, and La Malinche, the native maiden who became Cortés' mistress and interpreter. The Mexicans consider her a traitor and her name is a symbol for all that is bad in women.

In Yucatán the wicked woman is the x-tabai, a demon of the woods. She appears at times young, beautiful, finely clad, with loose flowing hair, to lure a man into the bush. If he cannot get away from her after she has revealed her true self, she chokes him to death. The x-tabai may also take the form of ceibas or other trees, so one must be cautious in passing them in the night, even on horseback, as the horse may see her and from fright throw his rider. She may also become a green and yellow snake with markings on its back, and stop up a man's nostrils with the tip of her tail. There is no use trying to shoot the snake because it cannot be killed and will only return to do harm.

In many of the villages of the highlands of Chiapas men tell the story of the wicked woman as an excuse for going home before dark. They know of men, among them their own brothers and friends, who have been enticed by a female into the surrounding ravines. She calls to them in the familiar voice of their wives or sweethearts, and they have been saved from death only by the timely arrival of the true wife or someone who has heard their cries for help. They generally reach home in a pitiful state, scratched and torn, bruised and bleeding.

Around Mexico City it is La Malinche that appears to men at night in the guise of an attractive woman to lure them to their doom.

In Mexico City itself the legend of La Llorona is still related. She was a pretty but humble maiden named Luisa, with whom a rich young man of high society fell in love. He did not marry her, but according to custom furnished a casita, a love-nest, for her, where they were happy for many years. His friends visited and respected her, and they had three children. Finally his family prevailed upon him to marry a girl of his own class. He told Luisa he was going to marry and she made a scene; he stopped visiting her. She was an uninvited guest at his wedding in the big Cathedral. She came home maddened with grief and sent a dagger into the tender bodies of each of her children, one after the other. Then horror-stricken, she ran wildly through the streets, calling for her little ones, sending terror into the hearts of all who heard her.

According to some of the chroniclers Luisa was tried and garrotted for her crime, and on that same day her lover Don Nuño de Montes was buried after having committed suicide.

This happened in the early days of the colonial period and ever since the Llorona roams the streets of Mexico City, wailing for her children and revenging herself on men. Sometimes she appears as a young, well-dressed, attractive woman. When she speaks to a man or he to her and he looks at her, he falls as if in a swoon and does not recover consciousness until the following day at noon. Once when she had her face covered with a veil, a man pulled it aside to look upon her and fell dead from fright. Instead of seeing the pretty face he expected to find behind it, he saw a horrible fleshless one.

Often in the dead of the night, when the winds blow down from the mountains that surround the Valley of Mexico, mothers hear the Llorona wailing for her children. Then they clasp their own to their hearts to protect them from the evil apparition.

No doubt the legend of the Llorona had its origin in some of those that have come down from pre-Conquest days, in which the goddesses Cihuapipíltin, those who died when their first child was born, returned to earth to harm children and adults. The crossroads were considered especially dangerous places for their attacks, and offerings were made to them at those points. It is also related that the Aztec goddess Cihuacóhuatl went about at night dressed in white with a cradle on her shoulders, wailing for her lost child. The sight of her was a bad omen.

The Llorona also haunts all the other big cities of the Republic.[28]

THE LEGEND OF THE CHINA POBLANA

The china poblana, the national feminine folk costume, is worn on occasions by citified girls and women of all social classes. It is the dress of those who dance the Jarabe Tapatío and of the charras who accompany the charros.

The traditional costume consists of a full red flannel skirt, reaching to the ankles, trimmed with designs of sequins, with about ten inches of the upper part green; a white, short-sleeved, embroidered shirt; a rebozo folded over the shoulders and crossed in front; many strings of bright beads, a colored ribbon bow on top of the head; red or green, high-heeled dancing slippers.

While the costume follows the conventionalized pattern, there are always differences in the materials and adornments. Actresses use colors other than red, while the charras and singers of ranchero folk songs wear a wide-brimmed felt sombrero.

The costume in itself is a perfectly normal Mexican creation and would not arouse any special interest if it were not that there seemed to be a need for explaining the name. *China* is both the feminine noun and adjective for Chinese, and poblana, the adjective of Puebla, which places the origin of the costume in Puebla, the capital of the state of that name.

The dictionary defines *china* as "maid servant." Some time at the end of the colonial period that is what maids were called, and men servants were called chinos. Later the name was also applied to gaily dressed girls who sold soft drinks and candies on the plazas. Some say the costume originated with them, but that does not account for poblana; nor does it satisfy the popular imagination. Hence a few incredible but very charming legends have been invented which may or may not have a basis of truth in connection with a Chinese Princess who became the China Poblana and introduced a costume similar in style to the present one.

One of the stories relates that in 1684, when the Mexican seas were infested with pirates, an English band of them captured a Chinese boat en route from Manila to Acapulco. On it was the young and beautiful Mongol Princess Mina. The chief of the pirates, a nobleman, took possession of the girl, but was only interested in keeping her valuable luggage. In Manila he sold her to a merchant, who took her to Acapulco and resold her as a slave to Captain Miguel Sosa, an honorable and well-to-do native and resident of the City of Puebla.

The first thing Captain Sosa did for the Princess Mina was to give her freedom. Then to compensate her in some measure for her misfortune, he bought her jewels and costly materials for a new wardrobe. Next he had her baptized, when she was given the name of Catarina de San Juan, after a young nun who had just died, daughter of friends of the Sosas.

Afterwards Catarina was put in the charge of a Mother Superior and her Father Confessor for her education. She became a devout Christian and led an exemplary life. She sold the pearls Captain Sosa had given her and bought dresses for poor children with the money; the rest of her jewels she gave to the Virgin of the Sorrows.

She never again wore extravagant clothes. During the cold months of the winter she wore a goatskin suit and other times the simple full skirt of red flannel, shirt, and rebozo. Her beauty, goodness, and humility were so appealing to everyone that the maid servants of the convents asked permission of the superiors to imitate her dress, as well as to use red for the skirt, which was granted them. Later the costume was adopted in many other places.

When Catarina died, she was buried with great honors in recognition of her virtuous life. High members of the church carried her coffin on their shoulders and all the clergy, sisterhoods, and many people accompanied them. All mourned the loss of Catarina, whom they affectionately called La China.[23]

Another less common legend has it that the China Poblana was a Hindu princess, born in 1609. Her name was Mirrha, meaning bitterness. When the Turks attacked the Kingdom of Indra Prastha, over which her father ruled, he took her with the rest of the household to one of the seaports, where he thought she would be safer; he was not aware that the place was constantly visited by Portuguese boats, manned by pirates under the guise of merchants.

One day while walking the streets of that city, the Princess Mirrha was separated from her younger brother and their attendants, and was stolen by the owner of one of the Portuguese ships. He took her aboard and made her change her rich clothing for the kind worn by the rest of the prisoners, thus making her one of them.

The boat then went to Cochin, where the authorities paid no attention to what the pirates carried on their boats. There the Jesuit Fathers baptized all the captives, giving Princess Mirrha the name of Catarina of San Juan. In Manila she was sold to a family for domestic work.

In those days the Spaniards of Mexico sometimes purchased slaves for their households. In accordance with this custom, the Marqués de Galves, who was then Viceroy, had sent word to the Governor of Manila, asking him to buy, if possible, "a pretty, graceful young girl slave" to send to him. At the same time, Captain Miguel Sosa and his wife had given a similar order to a Portuguese merchant who was going to Manila. The Governor was going to purchase the Princess Mirrha, but the merchant acted more quickly; he bought her at a low price and took her away secretly to his boat, arriving with her in Acapulco in 1620.

When Catarina arrived in Puebla, Father Aguila, one of her panegyrists, described her as "one of the loveliest and most perfect beauties of her day. Her skin was light rather than dark, her hair blond; she had a high forehead, bright eyes, straight nose; and the rest of her features were in harmony with her graceful elegance of body . . . and to all of this was added a strong desire to preserve her purity."

Catarina was a faithful, obedient servant to the Sosas, who taught her Spanish and gave her a good Christian education, but never adopted her. Years later they made her marry a Chinese slave, whose name was Domingo Suárez, called el chino by his masters, who were very fond of him. After her marriage the people began calling Catarina La China Poblana.

There are few details about the Princess Mirrha's later life, excepting that she refused to consumate her marriage with a person of lower rank and was wife in name only; that she lived a good, pious life, always helping the poor. It is said that she talked with the saints who granted her the power to cure, and had visions.

Other versions have it that Catarina tried to reconstruct her regal garments of regional materials, from which evolved the luxurious costumes of the Chinas of Puebla. One of them that is now on exhibition in the Puebla State Museum is said to be hers, but the data concerning its origin state that it was found in an old storehouse among clothes belonging to a troupe of actors of the last century.[24]

IXTLACCIHUATL AND POPOCATEPETL

Mexico's Two Famous Volcanoes

Ixtlaccíhuatl, "the white woman," lies on the highest point of the rim of mountains surrounding the Valley of Mexico, and near her stands Popocatépetl, "the smoking mountain." Both lord it over the countryside many miles around and can be seen from three states. Some days their snow-covered forms stand out stark and clear against the skies, while on others they are hidden from view. At dawn the rising sun touches them with a warm light, and in the evening they are lost in the play of light and shadow.

For those of us who live within view of their grandeur and beauty,

Ixtla and Popo, as we call them familiarly, have acquired human attributes; they seem like real people, like the lovers of the legend we so often hear.

Ixtlaccíhuatl, beautiful daughter of a powerful Aztec Emperor, was the only heir to his throne and glory. When her father became weak on account of old age, his enemies began to wage wars against him. He called to his aid the bravest of the young warriors of his tribes, and offered his throne and the hand of his daughter to the one who would vanquish his enemies. Among those who went into the fight was Popocatépetl, the bravest of all, who for years had been in love with the Princess and she with him.

The war was long, cruel and bloody. When it was about to end and Popocatépetl could return in triumph to claim his rewards, his rivals sent back the false news that he had been killed. The Princess then became victim of a strange illness. Neither the witch doctors nor the priests were able to cure her. She languished and died.

When Popocatépetl returned and found her dead, nothing could assuage his grief. He did not wish to go on living, so he constructed a great pyramid upon which he laid his beloved, and next to it another for himself, where he stands holding a torch to illuminate her eternal sleep.

During the years that followed, the snows enfolded the body of the Princess and covered that of the warrior, but it never extinguished the torch, which continues lighted, warm and everlasting, like the love of Popocatépetl for his Princess.

For the ancient Aztecs, Popocatépetl and Ixtlaccíhuatl were fertility gods, who together with all the other important deities were given fiestas with offerings and human sacrifices.

There were images of Ixtlatl in various of the Aztec temples, and one in a cave in the mountain on which she lies. Each image was surrounded by smaller ones to represent the surrounding hills. The one in the Templo Mayor of Tenochtitlán was made of wood and dressed in blue. On her head was a crown of white bark paper on which there were figures painted in black to indicate the forests; in the back there was a silver medallion from which white and black plumes projected and black streamers hung down. The face was youthful, with color in the cheeks. The image stood on an altar in a small chamber, adorned with rich cloth and other ornaments and was treated by the priests with great reverence and fear. They pronounced profound lamentations, long and elegant orations and prayers before it, accompanied by offerings and sacrifices.

For her fiesta, which lasted for two days, a female slave was dressed all in green, except for a white crown with black points to symbolize the sierra, the snow and woods. Afterwards the woman was sacrificed before the idol in the temple.

To the image in the mountain cave were taken two small children, either boys or girls, to be sacrificed. They were elegantly dressed and carried in canopies hung with rich cloth. At the same time all nobles and priests climbed to the cave with gifts of crowns of gorgeous plumage, beautiful women's garments, jewels with precious stones, and much food. Everyone fasted and prayed during the two days.

Popocatépetl or the Hill of Popocatzín was worshipped as the greatest of all the mountains, especially by the inhabitants of the region, many of whom lived on its slopes because of the richness of the land.

The people did not wait for his fiesta, but were constantly praying to him with offerings and sacrifices. His fiesta also lasted two days, for which there were images of him on the surrounding hills. These were formed of a masa (dough), made of amaranth seeds and corn, his with eyes and mouth. They were dressed with paper crowns and placed on a prominent place on the hill, where they received offerings of fresh ears of corn, food and copal. The priests and people climbed the hill-tops to light fires with which to burn the copal incense. Male slaves and children were sacrificed. All fasted and prayed.

On the last day the idols made of the masa were sacrificed and eaten. At the same time the priests looked for crooked branches, covered them with masa and, after performing ceremonies over them, gave them to the lame, to those who lacked an arm or were suffering from tumors or the contraction of tendons, who were thus obligated to furnish the masa for the coming year.

Similar ceremonies, taking place in our month of August, were performed for all the volcanoes in the country. These were called the tepeylhuitl, or the fiestas of the hills.[25]

NAMES—RIDDLES—SLANG—INSULTS—SAYINGS

Of these aspects of the lore I shall present only a sufficient number of examples to give an idea of what they are like. They are such an intimate part of the language and so idiomatic that they lose too much in transla-.tion. Very little has been done in collecting any of them, except the sayings.

Names of Drinking Places

Some of the pulquerías have already been mentioned in connection with their exterior wall paintings but here are a few more. El Paso de

Venus, The Passage of Venus; Cuatro Vientos, The Four Winds; El Tecolote, The Owl; Echate la Otra, Take Another One; La Gloria, Heaven; Detente, Hermano, Stop, Brother; Las Mulas de Don Cristóbal. The story about the last one is that once an owner of a pulquería named his place Los Caballeros de Colón or the Knights of Columbus. Some of the knights objected, so the next time they came by they saw the name changed to "The Mules of Columbus."

The names of cantinas, or bars, are just as imaginative as those of pulquerías. El Califa de León, The Caliph of Leon; Juan Sin Miedo, Fearless Juan; Aquí te Espero, Here I Wait For You; La Linterna Roja, The Red Lantern; Ora, Panciano—after a noted bullfighter—Come on, Panciano; El Toro Embolado, The Drunken Bull; La Bastilla, The Bastille; El Abanico de Pompadur, The Fan of Mme. Pompadour; La Lluvia de Oro, The Rain of Gold; El Reloj de Arena, The Sand Glass; La Madre Matiana, after a prophetess nun of the early part of this century. She is often recalled when something unexpected happens, in the phrase, Ni lo dijo la Madre Matiana, Not even the Madre Matiana said so.

Drugstores are usually named after saints, and La Esperanza, or Hope, is a favorite name for bakeries and groceries. In the village of Huixquilucan, Mexico, there are two butcher shops. One is called Los Granos de Oro, Grains of Gold, and the other Las Orquidias, Orchids. In both, as in all the others of the villages, the meat hangs on wire strings like clothes. They have funny old scales, and on their walls are niches with the patron saint, candles, and flowers.

Names on Push Carts

The itinerant vendors of ice-cream cones, sticks, and candies do not let themselves be outdone in the matter of names—Los Pajaritos de San Juan, The Little Birds of St. John; Las Desgracias de "Perl Jarbor," The Misfortunes of Pearl Harbor; Los Amores de Romeo y Juliet, The Love Affairs of Romeo and Juliet; El Carrito de los Niños, The Little Cart of the Children; El Palomar Bendito, The Happy Dove Nest; De los Niños Soy el Preferido, Of the Children I'm the Favorite.

There is no end to the fantasy and humor of those names. Some of the cheap eating places around the markets are sometimes named after famous restaurants. A favorite one is Sanborcito, the little Sanborn, after the noted American restaurant in Mexico City.

Names on Trucks and Busses

The names on these vehicles, both sentimental and humorous, transform them from moving mountains of steel into something human, intimate. They consist of current slang or slogans or a line or name of a song. A popular one during World War II was Volveremos, We'll Come Back! Others are—Aburrido me voy, I go on but I'm Bored; No creas, se sufre, Believe It Or Not, One Suffers; Mi amor eres tu, You Are My love; Ya voy llegando, I'm Arriving; Un Amor que se va, A Love That Is Ending; Aquí va tu Tarzan, Here Goes Your Tarzan; Pujando Pero Llego, Puffing but I get there.

The drivers of taxis, busses, and trucks, who drive like devils and are very superstitious, protect themselves by having a chromo or a small image of a saint hanging in their cars, usually of the Virgin of Guadalupe; sometimes it is a little niche with flowers and a tiny red electric bulb. And together with their saints and other safety charms are pictures of semi-naked women.

Nicknames

The natives give nicknames to their children to protect them from evil and black magic, but city people use them too. A person with blue or gray eyes, fair skin, and hair that is not jet black is always called "the blond or fair one," which is el güero for men and la güera for women. Either one is used instead of the first name by family and friends.

Some famous persons are often referred to by their nicknames—El Guerrillero del Norte, Pancho Villa; El Manco, or the one-armed man, is the late ex-President General Alvaro Obregón; El Varón de Cuatro Ciénegas, Venustiano Carranza; El Turco or the Turk, General Plutarco Elías Calles. The inhabitants of Xochimilco are called ranas or frogs because they practically live in the water. For a long time the well-dressed young men who stand about the streets and flirt were called los lagartijos or lizards; now they are called fifís, and the people in the provinces call them catrines.

Riddles

There are many riddles with local characteristics but they are the most difficult to translate. Here are a few from Mexico City:

Tito, tito, capotito, sube al cielo y pega un grito. Tito, tito, with a little cap, rises to the skies and shouts.—Firecrackers. Agua pasa por me casa, cate de mi corazón.—The alligator pear—a play on the name. I went to the market, bought little black things, which turned red in my house.—Charcoal. These three are typically Mexican but others are of Spanish origin.

The Maya riddles often begin with, Adivina, adivina lo que es, muchacho, Guess, guess, what it is, child. Here are two translated from the Maya: Water in the trunk and sun at the top.—Cigarettes. There's a little Negro who flies up into the air full and comes down hungry.—Firecracker.

Slang

The following expressions are used in Mexico City and elsewhere by citified people.

Vamos de vacilón or a vacilar. Let us go on a spree! (Vacilar, to vacillate, to stagger.)

Está echando ojo. He or she is flirting. (Echar ojo, to cast an eye on, to watch.)

No te hagas guaje. Don't play innocent. (Lit., Don't make a gourd of yourself.)

Some expressions are in sign language as well as in words, and one understands them.

Codo. Stingy. (Codo is the elbow. Double your left arm and touch the elbow with the right hand.)

I wasn't born yesterday. In Spanish: I already have my eye-teeth. (Point to them with your forefinger.)

I'm from Missouri. In Spanish: I'm Columbus—Yo colón. (Point with forefinger to the right eye.)

Hacer la barba means to flatter a person; literally, to fix one's face. (Rub your right cheek with the back of the right hand.)

Repiocha. Swell! (Pull your right hand down over your chin and make a quick circular motion below it.)

Insults

Many of them are like our own—fool, idiot, rascal. Among the worst are sinvergüenza, shameless one; cabrón, he-goat (when a woman puts horns on a man). Son of a bitch is often shortened to jijo. The above three are sometimes used good-naturedly and in fun. The very worst of all the insults is to tell a man to rape his mother (chingue tu madre). Men of all social classes use that, some more than others. Chauffeurs say it with their horns, and others whistle it.

Native boys and men who can scarcely speak Spanish use the last two expressions all the time. To them undoubtedly they lack the force of one born to the language, but they have spicy ones of their own. Their curses are also picturesque. A Maya one says, "May everything you eat turn into worms and devour your entrails."

Sayings

Innumerable sayings have been published in a thick book by Darío Ruben, but they lose much in translation. Many are Spanish and many of Mexican origin; some are like our own, but expressed differently because of the difference in the language.

El que tenga hambre, que se atice a la olla. He who is hungry let him stir the pot.

Cuando el tecolote canta, el índio muere. Esto no será verdad pero sucede. When the owl hoots the Indian dies. This may not be true but it happens.

Algo es algo dijo un calvo, cuando se tocaba un pelo. Something is something, said the bald man, when he felt one hair.

Por uno que madruga, hay otro que no se acuesta. For one who rises early, there is always another who has not gone to bed.

Gallina vieja hace buen caldo. An old hen makes good broth.

Sobre el muerto, las coronas. Over the dead, the crowns.

A la vista del amo, engorda el caballo. The horse gets fat when the master keeps an eye on him.

Cae más pronto un hablador que un cojo. A bluffer falls sooner than a lame man.

It's never so bad but it could be worse. Peor es chili y el agua lejos. It is worse with chili and the water far away.

A bird in the hand is worth two in the bush. Más vale pájaro en mano que cien volando. A bird in the hand is worth more than a hundred in the air.

All that glitters is not gold. Mucho ruido y pocas nueces. Much noise but few nuts.

Truth, although severe, is a real friend. One does not look a gift horse in the teeth. If you want to know a man, get him drunk. Children and drunkards tell the truth.

Out of sight, out of mind. Santo que no es visto no es adorado. A saint who is not seen is not worshipped.

A ceaseless talker. Habla hasta por los codos. He or she talks even through his elbows.

There's a limit to everything. No hay borracho que coma lumbre. Not even a drunkard will eat fire.

Clothes do not make the man. If you sigh in my presence, I know it cannot be for me.

Nothing ventured, nothing gained. Solo él que no monta no cae. Only he who does not mount, doesn't fall.

Every man has his price. Sola la cruz no roba. Only the cross does not steal (because it cannot move its arms).

¡Se me hace chico el mar para un buche de agua! The ocean is small for a mouthful of water! (The height of bragging.) [26]

NOTES

The numbers given below refer to books and other source material listed in the Bibliography, which follows.

Introduction

1) This introduction is based on reading the first three volumes of Sahagún, Landa, Diaz del Castillo, Joyce, Caso, Spinden, and others, and on the personal assistance of Dr. Alfonso Caso and Dr. Gordon Ekholm.

PART ONE

Houses and Ceremonies

1) 41
2) 42
3) 38. The belief that the cutting of wood is affected by the moon is probably widespread but it is seldom mentioned by investigators. Such a belief also exists in parts of Guatemala.

House Furnishings

1) 41, 42, 92
2) 38, Chap. III

Food

1) 99, pp. 598, 609-10
2) 93, p. 55; prepared in the same manner in Yucatán
3) 38, Chap. IV
4) Op. cit; 73 and 92

Pulque

1) 91, pp. 55, 109, 228
2) 59, No. 9, 1926, pp. 12-18. Tinacal customs communicated by Alejandro de Sela and Delfino Ramirez.
3) Communicated

Soft Drinks

1) 4

Smoking

1) 59, No. 5, 1926, pp. 18-21. Chamula custom communicated.

Chews

1) Communicated
2) See Peyote Pilgrimages and Fiestas, Part II.

Animals

1) 11, pp. 131-132; 73, p. 116; 92, p. 117; 99, pp. 636, 720

Agriculture and Ceremonies

1) Some of the customs communicated by José Ballesteros, former hacendado.

Pagan Ceremonies

1) 8 and 36
   92. The prayer was reconstructed into Spanish by Sr. Villa with the help of interpreter; into English by F. T.
   93, pp. 101-105 and 73, p. 128
   99, pp. 483-502

The Folk Arts

1) 59, 1933, VIII, 4-34
2) 59, 1929, Special mask number
3) 59, 1927, III, 5-17
4) 59, 1928, IV, 109-115
5) 59, No. 5, 1926, pp. 5-9
7) 99, pp. 571-645 and 55, pp. 196-235
8) Through the courtesy of Bodil Christiansen, I was able to see many of the costumes from the Sierra de Puebla and others belonging to her collection.
9) 56, pp. 164-180
   97
10) 94 and 96
11) This section on the Folk Arts contains descriptions of all the objects and techniques of "Mexican Popular Arts."

Markets
1) 32, Chap. XCVIII

PART TWO

1) In some villages men spend more than half their time on ceremonies and fiestas. 36, 38, 73, 92

The Family
1) Communicated

Clans and Kinship
1) Communicated by the authors of 38, 41 and 93

Godparenthood
1) 99, p. 718; 12, p. 22; 73, pp. 187-88; 93, pp. 142-3, 144

Education
1) 46, pp. 175-186
2) 59, 1928, IV, pp. 119-29

Government
1) Op. cit. Spec. Yaqui No. 1937, p. 126. 11, pp. 174-5

Religion
1) 93, pp. 97, 122. Data about talking boxes in Chiapas furnished by Calista Guiteras Holmes.

Birth and Infancy
1) 6, pp. 163-9
    11, pp. 233-35
    38, chap. XII
    52, p. 102-106
    55, pp. 175-6, 178, Vol. II
    59, 1928, IV, pp. 102-108
    63, pp. 74-76
    93 and 41
    99, p. 275

Marriage
1) 6, pp. 177, 180-192
    9, p. 38
    41, 42 and 93
    55, 92-97, Vol. II
    59, 1927, III, pp. 18-23
    59, VII, 1932, pp. 129-137
    64, pp. 243-5, Vol. II. About

Tehuantepec communicated.
73, p. 192
89, pp. 44-7
93, p. 146
99, p. 130

Love Magic
1) 59, pp. 17-20, I, 1925. Much communicated.

Medicine and Magic
1) 6, 202-207
    41, 42 and 93
    48, pp. 119-150
    59, pp. 17-21, No. 1, 1925; pp. 31-33, No. 2, 1926
    73, p. 118
    74, pp. 49-81
    93, p. 148
    99, pp. 148-153, 210

Death and Burial
1) 8, p. 59
    36, p. 64
    59, VI, 1930, devoted to death and burial customs
    59, Spec. Yaqui No., pp. 52-53
    73, pp. 198-204
    93, pp. 148-150
    99, pp. 147, 138-9

Religious Fiestas
1) From many sources.
2) Alabanza and music furnished by Concha Michel.
3) 59, No. 5, 1926, pp. 22-26
4) 59, 1927, III, pp. 203-210
5) Much data from an article written by Benjamin Villaran, Jr., for "Mexican Folkways" but never published.
6) 59, 1930, VI, pp. 38-46
7) 59, V, 1929, devoted to carnivals.
8) 99, pp. 75-96
9) 40, and from conversations.
10) 59, 1930, VI, 84-94
11) 6, p. 127

The Passion at Tzintzuntzan is described in "Mexican Folkways," No. 1, 1925. In writing about it for this book I was able to use Dr. Foster's notes on observations in 1946.

12) 92
13) 93, p. 121
14) 59, 1937, Spec. Yaqui No., pp. 34-44
15) 42
16) 59, 1933, VIII, pp. 56-76
17) 6, p. 125, and from Dr. Foster's notes of his study of Tzintzuntzan.
18) 59, 1926, No. 4, pp. 30-39
19) 38, Chap. XIV
20) 92
21) 93, p. 151
22) 59, 1925, No. 4, pp. 16-21; 1926, No. 10
23) 11, pp. 253, 293-4
    55, pp. 356-379
    99, pp. 403-411, 496

Children's Games and Songs
  1) 59, 1932, VII, pp. 107-110
  2) Op. cit. pp. 79-85
  3) Op. cit. pp. 63-74
  4) 61, pp. 35-37

Adult Games and Sports
  1) 59, 1932, VII, 56-60. 20, pp. 404-408
  2) 11, pp. 333-345, 364-65
     55, pp. 276, 282-293
     59, 1926, II, pp. 40-47
     The data about the trip to the Olympics was furnished by Enrique Aguirre, who accompanied as coach and manager.
  3) 10
  4) 59, 1932, VII, pp. 87-106

Charreadas and Bullfighting
  1) 1 and 76. Much of the data was furnished by Manuel Garcia Pa-

redes, a ranchero charro, and Alfredo Cuellar, a city charro.
  2) 68. Also much data communicated by the young writer Bernardo Jimenez Montellano, an ex-novillado, and Patricia Fent Ross, a writer and bullfight fan.

PART THREE

Music
  1) 57, Carlos Chavez, pp. 199-218
     59, 1937, Spec. Yaqui No., pp. 32-44
     59, 1927, III, Spec. Song No. 66
     78, I, Libro I, Chap. III and Libro II, Chap. V
     94
     96
     97

Dances
  1) 20, pp. 402-404
     32, Chap. XCIX
     78
     87, Chap. XI
  2) 13 and 53
  3) Music and much detail from 100. The data about the initiation and other details were furnished by a captain of a mesa in Mexico and never published previously. Historical origin, 33.
  4) 59, 1937, Spec. Yaqui No., pp. 52-63
     7, pp. 120-123, 126-31
  5) Op. cit, pp. 131-2, 111-112
  6) Op. cit, pp. 98, 112, 124
  7) 11, pp. 243, 273-4, 299-300, 315, 274-5
     55, I, pp. 33-344, 355
     59, 1927, III, pp. 218-234

9) Communicated
10) Communicated
11) Communicated
12) Text from 3, IV, pp. 155-186
14) 59, 1925, No. 2, pp. 8-10
15) 26, pp. 13-17. Text loaned by Donald Cordry and some data by Raul Guerrero.
16) 2, pp. 75-76
17) 20
18) 2, pp. 88-89. Some data and music furnished by Concha Michel.
19) 6, p. 144
20) Some data from manuscript on dances by Raul Guerrero.
21) Some data from Op. cit.
22) Communicated
23) 59, 1930, VI, pp. 84-94
24) First two communicated by Alfredo Barrera Vazquez; last one by Alejandro de Sela.
25) 27, pp. 52-61
26) From Raul Guerrero's mss.
27) The Tenancingo dance communicated by Concha Michel.
28) 59, 1930, VI
29) 59, 1932, VII, pp. 167-214
30) 73, pp. 109, 110, 124, 154-6, 158
31) 59, 1930, VI, pp. 110-116
32) 29, pp. 329-350

PART FOUR

Myths—Tales—Miscellanea

1) 18
   49, pp. 48, 50-51
   79, Chap. I
2) Op. cit., p. 243
   65
3) 92, pp. 155-157
4) 73, p. 210
5) 69. Recorded in Spanish and translated by M. R.
6) 24. Recorded in Spanish and translated by H. C.
7) Recorded in Maya and trans-
lated into Spanish by Alfredo Barrera Vazquez; into English by F. T. Published in Spanish in Coleccion Lunes, No. 29, 1946, Mexico.
8) Recorded in Spanish by Anne Chapman and translated into English by F. T. Published in French in the "Revue de L'Ifal," Nos. 4-5, 1946, Mexico.
9) 19. Paraphrased and translated into English by F. T.
10) Related to me in Spanish by a school teacher from Zacatecas.
11) 8, pp. 216, 218-219, 223
12) 55, II
13) Recorded and translated by D. C. Unpublished.
14) 45
15) 21, p. 62
16) 37. Recorded in Spanish and translated by G. M. F.
17) 59, 1933, VIII, pp. 36-45
18) Based chiefly on an article written by José Montes de Oca for "Mexican Folkways" but never published.
19) Communicated.
20) 59, 1928, IV, pp. 208-229. 41 and 73
21) 42. Recorded in Aztec and translated into Spanish by P. G. C. Into English by F. T.
22) Communicated by Pablo Gonzalez Casanova, Jr.
23) 78, I, Libro I, Chap. X; Libro X, Chap. XXVIII
24) 76, pp. 242-244, and 80
25) Legend communicated. Data on fiestas from 32, Chap. XCV.
26) Communicated by Roberto Gordillo, Enrique Gonzalez Casanova, Calista Guiteras Holmes and some sayings from 77.

BIBLIOGRAPHY

1. ALVAREZ DEL VILLA, JOSE. *Historia de la Charrería*. Mexico. 1941.
2. AMEZQUITA BORJA, FRANCISCO. *Música y Danza*. Mexico. 1943.
3. *Anuario de la Sociedad Folklórica de México*. Vols. I-IV. Mexico.
4. BATALLA, M. A. *This Week in Mexico*. Mexico City. March 24, 1945.
5. BEALS, RALPH L. *The Aboriginal Culture of the Cáhita Indians*. Ibero-Americano, No. 19. University of California Press. Berkeley. 1943.
6. ———. *Cheran: A Sierra Tarascan Village*. Smithsonian Institution Institute of Social Anthropology. Publication No. 2. 1946.
7. ———. *The Contemporary Culture of the Cáhita Indians*. Smithsonian Institution Bureau of American Ethnology. Bulletin 142. 1945.
8. ———. *Ethnology of the Western Mixe*. Publications in American Archaeology and Ethnology. Vol. 42, No. 1. PP. 1-176. University of California Press. Berkeley. 1945.
9. ———. *Problems in the Study of Marriage Customs*. "Essays in Anthropology in Honor of Alfred Luis Kroeber." Pp. 7-14. University of California Press. Berkeley. 1936.
10. BEALS, RALPH L. and CARRASCO, PEDRO. *Games of the Mountain Tarascans*. Reprint from "American Anthropologist." Vol. 46, No. 4. P. 517. October–December, 1944.
11. BENNETT, WENDELL C. and ZINGG, ROBERT M. *The Tarahumara, an Indian Tribe of Northern Mexico*. The University of Chicago Press. Chicago. 1935.
12. BEVAN, BERNARD. *The Chinantec*. Instituto Panamericano de Geografía e Historia. Publicación No. 24. Mexico. 1938.
13. BRETON FONTECILLA, CECILIA. *Fiestas del Corpus en Papantla, Veracruz.* "Anuario de la Sociedad Folklórica de México. Vol. IV. Pp. 1945.
14. CAMPOS, RUBEN M. *El Folklórica y la Música Mexicana*. Mexico. 1928.
15. ———. *El Folklórica Musical de las Ciudades*. Mexico. 1928.
16. CASO, ALFONSO. *Las Culturas Mixteca y Zapoteca*. Biblioteca del Maestro. Mexico. 1941.
17. ———. *Reading the Riddle of Ancient Jewels*. "Natural History." XXXII. Pp. 464-480. New York. 1932.
18. ———. *The Religion of the Aztecs*. Mexico. 1927.
19. CHACON PINEDA, NAZARIO. *Estatua y Danza*. Mexico. 1939.
20. CHRISTENSEN, BODIL. *The Acatlax qui Dance of Mexico*. Reprinted from "Ethnos." No. 4. 1937. The Ethnographical Museum of Sweden. Stockholm. 1937.
21. ———. *Notas Sobre la Fabricacion del Papel Indigena y Su Empleo para Brujerias en la Sierra Norte de Puebla*. Revista Mexicana de Estudios Anthropologicos. Tomo VI. Nums. 1-2. Enero-agosto, 1942. Mexico.

22. CHRONICLES. See Spanish Chronicles.

23. CLAVIJERO, FRANCISCO JAVIER. *Historia Antigua de Mexico*. Mexico. 1917. (Also in English.)

24. CLINE, HOWARD. *Lore and Deities of the Lacandón Indians*. "The Journal of American Folklore." Vol. 57. Pp. 107-115. April—June, 1944.

25. CODICES. The picture writings of the ancient Mexicans. There are some in existence from pre-Conquest times, while others were painted immediately after the Conquest. They are scattered through the various museums of the world, including those of Mexico.

26. CORDRY, DONALD BUSH and DOROTHY M. *Costumes and Textiles of the Aztec Indians of the Cuetzalan Region, Pueblo, Mexico*. 1940.

27.   . *Costumes and Weaving of the Zoque Indians of Chiapas, Mexico*. 1941.

28. COVARRUBIAS, MIGUEL. *Mexico South, The Isthmus of Tehuantepec*. New York. 1946.

29. CRUZ, WILFREDO C. *Oaxaca Recondita*. Mexico. 1946.

30. DAVIS, E. ADAMS. *Of the Night Wind's Telling*. University of Oklahoma Press. 1946.

31. DIAZ DEL CASTILLO, BERNAL. *The Discovery and Conquest of Mexico. 1517-21*. Translated with an Introduction and Notes by A. P. Maudslay. New York. 1928.

32. DURAN, PADRE FRAY DIEGO. *Historia de las Indias de Nueva España*. Mexico. 1880.

33. FERNANDEZ, JUSTINO; MENDOZA, VICENTE; LUNA, RODRIGUEZ. *Danzas de los Concheros en San Miguel de Allende*. Mexico. 1941.

34. FOSTER, GEORGE M. *Nagualism in Mexico and Guatemala*. "Acta Americana." Vol. II, Nos. I, II. 1944.

35.   . *Notes on the Populuca of Vera Cruz*. Pub. No. 51, Instituto Panamericano de Geografía e Historia. Mexico. 1940.

36.   .*A Primitive Economy*. Monographs of the American Ethnological Society. No. 5. New York. 1942.

37.   . *Sierra Popoluca Folklore and Beliefs*. "American Archaeology and Ethnology." XLII, 2. University of California Press. Berkeley. 1945.

38. FUENTE, JULIO DE LA. *Yalalag—A Zapotec Village in the Sierra de Juárez, Oaxaca*. (To be published 1947.)

39. GONZALEZ CASANOVA, PABLO. *El Ciclo Legendario del Tepoztecatl*. Revista Mexicana de Estudios Historicos. Reprint from Vols. I and II. Mexico. 1928.

40.   . *Cuentos Indigenas*. Universidad Nacional Autónoma de Mexico. Mexico. 1946.

41. GUITERAS HOLMES, CALISTA. *Cancuc. Field Notes on a Tzeltal Village in Chiapas*. Department of Anthropology, The University of Chicago. Chicago. (Microfilm) 1944.

42.   . *Chenahlo. Field Notes on a Tzotzil Village in Chiapas*. Department

of Anthropology, The University of Chicago. Chicago. (Microfilm) 1944.

43. HENDRICHS PEREZ, PEDRO R. *Por Tierras Ignotas.* Mexico. 1946.

44. HEWETT, EDGAR L. *Ancient Life in Mexico and Central America.* New York. 1936.

45. HURTADO, NABOR. *Los Huicholes.* "*This Week in Mexico.*" Mexico City. Aug. 31–Sept. 7, 1946.

46. IBARRA, ALFREDO, JR. *Cuentos y Leyendas.* Mexico, 1941.

47. *.Fogatas de la Revolución.* Mexico. 1946.

48. JOHNSON, JEAN BASSETT, *The Elements of Mazatec Witchcraft.* Reprint from the Ethnological Studies. IX. Pp. 119-150. Guthenburg Ethnological Museum, Sweden. 1939.

49. JOYCE, THOMAS ATHOL. *Mexican Archaeology.* London. 1914.

50. *. Maya and Mexican Art.* London. 1927.

51. KELLY, ISABEL. *Notes on a West Coast Survival of the Ancient Mexican Ball Game.* "Notes on Middle American Archaeology and Ethnology." Carnegie Institution of Washington. No. 26. 1940-43.

52. LANDA, FR. DIEGO DE. *Relacion de las Cosas de Yucatán.* In English. Introduction and Notes by Alfred M. Tozzer. Cambridge. 1941.

53. LARSEN, HELGA. *Mexican Indian Flying Pole Dance.* "National Geographic." Vol. LXXI. Pp. 387-400. March 1937.

54. LUMHOLZ, CARL. *Symbolism of Huichol Indians.* New York. 1900.

55. *. Unknown Mexico.* London. 1903.

56. McGEE, W. J. *The Seri Indians.* Part I. Washington, 1898. Seventh Annual Report of the Bureau of Ethnology.

57. MENDIETA, GERONIMO DE. *Historia Eclesiática.* Mexico. 1870.

58. MENDOZA, VICENTE T. *Romance y Corrido.* Mexico. 1939.

59. *Mexican Folkways 1925-1937.* Spanish-English magazine. Founded and edited by Frances Toor. Art Editor, Diego Rivera. (9 vols.) (Complete Index compiled by R. S. Boggs, University of North Carolina. Chapel Hill.)

60. *México-Leyendas y Costumbres, Trajes y Danzas.* Ed. Atoyac. Mexico. 1945.

61. OBREGON, LUIS. Recreación Física para Escuelas y Comunidades Rurales. Sec. de Educ. Pub. Mexico. 1935.

62. PARKES, HENRY BAMFORD. *A History of Mexico.* Boston. 1938.

63. PARSONS, ELSIE CLEWS. *Mitla, Town of Souls.* The University of Chicago Press. Chicago. 1936.

64. LA POBLACION DEL VALLE DE TEOTIHUACAN. 3 vols. Ed. by Dr. Manuel Gamio. 1922.

65. *Popul Vuh. Maya-Quiché Creation Myth.* Manuscrito de Chichicastenango Guatemala. Ed. by J. Antio Villacorta, C. and Flavio Rodas, M. 1927.

66. POZAS, RICARDO. *Field Notes on Chamula, a Tzotzil Village in the Highlands of Chiapas.* 1944.

67. PRESCOTT, WILLIAM H. *The Conquest of Mexico*. New York, 1934.

68. RANGEL, NICOLAS. *Historia del Toreo en México*. Mexico. 1924.

69. REDFIELD, MARGARET PARK. *The Folk Literature of a Yucatecan Town*. Reprinted from Publications, No. 456. Pp. 1-60. June 1935. Carnegie Institution of Washington.

70. REDFIELD, ROBERT and REDFIELD, MARGARET. *Disease and Its Treatment in Dzitas, Yucatán*. Reprinted from Publications, No. 523. Pp. 49-81. June 10, 1940. Carnegie Institution of Washington.

71. REDFIELD, ROBERT. *Tepoztlán. A Mexican Village*. The University of Chicago Press. Chicago. 1930.

72.   . *The Folk Culture of Yucatán*. The University of Chicago Press. Chicago. 1941.

73. REDFIELD, ROBERT and VILLA R., ALFONSO. *Chan Kom. A Maya Village*. Carnegie Institution of Washington. 1934.

74.   . *Notes on the Ethnography of a Tzeltal Community of Chiapas*. Carnegie Institution of Washington. 1939.

75. *Renascent Mexico*. Ed. by Hubert Herring and Herbert Weinstock. New York. 1935.

76. RINCON GALLARDO, D. CARLOS. *El Charro Mexicano*. Mexico. 1939.

77. RUBIO, DARIO. *Refranes, Proverbios, Cichos y Dicharachos Mexicanos*. Mexico. 1937.

78. SAHAGUN, FR. BERNARDINO. *Historia General de las Cosas de Nueva España, México*. 5 vols. (Portions have been translated into English and published by Fisk University.) 1938.

79. SELER, EDOUARD. *Gesammelte abhandlungen zur Amerikanischen Sprach— und Alterthumskunde*. Dritter Band. Berlin. 1908.

80. SODI DE PALLARES, MARIA ELENA. *China Poblana*. "Mexico, An Anthology." Pp. 412-415. 1945.

81. SPANISH CHRONICLES. See Introduction to Part IV and Nos. 32, 78, 87 of this Bibliography.

82. SPINDEN, HERBERT J. *Ancient Civilizations of Mexico and Central America*. New York. 1943.

83. STARR, FREDRICK. *Indians of Southern Mexico*. Chicago. 1899.

84.   . *In Indian Mexico*. 1908.

85.   . *Notes upon the Ethnography of Southern Mexico*. Proc. of Davenport Acc. of Nat. Sc. Vols. VIII, IX. Davenport, Iowa. 1900.

86. TOOR, FRANCES. *Mexican Popular Arts*. Mexico. 1939.

87. TORQUEMADA, JUAN DE. *Monarquia Indiana*. Mexico. 1870.

88. TOSCANO, SALVADOR. *Arte Precolombino de Mexico y de la America Central*. Mexico. 1944.

89. TOZZER, ALFRED M. *A Comparative Study of the Mayas and the Lacandónes*. New York. 1907.

90. *Twenty Centuries of Mexican Art*. The Museum of Modern Art. New York. 1940.

91. VAILLANT, GEORGE C. *Aztecs of Mexico*. New York. 1944.

92. VILLA R., ALFONSO. *Field Notes on the Tzeltal Municipio de Oxchuc, Chiapas*. 1944.

93. ———. *The Maya of East Central Quintana Roo*. Carnegie Institution of Washington. 1945.

94. ———. *Report on Music and Customs of the Coras of Nayarit*. Instituto Indigenista Interamericano. Mexico. 1944-46.

95. YURUCHENCO, HENRIETTA. *Report on Music and Customs of the Primitive Mexican Groups of the Highlands of Chiapas*. Instituto Indigenista Interamericano. Mexico. 1944-46.

96. ———. *Report on Music and Customs of the Huicholes of Nayarit and Jalisco*. Instituto Indigenista Interamericana. Mexico. 1944-46.

97. ———. *Report on Music and Customs of the Seris of Sonora*. Instituto Indigenista Interamericano. Mexico. 1944-46.

98. ———. *Report on Music and Customs of the Yaquis of Sonora*. Instituto Indigenista Interamericano. Mexico. 1944-46.

99. ZINGG, ROBERT MOWRY. *The Huichols: Primitive Artists*. New York. 1938.

100. ZOLORZANO, ARMANDO and GUERRERO, RAUL. *Boletín Latino Americano de Música*. Año V, Tomo V. Montevideo. 1941.

GLOSSARY

Because most foreign words have been defined in the text, only the often-repeated ones are included here, together with difficult popular names.

As an aid to pronunciation, it is well to remember that Spanish vowels have but one basic sound: approximately—a as in father; e as in met; i like the ee in meet; o as in toe; u like oo in food; y, when used as a vowel, is like the i. The consonants are practically like the English, with the following exceptions—g, when followed by i or e and j in all cases are pronounced like an aspirated h or like the German ch in Bach; h is always silent and is the only silent letter in Spanish; ll (in Mexico) is pronounced like a consonantal y in English. The r is similar to the one in thread and the rr is trilled more strongly. In Aztec words the x and j are interchanged when pronounced the same; but in some Aztec words, x is pronounced like sh and like s.

The phonetics used here are not scientific but based on easily recognized English sounds. The a will be represented by ah; the e by eh; the i by ee; the o by oh; the u by oo; and the gutteral g and j by h. Accented syllables will be marked with an accent, but as a general rule all words ending in consonants other than n or s are accented on the last syllable and in n, s, or vowels, on next to the last. Exceptions are marked.

acatlaxqui (ah-kaht-lásh-kee)—reed-thrower in Aztec.
aguamiel (ahgwah-mee-éhl)—the juice from which pulque is made.
aguardiente (ah-gwahr-dee-éhn-teh)—brandy or liquor.
ahijado (ah-ee-háh-doh)—godchild; fem. ahijada.
ahuehuete (ah-weh-wéh-teh)—an ancient sabine tree.
aje (áh-heh)—a worm from which oil is made for lacquer.
alabado (ah-lah-báh-doh)—song of praise.
alabanza (ah-lah-báhn-sah)—a religious song of praise.
alcalde (ahl-káhl-deh)—high village officer who acts as judge.
alférec, Pl. alfereces (ahl-féh-res)—an ensign; also an officer in the Chiapas fiestas.
alguacil (ahl-gwah-séel)—constable; also the man who asks permission for the bullfight to begin.
ancianos (ahn-see-áh-nohs)—old men or highly respected village elders.
ánimas (áh-nee-mahs)—souls, generally of the dead.
anizado (ah-nee-sáh-doh)—a liquor of Tehuantepec.
antojitos (ahn-toh-hée-tohs)—popular Mexican dishes.
arras (áh-rrahs)—the thirteen pieces of silver the groom slips into the hands of the bride during the marriage ceremony in the Catholic church.
arrieros (ah-ree-éh-rohs)—mule or burro drivers.
atole (ah-tóh-leh)—cornmeal gruel, sometimes flavored with chocolate.

autoridades (aw-toh-ree-dáh-dehs) —authorities; judges in a bullfight.

ayate, Mex. (ah-yáh-teh) —Otomí carrying cloth.

balams, (báh-lahms) —supernatural beings among the Mayas, who protect cornfields and villages.

balche (báhl-cheh) —the ritual drink of the Maya of Yucatán, fermented with the bark of the lonchocarpus tree.

barrio (bah-rée-oh) —a neighborhood of city or town, usually with a church and plaza of its own.

bastones (bahs-tóh-nehs) —canes.

bateas (bah-téh-ahs) —deep wooden trays, usually lacquered.

baules (bah-óo-lehs) —trunks.

bocamanga (boh-kah máhn-gah) —a lengthwise opening for the hand or head in the middle of a serape.

bolsas (bóhl-sahs) —fibre or woolen homespun bags.

bonuelos (boh-nwéh-lohs) —a big crisp pancake, fried in lard.

brasero (brah-séh-roh) —a charcoal stove in which the fire is started by fanning.

cabildo (kah-béel-doh) —place where the municipal council meets.

cacique (kah-sée-keh) —chief, leader.

caimán (kahee-máhn) —the alligator; a dance song of the huapangos.

calaveras (kah-lah-véh-rahs) —skulls, dead ones, dare-devils, scapegraces.

calendas (kah-lén-dahs) —religious parades in Oaxaca.

calzonera (kahl-sohn-éh-rah) —over-trousers, slit at the sides.

camisa (kah-mée-sah) —shirt, applied to those worn by both sexes.

canacuas (kah-náh-kwahs) —a Tarascan folkdance of the State of Michoacán, of pre-Conquest origin.

canastas (kah-náhs-tahs) —baskets.

canela (kah-néh-lah) —cinnamon.

cantinas (kahn-tée-nahs) —saloons.

carguero (kahr-géh-roh) —a man in charge of a fiesta.

casamentero (kah-sah-méhn-téh-roh) —a marriage-maker.

casa real (káh-sah reh-áhl) —royal house or Christian temple as distinguished from the pagan.

casita (kah-sée-tah) —little house; also love nest.

catrines (kah-trée-nehs) —citified men, who dress like dudes.

caudillo (kow-dée-yoh) —a leader of men.

ceñidores (sehn-yee-dóh-rehs) —long sashes. See fajas.

cenotes (seh-nóh-tehs) —the deep underground wells of Yucatán.

cerrados (seh-rráh-dohs) —closed (to new ideas).

chachalacas (chah-chah-láh-kahs) —birds that presage rain among the Mayas.

chamarra (chah-máh-rrah) —a man's short jacket, of wool or leather.

chapayecas (chah-pah-yéh-kahs) —long nose in Yaqui; name applied to the Pharisees.

charreadas (chah-reh-áh-dahs) —riding stunts performed by charros.

charros (cháh-rrohs)—Mexican horseback riders, who do cowboy tricks. Fem: charras.

chiapanecas (chee-ah-pah-néh-kahs)—folk dances and music of Chiapas.

chicha (chée-chah)—the ritual sugar-cane brandy of the Highlands of Chiapas. Also a soft drink made of chía seeds.

chilenas (chee-léh-nahs)—folk dances and songs of Guerrero.

chinquete (cheen-kwéh-teh)—the Otomí woman's type of skirt.

chiquihuite, Mex. (chee-kee-wée-teh)—petate basket without handles.

chirimía, Mex. (chee-ree-mée-ah)—a pre-Conquest type of clay or reed flute.

chirimoya (chee-ree-móh-ya)—a tropical fruit, soft and pulpy flesh around a big stone; outside green.

coleta (koh-léh-tah)—the false braid worn by the bullfighter.

coloquios (koh-lóh-kyos)—medieval mystery plays.

comal, Mex. (koh-máhl)—an earthenware griddle for baking and toasting.

comisario (koh-mee-sáh-ree-oh)—head of a community.

compadrazgo (kohm-pah-dráhs-go)—godparenthood.

compadres (kohm-páh-dres)—persons related through godparenthood.

comparsos (kohm-páhr-sohs)—group of entertainers that go about the streets during carnival time.

conchero (kohn-chéh-roh)—a dancer, who plays an instrument called a concha; that is a stringed instrument with an armadillo back; also the dance.

copitas (koh-pée-tahs)—cups; also drinks.

corridas (koh-rrée-dahs)—the regular bullfights.

corridos (koh-rée-dohs)—Mexican ballads.

corriente (koh-rrée-éhn-teh)—common.

costal (kóhs-táhl)—bag or sack.

costaleros (kohs-tah-léh-rohs)—men who carry bags.

costumbre (kohs-tóom-breh)—custom.

cotón (koh-tóhn)—a short, narrow serape, often woven of cotton.

cuadrilla (kwah-drée-ya)—a crew or the bullfighter's helpers.

curandera (koo-ráhn-déh-rah)—medicine woman; masc. curandero.

desencantado (dehs-ehn-kahn-táh-doh)—disenchanted.

doctrina (dohk-rée-nah)—the doctrine.

dorado (doh-ráh-doh)—gilded.

dueño (dwéhn-yo)—owner.

dulces (dóol-sehs)—sweets in the form of candies, candied fruit, and pastes.

ejido (eh-hée-doh)—a parcel of land.

empeyotado (ehm-peh-o-táh-doh)—when one has fallen in love through the magic of peyote.

enagua (eh-náh-gwah)—skirt.

enramada (ehn-rah-máh-dah)—a bower or arbor.

enredo (ehn-réh-doh)—a wrap-around skirt.

faja (fáh-hah)—a long wide sash, worn by both sexes.

fandango (fahn-dáhn-goh)—a dance; also a party.

ferias (féh-ree-ahs)—combination fairs and religious fiestas.

fiesteros (fee-ehs-téh-ros)—fiesta-makers of both sexes, of the northwest.

fiscal (fees-kahl)—the Christian official among the Huichols.

fonda (fóhn-dah)—a small, popular eating place.

gallos (gáh-yos)—cocks or the serenades at the hours when cocks crow.

gente de razón (héhn-teh deh rah-sóhn)—people with sense or citified people.

golpeador (gohl-peh-ah-dóhr)—striker in a ball game.

golpes (góhl-pehs)—blows.

guajolote, Mex. (gwah-hoo-lóh-teh)—turkey.

güaris (gooáh-rees)—women in Tarascan.

guayabera (gwi-ah-béh-rah)—a man's shirt of the style worn by charros.

güiros (gwée-rohs)—Cuban gourd instruments.

guitarra (guee-táh-rrah)—guitar.

guitarrón (guee-tah-rróhn)—a very large guitar.

guyaule, Mex. (goo-yah-óo-leh)—oak tree bark.

hacendado (ah-sehn-dáh-do)—owner of a large estate, called a hacienda.

hetzmek, Maya (héhtz-mehk)—carrying a child astride the hip.

hikuli (ee-kóo-leh). See peyote.

h-men (hmehn)—Maya pagan priest or shaman.

huapangos (wah-páhn-gohs)—songs and dances of the Huastecas.

huehuetl, Mex. (hweh-hwéhtl)—a vertical-cylindrical, pre-Conquest type of drum.

huipil, Mex. (wee-péel)—a straight, sleeveless, shapeless blouse.

Huitzilopochtli (wee-tsee-loh-póch-tlee)—the Aztec god of war.

indito (een-dée-toh)—little Indian man—both a term of affection and contempt, depending on how it is said and by whom.

ixtli (éesh-tlee)—maguey fibre.

jamaica (hah-mah-ée-kah)—a soft drink made with the jamaica flowers.

jarabe (hah-ráh-beh)—a syrup; also a folkdance.

jarana (ha-ráh-nah)—folkdance of Yucatán; also a small stringed musical instrument, like a ukelele.

jícaras (hée-kah-rahs)—small gourd bowls, generally lacquered or carved.

jorongo (hoh-róhn-goh)—a medium-size serape, generally worn folded over the shoulder; also open over the head.

juegos (hwéh-gohs)—games.

juez (hwehs)—judge.

juntarse (hoon-táhr-seh)—to join to live together without marriage.

Juros [sic] (hóo-rohs)—Jews.

ladinos (lah-dée-nohs)—citified people.

lavatorio (lah-vah-tóh-ree-oh)—the washing of a saint's image.

lumbre (lóom-breh)—fire, a light.

machete (mah-chéh-teh)—long, wide knife, curved or straight.

madrina (mah-drée-nah)—godmother.

maguey (mah-geh)—the century plant that furnishes pulque and fibre.

malacate, Mex. (mah-lah-káh-teh)—a spinning whorl.

mañanitas (mahn-yah-née-tahs)—birthday songs at dawn.

manda (máhn-dah)—a command; a self-imposed promise to a saint.

mano (máh-noh)—hand; applied to the long roller for grinding corn.

maravilla (mah-rah-vée-yah)—the marvel; a character in a Guerrero dance, los tlacololeros.

mariachi (mah-ree-áh-chee)—itinerant folk orchestra.

maringuilla (mah-reen-gée-yah)—the little Mary of the dances.

masa (máh-sah)—the corn dough for tortillas.

matachines (mah-tah-chée-nehs)—dancers of the matachine dance of the northwest.

matracas (mah-tráh-kahs)—rattles, especially those used at easter time.

mayor (mah-yóhr)—a superior village officer.

mayordomía (mah-yohr-doh-mée-ah)—a committee to care of images and organize fiestas. See mayordomo.

mayordomo (mah-yohr-dóh-moh)—keeper of saints' images and fiesta-maker; also a boss or overseer of workers.

mazorquitas (mah-sohr-kée-tahs)—little corncobs; mazorcas, big corncobs.

mecapal, Mex. (meh-kah-páhl)—tumpline, a band around the forehead, used to support a load that is carried on the backs by men or women.

mero (méh-roh)—the chief one.

mesón (meh-sóhn)—a place for housing horses, mules, burros and their drivers.

mestiza (mehs-tée-sah)—a woman of mixed Indian and Spanish blood; masc., mestizo.

metate, Mex. (meh-táh-teh)—a carved stone for grinding corn for tortillas.

mexicanos (meh-hee-káh-nohs)—Mexicans; name by which natives designate citified people.

mezcal (mehs-káhl)—the intoxicating drink of Oaxaca, fermented from maguey hearts.

milagros (mee-láh-grohs)—miracles; also those objectified in silver to hang near images in the churches.

milpa (méel-pah)—cornfield.

milpero (meel-péh-roh)—the man who owns and works a cornfield.

mitote, Mex. (mee-tóh-teh)—a Cora musical instrument, formed of an arc with thin rope.

mok santo (mohk-sán-toh)—the corn god of the Populucas of Vera Cruz.

molcajete (moh-kah-héh-teh)—mortar for pounding.

mole (Aztec, molli) (móh-leh)—a piquant sauce for meats and fowl.

mole de olla (móh-leh deh óh-ya)—beef with red chile sauce.

molino de nixtamal (moh-lée-noh deh nish-tah-máhl)—mill for grinding corn.

monigotes (moh-nee-góh-tehs)—big figures; boys who disguise themselves and walk on stilts during fiestas.

montera (món-téh-rah)—the pointed black hat worn by a bullfighter.

moros (móh-rohs)—Moors; also the name of a dance.

morrales (moh-rráh-les)—bags. See bolsas.

muleta (moo-léh-tah)—the small red cape, used by the bullfighter in the faena.

nagual (nah-gwáhl). See tona.

nealíka (neh-ah-lée-kah)—a Huichol symbol of the "eyes" of their gods.

negritos (neh-grée-tohs)—little Negroes; also the name of a dance.

nixtamal, Mex. (neesh-tah-máhl)—corn kernels soaked in lime water for grinding into masa for tortillas.

nopal (noh-páhl)—prickly-pear tree.

novilladas (noh-vee-yáh-dahs)—bullfights in which novilleros take part.

novilleros (noh-vee-yéh-rohs)—men in training for bullfighting.

Oaxaqueños (oh-ah-ha-kéhn-yohs)—persons living in the State of Oaxaca.

ocote (oh-kóh-teh)—pitch-pine, of which sticks are used for light.

ofrenda (oh-frénn-dah)—an offering to a saint or to the dead.

ofrezca (oh-fréhs-kah)—offer.

ojo (óh-hoh)—eye; also sickness from evil eye.

olinalaú (oh-lee-naw-láu)—a fine aromatic wood, used for making lacquered boxes.

otate, Mex. (oh-táh-teh)—a hollow reed.

padrecito (pah-dreh-sée-toh)—little father or priest.

padrino (pah-drée-noh)—godfather.

paixtle, Mex. (páeesh-tleh)—moss; name of a dance from Jalisco, whose costumes are of paixtle.

pále (páh-leh)—the Tzeltal name for a nagual in Cancuc, Chiapas.

panaderos (pah-nah-déh-rohs)—bakers; a dance song of the Huastecas.

panuelo (pahn-wéh-loh)—handkerchief or kerchief for the neck.

paraje (pah-ráh-heh)—small settlement.

partera (pahr-téh-rah)—a professional midwife.

pascola (pahs-kóh-lah)—a Yaqui dance; also a dancer of that dance.

pascua chica (páhs-kwah chée-kah)—the Pentecost.

pasión (pah-see-óhn)—passion; also a title of a man who pays for a fiesta among the highland tribes of Chiapas.

pastorela (pahs-toh-réh-lah)—a religious play in which shepherds take part, referring to the birth of Christ. See coloquios.

penitente (peh-nee-téhn-teh)—penitent.

peones (peh-óh-nehs)—those who help the bullfighter in the ring; also an unskilled, poorly-paid worker.

pepitas (peh-pée-tahs)—melon seeds.

petate, Mex. (peh-táh-teh)—reed mat, which serves as a bed and many other purposes.

peyote (peh-yóh-teh)—the sacred little cactus plant of the Tarahumaras and Huichols.

piloncillo (pee-lóhn-sée-yoh)—brown sugar.

piñata (peen-yáh-tah)—a clay jar, filled with sweets and toys; covered with a papier-maché figure and broken by someone blindfolded during the posada fiestas.

pinole (pee-nóh-leh)—powder of toasted corn, eaten dry or mixed with water.

pizcador (pees-kah-dóhr)—gleaner; fem., pizcadora.

pobrecitos (poh-breh-sée-tohs)—poor things.

popote (poh-póh-teh)—broom straw.

porra (póh-rrah)—gangs of fans at a bullfight.

posadas (poh-sáh-dahs)—lodging; also applied to the Christmas fiestas, which dramatize the journey of Mary and Joseph to Bethlehem and their asking for lodging on the way.

pozol, pozole (poh-sóh-leh)—corn dough, a native food; in Jalisco, a dish cooked with pork and chick-peas.

pulque (póol-keh)—brewed from the juice of maguey plants.

pulseador (pool-seh-ah-dóhr)—a pulse-taker or one who cures by taking the pulse.

puros (póo-rohs)—cigars.

quesadillas (kehs-ah-dée-yahs)—turnovers, fried in lard and filled with cheese, beans, potatoes, calabash flowers or huitlacoches.

quetzales (keh-tsáh-lehs)—tropical birds with beautiful plumes; also the name of a dance.

quexquemetl, Mex. (qehsh-keh-méhtl)—a cape-like blouse without sleeves.

quites (kée-tehs)—the passes with which a bullfighter takes the bull away from the horse.

ramilletes (rah-mee-yéh-tes)—bouquets, wreaths.

ranchería (rahn-cheh-rée-ah)—small settlement.

ranchero (rahn-chéh-ro)—rancher.

raspador (rahs-pah-dóhr)—a musical scraper; a stick with notches.

rebozo (reh-bóh-soh)—long straight scarf, used as a shawl by Mexican women.

red (rehd)—a net for fishing or formed into a bag.

refrescos (reh-fréhs-kohs)—soft drinks.

regidores (reh-hee-dóh-rehs)—councilmen.

retablos (reh-táh-blohs)—painted votive offerings to saints.

rezadores (rehs-ah-dóh-rehs)—professional reciters of prayers.

rodete (roh-déh-teh)—the hair formed into a roll with strands of wool.

rollo (róh-yo)—skirt of many yards of cloth, laid in pleats around the waist.

romance (roh-máhn-seh)—an early form of the Spanish ballad.

rosario (roh-sáh-ree-yoh)—rosary.

sacamisa (sah-kah-mée-sah)—to take an infant to Mass for the first time.

sacar la misa (sah-káhr lah mée-sah)—to take the Mass outside of the church.

sandunga (sahn-dóon-gah)—a song and dance of the Isthmus of Tehuan-tepec.

Santiago (sahn-tee-áh-go)—St. James.

santiguar (san-tee-gwáhr)—to make the sign of the cross or cure by blessing.

serape (seh-ráh-peh)—blanket.

síndico (séen-dee-koh)—a special office in Chiapas, filled by one who speaks Spanish.

sinfonía (seen-foh-née-ah)—symphony; a musical introduction played by the mariachis before each song.

soldadera (sohl-dah-déh-rah)—a woman soldier who follows her man to battle.

soldado (sohl-dáh-doh)—soldier.

son (sohn)—a dance; also the music for it.

sonaja (sohn-áh-ha)—rattle.

sonajeros (sohn-ah-héh-rohs)—dancers with rattles; the name of a group from Jalisco.

suerte (swéhr-teh)—stunt or trick.

tacos (táh-kohs)—a sandwich, with meat, cheese, or other fillings, wrapped in a tortilla.

tamarinda (tah-mah-réen-dah)—a soft drink made with seeds from the tamarind trees.

tapetes (tah-péh-tehs)—rugs or carpets.

tehuana (teh-wáh-nah)—a woman of Tehuantepec.

temazcal, Mex. (teh-mahs-káhl)—an aboriginal sweatbath.

tenanche (teh-náhn-cheh)—a woman who takes care of the images of female saints and virgins.

tenavari (teh-náh-vah-ree)—dried cocoons, filled with pebbles, used by Yaquis in their pascola dances.

tepache (teh-páh-cheh)—a soft drink made with pineapple, turned into a hard one by fermentation or mixing with pulque.

teponaxtli, Mex. (teh-poh-násh-tlee)—a pre-Conquest type of drum, hori-zontal and cylindrical.

Tepoztecatl (teh-pos-téh-kahtl)—a pulque god and legendary hero of Tepoztlán, Morelos.

tequila (teh-kée-lah)—an alcoholic drink, from a small agave plant, native to Jalisco.

tesgüino (tehs-gwée-noh)—corn beer of the Tarahumaras and Huichols.

tilma, Mex. (téel-mah)—a cape-like garment worn by men in pre-Conquest days. Now it applies to a short, narrow serape, with a hole for the head and generally belted in at the waist.

tinacal (tee-nah-káhl)—place where pulque is brewed.

tlacuil, Mex. (tlah-kwéel)—the indigenous hearth, formed of three stones which support a griddle.

tlapanco (tlah-páhn-koh)—sometimes called tapanco; a wide shelf for keeping things on and sleeping on.

tlatchli (tlát-chlee)—an Aztec ritual ball game.

tompeates, Mex. (tohm-peh-áh-tehs)—a round basket without a handle, woven of palm leaves.

tona (tóh-nah)—an animal guardian acquired by a child at birth.

topil, Mex. (toh-péel) —a village policeman and servant of the officials.

tostados (tohs-táh-dos)—tortillas, fried crisp and covered with meat, etc.

trago (tráh-goh)—a swallow; in Chiapas, intoxicating drinks.

trasteros (trahs-téh-rohs)—shelves for dishes or toys.

troje (tróh-heh)—corncrib or granary.

tuba (tóo-bah)—a soft drink, made from the sap of the cocoanut palms.

tule (tóo-leh)—reed.

tunas (tóo-nahs)—prickly-pear fruit.

tzeltal (tsehl-tahl)—an indigenous language of Chiapas.

tzotzil (tzóh-tzéel)—an indigenous language of Chiapas.

vacilada (vah-see-láh-dah)—lit. vacillation; slang, a laugh with the tongue in the cheek; a good time.

vaqueras (vah-kéh-rahs)—herdswomen; among the Mayas—the girls who dance the jaranas in the vaquerías.

vaquería (vah-keh-rée-ah)—herd or drove of cattle; the name given to a jarana dance, when the boys and girls who dance it are the herdsmen to the bulls.

vaquero (vah-kéh-roh)—herdsman.

vecinos (veh-sée-nohs)—neighbors—a term used by the natives when speaking of citified people.

velador (veh-lah-dóhr)—watchman.

veladora (veh-lah-dóh-rah)—the light which is always lighted on the altar.

vibuela (vee-bwéh-lah)—a small stringed instrument.

viejos (vee-éh-hohs)—the old men.

volador (voh-lah-dóhr)—a flyer; the name of the flying pole dance.

xicapexli (hee-kah-pésh-lee)—a painted gourd bowl in which women of the south carry fruit, balancing it on the head.

yuntero (yoon-téh-roh)—ploughboy.

Yuntzilob (yoon-tzee-lóhb)—the Maya supernatural beings, who watch over their needs.

zaca, (sáh-kah)—the sacred corn gruel of the Mayas.

zapateado (sah-pah-teh-áh-doh)—the Spanish form of clog dancing.

zempasuchitl, Mex. (sehm-pah-sóo-chitl)—a yellow flower like a marigold; the flower of the dead.

zip (seep)—the supernatural beings that protect the deer for the Maya.

INDEX